THE PANIC OF 1819

THE PANIC
OF 1819

THE FIRST GREAT DEPRESSION

ANDREW H. BROWNING

UNIVERSITY OF MISSOURI PRESS
Columbia

Publication of this volume has been supported with a gift from the
Kinder Institute on Constitutional Democracy

Library of Congress Cataloging-in-Publication Data

Names: Browning, Andrew H., author.
Title: The panic of 1819 : the first great depression / by Andrew H. Browning.
Description: Columbia : University of Missouri Press, 2019. | Includes
    bibliographical references and index. |
Identifiers: LCCN 2018043079 (print) | LCCN 2018044145 (ebook) | ISBN
    9780826274250 (e-book) | ISBN 9780826221834 (hardcover : alk. paper)
Subjects: LCSH: Depressions--History--19th century. | Financial
    crises--United States--History--19th century. | United States--Economic
    conditions--To 1865. | United States--Economic policy--To 1933.
Classification: LCC HB3717 1819 (ebook) | LCC HB3717 1819 .B76 2019 (print) |
    DDC 330.973/054--dc23
LC record available at https://lccn.loc.gov/2018043079

Typefaces: Bembo and Frutiger

STUDIES IN CONSTITUTIONAL DEMOCRACY

Justin B. Dyer and Jeffrey L. Pasley, Series Editors

The Studies in Constitutional Democracy Series explores the origins and development of American constitutional and democratic traditions, as well as their applications and interpretations throughout the world. The often subtle interaction between constitutionalism's commitment to the rule of law and democracy's emphasis on the rule of the many lies at the heart of this enterprise. Bringing together insights from history and political theory, the series showcases interdisciplinary scholarship that traces constitutional and democratic themes in American politics, law, society, and culture, with an eye to both the practical and theoretical implications.

Previous Titles in Studies in Constitutional Democracy

Lloyd Gaines and the Fight to End Segregation
James W. Endersby and William T. Horner

Aristocracy in America: From the Sketch-Book of a German Nobleman
Francis J. Grund
Edited and with an Introduction by Armin Mattes

From Oligarchy to Republicanism: The Great Task of Reconstruction
Forrest A. Nabors

John Henry Wigmore and the Rules of Evidence:
The Hidden Origins of Modern Law
Andrew Porwancher

Bureaucracy in America:
The Administrative State's Challenge to Constitutional Government
Joseph Postell

The Myth of Coequal Branches:
Restoring the Constitution's Separation of Functions
David J. Siemers

CONTENTS

ACKNOWLEDGMENTS

The idea behind this book gradually took shape over twenty years of teaching American history. I owe a debt of gratitude to my students in Oregon and Hawaii for their curiosity, interest, and good will. I also want to acknowledge my partners in teaching American studies over those years: the late Rosemary Stanberry, Kris Schuberg, and John Schlaefli. William Hausman and Clyde Haulman of the College of William and Mary offered valuable encouragement, as did Richard Scylla of NYU's Stern School of Business. Daniel Dupre (UNC Charlotte) reviewed the completed manuscript and made thoughtful recommendations for which I am grateful. The book is better for all of their suggestions; any errors are my own.

The staffs of a number of libraries and archives helped a great deal with tracking down obscure books, hard-to-find academic journals, and original manuscripts. I thank the kind librarians and clerks at the libraries of the University of Arizona, Portland State University, the University of Washington, Princeton University, and the University of Virginia, as well as those of the National Archives and the Library of Congress Manuscript Division. During a stretch when I was a long way from any other library, the excellent staff of the Jefferson County Library on Washington's Olympic Peninsula was particularly helpful with my many interlibrary loan requests.

The maps are the work of Chris Robinson. Those indicating the areas producing cotton and wheat are based on county-by-county statistics in the 1820 and 1840 censuses.

My editors at the University of Missouri Press have made this a more readable book in ways both large and small. I thank Mary Conley, Drew Griffith, and Barbara Smith-Mandell. In particular, Gary Kass has shown faith in this project from the start; I am more grateful to him than I can say.

Most of all I want to thank my brother, Jim Browning, whose years of experience covering the stock market for the *Wall Street Journal* brought unique insight to his many questions and suggestions, and my wife, Deborah Browning, who saw me through this as she has seen me through everything. They both read every word, and this book is for them.

THE PANIC OF 1819

INTRODUCTION

Two hundred years ago, the United States was stunned by the Panic of 1819—the first great depression, and of all the critical events in American history perhaps the least known and least appreciated. It introduced the American people to the pattern of boom and bust that has since become known as the business cycle; it was the first of the series of financial crashes and economic depressions (called "panics" in the nineteenth century) that have since recurred at regular intervals. It is no exaggeration to say that the Panic of 1819 changed the country profoundly, in ways that go well beyond the world of finance. Nevertheless, it was quickly forgotten as the country was once again swept up in what Hezekiah Niles, publisher of *Niles' Weekly Register*, called "the almost universal ambition to get forward." With little understanding of its causes, the country failed to learn its lessons and in less than twenty years plunged into the Panic of 1837.

The bubble of prosperity that led up to the Panic of 1819 also introduced elements of modern life that we can hardly imagine doing without: easily available consumer credit, real estate purchases with low down payments, a corner bank in every good-sized town, investment in the stock of corporations, and even the New York Stock Exchange itself, which opened in 1817. The ensuing panic gave the country its first experience of nationwide waves of bankruptcies, business failures, foreclosures, and unemployment; it began two centuries of condemning the poor as lazy, immoral, and self-indulgent—a disdain that would be directed at "Okies" in the 1930s and "welfare queens" in the 1980s. It inaugurated the endless debate over government regulation of business—essentially nonexistent until then—as well as the debate over free trade versus protectionism. It helped launch the mass-participation politics within which those debates and many others have taken place.

At the end of 1818 Southern cotton—the nation's most valuable export by far—lost half of its value almost overnight; in thirty key industries in

Philadelphia, three-quarters of the workers lost their jobs and the rest were paid one-fifth of what they had been; one-half of the real estate in Cincinnati wound up in the possession of the Bank of the United States; and the Bank employed Henry Clay to sue hundreds of debtors (including a United States senator) as well as the State of Ohio.

In 1819 the Supreme Court rescued the hated Bank from state attempts to tax it out of their jurisdictions: Chief Justice John Marshall's dramatic assertion of federal authority in *McCulloch v. Maryland* struck a blow at the heart of states' rights and strict construction of the Constitution. An anti-slavery movement in Congress had, at that very moment, precipitated a crisis by blocking Missouri's admission to the Union as a slave state. The fears of land speculators from Alabama to Missouri, the desperation of cotton planters who saw their survival threatened, and the resentment directed toward the Bank—now combined with distrust of the "overreaching" federal government—had much to do with the deep sectional divisions that followed, alienating West from East and South from North.

To speak of the "Panic of 1819"—a term not used until decades later—is to imply, misleadingly, a single, discrete event confined to a single year. There was no "Black Tuesday" in 1819. The country's financial institutions were not yet centered in one city, and communication was slow; Charleston learned at the end of January that English cotton mills had dropped their prices at the end of November, but word would not reach Mississippi or Alabama for several more weeks. The so-called panics of the nineteenth century—1837, 1857, 1873, 1893—were all multiyear economic phenomena, and the Panic of 1819 arguably began in 1815 as a regional depression in eastern commercial cities and mill towns, spreading down the Ohio River in 1816 and 1817; it evolved into a banking crisis in 1818 and became a full-blown national depression with the collapse of cotton prices in 1819 and a tide of business failures and bankruptcies that left no region unscathed. The sudden end of the western land boom left millions of dollars in unpaid debts, and hard times lingered in the South and West well into the mid-1820s.

Anyone who would understand the origins of the crisis must begin with the convulsions inflicted on the entire Atlantic world by the wars of Napoleon Bonaparte. Its roots go back at least to Jefferson's purchase of Louisiana from France in 1803; the $11.25 million in bonds that paid for that vast territory would come due—in gold or silver—fifteen years later. Just at the moment that the Industrial Revolution was creating a great English market for American cotton, the Napoleonic Wars threw up two great obstacles. First, revolutions in South America and Mexico, sparked by Napoleon's conquest of Spain and his installation of his brother as the new king, brought a halt to the mining of 80 percent of the world's silver and most of its gold. The second obstacle to trade was the blockade declared by Great Britain against France and its counterpart by France against Great Britain. As a neutral, the United States had thrived by carrying goods to both of the belligerents; now any further commerce threatened to bring the unprepared nation into war with one or both of the world's great military powers.

Jefferson's response, an embargo on all foreign trade, forced his agricultural nation to begin developing domestic industries. Their growth spurt was made possible by an equally rapid expansion of banking and by the innovation of limited-liability corporations, chartered by states and funded by the sale of stock. The greater number of those corporations were not manufacturers but the banks themselves, along with canal and turnpike corporations intended to get goods to market—and to help spur development of the thinly settled west. When the embargo failed to keep the country out of war, both manufacturers and farmers found a new market supplying the United States government in the War of 1812.

Wartime prosperity came at a cost. The United States had to endure the British invasion and burning of Washington, D.C., along with Tecumseh's War in the Northwest and the Creek War in the Southwest, both encouraged by Great Britain. Fortunately, Britain also found the cost of its prolonged wars so high that, after twenty years of Anglo-French conflict, Napoleon's surrender effectively ended British hostilities with the United States as well. But postwar Britain was hard pressed to absorb demobilized soldiers and sailors into its industrial workforce at the same time that military supply contracts were being terminated. The result was a decision to dump goods below cost on the American market, in a concerted effort to destroy nascent American manufacturing competition—to stifle infant industries in the cradle, in Lord Brougham's words. It had a sudden and devastating effect. In mill towns in New England and commercial cities along the Atlantic coast, economic depression began almost as soon as trade resumed. A moderately protective tariff in 1816 only briefly slowed the flood of imports, which rebounded the next year to record quantities.

Economic depression worked its way west through manufacturing towns like Pittsburgh and Lexington, Kentucky, but its initial impact was masked by a wave of land speculation that began once the Indian wars were over. Demand for western land was fueled by a combination of factors. In 1800 public land had been made available for 25 percent down with four years allowed to pay the balance; the minimum price had been set at two dollars per acre and had remained unchanged, despite rapid inflation. When Congress failed to renew the charter of the First Bank of the United States in 1811, hundreds of state-chartered banks had sprung up, all eager to lend. Then, in 1816—"the year without a summer"—record cold weather ruined harvests around the world and led to record high commodity prices; to avoid starvation, Europe was forced to import American grain and flour, while England paid higher and higher prices for American cotton to process into textiles and sell back to America. As speculators rushed to cash in, the land boom was on. First in Ohio and Indiana and then in Alabama, both the acreage sold and the prices bid at auction defied belief.

The insatiable demand created an enduring catchphrase: "doing a land-office business." Before the war, public land sales had averaged about 350,000 acres annually, and over the twenty years from 1796 to 1816, two new states had come into the Union. In the next six years there would be a new state every year. In 1815 over 1 million acres were sold, in 1818 sales exceeded 2.5 million acres, and in 1819 over 3 million acres were auctioned off at unprecedented prices, mainly in Alabama. It should have been obvious that a real estate/banking bubble was inflating, but the potential profits from wheat and cotton were irresistible. Banknotes—with next to nothing in the way of gold or silver to back them—could not be printed fast enough. Partly to impose some sort of order and partly with an eye to the Louisiana Purchase bonds (the first $3 million of which were due to be redeemed in 1818), Congress reversed course and chartered the Second Bank of the United States (BUS), 20 percent government-owned but 80 percent private. Its stockholders, in the United States and abroad, were all eager to earn dividends. Unwilling to deny them, for a year the Bank simply fed the borrowing frenzy instead of trying to restrain it.[1]

Manufacturing was still depressed when the commodity bubble began losing air. The 1817 harvests in Europe were abundant, and the high price of American wheat tumbled when Parliament forbade the importation of foreign grain. Land sales in the Northwest soon slowed in consequence. In the summer of 1818 the BUS, after a year of unrestrained lending, made a 180-degree change in policy; it now curtailed loans, demanded prompt repayment of outstanding debts, and refused to accept any bank's notes that were not redeemable in specie. Banks and businesses around the country began to fail. Then toward end of the year, British cotton mills, unable to keep paying high prices for raw cotton while selling yarn and cloth at a loss, abruptly switched from American cotton to a cheaper source in India. The Panic of 1819 arrived as word came from Liverpool that the price offered for cotton had dropped from over thirty cents per pound to under fifteen cents. Soon farms were being lost to sheriffs' sales, and city almshouses began to swell with destitute families.

It was popular at the time (and it has been ever since) to blame the second Bank of the United States for creating what people called "pecuniary embarrassments," "money pressures," or simply "hard times." The Bank had certainly made matters worse by pumping more credit into the market from 1817 through mid-1818; and although its switch to a policy of contraction was inevitable, it was dangerously sudden and continued without easing even after the severely deflated economy spiraled down out of control. But the Bank had not forced its customers to borrow so far beyond their means, and the orgy of speculation was itself inspired by unsustainable commodity prices that fell more abruptly—and further—than anyone could have foreseen. Some economists (including Murray Rothbard, who wrote the last book-length study of the Panic, in 1962) have blamed "central bank" intervention in a free financial market, but the BUS was hardly a central bank in the modern sense, and its intervention consisted of the same conservative policies that might be followed by any bank that was answerable to its shareholders; indeed, it was itself a part of the working of the free market. Secretary of the Treasury William Crawford wrote to assure the Bank's president, "The first duty of the Board is to the stockholders; the second is to the nation." Given that the Bank's charter required it to redeem its notes in specie, it would not have survived if it had continued to pay out silver while accepting the worthless paper of institutions like the notorious Owl Creek Bank, mocked in the press as "The Bank of Hoo! Hoo!"[2]

The Panic was too complex—and far too extensive—to blame solely on the Bank of the United States. There was plenty of blame to go around, but few were willing to accept any of it. Again and again, respectable people condemned bankrupts as irresponsible and extravagant—which some doubtless were—until they suddenly found themselves bankrupt as well. The Supreme Court struck down New York's bankruptcy statute as unconstitutional, but Congress refused to pass a national bankruptcy law, which the Constitution explicitly empowered it to do. Laid-off agricultural workers in the countryside tried to camp in the woods and live off the land; the middle class in the cities lost their income and wound up in debtors' prisons. Those least responsible for their own distress were the most frequently held accountable for it: the unemployed poor. Municipalities whose meager poor taxes were quickly spent refused aid to any but those willing to give up their freedom and enter the poorhouse; some churches provided winter firewood or soup, but charitable societies were more likely to dole out sermons on the virtue of thrift and the evil of luxury. The evangelical revivals of the Second Great Awakening rejected Calvinist predestination in favor of the possibility of salvation through personal conversion—but a corollary was the belief that people's poverty must be the result of their own moral failure rather than God's inscrutable will.

It is impossible to measure the damage done by the Panic of 1819—too few statistics were kept to allow detailed comparisons with later depressions—but the evidence that we do have is sobering. Contemporary estimates of nation-wide unemployment ranged from hundreds of thousands to millions, but in places like Pittsburgh and Philadelphia, where thorough investigations were undertaken, it appears to have reached 50 percent of workers. Of course the great majority of Americans were farmers, and before the War of 1812 most farms east of Ohio were owned free and clear. But the lure of cheap land, easy credit, and high profits had encouraged many eastern farmers to sell out and move west, even if only from Vermont to New York. Western land was a siren call that could not be resisted; people spoke of being "carried away" by the Ohio or Alabama "fever," and those who moved once would likely move again. Thomas Lincoln, father of the future president, was typical: born in Virginia, he moved his young family from Kentucky to Indiana to Illinois, always looking for better land. Nearly every farmer was in debt, often simply to a neighbor or relative, and court records are filled with both large and small landowners entangled in a net of promissory notes and informal agree-ments, suing their debtors in order to pay their creditors.

Wheat and cotton, the two great cash crops that had looked so promis-ing, lost half their value in 1818 and 1819, and millions of acres of newly purchased land were forfeited, often from the inability to pay a few hundred dollars on a loan. Nearly half of the public lands sold in Alabama wound up being relinquished to the government. The westward movement slowed to a trickle, and new western cities were especially vulnerable. In St. Louis half of the businesses closed and one-third of the people simply left. Cincinnati had been the fastest-growing city in America, but homes, stores, mills, hotels, warehouses, and coffee shops there were foreclosed upon. The Bank of the United States had to open a second Cincinnati branch devoted exclusively to managing its real estate.

From 1818 through 1823 the value of both imports and exports, which had been rapidly rising, fell more steeply than in any later depression. Except during the war years, the national debt had been steadily reduced by import duties; as they decreased, and as land sales slowed, federal revenue fell sharply; the 1821 fiscal year was the only peacetime year between 1804 and 1835 in which the national debt increased. Other long-term growth trends also reversed. Immigration from Europe had been steadily growing; British promoters came to America to scout opportunities for organized immigration, but they wound up warning immigrants to stay home, and ships left New York carrying disillusioned crowds of recent arrivals back to the old country, just as they would in 1932. Data is sketchy by which to measure Gross Domestic Product, but again the existing evidence is suggestive of deep decline, on a par with the Great Depression. In Pittsburgh, the value of manufactured goods fell to one-third of what it had been. It would take the city a decade to get back to the annual value of manufacturing reached in 1815, and Lexington's hemp-processing plants, which had produced naval stores like rope and canvas, never reopened. Since the economy of the United States was primarily agricultural and depended heavily on sales abroad, it is instructive to look at exports. Cotton, grain, and flour made up nearly 80 percent of exports, and between 1816 and 1823 the index of export values fell by more than half, even as the amount of cotton exported was actually increasing.[3]

The economy did eventually recover—in time for the next cycle of boom and bust in the 1830s. It is not so much that people quickly forgot the lessons of the Panic as that they failed to learn any. Everyone knew about the previous century's South Sea Bubble and Mississippi Bubble—European investment schemes that had blown up in the faces of gullible investors. But their victims were understood to have been the irresponsible wealthy, not the hard-working populace. The Panic of 1819 was different; it struck all economic classes and all regions. The country had seen nothing like this before, and there was so little context for understanding it that very little of practical benefit was learned. But the nation was also changing in ways that would not fade away with the memory of hard times, and the Panic of 1819 played a role in those changes. Widespread corruption in banking and government only intensified the public's distrust of both. The Bank, so welcome at first, had become the most hated of all institutions; eventually, antibank politics would help make Andrew Jackson the most popular president since Washington. First, however, the hostility to banks contributed to the demand for more public participation in politics, in states as diverse as Massachusetts, New York, and Kentucky. All six of the new states admitted from 1816 through 1821 came into the Union without any property-owning or tax-paying restrictions on voting, but the older states had been slower to give up those requirements. Before the Panic, popular voting was too low to be widely recorded; few eligible Americans voted—and most Americans were ineligible. In all states, the legislatures chose the U.S. senators; in half, they also chose the presidential electors. Held during the post-Panic depression, the presidential election of 1824 was the first in which popular votes were significant (or recorded for posterity), and by 1828, when Jackson was elected, nearly all adult, white males could vote—and did. Political parties, which had all but vanished in the so-called Era of Good Feelings, were stimulated by the debt-relief movement in Tennessee and Kentucky. Relief parties in the upper south, allied with Martin Van Buren's insurgent New York "Bucktails," became the core of the new Democratic Party. The shock of political and financial corruption, revealed by the Panic, was reinforced by the moral fervor of the Second Great Awakening; together they fueled the sudden rise of the Anti-Masonic Party and its successor, the Whigs. Soon a person's party affiliation would rival place of residence as a primary identity.

Sectional discord that would disrupt American life for decades to come was also awakened in 1819. Widespread anger at the Bank intensified the states'-rights backlash against *McCulloch v. Maryland*; both the West and the South saw the BUS as their oppressor, and their resentment was readily transferred to the federal government with which John Marshall's decision so closely identified the Bank. Southerners and westerners had speculated recklessly in public land when export crops were riding high. When prices fell, westerners called for canals to bring their produce cheaply to eastern consumers, while southerners could see no choice but to export twice as much cotton at half the price. And that required slave labor, suddenly threatened by the Missouri crisis. The Missouri Compromise quieted the bitter debate for a while, but the sectional divide would only grow worse, exacerbated by the depression that lingered in the South. The economic stress of the Panic deepened fault lines that would become chasms within a generation. The Panic helped create the East-West divide that put Andrew Jackson in the White House, and it deepened the North-South divide that led to secession and civil war.

The United States today is different in many ways from the America of 1819, and readers should be alert to the differences. To begin with, it was a much smaller country then. The 1820 census counted 9,638,453 Americans—about the population of North Carolina today. It was a nation of farms and tiny villages. The largest city, New York, was half the size of modern Fort Wayne, Indiana—and it gave way to farmland north of 14th Street, twenty blocks below the site where the Empire State Building now stands. Other than New York, there was no city with more than 65,000 inhabitants; seven of the largest twenty had fewer than 10,000. The U.S. government employed, outside of the post offices and the military, at most a few hundred people.

Statistics, then, must be understood accordingly, and estimates of unemployment must take into consideration the fact that over 15 percent of the workforce consisted of unpaid slave labor. Financial numbers in particular should not be viewed in a modern context. Today's steadily growing national debt (as of November 2018) exceeds $21 *trillion*; in 1822 it had jumped up to $91 *million* but was once again shrinking. Federal spending that year amounted to less than $20 million annually, compared to some $4 trillion at present. To move to a scale that is easier to comprehend, rent for a substantial house in Philadelphia before the Panic was $100 a month; after the Panic hit, a debt of less than one dollar could lead to imprisonment, and Massachusetts laborers were earning between fifty cents and a dollar for a day of at least ten hours' work. (The legal minimum wage in the state is today fifteen dollars per *hour*.) The highest paid artisans in New York earned twelve dollars per week when there was work, and the expenses of a working-class family came to six or seven dollars a week, whether there was work or not; today an experienced structural steelworker in New York would earn that much in less than fifteen minutes, and the Economic Policy Institute pegs the expenses of a family of five in Manhattan today at $2000 a week. The vice president of the United States (essentially a part-time employee in 1819) was paid $4000 a year— with no additional allowances; congressmen had no salaries but received six dollars per diem when Congress was in session, with the understanding that they paid all their own office expenses aside from rent and postage. (Snuff, on the House and Senate floors, was provided at no charge.)

Clearly there is no single multiplier to say how much more a dollar was worth two hundred years ago, but almost any dollar figure from 1819 must be understood as the equivalent of many times as much today: commodities like wheat and cotton are cheap today, only three or four times what they were then, but today's government spending or the income levels that define the very rich are over a hundred times as high. It cost five dollars to subscribe to *Niles' Weekly Register* for a year, the same as a single copy of the Sunday *New York Times* today. Building lots in Manhattan sold for $150 per acre (compared to as much as $2300 per *square foot* recently).

All such quantitative adjustments pose a challenge, but qualitative adjustments can be even more difficult. Many assumptions were simply different, from such predictable subjects as race and gender to less obvious ones like the ethics of nepotism or the habit of dueling. One difference in particular requires explanation: "money" in 1819 was simply not the same thing it is today. We take it for granted that money is something issued by national governments who guarantee its legitimacy. Prices may fluctuate, but few people seriously question whether a dollar bill—or more and more often, its credit-card equivalent—is actually worth a dollar. The Constitution speaks only of the federal power to "coin" money, but coins today are simply change, dropped into a tip jar to avoid rattling in our pockets against our cell phones. "Money" hasn't meant gold in the United States since 1933, when the final ten- and twenty-dollar gold coins were withdrawn; the last coin to contain any precious metal was the 1974 dollar (90 percent silver), minted six years after dollar bills ceased to be "silver certificates," exchangeable for silver dollars upon demand. The Bureau of Engraving and Printing began producing paper money—"U.S. notes"—during the Civil War, and for the last 150 years American money has meant government-issued bills and coins, although for half a century now we have happily accepted a "promise to pay" instead, in the form of bank-issued credit cards. Although a surprising number of Americans cling to the mistaken belief that there is a dollar's worth of gold in Fort Knox for every dollar bill that is printed, people who demand a return to the gold standard are often dismissed as eccentrics. The expression "sound as a dollar" may have fallen out of fashion, but the fundamental soundness of any given dollar bill is not questioned; if it suddenly were, "panic" might be an apt term for the reaction.

Until the end of the eighteenth century, money *did* mean gold or silver (called "specie") all around the world; idiosyncratic exceptions like wampum in North America or cowrie shells in West Africa were exotic curiosities. And what mattered was the *amount* of gold or silver, not the image stamped on it. The eight-reale Spanish dollar (popular in China) was preferred everywhere because it was very nearly pure silver, soft enough that you made change with a knife, slicing the coins into fractions called "cut money."[4] Banks, encountered only in big cities, were simply storehouses for bullion. A few governments resorted, in times of crisis, to "fiat money" (from the Latin *fiat*: "let it be")—paper bills with nothing in the way of gold or silver to back them. They were instantly discounted and rarely maintained for long. (Confederate money during the Civil War is a famous example.) England introduced the idea of banknotes; just what they sound like, they were messages written or printed on paper, in which a bank promised to hand over a given quantity of "real" money to the bearer. For large amounts, merchants found them much more portable (and easier to secure) than bags or chests of coins, although for everyday exchanges the common man still depended on small coins, barter, or even a handshake. Money was still gold or silver, but it could now be a paper *promise* of it too, and the value of the promise—of the banknote—depended on what one knew of the promiser: the Bank of England was trusted because everyone knew that the Bank of England had chests full of gold in its vaults. Thus, when the financial pressures of endless wars with France led the British government to order the Bank to suspend the exchange of precious metal for its banknotes, the public went along in the confidence that the gold was, after all, still in the vaults—even though the amount was far less than the face value of the notes in circulation.

There was, of course, a limit to the gold or silver being dug out of the ground; even before revolutions disrupted them, the mines of Spanish America could not keep up with the world's rapidly expanding economies. As towns and cities grew, barter became less popular—cobblers and landlords did not want to be paid with a bushel of wheat or a bale of wool. When the "market revolution" swept through America in the early nineteenth century, the need for currency became acute, but there was simultaneously less and less specie in circulation; it left the country in foreign commerce, especially with Asia, and the trade imbalance meant that purchased imports came back instead of gold or silver. Americans still remembered the disastrous effect of the fiat currency issued by Congress and some individual states during and just after the Revolution, so to meet the need for a "circulating medium" they turned to notes issued by banks. The First Bank of the United States, chartered by Congress in 1791, was nearly as solid as the Bank of England; with the federal revenues in its vaults, its notes were accepted everywhere at their face value. Then, after its charter expired in 1811, minimally regulated local banks proliferated throughout the states, all printing their own banknotes—and usually far in excess of any specie reserves they might have. The national mint turned out coins, but always too few—and, with the scarcity of specie, too valuable to spend; thus business was done with the notes of the various banks, more or less discounted depending on how far away or unfamiliar they were to the recipient. When the Second Bank of the United States was incorporated in 1816, its charter required that its notes be redeemable in specie. Therefore, they were always accepted as the equivalent of government coinage—"at par." The Bank's cashiers were understandably reluctant to accept deposits in the form of unfamiliar, distant banks' notes when withdrawals could then be made in gold or silver, especially when overextended local banks began refusing to redeem their own notes in specie.

The story of the Panic of 1819 is much more than a story of money, but money—whether deeply discounted or "good as gold"—is a central part of it. Today a tourist abroad may negotiate at a souvenir stand for the best exchange rate between dollars and the local currency; in 1819 almost every domestic transaction involved the exchange rate of dollars in one bank's money for dollars in another bank's, sometimes with different discounts for different banks in the same city. *Niles' Register* published a semi-serious anecdote of a customer who tried to redeem a certain bank's notes for silver; when they refused, he asked for notes from any other bank that would redeem; when refused again, he finally asked if they had any well-printed counterfeit notes for specie-redeeming banks. Still, banking was not the only problem. The overissue of paper "money"—banknotes—had much to do with price inflation, but it was not responsible for the high price of wheat when European harvests failed; the BUS decision to contract credit led to numerous business failures, but it did not cause the collapse of cotton prices when English mills turned to India for their raw material.

"The Panic of 1819" as a term may stand loosely for the hard times of a full decade, from 1815 to 1825. It was one of the great traumas of our nation's history, and it influenced developments that shaped our national identity, but no book has examined its national impact for over half a century. During that time a great many new resources have become available; the efflorescence of articles and monographs about the period has produced a wealth of information and interpretation, including new access to many primary sources essential to any understanding of the events. A significant number of sources still exist only in manuscript, but others have been made available online, by the Library of Congress and the National Archives in particular. The Panic was a national, public cataclysm, and the actions and reactions of government officials were well-recorded, starting with the *Annals of Congress* and the *American State Papers*. The journals of many state legislatures are invaluable sources as well. The limits to federal involvement in the economy, at least at the presidential level, are indicated by the near absence of references to the economic crisis in the annual messages of President James Monroe. Nevertheless, the great "pressure of the times" fills the memoirs and correspondence of public figures ranging from John Quincy Adams, Henry Clay, John C. Calhoun, and Andrew Jackson—all, by 1820, contenders for the 1824 presidential election—to former Presidents John Adams, Thomas Jefferson, and James Madison. Their private thoughts and public statements are preserved in published volumes of papers, works, correspondence, and memoirs.

Many less-familiar political figures were directly involved with the challenges of the crisis: Alabama's John Williams Walker, Kentucky's Richard Mentor Johnson, Massachusetts's Josiah Quincy, and Connecticut's Oliver Wolcott Jr., to name only a few. A surprising number of ordinary citizens closely followed the dense economic critiques that were published by the protectionist Matthew Carey, by the "Old Republican" ideologue John Taylor of Caroline, or by the Philadelphia financier and state senator Condy Raguet. Morris Birkbeck, James Flint, and Adam Hodgson were three perceptive Britons who traveled across America tracing the unfolding depression in their published letters home.

The many events of the day, important and trivial, were well-reported and editorialized upon by the hundreds of newspapers that were avidly read throughout the country. Published in now-vanished towns like Fort Claiborne and Kaskaskia or in the great eastern metropolises, they could be launching pads for ambitious editors who went on to the United States Senate (like Thomas Hart Benton) or became powerful presidential advisors (like Amos Kendall of the *Western Argus* or Duff Green, who followed Benton at the St. Louis *Enquirer*). Three papers in particular stand out, not only for their comprehensive record of what took place but for the influential editorials of their publishers: Thomas Ritchie's Richmond *Enquirer* (which Jefferson claimed was the only paper he read), William Duane's Philadelphia *Aurora* (as radical as the *Enquirer* was conservative), and the invaluable *Niles' Weekly Register* (published in Baltimore by Hezekiah Niles but read throughout the nation).

These were the public voices of an age when a single copy of a newspaper would pass through the hands of a dozen readers. But the most immediate sense of what the "hard times" meant can be found in the letters, diaries, business accounts, and court records of private citizens, many obscure at the time and nearly all forgotten now. A few, like Stephen Girard of Philadelphia or Stephen Duncan of Natchez, Mississippi, were so wealthy that the depression's worst blows could not ruin them; others, like Lucy Mack Smith (mother of the Mormon prophet Joseph Smith) led humble lives in small towns where the economy's vagaries really were what Jefferson called them: "waves of a storm [that] will pass under the ship." But for many, many people in cities or on farms, the "hard times" were a catastrophe that upended their lives: Llewellyn Jones, an aged veteran of Valley Forge who hanged himself in despair when cotton prices fell in Alabama, or John Piatt, Cincinnati's leading citizen and donor of its first public park, who died in debtors' prison at the age of forty.

Many other lives were cut short by the effects of the Panic, and even more hopes were dashed. The sad disillusionment of a nation resonates in the words of Patience Lippincott, called Patty by her family. With a three-month-old daughter she followed her husband to what he insisted was a "Terrestrial Paradise" in Missouri. Writing home to the brother she would never see again, she admitted that St. Louis "is a dissipated and disagreeable place to me" and closed her letter, "Let us remember that this world is not our abiding place. . . . We should not be immoderate in our desires for any earthly goal for all things beneath the sun shall fade and vanish away." Only a few months later her restless husband moved his little family again, to Illinois. There Patty died of malaria in the tiny village of Milton, which was entirely abandoned within ten years—another ghost town created by the Panic of 1819.[5]

THE LEGACY OF NAPOLEON
Embargo, War, and Peace

Washington, D.C., October 1800: At the beginning of October, the presidential campaign in the United States was sinking to its lowest level of slander and defamation. Thomas Jefferson's supporters called John Adams a "hideous hermaphroditical character, which has neither the force and firmness of a man, nor the gentleness and sensibility of a woman." Federalists labeled Vice President Jefferson "a mean-spirited, low-lived fellow, the son of a half-breed Indian squaw, sired by a Virginia mulatto father." Jefferson complained to his old friend Benjamin Rush that achieving the presidency would only leave him "a constant butt for every shaft of calumny which malice & falsehood could form." By mid-month, with the election of a Republican majority in the South Carolina legislature, Jefferson's victory seemed assured, and over the next eight years his gloomy prediction was indeed proven true. But on October 1st in the Spanish Palace of La Granja, an event took place that would lead to the single greatest success of Jefferson's presidency. The Treaty of San Ildefonso was signed and the vast Louisiana region, in Spanish hands since 1762, was returned to France. Three years later, the Senate would ratify Jefferson's purchase of Louisiana from France, thus doubling the area of the United States. The Orleans Territory became the state of Louisiana in 1812, but seven more years would go by before public land elsewhere in the Louisiana Purchase would be offered for sale by the federal government. When that section—the Missouri Territory—then applied for statehood, it sparked the crisis that Jefferson would call a "fire bell in the night." In 1820 he would acknowledge that "the knell of the Union [was] hushed for the moment" by the Missouri Compromise, but "this is a reprieve only, not the final sentence."[1]

Paris, April 1803: A year of fighting and thousands of casualties had left Gen. Charles Leclerc's army in Haiti worn down by fierce guerilla warfare and decimated by disease; Leclerc himself, Napoleon's brother-in-law, had

MAP 1. The United States in 1820. Map by Chris Robinson.

recently died of yellow fever. Although Toussaint L'Ouverture had been cap-tured, the slave rebellion he led showed no sign of giving up. With France's Caribbean empire in tatters, Louisiana had already lost its value as a granary for slaves on sugar plantations and seemed vulnerable to British invasion. On Monday, April 11, Napoleon met with his treasury minister, the marquis de Barbé-Marbois. The United States government had previously expressed interest in acquiring New Orleans, the new nation's only outlet on the Mississippi, but now the first consul spoke of selling the entire, undefined region of Louisiana. Barbé-Marbois later recalled that Napoleon reached his decision even as he spoke:

> They ask of me only one town in Louisiana; but I already consider the colony as entirely lost; and it appears to me that in the hands of this growing Power it will be more useful to the policy, and even to the commerce, of France than if I should attempt to keep it. . . . Irresolution and deliberation are no longer in season; I renounce Louisiana. It is not only New Orleans that I cede; it is the whole colony, without reserve. . . . Have an interview this very day with Mr. Livingston.[2]

Mr. Livingston was Robert Livingston, Jefferson's minister to France. From the end of the Revolutionary War there had been conflict over navigation rights on the Mississippi, the only practical route for exporting the produce of farmers west of the Alleghenies. With all of Louisiana once again French instead of Spanish, the choke point at the mouth of the river was suddenly in Napoleon's hands. To Jefferson it was clear: "There is on the globe one single spot, the possessor of which is our natural and habitual enemy. It is New Orleans." Livingston and James Monroe, who had just arrived in France to join him, had been authorized to spend as much as $10 million to purchase the city; if France refused to sell, they were to proceed to London to arrange a military alliance with England.[3]

The canny French ruler may well have guessed the Americans' fallback plan. The Louisiana Territory—untold millions of acres, at what turned out to be four cents an acre—was an offer they could not refuse, and there would be no alliance with England. Instead, nine years later England would be at war with both the United States and Napoleon. In the spring of 1803, however, Livingston and Monroe had to take matters into their own hands. Communications between Paris and Washington took two months by sailing ship, and Napoleon required a decision at once. Monroe was unsure—the asking price was half again what they were authorized to spend—but Livingston did not hesitate; he accepted the offer. They both signed the treaty on April 30 and signed the conventions arranging the payment on June 6. (President Jefferson did not learn what his representatives had done until July 3.) The first $3.75 million would be credited to the United States in return for its assumption of claims by American shippers against French privateers.

The remaining $11.25 million (60 million francs) would have to be paid in gold or silver—an amount that exceeded the entire specie reserves of the U.S. Treasury.

Clearly the money would have to be borrowed, and the only bankers who could arrange such a sum were in England and the Netherlands. France was at war with England; so too were the Dutch. The bankers, however, saw no problem; they were unusually cosmopolitan men. Hope & Company of Amsterdam had been founded by a family of Scotsmen, and Henry Hope had been born in Massachusetts and apprenticed as a banker in London. Baring Brothers, in London, had been founded by the sons of a German wool merchant. Thomas Baring had apprenticed with Hope & Co. in Amsterdam, and his nephew Alexander had an American wife. They were the multinationals of the early nineteenth century; the duc de Richelieu is supposed to have said in 1817, "There are six main powers in Europe: Britain, France, Austria-Hungary, Russia, Prussia, and Baring Brothers." In the present situation, Barings had the approval of the British government, which saw advantages in making Louisiana American. Thomas Baring noted that the prime minister "saw nothing in our conduct but to approve. He appears to consider Louisiana in the hands of America as an additional means for the vent of our manufacturers . . . besides other motives which we did not discuss directly, of a political nature." In fact, at the bank the bottom line always came first; during the War of 1812, Baring Brothers would even arrange the Americans' borrowing in Europe to finance their war with Britain.[4]

Washington, D.C., February 1804: After the Senate ratified the treaty of purchase, Alexander Baring spent the winter arranging the financing with Albert Gallatin, Jefferson's secretary of the treasury. The $11.25 million would be issued in 6 percent bonds (called "stock" in those days) to be redeemed in four installments, beginning in fifteen years. On February 13, 1804, Midshipman John B. Nicolson nervously signed a receipt for $7.5 million, Baring signed for the rest, and the freshly printed bonds were transported by ship to Paris. On April 28—one year almost to the day after signing the treaty—Barbé-Marbois delivered a quitclaim for Louisiana to Hope & Co., making the formal transfer of title. The first payment, in gold, would fall due in December 1818, when the president of the United States would be none other than Livingston's hesitant partner, James Monroe. The national funds were kept in the Second Bank of the United States, but despite years of prosperity the precious metal in its vaults would be far too little to redeem even the first moiety of the bonds. When the Bank decided to call in notes and curtail loans to raise the specie for that first payment, it would trigger the Panic of 1819.[5]

The French decision to sell Louisiana, and the long-term debt that the purchase created for the United States, were side effects of the Napoleonic Wars. Among many other international dislocations caused by those wars was the sharp drop in precious metal mined in Spanish colonies. It affected all of the Atlantic community, and its impact was felt as far away as China. A recurring theme in contemporary accounts of the "hard times" following the Panic of 1819 would be the scarcity of specie, felt from the highest levels of the financial world down to the small-town shopkeeper. A Scottish traveler in the Ohio valley, James Flint, reported on August 15, 1820, "A person who collected a salary to the amount of about eight hundred dollars, told me that he had received only five dollars of that in specie. You can easily perceive that under this state of things, very few will give specie to the tavern keeper, grocer, or others. . . . Specie is almost entirely withdrawn from the retail business." The Bank of the United States, facing its 1818 redemption of the first block of Louisiana Purchase stock, would be forced to buy $5 million in specie abroad, and after Langdon Cheves became the Bank's president in 1819, he would find it necessary to borrow another $2 million in specie in Europe; at the opposite end of the financial spectrum, small-town banks in Kentucky and Pennsylvania would issue paper notes in denominations as low as six and one-half cents.[6]

Both gold and silver coins continued to be minted by the United States— along with copper pennies and half cents—but between 1804 and 1834 the face value of gold coins would have been less than the value of the metal they contained, and even silver—the *de facto* standard for the nation—was too valuable to spend freely. On January 6, 1819, Treasury Secretary William Crawford replied to an inquiry from Congress about the Mint's ability to increase the number of coins. The assessment he forwarded from Robert Patterson, the director of the U.S. Mint, detailed the Mint's technical ability to manufacture coins but pointedly ignored the question of how much silver or gold might be available to it. In 1818, the year before the Panic, the Mint produced $242,940 in gold five-dollar half eagles and $1,070,427.50 in silver dimes and half dollars. In a country with a population of nine million, that came to just under fourteen cents per capita. Over all the years since independence, the Mint's total production amounted to barely $1.50 for each

American alive in 1818. By comparison, Albert Gallatin estimated in 1831, "In France . . . a country nine-tenths at least of the currency of which consist of precious metals, the estimates vary . . . from thirteen and a half to fifteen dollars a head." He believed that America in 1819 had only "about six dollars a head" in currency, and nearly all of that was in paper banknotes. In 1822, with recovery from the Panic just beginning, the Philadelphia financier Condy Raguet noted that $185,325 in gold had been coined the previous year, "Yet not a gold coin is anywhere to be seen in circulation."[7]

The problem of the "circulating medium" worried everyone. Secretary of State John Quincy Adams wrote in his diary on July 24, 1819, "I was swallowed up in calculation and meditation upon coins, currency, and exchange." He had just been called as a character witness on behalf of two French silversmiths in Washington, D.C., accused of having passed along counterfeit "five penny bit" coins. "The strongest circumstance against them was, that, being silversmiths, they should have received and passed off these pieces for genuine money, the bare inspection of them being sufficient to show that they were not of good silver." The best defense, he concluded, was that "being foreign here, they might know these pieces to be bad silver and yet believe them to be genuine coins," since small French coins were regularly debased. "I left the court-house before the jury came in with their verdict. They acquitted both the prisoners."[8]

Bad silver—or at least debased coinage—was not unfamiliar in the United States, despite the U.S. Mint's high standards. The reason was that most of the circulating coins were foreign. In 1806 President Jefferson had ordered a stop to the coining of U.S. silver dollars because they were being shipped to South America to be exchanged for Spanish eight-reale dollars ("pieces of eight") which were a little heavier. Those coins were then returned to the United States, melted down, and sold for a profit as bullion. As a result, only the lightest shaved-down Spanish dollars remained as the usual coin in circulation, along with fractional pieces of coins. (One-quarter of a Spanish eight-reale dollar was literally "two bits" when the coin was cut with a knife or hatchet to make change.) James Flint described these pieces to his readers back in Great Britain as "cut money, from which a portion of the metal has been fraudulently abstracted. The deficiency in weight prevents this part of the currency from being exported in direct payments, and nothing but the present depreciation of paper seems to prevent these remnants of silver from being disposed of as bullion."[9]

The most notorious aspect of the Panic of 1819 was the inability of banks to provide specie to redeem their banknotes, caused by the overall shortage of gold and silver. To Albert Gallatin, secretary of the treasury from 1801 to 1814, the reason for the scarcity was obvious. In 1831 he explained that "the diminution in the annual supply for the last twenty years [has] been exclusively caused by the convulsions attending the new American states"—the revolutions that broke out from Chile north to Mexico in response to the French invasion of Spain and the replacement of King Ferdinand with Napoleon's brother, Joseph Bonaparte.[10]

Gallatin estimated that since the discovery of the Americas, over $5.6 billion in gold and silver had been mined in the New World—compared with only $1.3 billion in all the rest of the world combined. Modern estimates agree that Bolivia, Peru, and Mexico—the colonies of New Granada and New Spain—were responsible for 85 percent of world silver production between 1500 and 1840. But when Napoleon seized control of Spain, the revolutions that swept across Spanish America wreaked havoc on silver mining. Coinage in the Mexico City mint, Spain's largest, fell from 24.7 million pesos in 1809 to 7.7 million in 1812; it would never exceed 10.1 million between 1811 and 1817. The Mexican states of Guanahuato, Queretaro, and Michoacan were the locations of the richest silver mines; they were also the cradle of the war of independence, and as early as 1809 work in the mines had come to a standstill. Over the next decade many mines were abandoned, and others operated only intermittently. As depreciated paper banknotes were losing much of their value in 1819, Thomas Hart Benton urged the United States to recognize the Mexican revolutionary government in order to get access to Mexican silver. Rather than offend Spain in such a long-shot bid, the government chose not to.[11]

Benton was not the only one concerned. As early as January 26, 1819, a committee of the New York State Senate listed the "causes of the embarrassed state of our country." First on their list was the "decrease of precious metals, in consequence of the agitation in Spanish America," and the following year Oliver Wolcott Jr., formerly Washington's and Adams's treasury secretary, wrote that "the scarcity of money has been further increased by the wars in Spanish America, which have prevented the customary supplies of gold and silver from the mines." But both the New York senate and Wolcott saw another cause as well, one that was also related to the Napoleonic Wars: "the vast exportation of specie to *Asia*." In the first two decades of the century, lamented Wolcott, because British trade was disrupted by war with France, "an active, though ephemeral commerce . . . swept a great capital of the metallic money from Europe and America, to Asia, from which it will not soon, if ever, return."[12]

The China trade, in pursuit of tea and silk, had been developed by Great Britain, but America took over the dominant share when war with the French and Dutch inhibited British commerce around the Cape of Good Hope. American trade with China grew from an average of seven ships annually between 1785 and 1800 to an average of twenty-four between 1801 and 1811. As the economic historian Yen-P'ing Hao notes, "Financing the tea trade was a perennial problem for American merchants because, quite simply, they possessed few items the Chinese really wanted to buy." What the Chinese really wanted was silver.[13]

China required a dependable measure of both quantity and quality of silver. American silver dollars would have been acceptable, but there were too few in circulation. The Spanish silver dollar was thus in demand both in China and in the United States—but it was worth *more* to Americans if they exported it to China. Consequently, American merchants found it necessary to engage in a new triangular trade. They would first sell American produce—cotton or grain—in Europe or South America, in return for Spanish dollars; these coins were then transported directly around the Cape to Canton (modern Guangzhou), where they were exchanged for tea or silk to be shipped back by the same route to New York. Until the Embargo Act put an end to the re-export trade, those goods could also be sent (profitably) across the Atlantic to London. In the ten years between 1805 and 1814, some $22 million in Spanish dollars acquired in exchange for American produce went to China without ever entering the United States. Another $29 million was shipped to China in the six years following the War of 1812—half of that in 1818 and 1819. Immediately after the Treaty of Ghent, while suggesting ways to improve finances now that peace had returned, Treasury Secretary Alexander Dallas could not resist one additional suggestion: "*The exportation of specie should be prohibited* for a limited time." The suggestion was ignored, as he expected it would be.[14]

Contemporary critics decried the damage done to American currency stability. Condy Raguet noted with dismay in 1823 that from independence up to that year, "nearly all [American] imports from China were paid for by an exportation of silver dollars . . . in addition to the supply required for the currency." Hezekiah Niles angrily editorialized in 1818: "So great is the present rage for the East India and China trade that Spanish dollars are at about a 9 per cent. Premium, over the best banknotes," so that merchants had a powerful incentive to keep them out of the domestic economy by shipping them to China. "American [silver] dollars are not quite so high, though extensively used in the traffic," being traded in South America for the preferred Spanish dollars. Niles roundly condemned "this traffic, in which we are altogether willing to wish that many may '*burn their fingers*,' for it is certainly disadvantageous to us." Within a very few months he would get his wish.[15]

Some historians point to yet another consequence of the Napoleonic Wars: the sudden demand for precious metals when Europe went back to a gold standard after the return of peace. Richard Ellis speaks of a "drain on specie reserves" because "Eastern Europe went onto the gold standard"; Clyde Haulman believes that "[a]ttempts by European countries to return to a specie standard in the years after 1815 further exacerbated the monetary problem in the U.S. These efforts meant nations were all trying to build up gold and silver reserves at the same time, thus placing intense pressure on the world's specie supply." And Leon Schur writes, "The world was struggling manfully to return to a specie standard. Every country was trying to build up its reserves of gold and silver."[16]

Here is what happened. The British government of William Pitt the Younger had been borrowing heavily from the Bank of England to fund its wars with France. On February 27, 1797, with barely £1 million in specie left, Orders in Council were given forbidding the Bank from paying specie for its notes "until the will of Parliament be known." Parliament's will would not be declared for another twenty years, and England was effectively off the gold standard.

The "drain of specie" from the Bank of England has usually been attributed to three causes: the instability of the British political environment, the military expeditions in Europe (including British subsidies of Austrian, Prussian, and Russian armies); and France's return to the gold standard after abandoning the Revolutionary paper *assignats*. In their 1935 *Fluctuations in American Business*, Walter Smith and Arthur Cole make the assertion—followed by most modern historians—that between 1797 and 1821 the currency of the world was "in a state of chaos." Politics in England were indeed unstable, and the armies of its shifting wartime coalitions were enormously expensive. But after giving up *fiat* paper, France had actually settled on a stable bimetal standard (like the rest of Europe) and monetary chaos was by no means constant.[17]

Napoleon's victories had brought to France war indemnities that built up specie reserves; the Louisiana Purchase added $11 million in specie when Hope and Barings sold the American bonds (largely to Napoleon's enemies, England and Russia). Indeed, throughout the Napoleonic Wars the franc was actually a stronger currency than the pound, with less fluctuation on foreign exchange markets. Through 1821 and beyond the franc was the currency of choice on the Continent; the pound sterling would come to dominate international trade on the whole, but the franc would remain "the most influential currency in Western Europe during the nineteenth century."[18]

Meanwhile in Britain, notes of the Bank of England became sufficiently trusted that there was little demand for gold coins when they were again offered in 1821. Once hostilities had come to an end in 1815, the government began to press the Bank of England to set a date for the resumption of specie redemption; the Bank dragged its feet, finding exchanges unfavorable, but after its initial experiments in 1816 with limited convertibility encountered no difficulties, Parliament finally passed a bill in 1819 to require full convertibility in May 1820. *Niles' Register* reported the decision to American readers on May 8, 1819: "Partial supplies of silver is [*sic*] furnished to the London banks by the Bank of England, and as the value of gold over banknotes had fallen, it was believed that some issues of it might soon be made with safety." Britain had grown comfortable with paper currency: there was virtually no demand for coin, and specie reserves were allowed to drop steadily again. Only then did Russia, Prussia, and Austria approach London to float bonds.[19]

Following the Congress of Vienna, most European nations (including Great Britain) did resolve to build up specie reserves. But in 1817, even as the newly chartered Second Bank of the United States was unsuccessfully demanding that banks in America resume the redemption of notes in specie—suspended in 1814—the Bank of England actually invited its recent allies to come buy gold and silver. Russia, Prussia, and Austria, whose treasuries had all been drained by their wars with Napoleon, acquired some £10 million in bullion from England during 1817 and 1818, and British surplus specie reserves dropped accordingly. The BUS was still able to purchase millions of dollars in silver and gold from England and Portugal in 1818 and 1819, even after the Europeans had got there first. The American specie shortage, like the inescapable debt for the Louisiana Purchase, was surely influenced by Napoleon's wars with Britain, but both had already done their harm before 1819.[20]

The wars between England, France, and their constantly changing cast of allies triggered other wars in addition to the revolutions that broke out in Spanish America. After two decades of uneasy relations with both France and England, the United States found itself drawn into the War of 1812 because of the conflicting demands of the two great adversaries. That costly, fruitless war led to the burning of the new national capital of Washington, D.C., and sparked yet further wars with the Shawnee, the Creek, and other tribes in the American West. Coming after the Embargo Act of 1807—President Jefferson's futile attempt to avoid outright hostilities—the War of 1812 proved devastating to the country's New England-based commerce with Europe. The Treaty of Ghent that brought the war to an end offered little more than a return to the *status quo ante*. Nevertheless, this war that appeared to accomplish nothing actually brought sweeping changes to the United States, initiating the bubble that would burst in the Panic of 1819.

The New England states were almost unanimous in their opposition to the war, to the point that the Hartford Convention in late 1814 seriously entertained secession. But there were inspiring naval victories on Lake Champlain, and the Vermont *Patriot* took a decidedly patriotic tone in the spring of 1815:

> What have we got from the war?
> The fear of our late enemy;
> The respect of the world; and
> The confidence we have acquired in our selves.

When the war ended, commerce with England (and the rest of the world) returned with a vengeance; in the interior, the Treaties of Greenville and Horseshoe Bend opened up vast lands to settlement, and the banks that had sprung up to fund the war were eager to lend to ambitious speculators. The war was followed by a period of seeming national unity that the Boston *Columbian Centinel*, on July 12, 1817, would memorably call the Era of Good Feelings. But beneath that superficial harmony lay regional conflicts and vulnerabilities that had only intensified during a decade of embargo and war.[21]

Napoleon's Berlin Decree in November 1806 forbade neutrals from trading with Great Britain; the British government responded in early 1807 with Orders in Council aimed squarely at the United States, directing the Royal Navy to seize ships that attempted to trade with French-controlled Europe.

Napoleon replied with the Milan Decree, declaring any ship that submitted to British search a lawful prize for privateers or naval vessels. He had little success enforcing his decrees—most French ships were bottled up in port by the British blockade—but Britain continued to stop American vessels, not only to prevent trade with France but to impress seamen who were suspected of being British subjects. On June 22, 1807, HMS *Leopard* fired a broadside into USS *Chesapeake* and seized four sailors, one of whom was hanged as a deserter from the Royal Navy. At that point, hoping to force England's hand by denying its commerce with America, Jefferson called for an embargo on all foreign trade, which Congress passed on December 22.

Jefferson's treasury secretary, the Swiss-born Albert Gallatin, warned that the embargo (and its successor, the Non-Intercourse Act) would be impossible to enforce. He wrote to the president, "As to the hope that it may . . . induce England to treat us better, I think it entirely groundless. . . . Government prohibitions do always more mischief than had been calculated." New England in particular found many ways to evade the law, from driving cattle across the Canadian border to smuggling by sea through Halifax, Nova Scotia. There was flagrant abuse of the embargo's "special permission" clause by Connecticut customs collectors happy to grant profitable exemptions. The dollar value of that illicit commerce can only be guessed at, but there is no question of the impact on legal trade: officially, between 1807 and 1808 exports fell from $108,343,150 to $22,430,960; inevitably, legal imports plummeted as well, from $138,500,000 to $56,990,000.[22]

The complete embargo lasted only until the end of Jefferson's second term in 1809. The incoming Madison administration replaced it with the Non-Intercourse Act, which simply prohibited trade with England and France. Those were by far America's two largest trading partners, but this restriction proved easier to get around than the absolute ban had been, and commerce recovered somewhat, with merchants sailing to South America, Asia, and any European ports that remained open. Still, in 1810 imports and exports were less than half what they had been in 1807, and the economy was suffering. One might suppose historian Douglass North to be speaking of the Panic of 1819 when he writes, "Collapse in domestic prices, widespread unemployment, and the passage of stay laws against the seizure of property in the southern states testify to the severity of the collapse"; in fact, he is describing 1807 to 1812. But even in New England not everyone saw the embargo as an unmitigated evil. In Salem, Massachusetts, William Gray—the greatest merchant of the period—supported it; on August 12, 1808, the Salem *Gazette* printed a letter in which Gray declared his belief that "existing circumstances rendered it prudent and necessary," even though, "Far from reaping profit from the Embargo my estate has declined ten per cent in value." Connecticut's Oliver Wolcott Jr. not only found the embargo necessary but, looking back in 1820, saw the net result as positive:

> The embargo, though injurious to some interests, was, in my opinion, advantageous to the country. It arrested [foreign] commerce, which had generally become a losing concern; it disengaged our merchants from a too-intimate connection with British finance, and compelled them to settle their accounts; it secured a great capital from the rapacity of a foreign nation; it disclosed the weak parts of our public policy; above all it was the cause of a great number of manufacturing establishments, which, though now inactive [in the aftermath of the Panic], can be easily revived with great benefit to the country.

Among those "manufacturing establishments" were textile mills that Wolcott and his brother had opened following the embargo.[23]

As early as 1810 Gallatin was explaining to Congress that there was a hidden benefit to the reduction of international trade: "A great American capital has been acquired during the last twenty years and the injurious violations of the Neutral commerce of the United States, by forcing industry and capital into other channels, have broken inveterate habits, and given a general impulse, to which must be ascribed the great increase of manufacturing during the last two years."[24]

The increase of manufacturing was indeed great, and Gallatin went on to acknowledge other causes in addition to the newly available capital: "The cheapness of provisions had always, to a certain extent, counterbalanced the high price of manual labor; and this is now, in many important branches, nearly superseded by the introduction of machinery." That combination of factors now fueled an expansion of the American economy—the beginning of the economic bubble. The cost of "provisions"—especially cotton, nearly all of which had previously been bound for England—was down thanks to the embargo. Wages had always been relatively high in America because it was so easy for laborers to move west and become landowners—never more so than between 1804 and 1820, when public land was available cheap and on easy terms. "The introduction of machinery," however, made all the difference. Eli Whitney had invented his cotton gin in 1793, and the jealously guarded secrets of Richard Arkwright's water-powered spinning frames had already been spirited out of England by a pioneer of industrial espionage, Samuel Slater. In 1790 Slater had promised Moses Brown, "If I do not make as good yarn, as they do in England, I will have nothing for my services, but will throw the whole of what I have attempted over the bridge."[25]

Before 1808 there had been only fifteen cotton mills in the United States: five in operation by 1804 (including the firm of Almy, Brown, and Slater) and ten more added between 1804 and 1808. Just one year later, sheltered from British competition by the effects of the embargo, eighty-seven new mills were in operation—an increase of nearly 600 percent. The number of active spindles grew from eight thousand to thirty-one thousand in a single year and by 1811 it had risen to eighty thousand. America, an almost entirely agricultural nation, suddenly had an industry—and investors were eager to get in on the boom.[26]

New England's shipping might be in the doldrums, but the middle states were humming. The *United States Gazette*, published in Philadelphia, described that bustling city a year and a half into the embargo:

> The embargo has as yet produced *comparatively* little inconvenience in this city and its neighborhood. During the last winter, we began to suffer from the domiciliary visits of laborers, *in forma pauperis*, who could not find employment and were obliged to beg; but generally the stores laid in by poor men before the embargo, were sufficient to keep want from their doors until the spring opened; since when the unexampled improvements in our city have given constant employment to eight or ten thousand of them.[27]

"Unexampled improvements" continued: from 1809 to 1811 the value of goods manufactured in Philadelphia jumped from $10 million to $16 million. The city was home to 273 looms, four woolen mills, seventeen carriage makers, twenty-eight soap and candle makers, seven paper mills, ten sugar refineries, twenty nail factories, twenty-four brush factories, and three glass works. Cotton processing machinery and steam engines were now being manufactured there as well. Another Philadelphia paper, *Prices Current*, devoted an article to the growth of manufacturing during the embargo. The editor—a loyal Republican—sent a copy to Jefferson "to prove that by the President's originating partial deprivations, he has ultimately bestowed on his country immense and imperishable benefits." Immense they may have been, if not quite imperishable. For the moment, however, editor Samuel

Relf could boast of the manufacture of carpets, calico cloth, shawls, bedspreads, earthenware, glassware, soap, lead shot, and a variety of chemicals.[28]

The embargo, so bitterly resented in New England seaports, created an environment in New York, Baltimore, and Philadelphia that seemed to promise freedom from economic dependence on Britain and improved conditions for both the rich and the humble. Historian Cathy Matson calls it "a ripe moment for merchants with capital, 'projectors' with plans for new enterprises, and banks with liberal credit to combine in a concerted drive for manufacturing." Charles Jared Ingersoll wrote *A View of the Rights and Wrongs, Power and Policy of the United States of America* in 1808:

> Who that walks the streets of Philadelphia and sees, notwithstanding a twelvemonths stagnation of trade, several hundred substantial and elegant houses building, and the laboring community employed at good wages; . . . who perceives, wherever he goes the bustle of industry and the smile of content; who under such circumstances, that is not too stupid to perceive, and too prejudiced to believe what he does perceive, can doubt the solid capital of this country?

Ingersoll, George Mifflin Dallas, Tench Coxe, and Matthew Carey founded the Philadelphia Manufacturing Society that year. Even as the Embargo Act and the Non-Intercourse Act were swept aside by a declaration of war in 1812, there was confidence that the country's capital would remain sound and its benefits imperishable. And the war itself, despite the fright when Washington, D.C., was burned, gave little reason to doubt that optimistic outlook.[29]

The declaration of war with England came as no surprise, but it nevertheless caused initial shocks in the economy. The inexperienced U.S. Navy, in warships like USS *Constitution,* had early victories over a shocked Royal Navy, but before long the vastly more powerful British fleet had imposed an effective blockade on American seaports, and imports which had briefly risen to $77 million by 1812 fell quickly to $22 million the next year and just under $13 million in 1814—a low for the entire nineteenth century. Exports fared even worse, falling under $28 million in 1813 and below $7 million in 1814, less than a third what they had been even during the embargo and barely 6 percent of the high point of 1807. The value of tobacco exports, which had already been declining, now dropped sharply, and while smuggling with Canada continued, the profitable West Indies market was no longer available.

With the effective British naval blockade, the American economy had become something of a closed system—albeit a leaky one, since smuggling never ended and foreign loans could still be found. Farmers no longer had access to the European market, but they could now sell to expanding domestic manufacturers; manufacturers had no foreign competition to deal with, and capital that was no longer invested in trade came to them instead. The wartime government bought from American manufacturers and borrowed from American banks, mainly in the Mid-Atlantic states. Tecumseh's War and the Creek War kept farmers from expanding westward, but domestic textile mills could handle no more than farmers' current production anyway—and *their* expansion was potentially limited by the number of American consumers. When the fighting finally ended and the system was thrown open, farmers could and did rapidly expand into the newly pacified Northwest and Southwest, eager to meet elevated European demand. Then manufacturers, suddenly competing with imports that Britain was dumping below market prices, would clamor for protective tariffs that farmers opposed. But from 1812 to 1815 mills, iron foundries, and other industries thrived in the hothouse environment.

An economic bubble had begun to inflate. As the first mills to open made impressive profits, investors were eager to follow, but by early 1813 the early windfalls were over; the cheap cotton had been bought up quickly, and prices were rapidly rising. James D'Wolf was one of the foresightful few: "Made very large profits 20 to 30 per cent per annum, both from the cause of having purchased a large stock of cotton at a low price, before our coasting trade was interrupted by the enemy, and the very high price of goods made." Others were not so successful, and most mills cut back production as profits slipped. The large firm of Almy & Brown, the only company whose records were available for Henry Stettler's *Growth and Fluctuation of the Antebellum Textile Industry*, curtailed production by 25 percent before the end of the war. Stettler's conclusion: "Increased competition and manufacturing costs more than offset the benefits of a war-related increase in demand."[30]

In New England mills continued to open, but only the innovative would succeed. Francis Cabot Lowell's first water-powered mill was up and running in 1814, its design stolen from English models but improved upon by Lowell and his successors. The Lowell mill became the great model for antebellum industrialization, but many other late-arriving mills failed, and with the coming of peace the number of new incorporations fell from forty-three in 1814 to fifteen "competitive" mills in 1815, six in 1816, three in 1817, four in 1818, and three in the panic year of 1819. Taking in all kinds of manufacturing, state legislatures incorporated 128 enterprises in 1814, seventy-eight in 1815, twenty-six in 1816, and a total of only twenty-eight in the next three years combined. Many failed before 1820. Even though manufacturing profits declined during the war, other outlets for capital investment (including trade, fisheries, and privateering) offered even less, "rendered unprofitable by the British blockade."[31]

One other economic activity prospered despite the blockade: smuggling. In 1820, Oliver Wolcott Jr. (whose cotton mills in Connecticut suffered from competition with untaxed, illegal imports) wrote,

After the war commenced the illicit trade became exceedingly pernicious. The imports were principally of British manufactures, for which payment was wholly in money [i.e., specie]. It was to arrest the progress of this trade . . . that the banks of New-York and Philadelphia suspended payment in money. If this measure had been adopted at an earlier period, a great capital would have been preserved to the country, which was worse than lost by checking the progress of domestic manufactures and diminishing the ability of the banks to support public credit.[32]

Smuggling may not have been the primary reason that domestic manufactures struggled, but there is no doubt that it contributed to the drain in capital, and not only in New England. In the words of Smith and Cole, "Wagon loads of silver dollars were finding their way to Canada in return for British Treasury bills sold in all our Atlantic seacoast cities," bills with which smuggled British goods were purchased. New York had once paid for its imports through the re-export trade; in 1807 nearly two-thirds of the city's exports had been re-exports, but from 1812 to 1814 all that was gone. Now specie was siphoned out of the city across the Canadian border or through a blockade that smugglers found to be porous.[33]

Both illegal and legal manufactured goods were also sold to the United States government. Stettler points out that in the state of New York, nineteen of twenty-three businesses that incorporated in 1813, and twenty-three of thirty-two the following year, were located upstate, "adjacent to a major theater of military operations." New England was happy to undertake lucrative government contracts. The government paid for war materiel with notes and drafts from the banks of the Mid-Atlantic cities, which piled up in Boston banks. But New England, dominated by Federalists who had depended on trade with England, was otherwise unwilling to support the war effort; in fact, the Boston *Gazette* threatened, "If James Madison is not out of office, a new form of government will be in operation in the eastern section of the Union." Madison was hanged in effigy in Augusta, Maine. Huge anti-war rallies were held in Boston's Faneuil Hall, and the Massachusetts House voted 406 to 240 to denounce the war as "awful" and "revolting."[34]

The Bank of the United States had been obliged by its charter to lend money to the U.S. government on demand, but its charter had expired in 1811, and the Bank had closed. With no revenue from import duties, and with no more BUS, the federal government faced the challenge of paying its bills for the War of 1812. Even the world's greatest financial power, Great Britain, had been forced by its French wars to suspend specie payment and swell its national debt to 200 percent of GDP. Gouverneur Morris, living in retirement at his Morrisania estate in New York, vividly remembered his struggles as Assistant Superintendent of Finance during the Revolutionary War. Now he wrote to his old Federalist colleague Rufus King that paying for the present war was like "the project of putting the world on an Elephant's Back to stand on a Tortoise and he on nothing."[35]

Morris and King had been delegates to the 1787 Constitutional Convention, where they had been among the most loyal lieutenants of James Madison, the convention's dominant figure. Madison had split with them—and with another former ally, Alexander Hamilton—when he opposed chartering the First Bank of the United States. In 1791 Madison had argued that the BUS was nowhere authorized by the Constitution, but twenty years later, after a term as president, he had changed his mind about its necessity. He and his treasury secretary (still Gallatin) had supported the 1811 effort to renew the charter; Henry Clay, who would later be one of the Bank's best-paid attorneys, was then a senator who voted against the bill, as did South Carolina Rep. Langdon Cheves, the future president of the Second Bank of the United States. Their votes were enough: recharter failed by one vote in the House and one in the Senate.

To fund the war—which Clay had vociferously demanded as a leading War Hawk—there was little for Madison and Gallatin to do now but borrow wherever they could, and borrow they did: $11 million in 1812, $15.5 million in 1813, $13 million in 1814, and $9.5 million in 1815, at 6 percent interest. In 1813 much of the bond offering was bought by the wealthy merchants Jacob Barker, John Jacob Astor, and David Parish, along with the Philadelphia financier Stephen Girard. United States bonds were sold on the European market by Baring Brothers Bank, of London, which had earlier arranged the financing of the Louisiana Purchase—once again, loyalty to clients overcame any qualms about patriotism. But it was banks in New York, Philadelphia, and Baltimore, paying with their own notes redeemable (for the moment) in specie, that bought the bulk of the bonds issued. As Smith and Cole note, "New England would have none of them. Opposition to the war was so strong in that quarter that the Boston *Gazette* urged its readers not to purchase war stocks."[36]

In 1790, before Hamilton persuaded Congress to charter the First BUS, there had been only three incorporated banks in the entire country: Philadelphia's Bank of North America, which had made the country's first initial public offering of corporate stock in 1781, and the Bank of New York and the Massachusetts Bank in Boston, both chartered in 1784. Their primary function was to extend short-term credit to merchants, covering them from the time they purchased cargo until the time they were paid for it. In 1791 the Bank of the United States had opened with $10 million in stock ($2 million paid in by the national government). It was the only truly national corporation in the country, and it dwarfed not only every other bank but every other business. The BUS charter required it to hold the deposits of the United States, pay all government debts on demand, and lend the government money when called upon. Specie was already scarce enough that gold and silver could never provide a circulating medium for commerce, and the Constitution prohibited the issue of paper money by states. Consequently, notes of the Bank of the United States became the *de facto* currency of the nation, the only paper money accepted in payment of federal taxes. Individual promissory notes also circulated widely, but they were risky—as Andrew Jackson learned to his lasting, bitter regret in 1796. Jackson had traveled to Philadelphia to sell several thousand acres of western land to a wealthy merchant and speculator, David Allison. Allison paid in personal notes, which Jackson promptly endorsed and used to purchase merchandise he planned to sell in Tennessee. But Allison's business failed, and he defaulted on his notes. Jackson was left holding the bag, personally liable for the promissory notes he had endorsed. It would be 1815 before he was free of the debts he had incurred because of the "paper system." In 1819, although Jackson by then had $22,000 in the

Nashville bank of his friend John Overton, he was forced to call in the notes of his own debtors in order to meet his obligations to his creditors after the Panic hit.[37]

In the vacuum left by the BUS closure in 1811, state banks proliferated rapidly. During the war years another eighty banks were incorporated—twice the rate of growth of the previous four years—and capital increased by 74 percent, to $115.2 million. The total number of banks by the war's end had reached 181 by a conservative count (although numbers as high as 208 have been claimed—the uncertainty stems from the problem that some banks received charters but never actually opened for business, while others opened without charters). That count does not include private banks like Stephen Girard's or banks like Ohio's notorious Owl Creek Bank, one of many joint stock companies that did not bother with the formality of a bill of incorporation by the legislature. During the War of 1812, after all BUS notes had been retired, the value of state banknotes in circulation rose from $2.3 million to $4.6 million.[38]

As the War of 1812 drove prices steadily up, circulating currency was suddenly in urgent demand. It is impossible to know how many unchartered banks came and went or how much paper they issued, but the explosion of banks incorporated by state legislatures is itself breathtaking. Pennsylvania's omnibus banking act of 1814 chartered thirty-seven new banks in a single stroke, nearly a tenfold increase in that state. They quickly placed $7,681,264 in banknotes into circulation—more than the total issued by all of the nation's banks in 1812. (At least ten of those Pennsylvania banks had previously operated without charters, which suggests that unincorporated banks were more common than is often thought.) New York doubled the number of its banks by 1818, Maryland went from six to twenty-four, and even the frontier territories of Indiana and Missouri chartered banks—the latter state's Bank of St. Louis operating (for security) out of a cellar dug into a hillside.[39]

Banking theory was primitive and largely unknown to many new bank directors; state regulations were sketchy. As the head cashier and president would vividly demonstrate in 1819 at the Baltimore branch of the BUS, bank officers could invent dishonest schemes faster than state legislatures could think to outlaw them. Most banks were run by directors with no banking experience; the majority were merchants, planters, speculators, or all three at once. Many directors held government offices. Their conflicts of interest were inevitable but not, at the time, illegal. From Massachusetts to Mississippi, locally influential men acquired bank charters, buying stock with promissory notes that were backed by nothing more than the value of the shares themselves. Bank stock might be resold at a profit, but most bank directors went in with the aim of lending themselves their banks' notes—and now they literally had a license to print money.[40]

Inexperienced bankers were irresponsible with both loans and the issue of banknotes, but the public demanded more of both. Much specie was leaving the country through smuggling, and none was coming in. Many small banks never intended to redeem their notes in specie—they had next to none of it—but by the spring of 1814 even sound, reputable banks like Philadelphia's Bank of Pennsylvania, Bank of North America, Philadelphia Bank, and Farmers and Mechanics Bank were feeling the stress; wholesale merchants were accepting payments "in hugely inflated forms of paper from the interior—notes that were then refused when merchants presented them at Philadelphia banks." Increasingly, specie reserves were siphoned into New England. The federal government borrowed from middle-state banks and then paid with their notes for war materiel in the Northeast. Boston banks were not only averse to lending to the government; they were also unwilling to leave open balances at the Mid-Atlantic banks that *were* making those loans. As a matter of policy, they returned all deposited notes at once to the issuing banks outside New England, demanding redemption in silver. The interstate balance of trade favored New England, and New England wanted to be paid in cash—in specie. As a result, the combined specie reserves of the Massachusetts, Boston, and Union banks (none of which made loans to the government) grew from $1,805,505.03 in January 1812 to $3,500,202.07 in January 1813, and to $3,954,510.87 in January 1814.[41]

Condy Raguet, himself a Philadelphia banker, described what happened: "The stoppage of specie payments . . . in 1814 commenced in Baltimore about the 27th of August, soon after the Battle of Bladensburgh and the capture of Washington, which events took place on the 24th of the month, and was followed by Philadelphia on the 30th and by New York on the 1st of September." Two days after the White House was burned by the British army, the big New York banks met as previously scheduled to discuss commercial credit. While the meeting was going on, word reached them that six Baltimore and Philadelphia banks had agreed to suspend specie payment: they would no longer redeem their notes in silver or gold coins. The New York bankers at first resolved not to suspend, but by September 2, when news reached New York of the attacks on Washington and Baltimore, they did so after all. *Niles' Register*, in March 1815, reported that specie redemption had by then stopped in Washington, D.C., Maryland, Pennsylvania, New York, New Jersey, Virginia, Ohio, and Kentucky. Sixteen or eighteen "less reputable" banks in New England, according to the *Register*, did not formally stop payment but "used the suspension as a pretext to pay or not pay, as circumstances direct."[42]

Smith and Cole, following such contemporary witnesses as Wolcott, maintain that "the invasion was, of course, merely the pretext for the suspension" that would continue for two years after the war had ended. "The main cause was the redistribution of the specie of the country, which gave New England an embarrassingly large share, while a minor cause was the drain of silver to Canada." New England bankers of this period are often characterized as more conservative in their practices, and it is true that they loaned mainly to investors they knew personally. Moreover, their banknotes were not circulated as freely because there were so many other notes locally available from banks in other regions. It was already clear that not all banknotes were of equal value. In 1814, notes of New England banks circulated at par; in other words, a ten-dollar note was accepted as the equivalent of ten dollars in silver and was received in payment of a ten-dollar debt. Elsewhere, silver was at a premium and banknotes were discounted. In New York or Charleston, a local bank's ten-dollar note would buy only $9.30 worth of goods. In Philadelphia, notes were at 85 percent of par, in Baltimore at 75 to 80 percent, "with every other possible variation in other places and states." Still, banknotes were the only available currency; under those conditions, no one who actually possessed silver or gold coins would be so foolish as to spend them. The big Boston banks did not suspend specie redemption, so New Englanders held onto those banks' more valuable notes. Banks everywhere continued to do business as usual, and as Daniel Webster and others repeatedly complained in Congress, their profits were "extravagant" even as suspension continued through 1815 and 1816.[43]

In the final months of the war, as American negotiators were seeking acceptable peace terms at Ghent, the government was having serious trouble selling bonds. In desperation, Congress doubled the direct tax and postage rates and increased inland revenue taxes, but all taxes together yielded only $4 million, and government spending in 1814 had reached $35.4 million. By the end of 1815 the national debt stood at twice its 1812 level. The Virginia conservatives known variously as the Richmond Junto or the Tertium Quid ("third thing"—neither Republican nor Federalist) continued to deny the constitutional authority of Congress to charter a bank, but many of their former allies—including Madison and the recently converted Henry Clay—sorely missed the BUS, with its dependable banknotes and government loans on demand.[44]

Clay and his fellow peace commissioners (John Quincy Adams, Albert Gallatin, James A. Bayard, and Jonathan Russell) signed the Treaty of Ghent on Christmas Eve 1814, although the distant fighting continued. The fastest way to send news was still to carry it in person; by the time ships brought news of the treaty to Washington in mid-February, the January 8 Battle of New Orleans had already made a hero of Andrew Jackson. News of peace was met with joy in some places, apprehension in others. The British commissioners at Ghent had abandoned their demands for a Native American buffer state between the Ohio valley and Canada—a disaster for the tribes there but welcome news for settlers in the Northwest. Tecumseh's confederation had already disintegrated with his death in 1813, and the Creek resistance in the Mississippi Territory was collapsing in 1814. While the end of the war was a relief for the West, it inspired much more ambiguous feelings in the cities along the Atlantic coast. Boston businessmen were torn between satisfaction at the resumption of transatlantic trade and worry over the future of New England's vulnerable new textile industry. Even as consumers welcomed the return of British imports, factories in the middle states dreaded the inevitable drop in their profits; only a month after the news of the treaty, Philadelphia prices had fallen more than 20 percent, beginning "a roller coaster of wild price fluctuations during 1816 and 1817—wilder than at any time between the Revolution and the Civil War." By the end of 1817 prices would be barely half what they had been at the beginning of 1815.[45]

On the other side of the Atlantic, British manufacturers were desperate for a market. The prospect of an end to the war with Napoleon led to a short-lived wave of exports to Europe, an exporting frenzy that, as Henry Brougham pointed out in Parliament, soon broke like the South Sea and Mississippi bubbles of the previous century. Europe was impoverished by twenty years of war and simply lacked the capacity to absorb very much of the backlog that filled the warehouses of the British manufacturers. America, emerging from a much shorter war relatively undamaged and eager to satisfy a pent-up demand for imports, looked like the only answer.[46]

In England 1815 was a year of turmoil. Initial optimism was shaken by Napoleon's return from Elba and the Hundred Days; following Waterloo, a speculative boom ended in credit collapse, business failures, and declining prices. By 1816 the economy was in deep depression. The iron and coal industries were idle, the wheat crop had failed, and there were intermittent riots by underemployed, underpaid laborers. To stave off a true workers' rebellion, it was imperative to keep factories operating, even as they lost money. On April 9, Brougham's words to Parliament were blunt: "It was well worthwhile to incur a loss upon the first exportation in order by glut to stifle in the cradle those rising manufactures in the United States which the war has forced into existence contrary to the usual course of nature." Brougham's speech would be widely reprinted in America.[47]

Anticipating the signing of the Treaty of Ghent, British ships had begun restocking the warehouses of Nova Scotia and Bermuda in late 1814. American commodity merchants were just as eager to put their exports back on the European market, where there was a much greater demand for American raw materials than for British manufactured goods. The news of the treaty reached New York in February of 1815; between March and September, $46 million in exports went out from that city and the other American seaports—but twice that value in British goods surged into the country. Imports came through Boston, Philadelphia, and Baltimore, but above all through New York, at prices that fell 15 percent the first year, another 20 percent the next, and still another 15 percent in 1817, despite the nation's first protective tariff in 1816. The total value of imports received in 1816—even at dramatically lowered prices—would not be matched until 1835.[48]

The flood of cheap goods was a blow to American manufacturers, but one that they were anticipating. (Tench Coxe bravely declared that "nothing can deprive us of our established manufacturers. They have passed the infantile stage and are now adult.") An equally powerful but unanticipated blow was the means by which they would be sold. Before the war, British goods had been purchased at wholesale by American merchants, whose business depended on the profits from their resale. A merchant named Abraham Thompson claimed credit for introducing a new system that bypassed the importers, to their dismay but to the delight of both consumers and British manufacturers. In a letter published by *Merchant's Magazine and Commercial Review*, Thompson boasted, "In the spring of 1815 I commenced the auction system in this city, in company with Mr. James Boggs, and during the remainder of that year, and the whole of 1816, the sales at auction and private sales were very extensive, and brought large numbers of purchasers, and many new customers, to the city of New York."[49]

Here was a double shock for New England. The new textile industry was being undersold at prices it could not match, and now Boston's dominance as a commercial port was being stolen by New York. Thompson had no sympathy:

From 1783 to 1817, Boston was the first importing city of the union, and the New York merchants purchased there most of their goods. . . . [F]rom 1812 to the spring of 1815, the period of the last war, Boston was comparatively a free port. It was supposed to be the policy of the British government not to blockade that port; but whatever may have been the motives or the causes it is certain that Boston during the war was comparatively well supplied with European and India goods, and that through that city New England received her supplies.

Now, in a shift that proved permanent, New York replaced Boston as the primary port of entry from Europe, and soon from India and China as well.[50]

Auction sales made it easy for importers to evade tariffs: goods were sold below cost to an agent of the manufacturer, who paid a correspondingly low tariff and then sold the goods at a higher price to a second agent, who then auctioned them. Bypassed warehouse owners lost rent, fewer clerks were employed, and the city lost revenue from merchants' licenses. The profits would be made from the price of the credit extended to auction houses themselves, to the retailers in the hinterland who sold the goods to their ultimate consumers, and to the wholesale jobbers who assembled shipments to those small-town retailers.[51]

For many in New York the city's new dominance of the import market came at too high a price. The New York *Evening Post* of January 11, 1817 printed a "memorial" by city merchants to the state legislature, a petition calling for a prohibitory tax that would end auction sales. Once again, the resourceful Abraham Thompson stepped in. He went to Albany and persuaded Governor Daniel Tompkins to let him draft instead a bill *reducing* the existing duties—with the result that now the India trade also abandoned Boston for New York, and state revenues actually increased, a result which, said Thompson, "aided materially the state of New York in in her payment of the canal debts" that were soon to come. The lower duties ensured lower prices that "drew merchants or purchasers from all parts of our widely extended country, which tended directly to enhance the value of houses, stores, and lots—multiplying the business of the shipper, importer, and jobber . . . and made our merchants princes."[52]

Baltimore merchants, led by the powerful firm of Smith and Buchanan, were divided on the auction system. Samuel Smith, who also represented

Baltimore in Congress, suggested a federal tax of 1 or 2 percent—the same tax New York imposed. He resisted proposals to set a higher rate. Philadelphia merchants, more strongly opposed, sent a memorial to Congress complaining of the "pernicious effects" of the auction system there. Cathy Matson notes that after Congress, in 1817, instead *repealed* the wartime 3 percent tax on auctions, "through the following months, sheriffs sold distressed and forfeited properties on a daily basis at the auction houses of Philadelphia, and increasing numbers of British auction agents advertised cheap goods for sale at the same sites." Only in Boston, the port that had lost the most business to New York auctions, were opponents successful—temporarily. Here, in one of the last outposts of the Federalist Party, merchants persuaded the selectmen and the General Court of Massachusetts (the state legislature) to begin seriously taxing auctions in 1819.[53]

Many of the smaller, less established, or less efficient mills were failing as the market was inundated by cheap imported textiles at auction prices; others reduced production or shut their doors to wait for the flood to subside. Cloth production in New England in 1816 fell to its lowest level since 1812. Between 1810 and 1815 the number of mills had nearly doubled from 76 to 140 within a thirty-mile radius of Providence—the national center of the textile industry—but the British dumping of cheap cloth caused many of those to close for good. Samuel Slater's mill there survived; so did the new Lowell mill at Waltham, Massachusetts, the country's most efficient. But below-cost imports were devastating to other new mills that had sprung up during the war. Output of "infant industries" around Philadelphia, including the recently established cotton manufactories, declined by 60 percent between 1815 and mid-1817.[54]

The newly formed Philadelphia Society for the Promotion of American Manufactures declared "a state of great depression" by the end of 1817. While the large coastal cities were the most conspicuous victims, the interior suffered as well. In Pittsburgh, a committee set up in December 1816 reported that "the manufacture of Cottons and Woollens [*sic*], Flint Glass and the finer articles of Iron, has lately suffered the most alarming depression." In the two years following the first wave of imports, the value of Pittsburgh's iron production fell from $764,200 to $525,616; brass and tin production from $249,633 to $200,000, and textiles from $115,500 to $82,000. Overall, the city's industrial output soon lost 14 percent of its value, statewide real estate values would soon fall by one-third—and the Panic of 1819 itself was still to come.[55]

Pittsburgh, at the head of the Ohio River, was already a major distributor to the more rural West. With a population in 1820 of 7,300 it was the country's twenty-third largest city, and two-thirds of its residents were supported by manufacturing. West of the Alleghenies only New Orleans and Cincinnati were larger. Lancaster, Pennsylvania, though smaller, had been connected to Philadelphia since 1795 by the Lancaster Turnpike, the nation's first long-distance paved road. In this Pennsylvania Dutch market town, investors had opened a small cotton mill at the very end of the war. They produced, on American-designed looms, a medium-coarse grade of cloth that was sold mainly to country stores and peddlers. Sixty miles from the nearest seaport, its relative isolation helped it survive the British dumping through 1815 and 1816, but such country mills often found themselves at the mercy of the big city merchants and importers, who controlled the extension of credit to inland retailers. After 1815 some country mills could not even place their goods in the very towns where they operated. In Massachusetts critics of both the auction system and the established merchants were hardly exaggerating when they railed against "a monopoly which is to be satisfied with nothing short of . . . the subjection of every country trader to the will of the importer."[56]

Credit, of several varieties, was a bone of contention. Baltimore merchants objected to "an immense stock of foreign merchandise" being sent "into the interior—generally on extended credits," with the result that "the interior of the country now stands largely indebted to the merchants of the seaport towns, while the latter are scarcely less in debt to foreign countries." More frustrating still than the greed of the importers was the apparent willingness of the U.S. government to facilitate a corrupt system; those same Baltimore merchants saw the root of the problem in the Treasury Department's policy of granting importers credit for customs duties instead of requiring payment in cash. In New York City, the center of importation, Ferris Pell and his brother Alfred operated Pells and Company, an auction house. The Pell brothers, cronies of Governor DeWitt Clinton, would eventually be indicted for securities fraud, but Ferris was an astute observer of the times. He wrote, "A disposition to gratify present wishes, by availing of credit, was universal [and] to perfect the delusion, the system adopted by the National Government, of giving long credit upon duties, acted as a potent auxiliary. . . . British agents poured in floods of fabrics; the revenue laws were fraudulently evaded; and the losses sustained by the fair merchant were dreadful."[57]

The impact of such fraudulent evasion—or at least delay—of the revenue laws was not lost on Alexander Dallas, who had become secretary of the treasury when Gallatin declined reappointment and became minister to France. The national debt had increased during the war from $45 million in 1812 to $119 million in 1815, and Dallas was not expecting any help soon from import duties. On February 20, 1815, with the news of the Treaty of Ghent, he wrote to the chairman of the House Ways and Means Committee, J. W. Eppes, "The West Indies trade will produce little and the European trade nothing, by way of revenue, before the first of May next. . . . [A] credit of eight, ten, and twelve months is allowed for the duties on merchandise imported from Europe and . . . a credit of three and six months is allowed for the duties on merchandise imported from the West Indies."[58]

Dallas was painfully aware of the need for increased revenues. Manufacturers were calling for prohibitive duties that would end the competition from imports—but would thus end revenue from import duties, which Treasury depended upon. Dallas's compromise, the Tariff of 1816, was an attempt to strike a balance between the two goals. It found broad support. Although Francis Lowell was one of the few cotton manufacturers who was still making profits, he lobbied Congress for a tariff on low-priced imported cotton. Lowell cannily advocated a minimum evaluation of twenty-five cents per square yard, regardless of any lower value that might be claimed on invoices, along with a minimum duty of six and one quarter cents per yard—just high enough to exclude the coarse cloth that competed with Lowell's own power-loom sheet cotton, but not enough to protect the slightly higher-grade cloth produced at the Lancaster mill or to keep out the English calicos that competed with Rhode Island's gingham.[59]

Secretary Dallas presented his tariff proposal to Congress in March 1816; the bill, incorporating Lowell's suggestions, passed on April 27. Its duties averaged 25 percent *ad valorem*, actually less than the duties that had prevailed during the war. It produced the revenue that Dallas had been counting on. Having put the Treasury back on the positive side of the ledger, a seriously ill Dallas announced his resignation. Two weeks before taking his place, his successor William Crawford wrote to Gallatin on October 9, "In many respects the nation was never more prosperous. American articles of almost every description bring the highest prices and many of the articles of foreign growth or manufacture are sold at first cost." In his initial Treasury Report on December 20, Crawford reflected the growing national optimism. He forecast that the 1816 revenue would be close to $47 million (the first three quarters having brought in $39 million—more than all of 1815) and he projected budget surpluses of over $8 million for 1818, 1819, and 1820. The following

October, he told President Monroe that it was time to abolish internal revenues. Congress agreed with him, and in April of 1818 Rep. Burwell Bassett reported to his constituents, "The situation of the treasury enabled us to take off all the internal taxes, leaving the means of reducing the public debt as rapidly as the conditions of the contracts would allow."[60]

The tariff had been cast as a defense of national economic security, and it had attracted bipartisan support, even in the South. The first American tariff to acknowledge a frankly protective purpose, it passed in the House 88 to 54, with even Federalists giving it a bare majority (despite Daniel Webster's opposition). Republicans voted for it by a margin of two to one, led by Speaker Henry Clay and opposed by John Randolph and the other Quids. The limited opposition in the Senate was made up of three Old Republicans from Virginia and North Carolina and four Federalists from New England and Maryland. John C. Calhoun, still a nationalist in 1816, was simultaneously backing a bill to charter the Second Bank of the United States. He saw both tariff and the Bank as questions of national security and economic independence. In some future war, Britain could cut off the delivery of essential goods; moreover, this was an opportunity to reduce the war debt. Calhoun and William Lowndes, also of South Carolina, argued that the tariff would protect both planters and manufacturers from the threat of cheap cotton products from India. "When our manufactures are grown to a certain perfection, as they soon will be under the fostering care of government . . . the farmer will find a ready market for his surplus produce; and what is almost of equal consequence, a certain and cheap supply of his wants. His prosperity will diffuse itself to every class in the community." The tariff would indeed succeed in keeping out competing yarn and fabric, but it could not protect southern planters from the eventual English decision to buy raw cotton from India. It would be the last tariff to win broad southern support.[61]

The tariff provided a limited degree of protection for manufacturers. The overall value of imports to the United States peaked in 1816, dropped off in 1817, and rebounded in 1818 before plummeting during the panic year of 1819 and continuing to decline each year until 1822. The Slater and Tiffany mill in Massachusetts had been forced to decrease its production after the war, but it would rise partway back in the years following the tariff: the 59,000 pounds of cotton yarn it sold in 1815 fell to 23,000 in 1816 and climbed back as far as 37,000 in each of the next two years. But the moderate tariff could not save others from closing for good. *Niles' Register* continued to publish demands for greater protection made by Matthew Carey's Philadelphia Society for Promoting Domestic Manufactures, and Tench Coxe, an inveterate protectionist, insisted that "a natural and practicable mean of diminishing that inconvenience [of cheap cotton imports] may be the prevention, by law, of the consumption of cotton goods, in the United States, made out of cotton produced by foreign soils and foreign populations." Southern planters listened, but after 1816 they would never again risk their export market or accept higher prices for the manufactured goods they needed. Pittsburgh, despite the tariff, would not begin to recover until 1823. Lexington, Kentucky, home of Henry Clay, had been a booming center of hemp processing and cotton bag manufacturing; it never regained its place as an industrial city, falling steadily behind Louisville, which became a steamboat hub on the Ohio. Georgia cotton would now be packaged for shipment to Liverpool mills in bags manufactured in Scotland—made out of Georgia cotton. More societies for the protection of domestic manufactures began to appear in 1817 in Delaware, Pennsylvania, and New York, and in 1819 even in the city of Cincinnati, which by then had been prostrated by the Panic and its ensuing depression. The following year, Matthew Carey would declare that the Panic itself had simply lifted "the veil that obscured the appalling vision of public distress" that had existed since 1815 in manufacturing cities.[62]

The years of embargo and war were over, leaving America free to expand west but deeply in debt, a nation with many more factories and many more banks, but without a sound currency. The cotton-exporting South and the commercial East had both been hit hard by embargo and war, but there had been some lasting changes: now New England bought southern cotton and sold its manufactures to the rest of the country on favorable terms. The large specie reserves of Boston banks had stopped growing when specie suspension became the rule elsewhere; *Niles' Register* was sure that in New England "many are now wallowing in great wealth, amassed by the 'smuggling trade' during the late war," but merchants and manufacturers were struggling, and unemployment increased in the large cities. The difficult years from 1807 to 1816 had sharply revealed regional differences that threatened to divide America into separate societies—maybe separate nations—even as the different regions were coming to depend more and more upon inter-regional exchange.[63]

The decade that followed the War of 1812 would bring in a Transportation Revolution and a Market Revolution, transforming American life. A Second Bank of the United States would be chartered—but so would hundreds of local banks of all degrees of reliability. The collapse of Indian resistance opened both the Northwest (Ohio, Indiana, Illinois, and Michigan) and Southwest (Alabama and Mississippi) to settlers and speculators, all eager to borrow in order to buy land where farmers might raise the crops that were— briefly—bringing record prices. Hopeful Americans turned their backs on the stagnant East and looked to the promising farmlands of the West; the 1820 census is the only one in history to report a *decrease* in the urban share of the population. The great westward migration would sweep both northern and southern settlers into the lands of the Louisiana Purchase—but millions of dollars in bonds from that purchase would soon be due, payable in gold or silver that the government did not have. And as the influx of settlers enabled the Missouri Territory to apply for statehood, America would face its first great crisis over slavery: Jefferson's "fire bell in the night."

The nation had survived what was already being called its second war of independence, and Americans faced the future with hope. The New York *Post* recalled in 1821 about wartime and post-war: "The general rise in prices stimulated the farmers to borrow in order to expand productivity; the merchant to extend more liberal credit; and the importer, to increase his orders. Individuals of every profession speculated; inflation thus fed upon itself." As the economy expanded on a tide of paper money, the threat of economic collapse was also growing, but—like Missouri—it seemed far away, beyond the horizon.

THREE REVOLUTIONS
Market, Transportation, Corporation

Speaking at length—as he always did—in support of the proposed tariff of 1820, Henry Clay compared the nation that consumed its own produce to the idealized household of his Kentucky friend and neighbor, former governor Isaac Shelby:

> You will behold every member of his family clad in the produce of their own hands, and usefully employed—the spinning wheel and the loom in motion by daybreak. With what pleasure will his wife carry you into her neat dairy, lead you into her store house. . . . What the individual family of Isaac Shelby is, I wish to see the nation in the aggregate become.[1]

Shelby had in fact become wealthy through interstate commerce in livestock, and he and Clay both raised hemp for the cordage and sailcloth industries. Clay, like modern politicians, was happy to invoke a nostalgic image of rural domestic virtue, but the self-sufficient farm was already becoming a thing of the past. By 1820 the United States was entering its second year of depression following the Panic of 1819. There had been hard times before in American memory, but this depression was different because the country was now different; subsistence farming was rapidly giving way to an interdependent network of commercial activity, more and more people were employed for wages, and members of the middle class were, for the first time, investing in corporate stock.

Rich investors like Robert Morris ("the financier of the Revolution") had been wiped out when a speculative bubble burst in 1797, but the impact of that crash had been limited to the major cities and the well-to-do. A financial crisis in 1792 had sent Hamilton's former assistant treasury secretary, William Duer, to debtors' prison, but it was not much felt outside of New York and was over in a month or two. The Mississippi Bubble and South Sea Bubble were still remembered for their insider trading and stockholder panics, but they had happened on the other side of the ocean, in a world where only the privileged felt their effects. They remained cautionary tales, but they were now nearly a century in the past.[2]

The economic "pressure" that hit big-city merchants and northern cotton mills in 1815 and 1816 spread down the Ohio River in 1817 and 1818, struck western land speculators and southern planters in 1819, and reached St. Louis and the Missouri Territory by 1820. It was an unprecedented nationwide depression in an increasingly complex economy: it hurt farmers, mill hands, shopkeepers, and stockholders in turnpikes and canal companies. The extent of the "hard times" was only possible because regions of the country and sectors of the economy were linked together as never before.

The successors to Washington and Jefferson's Revolutionary generation were going through their own revolution—three of them, in fact: two that have become familiar as the Market Revolution and Transportation Revolution of the antebellum 1800s, and a less well-known Corporation Revolution that helped make the other two possible. For the first time, cash income became a part of almost every American's calculations. The new economy made enormous fortunes, but its greatest effects were achieved in the more modest strata of society: the small farmers who became commodity traders and the artisans who became manufacturers all connected local markets to regional and national networks. The historian Joyce Appleby argues that they had a greater effect on the transformation of the economy than bankers or factory owners. She underlines the market's importance even to many of the rural poor "for whom the conspicuous material advances of their lifetime cemented their attachment to both the nation and its economic prosperity." To Richard Ellis, one of the first historians to draw attention to the Market Revolution, it is "the key development that explains the transition from what is known as Jeffersonian Democracy to what is known as Jacksonian Democracy in United States History."[3]

The boundaries between the agrarian and the incipient capitalist were fluid. Farmers moving into the Ohio valley began marketing their surplus by the third year after their first crop; in Missouri it was the same story, with farmers moving as quickly as possible from subsistence to commercial farming, selling everything from tobacco, hemp, and livestock to bacon, linen, and cowhides. Gottfried Duden, one of many Germans who emigrated to the region around St. Louis, wrote that it was "the ambition of every farmer in Missouri to produce his own necessities." At that point, ambitious farmers could sell their surplus and "spend their cash with a much easier mind for luxury articles, for things of one's fancy." It was a short step to becoming an Isaac Shelby.[4]

Industry was by no means limited to factories; more manufacturing still took place in homes than elsewhere. "Outworking" was the means by which most shoes were made and cloth woven in the 1810s and 1820s. Perhaps the ultimate elaboration of this practice was the method of making the popular palm-leaf hats that shaded farmers from the sun. Boston wholesalers would have the leaves shipped from Cuba or the Virgin Islands and then sell them to storekeepers in New Hampshire or Massachusetts. The storekeepers split the leaves and then sold them (on credit) to their rural customers; they, in their homes, braided the leaves into hats which they sold back to the storekeeper for store credit. The finished hats were in turn delivered to Boston merchants who sold them to the plantation market of the South—and back to the West Indies. Slaves on the sugar plantations in the Caribbean were wearing hats made from local leaves that had traveled five thousand miles to return to the place where they were grown.[5]

One way or another, most people in the early nineteenth century were working for or selling to someone else. There was a hazy line between the Massachusetts farmwife doing piecework for Boston hat merchants and the small-town children employed in Rhode Island cotton mills. The national ambition was to move west and acquire land—by one estimate, two-thirds of the increase in per capita output in the first third of the century was due to the expansion of western farming, which provided each farmer so much more land to cultivate that it seemed "to push the point of diminishing returns to the infinitely receding horizon." The agricultural prosperity of the West—above all the growth of staples for export abroad or sale to eastern cities—transformed Ohio, Kentucky, Tennessee, Alabama, Mississippi, Louisiana, the upcountry of South Carolina, and central Georgia. But in the East, where farmers were already running out of fertile soil, that per capita growth came from manufacturing, which employed semi-skilled workers, some as young as six years old. Southern New England, much of New York, New Jersey, and Pennsylvania, and the area around Baltimore became centers of feverish economic activity—a fever that would break by 1819.[6]

Samuel Slater, who had begun with the partnership of Almy, Brown, and Slater shortly after the Revolutionary War, soon had thirteen spinning mills, expanding from Rhode Island into Connecticut, Massachusetts, and New Hampshire, despite the competition from cheap British imports. The machinery that ran these mills was built on designs frankly stolen from England. Tench Coxe, Alexander Hamilton's deputy, sent an agent to England to procure machine plans; he was arrested. But Slater had slipped out of England under an assumed name, carrying detailed designs in his head. The New England mills, however, would not be simple copies of British factories. Francis Cabot Lowell had been touring Scotland shortly before 1812 when he met fellow American Nathan Appleton, who would become a partner in the Merrimack Manufacturing Company. Lowell and Appleton were horrified by the squalid working conditions in the mills they visited and feared that Britain was courting a workers' revolution. They returned to the United States prepared to pay higher wages in order to secure a reliable workforce.[7]

The first Lowell mill at Waltham opened at an inauspicious moment, just as the War of 1812 was ending and British imports were resumed. Nevertheless, the new company was a success. Lowell himself died in 1817, but the month after his death the Boston Manufacturing Company announced its first dividend for investors (17 percent), and over the next ten years its dividends would average 18.5 percent. These Boston Associates, as Lowell's successors became known, were the first in America to employ a power loom—most cotton on both sides of the Atlantic, though machine-spun into yarn, was then handwoven—and the first to practice vertical integration, controlling every step from purchasing raw cotton to selling finished cloth. When most American textile firms were retrenching, the Boston Associates' innovations brought increasing profits in 1817 and 1818, the result of efficiency: power looms saved two to eight cents per yard on the cost of labor.

Vertical integration of spinning mills and power looms required two or even three times the capital investment, but the western farmhand and the southern slave were soon to be clothed in the cotton cloth of New England's mills. Homespun was becoming a thing of the past in rural America; the time it took was not cost effective when power looms could replace it so cheaply, even allowing for shipping costs. Regardless of the paeans of Henry Clay, the Shelby women were no longer weaving clothes for their family—or their slaves—and the coat President Madison wore to his inauguration in 1816 was broadcloth woven in the mills of Connecticut's Naugatuck Valley.[8]

The region from Delaware to upstate New York was becoming an industrial corridor. Tench Coxe told the Senate in 1814, "Not a building for man, for cattle, nor for the safekeeping of produce or merchandise—not a plough, a mill, a loom, a wheel, a spindle, a carding machine, a firearm, a sword, a wagon, or a ship can be provided without the manufactures of the iron branch." The iron industry, spread up and down the Atlantic states but already centered in Pennsylvania, was a key component of the Market Revolution. In colonial times iron had been one of the industries that Britain had tried to monopolize from home; thus it was one of the first to grow after independence. By 1790 there were already eighty-four iron factories in the Mid-Atlantic region. It would take cotton mills until 1813—and a wartime boom—to reach that number. The iron industry had spread into northern Maryland, eastern and western Pennsylvania, southern New Jersey, and northern New York, following the deposits of ore and coal.[9]

The Market Revolution depended on sales as well as production. Cotton might be woven in Massachusetts or iron forged in Maryland, but it had to be sold to consumers in Virginia, or Ohio, or Louisiana. Producing only for the surrounding area severely limited growth. Dramatically improved transportation opened regional and even national trade routes, but there remained a troublesome obstacle: there was no national circulating currency. For a nascent market economy, money was suddenly crucial. In the eighteenth century, the great planters had lived on credit with London markets. Most Americans had needed actual money only to pay local taxes; otherwise, self-sufficiency was the norm. Storekeepers had accepted barter or, in the cities, had depended on the limited supply of British and Spanish coins. Between the demise of the First Bank of the United States in 1811 and the chartering of the Second Bank in 1816, silver coins had nearly vanished, and the only available currency was a motley assortment of local banknotes, with values that decreased with distance from the issuing bank. Because cotton exports through New York exceeded southern imports through New York, the balance came south in New York banknotes, which circulated at 3 percent below par even when the banks were redeeming them in specie, simply because of the distance.[10]

During the last year of the War of 1812, young Asa Sheldon took a shipment of shoes from Massachusetts to sell in New York—not a distant sale but a tricky one. As he recounts in his autobiography, "The difference between New York and Massachusetts money at that time was 16 per cent." Boston banknotes traded at par, while those from New York were discounted relative to specie. "But it was understood that New York merchants, in buying, expected to pay in New York money, as the banks had stopped specie payments." Sheldon made his sale, but when the buyer counted out the payment in New York bills, "I said, 'I can't take that, I must have Massachusetts money, or gold or silver . . .'"

"'How much pressure,' said he, 'shall I give on this money?'"

"'Sixteen per cent.,' said I. He straightaway counted out the cash, $24."

Sheldon spent his New York banknotes in New Haven, where he bought a load of flour. On the way home overland, he traded it for buckwheat at $1.00 per bushel, which he sold in Massachusetts for $3.50 per bushel.[11]

The Yankee trader could usually find a way to make a profit, but money itself had become a challenge. Allen Trimble, who would later become governor of Ohio, was accused of passing counterfeit bills in Abingdon, Virginia, while on his way to Kentucky. He was rescued by a storekeeper who reassured the accuser. "He said they were not counterfeit, but on Northern banks, and not so current as Virginia paper, and he changed one of them"—to the disappointment of "a crowd of rough looking men and boys who had collected to see the boy who had offered to pass counterfeit money, of which he had a great quantity (for that was the news spread through the town)."[12]

In the second quarter of 1817, with the new BUS beginning operations and state banks at least promising to resume specie redemption, price indexes in the four big seacoast cities finally came into agreement, and there was an eager and unified market for staple goods. Between 1790 and 1800 New York had grown by 83 percent, compared to only 43 percent for Philadelphia; by the mid-teens it was the first American city with a population greater than 100,000. New York had surpassed Philadelphia in exports by 1796, and thanks in part to the auction system, it also took over the lion's share of the import trade: 37 percent by 1821, while Boston, Philadelphia, and Baltimore shared 43 percent. That left only 20 percent of imports for Charleston, Norfolk, Newport, Salem, and all the other seaports. Southerners might export cotton directly to Liverpool from Charleston, Savannah, or New Orleans, but much went through New York—and nearly all their foreign purchases entered there, distributed by a burgeoning coasting trade. Ships arrived in Charleston from Philadelphia every ten days, but they came from New York twice a week. That difference, plus the risk of winter ice in the Delaware River, cost Philadelphia nearly all the cotton trade except for what was bought by local manufacturers.[13]

The cotton South was becoming the engine that drove the American economy. South Carolina senator James Hammond would not boast that "Cotton is King" until 1858, but it was already at very least the crown prince.

When cotton was sold to England (or New England), the income would pay existing debts and (in boom times like 1816 through 1818) might go partly into new land and new slave labor to work it, but at all times it left the South again in three ways. The first was the expense of transporting the bales, an unavoidable cost. Second was the purchase of foodstuffs for both slaves and their masters; more and more, plantations were devoted entirely to the profitable staple crops, and it was economically advantageous to buy food from the outside—wheat and corn as well as coffee, sugar, and other items that could not be produced locally. Third was the purchase of manufactured goods: cheap cotton clothing, shoes, and iron tools for the slave, luxury items for the planter. This demand for goods from outside a region that was growing more and more specialized prompted the expansion of both the coasting trade and the Mississippi riverboats. The South produced cotton (and to a lesser degree sugar, rice, and tobacco) and then relied on the rest of the country—or on foreign imports—for its material needs.[14]

In the interior, the rivers carried a vast freight of all kinds intended to meet those needs. Timothy Flint (a Baptist missionary, unrelated to the Scottish traveler James Flint) observed that the Ohio and Mississippi were becoming crowded with boats carrying downstream "the products and ingenuity and agriculture of the whole upper country of the west," including lumber from New York, pork, flour, tobacco, and hemp bagging (for cotton) from Kentucky, cattle and horses from Illinois, furs and lead from Missouri, and from everywhere corn, turkeys, apples, potatoes, and—to Flint's disapproval—"every kind of spirit manufactured in the region," especially corn whiskey and hard cider.[15]

But with growing financial "pressures," this interconnected market economy was feeling its vulnerability. A bewildering variety of local banknotes, some backed by specie but most not, appeared between 1816 and 1819; interstate buying and selling carried risks. Distance inevitability added to uncertainty. On January 23, 1819, on the eve of the Panic, *Niles' Register* noted, "Bills on New York are reported to be at 7 to 10 per cent. at New Orleans—and New Orleans bills are at 6 per cent. discount at New York! This is a thriving business for shavers!" And as the depression spread over the country, all but the most essential trade between the nation's most widely separated regions collapsed. Merchants in Indiana could not pay for the cotton cloth they had ordered from New England. The celebrated American clockmaker Chauncey Jerome arranged to send clocks from Connecticut to Louisiana in 1821, but the "peddlers came home the next spring without one dollar in money . . . indeed a bitter pill."[16]

The Market Revolution was only temporarily slowed by the Panic of 1819, urged on by the mechanical innovations of the Industrial Revolution. However, Thomas Cochran, in *Frontiers of Change: Early Industrialism in America*, offers this reminder: "The technological advances the country had recently seen—Rumsey's and Voight's water tube boiler, Evans's automated flour mill, Perkins's machine-made nails, Whitney's cotton gin—were so spectacular that one needs constantly to be reminded that the most important immediate spurs to development were in business incorporation, specialization, and transportation."[17]

By the end of the War of 1812 the age of the all-around merchant capitalist was already passing: exporters were shipping by common carriers rather than their own vessels, banking and insurance were taken over by corporations created specifically for those purposes, and industrialists were concentrating on the manufacturing process itself, letting others take responsibility for financing, transporting, and marketing their products. John Jacob Astor in New York, Alexander Brown in Baltimore, Stephen Girard in Philadelphia—the merchant princes of America—were already narrowing their attention to finance and investment. Fur trading had made Astor the richest man in the country, and his American Fur Company had achieved a near monopoly, but he would leave it to concentrate on New York real estate investment. Brown had quit the linen business to open Alex. Brown and Sons, America's first investment bank (which survives as part of the Raymond James financial empire). Girard, who had earlier sailed aboard his own trading ships around the Horn to California, bought up the stock of the First Bank of the United States in 1811. He abandoned commerce to manage the nation's largest private bank and came to the financial rescue of his adopted nation by arranging the purchase of Gallatin's bonds for the War of 1812 when it looked as though no one would. (*Forbes*, in 1998, ranked Astor as the third richest American in history and Girard as the fourth, after Rockefeller and Vanderbilt.)[18]

For the American public in the early nineteenth century, the most visible change occurred in the Transportation Revolution, the rapid decrease in time and cost of trade and travel. John C. Calhoun, 140 years before John Kennedy, exhorted his countrymen, "Let us conquer space"—to travel not to the moon, but from New York to Illinois or between Charleston and New

Orleans. Although Thomas Jefferson is still popularly associated with limited government, he too was eager to see his Louisiana Purchase connected with the rest of the country by federally funded internal improvements. Midway through his second term, Jefferson told Congress that he hoped "new channels of communication will be opened up between the states, the lines of separation will disappear, their interests will be identified and their union cemented by new and indissoluble ties." Jefferson authorized the building of the Cumberland Road in 1806, under the Constitution's provision for federal creation of post roads; formally named the National Road, it began in 1811 at Cumberland, Maryland, on the banks of the Potomac River, and seven years later reached the Ohio River at Wheeling, in what is now West Virginia. Gallatin, in so many ways Jefferson's right-hand man, proposed an even more extensive system of internal improvements that had the backing of Clay, Calhoun, and John Quincy Adams, but it was dropped following the embargo. Like Madison and Monroe after him, Jefferson believed a constitutional amendment would be needed to spell out the federal authority to undertake these projects, but he hoped one would be passed.[19]

Madison, in 1815, called for more defense spending, a Second Bank of the United States, and a protective tariff—all of which Congress would provide, in the name of national security—and he asserted "the great importance of establishing throughout our country the roads and canals which can best be executed under the national authority." On this too Congress delivered, but without the constitutional amendment that was Madison's prerequisite. Calhoun, still very much the nationalist who supported the tariff and BUS charter, led the passage of the Bonus Bill. It would place the $1.5 million "bonus," demanded from the BUS by Congress in return for its charter, in a permanent fund for internal improvements. To Calhoun's dismay, Madison vetoed the bill as unconstitutional, checking the South Carolinian's hopes to "bind the Republic together with a perfect system of roads and canals." If space were to be conquered, it now appeared that it would be up to private enterprise—and the individual states.[20]

Calhoun's model had been Virginia's Fund for Internal Improvements, for the benefit of which (along with the state school fund) Virginia demanded stock from every bank it chartered. Other states—famously New York, with the Erie Canal—would shoulder the responsibility for ambitious transportation projects, as would private or semi-public corporations set up elsewhere to build canals and turnpikes. But neither Congress nor Calhoun was prepared to give up entirely. In April 1818, under the Monroe administration, the House required the secretary of war (now Calhoun) and the secretary of the treasury (a much less enthusiastic William Crawford) to prepare a plan for opening and improving roads and canals, as well as a list of transportation companies in which the government might purchase stock. Henry Clay gave a major speech on the importance of internal improvements; Niles gave it four solid pages in the *Register* on October 24 and four more the next week. Finally, on January 7, 1819, Calhoun delivered his report (which Niles also published with approval):

> The interest of commerce, and the spirit of rivalry between the great Atlantic cities, will do much to perfect the means of intercourse with the west. The most important lines of communication appear to be from Albany to the lakes; from Philadelphia, Baltimore, Washington, and Richmond to the Ohio River; and from Charleston and Augusta to the Tennessee . . . The expense ought not to fall wholly on the portions of the country most immediately interested. As the government has a deep stake in them, and as the system of defense will not be perfect without their completion, it ought at least to bear a proportional share of the expense of their construction.[21]

Calhoun was anticipating Dwight D. Eisenhower's rationale for federal funding of the interstate highway system under the Defense Highways Act of 1956, but Monroe followed his predecessors in refusing to sign any legislation without first amending the Constitution. Moreover, federal revenues were falling and economic activity was decreasing with the Panic. New Jersey representative Ephraim Bateman wrote to his constituents in March 1819:

> The advantages derivable from that species of internal improvement which consists in good roads, good bridges, and canals, are incalculable, and worthy the fostering regard of wise government. . . . I nevertheless express a belief, that the probability of the U. States ever engaging in anything like an extended system of internal improvements, is daily lessening.[22]

Canal building would not hit its stride until the eastern cities came to depend on the farms of the western interior for food. But beginning around 1790 turnpike building boomed. When the Massachusetts delegation to the Continental Congress set out from Boston in 1774, the trip to Philadelphia required nearly three weeks; it took them two weeks just to get from New Haven to Trenton. By 1810 roads were so much better that the trip from Philadelphia to New York took only a day, and continuing to Boston required only one overnight stop on the way. Very soon there would be steamboat service up Long Island Sound to Fall River, Massachusetts, from which Boston could easily be reached by stagecoach in a matter of hours. By 1817 news was carried from Philadelphia to Richmond in five days, and on to Charleston in five more. Only a year after that, *Niles' Register* reported that President Monroe's message to Congress had been transmitted from Washington to New York—242 miles—in only twenty hours. It was set in print in Baltimore just four and a half hours after Monroe delivered it.[23]

Information was spreading more and more rapidly; between 1815 and 1830 the number of post offices more than doubled, from three thousand to eight thousand; nearly every village had at least a part-time postmaster. With postage rates averaging a penny for every six or seven miles, however, most of the mail between cities consisted of newspapers and business communication. (One measure of business decline after 1819 was the 10 percent drop in the number of letters carried by the Post Office over the next two years, the only exception to decades of increase.) By 1800 there were already twenty-four daily papers on the East Coast; the Post Office delivered complimentary copies exchanged by the editors at no charge. By 1822 it is safe to say that the United States had more newspapers than any other nation on earth, although not one had a paid circulation over four thousand. New York had 66 newspapers by 1810 and 161 by 1828; in 1820 the nation could boast 852 papers, most of them in towns with populations under one thousand.[24]

Predictably, transportation improved most quickly in densely populated areas. Massachusetts chartered over fifty for-profit turnpikes between 1797 and 1807, and New York chartered eighty-eight; together they built nine hundred miles of improved roads, all charging tolls. New Hampshire chartered twenty turnpikes; Vermont chartered twenty-six. Over a short period, the public invested nearly as much in proposed turnpike construction as the government had borrowed to fight the Revolutionary War; turnpike capital came to $7.5 million, and the total length of chartered roads reached 4,500 miles—of which perhaps a third were actually built.[25]

Even more ambitious, and nearly as important, were the long-distance roads meant to open up the West. Nine years before construction began on the National Road, the Ohio Enabling Act of 1802 promised that 5 percent of federal revenue from land sales in the new state would go to roads linking Ohio with the East. The Wilderness Road through Kentucky, the Georgia Road (Savannah to Knoxville), and the Federal Road in Alabama (from Athens, Georgia, through Mobile toward New Orleans) all carried travelers and trade west. The unfortunate truth was that roads across the Appalachian Mountains were cost-effective only for manufactured goods headed west; commodity prices were too low to cover the expense of sending wagonloads of raw materials east. But within roughly a hundred miles of eastern seaports there was still a net gain. So Pennsylvania chartered the Lancaster Turnpike in 1792 to serve the needs of prosperous southern Pennsylvania farmers. It was the first turnpike corporation chartered by a state, and was followed by the Germantown and Perkiomen Pike and the Cheltenham and Willow Grove Turnpike. All three paid their investors dividends of over 5 percent for decades. The goal of reaching the growing city of Pittsburgh inspired the creation of trunk roads in western Pennsylvania beginning in 1811, but as late as 1821 the nearly two thousand miles of completed roads in the state were mainly east of the Susquehanna River—within a hundred-mile radius of either Philadelphia or New York City. Many were as well-built as the road from Plattsburg to French Mills: "The bed of the road is composed of the best materials; it is raised several feet above the neighboring ground; wide and deep ditches are dug on either side, and the whole surface is covered with a thick stratum of gravel."[26]

The South was much slower to build roads; it was far more dependent on river transport, for produce could float downstream. The Virginia fund that inspired Calhoun was capitalized at $1,251,161 and was guaranteed all future bonuses from the extension, modification, or creation of bank charters—but Virginia was one of the states most reluctant to charter banks. Other states had actually anticipated Virginia: in 1806 Pennsylvania began subsidizing turnpikes by subscribing to the purchase of stock, and Maryland, in 1812, made the renewal of some bank charters conditional on investment in a fund to build a turnpike west to Cumberland. Turnpike corporations willingly obliged; the first offering of stock in the Lancaster Turnpike was oversold, and companies had no trouble courting investors, but the immediate profit was low compared to the long-term benefits. Even on a good paved road the cost of transportation remained high: twenty cents per ton per mile, when the shipping cost per ton downstream by river was only a penny and canal transport only two cents. Freight overland from Philadelphia to Pittsburgh (some 300 miles) was seven to ten dollars per hundredweight; continuing on by river from Pittsburgh to Shawneetown, Illinois, three times that distance, cost only one dollar per hundredweight.[27]

Canals actually served a number of useful purposes, even before the Erie Canal made its spectacular demonstration of the potential for long-distance shipping. In cities from Waltham, Massachusetts, to Louisville, Kentucky, they were the only practical way to get shipping around waterfalls. Richmond had dug a canal around the falls of the James River in the eighteenth century, admired by the duc de La Rochefoucauld Liancourt in his 1799 *Travels through the United States of North America*. George Washington had long dreamed of a canal to circumvent the Great Falls of the Potomac, even to reach the Ohio River. (On weekends, thousands now hike the towpaths in the Chesapeake & Ohio Canal National Historical Park.) In December 1818, only weeks before the Panic hit, *Niles' Register* reported that in North Carolina, "Preparations are making for a vigorous commencement of the locks and canal round the great falls of the Roanoke—which completed, will open an intercourse of several hundred miles, into very rich country." The Panic delayed the work, but the canal was completed in 1824, creating the town of Weldon where the locks were built. The same issue of the *Register* also reported the completion of improvements and the reopening of the Dismal Swamp Canal, a twenty-two-mile link between the Elizabeth River in Virginia and the Pasquotank in North Carolina. Observed Niles, "The reader by throwing his eye upon the map, will perceive the immense inland navigation . . . hereby opened."[28]

There were a number of blended private/public canal projects, including the Chesapeake and Delaware at the head of the Chesapeake Bay, the Dismal Swamp Canal at the bay's mouth, the Chesapeake & Ohio along the Potomac, and the Lewisville and Portland Canal in Maine. But no public or private canal came close to De Witt Clinton's pharaonic undertaking, the Erie Canal. Clinton persuaded the New York legislature in 1817 to build it entirely with public funds, and in 1825 he ceremoniously poured into New York Harbor a barrel of Lake Erie water, transported thence by canal barge. Hezekiah Niles regularly updated his readers on the progress of construction; he reported on October 24, 1818, that "the great canal in the State of New York, at present employs 5000 men and 2000 cattle," and he found space in his issue of February 20, 1819—an issue otherwise devoted to Congress's damning report on the misbehavior of the BUS—to copy a notice in the New York *Columbian* that sixty-three miles of canal were finished and another fifteen were half done. Six years later the completed canal was 363 miles long; the previous American record had been twenty-three miles. Its full length remains open today, although all the traffic is now pleasure boats.[29]

Canals, like turnpikes, were a conspicuous sign of the progress of transportation, but the most valuable waterborne trade continued to be transatlantic, and the greatest innovation there (before the advent of steam) was unspectacular but fundamental. In 1817 a group of Quaker merchants in New York City announced the revolutionary practice of scheduled bimonthly sailings between New York and Liverpool, departing on the first and sixteenth of each month regardless of wind, weather, or amount of cargo on board. Previously, ships owned by individual merchants had sailed only after they had assembled a sufficient cargo to make the voyage worthwhile. Now the Black Ball Line sailed on schedule, and cargo could be deposited up to a day before departure with the confidence that shipments would not be delayed while a ship's master waited in hopes of more. It was considered a newsworthy event in New York when one of the Black Ball ships, "the *Courier*, in coming out of Liverpool . . . met the *Pacific*, one of the line going into that part; and in coming into this port on Saturday afternoon, she met the *Amity*, another of the line, going out."[30]

Scheduled sailings were a change in transportation that, while revolutionary, might be overlooked by the general public. Nobody could overlook—or ever forget—the first steamboat they saw. Huffing and puffing, kicking up water with its paddle wheel, it was like nothing anyone had seen before. Roads and canals were of great utility, but they were not exciting sights in operation. A steamboat did things that were unheard of: it moved upstream, against the wind, blasting its steam whistle and belching smoke and sparks like a fire-breathing dragon. In fact, one of the steamboats on the Yellowstone Expedition in 1819, the *Western Engineer*, was designed to look like a dragon: "The bow of the vessel exhibits the form of a huge serpent, black and scaly, rising out of the water from under the boat, his head as high as the deck, darted forward, his mouth open, vomiting smoke and apparently carrying the boat on his back." The goal was to intimidate the native people as the expedition progressed through the territory of the Mandan and the Sioux, into the extremes of the Louisiana Purchase: "Neither wind, nor human hands are seen to help her, and to the eye of ignorance the illusion is complete, that a monster of the deep carries her on his back, smoking with fatigue and lashing the waves with violent exertion."[31]

Even without extravagant decoration, the plain facts of steamboats were attention-grabbing. Compare the relative impact of these three news items, printed on the same 1818 newspaper page:

> Pennsylvania: It is stated that a canal four miles long will unite the waters of the Schuylkill with those of the Susquehanna . . .

> The military road, opening from Plattsburg to French Mills . . . has been completed to the distance of thirteen miles.

> The steamboat *Vesuvius* has made the passage from Louisville to New Orleans, 1600 miles, in seven days, repeated.[32]

Vesuvius! Even the name was exciting. And 1,600 miles in a single week—unimaginable! But like the original Vesuvius volcano, steamboats did occasionally explode. In the twenty years from 1816 to 1835, forty such explosions took the lives of at least 353 people.[33]

The first American steamboat was built not by Robert Fulton but by John Fitch in 1787, two decades before Fulton's first commercial success on the Hudson. Fitch was ahead of the corporate revolution, and he could not find enough financial support to develop his invention. Twenty years later, "Fulton's Folly"—more formally *The North River Steamboat* but better known as the *Clermont*—had the backing of New York's wealthy Robert Livingston (Jefferson's agent for the Louisiana Purchase), and in 1807 it made the 150-mile trip upstream from New York City to Albany in about thirty hours. That time was remarkable, and it quickly got better; steamboats were a commercial success.

Steamboats impressed everyone. John Quincy Adams, while secretary of state, was fascinated by the numerous patent applications for various improvements in steamboat designs, spending an entire day in the Patent Office examining each of the scale models that had been submitted. He believed that a study of all the different models could lead to "inferences developing the moral and intellectual character of the nation itself and might . . . lead to inventions and discoveries as useful and important as any of those accumulated in that office." But while Adams (typically) mused about "the moral and intellectual character of the nation," others were thinking of ways to make money. Adams noted that "Fulton himself invented little or nothing but with the aid of Chancellor Livingston's fortune he made the inventions of others practically useful." Livingston's brother Edward had moved to New

Orleans shortly after the Louisiana Purchase and had become one of its most influential citizens; in 1811 Robert Livingston and Fulton obtained a monopoly from the Louisiana territorial legislature for their Ohio Steam-Boat Navigation Company's three boats, and Fulton declared, "The Mississippi is conquered."[34]

Fulton and Livingston were challenged by David French's Monongahela Ohio Steamboat Company, but the legislature extended their monopoly to 1817. The legislators were impressed by the way steamboats cut freight costs, declaring that they would soon create "an extensive commerce with the interior of the country." Just four months after the monopoly finally expired, a rival boat, the *General Pike*, became the first steamboat to arrive at St. Louis, taking twenty-five days upstream from New Orleans; by 1826 that would be cut to eight days. It would not be long before steamboats would go from New Orleans to Natchez in little over one day, and from Natchez to St. Louis in barely three more. By 1817 there were fifteen steamboats based in the southern interior; in 1818 that number doubled.[35]

Henry McMurtrie published *Sketches of Louisville* in 1819. He thought "the increase of the navigation and commerce of Louisville and Shippingport [its commercial suburb], since the year 1806, is, perhaps, unparalleled in the history of nations." In 1806 there had been two keelboats handling the trade; "whereas at the present moment there are twenty-five boats employed in that business, whose united burden is equal to six thousand and fifty tons!" Overall McMurtrie counted forty-one steamboats "employed on the Western waters" by 1819, and twenty-seven more "Now Building." Businessmen in Mobile built a steamboat for the Tombigbee River, to bring cotton out from interior Alabama. Two New Orleans merchants bought the steamboat *Louisiana* from Fulton and Livingston; they could take sugar upriver to Natchez and return with cotton for export. Resourceful entrepreneurs realized that wood-burning steamboats were a lucrative way to dispose of the trees being cleared from rapidly expanding cotton plantations in the Southwest; one planter near Natchez earned $12,000 in wood sales during his first year in Mississippi, before cotton had made him a cent. The next year he raised his first eighty bales of cotton, but he also sold another $10,000 worth of wood.[36]

Upriver, in Cincinnati, Louisville, and Pittsburgh, steamboat building was a thriving business. From 1811 until 1819, when orders abruptly stopped, fifty-eight were built for the southern interior. Steamboats dramatically changed the economy of the southern farmer. Cheap, quick upstream transportation lowered the cost of imported goods, significantly improving the farmer's purchasing power. When steamboats arrived on the Mississippi they cornered a great volume of upriver traffic that had previously come overland; it had been standard practice for Indiana and Illinois farmers (including the young Abraham Lincoln) to float produce down to New Orleans, sell their raft there for lumber, and *walk* five or six hundred miles back home. The entire trip took months, and so little merchandise could be carried back that tea sold in Illinois for sixteen dollars a pound. Steamboats reduced shipping costs in both directions, but the upstream reduction and the ability to take a single boat on a round trip were what really mattered.[37]

Oliver Evans, who had earlier patented a semi-automatic flour mill (and sold one to George Washington), designed with Richard Trevithick a high-pressure steam engine that was both cheaper to build and more powerful than the older, low-pressure engines. By the time Evans died in 1819, his Mars Works in Philadelphia had manufactured over a hundred of them. The new engines, however, were inherently more dangerous. In the next twenty years, 88 percent of the explosions were of high-pressure engines; most occurred on western rivers, but enough passengers on Hudson River steamers were fearful of explosions that boats powered by high-pressure engines began offering "safety barges," towed behind the steamboat for the timorous.[38]

Few passengers were deterred. The published fare from Louisville to New Orleans in 1819 was $75; the return trip, upriver, was $125—children and "servants" half price. The hard times after 1819 brought a drop in freight and, as a result, in freight charges, but they evidently made less impact on passenger travel. James Flint told his readers in September 1820, "In spring 1818 there were thirty-one steam boats on the Mississippi and Ohio; at present there are sixty on these waters. The increase in craft, together with the decreasing quantity of goods imported, has lowered freight from New Orleans to the falls of the Ohio [Louisville], from six cents to two cents per pound. The rates paid by passengers, however, are not reduced in the same proportion." Neither were the downstream freight rates; with the lower price of cotton, shippers knew that planters had to export even more now just to pay their debts. Despite the lingering effects of the Panic, the following decade would see another 190 steamboats built for the southern interior, an increase of 250 percent.[39]

The Market Revolution depended on a Transportation Revolution that tied Cincinnati to New York and Pittsburgh to New Orleans, and made it feasible for Boston merchants to import palm leaves from Cuba to make hats to sell in

Georgia, at a profit. That Transportation Revolution was itself made possible by a Corporation Revolution, a distinctly American surge in limited-liability joint-stock companies, which ensured that capitalizing a turnpike, a canal, or a bank would neither require nor jeopardize the fortunes of a few rich men.

There had been joint-stock companies in Europe since the Middle Ages. The British East India Company had become a byword for wealth and power; "John Company" was the de facto government for most of India, just as its North American counterpart, the Hudson's Bay Company, was for much of Canada. Such gigantic corporate monopolies, created by the Crown, were justified by the risk and expense of establishing merchant empires in distant places. They were few in number, and each was unique in its sphere; in all of Great Britain the only incorporated banks were the Bank of England and the Provincial Bank of Ireland. The distinctly American contribution to the history of corporations is twofold. First, each separate state asserted its own sovereign power to grant acts of incorporation by passing special legislation; indeed, the federal government's claim that it too could charter a corporation was controversial, the Bank of the United States being the sole case in question. Second, unlike the British model, American corporations were, before the 1830s, limited-liability companies exclusively. If an ordinary business could not pay its bills, an individual proprietor or member of a partnership risked losing everything he owned—and in 1819 many did. But if an incorporated bank should fail, leaving people holding thousands of dollars in suddenly worthless banknotes, none of its stockholders was personally obliged to pay those people a cent. Richard Sylla and Robert Wright have called the United States the first "corporation nation," and the easy availability of incorporated status to entrepreneurs contributed greatly to the rapid economic growth in the early nineteenth century.[40]

Louisiana after 1808 and New York after its general incorporation law of 1811 were the only states that did not require special legislation to grant a charter of incorporation, but state legislatures were usually happy to pass such acts. Charters enabled large undertakings like toll roads or textile mills to assemble the capital needed for start-up, by selling stock to many investors who were assured that whatever losses the company might incur, their own liability could never exceed the money they had put up to buy the stock. English banks (other than the Bank of England, which was in practice a branch of government) were simple partnerships. If a bank failed, so no doubt would each of its investors. That realization inspired conservative banking practices. In America, corporations were a marked exception to the prevailing ethical standard that the owner stood behind his business and took full responsibility for it, but their potential value to the community earned them that exception.[41]

Public acceptance of that limited liability was tested in 1819, as was the legal status of corporations in general and of the one and only federally chartered corporation in particular. The Supreme Court, in the *Dartmouth College* case, ruled that corporate charters fell under the constitutional guarantee of the sanctity of contracts. Chief Justice John Marshall declared, "A corporation is an artificial being, invisible, intangible, and existing only in the contemplation of the law"—but nonetheless legally real. A state could no more alter an existing corporate charter than it could interfere in any other contract. In *McCulloch v. Maryland*, a little later that year, the court found the incorporation of the Bank of the United States to be within the constitutional power of the federal government; in each case the court adopted the arguments of the corporation's counsel, Daniel Webster.[42]

The Bank of the United States (and corporations in general) did not find the public so supportive. As Hezekiah Niles bitterly editorialized, "Amidst all the distresses of the times . . . mercy or justice may as well be expected of a tyger in the desert, panting to slake his thirst in blood, as from unknown, and irresponsible associations of *mere* money makers. '*Corporations have no soul.*'" Thomas Ritchie, editor of the Richmond *Enquirer*, was no friendlier to the BUS than Niles, but his paper reported in June 1819 that it could find no instance of stockholders in any American corporation held liable for more than the amount of their stock subscription.[43]

Even in the conservative South there had been enthusiasm for corporations when the economy was still booming. Many planters owned shares and served on corporate boards or as officers of corporations. John Tayloe III of Virginia, heir to the vast Mount Airy plantation, owned stock in the Washington Bridge Company, the Potomac Steamboat Company, the Chesapeake and Ohio Canal Company, the Washington Tontine Insurance Company, and at least four banks; he was a director of the Bank of the Metropolis and of both the First and Second Bank of the United States and left $20,000 of BUS stock to each of his five daughters. Stephen Duncan, often said to be the wealthiest cotton planter in Mississippi, served as president of the Bank of Mississippi and joined forty other planters in Natchez to apply for the charter of the Natchez Steamboat Company in 1818.[44]

From the beginning, corporate stock was promoted as a good investment, a valuable asset that could easily be bought or sold. Dutch East India

Company stock had been sold on the Amsterdam Exchange since 1602. It didn't take long for stock markets to be set up in the economic centers of the United States. Although Boston was more partial to closely held family businesses, New York stockbrokers began buying and selling stock beneath a buttonwood tree that stood on Wall Street, and there twenty-four of them signed an agreement in 1792 to trade only with each other and to charge a commission of a quarter of one percent. The first stock they traded under the agreement was the Bank of New York. But two years before that, the Philadelphia Board of Brokers had been created by Matthew McConnell and nine other city merchants, including the brothers Clement and William Biddle. (Their nephew Nicholas Biddle would be the last president of the BUS, Andrew Jackson's adversary in the Bank War.) The Board of Brokers early on traded government debt, turnpike company stock, and the stock of the BUS; their founding president, McConnell, was one the First Bank's original directors, and cofounder Thomas McEuen was one of the original directors of the Second Bank. When Girard, Astor, and Parish formed a syndicate to buy government bonds and subcontract their sale during the War of 1812, thus performing the role the BUS would have taken on had its charter been renewed, much of that debt was sold by the Philadelphia Board of Brokers.[45]

Stockbrokers in New York recognized the advantages of Philadelphia's organized board and in 1817 sent a committee to Philadelphia, headed by William Lamb. Their sense of the situation was sufficiently urgent that Lamb postponed his honeymoon to make the trip. When the committee returned, the New York brokers decided to copy the Philadelphia rules, moved indoors to 40 Wall Street, and became the New York Stock Exchange. The NYSE, like the Philadelphia Board of Brokers, sold bank shares and stock in the marine and fire insurance companies that had sprung up following the war. The Second BUS opened for business in January 1817; the NYSE adopted its constitution in March. In April, the New York legislature voted to construct the Erie Canal, and that fall the Black Ball Line announced its first scheduled sailings to Liverpool. The economy was shifting into high gear.[46]

The stock markets did not play a central role in the Panic of 1819; there was no stock market crash, *per se* (and no one jumped out of the windows at 40 Wall Street—it was a ground floor office). Far more stock, especially outside of Philadelphia and New York, was sold privately than by brokers. But Rousseau and Sylla estimate that sale listings in newspapers of bank stock grew by 18 percent from 1790 to 1800 and by 12 percent from 1800 to 1809, with transportation stock listings growing rapidly in the latter decade. They see "a fundamental transformation in the way that the nation mobilized and allocated capital resources," and find evidence that "early capital markets met with success in raising funds for internal improvements such as turnpike roads and bridges."[47]

Contemporaries noted the same thing. The ambitious projector Elkanah Watson had proposed a canal from Buffalo to Albany as early as 1791, forming a company with Alexander Hamilton's father-in-law, Philip Schuyler, to build locks and canals in the Mohawk Valley. He founded the State Bank of Albany in 1803 and retired in 1807 to raise Merino sheep in Massachusetts. But he couldn't resist the stock market. An 1806 pamphlet entitled *Observations on the Real Relative and Market Value of the Turnpike Stock of the State of New York* was addressed to prospective investors:

> [I]n every item which goes to the inventory of our national wealth, turnpike stock in value (allowing our conjecture and calculations of internal commerce to be correct) is to city estates as two to one; to wild lands as five to one; to national stock [i.e., treasury bonds] as five to three (allowing six per cent. to be the medium use: it is less); to bank stock as one to one, to insurance stock as ten to seven, and to the medium profits of capital as twenty to thirteen.[48]

Despite Watson's carefully calculated assurances, turnpike stock did not pay off. From 1825 to 1855 six of the largest Massachusetts textile factories paid investors yearly dividends between 6 percent and 12 percent; the Massachusetts Bank averaged 6.5 percent from 1785 to 1855; and the Union Bank averaged 6.9 percent from 1795 to 1855. Three Boston insurance companies paid dividends between 1818 and 1855 averaging 8, 15, and 20 percent. But all that while most turnpikes lost money. An 1838 study concluded that New York turnpikes "have never remunerated their proprietors nor paid much over the expence [sic] of actual repairs." The state of Pennsylvania owned as much as $2 million in turnpike stock, but total dividends came to less than $5,000, an average of .025 percent per annum if spread over ten years.[49]

In the Panic of 1819, the New York financier Ferris Pell judged that turnpike stockholders "were generally sufferers." On the other hand, he continued, "the public were doubtless much benefitted. Intercourse was greatly facilitated, and the cordialities of life multiplied" by turnpikes. The stock owners weren't necessarily victims, either; the great majority of stockholders in the turnpikes were either farmers—whose produce traveled over them—or land speculators—whose property values they raised—or other individuals and firms interested in commerce over them. Henry Clay, the most public advocate of internal improvements, was candid:

> I think it very possible that the capitalist who should invest his money in them might not be reimbursed three per cent. annually upon it; and yet society in various forms might actually reap fifteen or twenty per cent. The benefit resulting from a turnpike road is divided between the capitalist, who receives his toll, the land through which it passes and which is augmented in its value, and the commodities whose value is enhanced by the diminished expense of transportation.

The Eastern Stage Company of Boston, for example, was profitable, although the turnpikes it traveled lost money. And by one estimate, in 1815 there averaged one tavern for every mile on the turnpike from Albany to Cherry Valley.[50]

Stockholders in turnpikes and banks often invested in those corporations because they saw them as essential means to *other* profitable activity. The same was true of steamboat lines. Some seventy cotton planters and other businessmen capitalized the Natchez Steamboat Company at $100,000; other planters set up the St. Stephen Steamboat Company in Alabama and the Natchitoches Steamboat Company in northern Louisiana. These companies typically sold stock at fifty or one hundred dollars a share, limited the number of shares any one investor could own, and elected officers and boards of directors. In addition to Stephen Duncan, the Natchez steamboat investors included David Holmes, Mississippi's first governor, as well as several magistrates and bank presidents—nearly all of them cotton planters as well. Seven of the directors who opened Nashville's Farmers and Merchants' Bank were also steamboat investors, as was the president of St. Stephens's Tombeckbe Bank, Israel Pickens, who would become the third governor of Alabama. Both steamboats and bank loans were essential to the development of the new, fertile cotton lands of the Southwest, and the cotton planters knew it. In 1820, despite the post-Panic depression, J. R. Poinsett, Stephen Elliot, John Wilson, and John Sullivan nevertheless announced the opening of the South Carolina Steam Navigation Company. Their potential investors all knew at least one of the four personally, or knew someone who did.[51]

By 1820, steamboat investment had already fallen behind the profit curve; two years earlier Fulton and Livingston had sold the *New Orleans* and *Vesuvius* to the Natchez Company after Louisiana ended their monopoly, and the rivers were growing crowded. Like the turnpikes and the New England cotton mills, steamboats were remunerative for those who got in first; when there were only six boats operating in the Northeast in 1811, all were highly profitable, but the later entries found it harder and harder to make money. Monopoly protected profits on the Hudson River for Fulton and Livingston—until *Gibbons v. Ogden* in 1824. A monopoly between Burlington, Camden, Philadelphia, and New Castle made money for Hoboken's John Stevens, but the western states were refusing to allow agreements to fix prices or restrict service, calling them conspiracies in restraint of trade. By 1822 Henry Shreve's Monongahela and Ohio Company, the biggest of the Ohio River steamboat companies, was nearly bankrupt; Shreve owed a total of thirty creditors $100,000. He eventually recovered, but other, smaller firms did not.[52]

On dry land, it took corporations to build the great bridges that spanned the Charles, Delaware, Susquehanna, Schuylkill, and Potomac Rivers (as well as many more modest bridges elsewhere). All charged tolls, of course, but so had the ferries they replaced—and the bridges were far faster, easier, and more dependable. In the decade from 1810 through 1819, 143 bridge companies were incorporated, along with nine new ferry companies, forty-nine canals, eighty-six "navigation" companies (steamboats and other water transport), and a remarkable 464 toll roads. "Mixed transportation" companies added another twenty-two. Transportation incorporation stalled during the Panic but then revived. Outside of New England, the decade of the 1820s saw nearly as many incorporations and the 1830s many more—reflecting the development of the Northwest and the arrival of the railroad, destined to become the king of transportation incorporation.[53]

Although transportation corporations produced dramatically visible, tangible results, financial corporations were ultimately at least as essential to the growth of the market economy, and manufacturing corporations were important, too. Transportation incorporation had increased by 44 percent in the 1810s, but when finance and manufacturing are added the total number of incorporations between 1810 and 1819 is more than double that between 1800 and 1809 and—everywhere but New England—greater than that between 1820 and 1829 as well. Sylla and Wright, who collected these numbers, ascribe the regional contrast to the large national increase in the second decade of transportation companies, not so much needed in compact New England. But it is also true that the economic downturn hit New England much sooner, with the 1815 dumping of imported manufactures causing factories to close; and the recovery began sooner there as well, making for a faster rebound in the 1820s. The first of the three "long waves of incorporation" before the Civil War had its arc from 1800 to 1821. The wave crested following the War of 1812 and then broke sharply; George H. Evans, in his exhaustive study of corporations in Maryland, New Jersey, New York, Pennsylvania, and Ohio, reports seventy-seven new charters in 1815, 105 in 1816, eighty-five in 1817, fifty-nine in 1818, sixty-eight in 1819, and only twenty-five in 1820 and sixteen in 1821. Across the country, state legislatures had incorporated twenty-six new factories in 1809, sixty-six in 1813, and 128 in 1814—mostly textile mills. Another seventy-eight were incorporated in 1815, despite the glut of imports. But the next three years would average only nine per year.[54]

Two instructive examples are the states of Pennsylvania and Ohio. The former stretched from the tidewater port of Philadelphia across some of the nation's most productive farmland, over the rugged Alleghenies to the growing manufacturing city of Pittsburgh on the Ohio River. There was no more diverse state, and Pennsylvania kept a competitive eye on both New York and Virginia, its two very large neighbors. In the first third of the century Pennsylvania chartered twice as many roads as Virginia, three times as many bridges, almost twice as many insurance companies, and nine times as many banks. Its transportation and financial incorporations also outnumbered New York's, although New York chartered more factories. Ohio, the next state to the west and the most rapidly growing state in the 1810s, averaged fewer than three incorporations annually through 1815. Then, epitomizing the nation, its legislature issued six times that number: eighteen charters in 1816 and eighteen again in 1817. The depression arrived there in 1818—in a sense it came down the river from Pittsburgh—and soon half of Cincinnati, which had been the country's fastest growing city, was in receivership. For the next seven years Ohio was back to averaging three incorporations per year, and it would be 1832 before the number again reached eighteen. During its burst of activity, this new, expanding state had chartered fourteen turnpikes and four bridges—but it had also incorporated eighteen banks, more than New York during the same period, even though the Empire State had more than twice its population and was home to the nation's largest city.[55]

In 1806 Elkanah Watson had declared, "Our national funds, our bank stock, the stock of our fire and marine insurance companies, turnpike stock, our active trading capital and real estate, compose the great mass of our country's wealth." That wealth, as it was exchanged, developed, and mortgaged, passed through an ever-increasing number of banks, whose own stock was traded more than any other variety. Rousseau and Sylla report a fact that seems to have surprised even them: "Everyone knows . . . that England was the financial leader of the nineteenth century [and] London and the Bank of England the center of the world's finances. . . . What everyone does not know is that as early as 1825 the United States, with a population still smaller than England . . . had roughly 2.4 times the banking capital."[56]

In newspaper listings of securities traded from 1810 to 1819, offerings of bank stock increased more rapidly than those for transportation or manufacturing stock. And it was loans from banks that financed most new businesses until they grew large enough to make direct public investment practical. In addition, Rousseau and Sylla note that "banks were able to attract deposits and capital through their ability to diversify and were thus instrumental in fueling early securities markets directly." And from 1817 to 1819, when investment capital was flowing into real estate above all, it was banks that made the land boom possible.[57]

An exiled loyalist, returning to Boston in 1808 after a quarter-century abroad, marveled at "the great number of new and elegant buildings" lining State Street; half seemed to be banks and insurance companies. But Boston was already being passed by larger cities, and as the middle states jockeyed for economic leadership, Baltimore, Philadelphia, and New York were competing fiercely to dominate exports from the west. When talk began of a New York canal from the lakes to Albany, Pennsylvania looked to strike a preemptive blow. In 1814 the answer to all questions seemed to be banks, so that year—in a paroxysm of incorporation—the legislature chartered forty-one banks with a combined capital of $17 million, nearly all of them west of Philadelphia. Of these, thirty-nine actually opened for business, and nearly half of those failed in the Panic of 1819; they helped to fuel the boom and—when their notes and loans suddenly lost their value—precipitated the bust.[58]

The explosion of banking was both a cause and an effect of the economic surge. Already in 1812, 44 percent of the country's five hundred largest corporations were banks; four years later banks were 56 percent, and out of 2,087 chartered corporations, 280 of the largest 500 were financial, claiming 71 percent of the authorized corporate capital. It is an indication of the nationwide character of the boom that ten different states could claim at least six of the five hundred largest corporations. Twenty-four of the biggest twenty-five were banks; the exception was the Globe Insurance Company.

Even the mega-banks were spread across the country: four of the ten largest were in New York, two in Massachusetts, and one each in Pennsylvania, Virginia, North Carolina, and Georgia.[59]

All told, twice as many corporations were created from 1810 to 1819 as in any previous decade. They provided the capital and built the infrastructure for the historic economic interconnection of East and West, cities and farms, that was the Market Revolution. Until that transformation took place there could have been nothing like the economic boom of the 1810s that touched almost all of American society; conversely, there also could have been no nationwide hard times like those of the ensuing bust. It would be nearly 150 years before historians began to speak of a Market Revolution, but both its cultural and economic effects (along with its dependence on banking) were described by Ferris Pell in 1819—the year that it all crashed:

> It cannot be denied that in those districts in which country Banks have been established animation has been infused. The faculties of the farmers have been brightened; their sense of the value of punctuality quickened; their social intercourse more free and frequent, and their ideas of life, and manners, and society, enlarged. Nor can it be denied that these institutions have been a channel through which a portion of the redundant Capital of our large cities, has found its way to the farmer; and have thus aided to break down those prejudices which have hitherto severed, and still continue to sever those two great interests.[60]

VOLCANO WEATHER

There were two volcanoes that gave their names to steamboats: Vesuvius and Etna. Shortly after the *Etna* was launched in 1816, the steamboat *Washington* exploded on the Ohio River. There would be no other volcanic names for steamboats, but not because of the unfortunate associations with explosion. (In fact, four years after the *Etna* sank on the Mississippi after hitting a snag, a new *Etna* was launched; it blew up on the Hudson). The explanation is more mundane: almost no one in America could name any other volcano.[1]

Mount Vesuvius had been notorious since the eruption of AD 79 that destroyed Pompeii, vividly described by Pliny the Younger. Etna, too, was familiar from classical history; it had also figured prominently in the popular *Baron Münchhausan's Narrative of His Marvelous Travels* (1786), and Vesuvius would soon be back in the public eye when Edward Bulwer-Lytton published his best seller *The Last Days of Pompeii*. It is safe to say that no American, not even professors of natural philosophy, had ever heard of a volcano called Tambora in the Dutch East Indies. Very few people would recognize the name today, although its 1815 eruption was the most violent in recorded history—ten times as powerful as the better-known Krakatoa in 1883, one hundred times the force of Mount St. Helens in 1980. Over the last few decades, however, it has become understood that an enormous cloud of sulfur dioxide, released when the upper third of Tambora was blown away, disrupted weather throughout the Northern Hemisphere. Coming after several years of already cooler temperatures during "a coincident depression in solar activity," the thick atmospheric haze led to weather extremes that caused famine in Europe and elevated grain prices in the United States. The chain of events following that distant eruption—including summer snow and unprecedented draught—helped persuade thousands of Americans to move west in search of greener pastures and to buy farmland on credit when the price of wheat suddenly rose.[2]

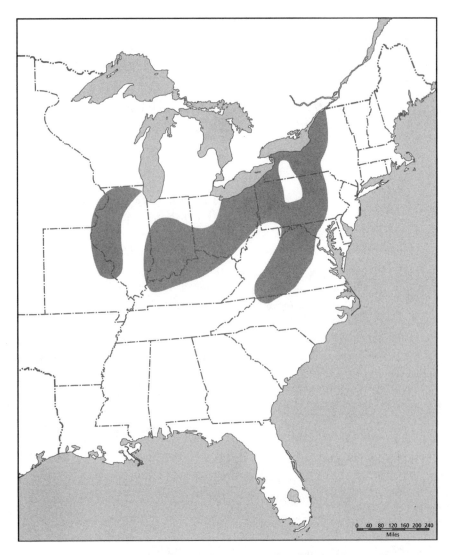

MAP 2. Primary Region of Wheat Production. Map by Chris Robinson

The year 1816 was not quite the coldest on record; data from before the twentieth century are incomplete and can be unreliable, and it appears the following winter was even colder. The entire stretch from 1812 through 1818 was remarkable for low temperatures, but in contemporary accounts it is 1816 that stands out as "the year without a summer." In Europe as well as North America, and in parts of Asia and South America, 1816 was remembered as the worst of a series of "cold and unaccommodating" years extending back to 1812, with crop failures and famine from Ireland to Tibet. The historian John D. Post sees it as a landmark in economic history:

> In the period from 1816 to 1817 there occurred an economic and social crisis which has remained obscured by the dislocations following the Napoleonic wars. The postwar readjustments were not the principal cause of the economic misery and social upheaval which appeared so soon after the return of peace. In addition, the bank panic and the depression of 1819 are largely unintelligible without reference to the more fundamental disturbances of 1816–1817. In essence, the distress of 1816–1817 had its origin in a subsistence crisis, an agricultural calamity of extraordinary geographic scope.[3]

That geographic scope, extending from China to Brazil, included both Europe and eastern North America. The year that New Englanders called "eighteen hundred and froze to death" was the last straw that sent farmers in search of better prospects to the south and west, but at the same time Europe's misfortunes also promised benefits for Americans. Thorp's *Business Annals* characterizes the European harvests of 1814 as "deficient," 1816 "a failure," and 1817 "below average"; Thorp records unusually high wheat prices in 1816, 1817, and 1819. New Englanders who went west were not simply fleeing their cold, unproductive homes; they were hoping to make their fortunes in the West, raising wheat for export to Europeans who were forced to choose between high prices and starvation. When harvests returned to normal and Europe stopped buying American grain, the Northwest land bubble burst and the Panic spread through Ohio, Indiana, and Illinois.[4]

Of course, no one in Europe or North America associated the perpetual haze and depressed temperatures with the eruption of a volcano in the East Indies. It is true that Ben Franklin, in Paris in 1783 to negotiate the end of the American Revolution, had speculated that Europe's "dry fog" and cold that year were the result of volcanic activity in Iceland, but that volcano was not far from busy shipping lanes and its continuous activity had been reported by numerous Scandinavian sea captains. Still, an exhaustive study of the log books of 227 sailing ships from 1815 through 1817 offers evidence of Tambora's impact on weather patterns around the world: colder Indian monsoons, below-normal air and water temperatures in the Galapagos Islands, severe draught in northeastern Brazil, and increased hurricane activity in the Atlantic. In Europe, however, the most serious consequence was a shift in the

North Atlantic Oscillation, the weather phenomenon that directs the track of storms. In 1816, it produced drastically increased rainfall and record cold weather. Central and eastern Europe suffered the worst harvests of the century (in some cases the worst in four centuries) along with widespread deaths of livestock. Ireland endured eight weeks of rain without a break, destroying the potato crop and leading to famine and a typhus epidemic. All across Europe, the recurring complaint was the failure of the grain harvest and the resulting high cost of bread.[5]

The prohibition of imported grain, designed to keep up prices and protect the incomes of England's large landowners, had been proposed in the House of Commons in 1813, but the next harvest was a poor one, and nothing was done. The average price of wheat in Britain in 1814 was seventy-four shillings four pence per quarter; peace and the abundant crop in 1815 brought it down to fifty-two shillings ten pence, the lowest price since 1804, and the powerful large landowners demanded relief. Parliament responded with the Importation Act of 1815, known ever after as the Corn Law, forbidding the importation of foreign grain unless the price of a quarter of wheat (eight London bushels, or one-quarter of a London tun) reached eighty shillings. It would remain in effect, except for brief suspensions, until 1846. But even without foreign competition, the price in 1815 remained below sixty shillings, in part because the postwar depression reduced wages and thus held down demand: the low-paid or unemployed working class could not afford as much bread.[6]

By late spring in 1816 it was clear that the coming fall's harvest would be terrible—Thomas Tooke called it a "lamentable deficiency in quantity and miserable inferiority in quality." In London the *Times*, restrained as always when discussing the British economy, acknowledged at the end of July that prices were rising on the Corn Exchange because of "the quantity of fine wheat at market being small and the weather continuing unsettled." Two weeks earlier the *Times* had reported the flooding on the Continent, a topic about which it felt free to speak in stronger terms: "Even if the weather were to take a favorable turn, the injury already sustained, and the calamitous consequences of a summer inundation cannot be repaired. . . . This appears certain—that an unusual scarcity and high prices of all provisions must be the consequence."

In May 1816 in West Dorset and Bury St. Edmunds there were attacks on mills and bakeries; the price of wheat had already risen 50 percent since

January, and unemployment was high. In June the Lancaster *Gazette* reported, "The atmosphere still seems as cold as in March or November." On June
6 it had snowed in Lancashire, "a circumstance not within the recollection of
the oldest person living in that neighborhood." The Ipswich *Journal* reported
"a considerable fall of snow" on July 6. That same day the *Royal Cornwall
Gazette* observed, "The extreme changeableness of the weather which has
prevailed so long still continues. Every flattering prospect of genial warmth
has been quickly succeeded throughout the spring, with the reverse of a
chilling and searching, or damp atmosphere, with the growing assurance of a
late harvest, so full of risk." At the end of August there was snow as far south
as Sussex, within forty miles of London, and "a considerable fall of snow in
Cambridge."[7]

That indefatigable diarist John Quincy Adams was minister to England in
1816. Both the weather in July and the people's reactions to it troubled him:
"The season has been so unusually and constantly cold that fires have been
kept without intermission in almost every house. . . . The weather has been
equally extraordinary over the greater part of Europe." He had read that an
Italian astronomer had predicted that the unusually extensive sunspots would
lead to "the total extinction of that luminary" and the end of the world on
July 18. "The effect and agitation of this story have been very considerable,
both in England and in France . . . [A]t Paris public prayers have been ordered
for favorable weather." Adams was dismayed that a woman in London had
"hung herself in a fit of melancholy at the prospect of the world's coming to
an end."[8]

The world did not end, and no further suicides were reported, but as autumn brought the predicted miserable harvest, violence was instead directed
outward. In October mobs attacked bakers and farm markets in Surrey, Sun-
derland, and Birmingham. Magistrates read the Riot Act and called out cav-
alry detachments. On November 15 eight thousand people assembled outside
London at Spa Fields. Since August the radical reformer Henry Hunt had
been disputing the optimistic government predictions of an abundant harvest. Now he urged the crowd to petition the prince regent for relief, calling
for a suspension of the 1815 Corn Law. The *Times* reported, aghast, that he
had referred to the nearby Coldbath Fields Prison as "the British Bastille."
That same issue noted that the temperature at York had dropped to twenty-
one degrees Fahrenheit, a circumstance that was reported (in a formula that
was becoming familiar) as "not remembered by the oldest inhabitant at this

early period of the winter." Finally, Parliament agreed to allow the importation of grain.[9]

Thomas Tooke, in his 1838 *History of Prices*, says the weather in England and France took a marked upturn after mid-1817, and crops flourished: "From a backward and sickly appearance they became luxuriant and promising. Prices consequently declined in both countries." But by that time thousands of Americans had been convinced that the export of grain and flour to Europe would make them rich; across the Old Northwest, the die was cast.[10]

America's own weather in 1816 has become the stuff of legend. It was not, in fact, the coldest year in American history—the three final months were too mild—but June, July, and August 1816 set cold-weather records that have never been broken. Thus 1816 truly was what it came to be called, the year without a summer. In America it was also, in marked contrast to Europe, a year of drought. It was the fifth of six consecutive abnormally cold years and the first of five consecutive abnormally dry years. Together, those facts made harvests abysmal. Since nearly all Americans were very locally focused, there was a strong tendency to see weather as a problem that could be cured by relocating; it was inevitable that so many people would decide to abandon the places where they had endured such a miserable stretch of weather. Samuel Griswald Goodrich, an editor at Hartford, Connecticut, and a popular author, later remembered, "Ohio—with its rich soils, its mild climate, its inviting prairies—was opened fully upon the alarmed and anxious vision. As was natural under the circumstances, a sort of stampede took place from cold, desolate, worn-out New England, to this land of promise." (Ohio did not keep that promise; the town of Dayton—newly founded by eastern land speculators and a popular destination—turned out to have the same mean annual temperature as New Haven, Connecticut.)[11]

All across the country January was cold, although February was slightly less frigid than usual. The problem was that it never warmed up. The Richmond *Columbian* of June 7 wrote, "This is an extraordinary spring. On Thursday last we had a frost in this city." The second week of June brought snowfall in Boston, still the latest that has ever happened; that week the thermometer dropped to twenty-four in Malone, New York. The Connecticut clockmaker Chauncey Jerome recalled that week forty years later in his autobiography: "I well remember the 7th of June. While on my way to work, about a mile from home, dressed throughout with thick woolen clothes and my overcoat on, my hands got so cold that I was obliged to lay down my tools and put on a pair of mittens which I had in my pocket." In Maine it snowed for three hours on June 10. The *Connecticut Courant* of June 25 reported, "A most severe frost destroyed the blossoms and even the leaves of the apple trees in certain directions, accompanied with ice . . . thicker in proportion, than any night last winter." And in Ohio, Goodrich's "land of promise," a visitor described a cold snap in June: "Dead leaves, in tufts, are hanging on the paw paws, and on most other trees—the first growth of the spring having been essentially destroyed. This remark will apply to much of the state where we traveled." He had come from Pennsylvania, where "fruit has been chiefly destroyed by the late frosts."[12]

July brought no improvement, with frost from Maine to Virginia on the 8th. On July 13 the Richmond *Enquirer* expressed the puzzlement and growing anxiety felt everywhere: "Our climate is far from having ripened to the summer heat; the nights and mornings are yet surprisingly cool." August offered a taste of summer (ninety-two degrees in Connecticut on the 18th) but bracketed it with frost in New England and a cold front that brought freezing temperatures as far south as Kentucky. August is typically the hottest month in Washington, D.C., but on the 30th the *National Intelligencer* reported "a temperature, such as is generally experienced in the latter end of October." Central Pennsylvania had heavy August frosts; so did Cincinnati.[13]

From Maine to South Carolina and west into Ohio, crops suffered severe damage. *Niles' Register* excerpted a letter from Erie, Pennsylvania, dated June 14: "It appears as if we shall have no crops in these parts—the corn has been all killed by the frost of the 9th, and until very lately Lake Erie was not navigable for the ice." Niles surveyed the country and concluded that in Louisiana "appearances were very alarming," that Pennsylvania would have "little grain and little fruit," and "there is little fruit to the northward of Pennsylvania." From Monticello, Jefferson wrote to Albert Gallatin, now minister to France, "We have had the most extraordinary year of drought & cold ever known in the history of America. . . . The crop of corn thro' the Atlantic states will probably be less than ⅓ of an ordinary one, that of tob° [tobacco] still less, and of mean quality."[14]

The *National Intelligencer* reported frost at Petersburg, Virginia, at the end of August—another "circumstance unparalleled in this part of the country"—and added, "What is equally extraordinary, we have had frost every month during the year." The freeze that week reached South Carolina, and in Danville, North Carolina, a farmer looked out over meadows "white with frost on Aug. 29 and 30." The frost, however, "killed nothing, as all was dead before" from the summer's drought. The *Carolina Courant* printed his account and allowed that "the people seem to be alarmed about their situation and considerable emigration is likely to take place."[15]

The summer was so dry that the Richmond *Enquirer* found the James River lower that it had ever been since the first colonists arrived in 1607. There were reports that one could walk across the Schuylkill near Philadelphia with dry feet, and that the Pee Dee, Waccamaw, and Black Rivers of South Carolina were lower than anyone could remember. (Newspapers had given up looking for new ways of saying "in the memory of the oldest inhabitant," but again and again they reported extremes that were without precedent.) Then the torrential rains of September arrived—probably a hurricane that stalled offshore—and "this unexpected visitation from Heaven added to the severe distress to which the country is otherwise reduced." The rains were hard enough to ruin the hay and clover crops, but once they had run off the water levels again dropped below normal. Drought in eastern North Carolina was so bad that many planters cut their green corn to feed their cattle, and "great numbers sold their property and joined the emigrants."[16]

Those who emigrated found that the drought was just as bad in the West; the Mississippi stopped rising a month earlier than normal at New Orleans; it was the lowest high water anyone had seen there. The drought continued for five years, suspending river traffic on the Ohio and Mississippi for extended periods. John C. Calhoun's 1817 corn and cotton crop was only half normal at his Bath, South Carolina, plantation; when he returned home from Washington in 1818, he found his cotton drought-stricken again. That year was likewise frustrating for Jefferson. With the price of wheat beginning to fall, he had been able to ship only fifty barrels of wheat to his mill at Richmond before the water level in the James again dropped too low for river traffic; by the time the water level rose, the price of grain had fallen much lower.[17]

Four years of cold, culminating in the disastrous weather of 1816, had persuaded many easterners to go west, but they encountered an added insult: the drought's low water was keeping them from getting there. In Hamilton, New York, on the Chenango River, a resident counted "three hundred families, besides single travelers, amounting in all to fifteen hundred souls"—more than the population of the entire county—"waiting for a rise in the waters to embark for 'the Promised land.'" But if they got as far as Pittsburgh they heard the familiar refrain: water levels lower than "oldest residents could recollect"; it was only the second time in history that the Ohio River failed to rise in the autumn. Niles reported in November that "all the goods that arrived at Pittsburg, since the middle of September, remain there, '*low water bound.*'" A month later, "three millions of dollars of goods were at Pittsburg," waiting for water to rise so that they might "descend the river, as well as a multitude of travelers and emigrants." This was no mere inconvenience; the Ohio River was the most economical way to bring manufactured goods from East to West, and farmers depended on both the Ohio and Mississippi Rivers to get their produce to southern customers and to the depot of New Orleans.[18]

The next year the Pittsburgh *Mercury* described wagons actually able to ford the Ohio: "the water in its channel being not more than 3 feet deep though its usual depth at high water is from 27 to 30 feet." The Shawnee-town *Illinois Emigrant* marveled, "It is astonishing to think that the Ohio, one of the largest rivers in the world—the Ohio, whose swollen waters presented a current fifteen hundred miles in length and from one to ten in width, and whose depths were almost unfathomable, should now be (comparatively) a small stream, fordable in many places, and literally seeking its way over pebbles to the great father of waters, the Mississippi."[19]

The father of waters was running perilously low as well. When Henry Clay tried to return to Kentucky from visiting New Orleans in 1819, the steamboat *Napoleon* could not proceed up the Mississippi without running aground, and he had to continue overland, missing a visit by President Monroe. In 1820, the final drought year, Timothy Flint found the Mississippi at the mouth of the Arkansas River lower than it had been in generations. "No steamboat was expected for some time, at least not until the river should rise."[20]

The rivers were not rising, but prices were. In Connecticut, Goodrich recalled the shortages:

> The crop of Indian corn was almost entirely cut off; of potatoes, hay, oats, etc. there was probably not more than half the usual supply. . . . At that time I made a journey into New Hampshire, passing along the Connecticut River, in the region of Hanover. It was then June and the hills were almost as barren as November. I saw a man at Oxford who had been forty miles for a half bushel of Indian corn and paid two dollars for it.

Such stories were becoming common, although it is hard to top Asa Sheldon's account from Massachusetts: "One man actually brought a large pig to David Hart [his neighbor] and exchanged it for a small one, and gave 50 cents boot money, because the little one would eat less during the winter." Far to the south, the cotton crop suffered, too. The Augusta (Georgia) *Chronicle* estimated that the crop would be only half of normal—but the price of cotton in Liverpool rose 50 percent from 1815 to 1817. Georgians and Carolinians eyed the rich lands of Alabama just going on the market, made their calculations, and began buying land.[21]

"Never has there been in America," declared Ritchie in the Richmond *Enquirer*, "especially in Virginia, so gloomy a prospect. It appears that it is more than probable that there will be very short crops of Corn, on account of which, people in general are much alarmed." The poor harvest was driving up prices in America, but prices in Europe were rising even higher—and American farmers were taking note. Ritchie urged his readers not to export wheat or flour since it was needed at home, but the temptation proved irresistible after Britain suspended the Corn Laws, allowing the importation of foreign grain. Jefferson shared Ritchie's concern. He had told Gallatin,

> The crop of wheat [in 1816] was middling in quantity, but excellent in quality, but every species of bread grain taken together will not be sufficient for the subsistence of the inhabitants; and the exportation of flour, already begun by the indebted and the improvident, to whatsoever degree it may be carried, will be exactly so much taken from the mouths of our own citizens.[22]

Virginia, Ohio, Pennsylvania, and New York were then the four largest wheat-producing states. As Jefferson feared, farmers in all four took note of the prices in Europe. In August 1816 Louis XVIII proclaimed that in France, "grain, meal of every kind, bread, and sea biscuit, may be imported free of duty, either by sea or land, till otherwise ordered," and by November, prices in England had risen so high that the importation of wheat and flour were at last permitted there, too. Wholesale wheat on the New York docks had risen from $1.41 per bushel in May 1816 to $2.00 in July and $2.50 by year's end. (No one dreamed that it would fall steadily through 1818 and 1819, to sixty-eight cents per bushel at the end of 1820.) While most American mills produced flour for local consumption, throughout the Chesapeake and along the Susquehanna, Brandywine, Hudson, and Delaware Rivers so-called merchant flour mills sprang up, dedicated to meeting the demands of Europe. Wheat farmers, like cotton farmers, looked to open western lands as they watched prices rise; in the next generation, the East would be left behind as

Ohio, Indiana, Illinois, and Wisconsin became the largest wheat-growing states.[23]

In October New England finally had its first steady rain since April; it helped put out forest fires. The last months of the year were mild, but emigration from New England continued unabated. A caravan of sixteen wagons emptied the town of Durham, Maine, carrying 120 people (led by the town's minister); they had agreed to purchase an entire township in Indiana. In a single month that autumn, 511 wagons, carrying 3,066 people, passed through Easton, Pennsylvania, heading west. Of those who remained behind, thousands subsisted on oats who had previously fed them only to their horses; fish, which in the past had been exported to southern Europe, became such a regular part of New Englanders' diet that 1817 became known as "the mackerel year."[24]

The mild fall proved to be a false promise, and the winter of 1817 grew bitter, east and west: the Potomac froze two feet thick, and the Ohio froze solid at Cincinnati—"a circumstance rarely, if ever, known before." As President Madison prepared to turn the White House over to President Monroe, he took a moment to write his old friend Thomas Jefferson, always eager for meteorological data: "As with you, the weather here of late has been remarkable both for the degree and the continuance of the Cold, and the winter for its dryness." That same week, according to *Niles' Register*, Philadelphia recorded two degrees below zero, New York seven below, Hartford fourteen below, Portland nineteen below, and both Hanover, New Hampshire, and Montreal thirty below.[25]

Three months later, in the middle of May, several towns in Vermont still had five inches of snow on the ground. Lucy Mack Smith, mother of the Mormon prophet Joseph Smith, recalled that this was the point at which her family gave up on Vermont. After three successive crop failures, her husband declared that "he would go to New York, where the farmers raise wheat in abundance." Their next harvest would feed them—when it came in—but until then, "Wheat was $2.70 per bushel and other things in proportion. 'How shall we,' said my husband, 'be able to sustain ourselves and have anything left to buy land?'" Mrs. Smith's answer was to join the market economy at once:

I had done considerable at painting oilcloth coverings for tables, stands, etc. Therefore, I concluded to set up a business, and if I prospered, I would try to supply the wants of the family. At this I succeeded so well that it was not long until we not only had an abundance of good and wholesome provisions, but I soon began to replenish my household furniture.

The Smiths contracted with a land agent to purchase one hundred acres at Palmyra, New York. "In a year's time we made nearly all of the first payment." They remained in Palmyra until 1827, when Joseph Smith and his followers moved on to Pennsylvania, Ohio, Missouri, and Illinois—as so many other Americans were doing.[26]

The Hallowell (Maine) *American Advocate* was among the many newspapers that took note of the stream of emigrants leaving New England. "Many ascribe it to the late cold season and are ready to sell their property for half what it cost, and migrate south." From Maine, "south" could be anywhere, but it was increasingly Ohio or Indiana. The year 1816 had also been cold west of the Alleghenies, but not so bad as in New England. The 1817/18 Chillicothe (Ohio) *Meteorological Register* struck a defensive note, not wanting to discourage emigrants: "The last year does not furnish a fair example of the meteorology of Ohio. The cold of the last winter exceeded by several degrees that of any former year since the settlement of the state." They needn't have worried. Nothing could dissuade the families who continued to vacate the East; like the Smiths, they were confident that they could make the first year's payment on a quarter-section of land where "the farmers raise wheat in abundance"—and by May 1817 the price of wheat in the eastern cities had reached the unheard-of level of $3.11 per bushel.

There were, of course, many explanations for the multitude who moved west after the War of 1812. The outbreak of war had not decreased the interest in the western territories, but it had made them dangerous places to live. With the cessation of violence—especially the end of the Indian wars— thousands set out for the land beyond the mountains. Between 1810 and 1820 the population of the United States grew by one-third, an increase of nearly 2.4 million, and most of that growth took place in the West. When the Panic of 1819 arrived, it would hit that region particularly hard.

The East grew much more slowly. New England had begun its settlement two centuries earlier; very little arable land was still uncultivated. No new settlers were adding to the population, and the cities' growth could barely balance the westward exodus from the countryside. In the first decade of the 1800s even the fastest-growing New England state, New Hampshire, added population at less than half the national average rate, a sluggish 14 percent. Farther south, Pennsylvania and North Carolina also lagged behind the country as a whole. Despite the rapid growth of New York City, the Empire State as a whole could do only 10 percent better than the national average, thanks in part to New Englanders taking their first step westward. On the other hand, Georgia—the least populous state at the 1790 census—more than doubled its population as cotton farmers poured into its western counties. That was better than ten times the rate of its more settled neighbor South Carolina, but it could not compare with the new territories to the west. Alabama's scattered population in 1810 was 8,000, but by 1820 it was home to 119,000 new settlers: a phenomenal growth rate of 1,322 percent. Illinois grew by 359 percent, Indiana by 488 percent, and even distant Missouri grew by 235 percent. All four, along with Mississippi (142 percent) would achieve statehood between 1816 and 1821. Ohio, thirteenth in population in 1810, was suddenly the sixth-largest state in 1820. A special census in Indiana revealed that it had added nearly forty thousand residents in only five years. Kentucky surpassed Massachusetts, and in 1820 Missouri, though not yet a state, was as populous as New Hampshire, Delaware, and Rhode Island combined.[27]

As recently as 1800, only a third of a million American citizens had lived west of the Appalachian Mountains. In 1820 the census counted two million. Never again would so large a proportion of the population live in settlements that were so new. Some were pushed west by failed crops and cold weather; some were pulled west by the lure of rich farms and high prices; and some were simply swept up in the enthusiasm that was so often spoken of as a contagious disease. So many more besides the Smiths left Vermont that the Green Mountain State actually shrank between 1815 and 1820—young adults of childbearing age were deserting the state. Gershom Flagg was one of them. On February 1, 1818, he wrote home to his parents:

> Altho you say the Ohio feever is abated in Vermont—the Missouri & Illinois feever Rages greatly in Ohio, Kentucky, and Tennessee and carried off thousands. When I got to Ohio my Ohio feever began to turn but I soon caught the Missouri feever which is very catchin and carried me off. I think most probable I shall return if my life & health is spared a year from next spring but it is very uncertain whether I stay in that country. Surely nothing except my friends would tempt me ever to see Vermont again.[28]

Eastern states worried that their young men and women were falling victim to the Ohio, Missouri, Mississippi, or Alabama "fevers." They tried without success to hold on to them. Gov. Oliver Wolcott of Connecticut urged prospective emigrants to reconsider; in his inaugural address, he asked the legislature to help finance more mills to provide more jobs in the state. The New York *Columbian* warned its readers, "By rendering it in the interest and happiness of the population to stay at home is the only way to check the rage" to move west, but the New York Emigration Society replied that it had become "expedient for many persons now living in New York and elsewhere to change their place of residence and mode of employment and that views of such persons are generally diverted to the new lands of western states, as affording more certain means of subsistence."[29]

New York City was still growing, but throughout the country barely 7 percent of the people lived in communities of 2,500 or more. Almost half of that "urban" population lived in the six largest cities: New York, Philadelphia, Baltimore, Boston, New Orleans, and Charleston. Neither the re-export trade nor the shipping industry recovered their profitability after the War of 1812, and manufacturing continued to struggle under the flood of cheap imports. Baltimore, New Orleans, and the new western metropolis of Cincinnati (population 9,000) were the only cities that boomed after 1815—Baltimore because it was the major port for exporting wheat and flour. The old cotton port of Charleston declined, but New Orleans took off; in the 1820s it would be second only to New York in the value of its exports. Cincinnati's growth, nearly 300 percent from 1810 to 1820, showed what inland cities could do in the age of steamboats, canals, and turnpikes, but its collapse when the Panic began was also a reminder of how precarious the western prosperity really was, and the population of St. Louis would shrink by one-third after the Panic. The decade of 1810 to 1820 remains the only one in which the percentage of town and city dwellers actually declined; there were too few opportunities in town and an unmatched opportunity to achieve the dream of being an independent freeholder in the vast lands available on credit in the west.[30]

By the end of 1816 the tide of emigrants was approaching its flood. The Zanesville (Ohio) *Messenger* marveled, "On some days, from forty to fifty wagons have passed the Muskingum at this place. The emigrants are from almost every state north or east of the Potomack, seeking a new home in the . . . territories of the west." Those who did not travel entirely by wagon hoped to float west on rivers. Thomas Douglas and his family migrated from Connecticut to Madison, Indiana. (Every western state had both a town and a county named for Washington, Jefferson, and Madison; Adams was occasionally overlooked.) The Douglases took a stagecoach over the turnpike as far as Pittsburgh, where they were dismayed to find the steamboat they planned to board was "hard and fast on a sandbar at Beaver, a few miles below Pittsburg." Water levels were dangerously low, but Douglas bought a flatboat and managed to float his family down the shallow Ohio River, skirting rocks and gravel bars.[31]

Many years later John Jay Smith remembered his own 1819 journey, "by the beaten track to Pittsburg, thence to Cincinnati by the lower route, then a wilderness, and much of it a quagmire." At a rough tavern he encountered Henry Clay heading east, who regaled the emigrants with tales of "perilous adventures and hair-breadth escapes with the Indians and the animals of untrodden forests." The migration pressed on from Pennsylvania into Ohio, even though much of the state consisted of vast tracts of wilderness, still occupied only by the Shawnee and Miami. The brand-new town of Dayton had been laid out by its promoters in the midst of that undeveloped area, where a group of merchants, manufacturers, and land investors founded a corporation to build a toll bridge over the Miami River. James Kimball, who left Salem, Massachusetts, for Ohio, "never imagined the migration so great as it is." He was amazed by the numbers "from all parts of the world crowding on board the boats, arks, and rafts with their families," moving inexorably west.[32]

If the immigration was not quite from *all* parts of the world, it did include many from Great Britain, France, and Germany. A New York newspaper counted 2,050 immigrants arriving from Europe just in the final week of August 1817. The great exodus from Ireland was still a generation in the future, but among the travelers going west were a number of advance scouts from England and Scotland, sizing up the prospects for the many in Britain—members of the middle class as well as factory hands and farmers—who were looking with interest at the new world. James Flint was one of them. As he surveyed the assortment of travelers working their way west, "some sleeping in the woods, pushing all their belongings in wheelbarrows, or riding in Conestoga wagons," he was struck by their variety: "The Canterbury pilgrims were not so diversified nor so interesting as these." The Englishman Morris Birkbeck, also reporting to British readers, made the much-quoted observation, "Old America seems to be breaking up and moving westward":

Several branches of what has properly been called the current of emigration, being here united, strangers from the eastern country, and from Europe, are passing in an unceasing train. An intelligent gentleman, at [Chambersburg,

Pennsylvania], informed me that this stream of emigration has flowed more copiously this year, than at any former period; and that the people moving westward, are ten times more numerous than they were ten years ago.

But Flint sensed something ominous in the throng that drove relentlessly on, abandoning their old homes; at the end of September 1818 he wrote from Pittsburgh, "Emigrants continue to flock westward. . . . At first view, this great migration leads to the conclusion, that oppression, and the fear of want, are in extensive operation somewhere to the eastward." Meanwhile, somewhere to the westward, 7.5 million acres of public land had already been sold on credit in Ohio, Indiana, and Illinois, with almost half of the $16 million purchase price still outstanding—and now the price of wheat was falling.[33]

The population was surging west beyond Ohio. Late in that fall of 1818, *Niles' Register* marveled, "In the state of Indiana, a wilderness a few years ago, 12,000 voters were polled at the last Congressional election." At Fort Claiborne on the Alabama River, Niles continued, "Two years ago there was but a single hut on the place where a town now stands, which is computed to contain *twenty-seven hundred* inhabitants!" (Steamboats made Fort Claiborne a shipping center, but the railroad would bypass it, and today it is a ghost town.) The St. Louis *Gazette* had boasted that "Missouri and Illinois exhibited an interesting spectacle" in 1816: "A stranger to witness the scene would imagine that Virginia, Kentucky, Tennessee, and the Carolina's [*sic*] had made an agreement to introduce us as soon as possible to the bosom of the American family. Every ferry on the river is daily occupied in passing families, carriages, wagons, negroes, carts, &c. &c.—respectable people, apparently able to purchase large tracts of land." In December 1818, even as he published warnings of economic downturn, Hezekiah Niles was still impressed: "The emigration is wonderful—and seems likely to acquire new power." A month later he noted, "The emigration to Missouri is so great as to furnish a home market, at very high prices for all provisions, raised in the territory—thus wheat is $1 a bushel, beef at 6 [dollars] and pork at 5 per cwt—corn 50 cents per bushel, & c." But those prices were substantially lower than export prices had been a year earlier, and now the price of cotton had begun to fall as well.[34]

Emigration to Missouri remained "wonderful," but "fear of want" had begun to follow those pilgrims down the Ohio River, and property owners in the boomtown of Cincinnati were beginning to default on mortgages.

Hidden at the end of Niles's otherwise positive article on the first Missouri land sale, in October 1818, was the note that when the sale closed, only 35,000 of the 700,000 acres available had been sold. "[A]lthough part of the tract brought four, five, and six dollars per acre," most went for the minimum price. "Many tracts of hickory land were offered at two dollars, which nobody would take." The sale of lands at the much-vaunted Boon's Lick was postponed.[35]

By the beginning of 1819 the British advance men, at first so enthusiastic about the prospects they saw, had become disillusioned. They admonished would-be emigrants to beware: "Gain! Gain! Gain! Gain is the beginning, the middle, and the end, the alpha and omega of the founders of American towns. . . . Hundreds of these speculations may have failed." So warned Birkbeck, who had himself founded the Illinois community of Wanborough for English immigrants. The same disillusionment was voiced by yet another English traveler, Joseph Biggs:

> A speculator marks out the plan of a city with its streets, squares, and avenues, quays and wharves, public buildings and monuments. The streets are lotted, the houses numbered, and the squares called after Franklin and Washington. The city itself has some fine name, perhaps Troy or Antioch. . . . All this time the city is a mere vision. Its very site is on the fork of some river in the far West, 500 miles beyond civilisation, probably under water or surrounded by dense swamps. Emigrants have been repeatedly defrauded out of their money by transactions so extremely gross as hardly to be credited.[36]

As early as 1811 Rep. Jeremiah Morrow had warned that the credit terms of the Public Land Act of 1800 would "engender disaffection of the most dangerous kind—disaffection nerved by the powerful motives of interest. And as it regards purchasers, the credit at present allowed often induces individuals to make purchases beyond their means." When the prices of first wheat and then cotton began to fall, taking land prices down with them, there were plenty of voices saying, "I told you so." On March 4, 1819, New Jersey congressman Ephraim Bateman wrote to his constituents:

> Too hurried an accession of population has not been favorable even to the west, as it has introduced a spirit of speculation, along with an immense mass of foreign goods, which they had better done without, and produced very heavy and

embarrassing debts to the Atlantic cities for those goods, and to the government for land, as evinced by the deplorable conditions of the local currency. There are at this time upwards of 12 million dollars due to the government for land, 7 millions of which from beyond the Ohio. There is every reason to believe that, unless the system of extended credit be discontinued the amount will annually accumulate, and at no distant day produce such an odious relationship, that of creditor and debtor between the government and a portion of the people, as to be productive of serious consequences.[37]

How had the United States come to this "odious relationship . . . of creditor and debtor" with so many thousands of its citizens? It had not begun that way. In the difficult days after the Declaration of Independence, the thirteen states in Congress assembled had written the Articles of Confederation, but Maryland, which had no western land claims, had refused to confederate with the others until they ceded their own claims to the federal government. As one by one the states gave up their extravagant and conflicting claims, Congress found itself in possession of a vast expanse of utterly unexplored land beyond the mountains.

After Washington became president, U.S. sales of public land took place, but they were directed toward wealthy investors who could pay cash. With the development of the political parties, a Federalist congress was not eager to enlarge the population of the Republican-leaning west. The Land Act of 1796 set a minimum price of two dollars per acre (with higher prices possible at public auction) and a minimum purchase of 640 acres: a square-mile section of a thirty-six-section township. The price tag of at least $1,280 was far beyond the means of most would-be settlers at a time when farm labor paid about eight dollars a month (with board) and the best-paid mill workers earned fifty cents per day. Only 5 percent ($64) was required at purchase, but $640 was due in just thirty days and the balance within a year—too soon for a first crop to be made on land that had first to be cleared.[38]

Sales were predictably slow. After Hamilton left the Treasury Department, the new secretary, Oliver Wolcott Jr., wrote to Virginia's Rep. John Nicholas in 1797: "The whole of the sections were repeatedly exposed to sale, at Pittsburgh, but without success." Hostile Indian tribes at first discouraged settlements, but the Treaty of Greenville removed that threat from the southern two-thirds of Ohio and squatters moved in, looking forward to a sale of cheap government land.[39]

By 1799 the Northwest Territory had grown to the point that it could send a nonvoting delegate to Congress. The territorial legislature chose a young veteran of the Indian wars, a signatory of the Treaty of Greenville: William Henry Harrison's fame as the hero of Tippecanoe was yet to come, but he was the son of a signer of the Declaration of Independence and the son-in-law of a major land speculator, John Symmes. Although a territorial delegate could not vote in Congress, he could propose legislation; in April Harrison introduced the Land Act of 1800. Although the Federalist party remained in control until the fall election, congressional leaders could tell which way the wind was blowing, and Harrison's bill passed a month later with almost no debate and without a roll-call vote in either house.

The new law left the minimum price at two dollars per acre (twice what Harrison's father-in-law was asking), but it made two significant changes. First, the minimum purchase was cut in half, to 320 acres, making the cost of a farm a little less daunting. But the second, history-making innovation was the introduction of credit from the federal government: one-quarter of the price would be due in forty days, another quarter in two years, the third quarter in three, and the final payment in four years. Interest was set at 6 percent, with a discount if any of the last three payments was made before it was due. Suddenly any working man who could save up $160—only twenty-two cents a day over two years—could purchase 320 acres in Ohio, to be paid off as his first three crops came in. Or an investor with a little cash could make the minimum $160 first payment for a half-section, then subdivide it and sell four 80-acre farms (the size Abraham Lincoln's father purchased in Indiana) at $2.50 per acre—a reasonable premium for a more affordable smaller property. With the proceeds he could buy five more half-sections and repeat the process, and do it yet again with twenty-five half-sections before the second payment was due on the initial purchase. He could thus realize a profit of nearly $5,000 on an initial outlay of $160—a rate of return of better than 3,000 percent in one year! It sounded too good to be true, but it worked until the pool of buyers began to evaporate in 1818. A fifth-year grace period was part of the 1800 Act, and Congress would vote a total of twelve extensions between 1812 and 1820. In 1804 the minimum purchase was halved again to 160 acres, so the process was now open to anyone with eighty dollars—less than a farmhand earned in a year, after his board.

Over the next sixteen years the bulk of Ohio, Indiana, Illinois, Mississippi, Alabama, and much of Missouri would be sold on those terms, usually auctioned for more and often for much more than the minimum price per acre. Inevitably, large debts grew to the federal government—especially from speculators—and local banks loaned millions of dollars to enable buyers to make their debt payments and to finance resales. The 1800 law set up four land districts in Ohio, with offices at Cincinnati, Chillicothe, Marietta, and Steubenville. By 1812 there were eighteen offices, with land districts added in the Mississippi Territory in 1803, Indiana, Illinois, and Michigan in 1804, Missouri in 1809, and Alabama and Louisiana in 1811.[40]

When Jefferson was elected president in 1800, he appointed Albert Gallatin secretary of the treasury; Gallatin would hold the office until halfway through James Madison's second term, making him the longest-serving treasury secretary in history. With experience speculating in both Virginia land warrants and acreage in western Pennsylvania, Gallatin had continually supported the sale of smaller tracts to actual settlers during six years in Congress. After Jefferson doubled the national domain with the Louisiana Purchase, Gallatin went to work organizing the new lands for eventual sale. (There was as yet no General Land Office or Interior Department.) To the magnitude of the task was added the complexity of numerous conflicting French and Spanish land grants; the Mississippi River was lined by French-speaking towns, and it was said that on both banks the land claims "overlapped like shingles on a roof."[41]

Jefferson and Gallatin were eager to add new Republican states; they also planned to raise revenue from public land sales. After the embargo cut deeply into customs receipts, Gallatin hurried the Mississippi Territory lands onto the market, even before the many conflicting land titles were cleared up. He wrote to Jefferson, "The importance of carrying the land system into operation there, for the purpose of quieting the people and encouraging population, had induced me to adopt that mode rather than to delay the sales several months longer, in order to wait for the surveyors' returns." Jefferson hoped that land revenues would eliminate the national debt; Madison, his successor in office, believed the proceeds might be used to purchase slaves from their owners as a "sufficient, fair, and efficacious means of gradual emancipation." Both would be disappointed.[42]

Even before the land rush that followed the War of 1812, the task of surveying and selling the public lands was overwhelming. In 1812 Josiah Meigs was appointed surveyor general. He had been a professor of physical science at Yale and the president of the University of Georgia. Two years later he exchanged offices with Edward Tiffin and became the commissioner of the

General Land Office, a position he would hold until his death in 1822. The policies he would carry out under three presidents had already been set by Gallatin. Each office was run by a register, who kept track of sales and took custody of funds, and a receiver, whose job it was to calculate payments and interest due—a nearly impossible task, given the numerous unscheduled, partial, or delayed payments. They had the assistance of up to four clerks, whose qualifications and reliability were the subject of constant complaints. The officers were expected to reject not only counterfeit banknotes but also any notes that would not be accepted at par by those banks that the secretary designated as Banks of Deposit. Thus, the officers of any given land district had to know the current conditions of more than fifty banks whose notes might be submitted by purchasers; that task was so daunting that little effort was made between 1814—when most banks suspended specie redemption— and 1817, when redemption was theoretically resumed. Gallatin directed the receivers to remit banknotes through the U.S. Mail, after first cutting them "in two equal parts in order that each half may be forwarded by a different mail," for security.[43]

Gallatin also initiated the practice of employing senators, representatives, and territorial officials to inspect all land offices annually. From the beginning the inspectors were selected from among the political allies of the secretary, an invitation to corruption. William Crawford would later expect his inspectors to promote his campaign for the presidency, but Gallatin worried constantly about his officers' reputations. He told Jefferson, "My best endeavors, knowing the abuses committed in almost every State, had been exerted, and, I think, with success, in preserving the purity of our land offices." Registers earned only $500 in annual salaries, but they also received commissions on sales in which millions of dollars might pass through their hands in a matter of days.[44]

The coming of war in 1812 created chaos on both the northwestern and southwestern frontiers. Until the peace returned in 1815 no further surveys were attempted, and sales of already-surveyed lands slowed: in the Southwest 144,873 acres in the Mississippi Territory (which included Alabama) had sold in 1812, but only 30,261 in 1813 and 41,272 in 1814. In the Northwest, however, even the threat of Indian depredations, backed by the British, did little to deter land-hungry settlers. Sales dropped off in 1812 as a result of Tecumseh's War, but they rebounded the next year to levels above those of 1811; then in 1814, after Col. Richard Mentor Johnson claimed to have personally shot Tecumseh at the Battle of the Thames, sales almost doubled. (Johnson would be elected senator and then vice president on the dubious campaign slogan, "Rumpsy-dumpsy, who killed Tecumpsy?")[45]

As soon as the war began, hoping to encourage enlistment, Congress set aside six million acres for military bounty lands: two million each in Illinois, Michigan, and Missouri. Speculators offered to buy up the patents as soon as they were issued, but by 1814 the lands had not yet been surveyed (and when they finally were, the surveys revealed that much was unfit for cultivation). Meanwhile Congress temporized by authorizing preemption in 1813 in Illinois and in 1814 in Missouri. This halfway step gave settlers the right to claim land in advance for purchase at the minimum price after it was surveyed— if they had already improved it. An unintended consequence, reported by the register at Vincennes, Indiana, was the "delusive hope of obtaining preemption rights" in other territories as well, which encouraged squatters in Indiana. Prospective landowners were still champing at the bit. As wartime government contracts brought prosperity to Ohio farmers, William Reynolds, register in Canton, Ohio, wrote to Commissioner Tiffin in 1814 that "applications for new lands are numerous," and John Badollet at Vincennes tersely reported "the Indians harmless & we in a state of tranquility." Badollet later declared that "the apprehension of Indian hostilities had but a limited influence on the number of emigrants and is not likely to impede the proposed sales."[46]

By the beginning of 1815 there were eighteen land offices; over the next four years twelve more were added, from St. Helens in Louisiana north to Terre Haute, Indiana. The land officers were all prominent citizens: John Brahan of the Huntsville office had been a general under Andrew Jackson at New Orleans; Badollet at Vincennes was a childhood friend of Gallatin from Switzerland. Land office registers would later be elected governors of Alabama, Illinois, and Missouri. Several officers in Alabama, Indiana, and Missouri were also presidents of banks there, which might today suggest conflict of interest but seemed a perfectly natural combination at the time.

The unleashed demand for western lands required both credit and currency from local banks; as they were deposited in government accounts, the steady flow of banknotes from west to east would create serious problems. Receipts at the land offices came primarily in the form of depreciated notes issued by western banks. (Outside New England there had been no notes redeemable in specie since 1814.) Most federal spending during and after the war took place in the East, where local notes traded closer to par. The Treasury Department was thus losing money by taking in depreciated western banknotes from land sales and paying out at eastern exchange rates. When the Second Bank of the United States was created in hopes of regularizing the currency, it could not keep up with the multiplying western banks; at first it didn't even try.[47]

All told, between 1812 and 1821, more than 3.75 million acres were sold in Ohio, more than in any other state. In 1817 Indiana's Vincennes land office led the nation in sales, with Jeffersonville not far behind. That March the Vincennes receiver, Nathaniel Ewing, reported to Meigs, "The Public sales taking place so near the end of the year and the great quantity of land sold, more than could have been calculated in the time allowed by Law, occationed [sic] a hundred mistakes in our books, which has taken all winter to correct." The previous December Vincennes register Badollet had written to warn the commissioner that accounts would be delayed because of "the extraordinary quantities of land sold at the public sales [and] the number of persons thronging the office." In July 1817 he added, "For a considerable time the applications were so numerous that it was impossible to record them as rapidly as they came in."[48]

Sales in Illinois in 1818 challenged those of the previous year in Indiana, although much of the territory had yet to be ceded by the Indian tribes. Morris Birkbeck, writing from the "English Prairie" there, observed that each new emigrant brought "a little store of hard-earned cash for the land office of that district; where they may obtain a title for as many acres as they possess half-dollars, being one-fourth of the purchase money"—as long as they could find land selling for the minimum. The territorial capital Kaskaskia, on the Mississippi River, was an old French colonial town with a population of seven thousand. Kaskaskia boasted two newspapers, the *Herald* and the *Western Intelligencer*; according to the latter in early 1818, "Almost every person has to a greater or less degree, become a dealer" in western lands. That year, in just the first three quarters, the Shawneetown office sold more than 200,000 acres. The population by 1818 was great enough to make Illinois a state. But that autumn, when the Corn Law went back into effect in Britain, grain prices fell to $1.45 per bushel and land purchases stalled. By then the Bank of the United States had reversed its liberal lending policies and was calling in debts; money was suddenly scarce. The *Herald* wrote that September, "The [Bank of the] United States' branches are drawing the cord tighter and tighter; they are limiting the number of banks whose notes are receivable for lands."[49]

Now the economic climate was feeling a chill across most of the country, but optimism continued longer in Missouri. Three years before the Tambora eruption, the territory beyond the Mississippi River had suffered a geophysical shock of its own: in mid-December 1811, a fault deep underneath the region had snapped. The violent earthquake, with its epicenter near the village of New Madrid, was felt as far away as New York City; it knocked down chimneys in Cincinnati and awakened sleeping people in Charleston, South Carolina. Modern estimates put its strength at 7.5 to 7.9 on the Richter scale, with aftershocks in January and February that were nearly as powerful; no stronger quake has ever been recorded east of the Rocky Mountains. Eyewitnesses described the current running backwards in the Mississippi and land undulating like ocean waves. Had it happened a century later, thousands of people would have died, but because Missouri was so thinly populated—and masonry structures nearly nonexistent in the immediate vicinity—only one fatality can with certainty be ascribed to the earthquake, although there may have been drownings on the river as boats were swamped.[50]

Farms and small towns were ruined, and in Washington, D.C., where some had felt the shaking a thousand miles away, Congress voted to provide warrants to all those affected, allowing them to exchange their devastated land for any public land in the territory. The result was nearly as chaotic as the quake itself. Congress had neglected to make the warrants nontransferable, and there was a brisk business in buying them up at a discount. Fast-moving speculators took advantage of many residents who had not yet heard of the warrants, buying up their ruined property for a song. On the other hand, some canny property owners sold their land multiple times to would-be sharpers who were left to argue over who got the warrant. Congress also failed to specify which public land could be exchanged, with results that might have been predicted.

Throughout the settled regions of Missouri, strangers showed up in towns like Boonville and Franklin, laying claim to preemptory settlers' city lots—land that had been improved but not yet purchased, as the territory had been kept waiting for sales to begin. Some claimed entire village commons. One bold owner of a New Madrid warrant claimed the sandbar that lay between the city of St. Louis and the low-water mark of the Mississippi River, with the intent of charging a toll for river access during the dry season. Secretary Crawford eventually ruled that the oldest claims would have preference, but the New Madrid warrants, like the Yazoo scrip that would shortly appear in Alabama, added one more layer of complexity, and the confusion contributed to the delay. By the time the first sales finally got under way, the Panic of 1819 was already looming over the eastern horizon.[51]

Settlers, preemptive or armed with warrants, had not waited. To the Boon's Lick region, along the Missouri River, "in the winter, spring, summer, and autumn of 1819 they came like an avalanche . . . faster than it was possible to provide corn for breadstuffs." Once the sales built up steam, the Franklin office auctioned off acreage comparable to the amounts sold in Huntsville or Vincennes, but at nothing like those prices; the February 1819 sale totaled 249,347 acres, but the price averaged only $3.85 per acre, not much more than the minimum. By the fall of 1820 the effect of the Panic was obvious: Missouri offices that had sold 892,047 acres for $2.5 million in 1819 could sell only 75,792 acres for $137,188 in 1820. (By then the minimum price had been reduced by Congress to one dollar per acre.) Optimism had fled.[52]

A major obstacle in 1820—the refusal by the Bank of the United States and the land offices to accept the notes of a growing number of banks—was hardly news to Crawford; he, after all, was the one who ultimately decided which banks' notes would be "land office money" and which would not. And he was hearing about it from all the offices. The surveyor general of the St. Louis office, William Rector, wrote in the fall of 1819 to ask if instead of paying his deputies out of the receipts from the office, the government would send funds from Washington: "Much of the money that has been received in payment for public lands is not now Bankable." And in 1820 at Huntsville, Alabama, where land remained in greater demand than elsewhere, the local newspaper complained that "the hardness of the times and the extreme difficulty of getting land office money, which is now 15 per cent. above the currency of the country [i.e., local banknotes] no doubt depress the price."[53]

By the end of 1818 the great land fever was cooling off just as the climate began warming up. The weakness of postwar American manufacturing had already depressed the economy in the East, and now the West was discovering the consequences of real-estate speculation. The monetary frustration felt throughout the region was summed up by Nathaniel Ewing in January 1819. Writing not in his capacity as land office receiver but as president of the Bank of Vincennes, he told Secretary Crawford, "The present situation of the western people is distressing: they cannot get for their produce one dollar of the kind of money that will be received in payment of their debts due to the United States." But there was a more fundamental problem, as Crawford reported to Congress: "In the early part of 1819, the prices of all articles produced in the Western States fell so low as scarcely to defray the expense of transportation to the ports from whence they were usually exported to foreign markets." He was right; cotton was just barely worth the cost of shipping, and wheat and hemp no longer were.[54]

Those who prefer to see the Bank of the United States as the primary culprit have generally blamed falling prices on the tight money policies of BUS president Langdon Cheves, but the prices of some commodity exports had begun to fall while his predecessor, William Jones, was still pursuing an expansionist policy. Irresponsible state-chartered and private banks certainly had much to answer for, and the BUS did much to make a bad situation worse; by the time Andrew Jackson told Nicholas Biddle, "I do not hate your bank any more than I hate all banks," most Americans felt the same. The hostility with which banks would long be viewed was by no means undeserved. But it is impossible to understand the evolution of an urban, eastern recession into a national depression without tracking the rise and fall of the export commodities—above all, wheat and cotton. Speculators in the Northwest bet fortunes that the price of land would rise, but it rose there only while the price of wheat was rising. There was no single cause of the collapse of America's postwar economy, but among the largest of the contributing factors was the desire to get in on the commodity export boom—and the inability to escape when that boom turned to bust.[55]

Because the rising debt for western lands closely correlated with rising export commodity prices, the number of victims of the Panic of 1819 multiplied when land buyers—farmers as well as speculators—were unable to pay the remaining half or three-quarters due on their purchases after precipitous drops in prices robbed them of the income they were counting on. The land boom had not been initiated by any change in credit policies at the General Land Office; more buyers simply wanted land suitable for growing wheat and cotton because they saw prices going up and transportation costs coming down. As Arthur Cole long ago observed, "a steady volume of [land] sales, or even a volume that increased somewhat in size as the years went by, could be attributed simply to the westward trend of population, [but] the peaks reached in 1818, 1836, and 1854–55 stand out with marked prominence." Three times before the Civil War the volume of public land sales reached its greatest heights: just before the Panics of 1819, 1837, and 1857. Each peak followed a rapid rise in commodity prices, and each downturn began soon after those prices fell. Cole finds that immigration figures do not correlate with those peaks; growth of internal improvements does only somewhat; but the clearest explanation is "rising commodity prices followed by drops."[56]

There had been a growing domestic market for wheat during the War of 1812, and land sales in Ohio had been quick to respond in 1814 and 1815. But it was the miserable harvest of 1816 that caused grain prices to spike at home and abroad, and the sudden expansion of the European market encouraged more farmers (and speculators) to purchase western land. The extreme weather of 1816 certainly affected North America as well as Europe, but American drought proved less calamitous than European flood, and despite their own crop shortfalls, American farmers (as Jefferson feared) found export prices irresistible. As late as October 18 the British prime minister, Lord Liverpool, was assuring John Quincy Adams that although the harvest "had been particularly bad, there would turn out to be enough for the consumption of the people," but in November wheat that had sold for fifty-two shillings the previous winter was commanding ninety-eight shillings, and the Corn Law was finally suspended: wheat, rye, barley, and "Indian corn" were admitted duty-free.[57]

The ports remained open through the following November, and 316,000 quarters of American grain were imported. Then the government closed them again, insisting that the 1817 harvest would be sufficient to bring prices down. It was not, and after only three months there was no choice but to suspend the law again. In America export prices surged (along with land sales in the Northwest), but the British closed the ports once more in September 1818, reopened them in November, and then closed them in February 1819, just as the Panic was sinking in on the United States. They would remain closed, thanks to harvests that were at least average, until 1823. *Niles' Register* reported that British imports of American flour fell from 540,000 barrels in 1817 to 43,000 barrels in 1819.[58]

Export prices for wheat had hit $2.53 per bushel in New York at the end of the volcano year of 1816; they remained over $2.40 through June 1817, as Americans headed to the Northwest to clear new farmland, buying $2.7 million worth on credit in 1816 and another $3 million in 1817. In the summer of 1817 wheat prices began to drop, falling to $1.94 at the end of that year and $1.72 at the end of 1818. As the price of wheat declined (to ninety-nine cents per bushel at the end of 1819), so did the land rush. By the end of 1820 wheat was selling for only sixty-eight cents per bushel, barely a quarter of its price when land fever took hold. The problem was not simply diminished demand; thanks to the incentive created by the high prices—and the need to raise crops in order to pay off the new lands—supply was at an all-time high.

More than seven million acres had been bought in the Northwest; most of it had been planted in wheat, corn, or rye, and by 1818 there was a glut.

The western states were above all the breadbasket of the South. Eastern farms supplied eastern markets, and Pennsylvania and Virginia wheat could more cheaply be exported abroad, through Baltimore; Ohio, Indiana, and Illinois sent wheat down the Ohio and Mississippi Rivers. The growth of the market for western crops was tied to the expansion of the cotton economy. As the populations of Alabama, Mississippi, and Louisiana grew rapidly, the quantity of grain and flour shipped downriver increased. In Alabama and Mississippi, the rise and fall of land sales followed the rise and fall of the price of cotton at Liverpool, the primary port of entry into England; there were record-setting southern land sales in the fourth quarter of 1818, and cotton had been at its sustained high from the end of 1817 through the first three quarters of 1818. But when cotton export prices fell, the price of grain fell with them. In the wake of falling cotton prices, southern agricultural fairs, magazines, and county agricultural societies began to emphasize local production of foodstuffs. The dollar value of all produce received in New Orleans from the interior had risen from $8.7 million in 1816 to $13.5 million in 1817 and $16.8 million in 1818—but it fell to $12.6 million in 1819 and $12 million in 1820. It would not return to its previous high, despite increasing quantities, until 1824. In many ways, a critical element of the Panic of 1819 was the boom and bust of the cotton South.[59]

ALABAMA FEVER
"I Must Go West and Plant"

As commodity prices began their fall, the stream of emigrants from the Northeast to the Northwest slowed. But the Old South continued to send thousands to the fertile lands to its west. Family members of James Madison were among them. His sister Frances and her husband moved to the new county in Alabama that had recently been named for her brother, where he had himself bought land. Nearly all of Madison's Taylor cousins (except the president's critic John Taylor of Caroline) decamped for Kentucky, and his private secretary, Edward Coles—his closest friend after Jefferson—moved to Illinois, in order to free his slaves. Madison remained in Virginia; so did Jefferson, who would be ruined there in the Panic of 1819.[1]

North Carolina also seemed to be emptying westward. Judge Archibald D. Murphey told the state Senate, "It is mortifying to witness the fact that thousands of our wealthy and respected citizens are annually moving west in quest of that wealth which a rich soil and a commodious navigation never fail to create in a free state; and that thousands of our poorer citizens follow them, being literally driven away by the prospect of poverty." (Murphey borrowed heavily to invest in North Carolina real estate and canal development and was ruined when the BUS called in his loans.) The Raleigh *Star* noted in 1816 that in the western part of the state, "Great numbers are disposing of their property, and preparing to emigrate to the West and South." In the eastern part of the state, the young planter James Graham employed a familiar metaphor when he wrote to Thomas Ruffin in 1817:

The *Alabama Feaver* [*sic*] rages here with great violence and *carried off* vast numbers of our Citizens. I am apprehensive if it continues to spread as it has done, it will almost depopulate the country. There is no question that the feaver is contagious . . . for as soon as one neighbor visits another who has just returned from the Alabama he immediately discovers the same symptoms which are exhibited by the person who has seen the alluring Alabama. Some of our oldest and most wealthy men are offering their possessions for sale and desirous of moving to this new country.[2]

James Henry Hammond stayed behind in South Carolina, but he was sorely tempted: "Nearly every one of the young men with whom I was brought up" had left for either Alabama or Mississippi. "I have been trying to get over my desire for a western plantation, but every time I see a man who has been there it puts me in a fever . . . I must go West and plant."[3]

The Alabama Fever broke out after the Battle of Horseshoe Bend in 1814, when Andrew Jackson forced the defeated Creeks to cede 23 million acres to the United States. As cotton prices reached unimagined heights over the next four years, some $16 million worth of land was sold in Alabama alone. Then British cotton mills turned to India for their supplies. When cotton prices collapsed at the end of 1818, and speculators realized that they could not pay their debts to the Land Office, the Panic of 1819 became national.

Before Jackson's treaty with the Creek nation, only the southern and northern margins of Alabama had been open for settlement, ceded by the Choctaws in 1802 and 1805 and by the Cherokees in 1806. After the Great Creek Cession, there were further forced Choctaw and Chickasaw cessions in 1816, so that three-quarters of the present state and much of Mississippi rapidly became available for purchase. The arc of migration (and speculation) can be traced in the receipts of the Alabama land offices:

1816	$398,000
1817	$1,718,000
1818	$8,676,000
1819	$4,148,000
1820	$1,067,000[4]

Treasury Secretary Crawford presented his report to Congress in 1818, at the end of December. A year earlier, he noted, sales in the state of Ohio and the territories of Indiana, Illinois, and Michigan had exceeded $3 million; $825,000 had sold in Mississippi in 1817 and the same in Alabama. Now, in just the first three-quarters of 1818, the Northwest sales had reached $2.5 million, and Alabama had already sold $3.2 million, more than the rest combined—with the enormous sales from Huntsville in the third quarter not even included.[5]

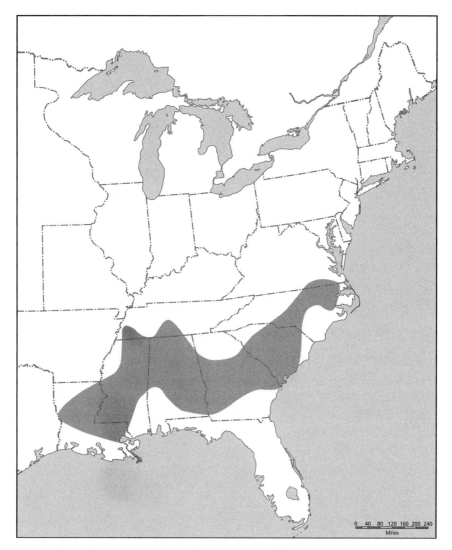

MAP 3. Primary Region of Cotton Production. Map by Chris Robinson.

Senator Charles Tait was one of Crawford's Georgia friends. As the thousands of acres of rich land sold at Huntsville in 1818 to 1819 made national news, he wrote to congratulate their mutual friend John Williams Walker in Alabama on "the most wonderful accounts of their fertility" that were circulating in "the older states." The unprecedented sales were reported with wonder in *Niles' Register* on September 19, October 17, and November 14,

1818; in the *National Intelligencer* on October 9, November 9, November 30, and December 4, 1818; in the (envious) Kaskaskia (Illinois) *Western Intelligencer* on October 2, and in the (hopeful) Missouri *Gazette* on October 9 and November 30.[6]

The pace and scale of the Alabama land sales took the Treasury Department by surprise. In April the Huntsville register, John Read, alerted the Land Office, "The lands sold will probably average higher than any lands of the United States ever sold. . . . There appears to prevail something like a land mania." The minimum price set by law was two dollars per acre; in September 1818, "The highest quarter section was bid off by a respectable planter at one hundred and seven dollars per acre." But each auction brought more astounding news. "The sale of public lands at Milledgeville during the week ending October 27th, amounted to more than seven hundred thousand dollars—a larger sum than the entire sale held at that place last year," *Niles' Register* reported in November. "The whole amount of the sales of land in Alabama, at the late offering of them, it is stated, will exceed three millions of dollars." By the end of that year, the total exceeded $8.6 million.[7]

The Pittsburgh *Gazette* was incredulous that "wild land" in Alabama was selling for "30 dollars an acre, when better land lying within 12 or 15 miles of Natchez could be purchased for from 10 to 20 dollars an acre." The paper had its suspicions: "We are now satisfied that it was a trick played off on the government [by] speculators previous to the sale" conspiring to bid up the price to eliminate competition, "but when payment came to be demanded, the bidders had disappeared. . . . The persons who had laid the plan then appeared, and agreed to buy the land at congress price [i.e., two dollars]!" The high bids, as it turned out, were real enough, but so was speculation—and occasional trickery. One particular combination was put together by the "Broad River Group," a loose affiliation of old friends and associates of the secretary of the treasury. Another was based in South Carolina, and a third was made up of Tennesseans—including Andrew Jackson. All were suspected of the kind of chicanery the *Gazette* described. The Fort Claiborne *Courier* editorialized, "We presume that the gentlemen speculators formed their plans on the commonly received principle, that the public is a goose, and that while its enchanting plumage offered so many temptations to pluck a few feathers, no other danger was to be apprehended than that of being *hissed at*."[8]

The *Courier* hissed, but Crawford's Treasury Department was slow to react. The Alabama land offices forwarded letters of concern, but the secretary, his loyalties divided between his speculative friends and Treasury's interest in high prices, returned them with the annotation, "Needs no attention." Not until July 1820, when the rush was over—and only after at least one land office receiver had acted on his own initiative—did Crawford finally direct officers to "counteract combinations by bidding against them." A year before that Niles had warned, "Care should be taken to guard against the sales of any extensive tracts which the current emigration may not require, whilst every reasonable facility ought to be extended in favor of actual settlers—to check speculation thereon and forbid monopoly."[9]

The actual settlers Niles worried about kept on coming. By 1820 Alabama's burgeoning population reached 75,488: 42,176 whites and 33,272 African American slaves. In the year 1818, seven new counties were organized there, and Mobile began its rise as one of the country's fastest growing seaports, destined to join (briefly) New Orleans and New York in the top three exporting cities. South Carolina and Georgia would remain the leading cotton-producing states for a few more years, but they could grow only three hundred pounds per acre; Alabama's rich, dark soil yielded eight hundred or even one thousand pounds per acre. Mississippi, in Alabama's shadow despite a head start, nevertheless doubled its own population, even though two-thirds of the state remained in the hands of the Choctaw and Chickasaw tribes. In 1819 the state's cotton production also doubled from the preceding year, ahead of Alabama where land was still being cleared. By 1819 the crop in Mississippi would be worth $3 million, but—thanks to the then-falling prices—that was very little more than 1818 had brought for half as much cotton.[10]

It was not only southerners who flocked to Alabama and Mississippi. Francis Corbin was right when he told James Madison, "We see no Foreigners of any Note or Mind coming to settle" in the South; the institution of slavery repelled many, and big cotton plantations were expensive. But Yankees were not deterred. Among the Pennsylvanians who settled in and around Natchez in the early 1800s were Samuel Postlethwaite (who came in 1802), his nephew Stephen Duncan (in 1808) and Duncan's friend Thomas Butler (also in 1808). In the small social circle of Natchez planters, Duncan and Butler married two daughters of Abraham Ellis, and Ellis's brother-in-law, William Mercer, joined Postlethwaite in founding the Bank of Mississippi in 1809. Postlethwaite succeeded Mercer as its president in 1815, and Duncan would follow him in 1825. (All were investors in the Natchez Steamboat Company as well.) Duncan had become a bank director in 1816, just in time to take out large loans to procure cotton land. As a director, he not only got below-market rates but was under no pressure to repay loans, even during the Panic of 1819.[11]

A complication unique to the Southwest was the "Mississippi stock" or "Yazoo scrip." In 1796 Georgia's Federalist state government, in a cloud of bribery and influence peddling, had sold off some 35 million acres of the state's far western Indian reserves along the Yazoo River (now part of Mississippi). Outraged Jeffersonians had then passed legislation to rescind the sales and cede the land to the federal government, along with the rest of the state's western claims. The speculators sued, and in 1810 the Supreme Court declared that the rescission had been unconstitutional, but it was too late by then to undo it. After four more years of contention, Congress voted to resolve the controversy by giving $4 million from Mississippi land receipts to the dissatisfied claimants. The award was made in scrip that could be used only to purchase federal land in Mississippi or Alabama. As always seemed to happen, most of the scrip was bought up by speculators at discounts of 40 to 60 percent. Of the $1.5 million in down payments made at the 1818 Huntsville sales alone, two-thirds came in Yazoo scrip. Buyers kept little of it in reserve for future payments; they were counting on high cotton prices and continued demand to take care of the future.[12]

Aside from the scrip, purchasers usually paid with an ever-expanding array of different banknotes, issued by the banks that were proliferating in small towns as well as big cities. Crawford gave preference to some over others—often out of caution although sometimes, apparently, out of political favoritism—but he spoke to Congress of the new banks in general with disdain in February 1820:

> Banks have been incorporated, not because there was capital seeking investment; not because the places where they were established had commerce or manufactures which required their fostering aid; but because men without active capital wanted the means of attaining loans which their standing in the community would not command from banks or individuals having real capital and established credit.[13]

Many of the new banks merited Crawford's scorn, although others were created by individuals of the highest standing and credit in their communities; and when the Second Bank of the United States opened for business, its initial lending practices were every bit as irresponsible. Despite the disapproval Crawford voiced in 1820, in 1817 and 1818 he had been eager to sell the public lands, and countless farmers and investors had been eager to buy them. Without banknotes there could be no sales, and without loans there was no way to get banknotes into the hands of buyers. In Alabama, where sales were so overwhelming and immigration so rapid, newly created local banks at least offered an alternative to the dozens of distant Kentucky and Tennessee banks whose unfamiliar notes ranged in value from the uncertain to the utterly worthless. In 1818 Crawford acknowledged the soundness of some local banks when he lamented the challenge of discerning them from the notorious "Owl Creek" variety: "The doubtful state of the currency, in most parts of the country resulting from the excessive multiplication of banks by the states, renders it extremely difficult to discriminate between those that are really solvent from those that are not so."[14]

Crawford wrote those words to John Taylor, the receiver at Milledgeville, Georgia, whose office made the first great Alabama sales. Crawford had installed as register at that office his friend Alexander Pope; Pope's cousin was LeRoy Pope, a founder of both the Planters and Merchants Bank at Huntsville and the Indian Creek Navigation Company, whose steamboats took cotton down the Tennessee River to New Orleans. LeRoy, like Crawford a Virginia native who had moved to Georgia, was one of the two most powerful men in the territory. His rival was Israel Pickens, the founder of the Tombeckbe Bank in the southern part of the state and the register of the St. Stephens land office. Crawford would not have questioned either man's "standing in the community," but both founded their banks with the clear intention of personally borrowing from them in order to buy cotton lands and get that cotton to market.

Sales of the Great Creek Cession began at Milledgeville, in central Georgia, in August 1817. Alexander Pope and his clerk would announce the auction of one township—thirty-six square miles—each day from 9 a.m. to 2 p.m.; Pope and his receiver, Taylor, would spend the rest of the hours until dark settling accounts with the day's successful bidders. General Land Office rules called for taking a deposit as each sale was made, but Pope assured Commissioner Meigs that if that policy were followed, "I am persuaded that without five or six competent clerks not more than 12 or 15 Sections could be conveniently sold in a day," and he was struggling with "the impossibility of procuring competent Clerks at any price." He tried to catch up in the evenings instead and sold land three times as fast. In 1818 the Milledgeville office would auction off 292,526 acres for over $1.2 million. Pope could not resist buying several tracts for himself.[15]

Not all the land office receivers and registers who bought land were out to make their fortunes. Land officers who were concerned for either the federal revenues or the actual settlers sometimes found it necessary to bid against combinations of speculators, even before Crawford approved the tactic. Their hope was to keep the combines from snapping up huge tracts at the minimum price and then—often that same afternoon—reselling sections at much higher rates to prospective farmers who could not bid on such large quantities. According to John Coffee, surveyor of public lands at Huntsville, "A plan was proposed by some of the capitalists around Huntsville to form a company . . . to purchase all the land, or as much as they could," by intimidating the competition or bidding on entire townships. Coffee testified to Congress that he, register John Read, and receiver John Brahan had agreed:

> We felt it a duty, by all means within our reach, to oppose the plans of the company, and prevent them if possible from purchasing the lands at the minimum price or below its real value, and thereby speculate upon the government, and on those persons who were desirous to purchase for actual settlement. . . . General Brahan took an active part in bidding against the company, and of course became the purchaser of several high-priced tracts the first day. . . . I know at the time he had a large sum in [Yazoo] scrip, and toward the close of the sales I heard the General remark that his commission would be worth something like thirty thousand dollars, which in addition to his scrip, he thought would pretty well cover his purchases.

Madison County judge Henry Minor confirmed that "General Brahan bought to a very large extent at those sales; and that from all I saw or heard, I believe that his active bidding had a considerable effect in enhancing the prices. I have been informed, and believe, that he has since sold land certificates to a large amount, bought at these sales, at a discount of fifty per cent." Brahan did not in fact have sufficient funds, and the Panic of 1819 prevented his selling all the land he had contracted to purchase. Crawford—whose friends were among the speculators Brahan frustrated—fired him. By the time of his death in 1834, Brahan had repaid the Treasury Department, and Congress voted financial relief to his widow in acknowledgment of his financial loss.[16]

Brahan was a Jackson man—another reason for Crawford's hostility, for he and Jackson were already rivals and bitter enemies. Jackson himself owned shares in at least two land companies and had combined with several other Tennesseans in May 1818 to buy land on behalf of Philadelphia investors; his biographer Robert Remini believes he made as much as $100,000 from land investments, the equivalent of millions today. Nonetheless, the hero of New Orleans and Horseshoe Bend was revered in Alabama; when he appeared in Huntsville in November to bid on a tract, no one would bid against him. He paid the minimum two dollars per acre for a section surrounded by others that went for forty dollars or more per acre; embarrassed, he declined to make any more bids. Jackson and his friends were none too scrupulous in private, but they accused Crawford's friends in the Broad River Group of crossing the line of what was acceptable. James Jackson (no relation) wrote to the general from Huntsville in February 1818, explaining the process Crawford's old neighbors Thomas Bibb and Waddy Tait (or Tate) planned to employ:

[They would] take in the persons who possessed funds, by the strength of which all other purchasers (or as they called them sharp-shooters & quarter-section men) were to be beaten fairly out of the market, the lands gotten for little or nothing—the Company was then to have a second sale, by way of dividing up the property. . . . I declined to have anything to do with them first because there was too much illiberality in the rich combining to push out of the market those who were unfortunate enough not to have funds, second because I dislike these large combinations, and thirdly because I had no confidence in the greater part of those conserned [sic].

Six years before the two adversaries would compete for the presidency, southerners were already dividing into Jackson and Crawford men.[17]

The sales at Huntsville in 1818 set records and helped popularize the expression "doing a land office business," as a description of any wildly successful commercial undertaking. Back in Washington, officials could not envision the frenetic activity. When Crawford told the Huntsville office that he was "extremely dissatisfied on account of your neglecting to settle your accounts, that no longer delay is admissible," register John Read replied, "I hope the Honble Secretary examines well the reports of the business done here during the Public Sales & for some time after, that it will serve as some sort of apology for my suppose [sic] neglect of duty."[18]

The Alabama Fever sales proved to be the high-water mark for the land mania, occurring just as cotton was peaking in Liverpool at nearly twice the price it had been three years earlier (and soon would be again). They followed sales in the Northwest that set what had appeared, until Alabama, to be unbeatable records. In both regions, sales slowed once the Land Office began severely restricting the number of banks whose notes would be considered "land office money"—and after the Bank of the United States began contracting credit. Crawford understood the problems that his policies and those of the BUS were causing, but neither he nor the BUS saw any other choice; too many local banks throughout the West had issued too many banknotes with absolutely no prospect of redeeming them in specie. And even if sound currency had been available, there was the stubborn fact that foreign commodity prices were falling for reasons that had nothing to do with American currency.

Demand by English mills had created a rapid rise in the price of cotton, and the freakish weather of 1816/17 had done the same, briefly, for grain; together those factors had added urgency to the westward movement of so many Americans. A profusion of banknotes had enabled speculators and settlers to make the low down payments that were all that the government required for public lands, and loose credit from the issuing banks had made banknotes easy to obtain. By late 1818 those banknotes might be worth half or less their face value, but the banks (and especially the Bank of the United States) still expected their loans to be repaid. Grain prices fell steadily after 1817, and cotton prices dropped precipitously at the end of 1818. Domestic demand for wheat was steady, but better weather and new western farms increased supply, and the foreign market was greatly reduced once the Corn Law was back in effect. Domestic demand for cotton was weak because few American mills could compete with underpriced British imports, even after the tariff of 1816. The foreign market was about to collapse when British manufacturers switched to cheaper cotton from India, and a million new acres planted in Alabama and Mississippi meant the fast-increasing supply would keep prices down even after the British switched back. Moreover, the fall in cotton prices would be felt throughout the American economy. The Southwest bought flour from the Northwest. Products shipped down the Mississippi to New Orleans included eastern manufactured goods sent overland through Pittsburgh, in addition to the products of that city's own factories. The western and southern states were major markets for American manufacturers, and demand in both regions depended—directly in the South and indirectly in the Northwest—on the cotton export market. Thus, cotton was the single most important factor in both the expansion and the subsequent contraction of the entire American economy. It amounted to 39 percent of all exports in the period from 1815 to 1820, on the way to reaching 59 percent by 1840 to 1860. When the price of cotton rose, the American economy expanded; when it fell—as it did in 1819—all of America suffered.[19]

South Carolina and Georgia generally shipped their cotton from Charleston or Savannah to England, often by way of New York. Cotton from southern Alabama and southern Mississippi went out of Mobile (sometimes on through New York), while cotton from the northern parts of those states, as well as Tennessee, was shipped down the Tennessee or Yazoo Rivers to New Orleans and thence directly to England. When the cotton was sold at Liverpool, it was not paid for with gold or silver to be shipped back to the United States. Like the United States, England was operating on its own paper currency, the notes of the Bank of England. Cotton, therefore, was paid for in bills of exchange, which in turn were used by merchants to purchase goods in London, to be exported to the United States. At each step, commissions were charged and profits taken. Even after the tariff of 1816, America's imports exceeded its exports, so the bills of exchange were not sufficient to meet the need to purchase British goods. Since American banknotes were useless in Britain, there was no alternative but to pay the difference in specie. Officially, England was on a gold standard, but available coins (Spanish or American) were primarily silver. Thus, differences in the balance of trade required silver to be exchanged for gold (in America or in Europe) which was then shipped to England. All of this meant an additional 10 percent cost. For that reason, bills of exchange in London could command a 10 percent premium—which explains why New Englanders had shipped silver to Canada to buy them, in order to acquire imports—war or no war—from England.[20]

America's primary export, cotton, came from the South, but nearly all imports arrived through northern cities on the Atlantic coast. Any cotton planter whose personal balance of trade was positive (buying fewer imported goods than the value of his cotton) was paid the difference in New York banknotes, which were inevitably discounted in the South, hundreds of miles from the issuing banks. A planter in Alabama was well aware of the price paid for cotton in Liverpool, although he was always several weeks behind. He could see 10 percent of his profits skimmed off by the premiums on bills of exchange and another 10 percent lost to the discounts on banknotes. It is no wonder that southern planters resented the middlemen along the way.

Land and slaves were the *sine qua non* of southern society; when a poor boy like Andrew Jackson made good, his first instinct was to buy land and slaves. Most planters who had not pulled themselves up by their bootstraps, as Jackson did, had been educated in the Greek and Roman classics at schools like Moses Waddel's academy, which prepared Calhoun for Yale and John Williams Walker for Princeton. Reading Virgil, Livy, and Plutarch, they found their models in Roman landowners: aristocratic farmers like Cincinnatus, who walked away from his plow to become dictator and save Rome— and then returned to resume plowing where he had left off. Their more recent, Revolutionary American heroes were fellow southerners, self-styled "farmers" like Washington, who was often called the American Cincinnatus. Thus, even more than in England, in the cotton South only landowning had social status. The professions lacked the essential prestige of planting, and gentlemen who practiced law or medicine made it a point to own land and slaves as well. Commerce was left, at least in public, to Yankees. Merchants were social inferiors in the eyes of the upper classes and predators in the eyes of the poorer farmers. The wealthy planter might be arrogant, but he did not make his profit off his neighbor; bankers and cotton factors clearly did.[21]

A land rush was inevitable when the availability of rich new soil was coupled with the escalating price of cotton. In England, the homeland of technological progress, factories continually demanded more raw material, and as the historian Eric Hobsbawm famously declared, "Whoever says industrial revolution says cotton." England's increasingly mechanized mills had been starved for cotton during the War of 1812. After peace returned in 1815 and the army and navy demobilized, Britain faced the threat of revolution if large-scale unemployment was not prevented; preservation of the social order required full factory employment, which meant textile exports must be kept up—even, if necessary, at a loss. Raw cotton imports therefore more than doubled in the first year of peacetime, reaching 125 million pounds in 1817 and 177 million pounds in 1818.[22]

By no means all of the cotton came from the United States; even as late as the 1850s nearly a quarter of British cotton imports came from somewhere else. Before the cotton gin, Britain had imported no North American cotton at all; it came in from other British colonies or from colonies of France, the Netherlands, and Portugal. As much as 25 percent was purchased in the city of Smyrna in the Ottoman Empire. In the 1780s Liverpool customs officials refused to acknowledge that cotton was even grown in the United States, but in 1801 almost 10 percent of imported cotton was purchased from the United States, and by 1807 half came from the American South, primarily Georgia and South Carolina.[23]

From 1816 to 1818 American cotton production averaged 125 million pounds per year, with most going to England, a little to other European countries, and a small fraction remaining for the home market. From 1819 to 1821 annual production averaged 170 million pounds, exceeding 200 million pounds from 1822 to 1824. Such quantities obviously relied on the British market. It took only two or three years to go from raw land to cotton crops in Alabama; as new fields began to produce, southern Alabama's crop increased from an annual average of 5.5 million pounds between 1818 and 1820 to 23 million pounds between 1822 and 1824; it would average 40 million pounds per year between 1827 and 1829. Northern Alabama, separated both socially and economically from the southern part of the state, had been almost entirely unsettled before 1810, but by 1820 it had a free population of 27,352 and an enslaved population of 11,541. Its "Big Bend" of the Tennessee River, where land began to be sold in 1817, produced an estimated 15 million pounds of cotton in 1821, and the rest of the northern region added another 10 million. New Orleans, the cotton depot for Tennessee, Mississippi, and northern Alabama, went from shipping 18.5 million pounds in 1816 to exporting 80 million in 1822.[24]

At any other time such an increase in cotton supply would have meant an instant collapse of prices, but thanks to the extraordinary demand in England, the first few years of increased supply were accompanied by increased prices. Late in the war (November 1814) the wholesale price at blockaded Charleston had sunk as low as nine cents per pound, but within six months of the peace it had doubled; by December 1815 it was at twenty-five cents, and during 1816 and 1817 it averaged twenty-eight. It was then that land sales at Huntsville began to set records and cotton production from existing plantations increased. From January to November 1818 the price was never less than thirty cents per pound.

As long as the price of cotton was high, so was the price of Alabama land—and the demand for it. When cotton sold for thirty cents per pound and the cost of growing it was about half that, the annual profit averaged $130 per acre. Under those conditions a price of $50 or even $75 per acre in 1818 seemed like a bargain. From 1815 to 1819, the relative shares of tobacco, rice, and forest products declined in the export market; wheat and flour fluctuated with the Corn Law, never exceeding than 16 percent of exports; but cotton accounted for as much as 40 percent of all American exports by value. While American mills struggled to compete—some more successfully than others—the English demand for raw cotton seemed only to grow. Like shares of stock in 1929 or real estate in 2007, it seemed the sky was the limit. Exports of cotton to England kept growing, to 51 million pounds in 1816, 61 million in 1817, and 68 million in 1818, but the price increased just as quickly.[25]

It was too good to last. By the fall of 1818 there were darkening clouds on the horizon, and warnings began to be sounded. They came from one of the early boosters of the American cotton industry, Tench Coxe, a prolific (some might say compulsive) writer on political and economic matters. Coxe strongly supported protective tariffs and domestic consumption, and he was worried about what seemed a dangerous dependence on exports. In 1817 he had published an essay called "The Cotton Culture, the Cotton Commerce, the Cotton Manufactures." Late in 1818 he published an "Addition" to it that sounded an ominous note: "The continuation of so good a price for cotton wool (which sensibly declined in England in September) is owing, undoubtedly, to the power and improvements of machinery, and the substitution of cotton for linen, wool, leather, and silk, in modern manufactures. But these two causes have their limits." Prices slid 20 percent in December 1818 and fell fast in the new year until they settled at fifteen cents. Cotton had lost half its value, and there the price would remain, wavering up or down no more than four cents, until 1823, when oversupply sank it as low as 8½ cents per pound, a quarter of its 1818 high.[26]

In 1816 the directors of the East India Company had shipped Whitney cotton gins to Bombay. As the profits on exports to the United States shrank to nothing, England was actively looking for other, cheaper sources of cotton than the American South. In the first nine months of 1817 England imported 175,650 bales from the United States—along with 65,850 bales from Brazil, 36,750 from the West Indies, and 72,830 from India. In the first nine months of 1818, American cotton imports had increased by 20,000 bales, but Brazilian imports were up by an additional 62,000 and Indian by 103,000. Late in the year Coxe was warning Americans that

"the advance in the cotton trade from Hindoostan to Europe is wonderful. . . . [A]s our greatest export of any two successive years has been 135,000 bales for each year, to Great Britain, and as the East Indies are now making them up 220,000 bales

in the current year, 1818, for the British market . . . the year 1819 seems likely to bring the whole subject of our cotton crop, capacity and consumption, into the most serious consideration and trial."[27]

Supply had finally caught up with demand. Coxe's contacts in England were good, and his figures were accurate. "The cotton market of England, in September [1818], after the return of the spinners to their work, was languid, and prices declining: stocks of cotton great, increasing, and likely to be very heavy by the first of January 1819. There is every prospect of reduced prices." As sales of British textiles slowed in a listless European economy, Coxe warned that "the accumulation of cotton in the British and European markets, arising from the increased cultivation, and especially from the vast importations from India, is expressly noticed in British letters to this country by some of the last vessels."[28]

Niles' Register would shortly begin publishing some of those letters; the paper noted that one from Liverpool, dated December 11, "strikes at the consumption of our great staple with exceeding force":

Whereas the stocks in Liverpool at the close of the year will probably be about 45,000 bales of American cotton instead of 19,000 bales at the close of last year . . . [a] scarcity of money (which is now considerably felt) is likely, in our opinion, to have a material effect on the market, and keeping down the prices of all descriptions of property.[29]

Another letter, dated February 16, was even more direct:

Upland [cotton] is now selling at 15 to 16½ d. per pound. The importations have been greater than we expected—and we have accordingly to recommend to you, not to ship that sort, unless you obtain a good quality at 20 cents. . . . P.S. 23rd February. Since the foregoing was written, cotton has declined one half penny per pound, in consequence of which we would recommend you not to ship at a higher price than 18 cents.

The writer went on to note that the Corn Law was once again in force, so that wheat and flour would be excluded at least until May, and probably until August 1819. As it turned out, the exclusion continued until 1823.[30]

Throughout the spring of 1819 news from Britain continued to be grim. On March 28, "The [London] *Gazette* of last night contains a list of *thirty* bankrupts; some of the houses have been established nearly a century." On April 9, "Great numbers of woolen and cotton weavers are said to be out of employ in England, on account of the diminished demand . . . and fears are entertained for the public peace." Ferris Pell, in New York, warned that "the Bank of England is abridging its circulation [of banknotes] and diminishing the nominal value of every species of property." The Boston *Weekly Report* told its readers that the Bank of England had "reduced its circulation by . . . about forty million dollars" and "the extent to which this depression will go is as yet uncertain—nor is it in the power of any body to foresee it." Several banks in England were reported by Niles to have stopped payment on July 12, 1819, and "Several very large meetings of the laboring classes have been held . . . The distress of these people seems to be exceedingly great."[31]

Britain was falling into an economic depression of its own, and a financial contraction combined with a supply surplus to send cotton prices still lower: fifteen cents per pound in April, fourteen in May, and thirteen in June, falling below the cost of production before edging back up to the break-even point in the autumn. The *value* of American cotton exports fell from $31 million in 1818 to $21 million in 1819, even as the *amount* substantially increased. In 1820, when British mills abandoned their Indian sources, almost 50 percent more cotton was exported to England than in 1819, and yet the value of the 1820 exports was a million dollars less. The Augusta (Georgia) *Herald* dolefully acknowledged:

> The distressing accounts from Great Britain and the continent of Europe, appear to have at length convinced the planters, as well as the merchants, that the staple produce of our state, has really been above its actual value. More than three thousand bales of cotton are stored in this city, for which 23 or 24 cts. per lb. has been refused, which would not now sell for 15 cts.
>
> Speculations to an immense amount have been entered into, upon a mere hope of a profit, and the consequences must be ruinous: indeed, the extent of the evil can scarcely be imagined. Men, who six months ago were wealthy, have hazarded their fortunes upon a speculation which has failed; although they are not actually insolvent, yet their losses, consequent upon the sudden decline of cotton, has [*sic*] swallowed up the profits of years of industry.[32]

The Philadelphia *Aurora*, through which William Duane had long promoted protection of domestic industry and opposed dependence on imports, took a self-righteous tone: "Let the American people now turn to the spindle; the day is near at hand when the cotton planter will earnestly desire his cotton to be sold in domestic mart only. . . . We are going to have sad times, and plenty of goods under the hammer at any price they will bring." Duane's prediction of hard times was right, but he was wrong about the lesson the planter would learn. As it turned out, England's downturn was neither so long nor so severe as America's. Mill owners had never expected to replace superior American cotton permanently with an alternative that they acknowledged was inferior, and once the Indian imports had done their work in driving down prices, English mills returned to American cotton. (Not only were supplies from India understood to be of poorer quality, but resentful Indian subjects of John Company sometimes went out of their way to contaminate shipments with sticks, stones, and even dung hidden in the bales.) On May 25, 1819, the banker Alexander Baring told the House of Commons, "An article which has lately come in great abundance from India, cotton, will probably not come at all since the cotton of America is reduced to its present rates." His prediction was more accurate than Duane's; in 1822 only 4 million pounds of cotton was imported from India, compared to 142.5 million from the United States. By then the price of cotton had fallen yet again to a new low, but John C. Calhoun, a substantial planter, took note that consumption was again "enormous" and was relieved that competition from India had almost disappeared.[33]

The glut of overpriced cotton had done its damage, damage not limited to the cotton planters. Coxe had pointed out that because the cotton industry "employs a large portion of our population [and] forty millions of dollars are nearly half our whole annual exports of the latest year . . . the markets of rice and other grains, cattle, and tobacco will languish, when cotton shall decline in price." They did. Tobacco export values fell by one-eighth, and wheat exports declined from $18 million in 1817 to $12 million in 1818 and $6 million in 1819; sales of wheat farmland fell off faster than those of southern cotton land, and speculators in the Northwest were ruined. As European harvests improved, Russian wheat exporters suffered the same losses, and— as dominoes fell across thousands of miles—in 1819 there was a 50 percent drop in American exports to Russia of iron, hemp, and sailcloth (woven from hemp: "canvas" is an old French corruption of the Latin "cannabis"). Virginia, where wheat had displaced tobacco as the most valuable crop, suffered a loss of 56 percent of the value of its exports, not only from lower prices but from a continuing decline in quantity; total inspections of flour for shipment dropped about 40 percent from 1819 to 1822.[34]

The prices of America's two greatest exports, cotton and wheat, fell because of the rise in supply and drop in demand; other prices were doubtless influenced by a general deflation as the money supply contracted. But one other commodity's price directly followed that of cotton: slaves. Virginia had become, to the embarrassment of some of its prominent residents, a leading exporter of slaves to cotton plantations. Francis Corbin had written to his friend James Madison, expressing his regret that it was now "Our Negroes, upon whose increase ('miserable dictu') our principal profit depends." Between 1810 and 1820 at least fifty thousand slaves were taken from the Chesapeake states to the new Southwest; the English abolitionist Adam Hodgson, traveling through America between 1819 and 1821, estimated that "from Maryland and Virginia alone, from 4000 to 5000 per annum are occasionally sent down to New-Orleans; a place the very name of which seems to strike terror into the slaves and free Negroes of the Middle States." The slave population was being relocated; Virginians had owned 45 percent of all southern slaves in 1790 but only 28 percent in 1820.[35]

The price of slaves closely tracked that of cotton both on the way up and on the way down: slaves sold for more in New Orleans than in Virginia, reflecting the proximity to the cotton fields, but a field hand in New Orleans who would bring $1,200 or even more before the Panic sold for only $700 in 1823. As the depression deepened, the price of slaves in Virginia dropped 37 percent between 1819 and 1822. The *Kentucky Gazette* reported in the fall of 1819, "Slaves which sold some time ago, could command the most ready money, have fallen to an inadequate value. A slave which hires for $80 or $100 per annum, may be purchased for $300 or $400." The following spring, Hodgson wrote from Natchez to his British readers, "When cotton rises the value of negroes advances in almost the same proportion. Indian corn, the primary article of subsistence, follows, but at a little distance, because it can be imported from other states, and land [follows] at a still greater [distance], because almost any planter possesses more than he actually cultivates. Corresponding effects are produced by a fall of cotton in foreign markets." In the winter of 1820/21 Hodgson, by then in Virginia, reported that "Slaves . . . in Norfolk are now worth on an average 300 to 400 dollars each." That was half the 1818 price.[36]

When cotton and land were in the greatest demand in 1818, the uncle of a young Mississippi planter named Samuel Steer had advised him to purchase shares of the Bank of Mississippi. Steer replied, "While cotton can command from 20 to 30 cts. per lb. Negroes will yield a much larger income than any bank dividends." He added, "For a young man just commencing in life, the best stock in which he can invest is, I think, Negro stock." His was a widely held belief: between 1790 and 1810, as Georgia cotton production grew from 3,138 bales to 117,824, the state's slave population grew from 29,000 to 105,000.[37]

Adam Hodgson, like many English visitors to America, was morally opposed to the institution of slavery and "the horrid atrocities that it gives birth to, even under a government pre-eminently free." But he could speak dispassionately about slavery while predicting that the dropping price of cotton—rather than moral pressure—might put an end to it:

> It is one of the inconveniencies to which slaveholders are exposed (especially where the range of articles to which the climate is favorable is limited) that they are constantly liable to a great extinction of capital by a reduction in the foreign market of the articles they produce. . . . The depreciation may proceed so far that the labour of a slave is worth so little more than his maintenance as to afford no recompense to his owner for his care and superintendence.[38]

A number of southerners agreed; the Jeffersonian view of slavery as a still-necessary evil which was "on the path to ultimate extinction" had not yet been replaced by the argument that it was a positive good; even Calhoun would not take that position until 1837. Madison and his correspondent Corbin shared a moral repugnance toward slavery even as they continued to hold slaves. In the same letter in which he decried Virginia's participation in the slave trade, Corbin (like Hodgson) expressed his hope that the economic depression would push slavery to collapse under its own weight: "I think slavery is working its own cure. Under the best management, with daily vexation and never ending violence to our feelings, it does not afford two per ct. upon our Capital, and often brings us into debt." Besides his pragmatic belief "that slavery and [wheat] farming are incompatible," he was also hopeful that the crisis over Missouri would bring the issue to a head: "We must either abandon the pure morality of Republicanism, or the gross and glaring immorality of slavery."[39]

Hodgson and Corbin, however, were overlooking two critical factors. First was the reality that in the cotton South slave owning was not only a practical necessity but a social one. The economic historians Samuel Williamson and

Louis Cain have recently calculated that the "labor income value" of a slave rose more steeply from 1817 to 1820, as thousands of acres were newly planted in cotton, than at any other period in history—by more than 125 percent over three years. However, "as a signaling device of [social] status," a slave's "status value" in dollars increased even faster, by 150 percent. As a proportion of the total national wealth, "the value of the slave population in 1819–20 has never been matched."[40]

Second, southwestern planters could still afford to continue raising cotton with slave labor; indeed, they could not afford to do otherwise. The vast lands purchased at Huntsville in 1818 had not produced their first crop when the price of cotton fell, but the land and the slaves were there, and the only way to survive lower prices was to plant even more cotton. While increased supply would continue to drive prices down, demand eventually had to grow again; in 1819, despite a *price* drop of 50 percent per pound, the *value* of U.S. cotton exports dropped only 30 percent—compared to 42 percent for overall exports—and it began to rise again as soon as 1820. It was a matter of accepting lower, sometimes marginal, profits and putting faith in volume. The national cotton crop that had averaged 125 million pounds annually from 1816 to 1818 grew to an average of 170 million in 1819 to 1821 and over 200 million in 1822 to 1824; the increase in supply kept the price from recovering, but the fertile soil and slave labor were so productive that planters could break even as long as they kept expanding. When land sales in Indiana and Illinois decreased by nearly two-thirds in 1819, the frenetic Alabama sales slowed only by half; the 1819 sales in Cahaba, Alabama—even after the drop in cotton prices—still brought in nearly $3 million.[41]

Hodgson and Corbin were mistaken in their predictions, and the internal slave trade slowed only briefly; Virginia and Maryland continued selling thousands of slaves each year to Alabama, Mississippi, and Louisiana. In 1821 Supreme Court Justice Bushrod Washington, nephew of the former president, sold fifty-four of his ninety slaves to the Southwest, and in April 1820 the congressional gadfly John Randolph of Roanoke, unwavering enemy of tariffs, internal improvements, and all forms of "encroaching federal power," placed a notice in the Baltimore *Federal Gazette* and other newspapers:

MISSOURI—*To Southern and Western Planters, For Sale*—One Hundred prime Virginia born SLAVES, the property of a planter who is contracting the scale of his business and does not choose that ALL the produce of his land and labor should go into the pockets of manufacturers or fund holders. These slaves will

be sold all together, or in families, to suit purchasers—Conditions—CASH and
removal, not south of the State of Georgia.

After his death in 1833, all of Randolph's slaves (numbering 383) were eventually freed in accordance with his will, and resettled in Ohio. But during the
decade of the 1820s at least 155,000 slaves were brought into the Southwest
from eastern states to expand the production of cotton.[42]

No future land sales would ever match those of 1818, but in 1820, when Illinois land offices sold only $87,000, Alabama sales were still over $1 million,
even though cotton sold for only seventeen cents per pound. It would take
a long time for that price to rise. The supply curve for cotton, as Douglass
North has pointed out, was steep: "The large increase in output . . . caused
a tremendous shift to the right in the supply curve and the beginning of [a]
lengthy period of digesting the increased capacity." Even with the rapidly
rebounding demand in England, it took another decade for demand to catch
up to supply. By the time it did, the lessons of 1819 were already being forgotten. If anyone should have learned from the Panic of 1819 it was Nicholas
Biddle, who replaced Langdon Cheves as president of the BUS. But after
Biddle lost his Bank War with Andrew Jackson, he destroyed his own fortune in a misbegotten attempt to corner the cotton market in 1836 to 1837.
He purchased enormous amounts of cotton through his family's Liverpool
affiliate, Humphrey and Biddle, with the plan of holding it back from English
manufacturers and forcing up prices. But when the price fell instead in the
Panic of 1837, English mills refused Biddle's cotton and he was ruined. He
was sued by the investors in his scheme, arrested, and charged with criminal
conspiracy. Like the BUS officers who faced similar charges in 1819, Biddle
was acquitted—but by then the country was once again plunged into a deep
depression.[43]

Both steadily rising cotton prices and surging grain prices after the "volcano
weather" of 1816 lured Americans to buy millions of dollars of land with
loans that, after 1819, many could not repay. In his 2013 *Nation of Gamblers:
Real Estate Speculation and American History*, economist Edward Glaeser notes
that the 1817/18 economic boom was "fueled by optimism about . . . England's demand for American cotton," and he attributes the 1819 bust to the
failure of that cotton market; Madison came to the same conclusion in 1821,
telling Richard Rush that "a surplus . . . for which foreign demand has failed
is a primary cause of the present embarrassment of this country." As North

points out, "Direct income from the cotton trade was probably no more than 6 percent of any plausible estimate of national income [but] it set in motion the whole process of accelerated expansion [and] . . . was the key industry in both the expansion and subsequent collapse and readjustment." Both North and Arthur Cole have demonstrated the close connection between wheat and cotton prices and the land booms in the years before the Panics of 1819, 1837, and 1857.[44]

In just the four states of Alabama, Ohio, Indiana, and Illinois, $25 million worth of land was sold in 1817 to 1819 at 25 percent down; three-quarters of that debt remained unpaid when prices collapsed, money contracted, and buyers began begging the federal government to accept unimproved lands back in return for debt cancellation. The victims were not all speculators; actual farmers and settlers were hurt, especially in the Northwest. The larger southern planters coped by selling more cotton at lower prices, but everywhere land speculators were becoming desperate—and as the *Western Intelligencer* had pointed out, it seemed that everyone in the West had, "to a greater or lesser degree, become a dealer" in land.[45]

The economist Murray Rothbard divides the blame for low export prices between the improved European harvest of 1817 (true for grain, but not for cotton) and a business contraction in Britain during the following year. But overall British imports of cotton actually increased substantially in 1818 and declined only briefly in 1819 once a surplus had piled up. By then the high price of American cotton had been successfully attacked by British importers who temporarily shifted to Indian cotton, tolerating its inferior quality just long enough to force the price down—much as British exporters had bitten the bullet in 1815 when they dumped products below cost, in an attempt to destroy American manufacturing. Neither strategy could be sustained in the long run, but their combined effect on the American economy was dire.[46]

Rothbard also blames the contraction of the American money supply that occurred just as debtors across the country were in sore need of liquidity, certainly another cause of falling prices. The economy at the beginning of 1819 was descending into a vicious circle—or a perfect storm. Huge debts for land made farmers especially vulnerable to the falling price of their produce, and cotton planters bought still more land in order to raise more cotton to compensate for the lower prices. The flood of cheap, auction-priced British goods after the return of peace dealt a blow to both American manufacturers and merchants, leading to lower wages and the unfamiliar specter of unemployment. Consumers, with reduced incomes, bought less and looked for the lowest prices, which usually meant imports. The postwar European demand had opened up a tempting export market for wheat and cotton, but the rush to take advantage of high export prices created a surplus that drove those prices back down. And just as corporate investors, speculators, and farmers were scrambling to pay their debts, much of the available currency was suddenly rejected by the largest creditors—the General Land Office and the Bank of the United States.[47]

The causes and the effects of the monetary contraction by the BUS must be examined, but first it is necessary to understand the process of monetary *expansion* that inflated the financial bubble in the first place. The Bank of the United States bore its share of responsibility for that as well, but it was above all the consequence of the hundreds of banks that proliferated in the years from 1812 to 1819. They seemed to spring up like mushrooms—practically overnight and often in the dark—and like mushrooms, they could be dangerously difficult to distinguish between.

BANK EXPANSION
"Frothy Bubbles"

Nobody liked banks, because nobody trusted banks—least of all the bankers themselves. Spencer Roane, chief justice of the Virginia Supreme Court of Appeals, declared that "banking is an evil of the first magnitude." In the wake of the Panic of 1819, Virginia governor Thomas Mann Randolph told his state's legislature that rather than promoting economic growth, banks "beyond all doubt have a strong tendency to prevent permanent advances by capitalists for the promotion of useful industry, and facilitate and encourage those employments of money least beneficial to the general interest of society." The legislature agreed, and Virginia would charter no new banks for the next fifteen years, until the conclusion of Andrew Jackson's war on the Bank of the United States.[1]

Nobody trusted banks because nobody trusted paper money. The hostility was deeply rooted. Washington had warned in 1786, "Paper money has had the effect . . . that it will ever have: to ruin commerce, oppress the honest, and open the door to every species of fraud and injustice." Two years later Jefferson declared, "Paper is poverty. It is only the ghost of money, not money itself," and in 1809, John Adams flatly stated, "Every dollar of a [paper] bank bill that is issued beyond the quantity of gold and silver in the vaults represents nothing and is therefore a cheat upon somebody." The Founders' generation remembered the paper issued by the states after the Revolution, which had created terrible inflation and led the Constitutional Convention to specifically authorize the United States to *coin* money—but to say nothing about *printing* it.[2]

As the feverish economy heated up after the War of 1812, the aging Jefferson continued to rail against the "bank paper" foisted on virtuous farmers by the banks of the corrupt cities: "It never was, and is not, any confidence in their frothy bubbles, but the want of all other medium which induced, or now induces, the country people to take their paper." And as the Panic was spreading across the country in 1819, Adams wrote to Jefferson that while shaving gold coins was obviously criminal, "a theft of greater magnitude and still more ruinous is the making of paper. It is greater because in this money there is absolutely no real value. It is more ruinous because by its gradual depreciation . . . it produces the effect which will be produced by an infinity of successful deteriorations of coin." Real money was gold or silver. Years before, James Madison had written notes for a speech to the Virginia Assembly, attacking paper money that was "destroying that confidence between man & man, by which resources one may be commanded by another." Since opposing Hamilton's Federalist banking proposals, he had come around to the necessity of a national bank; but his cousin John Taylor of Caroline remained an Old Republican and a leading anti-bank theoretician. In 1814, as state banks were suspending the redemption of their notes in silver, Taylor argued that paper money "invariably impoverishes all the laboring and productive classes" and declared that "a paper system, in any form, will rob a nation of prosperity without giving it liberty; and by creating and enriching a speculative interest, will rob it of liberty without giving it prosperity." (Taylor had learned rhetoric from the speeches of his neighbor Patrick Henry.)[3]

The evils of paper money were an article of faith long before the Panic struck, but that financial crisis would confirm the orthodox belief. In November 1818 Jefferson wrote again to Gallatin, in Paris: "The flood with which [banks] are deluging us of nominal money has placed us completely without any certain measure of value, and by interpolating a false measure, is deceiving and ruining multitudes of our citizens." It would soon ruin him; he was deeply in debt to banks and about to go deeper. The author of the lengthy *Cause and Cure of Hard Times*, under the Jeffersonian pseudonym of "Seventy-Six," blamed the Panic on "paper gold, and paper land, and paper houses, and paper revenues, and paper government."[4]

Reacting to the Panic, when gold and silver were nearly impossible to get and most banknotes badly depreciated, there was a movement (especially in the West) for abandoning specie entirely—for adopting a national currency with no connection to precious metal, what is now generally known as *fiat* money. On January 9, 1819, *Niles' Register* darkly warned, "The curses of the paper system are falling heavily upon the people—and to *relieve* them, powerful efforts are making to seduce congress to become manufacturers of paper money. Scheme follows scheme, and project is heaped upon project—some of which out-do Law's famous Mississippi ballooning in France, or the not much less celebrated South sea bubble in England." Like so many others, Niles could not resist drawing the parallel with the great swindles of the previous century. And like Jefferson, Niles viewed the collapse as the work of city sophisticates, impoverishing the honest but innocent country folk: he anticipated "the day of settlement—WHICH EVERYBODY KNOWS MUST COME" and warned that "persons residing in town have generally a very faint idea of the distress that prevails in some parts of the country."[5]

Secretary of State John Quincy Adams, his attention focused on difficult negotiations with Spain, mentioned the growing financial unrest in his diary only after occasions when Treasury Secretary Crawford brought it up, but it gradually began to penetrate his consciousness. A week after his testimony on behalf of the French silversmiths, he wrote in his diary about a conversation with John C. Calhoun, who had earlier led the campaign to charter the Second Bank of the United States: "I called on Mr. Calhoun, the Secretary of War, at his office. . . . He thinks we shall unavoidably come within a year to a paper-money currency, and I believe he judges rightly. We shall come to it, and to all its unjust and cruel consequences—the last of which to be dreaded is a civil war between debtors and creditors."[6]

Adams had recently returned from his post as minister to England, and he was one of many who associated paper money with Great Britain, which had not been redeeming notes in specie since 1797. Another was William Duane, the Irish immigrant who published the *Aurora* in Philadelphia. Duane had once been an advocate of paper money, but he warned shortly before the embargo that "the *paper money*, the *mercantile*, and the *banking* system" would take America down the path of England, where "poverty, stupidity, disease, and vice have suspended industry, intelligence, health, and innocence." At the beginning of 1819, South Carolina attorney general Robert Y. Hayne wrote to his friend Langdon Cheves, who was about to take over as president of the BUS, "It seems to me that the final result will be the stoppage of specie payments by all the banks and then we will find it necessary to follow the example of Great Britain and deal on paper. The time is approaching rapidly when gold or silver will be regarded as merchandise only and bill will become the current coin."[7]

Niles dunned subscribers (on his front page) to pay up—but only in notes redeemable in specie. He never missed an opportunity to suggest that paper bills were no different from counterfeits; employing a favorite device, the anecdote ascribed to a distant and anonymous correspondent, he reported,

> A gentleman residing in Missouri, on our returning to him a counterfeit bill, observes—"that most genuine bills are as really counterfeit as any other!" Indeed, some of the deceptions are worthy of sleight-of-hand-men. A person this day paid us a note, which he received as having been issued at Philadelphia— and so it was; but unfortunately for him, it was "*New* Philadelphia;"—the "new" printed very small and the "Philadelphia" very large—*ad captandum* ["to ensnare the vulgar"]! Is this right? Is it indeed *lawful*?

Niles also enjoyed repeating stories of counterfeit paper circulating in locales as disparate as Kentucky and Boston and warned of altered denominations on bills from New York.[8]

Jefferson saw the same equivalency; he told Gallatin that when paper money was proffered, "no man will receive it but to pass it away immediately," the same reaction that the merchant John Neal had to the counterfeit bills that he estimated made up 10 percent of his receipts. Neal quoted a local proverb: "If you buy the devil, the sooner you sell him the better," and he passed along counterfeits as quickly as possible. Allen Trimble recalled, "It was almost impossible for a man of business not to have a counterfeit bill occasionally in his possession, and it was considered by many persons not improper to pass them off, and no exception by public opinion taken to such acts." Banknotes of dubious value were, as Jefferson said, treated much the same; the industrialist Ichabod Washburn seems to have felt worse about using an "uncurrent five dollar Ohio Bank Bill" than most of his contemporaries did about passing counterfeits. He had been on a trip through Massachusetts while still a young apprentice and was surprised that a tavern keeper took the bill and gave him $4.50 in change—but he made a point of avoiding that tavern on his return trip. Almost everyone agreed that paper money was dangerous, untrustworthy, and immoral—and almost everyone agreed that they could not do without it. Banks, while just as suspect, were just as necessary.[9]

The problem was that the modern market economy required cash. Barter might still work on the frontier, but urban commerce had long since abandoned it. Cotton planters ultimately exchanged their crops for the manufactured goods they needed, but several intermediate paper steps were required. You could not purchase land or slaves with bales of cotton or pay turnpike tolls with bushels of corn. Bushels of gold and silver were equally impractical:

the quantity of specie needed to pay for a house or a power loom was not merely cumbersome, it was simply unavailable. And a growing economy demanded credit as well as cash, banks as well as banknotes. Time and distance made commercial credit indispensable; the cultivation of staple crops in America had depended on credit since John Rolfe introduced tobacco planting in 1619. A crop required a season between planting and harvest, and buyers were many miles (and weeks) away. Credit was necessary to purchase a cargo that would not be paid for until it reached a far-off port. An expanding economy required credit to invest in future returns, and a geographically expanding population required both cash and credit to purchase new land.

Without banks, the American economy would have remained in the eighteenth century, dependent on a purely local exchange or at the mercy of foreign creditors. Corporations were an engine of growth, but if they were to be transformed from the royal monopolies of merchant-adventurers into businesses that built and operated bridges, factories, and—very soon—railroads, they would need cash to pay labor and credit to make capital investments in land or machinery. And their customers would need cash to purchase their services and products: barter would not serve for steamboat fares or calico cloth by the yard. Andrew Jackson, the epitome of the new American, still insisted that only gold and silver were legitimate money—hence the Bank War and Specie Circular of his presidency, after he was swept into office on an anti-banking tide that accused financiers of enriching themselves from the labor of more honest men. But Bertrand Russell, in his history of the nineteenth century, states the underlying reality:

> Jackson and his supporters were all anxious to profit from the opportunities for growing rich that existed in the West. Those who owned slaves saw nothing objectionable in appropriating the results of their labor, and those who speculated in real-estate did not wish to lose the chance to gain when their land increased in value. . . . So long as the kinds of gain they desired for themselves are permitted, so long the banker's kind of gain must also be permitted. Jackson, therefore, could only decree that banking be badly done, not that it should cease altogether.[10]

The rapid expansion of banks and bank credit at the beginning of the nineteenth century did not cause the Panic of 1819, but neither the economic boom nor the inevitable bust could have happened without it. Farmers could survive a drop in commodity prices if their land was not mortgaged, and merchants could get by if they had not borrowed to acquire their inventory—or accepted too many risky banknotes in payment. (Unemployed wage-earners were simply out of luck.) But more and more farmers had felt the need to borrow in order to move beyond mere subsistence, and merchants really had no choice about either borrowing or extending credit if they wished to do business.

In the first two decades of the nineteenth century, American banks grew like cancers, were begotten like bastard children, or descended upon the land like locusts—all of those figures of speech were employed at the time and all, at some point, seemed apt, but it is true that the new bankers and their customers were alike inexperienced, and as the economy ballooned, they were all equally eager to "get forward." At the close of the Revolutionary War, there was only one bank in the new United States of America: Philadelphia's Bank of North America, chartered in 1781. A second opened in 1784 in New York City and a third shortly thereafter in Boston. By 1800 there were twenty-nine—almost a tenfold increase in banks, but with only a sixfold increase in capital. Ten years later the number had grown to ninety, and ten years after that (in 1820) there were more than three hundred. Those Federalist-chartered banks before 1800—including Hamilton's original Bank of the United States—were located in commercial Atlantic cities. Their customers were primarily merchants, and their loans, limited to thirty, sixty, or at most a hundred days, were rarely renewed. But after 1800, new Republican banks began targeting farmers. No longer restricted to seaports, they started to offer loans for periods of two, three, or five years—long enough to buy land (and slaves) and to get in a crop or two before the loan was due. More and more often, they allowed borrowers to extend their loans, renewing them when they reached their terms instead of paying them off.[11]

States quickly came to view credit as necessary to their growth, and they chartered more and more banks in order to help their commerce compete with that of neighboring states. Virginia, which in a few years would become the center of hostility to banks, was initially eager to charter them. Baltimore, by 1800, was clearly surpassing Norfolk and Alexandria in its import and export traffic. To many Virginians, Baltimore's banks appeared to be the key to expanding the economy of its hinterland. Norfolk had one of the best natural harbors in the Mid-Atlantic, but no banks; the Virginia Assembly provided them by requiring its state-chartered banks to open branches there, at the same time that it began requiring any new banks to pay into the state's Fund for Internal Improvements, to enlarge its distribution network. Other states followed that example. Pennsylvania had four state-chartered banks before 1810, but as New York moved ahead of Philadelphia in its commerce—soon boasting seven chartered banks with over a million dollars in capital—the Pennsylvania legislature responded by chartering forty-one banks in a single piece of legislation in 1814. (It is not certain how many of them actually opened for business; some clearly did not.)[12]

The small state of New Hampshire had ten banks, in six different towns, by 1813. By 1818 booming Ohio had twenty-six banks. Kentucky, home of the commercial cities of Lexington and Louisville and surrounded by thousands of potential borrowers buying land in adjacent states and territories, found itself with only one bank (opened in 1806), so in 1818 the legislature chartered forty more banks—thirty-three in one act. The bemused editor of the Cincinnati *Liberty Hall* commented, "A new idea has sprung up that the only way to destroy the monopoly of banking is to make it universal." (The new banks lasted less than two years; once the Panic hit Kentucky, only sixteen remained open through 1819, and the next year the state rescinded their charters in favor of a single state-owned Bank of the Commonwealth.) The western land bubble that was making everyone "to a greater or lesser degree" a real-estate dealer now seemed to be mass-producing bankers. The Methodist circuit rider James B. Finley remarked, "Everybody went to banking . . . Tavern-keepers, merchants, butchers, bakers [became] bankers." Regulations were few and financial theory rudimentary, and banking experience was nonexistent. Niles sniffed that all you needed to start a bank were paper, plates, and presses; that was only barely hyperbole.[13]

It is impossible to say how many banks were operating around the country; they were springing up everywhere, many without the formality of a state charter. In the little state of Rhode Island the number more than doubled in the three years leading up to 1818, from thirteen to at least twenty-seven. Nationally they grew by at least 30 percent in those same three years. The historian Harlow Unger believes there may have been more than a thousand banks before 1820, although he offers no evidence for that unusually high number. J. Van Fenstermaker and Warren Weber have both made scrupulous studies of state-chartered banks but arrive at different numbers; Fenstermaker lists 341 in 1820, but Weber believes 329 is a safer number (including sixty-five branch banks); he thinks Fenstermaker overestimates by counting banks that were chartered but never opened or whose closings were not reported. By Weber's conservative count there were, in 1819, at least 264 state-chartered banks legally issuing banknotes in twenty-two states, three territories, and the District of Columbia. Albert Gallatin, at the time, counted 212—with capital ranging from $45,000 (in Vermont) to $12.8 million (in Pennsylvania)—but he certainly missed some of the smaller ones. None of these estimates except Unger's takes into consideration the numerous unchartered banks. Banks were simply opening and closing too quickly for any accurate census. By Fenstermaker's numbers, Tennessee chartered ten banks in 1817, six of which closed in 1819; Washington, D.C., chartered five banks in 1817, but in 1820 only three remained open; of Pennsylvania's forty-one chartered in 1814, fifteen failed by 1824; and none of the three banks chartered by Illinois between 1816 and 1819 was still operating in 1821.[14]

Secretary Crawford had plenty of company in disapproving of the proliferation of banks outside of large commercial cities. But while Crawford believed that banks were opened by men of too little standing in their communities, others complained for the opposite reason. New Jersey's Rep. Ephraim Bateman (whose state, with no large city, had nonetheless chartered nine banks before 1812) wrote his constituents an open letter in the *New Jersey Journal* in early 1819:

> Inland towns and agricultural districts are seldom benefitted but often injured by [banks]—in the country they are apt to encircle round them a kind of monied aristocracy, who hold in their hands in too great a degree the destinies of the adjacent country, made dependent on, and sometimes subservient to, a directorship, located in those towns. A slight knowledge of human nature is sufficient to convince that those directorships may readily become dictatorships—so potent is money even in the shape of banknotes.[15]

Banks were opening in "inland towns and agricultural districts" because that was now where they were needed. The function of banking was changing rapidly. Banks chartered to provide short-term credit to importers and exporters—or to lend money to the governments that had chartered them—had never expected that their loans would grow into long-term obligations. But Davis R. Dewey, in *State Banking Before the Civil War*, identifies the changes that began to take place:

> A few banks continued to confine their credit to thirty- and sixty-day instruments, or said they did; but by 1800 probably, the majority had begun to lend for longer periods. Three month, four month, and six month maturities

increased. Moreover, it was no longer a firm expectation, as it had originally been, that promissory notes would actually be paid at maturity, for renewals were becoming a matter of course. In spite of these essential changes in credit practices, the tradition of short-term credit continued to be held in pious respect and bankers liked to pretend that they were faithful to it.[16]

The practice of banking was diverging from what theory had existed. Commercial cities were no longer limited to the east coast; boomtowns like Pittsburgh, Cincinnati, Louisville, Lexington, Rochester, St. Louis, Nashville, Milledgeville, and Huntsville were appearing in the interior, and the distant port of New Orleans surpassed Boston in the value of its exports. Following the example of the Bank of England, Hamilton in 1791 had adopted for the Bank of the United States a restriction on the ratio of bank liabilities to paid-in capital, and the Bank of New York promptly did the same. In New York the ratio was soon fixed at 3:1; in conservative Boston 2:1 was preferred, but then Virginia allowed 4:1, and gradually the prevailing ratio approached 10:1. Such restrictions were designed to ensure a safe specie reserve, and the (theoretical) short-term loans were meant to provide a steady replenishment of that specie. But the disruptions of the Napoleonic Wars and the War of 1812, along with the demands of the market economy, gave banks new priorities. Everyone needed more currency, and everyone wanted more credit.[17]

Publicly, the call was for conservative practices. Pennsylvania's Rep. Samuel Ingham told Congress in 1814 that although banks might make loans equal to their entire capital, "It is, I believe, unusual for the large state banks to issue, in paper, more than one third or at most one half of their capital." Moreover, he insisted, "No bank conducted with integrity ever did issue notes to the amount of its capital; and no bank that has any regard to its reputation will ever dare to do it." If that was so, a great many banks were disregarding their reputations. Gallatin estimated that between the closure of the First Bank of the United States in 1811 and the chartering of the Second Bank in 1816, banknotes in circulation increased from $28 million to $68 million, while Rousseau and Sylla have shown that paid-in capital actually *decreased* between 1814 and 1817, even though the number of state banks was rapidly rising.[18]

In the face of growing demand for both note issue and loans, banks were relaxing their former restrictions. One reason was the competition. At the same time that farmers were pressing banks for longer loan terms, the U.S.

Treasury was offering four-year credit (with multiple extensions) for the purchase of public lands, with only 25 percent down. Today's banking regulations frown on the use of borrowed money for down payments, but there were no such scruples two hundred years ago, and borrowers clamored for bank loans to provide those down payments, loans that speculators expected to repay quickly as they resold their purchases for immediate profits. Moreover, the state-chartered banks were not the only source of banknotes: there were private banks, mutual savings banks, and insurance companies, all engaged in banking without charter or regulation. From his list of active banks before the Panic, Weber says, "The numerous 'private banks' that existed during this period are . . . excluded because they were not chartered and could not legally issue notes." That is not quite true. Most state restrictions on note issue date from after 1815, and existing banks were often exempted. Before 1815 only four of the eighteen states—Massachusetts, New Hampshire, New York, and Maryland—required that banks be incorporated by the state, and only Rhode Island, Virginia, and Pennsylvania forbade note issue by unincorporated banks. New Jersey and Ohio passed similar laws in 1815, but Ohio gave a three-year exemption to banks already in operation—and most of those banks simply ignored the restriction at the end of the three years. In 1816 the Cincinnati *Western Spy* observed that Ohio also limited banks to lending no more than three times their paid-up stock but noted that both laws "seem generally to have been forgotten." As late as the 1830s there was no restriction at all on who could issue notes in Connecticut, Delaware, Kentucky, Tennessee, South Carolina, Alabama, or Mississippi.[19]

Smith and Cole acknowledge that "certain of the currency difficulties of the period [1790–1820] were due more to excessive note issue by unincorporated banks than to the mistakes of chartered banks; but concerning these private institutions there are, of course, no statistics." Not all of them were irresponsible; Stephen Girard had bought the offices and equipment of the First Bank of the United States when its charter expired, and he reopened it as a private bank in 1812 with a paid-in capital of $1.2 million. (State law forbade unincorporated "associations" from issuing notes, but Girard had no associates—the bank belonged to him alone, and so the law did not apply.) In Tennessee, where there were no legal prohibitions, Yateman, Woods, and Co. operated a private bank for years; it was one of the state's strongest banks until it went down in the Panic of 1837.[20]

A few private banks had solid reputations, but others issued banknotes with no intention of ever redeeming them. The former, in Ohio, included the Bank of Xenia and John H. Piatt and Co. of Cincinnati, two of the most trustworthy banks in the state; the latter's notes had depreciated only 4.5 percent in late 1818, before its sudden failure in 1819. At the other extreme was the Granville Bank. John Kilbourn, editor of the Ohio *Watchman*, told his readers that he esteemed its officers "in their private capacity," but as bank directors they were "a pack of knaves and swindlers." It failed in 1817, reopened, and failed again in 1837. The low regard in which these banks were held was so widespread that one resident of Chillicothe is said to have called another, at whom he had lost his temper, "a d____d UNCHARTERED son of a b___h"; evidently, "It became fashionable at the Capital to apply the term unchartered to all evil doers." The most notorious of them all was Ohio's Owl Creek Bank, which Hezekiah Niles made nationally infamous, mocking it at every opportunity in the *Register* as "the Bank of Hoo! Hoo!"[21]

The Owl Creek Bank, and others like it, pumped out banknotes in very small denominations: surviving examples range from ten dollars down to six-and-a-quarter cents. For reasons that will shortly be obvious, few of its records have been preserved, but a stock ledger and a transfer book dated 1816 to 1820 are in the Western Reserve Historical Society collection. The bank continued in operation in the town of Mount Vernon, flouting state law, until 1837.[22]

There were dozens of stockholders, but the Owl Creek Bank was not incorporated by the state. Thus all were individually liable when the bank was finally sued in 1829. Living up to its name, the bank proved to be a fly-by-night operation: under cover of darkness, its flimsy building was broken into and the box containing the bank records was removed. It was later found in the woods outside of town, "broken open and the books and papers scattered about with several of the names of the stockholders obliterated."[23]

Owl Creek was the most notorious of the "paper mills," but an earlier example in Rhode Island introduced a number of the schemes that unscrupulous bank operators would employ. In the first decade of the 1800s Andrew Dexter Jr. built the Boston Exchange Coffee House—at seven stories, the city's tallest building. To help pay for its construction he operated the Boston Exchange Office, hiring "runners" to buy up discounted notes of out-of-town banks and present them at the place of issue to be redeemed at face value. (Banks had not yet suspended specie payment.) At some point it occurred to him that the process could be made to work in reverse, at least for a while. He cast his eye about and settled on the small, disorganized Farmers Exchange Bank in Glocester, Rhode Island, some sixty miles from Boston.

Dexter quietly bought up stock from eleven bank directors and then paid them out of the bank's assets—including their own promissory notes, put up in lieu of cash when they had originally bought their shares. As the primary shareowner, he took the opportunity to become the bank's primary borrower as well; the language of his loan agreements specified that he would "not be called upon to make payment until he thinks proper, he being the primary stockholder and best knowing when it will be proper to pay."[24]

Dexter's plan was to issue as many banknotes as possible and distribute them as far from Glocester as possible, delaying their return for redemption as long as possible. He arranged to exchange notes first with a similarly shady bank in Pittsfield, Massachusetts, and later with an even more distant bank in Marietta, Ohio. His specie reserves seem never to have exceeded $200, and may have been as low as $45, but he eventually issued $800,000 in notes. He complained that the bank's cashier, an unhappy Quaker named William Colwell, didn't—or couldn't—sign notes as fast as Dexter could print them. (He had the plates and press in Boston, but Colwell manned the bank in Glocester and had to sign each note there.) "I am sorry," Dexter wrote to him, "You have signed no more bills, and beg you to sign twice as many more during the next week. I wish you would work day and night so as to sign if possible $20,000 a day." He meant day and night literally, directing Colwell to sign notes after midnight, behind closed doors, so that no one would see how many notes were being produced. By 1808, when enough notes had worked their way back to provoke complaints, Dexter was gone. He fled to Nova Scotia, taking the books with him. In response to Dexter's swindle, Massachusetts passed a law in 1809 imposing a penalty of 2 percent per month on notes that banks failed or refused to redeem in specie. Daniel Webster insisted on such a clause in the charter of the Second BUS, where it applied to both notes and deposits. Similar laws were passed in Pennsylvania and Maryland in 1814 and New York in 1816, ordering that charters be forfeited should banks fail to redeem.[25]

Banks nevertheless found ways around the laws—in the interest of self-preservation, as notes were circulating more and more widely at steeper and steeper discounts after the 1814 suspension of specie redemption. The Jersey Bank, of Jersey City (which loaned money to Thomas Jefferson when the BUS hesitated), stated in fine print on its notes that they were payable "on demand at the Ontario Bank, State of New York"—three hundred miles away in the town of Canandaigua. The Jersey Bank appears to have closed in 1838 just as the legislature was preparing to repeal its charter, but some of its notes still survive. The Bank of Darien, in Georgia, issued notes that were widely used to pay for Alabama land; when it was finally forced to redeem them, it required the bearer to swear before a justice of the peace, in the presence of five bank directors, that he was the owner of the note and not the agent of a third party. No matter how small the denomination, the bank charged a fee of $1.37½ for each note presented.[26]

With few banks outside New England redeeming notes in specie, most banknotes were circulating below par—at less than their face value. There was always a risk in accepting out-of-state banknotes, so their face value was naturally further discounted: the more distant the issuing bank, the higher the discount. Local banknotes were always preferred, but out-of-state notes were rarely rejected outright. Northern Alabamians had their own Planters and Merchants Bank at Huntsville but just as often used Tennessee and Kentucky notes; southern Alabama preferred the Tombeckbe Bank (St. Stephens) or the Bank of Mobile, but freely used South Carolina and Georgia paper.[27]

Alabama's banks illustrate one of the main reasons inland banks were multiplying: all three of them were created explicitly to meet the needs of the booming land sales in 1817 to 1819. Tiny St. Stephens, near the Gulf coast, happened to be the location of the first land office opened in the state. The new land office's register, Israel Pickens, had written to Crawford, "On the new surveys coming into the market, and after the land office is brought from Milledgeville into the heart of the country, the effect produced on the land market by the facility of procuring loans in the country may be easily imagined."[28] Being an imaginative man, Pickens opened the Tombeckbe Bank there. He was not a close friend of Crawford, but LeRoy Pope was; Pope founded the Planters and Merchants Bank in Huntsville when a second Alabama land office opened there. The shareholders of these banks would never have invested in bank stock if they had not expected to borrow more than they put in (paying for their stock with promissory notes much more often than specie). They would have invested directly in land and slaves instead, but the purpose of the banks was the multiplication of capital—providing plentiful money, on generous credit, that could *then* be invested in land and slaves.

In state after state, just as New Jersey's Bateman had indignantly observed, the powerful elite founded their banks and took full advantage. In 1818, with cotton at an all-time high and statehood freshly granted by Congress, the Bank of Mississippi was rechartered as the Bank of the State of Mississippi, with Samuel Postlethwaite continuing as president and Stephen Duncan still on the board of directors. Just as elsewhere, directors' perquisites included special interest rates. Loans during the period were offered to the public at a remarkable range of interest rates, reflecting strength of credit or personal connections—anywhere from 3.5 percent to 36 percent. Most large borrowers counted on personal acquaintance with board members and thus paid the lower rates. Major stockholders like Duncan not only earned dividends but also borrowed the full face value of their shares (or more) at below-market interest. Unsecured and automatically renewed every two or three months, these loans could be used to buy not only the usual land and slaves but additional shares of bank stock as well. Although Mississippi law limited banks to selling ten shares of stock every ten days to any individual, Duncan circumvented the law's intent by buying large quantities of stock from other investors, and thus quickly amassed controlling interest. In one example of the opportunities available to board members, Duncan borrowed money at 6 percent, which he turned around and loaned to Theodore Stark at 10 percent—still a lower rate than that offered to the public; Stark was a friend, but business was business.[29]

Of course it was all too good to be true. Through 1816 into 1817 finance was entering never-never land: loans that would never be repaid and banknotes that would never be redeemed, issued by banks that might be unknown outside of their own neighborhoods (where they were often distrusted). In 1817 the protectionist critic Matthew Carey, himself a director of the Bank of Pennsylvania, warned of "the flood of wretched, depreciated paper currency which has overspread the country." Benjamin Morgan, about to be named a director of a BUS branch, had complained to Pennsylvania's Rep. John Sergeant the previous year of "the evils we experience from the excessive issue of bank paper," and the Washington (Pennsylvania) *Reporter* condemned "a flood of paper," issued by western Pennsylvania banks "to accommodate the public, without any intention of redeeming it." These were expressions of concern from relative conservatives in the East, but even ambitious westerners, who most benefitted from the new banks, were growing worried.[30]

In Missouri purchases of eastern manufactured goods exceeded the value of the territory's exports, sending both specie and the more trustworthy banknotes inexorably eastward; soldiers at Fort Bellefontaine and federal officials in St. Louis insisted on being paid in treasury warrants rather than the depreciated banknotes from Ohio, Kentucky, and Pennsylvania that were so commonly seen. Territorial pioneer John Mason Peck called those notes "shinplasters . . . the droppings of that first generation of banks instituted in the West without any adequate specie basis. Their leaves were scattered over the frontiers like the leaves of trees by an autumn frost, and the price of every article of necessity was higher in proportion." In 1816 the Territory of Missouri chartered its own Bank of St. Louis (located in the back room of Riddick and Pichard's general store on Main Street), hoping to create a more trustworthy local currency. As happened so often, they were disappointed. The bank took furs and lead as security for loans and printed paper notes called "beaver bills" because they bore the image of a trapped beaver (and replaced the region's traditional currency, beaver pelts). The bank promised to redeem notes in specie—a novelty in the West—but found itself quickly in trouble when the head cashier, John B. N. Smith, created a complicated scheme to deprive the bank of its assets, making unsecured loans to favored real-estate speculators, including a number of his friends in Kentucky as well as some of the bank's directors. The bank closed in July 1819, a casualty of the Panic.[31]

Among the unhappy directors were Thomas Hart Benton and St. Louis's leading citizen, Auguste Chouteau. They resigned in 1817 to form a group of eighty-three investors, including other disillusioned stockholders, who opened the competing Bank of Missouri in the cellar of Chouteau's home. With a subscription of $78,000, the bank was incorporated by the territory, its declared purpose to "repel the influx" of notes from Kentucky, Ohio, and other western states, something the Bank of St. Louis had failed to do. The Bank of Missouri became a United States depository in 1818, and 90 percent of its $750,000 in deposits were either land office receipts or other federal funds, including the payroll for Fort Bellefontaine. Although it was never accused of the worst of the shady dealings that ruined its competitor, this bank too made unsecured loans to directors, which they were unable to repay after the Panic hit. In 1821, farms in Missouri that had fetched $10,000 three years earlier could not be sold for $1,000, and the state legislature passed a stay law preventing foreclosures, whereupon the Bank of Missouri went out of business.[32]

James Flint's letters to England blamed the problems on westerners' lack of sophistication. "That the present disorders in banking are not extended over the whole of the United States is manifested by the tables of exchange periodically published at New York. These show that the depressions of money are chiefly confined to the western country, where the substantial capital is small, and where (there is reason to believe) a large portion of the people are less acute." John Quincy Adams certainly agreed with that assessment, and he congratulated his fellow New Englanders on being "less licentious in their banking practices, the banks in Boston never having suspended specie payments, not even during the last war." This was true but somewhat disingenuous, given those banks' behavior during the war. Connecticut's Oliver Wolcott had little good to say for Boston banks as a rule, but he too decried the irresponsible expansion of banks outside the region:

> After the banks suspended payments in specie, the public expenditures rendered the current money too abundant. A great number of banks were also established by men who possessed neither capital nor experience, the credit of which rested solely on the breath of public opinion. . . . Though many banks have failed, few of those which possessed any considerable sums of metallic money in proportion to their issues of paper, and which have been honestly managed, have yet forfeited their credit.[33]

Banking historians like Bray Hammond and Walter Smith have praised the "conservative practices" of the New England banks, but Fenstermaker acknowledges what Wolcott knew very well: "New England banks . . . were able to maintain specie payments for three reasons, two of which were not especially patriotic." First, they declined to lend money to the federal government during wartime. Second, they acquired stocks of specie through New England's willingness to trade with the enemy—and by demanding specie to redeem the more southern banknotes that the federal government spent in New England for war materiel. Finally, illustrating Gresham's Law ("bad money drives out good"), the New England public hoarded the undepreciated notes of New England banks, choosing to spend the widely circulated notes from New York and Philadelphia rather than the more valuable Boston notes that were still backed by specie—thus making it easier for those Boston banks to continue promising to redeem in specie.[34]

There is no question that New England banks were more conservative in their lending practices, generally making loans only to individuals with whom their officers had business—or family—relationships. The New England economy was made up of a smaller group of wealthy, connected individuals and was longer established than the newer, developing economy of New York or Baltimore—characteristics that made it safer but less dynamic. In New England, capital entered the economy through loans to insiders, especially the powerful group who came to be known as the Boston Associates—Appletons, Lowells, Lawrences, and others who were making the gradual, cautious transition from shipping to industry. For example, when the Massachusetts Hospital Life Insurance Company (dominated by Associates) decided to invest in textile mills (owned by Associates), it classified its investments as personal loans made with textile shares as collateral. Those investments might return lower profits than some others would have, but they enabled the Associates to invest their trust funds (managed by Massachusetts Hospital Life) in their own businesses. Massachusetts banks followed similar patterns of lending, ownership, and control.[35]

By maintaining a narrowly regional focus—and making fewer real-estate loans, there being less land available in New England—banks in Massachusetts in 1820 had notes in circulation totaling only $3,841,266, backed by specie reserves of $2,049,741.23. Flint had pointed out that western currency suffered the worst depreciation, and *Niles' Register* reported on October 1, 1818—when some Pennsylvania and Ohio banknotes were discounted as much as 50 percent—that New Hampshire, Connecticut, and Rhode Island banknotes were discounted only 0.5 to 1 percent, while Massachusetts notes circulated at par or at most a 1 percent discount. Niles concluded with a reminder, emphasized by a pointed finger: "☞ It is understood that all those banks pay specie!"[36]

In fact, New England banks had begun policing themselves. About the same time that South Carolina's Attorney General Hayne was objecting to Virginia banks' habit of buying up his state's depreciated notes to present for redemption in specie, the Suffolk Bank in Massachusetts sponsored a consortium of Boston banks to do the same thing to less-conservative banks in western Massachusetts. Suffolk offered those banks an ultimatum: participate in a regulated, organized system of note redemption, or face crippling unannounced calls on their notes. The "country banks" protested and delayed, but eventually they gave in. There had earlier been widespread demands for the same kind of control on the national level; even those who had killed the First Bank of the United States were finally ready to charter a second one for that very purpose.[37]

During the dark days of 1813 and 1814, the nation had sorely felt the absence of the First Bank of the United States. The Madison administration, desperate for cash to prosecute the War of 1812, made repeated efforts to charter a

Second BUS that could lend the government the money it so badly needed. Federalists like Webster who had supported the First Bank now joined forces with hardline Old Republicans like Randolph to block half a dozen bills that came forward to charter a Second BUS—the former because they opposed the war and wanted to prevent administration access to funds, and the latter because they had not given up their old conviction that the Constitution nowhere authorized Congress to charter a bank. But many former opponents had come around to the belief that because a central bank (although they did not yet use that term) was essential to the nation's war effort, creating one must after all be included among the "necessary and proper" powers of Congress. One of the converts was Speaker of the House Henry Clay, whose single vote had been enough to defeat the renewal of the Bank's charter in 1811. Clay was an energetic advocate of the War of 1812, and his fellow War Hawk, John C. Calhoun, took the lead in the effort to charter a new Bank of the United States. (Ironically, Webster would later join Clay as a well-paid attorney for the BUS and an eloquent defender of the powers of the federal government, while the once-nationalist Calhoun would, in future years, take up the cause of states' rights—condemning the Supreme Court's approval of the BUS charter, in retrospect, as an instance of federal overreach.)

When the war ended in 1815, the case for the BUS shifted from providing war loans to protecting the national credit and currency—still an argument for national security at a time when Britain had simply evolved from a military adversary to an economic one. In the absence of the BUS, as wartime domestic commerce had increased, unregulated state banks had multiplied. Estimates of the total state banknotes in circulation in 1816 range from $68 million by the former treasury secretary, Gallatin, to $110 million by Crawford. Gallatin's figure is probably more accurate, but as with estimates of the number of banks themselves, there is no way to be certain. Even by Gallatin's conservative estimate note issue had more than tripled since 1811, reaching a level between 1816 and 1818 that would not be matched until the 1830s, by which time the population had increased by more than 30 percent. Moreover, since 1814 almost none of the more than $60 million in notes issued outside of New England had been redeemable in gold or silver. Richard Sylla has not found the term "central bank" applied to the BUS before the Bank War of the 1830s, but it is clear that a central bank was what more and more people wanted. Through late 1815 and into 1816 six men came to figure most prominently in the successful charter of the Second Bank of the United States: the merchant/financiers Stephen Girard, John Jacob Astor, David

Parish, and Jacob Barker; the new treasury secretary, Alexander Dallas; and the South Carolina congressman John C. Calhoun.[38]

In 1813 Dallas, then U.S. attorney for the Eastern District of Pennsylvania, was helping Gallatin raise funds for the War of 1812. Girard, Astor, and Parish had met with him and agreed to buy $9 million in government bonds; Barker had agreed to place a $5 million loan and, when he found few investors willing to join him, argued in the *National Intelligencer* (March 16, 1814) that a national bank was now necessary for the nation's survival. All four were prepared, with the help of the New York financial community, to put up the necessary capital to launch the Second BUS. Calhoun and Dallas had previously made competing and unsuccessful attempts to get a bill through Congress and into law, and Dallas had failed in 1815 to get big-city banks to cooperate in equalizing exchange or in creating a circulating currency based on treasury notes. The Bank of North America had been unable to persuade other Philadelphia banks to resume specie redemption, and in February 1816 the smaller Pennsylvania banks, meeting at Harrisburg, agreed to accept in principle a limitation of their discounts (that is, their lending) but still refused to redeem notes in specie. At that point, Calhoun and Dallas finally decided to cooperate in order to pass a bank charter in Congress.[39]

Calhoun opened the campaign by declaring that since the extinction of the First BUS, the face value of banknotes had increased from $80 or $90 million to as much as $200 million (almost twice Crawford's generous estimate and more than three times Gallatin's). Little of that amount was supported by silver reserves. "This excess was visible to the eye," said Calhoun, "and almost audible to the ear; so familiar was the fact, that this paper was emphatically called *trash* or *rags*." Government contracts promising payment in gold or silver were being paid in depreciated state banknotes, and taxes—which the Constitution required to be equally assessed throughout the nation—were paid in notes of widely varying value, so that "the people in one section of the union pay perhaps one-fifth more of the same tax, than those in another." He continued,

> For gold and silver are not now the only money; whatever is the medium of purchase and sale must take their place; and as bank paper alone was now employed for this purpose, it had become the money of the country. A change, great and wonderful, had taken place . . . which divests you of your rights and turns you back to the condition of the Revolutionary war, in which every state used bills of credit, which were made a legal tender and were of various values.

Then Calhoun offered the clincher: to end the tyranny of paper, a national bank's first rule "would be to take the notes of no bank which did not pay in gold and silver."[40]

Dallas and Calhoun together wrote the new BUS's charter, basing it closely on the 1791 charter of Hamilton's First BUS. Calhoun introduced his bill in Congress early in 1816, and this time it moved inexorably to passage. Acknowledging the inevitable, the acerbic Randolph commented, "Every man you meet, in this House or out of it . . . is either a stockholder, president, cashier, clerk, doorkeeper, runner, engraver, paper maker, or mechanic, in some way or other, at a bank."[41]

In March the final vote in the House was close, heavily partisan, and broadly regional. New England and the four middle states (New York, New Jersey, Delaware, and Pennsylvania) were divided 35 to 45 against the bill; the nine southern and western states voted in favor, 45 to 26. The next month, more than half of the pro-Bank votes in the Senate came from southern and western states as the charter passed in that chamber 22 to 12. Webster, now representing Massachusetts, was unable to prevent the bill's passage, but he was able to secure a joint resolution requiring that all taxes be received only in notes redeemable in specie, and the new Bank of the United States would come into existence with the challenge of making that possible—and soon.[42]

Suddenly, Niles was fearful not of too much credit but of too little. A week after Madison signed the Second Bank's charter, the *Register* warned,

> If only half the evil that is anticipated by intelligent gentlemen be felt, we shall have 'such times' as the present generation has never seen. The embargo or the war, with all its real or imaginary train of distress was nothing to what is anticipated now, from the necessity apparently existing that the banks should suddenly withdraw their accommodations [i.e., their flexible loan-renewal policies] to meet forced requisitions of specie; at a time when foreign trade is much against us. . . . It may safely be said, I believe, that our imports have exceeded our exports by at least one hundred millions of dollars for the past year; this excess, with the duties & c. accruing on the goods here, essentially depends on credits and accommodations. Can these credits and accommodations be withdrawn at once?[43]

The answer was clearly no. The president of the new Bank, once it was up and running, would inform Crawford that he was "not at all disposed to take the late Bank of the United States as an exemplar in practice: because I think its operations were circumscribed by a policy less enlarged, liberal, and useful than its powers and resources would have justified." Far from restricting the expansion of credit and accommodation by state banks, the new BUS would follow the "enlarged, liberal" policy of enthusiastically extending its own credit. The ambitious head cashier of the Baltimore branch had already taken the initiative to write to Crawford on his own, drawing the same contrast with the previous BUS: "Instead of extending its operations so as to embrace every real demand of commerce, instead of expanding its views as the country and its trade grew, [the First BUS] pursued a timid and faltering course." The cashier had big plans, with nothing timid about them; his name was James M'Culloh, although a court reporter's error would make him known to history as "McCulloch" in the Supreme Court case of *McCulloch v. Maryland*. When he and the Baltimore branch president were later indicted by the state of Maryland for bank fraud on a truly "enlarged, liberal" scale, his name would be spelled correctly.[44]

Before the new bank could commence operations, it had only twenty days to sell the stock that was intended to provide its capital. The U.S. Treasury would pay in $5 million, but the rest of its $35 million capitalization had to come from private subscribers, at $100 per share. Subscription was slow, and as the time limit approached, the Bank found itself $3 million short. Once again, Stephen Girard stepped up; he bought the entire amount, some of which he then sold to Astor. He did this, he later explained to David Parish, for two reasons: "to promote the early operation of that indispensable institution" and to avoid the "increase of a multiplicity of proxies." He had reason to be concerned: the charter limited any one shareholder to no more than thirty votes in electing board members, no matter how many shares he owned, and Girard was aware that unscrupulous operators were already taking steps to get around this limit by having themselves designated as attorneys to vote the proxies of any number of supposed "owners." George Williams, a director of the Baltimore branch who would soon join M'Culloh in raiding the branch for hundreds of thousands of dollars, controlled 1,172 shares in the names of 1,172 individuals who probably had no idea they owned bank stock.[45]

With the initial stock installment paid in, the main office of the Second Bank opened in Philadelphia on January 7, 1817. Like the First BUS, its charter ran for twenty years, and it would be governed by twenty-five directors. On the advice of Treasury Secretary Dallas, Madison had already appointed the five to be chosen by the government, all Republicans: Stephen Girard,

John Jacob Astor, Pierce Butler, James A. Buchanan, and William Jones. The directors elected by the stockholders were evenly divided, ten Republicans and ten Federalists. They elected Madison's choice, William Jones, as president. Jones was the former secretary of the navy and had been acting secretary of the treasury after Gallatin left for Europe; Astor and Girard were the two richest men in America. Butler, who had served with Madison at the Constitutional Convention, was an enormously wealthy South Carolina planter who preferred to live in Philadelphia, and Buchanan was a partner in the venerable Baltimore merchant house of Smith and Buchanan. Astor had proposed Buchanan for president of the Second Bank, but he would instead be appointed president of the Baltimore branch, where his reputation would be destroyed by his complicity with M'Culloh and Williams.[46]

Girard looked over the new board with dismay; he was unimpressed by Jones, and too many of the others struck him as untrustworthy, including Williams and Dennis Smith, the president of Baltimore's Mechanics' Bank (to which Smith was personally in debt for $800,000). On the day that the Bank opened for business Girard wrote, "If I live twelve months more I intend to use all my activity, means, and influence to change and replace the majority of directors with honest and independent men." When he failed to accomplish that goal by the end of the year, he resigned, still by far the Bank's largest stockholder although his thirty votes were far too few to make a difference.[47]

After Congress concluded an investigation of the Bank in early 1819, Jones too would resign. Historians have treated him harshly: Robert Remini calls him "venal and cunning," Sean Wilentz describes him as a "deft political self-promoter," and Robert Wright says that under his leadership the Bank "proceeded to run the economy into the ground by first extending far too much credit, then quickly restricting it." Wright may be correct, but it is not clear that a different president could have avoided the crash; Jones's successor, Langdon Cheves, is praised by Ralph Catterall and Bray Hammond, but his aggressive policies actually made a bad situation worse—as William Gouge acidly observed, "The bank was saved and the people were ruined." Jones was a self-made merchant, a naval veteran of the Revolution. After a single, uneventful term in Congress he did not seek public service again, but he quickly found himself in it against his will and to a degree that must have seemed nightmarish. He resisted several offered appointments but at last agreed to be secretary of the navy in 1813; at once he also found himself, despite his objections, delegated to step in for Albert Gallatin at the U.S. Treasury when the secretary was sent to Russia that year. Gallatin, who had held office since 1801 and would not give it up until February 1814, was reluctant to cede his authority to a novice he barely knew; he made it clear he expected the acting secretary to do as little as possible and left him no hints about how to go about paying for the war. Jones nevertheless arranged the loans that kept the finances afloat; Madison's biographer Richard Ketcham is more charitable than most in his assessment of the acting secretary: "The faithful Jones . . . performed services for nearly two years that few other men in the country could have rendered."[48]

For good or for ill, Jones became president of the BUS, despite Gerard's disapproval; Wilentz says that Gallatin was "so aghast at Jones's elevation that he never thereafter spoke to Alexander Dallas" (although he had little opportunity, since Dallas died only five months after Jones was elected, and Gallatin was out of the country). Madison's confidence must have been based on Jones's wartime service at the Treasury Department; the Bank's new president, in sharp contrast to the Barings, Hopes, or Rothschilds in Europe—but just like most American bank presidents in this period of banking explosion—had neither experience nor training as a banker. Jones faced immediate challenges. Under the terms of its charter the BUS should have had at least $4.5 million in specie reserves at its opening, but even three months later it still had only $1,811,839, and as late as July 1817, when the third and final installment from its stockholders should have brought its supply of gold and silver up to $7 million, its specie reserve was "the pitiably inadequate sum of $2,129,368."[49]

How could this have happened? Jones eventually informed Crawford that the stockholders had followed the example of investors in the state banks: although the charter required that their stock be paid for in specie, the bulk of the second and third installments had been made either in the Bank's own notes or else—like the first installment—in notes from banks that had *promised* to resume payment in specie, although none of them was yet doing so. (Moreover, Jones later had to admit that stock payments were recorded as received in BUS notes before the earliest date at which the charter permitted the Bank to issue any.) As Niles indignantly reported on January 2, 1819, "Of course, the notes and checks of the Bank of the United States and the notes of the banks actually paying specie, were indiscriminately received, with gold and silver, in payment of the cash part of the installment." Girard was absolutely right to distrust his fellow directors, and the Bank that was meant to stanch the flood of paper had itself set sail on the same tide.[50]

Specifically, the charter had required that 25 percent of any stock purchase be made in specie and 75 percent in either specie or government bonds. That was plainly stated; there was no other legal alternative. But both specie and bonds were at a premium of up to 8 percent in 1817, and the Bank directors agreed to accept (from themselves) promissory notes backed by nothing more than the stock for which they paid—obvious fraud from a modern perspective, but a common practice at other banks at the time. As would become abundantly clear, there were few laws on the books to cover bank fraud or even embezzlement, and little in the way of legal precedent. Bank historian Davis Dewey believes the Second Bank opened with $2 million in specie, $14 million in bonds, and $12 million in promissory notes; Bray Hammond thinks even that estimate is too optimistic. What was clear was that the BUS badly needed to acquire specie, and so the Bank—chartered to protect national security against the economic threat of England—sent one of its directors to England to borrow or purchase $5 million in gold and silver.[51]

John Sergeant, who was also a Federalist congressman from Pennsylvania, traveled to London on the Bank's behalf. In March 1817 he concluded an agreement with Baring Brothers and Reid, Irving & Co., to deliver $3,195,000—half in Spanish dollars and the other half in either silver or gold—to the United States within six months. Given the world shortage of specie, the terms proved impossible to meet, and even after twelve months less than two-thirds had reached the Bank. This was the inauspicious beginning of what would eventually amount to $7.3 million in specie imported by the BUS in less than two years—$675,000 in gold from Lisbon and London, and the rest in silver, chiefly from France and the British colony of Jamaica. But the specie was flowing out much faster than it came in; Astor, now the president of the New York branch, worried in November 1817 that the parent Bank had only $245,000 in its specie reserves, and six months later the reserves were still no larger, despite the imported millions.[52]

Although it was incapable of maintaining its own specie reserve, the BUS had committed to bringing the other banks back to specie redemption. Isaac Thomas, congressman from Tennessee, had defended his vote for the Bank charter in March 1816, telling his constituents in a florid mix of metaphors that the existing banks were "cancerous ulcers seated on the political body" that had "swallowed up the precious metals, gorged the country with their

notes," leaving it up to the BUS "by diffusing through the country an appreciated paper" either to "coerce the state banks to resume specie payment or
stifle the profits of this business." Alexander Dallas had tried and failed to use
persuasion to get banks to resume specie payment earlier in 1816; he could
not get state banks to agree even to redeem notes under five dollars. The
banks had refused, asking for the aid of the not-yet-opened Second BUS and
demanding an extension until July 1817. Dallas's successor, Crawford, threatened to withdraw all government funds (some $11 million) from banks that
would not resume by February 20, 1817, but the banks called his bluff, and
bluff it turned out to be. Jones was finally able to get the big eastern banks to
agree to the February date for resumption by promising that by July the BUS
would have loaned a minimum of $2 million in New York, $2 million in
Philadelphia, $1.5 million in Baltimore, and $500,000 in Virginia—in notes
that were, of course, redeemable in specie, as the Bank's charter required. In
an additional, unfortunate compromise, Jones also agreed that a bank need
not actually pay out gold or silver, even after July, so long as it paid with
notes of other banks that were part of the agreement. As the banks realized,
this meant that if enough of them *promised* to resume paying in specie, none
of them would actually have to do so—at least not to the BUS. While the
Bank kept its side of the agreement, the Baltimore and Philadelphia banks
had trouble keeping theirs, and smaller Pennsylvania banks came up with
various schemes to avoid specie redemption entirely. By December Crawford
had to admit to Congress that most Pennsylvania banks only "ostensibly pay
their bills in specie."[53]

Acquiring specie and imposing order on the state banks were not Jones's
only challenges. As early as May 1817 he had come into conflict with Crawford over the acceptance by the Second Bank of land office receipts that came
in the form of western banknotes, deposited at the eighty-nine designated
state banks of deposit Treasury had used before the BUS opened. Crawford,
who mainly thought of the Bank in terms of the services it could provide
to the Treasury Department, was eager to get those receipts into Treasury's
BUS account, but Jones was genuinely concerned about maintaining some
kind of discipline. He told Crawford, "The receipt of the paper of the country banks may be a measure of necessity on the part of the Government, but if
the interest of the public shall render the measure expedient, the public, and
not the bank, it is respectfully conceived, ought to sustain whatever loss . . .
may be incurred." He feared—correctly—that the Bank would be unable "to

enter into a sound discrimination" between solvent and insolvent banks. He also suspected—again correctly—that the banks hoped "by this ingenious kind of transmutation, [to] convert their paper into solid coin."[54]

Crawford now threatened to withdraw Treasury deposits from the branches of the BUS, but this too was no more than empty bluster. Jones offered a compromise. He would agree to take the receipts as "special deposits" that would be creditable back to the sending banks only in their own banknotes. The much-maligned Jones was behaving conservatively, but Crawford continued to insist that he "show great leniency to small banks" since "the Treasury has too deep an interest in their credit at this moment to be willing to see them sink." Crawford's interests were tax revenues and land sales; his worry was that in areas of the country where there was no branch of the BUS, the Treasury Department depended on local banks for the deposit of its receipts. Those areas included the states of Tennessee and Indiana and the rapidly growing territories of Mississippi, Alabama, Illinois, and Missouri, as well as the western parts of North Carolina, South Carolina, and Georgia. Between Lexington, Kentucky, in the North and New Orleans in the South—a distance of seven hundred miles—there was no branch of the BUS west of the mountains.[55]

Even so, distribution of the Bank's branches was still skewed to the West and the South. The First Bank of the United States had limited its branches to Washington, D.C., and seven coastal cities, all but New Orleans on the eastern seaboard. The Second Bank would serve the rapidly growing interior. Besides the main office in Philadelphia, branches were opened in Augusta, Georgia (which soon closed) and Savannah; New Orleans; Charleston; Fayetteville, North Carolina; Norfolk and Richmond, Virginia; Baltimore; Washington, D.C.; Lexington and Louisville, Kentucky; Chillicothe and Cincinnati, Ohio; Pittsburgh; New York City; Middletown, Connecticut; Providence; Boston; and Portsmouth, New Hampshire. There were only four branches to serve all five states of populous, commercial New England, but two each in Pennsylvania, Ohio, Kentucky, Virginia, and (initially) Georgia; one each in New York, Maryland, Louisiana, North Carolina, South Carolina, and the District of Columbia; and none in New Jersey or Delaware. Ten out of nineteen were south of the Mason-Dixon line and six were west of the Alleghenies. (It was BUS policy not to open branches in territories before statehood.)

Each branch was legally designated an office of discount and deposit, with no branch limit on loans. As a result, branches in the South and West

MAP 4. Offices of the Bank of the United States, 1817–1826. Map by Chris Robinson.

were soon lending ("discounting") money extravagantly. In June 1818 the Cincinnati branch loaned over $1,800,000; the Lexington branch lent out $1,619,000 that same month. For months Jones and the other directors did nothing to discourage the undisciplined practices of the western branches, whose directors were motivated by the local clamor for loans and seem to have been completely blind to responsible banking practice. The branches renewed loans over and over, made long-term mortgage loans (against BUS policy), and issued drafts and banknotes far in excess of their own reserves. When the main office finally did instruct the western branches to start restricting loans, the local officers proved not only incompetent but disobedient. Still, the congressional investigating committee would conclude that "such was the want of firmness or of foresight in the parent board, that, after finding its repeated remonstrances disregarded, it never removed one of the offending directors and took no effectual steps to control them."[56]

The editor of the *Journal of Banking*, William Gouge, looked back ruefully in 1833: "The first months of 1818 were the golden age of the western country. Silver could hardly have been more plentiful in Jerusalem in the days of Solomon than paper was in Ohio, Kentucky, and the adjoining regions." Paper was plentiful indeed, but silver was manifestly not. The notes issued in such quantity in the West inevitably followed "the course of exchange" to the eastern branches, where they were presented for redemption; every BUS branch was required to redeem the notes of every other branch. With the constant drain of silver, in March 1818 specie began to command a premium relative to BUS notes; it rose to 4 percent in June and 6 percent by November. A vicious cycle had begun: brokers (and other banks) bought up BUS notes, presented them for redemption in silver, sold the silver (at the premium) for more BUS notes, redeemed them, sold the silver, and so on, over and over. The eastern branches were running out of silver and once again had to acquire it abroad, "at usurious rates." The Bank was "bailing water with a sieve," as its historian Ralph Catterall puts it, and Jones finally realized the trouble he was in.[57]

Jones wrote to Crawford on June 23, 1818, "The fact is, that the bills of the bank are sought after with avidity by banks, brokers, and India traders, in order to draw the specie, which they find it impossible to procure elsewhere but in a partial degree and with great difficulty." Crawford had to admit to an angry Congress that, despite the promises made in 1816, convertibility of banknotes to silver had proven to be "nominal only, in most of the country," but he expressed confidence that it was finally "becoming real wherever it is ostensible." In fact, the opposite was happening. The Bank had opened in January 1817, when specie was at a 14 percent premium in Boston and New York and at 6 percent in the West; the premium did decrease, but if banks had actually resumed specie redemption it should have disappeared. In May, Niles reported that "though our banks ostensibly pay specie, it is almost as rare as it was some months ago to see a dollar. 'Paper does the business' still." In July, the variation among different banknotes' value was greater than it had been in February; in October, Spanish dollars still sold at a premium, and that month Jones had to admit to Crawford that banknotes from "the interior of Pennsylvania have as little of the quality of money or credit" as they had the year before. After the BUS had been operating for ten months, the premium for specie at New York was back up to 7 percent.[58]

The Bank of the United States was the largest corporation in the country, the only truly national business. It held the federal funds from taxes and land sales and handled federal financial transactions. Its banknotes—always redeemable in specie—were effectively legal tender, unlike any other bank's notes. It had been chartered with an obligation to regulate a financial system that lacked any kind of order, and yet during the first year of operation its directors appeared to see themselves as no different from the officers of any other bank, making incautious loans to other banks, to businesses, and to individuals—notoriously, to select politicians, editors, and, of course, themselves. The Bank's first historian, over a century ago, marveled that the directors, rather than considering it their primary duty to rein in an out-of-control financial system, assumed "that they were bound to secure large dividends, a most remarkable criterion by which to regulate the business of a bank." And indeed, in January 1818, with its specie reserves evaporating, its assets losing value, and its liabilities growing, the BUS nevertheless declared a 4 percent semi-annual dividend to its stockholders.[59]

Two months after his fellow directors voted themselves that dividend, John Jacob Astor wrote to Albert Gallatin that the Bank had made money so cheap "that everything else has become Dear, & the Result is that our merchants, instead of shipping produce, ship Specie, so much so that I tell you in confidence that it is not without difficulty that specie payments are maintained. The different States are going on making more Banks & I should not be surprised if by & by there be a general Blow-up among them." By and by would come sooner than he guessed.[60]

BANK CONTRACTION
"The Axe Must Be Applied to the Root of the Evil"

The metaphor of the elephant in the room is not a new one; in 1814 Russia's most popular fabulist, Ivan Krylov, published "The Inquisitive Man," which revolves around an elephant that goes unnoticed in a museum full of tiny exhibits; Dostoevsky later presumed that all his readers were familiar with the tale. Mark Twain employed the same concept in his story "The Stolen White Elephant." In 1817, at the Bank of the United States, the elephant in the room was the Louisiana Purchase debt.[1]

Over $4 million in Louisiana bonds would come due in 1818 and 1819—most owed to foreign creditors, and all promised in specie. The *National Messenger* reminded its readers,

> The Louisiana Convention has been sixteen years upon the statute books. It must, therefore, have been known to every one that the first installment of the Louisiana debt was payable on the 21st of October, 1818. It was equally known, that this installment could not be less than three millions of dollars. . . . The measure, therefore, has not come upon the community by surprise.[2]

Crawford's treasury report of December 1817 contained a reminder, had one been needed, that the first installment of the loan would soon be due from the government's account at the Bank of the United States. But eighteen months into William Jones's presidency of the BUS, in the summer of 1818, it was obvious that the Bank's specie reserves were vanishing; it did not have the silver in its vaults to make the payment. The Bank saw no choice but to demand some of the millions of dollars that were owed to it—in specie—by the hundreds of state banks whose notes made up the bulk of its deposits. Its directors now tried to stop the hemorrhage of the Bank's specie and to curtail loans that had been continually extended. Most historians conclude that in so doing the BUS precipitated the Panic of 1819. A century ago

Ralph Catterall already considered that to be the consensus, but he qualified it slightly: "Its curtailment had, indeed, precipitated the panic, for which, however, it was hardly more responsible than was Noah for the flood." The Bank's policy of contraction created monetary deflation, with a suddenness and to a degree that the secretary of the treasury rightly called unprecedented in world history. The amount of currency in circulation shrank to half of what it had been before the BUS was chartered; prices (and employment) not only fell but remained low for years—a depression that lasted from 1818 until the mid-1820s in much of the South and West.[3]

As soon as the policy of contraction was announced, the Bank and its president became the scapegoats for the hard times the nation experienced. The assignment of blame, however, has been muddled to this day by critics' inability to agree on whether the Bank's error lay in imposing restrictions so abruptly or in not doing so sooner. Nicholas Biddle reminded Congress, more than a decade after the fact, "The situation of the first administration of the bank was extremely difficult and delicate. They had to achieve the most critical of all financial operations—the passage from a vitiated to a sound currency." Moreover, "from the first hour of its creation" the Bank "was urged and goaded by the Government into an enlargement of its business . . . and this fault, if fault there were, belonged rather to the Government than to the Bank." Jones had to deal not only with the recalcitrance of hundreds of banks around the country but with the inconsistency and unreliability of Treasury Secretary William Crawford. John Quincy Adams, who worked with Crawford daily, confided to his diary, "Those [challenges] incidental to the Treasury are in a state which would give an able financier an opportunity to display his talents; but Crawford has no talents as a financier. He is just, and barely, equal to the current routine of the business of his office. His talent is intrigue . . . I do not think him entirely unprincipled; but his ambition swallows up his principle."[4]

Biddle also told Congress that in 1817 the government deposits in the BUS came to nearly $25 million, "consisting in a great degree, of the notes of distant banks professing to pay specie," and that the Bank agreed to treat those various notes as equivalent to its own, "which could not fail seriously to derange its operation." Jones had resisted when Crawford urged that policy, but after the secretary, under pressure from the surrounding banks of Virginia and Maryland, insisted on it in May of 1817, he capitulated. Jones has been faulted for lax supervision of the BUS's western branches, which through 1818 repeatedly paid customers with other banks' notes from their vaults instead of in their own issue, but Crawford, in an 1823 letter to Biddle, admitted that he encouraged this practice. And on various occasions in 1818 and 1819, after the BUS had finally begun its effort to impose discipline, Crawford's Treasury Department propped up uncooperative western and southern banks by making federal deposits in them, rather than in the BUS.[5]

Jones is also criticized for failing to keep the BUS branches' lending under tighter control. He feared that if the central board suggested a maximum amount of money for each branch to lend, some branches might take that as encouragement to lend to the maximum. In late 1817 he told the Savannah branch, "The Bank of the United States is integral in its organization, but indivisible in its interests . . . and the apparent interest of any particular office must necessarily be subordinate to the general interest," and in early 1818 he instructed the Charleston branch president, "Your board will please observe, sir, that it is no part of the parent board to give a definite capital to the respective offices, to be employed for the benefit of their respective districts." Soon it was evident that many branches, particularly in Kentucky and Ohio, took that policy to mean that they might lend without limit. By summer, the branches at Lexington, Louisville, and Cincinnati had each extended well over $1 million in loans that showed every sign of being renewed indefinitely.[6]

A sore spot from the beginning had been the requirement that every branch redeem the notes of any branch. In the summer of 1817, Crawford had written to Jones, "In referring to the causes which had the most decided influence on calling the United States Bank into existence, the inconveniencies resulting from the inequality in the rate of exchange between the different sections of the union stand eminently prominent." Crawford continued to maintain the fiction that state banks actually *were* redeeming in specie, while the BUS continued depleting its reserves by paying silver at eastern branches for the notes issued by western branches. He had warned Jones, "Whenever the bills of the bank and its offices shall not be discharged in specie, without reference to the place of issue, the existence of a currency of universal circulation and universal value, distinct from specie, will cease." In essence, he was insisting that the emperor would not be naked unless the BUS admitted that he was. For eighteen months that illusion was kept up, but at a cost to the Bank of over $5 million in specie borrowed abroad. It could not last; even the money brokers who were milking the BUS for silver realized that, and in the summer of 1818 they began to charge a 2 percent premium for silver against even BUS notes.[7]

In July the Bank's directors faced reality and voted to begin contracting, both by redeeming the state banknotes that filled the branches' vaults and by curtailing the loans they had made—starting in Cincinnati, where loans outstanding exceeded $1.8 million. They gave the branch office instructions to begin collecting balances due from three Cincinnati banks at the rate of 20 percent each month, effective immediately. At the same time, they resolved to curtail the loans outstanding at the branches in Philadelphia, Baltimore, Norfolk, and Richmond (where one of the chronic debtors was Thomas Jefferson) by a total of $5 million. The goal was to achieve some balance between the southern and western branches that had extended loans extravagantly and the northeastern branches that were exhausting specie by redeeming the other branches' notes.[8]

On August 28, with Boston and New York specie reserves practically gone, the BUS directors voted to stop requiring each branch to redeem the notes of all branches. While the curtailments in July had shocked the West, this news stunned the entire nation: there could be no clearer signal that the BUS, created to strengthen the nation's financial system, was itself in serious trouble. The decision, according to Rep. John C. Spencer, was one of the chief reasons his committee was appointed to investigate the Bank. Even Rep. John Sergeant of Pennsylvania, the Bank's director who had gone to London to seek specie, spoke in the House of "an almost universal clamor" against the decision. Niles was predictably outraged, writing the next week, "The last vestige of a balance in favor of the people for the immense advantage bestowed to very 'belzebubs in speculation' is wrestled from them with a degree of impudence equaled only by its violation of every principle of common justice, if not common honesty." Similar reactions appeared in the *National Intelligencer*, the Philadelphia *Aurora* and *Enquirer*, the Pittsburgh *Statesman*, and the Westmoreland (Pennsylvania) *Republican*. Two weeks later, Niles complained that with "more than one hundred dollars in small notes" of the various branches of the BUS in his hand, he "could not pay the postage of a few letters" in Baltimore.[9]

The furor over the policy of contraction was soon followed by dismay that it was not working. Local banks began calling in loans from their debtors, but they could not meet their targets; in fact, the Cincinnati banks owed the branch office more in October than they had in July. The three banks—the Miami Exchange Co., the Farmers and Merchants Bank, and the Cincinnati Bank—were indignant in their own defense. They charged that the BUS branch had failed to issue any banknotes, forcing local banks to provide all the currency for the public; most of the notes the Bank was now presenting for them to redeem had come in as land office receipts. And that failure to issue notes now made it difficult for their own borrowers to repay the loans made over the past two years. On August 20 the three banks made a joint protest that the curtailment "had excited much astonishment and no small degree of alarm." Given that the BUS had "a full knowledge of the circumstances of the western country, and of the manner in which the debts had been contracted, it can be viewed only as the commencement of the scene of ruin and distress to the community which the enemies of the institution have so often predicted."[10]

At the end of October the BUS informed the three banks that it would provide no further credit to them until their balances due were paid; the banks responded by suspending specie redemption. All across Ohio a rebellion was already under way as the BUS sent agents to demand payment on banknotes. In June, the Farmer's Bank in Canton had redeemed a quarter of its notes in specie and then refused to continue. The German Bank in Wooster flatly refused; it probably had no specie in its possession. When the Bank's agent arrived at Cleveland, the directors of the Commercial Bank of Lake Erie convened a hasty meeting and voted to refuse specie payment, even as the cashier was counting out silver coins and the BUS agent was arranging transport for them. On the east side of the Ohio River, the Virginia Saline Bank in Clarksburg (now West Virginia) made an effort to comply, obtaining judgments against its own debtors for more than enough to satisfy the BUS demands, but one of those judgments was against the clerk of the county court, and he refused to sign the order to execute the judgments. The frustrated Bank agent reported that the Clarksburg tavern keeper refused to accept Saline banknotes for his bill.[11]

The public was clearly on the side of the local banks, and the BUS now acquired its reputation as "the monster" and "the money power." For months the Bank had refrained from presenting some $500,000 to $800,000 in banknotes from South Carolina banks, accepting the promise that the banks would pay specie if demanded. When the Charleston branch was at last ordered to make that demand—20 percent of the notes by October—the branch president wrote to Jones, "We understand that the banks of the State will apply to the legislature now in session, to tax or otherwise embarrass us. . . . The banks, if called on too hastily for specie, will no doubt unite to refuse, and rely on the confidence of the community as their shield. In this extremity of the Union, there is reason to fear that they would be shielded."

John C. Calhoun was still on the side of the BUS, but his home state was already threatening the same resistance to national authority that would reappear under his leadership in the Nullification Crisis of 1832.[12]

Community opposition was no idle threat; Crawford, who opposed contraction and continued to pretend that banks actually were redeeming notes in specie, later told Congress,

> The extreme diffusion of bank stock among the great body of citizens, in most of the states, had produced . . . forbearance among individuals. To demand specie of the banks, when it was known they were unable to pay, was to destroy their own interests. . . . In favor of forbearance was also added the influence of the great mass of debtors. To this portion of the community all other evils were light when compared with the imperious demands of the banks.[13]

Slowly, the BUS collected its loans—enough to damage local economies, but not enough to solve its problems. In July total loans outstanding had amounted to over $52 million; by late autumn the figure stood at $44 million, a decrease of 15 percent; BUS notes in circulation had meanwhile shrunk from $9 million to $7.3 million, a decrease of almost 20 percent. Since the Bank demanded either specie or its own notes in payment, it was growing more difficult for debtors to repay those loans. As BUS notes remained redeemable in silver, its specie reserve kept eroding, despite all the efforts to force state banks to convert their own notes to specie. Then the long-anticipated blow fell: the Treasury Department called for a transfer of $2 million in specie from the BUS to make the first scheduled redemption of the Louisiana Purchase loan and discovered that the Bank simply did not have it.[14]

James C. Fisher, a director who would become the Bank's interim president, explained what happened next in a letter to New York's Senator Rufus King: "The Directors for a time did not know what answer to give—however, by prudent conduct they avoided paying the specie and made an arrangement to pay by bills [of exchange] on London which saved the Bank." Owners of Louisiana bonds were willing to make the concession; even BUS notes had depreciated against silver by now, but London bills of exchange were still as good as gold—and for most of the creditors, more convenient. Sergeant's mission to Europe in 1817 had produced a contract with Reid, Irving & Co. and once again with Baring Brothers (one of the two largest owners of Louisiana stock) to send $3.195 million in Spanish dollars to Philadelphia no later than January 1819. Deliveries—eventually totaling less than two-thirds of the agreed amount—had begun in July 1817, in silver arriving from Lisbon, Gibraltar, Livorno, Kingston, and London. Thomas Wilson & Co. delivered $675,000 in gold and about $3 million in Spanish silver in a second loan in 1818, and Thuret et Cie. of Paris provided $500,000 in silver; yet another $940,000 was then procured in Jamaica. It had made no difference—as soon as the specie came in, it went out over the counter to redeem BUS notes.[15]

At the same time that it chartered the First Bank of the United States, Congress had created the Commission of the Sinking Fund, charged with paying off the national debt at the rate of $10 million per year out of the budgetary surplus. The commission was made up of the secretaries of Treasury and State, the attorney general, the chief justice, and the president pro tempore of the Senate; it usually met with the quorum of Secretary Crawford, Secretary Adams, and Attorney General William Wirt. In 1818 the commissioners agreed to purchase $1.3 million in Louisiana stock as part of the regular debt reduction, thus decreasing the amount to be redeemed. On October 12, nine days before the Louisiana Purchase redemption was due, Adams was in Philadelphia, where he dined with William Jones and three younger men—Charles Jared Ingersoll (U.S. attorney for the city), George Mifflin Dallas (son of the late treasury secretary), and John Connelly, about to join the Bank's board of directors. Judging from Adams's diary entry for the date, the arrangements to take care of the Louisiana creditors had all been made; Jones betrayed no sign of any uneasiness, and the subject of the Louisiana loan evidently never came up. Adams, in his diary, reproached himself for "having talked too much at dinner . . . I [cannot] always (I did not this day) altogether avoid a dogmatical and peremptory manner, always disgusting, and especially offensive in persons to whose age or situation others consider some deference due." His companions may not have noticed; Jones was probably relieved that a crisis had been avoided, and his fellow directors were about to reelect him to another term as the Bank's president.[16]

Just one week later Crawford broke the news to Adams that the economy was in deep trouble; Adams's diary entry of October 19, 1818, marks his first realization that the nation's finances were in serious jeopardy. (His diary entries on the economy nearly all appear immediately after he and Crawford have spoken. Crawford, careful to be optimistic in public utterances, seems to have given vent to his worst fears when talking privately with Adams, so that the latter usually came away shaken.) Crawford revealed that the BUS planned to liquidate $400,000 in United States bonds—part of the Bank's original capitalization—and he admitted that the Treasury Department did not have the funds with which to buy back the stock itself. That same month the Bank authorized the purchase of yet another $1.5 million in specie abroad. During the eight months of the Bank's contraction it had managed to collect $2,614,441 in specie from state banks; from its opening in January 1817 through the end of December 1818, it had been forced to import $6.5 million in silver and gold, with a total premium and service cost of another half million; in January, it would borrow $2 million more in specie from Barings, at an interest rate of 5 percent.[17]

As the turbulent year came to a close, *Niles' Register* reported that the total debts due to the Bank (in loans or in unredeemed notes) came to nearly $55 million. Demand deposits in the BUS totaled over $13 million, of which nearly $4 million belonged to individuals and the remainder to the U.S. government or "other public officers." Less than $8 million was "from banks paying specie" or in "notes of banks paying specie on hand"—and more than 10 percent of the total was owed to the Cincinnati branch; only the central Philadelphia office and the Charleston branch were owed more. The *National Intelligencer* had published the amounts of the loans outstanding that month at the different branches. The central bank and the Baltimore branch had each loaned over $8 million; Charleston, Richmond, and New Orleans each had loans of over $2 million out; New York, Cincinnati, Lexington, and Washington, D.C., had each loaned over $1.5 million; and Pittsburgh, Norfolk, Savannah, and Louisville had each loaned over $1 million. Ironically, only the eastern branches, which had been paying out specie to redeem western branch notes, had succeeded in curtailing their lending or calling in notes; the branches below the Mason-Dixon line and west of the Alleghenies were as badly extended as ever, their deposits made up of notes from banks that were now increasingly suspending payment in specie.[18]

January brought one blow after another. That month the price of cotton at Charleston fell sharply on news from Liverpool buyers. Spencer's investigating committee delivered a stinging report that, while it stopped short of recommending repeal of the Bank's charter, was harshly critical of its practices. On the 30th *Niles' Register* reported, "William Jones, Esq., has resigned the presidency of the Bank of the United States. . . . Mr. Jones has lately been afflicted with the erysipelas, or St. Anthony's fire, which has for several days closed both his eyes." Niles managed to resist commenting on the aptness of the ailment of this unfortunate man, who has ever since been accused of closing his eyes to the mismanagement of so many of the Bank's offices. Fisher, a conservative Philadelphia Federalist, was elected temporary president. Once again he shared his thoughts with Rufus King:

> I am perfectly in accord in sentiment with you, that unless the Speculative Directors resign or are put out of the Bank, it will injure the National Credit. I am happy to say that the last election for Directors has been so managed as to leave out all the speculators except two or three, and they have lost all their influence, so that if the Bank can now be placed on safe ground it may yet prove of immense benefit to the country.[19]

The autumn election of directors had threatened to remove Williams and Buchanan, who had been using huge amounts of the Baltimore branch's money to speculate in Bank stock; a significant part of Baltimore's $8 million in loans had been made to them and to head cashier James M'Culloh. The Baltimoreans controlled enough votes (including those of the more than one thousand individual stock owners whose single shares Williams voted) that they survived for the time being. At the same meeting the stockholders had also turned back a movement to replace Jones with Langdon Cheves, a director of the Charleston branch, but they had elected Cheves to the national board. When Jones then resigned, Cheves was the obvious choice. Three weeks after announcing Jones's resignation, Niles reported that Cheves would be the new president, "if he consents to accept the office." The same article reported that President Monroe had appointed five new directors to represent the federal government; one was Nicholas Biddle, who would succeed Cheves four years later and serve as the Bank's president until its charter expired in 1836.[20]

Cheves was forty-three years old, a former congressman from South Carolina who had replaced Henry Clay as Speaker of the House in 1814; like Clay, he had voted against rechartering the First BUS but had supported chartering the Second BUS. In 1815, he had been offered the position of secretary of the treasury but had declined. After his term as president of the Bank he resisted efforts to get him to join the crowded field for the 1824 presidency of the United States; it is unlikely that his association with the Bank would have won him many votes. He retired to private life on his Carolina plantation, Lang Syne—where, according to Professor Joseph LeConte of the University of South Carolina, who visited him there, he occupied himself by working out a theory of evolution nearly the same as that which Darwin would publish years later.[21]

Cheves liked to claim that he had been drafted to take charge of the Bank in its hour of need, unaware of what he was getting into. He later told stockholders, "When I was invited, and consented to fill the station I now hold, I was alike ignorant and unapprehensive of the situation." He was not being completely honest. In an uneasy series of hedging phrases he then acknowledged, "I had held, it is true, shortly before, to oblige my friends, a place in the board of the office at Charleston, at which I occasionally attended." Stephen Girard had been determined to purge the board of directors of both the incompetent and the corrupt. He reported the unsuccessful attempt at the fall meeting to replace Jones with Cheves in a letter to John Stoney, one of Cheves's fellow directors at the Charleston branch: "Jones's supporters carried the election by a great majority. I sincerely hope that Mr. Cheves will take his seat at the board until the next election when with the aid of his friends it is probable that in 1820 he will be elected President of the Bank of the United States." The election had come much sooner than Girard or anyone else had expected.[22]

For three months, until Cheves first convened the directors in April, the Bank was treading water—continuing Jones's strategy of gradual curtailment and note redemption but still suffering from too many loans and too little specie. March brought the welcome news that the Supreme Court, in *McCulloch v. Maryland*, had fully endorsed the Bank's constitutionality and denied the states' power to tax it, but the BUS was still in trouble. Cheves later wrote to the Bank's stockholders, giving them his version of the crisis he had inherited:

> I was satisfied that there was a great want of financial talent in the management of [the Bank]. But I had not the faintest idea that its power had been so completely prostrated, or that it had been thus unfortunately managed or grossly defrauded. I never imagined that when it had, at so much expense and loss, imported so many millions of specie, they had been entirely exhausted, and were not yet paid for; nor that the Bank was at the point of stopping payment.

It is unlikely that Cheves was that completely in the dark, but it is certainly possible that he was genuinely shocked to learn how dire the situation actually was. (Cheves maintained that he was unaware in April of the losses the

Baltimore office had incurred thanks to Buchanan, Williams, and M'Culloh; this is also highly unlikely, since the Spencer Committee's report in January had made it clear that there was chicanery at that branch.) He told the stockholders,

> The specie in the vaults on the 1st of April, 1819, was only 126,745 dollars 28 cents, and the Board owed to the city banks, deducting balances due to it, an aggregate balance of 79,125 dollars 99 cents.
>
> It is true that there were in the Mint 267,978 dollars 9 cents and in transit from Kentucky and Ohio overland 250,000 dollars [the fruits of Jones's pressure on the West]: but the Treasury dividends were payable on that day to the amount of 500,000 dollars.

The wagons full of specie from the West "arrived very seasonably the next day, or a day or two thereafter."[23]

Anyone less self-confident than Cheves might have turned around and gone back to Lang Syne; even he may have been tempted. The Bank still owed Baring Brothers and Thomas Wilson nearly $900,000 for the specie bought in 1818. Some $6 million of its banknotes remained in circulation (redeemable, of course, in silver) "at a time, too, when the scarcity of money called forth every disposable dollar, and therefore created demands on the Bank for an unusual portion of the ordinary deposits and circulation." If these worries were not enough, Cheves discovered an ingenious practice by merchants at the major importing cities that was steadily draining what specie remained in the branches there. The Bank had to take in the import duty bonds paid at Boston, New York, and Philadelphia, bonds that "were demanded the next day, in Philadelphia, and at the same time, in every office of the establishment, at the discretion of the officers of the Government." Importers were required to pay duty bonds on everything they brought in but were then issued certificates called "debentures," entitling them to refunds on goods that were re-exported. To his dismay, Cheves discovered that the bonds were being "paid at one counter" in distant banks' bills, while "the debentures, which amounted to one million dollars every three months, were demanded and paid at the other, in specie or its equivalent." The importers were converting paper into silver, at the Bank's expense. Meanwhile, the Bank was indeed struggling to survive: "The southern offices were remitting tardily, and the western not at all. All the resources of the Bank would not have sustained it in this course and mode of business another month!! Such was the prostrate state of the Bank of the nation, which had, only twenty-seven months before, commenced business with an untrammeled capital of twenty-eight millions of dollars."[24]

Cheves was being more than a little disingenuous; the bank's initial capital, badly diluted from the start with IOUs, had hardly been "untrammeled," but the outlook in early 1819 was nonetheless grim. Financiers and politicians alike waited apprehensively to see what Cheves and the new directors would do. In April, unwilling to wait, Crawford urged Cheves to continue the policy of contraction: "The axe must be applied to the root of the evil"—i.e., the overextension by the banks. He went so far as to recommend that the Bank reduce its liabilities to the point that they were no higher than its specie reserves; Cheves politely ignored that suggestion. In Washington, Adams recorded in his diary a potentially embarrassing invitation at this moment to become a director of the Bank of the Metropolis in Washington. He was flattered and at first intended to accept, but the following day he declined, noting that "as the Bank of the United States is a subject of great public agitation at this time, there might be some impropriety in me assuming the special relation of a director to one of the banks." This is the first time his diary acknowledges any "agitation," but just a week later he was forced to confront the unfolding crisis.[25]

Adams's diary entry for April 5, 1819, is taken up by his account of letters received from Cheves and from Rep. Samuel Smith, the chairman of the Ways and Means Committee and the senior partner in Baltimore's most influential merchant firm, Smith and Buchanan. Cheves had sent a letter to Crawford that the secretary shared with other cabinet members, looking for their suggestions on what to do. In it Cheves laid out the "distressed state of the Bank and the commerce of the country generally" in terms very much like those he would later use to the stockholders. It would be "utterly impossible" to continue supporting specie payment through the spring, and equally impossible to make the 1819 redemption of the Louisiana Purchase bonds without yet another specie loan from Europe. Hoping to stop losing specie through debentures, he wanted the Bank branches to refuse notes from each other even for deposit in government accounts. Crawford told Adams he feared the merchants whose revenue bonds were due would "tender payment in the bills of distant branches, and then wait the event of a lawsuit, which would embarrass and delay the receipts of the revenue"—always Crawford's first concern. Smith's letter urged that the redemption of Louisiana Purchase bonds, even though required by law on October 21, be postponed since, "as it must be made in specie, [it] proves to be among the most distressing drains that have been suffered." Adams acidly observed that Smith was himself one of the largest speculators in BUS stock "and an exporter of specie to India by the half million at a time." Adams's final thoughts of the day were his first reflection that "the state of the country, circulation, and exchange . . . and the widespread corruption of the state banks . . . [is] perilous in the highest degree, and threatens to terminate in a national convulsion." But he and Crawford, after much hand-wringing, left it to Cheves.[26]

Cheves was getting his ducks in a row in preparation for his first meeting with the Bank's directors the following week. There he hit the ground running and quickly got the directors to agree to six "Principal means of relief":

1. To continue curtailments previously ordered.
2. To forbid offices, at the South and West, to issue their notes when the exchanges were against them [i.e., when local banks were not paying specie].
3. To collect the balances due by local Banks to the offices.
4. To claim of the Government the time necessary to transfer funds [received for revenue].
5. To pay debentures in the same money in which the duties on which the debentures were secured, had been paid.
6. To obtain a loan in Europe for a sum not exceeding 2,500,000 dollars [the amount of the scheduled Louisiana redemption], for a period not exceeding three years.[27]

Cheves barely paused to catch his breath. Nine days later he was in Washington, warning Crawford in person of the precarious state in which he found the Bank. Crawford, Wirt, and two of the Bank's own lawyers were convinced that, while a branch of the BUS might legally refuse to redeem another branch's notes for the general public, "*the Government* was bound to receive in payment of duties the bills at one branch which are issued and on their face made payable at another." Adams noted that Crawford's concern was still the delay a possible lawsuit might create in the collection of revenue, along with his fear "that the refusal to receive the bills would excite clamor against the Government." The next week Crawford confided to Adams that there had been "great deficiencies in the [import duty] receipts from Norfolk" for February and March, and "from the Western country the receipts from the sales of lands had very greatly fallen off, and were dwindling down to nothing." As was beginning to happen more and more frequently, Adams came away from their conversation fearing "a crisis which will shake the Union to its center. I see violent and threatening symptoms of the disease, without knowing where to look for the remedy."[28]

Crawford may have known no remedy either, but he was eager to employ any treatment he could. In early May he convened the Sinking Fund Commission and presented a plan. His proposal, adopted by the commissioners on May 5th, was for the government to make another purchase of just over a quarter of the Louisiana Purchase debt from the bondholders, ahead of the redemption date, with new treasury bonds. Not only would he reduce the sum needed in specie on October 21 by 27 percent, but he would save the interest that would be due in the interval. This resolution, not immediately made public, came two weeks before *Niles' Register* reminded its readers, "*Louisiana Stock.*—Fifty-four per cent. of the balance due on this stock will be paid to the holders on the 21st of October next, and no interest will be paid on that portion beyond that day."[29]

In June, Crawford again convened the Sinking Fund Commission to finalize the stock purchase ahead of the redemption, reminding them that "as that payment may be called for in specie, every portion of the stock purchased for the public reduces the amount which will be payable to individuals" out of the Bank's specie reserves. (Another European loan was proving difficult, although that information had not yet come back across the Atlantic.) Crawford also reminded the others,

> Pressure of embarrassment among the people, arising from the depreciation in the value of exports, from the excess of our own importations, from the extravagant multiplication of banks and the unprincipled manner in which many of them were managed . . . [is] increasing from day to day. The failures of banks in every part of the country are numerous; those of individual merchants in our principal seaports still more so.[30]

The most shocking of the individual merchants' failures had occurred a month earlier when Smith and Buchanan failed in Baltimore. Adams wrote in his diary—after yet another depressing talk with Crawford—that "the staple production of the soil, constituting principal articles of export, are falling to half and less than half the prices which they have borne, the merchants are crumbling to ruin; the manufactures perishing, agriculture stagnating, and distress universal in every part of the country." His entry concluded—it was Crawford's constant theme now—"There will be a great falling off of the revenue of next year." Adams was never a sanguine character, but none of the evidence that summer gave anyone cause for optimism.[31]

Distress was indeed nationwide, but it was nowhere worse than in Ohio, where the Bank's contraction had taken such a toll. Chillicothe's *Scioto Gazette* dolefully reported on May 14, "On Friday morning last two wagons loaded with specie, from the U. States bank in this place, took up the line of march for Philadelphia. The amount of specie which has just left our state, is estimated at from $125,000 to $140,000." *Niles' Register* followed this on June 26 with the observation that "$800,000 in specie have been drawn from Ohio within the past twelve months, for the bank of the United States."[32]

Some officers of the western branches considered themselves among the victims of Cheves and his directors. The former cashier of the Cincinnati branch, Gorham A. Worth, wrote to branch director Thomas Sloo Jr., "Mr. Cheves is at present Lord of the ascendant, and deals damnation round him! All of the *Old System* is to be changed—right or wrong—and though a man of some talent, [Cheves] is too crooked a Devil, and has too much malice to perceive or pursue the Interests of the Institution. If he is not over ruled, the Bank is damn'd!" Nearly five hundred miles up the Ohio River, the Pittsburgh branch had issued no notes before 1819, making use of those of state banks instead; its directors were watching their specie reserves drop from $64,035 in June 1818 to $29,324 in December. A year later, they would be down to $12,656 as the specie was steadily drawn east by the Bank's contraction policy.[33]

With autumn approaching, the Louisiana loan remained a sword of Damocles hanging over the Bank. It was becoming clear that no specie purchase from Europe could be arranged in sufficient time and sufficient amount to solve the problem, even after the Sinking Fund Commission bought up a quarter of the Louisiana stock. Once again creative thinking was necessary to avoid defaulting on the nation's debt. Details of the solution were revealed fourteen years later during the epic struggle between the BUS and President Andrew Jackson. In 1833, the *Report of the Bank of the United States to the Committee of Ways and Means of the House of Representatives* explained that Cheves had "laid before the board a private correspondence between him and Edward Jones, Esq., Chief Clerk of the Treasury Department" (no relation to William Jones). Either Crawford or (more likely) his clerk had come up with the idea of asking "whether the Bank can advance the amount to the holders of the stock"—in BUS notes—in order "to save the public credit, and to satisfy the holders."[34]

That was what happened. The Bank agreed to advance $1.5 million to stockholders and withhold the stock until the government had the funds to pay for it. The *National Intelligencer* outlined the plan in September: "The Bank of the United States has assumed the payment of that portion of the Louisiana debt redeemable in the next month, and . . . foreign holders have cheerfully consented that the payment by the Bank . . . shall be deferred for three years, the Bank paying them the same rate of interest as they have received from the government." On October 20 the Bank charged against the Treasury Department $1,852,578, for payments that were owed to various creditors (more than $1 million to Barings and Hope) on stock that was "in the meantime . . . held by the bank under the agreement acceded to." Disaster was again averted, and that month the relieved Bank took the first step toward relaxing its policy of refusing to pay notes of all branches at any branch: it announced that five-dollar notes would now be exchangeable at all offices.[35]

Cheves had piloted the Bank through potentially fatal shoals, but at serious cost to the country's banks and to many individuals' finances. Roger Taney, the fourth of Jackson's five secretaries of the treasury, later calculated that to collect $1 million from state banks under Jones's and Cheves's contraction policies, the BUS must have decreased note circulation by $4 or $5 million; banks in turn had to call in at least that much in depreciated notes from their own borrowers in order to pay the Bank. Every dollar successfully collected by the BUS was multiplied by four or five in its cost to the state banks and their debtors and in the damage to local economies.[36]

Cheves continued to insist on strict policies of curtailment and banknote demands, past the point of diminishing returns. In the six months of Jones's initial contraction, demand liabilities of the Bank (circulating notes and both private and public deposits) had decreased from $22 million in 1818 to $12 million in the spring of 1819, when Cheves took over. In the following year they declined only another $2 million. Notes outstanding, in particular, had fallen from $10 million in the summer of 1818 to $8.5 million in the fall (when Jones tightened the screws in Ohio), to less than $5 million in the next summer; they would decline only another $1.4 million by January 1820. Meanwhile, with land sales grinding to a halt in the Northwest and slowing in the Southwest, deposits fell from $9 million in the autumn of 1818 to under $3 million by the time Cheves took over. Most of the Bank's reduction in exposure had already taken place before Jones resigned as president in January 1819—and before the collapse of cotton prices that same month. But Cheves continued the contraction even after the nation's two largest exports—cotton and wheat—had plummeted in value and tax revenues from imports had dropped from $21.3 million to $16.6 million. Looking back from 1833, William Gouge would make his oft-quoted observation, "The Bank was saved and the people were ruined." A century and a half later, the historian Sean Wilentz comes to much the same conclusion: "By clamping down even harder through 1820 [Cheves] contributed to turning what might have been a sharp recession into a prolonged and disastrous depression." In the process, however, he "accumulated a huge horde [sic] of specie in the BUS."[37]

Despite the disruption of the Mexican mines, despite the exports of Spanish dollars to China and the trade deficit with Europe, a fair amount of silver had been out there—in the vaults of the state banks, in people's strongboxes, or hidden under floorboards. Now it was moving into the coffers of the Bank of the United States. In July 1817 the BUS office at Philadelphia had reported $340,802 in specie holdings; a year later, despite all the infusions from Europe, the figure was only $598,552; but by June 1819 it had risen to $1,212,411. Crawford—whose estimates must always be taken with more than a grain of salt—thought that as of September 1819 there was still about $12.5 million in specie in the possession of the nation's banks, in addition to $3.25 million at the BUS offices overall. His guess was "perhaps" another $4.5 million in the hands of individual citizens or businesses, for a total of about $20 million in silver and gold. He also estimated that $45 million in variously depreciated banknotes remained in circulation, down from the $68 million Gallatin believed had been circulating in 1816. The Bank continued to amass specie, reaching $8 million by the spring of 1821—three times the highest figure it could claim at any point in 1818—although the nation's circulating currency had shrunk by half.[38]

Early in 1818, when specie was still flowing *out* of the BUS, a premium for silver had appeared against the Bank's notes: 2 percent in March, 4 percent by June, and 6 percent by November. As inflation gave way to deflation in the Panic, the premium dropped back to 2 percent in June 1819, and BUS notes were once again at par with silver by April 1820. But the notes of western banks, especially in Tennessee and Kentucky, would remain well below par, and those banks would not redeem in specie for several years to come. While inflation prevailed, silver had been too valuable to spend, and both banks and individuals had squirreled it away. When the BUS, under first Jones and then Cheves, had contracted to the point of deflation, hoarders found that they had not held onto enough to save themselves—or many of the banks to which they were in debt.

It is impossible to say how many banks failed in the wake of the Panic. In 1830, Gallatin declared that at least 165 banks had failed since 1811. Since Weber and Fenstermaker believe that no more than 400 were chartered by 1819, and very few failed before the Panic, that suggests a proportion comparable to the wave in the early 1930s—perhaps 40 percent. (For comparison, the FDIC lists 525 failures in the Great Recession between 2009 and 2015—6 percent of some 8,300 insured institutions.) "The capital of 129 of these amounted to more than twenty-four millions of dollars stated as having been paid in; the whole amount may be estimated at near thirty millions; and our list may not be complete." It could not have been—any number of small, unincorporated banks had closed without any formal notice or record. Allowing for $110 million capital in banks still in operation in 1830, Gallatin figured that one-fifth of the nation's bank capital had been lost. That capital (not all by any means in specie or government bonds) had grown rapidly during the War of 1812, and the circulating currency had expanded even faster. From the beginning, however, the scarcity of silver had limited the banks' ability to redeem their notes, and in 1814 under the stress of having New England banks siphoning off what silver they had, most banks had suspended redemption and their notes had depreciated as low as 15 to 20 percent below par.[39]

Shortly after that the BUS was chartered with the intent of stabilizing currency, and in 1817, with nearly all banks "nominally" redeeming in specie once more, notes were at par nearly everywhere. After a year of BUS contraction, however, more and more banks were again refusing to redeem their notes in specie, and the national currency was less stable or predictable than it had been five years earlier. Niles, in the summer of 1819, evaluated the currency reaching Baltimore and reported depreciations from face value in the nation's third busiest commercial city ranging from 1 to 6 percent for New England banks to anywhere from 20 to 60 percent for those in Virginia, North Carolina, western Pennsylvania, Indiana, Illinois, and Missouri.[40]

It would get worse.

When the BUS began its contractions the previous summer, reactions had ranged from bafflement to outrage. The president of the Bank of Wilmington and Brandywine had replied to the BUS demand for specie in a puzzled tone: "It was very unexpected that you had any of the notes of this bank, and under the existing difficulties of making present pay, I feel at a loss in giving a promise to comply with the redemption of that amount by October next." The BUS agent reported that the furious president of the Commercial Bank of Lake Erie in Cleveland had declared "that the Bank of the United States has converted their offices into brokers' shops, and that he considered it a duty that he owed to society to resist their encroachments; that he would publish to the world the reasons for his refusal to pay, and call on the other banks to act in the same manner, and to form a coalition against the Bank of the United States, and whether they joined in it or not, that the bank would at all events resist all in their power."[41]

By November 1818, with their backs against the wall, the Cincinnati banks stopped payment on their notes; western Pennsylvania banks followed in December. The Bank of Kentucky, the state's oldest and strongest, stopped paying specie on November 30, and the state's other banks had all suspended by January, their notes now discounted by 20 percent or more. Amos Kendall, then the editor of Frankfort's *Argus of Western America*, blamed the BUS for wreaking financial havoc in Kentucky. "It found there a sound local currency, issued by a bank managed with signal caution, ability, and skill. It was mainly instrumental in driving that currency out of circulation without furnishing a substitute, and compelling the bank which issued it to stop payment." Later, as an influential member of Jackson's Kitchen Cabinet and the author of his veto message after the Bank's recharter passed Congress, Kendall's lingering bitterness toward the BUS would reinforce his president's own hostility.[42]

As *Niles' Register* surveyed the damage at year's end, it concluded that the Cincinnati banks' suspension "has filled all the western country with distress and alarm. . . . [O]thers may be expected to do the like, for specie is drawn from that quarter by waggon loads." Niles blamed the BUS for having "peremptorily required [the banks] to pay—and they could not pay the branch and have refused to pay anybody." The article concluded with a shrill warning: "The mammoth will not bear a rival, or suffer any other bank to exist but itself—if it can prevent it, to secure a monopoly of the whole money concession of the United States. When that comes to pass—God help the people."[43]

Events had gotten ahead of Niles; other banks in Ohio had already followed the example of Cincinnati. Allen Trimble wrote home from the state capitol on December 9, 1818, to advise his brother which banks could still be trusted. The boy who had been accused of passing counterfeit money on his way to Kentucky was now a state senator, but he was still bedeviled by uncertain currency: "I have seen the Treasurer of the State and learn from him that he is now taking Western Reserve [Bank] notes in payment. You need not fear taking them. New Lisbon is not taken, but it is said they exchange other paper for their notes. . . . The banks have stopped specie payment throughout the state except old Chillicothe."[44]

By the end of 1818 every bank in Vermont had closed; Niles reported that most Pennsylvania banks beyond the Alleghenies were "in such a predicament that their notes are, at present, *without price* in the money-market on the seaboard." Ohio banknotes were no longer accepted in Baltimore at any rate of depreciation. In December, the *National Intelligencer* reported that after the venerable Bank of Kentucky suspended specie payments, "representatives of ten of the *independent banks* of Kentucky, as they are called—that is, the banks chartered, 35 in number, during the last winter . . . unanimously resolved, to 'recommend to their respective institutions, to suspend the payment of specie.' This is stopping payment wholesale."[45]

Writing from Lexington at year's end, James Flint summarized for his British readers the chaotic state of banking in America:

There is here much trouble with paper money. The notes current in one part, are either refused or taken at a large discount, in another. Banks that were creditable a few days ago, have refused to redeem their paper in specie or in notes of the United States' Bank. In Kentucky, there are two branches of the United States' Bank, thirteen of the Kentucky bank, and a list of fifty independent banks, some of which are not in operation. In the state of Ohio there are thirty chartered banks, and a few which have not obtained that pernicious distinction. In Tennessee, the number of banks, including branches, is fourteen. The total number of these establishments in the United States, could not, perhaps, be accurately stated on a given day. The enumeration, like the census of population, might be affected by births and deaths. The creation of this vast host of fabricators, and vendors of base money, must form a memorable epoch in the history of the country . . .

When the sick system dies, the public will see the full amount of the penance they have to suffer for their credulity.[46]

The public had been in a state of denial. The English economist David Ricardo was puzzled that Americans tolerated such a flimsy, tottering banking system; Condy Raguet, the Philadelphia financier and legislator, gave him the same explanation that Crawford had offered: "The whole of our population are either stockholders of banks or in debt to them. It is not in the interest of the first to press the banks and the rest are afraid. This is the whole secret." Raguet, obviously frustrated, continued, "An independent man, who was neither a stockholder or debtor, who would have ventured to compel the banks to do justice, would have been persecuted as an enemy to society."[47]

On through 1819 the contraction continued, and across the country more and more banks first announced specie suspension and then closed their doors. Now the public response ranged from blind confidence to bleak despair, with occasional flashes of black humor. In the spring John Quincy Adams wrote in his diary that "the bank bubbles are breaking . . . the merchants are crumbling to ruin, the manufactures perishing . . . there seems to be no remedy but time and patience, and the changes of events which time effects." But a month later, the Albany *Argus* declared, "We are satisfied the present alarm is unreasonably great. Stopping payments and the insolvency of a bank are very different things, and the last is by no means a consequent inference of the first." Attempts to charter new banks continued in Georgia (where the legislature refused), Vermont (where the legislature agreed, but the newly chartered banks failed to open), and Maryland. The Maryland proposal elicited this suggestion from Niles: "We would advise the House of delegates to refer it to the attending physicians at Baltimore Hospital, whose skill in the management of insane persons is highly spoken of."[48]

The expedient of banks' redeeming their notes in the notes of other banks was widely disapproved but inescapable. James Flint remarked, "So long as a credulous public entertained full confidence in banks, bankers gave in exchange for their paper, that of *other banks, equally good with their own.* The same kind of exchanges are still offered now, when the people are very suspicious." The practice inspired another of the Niles's apocryphal tales from a distant correspondent: when a "pretty slick Yankee" arrived in Cincinnati from Pittsburgh, he brought $1,000 in notes of Piatt's Bank to the bank's office and asked for specie. When it was refused, he asked for notes from any specie-paying bank. Refused again, he said he would rather have notes from Owl Creek (Niles's favorite whipping boy, "the Bank of Hoo! Hoo!"). Indignantly refused, with protests at the insult, he finally asked if they could at least exchange "any well executed *counterfeit* notes on any good banks."[49]

In the West, the rising and falling local banks had been symbiotic with the rising and falling federal land sales—which, in turn, had tracked the prices of wheat and cotton. Here again Crawford found himself walking a tightrope, trying to maximize sales on the one hand while assuring the integrity of the currency on the other. As early as 1816 the new secretary of the treasury had written to the newly elected president of the Bank, "The public revenue from the sale of public lands is accumulating in Ohio and Kentucky, but the currency is so bad that it is useless anywhere else." He confessed to Biddle six years later that he had then advised Jones to just get rid of suspect local banknotes over the counter to the public, as quickly as possible. After the Bank's contraction policy pushed western banks to suspend specie payment, he had taken on the thankless task of decreeing which banks' notes would be "land office money" and which would be refused—inevitably laying himself open to not-undeserved charges of playing favorites. Late in 1818 he wrote plaintively to the receiver at the Milledgeville office in his home state of Georgia, "The doleful state of the currency, in most parts of the country, resulting from the excessive multiplication of banks by the States renders it extremely difficult to discriminate between those that are really solvent, [and] those that are not so."[50]

In Alabama, where land continued to sell if acceptable money could be found, Crawford's order to refuse the notes of so many banks began "to operate with great severity upon the people of this country. . . . All confidence in the paper currency of the country appears to be lost by the people at large." Crawford's approved banks seemed to be taking advantage of their favored status to resist efforts by the BUS to collect from them. In June 1819 Cheves pointedly reminded Crawford that some western banks that he had designated receiving banks for land receipts were refusing to pay the BUS specie on demand. Singling out the Bank of Vincennes, whose president happened to be a Crawford-appointed land office register, Cheves wrote, "If our demand shall not be met in an available shape as is possible [i.e., specie or BUS notes], from mere indifference to our claims, if from no other cause, it would be a particular favor to the bank to have your sanction of our demand, as it would no doubt have a considerable influence."[51]

Neither of the banks in Missouri was paying specie. The last bastion in the West, the Bank of Chillicothe—Trimble's trusted "Old Chillicothe"—threw in the towel in June 1819, refusing to redeem in specie any longer. But now even banks along the East Coast were suspending as well. North Carolina banks stopped paying specie at the end of May; South Carolina banks suspended and would not resume until 1823. The bills of Baltimore's City Bank were no longer taken as "current money" in June, and several banks in Georgia and Pennsylvania stopped payment. By August two of Tennessee's three largest banks had gone out of business, and the remaining banks' notes were taken only at half their face value. Baltimore banks were experiencing shocks, although the banking hubs of Philadelphia and New York City—with stronger specie reserves and proportionately less money in outstanding loans—were weathering the storm. By midsummer the same could not be said for the rest of Pennsylvania and New York. "Country banks" in both states began to suspend payment, and the Farmers and Mechanics Bank in Pittsburgh shut its doors.[52]

The New York Senate *Journal* for the 42nd session, 1819, recorded that the banks in New York City alone had called in $15,030,000 in loans. State governments were under pressure to act but could rarely decide on a course of action that promised to do more good than harm. In 1819 Maryland and Pennsylvania voted to void the charter of any bank refusing to pay specie on demand; New York adopted a new constitution in 1820 that required a two-thirds vote of the legislature for any future bank charters. Legislatures, trying to do the right thing, sometimes reversed themselves almost overnight. The Maryland legislature, on February 15, 1819, passed a law against banks that refused to pay in specie. Only two days later, it passed a law against persons who demanded payment in specie. The first act was "to compel . . . banks to pay specie for their notes, or forfeit their charters." The second, after a brief reconsideration, was intended "to relieve the people, of this state, as far as practicable, from the demands on the banks of this state for gold and silver by brokers." Pennsylvania went through the same back and forth the following month, ordering banks to pay specie but then targeting brokers "habitually in the practice of receiving or buying notes at less than nominal values." Banks themselves took direct action in self-defense: the State Bank of North Carolina, the Bank of New Bern, and the Bank of Cape Fear sent agents to New York to buy up their own notes in order to retire them and agreed in June not to redeem their notes in specie to brokers—although they continued to require their debtors to pay *them* in specie. Thomas Ritchie, in the Richmond *Enquirer*, condemned the decision. He pointed out that North Carolina banknotes would be hugely depreciated in Virginia if customers did not believe they could sell them to brokers. There seemed to be no response banks or legislatures could make that did not have unintended consequences.[53]

On through the fall and winter banks continued to suspend specie payment. In September, after more than a year of contraction, *Niles' Register* listed sixteen banks in Kentucky as "doubtful" and six whose notes "are believed to be good," but none as paying in silver. The Philadelphia *Democratic Press* published the names of ten in Kentucky among a "legion of banks which have stopped payment." By October Niles could find only "two or three independent banks" whose notes could be trusted. "Many of them have forfeited their charters, and others are wisely preparing to wind up their affairs. It will require many years of industry and economy to repair the depredation which these institutions have caused. . . . Experience is a dear school." At the end of the month two more banks in Kentucky had given up, and another was redeeming its paper in notes of the Bank of Kentucky, "payable one year after the date." In Pennsylvania, the other state that had chartered banks *en masse*, "the greater part of this lot has gone or is going. A few, prudently conducted, have maintained an honorable reputation. But the majority appear to have striven only to excel in acts of speculation—by which we mean FRAUD."[54]

As the new year of 1820 began, notes of all surviving banks outside of the four largest cities were still depreciated. The only banks still open in Tennessee and Kentucky were the oldest, most conservative institutions whose notes were nevertheless discounted 15 percent in the eastern cities—and a failing handful whose notes were everywhere rejected on sight. Any Ohio bank that might pay specie to individual customers (none would pay it to the BUS) was still discounted 10 percent; the rest suffered depreciation of 15 percent or more. In Baltimore, even some Maryland and District of Columbia banknotes were depreciated 12 percent, 50 percent, or "almost 100 percent." Vermont had no banks, Missouri would see both of its banks closed within a year, and Indiana and Illinois were headed in that direction. Because the BUS branch in Savannah was not issuing banknotes, it had been treating local Georgia notes as the equivalent of specie. In May 1820, fearing to provoke a storm of controversy, it announced that it would be presenting them for collection, but only the amount above a "cushion" of $100,000 in its deposits. After a tentative compromise by the Georgia banks, relations collapsed, and the Planters' Bank of Savannah and the Bank of the State of Georgia refused to do any business with the BUS, including redeeming their notes. It was at this point that the legislature repealed its penalty for nonredemption of banknotes—but only when the BUS was the one seeking redemption. The conflict reached the Supreme Court in *Bank of the United States v. Planters' Bank*, over the legal question of whether the banks could be sued in federal courts, with the court finding for the BUS.[55]

By Weber's very conservative count, at least fifty-one state-chartered banks had now failed, and another twenty-four would close by November 1822. Many more closings went unreported in either newspapers or state records, and Thomas Greer, writing in the *Indiana Magazine of History*, thinks the failures between 1819 and 1823 numbered at least eighty-five. Gallatin's estimate was higher still: eighty-six just in Kentucky, Tennessee, Pennsylvania, and Ohio, and twenty in "conservative" New England. Eighteen state-chartered banks with a combined capital of $2 million failed in Ohio, along with an unknown number of "d—m'd unchartered rascals." (Owl Creek held on.) Banknotes in circulation had decreased to less than half what they had been in 1816.[56]

In February 1819, Crawford made his "Report on Currency" to the House of Representatives. He began by declaring that "the multiplicity of local banks, scattered over the face of the country, in particular parts of the union . . . by the depreciation of their paper, have levied a tax on the community, within the pale of their influence, exceeding the public contributions paid by them." After his many assurances, he finally had to admit that three years after the Bank of the United States opened with its promise to restore a sound national currency, "the great mass of the currency is not even ostensibly convertible to specie at the will of the holder," and that during "the greater part of the time" since specie resumption was promised, "the convertibility of banknotes into specie has been rather nominal than real in the largest portion of the Union."[57]

Crawford told Congress that perhaps $4.5 million in specie was in circulation and probably $3.25 million was in the vaults of the BUS. (The Bank was still doing its best to keep that specie *out* of circulation; the elephant, however, had left the room, and the Louisiana loan would pose no further threat.) Crawford criticized merchants who had continued to ship silver dollars to China: "The amount exported [from 1815 to 1819] was very great, and seriously affected the amount of circulation, by compelling the banks to diminish their discounts." This last charge was doubtful; the outflow of specie contributed to the reluctance to redeem paper with silver, but the banks had shown no sign of decreasing their lending until the BUS began calling in their notes. Crawford had just blamed the state banks for their overissue of currency, creating the postwar inflation; now, he had to acknowledge the painful effects of deflation that spring caused by the BUS contraction: "All intelligent writers upon currency agree that where it is decreasing in amount, poverty and misery must prevail. The correctness of the opinion is too manifest to require proof. The united voice of the nation attests to its accuracy." And he acknowledged that what would become known as the Panic of 1819 was without precedent: "As there is no recorded example in the history of nations of a reduction of the currency, so rapid and so extensive, so but few examples have occurred, of distress so general and so severe, as that which has been exhibited in the United States." Circulating currency in 1819 amounted, by his estimate, to $45 million—down from $110 million four years earlier. Now Crawford made the unwelcome prediction that it must decline still further before it would be sound, and the nation would "continue to suffer until this is effected." He continued,

The reduction exceeds fifty-nine per cent. of the whole circulation of 1815. The fact that the currency of 1815 and 1816 was depreciated, has not sensibly diminished the effect upon the community of this great and sudden reduction. Whatever was the degree of its depreciation, it was still the measure of value. It determined the price of labor, and of all the property of the community. A change so violent could not fail, under the most favorable of auspices in other respects, to produce much distress, to check the ardor of enterprize, and severely to affect the productive energies of the nation.[58]

The united voice of the nation attested to the accuracy of *that* conclusion, also too manifest to require proof—and still more dangers were appearing. When John Quincy Adams looked ahead to 1820, the outlook was grim:

The Bank, the national currency, the depression of manufactures, the restless turbulence and jealousies and insubordinations of the State Legislatures, the Missouri slave question, the deficiencies of the revenue to be supplied, the rankling passions and ambitious projects of individuals, mingling with everything, presented a prospect of the future which I freely acknowledge was to me appalling.[59]

HARD TIMES IN THE EAST
"A Long Continuation of Distress"

The *Oxford English Dictionary* suggests that the application of the word "panic" to a financial crash dates from the Panic of 1825 in England, citing Charles Knight's *Popular History of England*: "This pecuniary crisis universally obtained the name of 'The Panic.'" Jessica Lepler, in *The Many Panics of 1837*, can find no such application of the term in America before the New York *Times* in 1857. "Panic" would become the standard term for such an event in the second half of the nineteenth century—the Panics of 1857, 1873, 1893—only giving way to the less-dramatic "depression" after 1929. The eighteenth century had introduced "bubble" as a term for the rapid but insubstantial expansion of financial hopes. Bubbles inevitably burst; the American pronunciation—"bust"—and its counterpart, "boom," are said by the *OED* to date from the 1860s or 1870s.[1]

It has not previously been noted by historians of either economics or language, but Thomas Jefferson may actually have been the first to apply the word "panic" to a financial upheaval, and he did so in 1819. Writing to Richard Rush on June 22, 1819, he described the economic conditions that year by saying that "at present all is confusion, uncertainty and panic." However, no other contemporary accounts from the period around 1819 mention "panic"; most often they speak of "pressure," leading up to "embarrassment" or even "evil," followed by the simple and direct "hard times." "Panic" might be a fair description of the sudden hysteria that swept through the City of London in April 1825 or Wall Street in October 1929, but it is really a misleading term for either the economic collapse of 1818 to 1819 or the nationwide depression in the years that followed. What happened was more like a Mississippi flood; it inspired feelings of dread or despair as it came inexorably on, but there was rarely a moment of sudden shock or surprise—or there should not have been, for anyone paying attention.[2]

Of course, confusion, uncertainty, and even panic could describe what Jefferson personally experienced in his retirement at Monticello—not a detached spectator, but suddenly a casualty of the hard times. His mounting debts and the unexpected failure of a friend whose notes he cosigned would force his heirs to sell his beloved mountaintop plantation. The view there was directed westward: Jefferson, who had sent Lewis and Clark as far as the Pacific, was always keenly interested in the land west of the mountains, much of which he had added to the nation through his Louisiana Purchase. In 1819, even as his own finances were collapsing, his attention was focused on the crisis unfolding in Congress over slavery in Missouri, which he called "a fire bell in the night" for the Union. His favorite correspondent in old age, the irascible John Adams, shared his concern, but Adams was not so worried about Missouri as he was discouraged by what he took to be the self-evident truths of the pursuit of financial happiness: "Will you tell me how to prevent riches from becoming the effects of temperance and industry— Will you tell me how to prevent riches from producing luxury— Will you tell me how to prevent luxury from producing effeminacy intoxication extravagance Vice and folly."[3]

Adams was not the only one who thought the economic collapse was also a moral collapse. Thomas Astley, a director of the Bank of the United States, was an Englishman by birth who had emigrated to Pennsylvania. In the spring of 1820, as the depression was deepening in Philadelphia, Astley wrote an open letter to a friend in Great Britain, printed in London newspapers:

> On the first day of my arrival in Philadelphia [before the war] I walked round among correspondents whom I had before known by name. I was at home amongst them, and I would, without the least hesitation, have sold them goods to the amount of 100,000 pounds. Now I do not know the persons doing business, and there is not one among them whose order I would take for £1000! What a difference! A long continuation of distresses in the commercial world has had a bad effect upon the morality of the country.[4]

Hezekiah Niles, in Baltimore, considered Astley's letter disloyal. He called its author an ingrate "whom we have tenderly nursed within our own bosoms," but his *Register* had been even harsher in condemning unprincipled businessmen and gloomier in describing the economic distress. A year earlier, on April 10, 1819, Niles was already writing,

> From all parts of our own country we hear of a pressure on men in business, a general stagnation of trade, a large reduction in the price of staple articles. Real property is rapidly depreciating in its nominal value. . . . Many highly

respectable traders have become bankrupts, and it is agreed that many others must "go"; the banks are refusing their customary accommodations, confidence amongst merchants is shaken . . . but worst of all is, that those whose opinions deserve to be respected, tell us these things are only the beginning of evils! If so, what will the end be?

And six weeks later he added, "We are well assured that there will be a terrible smashing among the people—extensive bankruptcies among the merchants, and great sacrifice of the hard-earned property of the farmer and planter. Again, we say, let it go on—'seeing is believing, but feeling has no fellow.'" By October 1819, the *Register* would report 50,000 unemployed in Baltimore, Philadelphia, and New York.[5]

Matthew Carey, observing from Philadelphia, estimated that three million people—a third of the nation—were directly affected by the Panic of 1819 and the ensuing depression. Land in that city that had commanded $150 per acre in 1815 went for $35 in 1819. In New York, property values fell from $315 million in 1818 to $256 million in 1820, and in Richmond real estate lost half its value. By way of comparison, only the Panic of 1893 and the Great Depression in the 1930s saw a greater percentage drop in the GDP; the "hard times" that began in 1815 in the East and lasted into the mid-twenties are vividly revealed in the collapse of per-capita GDP. The 1814 figure of $133.35 dropped abruptly to $111.32 when cheap imports undercut mills and merchants in 1815. It continued to fall steeply through the teens, finally bottoming out in 1824. The $69.83 figure for that year was the lowest in thirty years; per-capita GDP would never be that low again. While there are only estimates for unemployment during these depression years (when most people were still self-employed farmers), it may have reached 20 percent of the wage-earners nationally, a rate surpassed only in 1932 to 1934. The year 1821—a low point in the nation's buying power—was one of only three years before 1860 in which the value of imports did not exceed that of exports, and 1821/22 was the only time between 1815 and 1835 in which the national debt was not reduced.[6]

Over the decade between 1814 and 1824 the per-capita GDP (and purchasing power) declined by nearly half. It is little wonder that people could not repay debts they had incurred during times of high prices. For an individual to fail in business was itself nothing new; a study of 217 autobiographies and memoirs between 1775 and 1800 concludes, "Most who seized the opportunities opening up in trade and manufacturing failed in their careers at least once, some being totally wiped out." But after 1819, bankruptcy—formerly viewed as one of the natural hazards of economic life—took on a new stigma of moral failure it had not had before. In 1818, as business failures quickly began to increase, Niles joined a chorus calling for a uniform federal bankruptcy law—something specifically authorized by the Constitution but on the books only between 1800 and 1803, and then as an involuntary bankruptcy statute. Niles's reasons, however, did not include sympathy for the failed businessman. He believed such a law "would operate on *incorporations* as well as individuals, and be the very thing to shut up every swindling or ill-directed banking institution, causing the whole race of money-makers to be exceedingly cautious."[7]

In 1819 John Marshall's Supreme Court declared a state bankruptcy law to be an unconstitutional usurpation of a federal power. In the case of *Sturges v. Crowninshield,* a divided court overturned the New York insolvency law. Immediately after the decision Niles predicted that "congress will do something on this matter in the coming session." But Congress refused to do so; a bill introduced in the Senate was defeated 23 to 15, without a single supporting vote from the West, where the conflict between debtor and creditor was reshaping politics. Now Niles declared, "The Senate's rejection of the bill to establish an uniform system of bankruptcy, as congress is *specifically* empowered by the constitution to do, will severely oppress that numerous part of the community who have recently been, or now are, interested in trade or commerce"; later he would estimate that $100,000,000 in mercantile debts to Europe were wiped out by bankruptcy from 1819 to 1820. That may be an exaggeration, but modern estimates are at least $70,000,000.[8]

Bankruptcy laws had a special urgency in an era when imprisonment for debt was still common. Five years before the young Charles Dickens's family would move into London's Marshalsea Prison because of his father's debts, James Flint assured his British readers that in America, "We know of no example here of imprisonment for a debt of a shilling, or for a supposed fraud of one penny"—but very soon there would be imprisonments for less than a dollar. In 1820, Hannah Crispy would be imprisoned in Boston, along with her nursing infant, for failure to pay a twelve-dollar debt. After twenty days the child died, but the creditor refused to discharge Crispy unless he was paid, whereupon the district attorney "discharged her on his own responsibility, to attend the funeral." Richard Mentor Johnson, himself pursued by creditors, succeeded in persuading his state of Kentucky to end imprisonment for debt in 1821. The following year he introduced a Senate bill to end the practice nationally, citing the heartrending experience of Hannah Crispy. It failed, was reintroduced in 1824, and failed again. The effort was repeated in 1828 and then given up.[9]

As business owners sank into failure, employees faced wage cuts and unemployment. In the summer of 1819, Niles reported that "most of our manufactories have stopped or are about to stop, and every branch of mechanical industry is reduced from one third to one half of its recent amount." By late fall, the nation was experiencing an unprecedented phenomenon that would become too familiar: "Multitudes of people, both able and willing to work, who have no means but their industry, are unable to find employment." Flint, traveling through the recently prosperous Ohio valley, pointed out that a farmer could not "pay 125 cents per day to the labourer, and sell his corn for 25 cents per bushel, nor can the labourer work for a small hire while he pays two and a half, or three dollars a-week for his board, and an extravagant price for his clothing." He passed along the estimate in August 1820 that half a million were unemployed, but admitted that there was no way of counting. Although prices gradually began to rise in 1821, wages of laborers kept falling. From New England on down the coast to Georgia, the East was in the grip of depression.[10]

People regularly spoke of the nation's economic troubles in metaphors from physical illness: a "dropsical fullness" of paper currency and the "fevers" of migration and land investment gave way to financial "disease" for which no cure could be found. In the early nineteenth century, physicians had few remedies to offer their patients beyond bleeding or powerful emetics, and John Quincy Adams was convinced that for the nation's economic ills, "there seems to be no remedy but time and patience." As he watched the depression spread across the country in June 1819 he confided to his diary,

> The disease is only disclosing its first symptoms. New England scarcely yet feels it. They produce none of the great articles of export, which have sunk within a few months in the fading market to half-price: cotton, tobacco, rice, wheat, and flour. But as commercial and navigating, it will reach them by reflection from the South and West. The profits of commerce and shipping must fall after the price of the exports has been so much reduced as necessarily to reduce in turn the quantity of imports. The distress in this quarter will therefore come later, but it will come.[11]

New England did appear better off, in some respects, than the rest of the country; the banks there would actually expand their notes (slightly) from 1818 to 1821, in response to the decrease in out-of-state banknotes, and the Lowell mill at Waltham remained profitable. But Adams had been out of the country for most of the years between 1809 and 1819 while New England was becoming more industrialized, and he had not seen firsthand the effect on both commerce and manufacturing there of the flood of cheap imports. In Massachusetts, commercial capital lost 25 percent during 1819, and the U.S. Treasury brought suit against merchants for $3 million in unpaid tax revenue. In parts of the Northeast, the depression that gripped the nation in 1819 had actually begun in 1815, as cotton mills shut down and investments in all but the most efficient factories were lost. In 1813, 1814, and 1815 Massachusetts had incorporated sixteen, thirty-one, and twenty-one new textile firms; in the next five years, 1816 to 1820, the state incorporated six, none, two, none, and two. In all of New York and New England, 1813 to 1815 had seen 194 incorporations; in 1816 to 1820 there would be only thirty-five. David L. Dodge had opened a new mill in Bozrah, Connecticut, in 1813. By 1819 he had undergone "a great reversion in business, mainly from the great influx of foreign goods which followed the return of peace." Three of his stockholders had become bankrupts, and the mill would close in 1824. He mournfully concluded, "None but the new factories with modern improvements in machinery could sustain themselves."[12]

Even as Adams was recording his belief that New England was not yet suffering, Oliver Wolcott—the mill owner who was now governor of Connecticut—was preparing his *Remarks on the Present State of Currency, Credit, Commerce, and National Industry*. He saw a different picture: "The present embarrassment extends to men who have been prudent in the management of their affairs, and embraces alike the industrious farmer, mechanic, manufacturer, and merchant; the borrower and lender; in short, every description of men, except the mere hoarders of money." In Adams's home state of Massachusetts, where sixty-eight textile firms had opened during the War of 1812, twenty-four went out of business between 1816 and 1820. In Rhode Island, perhaps two-thirds of the textile businesses suffered losses over those years. Wolcott was inclined to attribute "the general stagnation of commerce and industry" to the "unavoidable connection which has long existed between our system of commerce and revenue, and that of Great Britain," but there were other causes at work as well. Rural America was the great market for New England's main product, coarse machine-made cotton cloth. When the

South and West were hit by lower prices for wheat and cotton, that market fell off. The price of "brown shirting" dropped ten cents from the 1818 high of thirty-four cents. Slater and Tiffany's cloth sales declined by 15 percent in 1819. The Troy Company of Fall River was unable to collect "that old debt for Indiana money" in December 1818, and by the following March it had over $10,000 overdue for sales in the West—a sizable deficit for a company whose net profits never exceeded $9,000 between 1818 and 1823. Troy told its Philadelphia agents not to sell over the mountains except for trustworthy currency at or near par, "for we had much rather our goods remain unsold than to have them sold and never receive pay."[13]

The governor of Massachusetts began each year with an address to the General Court (as Massachusetts called its legislature). In January 1819 Gov. John Brooks warned that the state was already going through "times of peril and extreme pressure." The next year, he devoted half of his address to the continuing depression and to embarrassments "which had led to increases in pauperism, crime, and the cost of poor relief." Boston's *Columbian Centinel* of June 26, 1819, reported that "complaints of Hard Times appear universal," and the Boston *Patriot* noted that the city in September "presents a dull and uncheery spectacle—silence reigns in the streets and gloom and despondency in every countenance."[14]

The gloom would be slow to lift. Thirty-five hundred in Boston were imprisoned for debt between 1820 and 1822. Many more barely escaped jail. Since so many who were creditors to some were also debtors to others, chain reactions were common. Asa Sheldon, the Yankee trader who had earlier profited from the difference between Massachusetts money and other states' paper, recalled years later his experience in 1819:

> Still owing large debts and hard times coming on, creditors pressed their claims. I could not collect my debts fast enough to satisfy their demands, and failure unavoidably ensued. My real estate was resigned into the hands of fourteen of my largest creditors, and the property appraised off at a very low rate, but sufficient to cancel all my debts excepting $34. Had this $34 been paid, it would have cleared me from their debts; but I had no heart to ask anyone to lend it to me.[15]

Sheldon was what was just becoming known as a "self-made" man, an entrepreneur who had made his money by taking risks; only thirty-one years old in 1819, he was confident that he would bounce back. David Stoddard

Greenough Jr. was a different story. He was an attorney, also in his early thirties, a member of an old and prominent Boston family. More than anything, he was horrified at the thought of public disgrace if his bankruptcy should become known. His friend and Harvard classmate Benjamin Guild counseled him, "Your situation is not in the least suspected and if . . . it can never be known, you will be able by your industry and your character to acquire a sufficient support for yourself." On the other hand, "If it once becomes the subject of doubt and conversation it will be much more difficult for you to do anything to support yourself hereafter." Rather than depend on his own industry and character, Greenough laid his failure before his father, who paid off his creditors. The shame was so intense, even without public exposure, that Greenough could not face it even in his diary; the only entry after June 16, 1818, until January 1, 1824, is this note: "Many unpleasant occurrences are consequently omitted."[16]

Earlier panics had injured only well-to-do investors; in 1819 the humble suffered along with the well-to-do. Massachusetts agricultural laborers' wages had risen from $0.60 per day in 1811 to as much as $1.50 per day in 1818, but in 1819 they fell to $0.53. Many now were grateful simply to exchange work for room and board. Oliver Wolcott thought that if New Englanders were suffering less than westerners, it was not because their banks and businesses were more responsibly run, but rather "owing to a more dense population and varied industry, by which people are enabled more conveniently to supply their mutual wants, by a barter and exchange of commodities." But barter was not enough. Although New England's recovery was under way by the end of 1821, in 1822 Josiah Quincy told the Grand Jury of Suffolk County that there were still seven hundred men, "for whom work cannot be obtained," on the books of the Boston Employment Society. "These men long for work; they anxiously beg for it; yet it is not to be found."[17]

To a visitor, New York seemed bustling in 1818; when he entered the harbor, James Flint found it difficult to see the buildings through "the forest of masts in front of them." After touring Long Island, he advised his readers that "the high price of land prevents emigrants from settling here." Still, he reported with satisfaction that wages were a dollar a day and board only two or three dollars a week, so that a wage-earner who was tempted by westward migration would find that "it is in his power to banish every appearance of poverty, and to save some money, provided he is disposed to economy.[18]

New York had begun to recover some prosperity after the first blow from cheap imports, but it did not last, either in the city or upstate. On the first of May 1819, six New York merchants closed their doors. Business failures were becoming a daily occurrence. That month George White's New York *National Advocate* reported,

> The pressure of the times is now beginning to be most severely and dangerously felt. In New York, four or five highly respectable mercantile houses have stopped payment and there is reason to fear that the evil will be increased. The rage for speculation has carried them beyond their depth, added to which the extraordinary state of commerce with Europe affords no hope of better prospects.

Imports were beginning to decline; exports through the port of New York—wheat from upstate and cotton shipped on from Charleston—were dropping in value, and falling freight rates were hurting shipping companies. Investments in canals and toll roads were unprofitable, and those who had speculated in bank stock were watching its value shrink. Jacob Barker had helped fund the BUS in 1816; in June 1819, Barker temporarily closed his exchange bank in Manhattan after the failure of the Washington and Warren Bank, which he also owned, in the town of Sandy Hill. Barker paid off the Washington and Warren notes in specie—at seventy cents on the dollar—but Niles reported, "Jacob Barker's [Manhattan] bank is shut up this day, in consequence of a heavy run upon him yesterday to meet the Washington and Warren banknotes . . . there is a great mob around his *closed* bank, and constables are fixed to prevent its being gutted, as many fear will be the case."[19]

New York real estate prices, which had only recently struck Flint as too high for immigrants to consider, were falling steeply for both city lots and country acreage. Through 1819 and 1820 New York City's Common Council was deluged by petitions seeking postponement of property taxes because of the "extreme pressure of the times," citing the general lack of money and the failure of tenants to pay rents. The revenue shortfall forced the city to cut back steeply on spending: support of the city almshouse was cut by 20 percent despite the rapidly growing number of inmates, expenditures on docks and roads were cut by more than 25 percent, and the mayor's salary was reduced from $7,500 to $5,000. The council noted with dismay that the city had never been in debt before 1810, but it owed $600,000 in 1819, and the City of New York entered the summer of 1820 with a deficit of $1,166,023.20.[20]

A familiar pattern of events unfolded: creditors who could not collect on accounts that were due to them had to default on their own debts. Attorney

Richard Varick wrote to Abraham Van Vechten in April to complain that his difficulty collecting from clients meant he could not pay his own bills, now twelve months past due. Henry Meigs, son of the Land Office commissioner Josiah Meigs, was also an attorney and had just been elected to Congress; he too complained about the difficulty of collecting legal fees of fifty dollars even from the wealthiest clients. Many New Yorkers were finding, just as the New England textile mills were, that economic distress in Ohio or Indiana was taking its toll on them. A client retained Thomas L. Ogden to defend him for nonpayment of $1,200 to LeRoy Bayard & Co.; he explained that he had been counting on payments due to him from the Northwest, "which everyone knows lacks money," and was thus unable to pay Bayard. In July James Murray told his wife that their neighbor Thomas A. Morris, son of the Revolutionary War financier Robert Morris, had failed owing $150,000: "There is little to pay it with." And Herman Melville's namesake uncle Herman Gansevoort had to admit to his brother Peter that he could not pay the money he owed him unless he could collect from his own debtors.

New York depended on exports as well as imports, and as the prices of wheat and cotton fell, exports brought in less and less. Of course prices were falling for consumers, too, but not as fast as their incomes; the *Evening Post* complained that butchers' prices for beef were still high, a complaint echoed a year later in the *Advocate*. All wage earners were struggling; even the clerks at the BUS branch office had their pay cut as much as two-thirds. There was no organized labor in the modern sense—the journeymen's benevolent societies, predecessors of labor unions, functioned primarily as fraternal organizations, planning parades and collecting for sick members—and strikes were still a novelty, but in 1819 both the masons and the tailors did strike, the latter upset because master tailors were hiring lower-paid women as "slop workers," making cheap clothes in set sizes. (Significantly, the number of secondhand clothing shops increased during the depression years; in northern cities they were largely owned by African Americans.)[21]

Membership in journeymen's organizations declined through the depressed years as the growing unemployment made coordinated action harder. Out of 102 members of the Society of Shipwrights and Caulkers, thirty-eight were expelled between 1819 and 1821 for nonpayment of dues. An English traveler reported "500 shoemakers out of employ and an equal proportion of hands in almost every other branch of business." When Niles estimated that ten thousand able-bodied men were unemployed in New York, "wandering the streets" in search of work, the New York *American* challenged that figure on the grounds that if each one had a wife and three children, nearly half the population would be walking the streets; the *American* overlooked the number of women and children who were themselves working to support their families, and who were less likely to be laid off because, like the female "slop workers," they could be paid less for the same work.[22]

The distress extended beyond New York City. Niles reported a sheriff's sale in western New York of forty-three tracts of land, "many listed as farms on which the owners reside," along with ten postponements of sales and notices of the auctions of farms belonging to yet another ten people in default of mortgage payments. The western part of the state had been developing rapidly, spurred by the plans for the Erie Canal; when Anne W. Cary, daughter of a Granada sugar planter, had visited Rochester in 1818 she was shown an acre of land worth $30 in 1812 that had recently sold for $6,000; even then land values were dropping, and the state real estate valuations for tax purposes had declined slightly from 1817. In 1819 valuations fell from $315 million to $282 million, despite the continuing development of western towns and farms: "The whole productive labor of the people of this great state, as applied to the clearing of new lands, the improvement of farms and building of new houses . . . has been insufficient to prevent a *general* depreciation of property." By 1820, things were worse. Samuel Hopkins, president of the Genesee Agricultural Society, gave a speech that October:

> My first wish would be . . . to speak in a tone that would rouse the tenants of every log-home in these counties and make them stand aghast at the prospect of families naked—children freezing in the winter's storm—and the fathers without coats or shoes that would enable them to the necessary labors of the inclement season. . . . Last year we talked of the difficulties of paying for our lands; this year the question is, how to survive.[23]

The depression was arguably even more severe farther to the south and the west. As banknotes lost value and bankers demanded loan repayment in specie, Matthew Carey, the Philadelphia banker and publisher, observed, "Merchants who have stood for forty years, as well as those who have made a forty days trade of it, are tumbling like rows of bricks." Only recently Carey had been an advocate of expansionist banking, declaring, "Liberality is nine times out of ten a sound policy in banking." In 1818 and 1819, however, Pennsylvanians were holding overexuberant banks responsible for the "pressures" and "embarrassments" that they were feeling. The Greensburg *Republican* took the position that speculators were themselves less at fault than the bankers who had "*induced* and *enabled* many persons *to forsake their honest* and laborious pursuits for the purposes of trade & speculation." After a lengthy investigation led by Condy Raguet, the Pennsylvania Assembly reached much the same conclusion. Westerners might blame the BUS for its relentless policy of contraction, but the Raguet Report put the onus for the people's distress squarely on the state banks, for their irresponsible expansion—Carey's "liberality." Raguet's committee concluded, "The cause is to be found chiefly in the abuses of the banking system, which abuses consist *first* in the excessive number of banks and *secondly* in their universal bad administration."[24]

In Pennsylvania, the "New School" Republicans were commercially oriented and had happily supported the banking establishment when they came to power in 1817. Led by Gov. William Findlay, they had appeared to be the wave of the future and were credited with bringing a temporary prosperity after the postwar manufacturing slump. Now, as the economy took a much deeper dive, there were more and more complaints about government run by what William Duane's *Aurora* called "a few lawyers of questionable character" and "a host of bank stock holders and bank directors." The New School faced determined enemies: the publisher's son, William John Duane, who would later be the third of Andrew Jackson's five treasury secretaries, was no more fond of banks than was Jackson. In 1819, newly elected to the Pennsylvania Assembly, he too led a committee to investigate the state's economy. Duane's committee agreed with Raguet's finding that "distress is general," but assigned wider blame. Its conclusions: "That embarrassment is Universal; that the sordid and avaricious are acquiring the property of the liberal and industrious; that so much property is exposed to sale under execution that buyers cannot be had to pay more for it than the fees of office." On one hand, Duane called for a constitutional amendment to ban the Bank of the United States, and on the other, he blocked Findlay's attempt to expand state paper money loans to help debtors. Moreover, he encouraged the state to revoke the charters of the improvident banks it had lately chartered.[25]

There had been clear signs well before 1819 that Pennsylvania's economy was in trouble. The manufacturing city of Pittsburgh had been an early victim of the wave of imports from Britain. Philadelphia, too, now suffered from being more dependent on manufacturing than New York, and the city had fallen farther behind its northern competitor as an export depot for wheat and cotton. Flint had sensed the difference: "On approaching Philadelphia I felt disappointed in seeing shipping so very inferior to that of New York; and the houses fronting the river are old and irregularly placed, so that the idea of a port declining in trade immediately occurred." Output of the city's industries, including the new textile factories, declined 60 percent from early 1815 to 1817. By 1818, it seemed to Flint that "Philadelphia does not abound in manufacturing establishments. The predominance of British goods has shut up many workshops that were employed during the late war." He did note paper mills, foundries, and two lead-shot factories, and he was impressed by "a mill for cutting brads, which produces no less than two hundred in a minute." But Flint struck an ominous note:

> Philadelphia is in various respects well-adapted to manufacture; if the facilities which it presents for its advancement are neglected, the city must decline, as the trade of New York and Baltimore is making rapid progress. The new road from the latter city to the Ohio and the extensions of carriage, by steamboats through the Mississippi and the Ohio, are all circumstances which tend to supersede Philadelphia as a market and a thoroughfare.[26]

Flint had accurately identified Philadelphia's weakness, and in the following year, as the price of wheat fell from $2.50 to $1.00 per bushel, even Pennsylvania's own wheat crop was more likely to leave the state through Baltimore or New York. Girard wrote to a Paris merchant house, "Our maritime and inland commerce is in a deplorable situation. Nothing but losses, sacrifices, and failures surrounding us. These calamities may partly be attributed to the great facility which our Company Chartered Banks have offered to several of our merchants, traders, and mechanics who with their fictitious capital have acted imprudently." And to a New York merchant house he wrote that spring, "I am sorry to hear of the several failures which have taken place in your city. *This* place [Philadelphia] is in a like situation & I am afraid that many will continue that mode of ending up until they have paid the capital borrowed of our banks."[27]

Girard's prediction was correct. In 1819, 3,516 actions for debt were filed in Philadelphia, an increase of more than 150 percent from 1816; half of their targets wound up imprisoned. And the depression only deepened as 1819 gave way to 1820 and 1821. On October 20, 1821, Robert Waln wrote to tell his brother-in-law Gideon Wells, "This last shock has . . . nearly overcome me. . . . The last cup of bitterness was administered by hands which for many years had been sustained and supported and encouraged by me with more than Brotherly and paternal affection. The path before me is dreary." Waln was yet another merchant who could not collect what was owed by western debtors, with the result that his Philadelphia business failed.[28]

Still no one seemed to believe that the misfortunes of others could soon become their own. In 1821 Waln's neighbor Rebecca Gratz told her sister that his failure was the just deserts of extravagant living, but very soon her own family was struggling to hold on. By the time her brother's business failed and she was forced to give up her Chestnut Street mansion for a house half its size, experience had made her more philosophical; now she told her sister, "We must not expect to always have the things we wish for in the world, but . . . make the best of what we have." The economic collapse that had moved downriver from Pittsburgh to the West now rippled back to Philadelphia in many different ways. Steamboat companies went out of business in Natchez and Louisville: Joseph Hornor, a hardware merchant in Philadelphia, lost his investment in the *Maid of Orleans*. When Hornor's partners could not sell the boat to cover their debts, he demanded payment from his own debtors. He was shocked when they replied with excuses. But in 1821 *his* creditors foreclosed, and suddenly the shoe was on the other foot. He lost everything and complained, "I have struggled very hard to get along, and have sacrificed all my comforts in the trial. If I fall it will not be my fault."[29]

Carey, the former proponent of liberality in banking, received a letter from J. M. Connor, a fellow member of the Hibernian Society, asking for thirty-five dollars to pay his way out of debtors' prison. On June 21, 1819, Connor wrote, "God knows that to a sensitive and honorable man in a place like this, it is productive of the most agonizing mortification." There is no record of whether Carey sent the thirty-five dollars, but since he kept the letter it seems likely he did. There were more than 1,800 other inmates in Philadelphia's debtors' prison that year. The state abolished imprisonment of women for any debts incurred after February of that year, but all other categories of debtors remained vulnerable to the extreme; Niles reported that on March 15, 1820, a deputy constable brought the corpse of a debtor to the jail at the town of Westchester, having seized it on the way to the grave. The sheriff, understandably, refused to receive the prisoner. There were 286 debtors jailed in Alleghany County and another 221 in Lancaster County. Many more debtors escaped imprisonment but still lost everything; the Raguet Committee counted 14,537 actions for debt across the state in 1819—twice the entire population of Pittsburgh—and did not include those brought for small amounts before a justice of the peace.[30]

Homes, farms, and businesses were all liquidated to pay debts—but, as a result of the banking contraction and the consequent decrease in circulating currency, prices had deflated to the point that everything sold for a fraction of its earlier value. The *Aurora* of September 16, 1819, told of a landowner near Easton who was forced to mortgage a property for $2,500 that he had bought for $12,500—and then lost it at a sheriff's sale. The same issue reported that a druggist's stock was seized when he could not pay the rent for his pharmacy; his landlord sold for $400 what "in ordinary times" was worth $2,000 wholesale or $10,000 retail. It was true that in the area around York, farms that had sold in 1818 for $260 an acre were still selling for $200—"the fatal effect of the paper system having been almost entirely averted from the district, either by the prudence of the Bank Directors, or, what is more likely, the inveterate habits of the German farmers, which did not readily become reconciled to a flimsy substitute for gold." The English traveler Adam Hodgson made that observation and noted this contrast: "The farmers in the county of Lancaster, unlike those of York, are, I am told, deeply in debt; the treacherous paper system having been incautiously admitted." Farther west in the state, the *Register* reported a sheriff's sale of twelve farms, five mills, and several tracts of land, as well as "the sale of a farm in Pennsylvania, by the sheriff, for nine thousand dollars, at the instigation of a neighboring bank, which was worth at least *twenty-five thousand*." But Niles held the borrowers in part responsible for their own suffering: "These people are greatly to be pitied; but their imprudence is as reprehensible as the authors of their wrong are detestable."[31]

It was more difficult to hold the urban poor responsible for their lack of work. By the end of 1819 there were as many as 20,000 Philadelphians reported unemployed, out of a workforce of perhaps 64,000. Flint reported that an estimate of 15,000 out of work had been sent to President Monroe, and said there were twenty applicants in that city for every job that opened. He believed there were 350,000 out of work nationally but added, "It is not pretended that these enumerations are derived from accurate data, or that they are even very close approximations to the real numbers; but taken in connection with other well-known facts, they may be received as evidence that the evil exists to a very considerable extent."[32]

The city of Philadelphia, however, was determined to find out just what that extent was. One committee after another examined the evidence that it could gather. The Philadelphia Society for the Promotion of American

Manufactures set up a fact-finding committee that counted at least 12,000 unemployed in the city in September 1819, with the rest of the labor force working for wages that had been reduced by 80 percent. Another citizens' committee, once again headed by Condy Raguet, identified sixty different branches of manufacturing in Philadelphia and looked carefully into thirty of them, finding that employment in these occupations alone had declined from 9,672 in 1816 to 2,137 in 1819, and that total weekly wages had decreased from $58,000 to $12,000. *Hazard's Register of Pennsylvania* recorded employment in cotton spinning and weaving down from 2,325 to just 149. The number of people with no means of sustenance grew. The *Aurora* reported that the almshouse had held between 736 and 778 paupers each year from 1813 to 1818; in 1819 it held 934, a 20 percent increase. Carey declared, "Resources of both [citizens and government] exhausted; both marching to poverty . . . in the same road, on the same principles; their expense exceeds their receipts." The expenses of the city itself by October 1819 exceeded receipts to the point that the Corporation of Philadelphia was $1.2 million in debt.[33]

Like debt, poverty spread well beyond the big city. Rural Bucks County began the year 1820 with ninety-one adults and fifty-six children in its poorhouse, and fifty-nine others receiving "outdoor" relief from the county. Hodgson was struck by the number of unemployed laborers in the countryside seeking work in exchange for food: "Five out of ten may wander about for weeks or months, in the agricultural districts of Pennsylvania, without finding employment, or means of supporting themselves by their labour. . . . In the neighborhood of Philadelphia, I heard of *many* instances of less skillful labourers making similar applications in vain." Woodcutters' wages averaged thirty-three cents per cord over the first half of the century but fell to ten cents per cord in 1821 and 1822; unskilled turnpike laborers earned seventy-five cents a day in early 1818 but only twelve cents a day in 1819. Some may have been among the desperate people Niles described as "land privateers" (they called themselves "turnpikers") in Pennsylvania who stopped coaches—even U.S. Mail coaches—to demand a toll, threatening to shoot those who would not pay.[34]

Iron furnaces and forges in Pennsylvania and New Jersey that had operated since the eighteenth century were shutting down. Cumberland Furnace, opened in 1799, was mortgaged to a bank in 1821 and then foreclosed upon. Dale Furnace in Berks County had been built in 1791; tax records show a new owner in 1820, who abandoned the property in 1822. Joanna Furnace had been operating since 1791 but closed in 1821, and George Ege, who had built Reading Furnace in 1792, lost it to creditors in 1824. Hanover Furnace, in Burlington County, New Jersey, which opened in 1791, had reached its peak activity during the War of 1812, when it produced cannons and cannonballs; it closed in the early 1820s.[35]

Pittsburgh was much smaller than Philadelphia, but its economic suffering was proportionally greater. Early in 1817 Zadock Cramer's *Pittsburgh Almanack* had still boasted that local manufacturing "has almost rendered us independent of the eastern states," and Flint, passing through Pittsburgh on his way west, had been impressed that "a considerable degree of industry is manifested by the bustle that pervades this town." He listed four iron foundries, six glass factories, two woolen mills, two cotton-spinning factories, two steam-engine makers, a chemical factory, a nail factory, and numerous smithies, altogether employing over 1,500 people in a city of 7,000. He noted a 330-ton steamboat nearly completed but kept from launching by water levels "lower than they have been for many years past," levels that also kept merchants and migrants from getting downriver. Less than four months later the bustle was gone; in early February 1819 the Pittsburgh *Gazette* found that "the general pressure seems to encrease [*sic*], the gloom which overhangs us becomes darker and darker; the mechanical and manufacturing community is languishing into annihilation"; and a year later the *Gazette* reported that industrial employment, which had reached 1,960 in 1815, had fallen to 672. In the glass factories it had dropped from 169 to 40, in the steam engine works from 290 to 24, and overall industrial income had plummeted from $235,000 annually to $35,000. Carey found 1,238 unemployed in 1819, corroborating the *Gazette*'s figures—65 percent out of work. By his accounting, the "amount of work done" in the city declined from $2.6 million in 1816 to $830,000 in 1819; for the same period, he believed "work done" in Philadelphia had lost $7 million. Over just six weeks in the summer of 1819, 115 people went to jail for debt in Pittsburgh; two-thirds of them owed less than ten dollars, and one man—belying Flint's earlier assurance—was jailed when he could not pay a debt of eighteen and three-quarters cents.[36]

To those who accused him of exaggerating the suffering (and thus discouraging immigration) Matthew Carey replied, "I respectfully ask those fastidious gentlemen, whether 'numerous families being deprived of the common necessities of life'—the 'prisons overflowing with insolvent debtors'—and 'vast numbers of industrious farmers being driven from their homes and forced to seek in the uncultivated forests of the west, that shelter of which they have been deprived in their native state,' be not as complete proofs of misery as can be exhibited." Carey was quoting from the recent report of the Pennsylvania Senate.[37]

It seemed as though economic and natural forces were conspiring: in the summer of 1820 Philadelphia was hit by an outbreak of yellow fever, its worst since 1792. Quarantines were imposed, and New York City refused to admit anyone who had been in Philadelphia within thirty days. Among those excluded was Joseph Bonaparte, brother of Napoleon and not long since king of Naples and Sicily as well as Spain. Bonaparte was now an emigré living in New Jersey. On his way from Philadelphia to the fashionable resort town of Saratoga, he was forced to travel along the west bank of the Hudson; New York City had turned him back at the ferry dock. Joseph Stoney wrote from South Carolina to commiserate with his friend Girard. He had been reading the Baltimore and New York newspapers and was shocked by the lack of sympathy shown to Philadelphians at the time:

> I regret extremely to find that Baltimore and New York instead of taking the most deep and friendly interest in the health and prosperity of your city (if I may judge of the people by their organs the public papers) almost appear happy in having the opportunity to proclaim to the world, your misfortunes. Whether the prosperity, wealth, or enterprise of your city is the cause of the jealousy . . . their conduct in this particular respect must be viewed with horror and contempt.[38]

The reaction was not really surprising. There was little love lost between Philadelphia and New York since the latter had eclipsed the former as the nation's largest and wealthiest city. The two had competed to become the nation's capital until the creation of Washington, D.C., ended the dispute, and Philadelphians did not hide their belief that New Yorkers were crass and grasping. Philadelphia did not feel much brotherly love for its brash competitor to the south, either. At a time when other eastern cities were slowing their growth or stagnating, Baltimore had been an exception, building new textile mills and successfully taking over the export of Pennsylvania's wheat crop via the Susquehanna River. The Baltimore branch of the BUS had been the busiest of all the BUS branches, and the congressional committee's report had revealed that it had lost even more than Cincinnati in bad loans, making it the most profligate as well. But Maryland's new textile industry had suffered along with New England's, and in 1819 the price of cotton twist yarn in Baltimore fell by 25 percent from sixty cents per pound to forty-five cents;

it would take years to work its way back up as far as fifty cents. Losses among Baltimore's ambitious merchants were worse still.[39]

On May 24, 1819, John Quincy Adams's diary records "the news that the houses of Smith and Buchanan, Hollins and McBlair, Didier and D'Arcy, four Williamses, and many others, this day failed. Smith and Buchanan have been for many years the greatest commercial house in Baltimore, the others have all been in immense business, but bank speculation is what has broken them down. They will undoubtedly drown numberless others with them." All of the merchants had watched their profits disappear as wheat exports decreased and European imports in turn diminished. Now it was revealed that Buchanan, Williams, and M'Culloh had bet millions of the Bank's dollars that Bank stock would continue to appreciate; when the opposite happened, and contraction led to deflation, they were ruined, and the money they had borrowed was lost by the Bank. Adams was scandalized: "The moral, political, and commercial character of the city of Baltimore has for twenty-five years been formed, controlled, and modified almost entirely by this House of Smith and Buchanan, their connections and dependents. It may be added that there is not a city in the Union which has had so much apparent prosperity, or within which there has been such complication of profligacy."[40]

Adam Hodgson passed through Maryland on his way from Virginia to New York. He was shown the sights and was told the stories that were repeated in every American town or city: "A house and store in Baltimore were pointed out to me, in the principal commercial street, which about 1816 were let for 2000 dollars per annum, but are now let at only 600. This is an extreme case, but taking the city generally, it would probably be correct to estimate the decline in rents at from 40 to 50 per cent." This was a stranger's introduction to the city. For Hezekiah Niles, Baltimore was home. His lead story on October 30, 1819, began in all caps:

HARD TIMES!—Considering the general depression of business and the deranged state of the currency in many parts of the United States—the editor has not, for a long time, said much about *his own* affairs. . . . the [subscription] receipts at this office for September and October (our harvest months) have hardly amounted to one third of the sum paid to us in the same period of last year.

Three months earlier the *Register* had noted that one subscriber apologized for not paying his bill, explaining that factories he had built at a cost of $150,000 had just gone, at forced sale, for $20,000. Niles, surveying his home town, was badly discouraged by what he saw around him. He felt Baltimore's losses personally—these were his neighbors—but he also knew that what he saw was repeated all around the nation. In mid-1819 he poured out his emotional reaction:

> It is sickening to the heart to see the lists of persons who are published weekly in the Baltimore papers, as making applications for the benefit of the insolvent laws of Maryland. The amount of debts due by them is enormous. A similar work is going on in all the large cities and towns of the United States. They who were a little while since 'the tip of the top' and residing in palaces are thus engaged in settling their debts and dragging many sober and discreet mechanics and tradesmen along with them.

In October he reported that the Baltimore *Federal Gazette* contained "*six* solid, formidable columns of advertisements by order of the commissioner for conferring the 'insolvency laws' of Maryland—in all about sixty [individuals] several of whom are those who until recently counted their affairs by hundreds of thousands or by *millions* of dollars."[41]

As businessmen failed in Baltimore, their employees, too, were left to scramble. In August, when twenty thousand "able bodied men" were "daily seeking work" in the much larger city of Philadelphia, Niles reported that "in Baltimore there may be about 10,000 persons in unsteady employment or actually suffering because they cannot get into business. We know of several decent men, lately 'good livers,' who now subsist on such victuals as two years ago they would not have given to their servants." How those servants were now faring was left unsaid. As early as October 1817 the Baltimore *American* had declared, "Misery could not be exhibited in a more condense form than it is in the suburbs, lanes and alleys—the huts, hovels and dens of Baltimore." In 1819 both measles and yellow fever added to the misery; nearly five thousand, who could, simply left the city, but the poor, "condense" as they were, had nowhere else to go. An anonymous physician wrote to the mayor, calling his attention to the residents east of Hartford Run who were largely without jobs or incomes: "Commerce is the main spring of this City. . . . But this same business which diffuses life, vigor, and activity to this whole City, brings down upon this part of the City most of these poor. They have all been, more or less, directly engaged in commerce, and have felt its depressed spirit comparatively speaking, a thousand fold more than the merchants."[42]

The depression deepened through 1820 and 1821. In September 1820 Niles observed, "A mechanic is hardly half his time employed, or at reduced wages, and must therefore limit his expenditures"—slowing down the retail recovery. In 1822 the firm of Alexander Brown and Sons, the greatest surviving mercantile house, told *Degrand's Boston Weekly Reports*, "To give you a description of the public feeling in this place . . . wd. be impossible. The question is who is not failed." That year a writer for the *Federal Gazette* was appalled by the number of beggars in the street, and found "every feeling of my soul harrowed up by a sight most shocking to humanity, age in rags, in want, in pain, homeless, friendless, penniless. To have this is unacceptable in our State, and an infinite inconvenience to its citizens." His soul may have been harrowed, but his solution was to demand enforcement of anti-vagrancy laws. New York had formed its first Society for the Prevention of Pauperism in 1817, and Philadelphia's Provident Society for the Employment of the Poor would finally appear in 1824. The Baltimore Society for the Prevention of Pauperism was organized in 1820, as the depression there intensified. In recent years, Baltimore had typically spent little on its poor—1818 was the first year that its spending on relief exceeded the amount spent before the Revolution—but from 1817 through 1821 the almshouse annual budget rose from $14,000 to $20,000 and the average number of inmates doubled; about a fifth were children. In addition to the dozen soup kitchens that opened in 1819, there was a medical dispensary for "the deserving poor" on Chatham Street. It had seen only a few hundred patients in 1804 when it first opened, but it served six thousand in 1822.[43]

Many of Maryland's urban unemployed tried their luck in the countryside. At harvesttime in 1820, Niles wrote, "It appears to me probable that from 20,000 to 40,000 able laborers [nationally] are now thrown from the mechanical into the agricultural classes per annum, from the diminished demand for their several kinds of work." Those in Maryland fared no better than their counterparts in Pennsylvania did, and in at least one case, they went into partnership together. William Fry, an out-of-work laborer in western Maryland, was accused of stealing horses. He testified that "about the middle of March I left the neighborhood of Harper's Ferry, where I had spent the winter, and came to Frederick town to look for work." There he met Harry Carin, who claimed to be a farmer from Harrisburg, Pennsylvania. "He offered me good wages and steady employment if I would go home with him, and being out of employment and destitute for a house, I readily accepted." But Carin had actually been traveling through Virginia and Maryland stealing horses and persuaded Fry to join him. Both were convicted. The people in rural Maryland had little work to offer the impoverished townsmen who appeared among them; there was too little work even for the locals, who resorted to whatever expedients they could to support themselves. James Brightwood, of Frederick County, was arrested for selling unlicensed liquor at a shooting match he had organized in the winter of 1821/22. His friends petitioned the governor, pleading that he was simply trying to provide for his "wife and four small children . . . altogether dependent upon his labor, he has no property whatsoever." City-dwellers who were also foreigners had twice the difficulty. A Swiss immigrant, Jakob Rutlinger, had no luck seeking work in Baltimore in 1823 but was even more at a loss in the countryside. He felt like "someone who can't skate and is chased out onto the slippery ice."[44]

There is still a tendency to minimize the impact of early economic downturns in the nineteenth century, to believe that those who lost jobs could simply return to the farm until the economy improved. But reality was not that simple. Most had no farm to return to, and "hard times" pursued any urbanite who tried to live off the land. Flint met many of them headed west with no particular destination. In August 1820 he told his readers,

> In my letter of 26th June last, I mentioned that mechanics were leaving the towns of the western country, becoming cultivators in the backwoods. In many cases their former habits are such as are not well calculated to reconcile them with their new situations. It appears evident that such people, placed in the forests, cannot for some time produce sufficient to exchange for such foreign luxuries as they formerly consumed, and such articles of imported dress as they have been accustomed to wear. The former may easily be dispensed with, but for the latter a substitute must be provided.

Flint understood that "uncleared woods are not suitable pasture for sheep"— and few of the unemployed carried spinning wheels and looms.[45]

On down the coast, the southern states escaped the worst unemployment simply because their cities were fewer and smaller, and people were more likely to be farmers. But in places like Charleston and Richmond businesses were also failing and people out of work; during the depression years free blacks like David Walker left Charleston for Philadelphia or Boston partly because of the repression following the Denmark Vesey conspiracy in 1822, but also because there were fewer jobs for artisans like the shoemakers, tailors, carpenters, and plasterers who led the membership of the African Methodist Episcopal Church—and made up the majority of the free blacks brought to trial along with Vesey.[46]

In the rural areas farmers were caught between crops that did not pay and loans that could not be repaid. Virginia's most famous farmer, the proprietor of Monticello, wrote to John Adams in November 1819:

> The paper bubble is then burst. This is what you and I, and every reasoning man, seduced by no obliquity of mind, or interest, have long foreseen. Yet its disastrous effects are not the less for having been foreseen. We were laboring under a dropsical fullness of circulating medium. Nearly all of it is now called in by the banks who have the regulation of the safety valves of our fortunes and who condense or explode them at their will. Lands in this state cannot be sold for a year's rent: and unless our legislators have wisdom enough to effect a remedy, by a gradual diminution only of the medium, there will be a general revolution of property in this state. . . . I do not know particularly the extent of the distress in other states, but Southwardly and Westwardly I believe all are involved in it.[47]

The collapse of cotton prices had indeed staggered Georgia and South Carolina, still the leading producers. Hodgson traveled across Georgia in the spring of 1820. When he stopped at an inn in western Georgia, "The first question my landlady asked was the price of cotton in Augusta, a question which was eagerly repeated wherever I stopped." That price would remain unchanged all year: half of what it had been in 1818. Hodgson's voluble innkeeper told him that "there was an academy to which her daughter went when cotton was thirty cents a pound; that she paid three hundred dollars per annum simply for board, and fifty more for learning the *pi-a'-no!* but that, as cotton had fallen to fifteen cents, she could not afford to buy an instrument, and supposed her daughter must forget her music."[48]

The Southeast was already in decline before the Panic. Between 1815 and 1820 rice exports, important to South Carolina, had remained flat; farther north, tobacco exports were diminishing in price and in volume. Douglass North cautiously acknowledges, "It is likely that per capita income declined between 1819 and 1823" in the Old South, despite the greatly increased acreage planted in cotton. Cotton planting was generally moving west, and west Georgia cotton had begun to be shipped out of Mobile rather than Savannah or Charleston. A. G. Smith, in his *Economic Readjustment of an Old Cotton*

State, estimates that net emigration from South Carolina, which long remained depressed by low prices, was nearly seventy thousand in the decade following 1820: "Small farmers with higher costs were most affected and contributed largely to this migration, although some large planters migrated west with their slaves." The census of 1820 would reduce southern influence in Congress: although the size of the House of Representatives was enlarged by 15 percent after the census, from 185 to 212, South Carolina's representation remained static at nine and Virginia's actually slipped from twenty-three to twenty-two—the only state up to that point to suffer a *loss* in representatives. (Pennsylvania at the same time gained four seats, and New York added nine.) The national importance of South Carolina and Virginia was declining along with their share of the population.[49]

Virginia lost a million emigrants to the West between 1800 and 1850, more than any other state. Many of the most ambitious and articulate sons of the Old Dominion had left home to seek their fortunes farther west—men like Henry Clay, William Henry Harrison, Zachary Taylor, Sam Houston, Edward Coles in Illinois, and two of Alabama's leading citizens, LeRoy Pope and his son-in-law, John Williams Walker. Of the forty senators in the Fifteenth Congress, eleven were natives of Virginia, representing six slave states and three free states. Among the South Carolinians who also had left was the best known and most admired man in Tennessee—Andrew Jackson. In the post-1819 depression, those who stayed behind in South Carolina were finding the state's economic importance waning along with its political influence. Many of them could remember when Charleston had been the southern stronghold of Federalism, the biggest, busiest city south of Philadelphia, with dreams of rivaling Boston as a great seaport. But the city had stagnated instead; exports of cotton moved to Mobile and New Orleans as the Southwest's first crops began to come in. Imports, even those intended for southern plantations, were now arriving in New York, not Charleston, and it made no economic sense for transatlantic shipping to come nearly empty to Charleston in order to pick up its cotton. From 1810 to 1820, Charleston managed a net growth of sixty-nine residents. It seemed that the proud southern city might soon be little more than a stop for the coasting trade.[50]

South Carolina was the home of Langdon Cheves, and an important bloc of other BUS directors and shareholders had plantations there. John Stoney, who acted as Stephen Girard's agent, was one of them. In 1819 he wrote to the Philadelphian with discouraging news. "The monied planters, alarmed at the great depression in January, turned their attention to the purchase of land and negroes and I am aware have invested all their disposable funds, for at least twelve months in that way, so that the only purchasers of stock are guardians of estates, Public Institutions, and Capitalists investing their dividends." The BUS stock that Girard hoped to sell in Charleston could not possibly bring the $115 a share that he sought—and "great anxiety to sell" was being shown by New York and Baltimore agents as well.[51]

Charleston businessmen faced the same difficulties their northern counterparts faced: imports and exports were falling off, and money that had been easy to borrow when times were good was hard to repay now that times were bad. But the stigma of personal failure was, if anything, even more intense in the South, and some bankrupts went to great lengths to hide their collapse. John White was a Charleston merchant who lost not only his own money but his brother's savings as well. When the brother died in the yellow fever epidemic, White moved north and concocted a fantasy in which he had been successful in South Carolina, but his brother had become ill, moved to France, and entered a monastery. When the elaborate hoax fell apart, White confessed that his income had been "inadequate to my wishes; unfortunately for me, I began to speculate. . . . God Knows I strove for success, but I could not command it."[52]

North Carolina, that "valley of humility between two mountains of conceit," had never had the economic or political clout of South Carolina or Virginia, but it could not escape the Panic of 1819. Archibald Murphey criticized North Carolinians who abandoned their state for the lure of Alabama. While serving in the North Carolina state senate (1812–18), he had supported unsuccessful attempts to repeal the statute of imprisonment for debt; he did not dream that in the following decade he would find himself a victim of that severe law. Murphey was an early advocate of internal improvements and encouraged those who had capital to invest in the future of North Carolina instead of buying land elsewhere. He boasted of having bought land for $5,000 in 1815 that he sold for $22,100 two years later. He had himself invested in several canal projects and had purchased a resort hotel complete with mineral springs, all in his home state. But he had borrowed to make those investments, and by 1819 his debt was approaching $100,000. In the hard times that followed, his tobacco lands lost their value, canal construction stopped, and too few people could afford resort vacations. Murphey was a man of integrity, and he had assumed the debts of several relatives in order to save them from debtors' prison. He put his property—six thousand acres of plantation land, nine town lots, his hotel, and forty-three slaves—in a trust, to be sold as his debts came due. He resigned from the North Carolina Superior Court, and it is a testimony to him that his friend and former law clerk, Thomas Ruffin, also left the court and returned to private practice in order to pay a debt contracted by Murphey. The North Carolina economy remained flat through the coming decade; after years of struggling to pay his creditors, Murphey was finally arrested in 1829, seized in the midst of arguing a case in court. He spent twenty days in jail for debts he had managed to reduce to $2,128. He wrote to Ruffin, "To be harassed by my creditors is worse than Death to me. . . . I must get out of the way of these men if I can. . . . Now the cup of my Humiliation is full to the Brim. After a life of incessant Toil, and as I hoped, of honorable exertion, to be degraded in the World and pointed at even by the Common Vulgar, is a condition to say the least of it, not to be envied."[53]

Virginia was the premier southern state; it still stretched from the Atlantic Ocean to the Ohio River, and until the 1820 census it remained the most populous of all the states. All but one of the nation's presidents had been born there, and the exception, John Adams of Massachusetts, was a rarely mentioned Federalist anomaly in a country now overwhelmingly Republican, the only president who had failed at reelection. In 1819 the Virginian James Monroe's own reelection was a foregone conclusion (he would receive all but one of the electoral votes in 1820), and the two leading contenders already looking to succeed him were both Virginian by birth. But Crawford had left Virginia for Georgia and Clay for Kentucky—uncomfortable reminders that Virginia's sons and Virginia's influence were both departing.

Although her glories were now spoken of in the past tense, Virginia was ironically the most modern of the southern states. The great landowners had realized in Washington's time that tobacco's potential had already been reached, and (to use their own terminology) many had since switched from "planting" to "farming," so that Virginia vied with Pennsylvania to be the leading producer of wheat. Virginia's commercial and industrial ambitions gave the state more in common with Maryland to its north than with North Carolina to its south. It was still predominantly farming country, but Thomas Jefferson, who had famously called farmers "the chosen people of God, if ever he had a chosen people," was operating a slave-run nail factory and leasing out an automated flour mill he had built, hoping the profits might offset his losses in both tobacco and wheat as prices kept falling.[54]

The Old Dominion had no city on a par with Charleston, but it had four of the twenty-five largest cities in the 1810 census—only Massachusetts could claim more—and its urban population was proportionately greater than that of any other southern state. Alexandria had sprung up in the middle of the last century, directly across the Potomac from the future site of the District of Columbia. Created as a tobacco depot, the city had made a smooth transition to wheat export. It was a thoroughly commercial town, home to a number of banks whose currency had begun to depreciate, although none of them had yet failed. Now the effects of the Panic were being felt there. In 1820 a wharf and warehouse, recently built at a cost of $17,000, sold at auction for $1,250. Norfolk, situated on an unparalleled natural harbor, was another mercantile city that still imagined itself a competitor of Baltimore. But Norfolk's growth had stopped during the war, and the 1820 census would find it even smaller than it had been ten years earlier—an unhappy distinction that Charleston escaped by the slimmest of margins. In 1819, Crawford worried when Norfolk became the first seaport to collect decreased import duties.[55]

Virginia had two inland cities that were more vibrant places: Petersburg at the falls of the Appomattox and Richmond at the falls of the James. Like other settlements at the fall line, they had from the beginning been both mill towns and transportation hubs. Both cities resembled Pittsburgh or Albany more than Savannah or Charleston, with flour mills and sawmills, small factories, and even Richmond's Tredegar Iron Works, unique in being operated with slave labor. Only twenty miles away, Petersburg was then and remains today in the shadow of Richmond, but in the first decade of the century it had grown by 60 percent, and at the time of the embargo it had boasted 307 merchants licensed to sell imports from abroad. By 1817 that number had grown to 485, but many would close in the 1820s. There had been plans to set up the state's first cotton mill in Petersburg, but they were put on hold when the depression brought activity to a halt. Hundreds of clerks and mechanics there lost their jobs in the wake of the Panic.[56]

The real value of Virginia's commodity exports dropped 36.8 percent between 1818 and 1821, thanks to the reimposition of England's Corn Law and the depressed economies of both Europe and America. When agricultural exports declined, so did the value of land and slaves. Two of the largest mills in Richmond saw their realty assessments fall from $80,000 in 1818 to $40,000 in 1819, and then to $20,000 in 1820. Clyde Haulman, in his *Virginia in the Panic of 1819*, compares the losses incurred then by Richmond merchants to their losses during the Revolution, those by retail stores to losses during the Great Depression, and those by small businesses to losses during the recession of the early 1980s. (He wrote just before the recession of 2008.) The business downturn in Europe was bad—in 1819 bankruptcies increased 33 percent in Paris and 56 percent in London—but Virginia's was proportionately worse: Richmond bankruptcies increased that year by nearly 70 percent. In the *Enquirer*, Ritchie surveyed the Commonwealth at year's end: "The iron business languishes, the wagon shops are shut up; taxes cannot be paid in the required money; the flinty creditor asks Virginia paper or gold or silver for his debt; the debtor, unable to raise either, gives up his land, and ruined and undone, seeks a home for himself and his family in the Western wilderness."[57]

Ritchie had warned against the bank expansion. In 1818 the *Enquirer* had printed Aesop's fable of the fox and the goat, in which a fox jumps into a well for a drink, finds he cannot get out, and calls to a goat to climb in and help him. The fox jumps onto the back of the goat and out of the well, but when the goat asks how *he* will get out, the fox replies, "If you had only as much brain as beard, you would never have jumped into a well without thinking how you were to get out." The paper announced the moral of the fable: "Never do you go into a Bank without seriously thinking how you are to get out of it." By the following spring Ritchie's fears seemed well-founded:

> We understand that the office of the bank of the United States, in this city, not only refuses to receive the notes of other branches of that bank (as has been long known to the public) but also refuses the notes of the branches of the Virginia state banks in every case and even in certain cases of the mother bank in order to prevent its notes from being drawn out for the purpose of remitting to the northern towns, where they are worth rather more than the notes of the state banks, in consequence of being taken in payment of custom house bonds.

Two weeks later Ritchie generalized, "Never did a thicker gloom hang over the monied transactions of this land. The state of the markets, of trade, of the interests of manufacturers, of the precious metals; there is scarce an individual in this country who does not feel some interest in these questions."[58]

Two years later there was no sign of recovery in Virginia. Hodgson, on his way north, wrote, "The depreciation of real estate throughout the Union is perfectly astonishing, and sales are occasionally forced at sacrifices almost incredible. . . . In Richmond, where the disastrous results of Bank mania have been pre-eminently conspicuous . . . real estate has fallen from 50 to 75 per cent." It was comparable to the calamity that had befallen Cincinnati: "It is estimated that more than half of the city and its immediate vicinity is mortgaged to the banks." Writing from Norfolk, Hodgson was put in mind of Maryland's port city: "In Baltimore, about one-third is similarly situated, and property is only prevented from exhibiting a depreciation nearly equal to that of Richmond by the policy adopted by the banks of holding it in expectation that its gradual advance will pay them a better interest for their money than could be obtained from investments or discounts, if they were forced to sell."[59]

The more solvent banks might have had the luxury of waiting until prices rose; farmers did not. Very few farmers would have received as much consideration as the master of Monticello, but Jefferson's nightmare experience with banks could stand for that of many farmers, in Virginia and across the country. It is therefore worth recounting at some length.

Jefferson had begun borrowing from the BUS as soon as it opened an office in Richmond. Already chronically in debt to creditors ranging from the house of Van Staphorst in Amsterdam to local merchants in Charlottesville, in June 1817 he borrowed $3,000 from the BUS, adding another $3,000 the following spring. These loans were arranged by the branch president, former governor Wilson Cary Nicholas, whose daughter had married Jefferson's grandson Thomas Jefferson Randolph. At the end of April 1818 Nicholas—speculating in western lands—asked Jefferson in return to cosign two of his own notes, totaling $20,000. Later that year, when Jefferson asked the Richmond branch to renew his loans, he discovered that the Bank had begun contracting credit; all renewed notes would be curtailed by 12.5 percent, and he would have to pay that difference first. He told his agent, Patrick Gibson, "That notification is really like a clap of thunder to me." Jefferson must have been further worried when, in September, Nicholas asked him to renew his endorsement of the two notes, but he did so without comment. In February 1819 Gibson delivered the bad news that the price of wheat was still falling and the Bank was further curtailing his loans. Jefferson tried to sell land to pay the Bank but was shaken to discover how low the price of land had now sunk and how little demand there was at any price. He could find no buyer.[60]

Three weeks later, he received a letter from Nicholas:

> Mr. Gibson has stated to me your wish to obtain a loan favor [sic] the Bank of the U.S. (at this place) of an additional sum. From particular circumstances there is a great unwillingness at this moment to make loans for a longer period than sixty days. I have therefore advised him to let the application be made at

the Farmers Bank, where my brother [Philip Nicholas, the Farmers Bank president] thinks it would be obtained without any difficulty.[61]

As the nation's economy spiraled out of control that spring, so did Jefferson's debts. After he wrote to Nicholas, thanking him for his help with "my little money embarrassments," Nicholas had to reply that, "on account of the uncertainty of what could be gotten from the bonds," he had also directed Gibson to the New Jersey Bank "so as to take the chance at both." He added, "Your note was done there for over half the sum, on that day it wou'd not have been done for any other man for any part."[62]

Jefferson gratefully accepted the loan on those terms, and Nicholas picked that opportune moment to ask for yet another renewal of Jefferson's endorsement on his $20,000, "by the first mail. I ought to have [requested] it by the last mail but it escaped me." Even as he did so, he posed the question that was on everyone's mind: "What can be done to alleviate the suffering of the country at the present moment? So the question is asked by every man I see, but no man answers it. Will the people have such dreadful sacrifices as they are threatened with?"[63]

In the cases of both Jefferson and Nicholas, the answer was inevitably yes—they could not escape. Perhaps Jefferson was uneasy when he read Nicholas's letter (he should have been), but he nevertheless endorsed the notes once again. He now had at least five loans of his own from three or four different banks and little prospect of repaying them. All too soon Nicholas wrote to warn him that his loan from the BUS would be due in less than a month: "I fear the money will be expected to be paid. I hope you will pardon the liberty I take in reminding you of this circumstance." Like Nicholas, Jefferson seemed to deflect his own troubles by remarking on the universality of hard times.

The sudden suspension of all demand for either produce or property, by withdrawing from the market those who have capital as well as those who have none, produces a distress in the country of which I have never seen the equal. The solidest man can neither collect nor pay a dollar, & the collection of taxes seems impossible. Unless the legislature devises means to give time to let the country down gently from the precipice to which their unwise policy has advanced it, there will be a great revolution in private fortunes even the most solid: for small debts will sweep away large masses of property.[64]

Jefferson's fortune was certainly not the most solid and his debts were not so small; he surely feared that the "revolution of property" of which he often spoke would include his own. It must have been with a sinking feeling that he read Nicholas's request the next day that he yet again endorse the notes. This time, in a fervent tone that ought to have triggered some concern, Nicholas gave Jefferson "the strongest assurances, that whether I live or die, neither you nor yours, shall ever receive the slightest inconvenience from your goodness to me." Perhaps he meant it when he wrote it, but a month later Nicholas's financial juggling all collapsed, bringing down Jefferson's fortunes with it. On August 5, 1819, Jefferson read these words: "It is with the greatest pain & mortification I communicate to you that I was obliged to suffer a protest the day before yesterday. . . . I will tomorrow convey my property to trustees to oversee the payment of my debts and particularly my endorsers. If I could have possibly foreseen such a state of things, nothing cou'd have induced me to embarrass you."[65]

Jefferson truly was thunderstruck; it took him several days to pull himself together enough to reply tersely, "A call on me to the amount of my endorsements for you would indeed close my course by a catastrophe that I had never contemplated." It now fell to the miserable Nicholas, president still of the BUS branch, to tell Jefferson that the notes would indeed be called in unless he could find some third party to add his endorsement; Jefferson replied that he would put his Poplar Forest plantation in trust to his grandson, Nicholas's son-in-law, who agreed to endorse the bonds.[66]

Wilson Cary Nicholas was the brother-in-law of Samuel Smith, the senior partner of Smith and Buchanan who had been ruined by Buchanan's speculation in BUS stock a few months earlier. Now he was brought down by his own speculation in western land—a sure thing that had turned into an unsalable commodity. Despite liquidating all his Virginia property (for which, as Jefferson had already discovered, there was so little demand) Nicholas could not pay his debts; a broken man, he died within the year at the home of his daughter Jane Hollins Randolph and her husband, Thomas Jefferson Randolph. "Jeff" Randolph had for some time been trying to sort out his own father's mismanaged finances; now the young man (he was not yet twenty-seven) took on his father-in-law's as well, and in 1821 he would accept control of those of his grateful grandfather. He managed to hold onto Monticello while his grandfather still lived, paying the BUS $1,200 in interest annually, but in 1828, to pay off the last of Thomas Jefferson's debts, he would have to sell it—although he, his wife, his father-in-law, and his grandfather are all buried there.[67]

Thomas Jefferson may have died the best-known victim of the Panic of 1819, but he was by no means the last one; painfully slow recovery began in Virginia in late 1821, but depression dragged on through the next several years in the western part of the state, which was closely tied to the Ohio River valley's sluggish economy. Another planter, James Madison, was also trying to cope with the fallout of the Panic and its lingering depression in Virginia. Madison was a more practical farmer and was far more frugal than Jefferson, but he was burdened by a wastrel stepson. Payne Todd was only two years old when his widowed mother became Dolley Madison, but between 1813 and 1836 his stepfather would spend about $40,000 for Todd's gambling debts and other extravagant expenses, which Madison tried to hide from the young man's mother. That was an enormous sum under any circumstances, but disastrous for a farmer during Virginia's continuing agricultural depression. In April 1825, while Randolph was still paying interest on Jefferson's BUS loans, Madison wrote to the Bank's current executive officer, Nicholas Biddle. Explaining that he had endured an unprecedented nine crop failures over ten years, combined with low prices and a stagnant overseas market, the former president applied for a loan of $6,000.[68]

In a response that can only be described as mealymouthed, Biddle wrote back, "The early misfortunes of the Bank of the U. States . . . have thrown upon it a great mass of real property. . . . Under these circumstances, it has become for many years past, an established part of the policy of the Bank to avoid all loans for indeterminate or long periods and all loans on the security of real estate." The Bank, which by then was well on its way to amassing $6 million in specie reserves through its severe, continuing contraction, rejected Madison's application, "constrained by a sense of duty to the interests confided to them" by the stockholders—who throughout the depression years never received less than 2.5 percent in semiannual dividends.[69]

Madison stiffly pointed out that his application had *not* been for a loan of "a very long or indefinite period, or on landed security merely. It did not Preclude a limitation to a year or two, nor the usual personal security along with the real." Nonetheless, he would not pursue the application further. When in 1833 Biddle faced a test of strength with Andrew Jackson and learned that the president of the United States had more power than the president of the Bank, the elderly Madison was no longer making public statements. He would probably have been too discreet, in any case; he always was. But in the hard times following the Panic, even where the two most famous men in America were concerned, the Bank had left no doubt that *it* was making the decisions.[70]

CHAPTER EIGHT

HARD TIMES IN THE WEST
"Reflections Which Almost Unmans Me"

Depression moved west the same way the settlers had, over the Appalachians and down the Ohio River into Kentucky, through the wheat-growing country of Ohio and Indiana and the boomtowns of Cincinnati, Louisville, Lexington, and St. Louis, and into the unbelievably fertile land of Alabama and Mississippi. The woolen mills and hemp factories felt it first, undercut in 1815 and 1816 by cheap imports just as industries had been in Pittsburgh or Rhode Island. Then wheat farmers were hit by the falling prices when the Corn Law closed the British market in 1817. After wheat became unprofitable, land sales slowed—and when the Land Office restricted the money it would accept, sales nearly stopped in the Northwest. The BUS contraction seemed like the death knell of Cincinnati, although thanks to the Ohio River traffic, Cincinnati and Louisville would recover in a few years. Lexington's "infant industries" would not—they were effectively strangled in the cradle. As Thomas Hart Benton declared, "All of the flourishing cities of the West are mortgaged to the money power. They may be devoured by it at any minute. They are in the jaws of the Monster. A lump of butter in the mouth of a dog—one gulp, one swallow, and all is gone."[1]

The collapse of cotton prices, combined with the disappearance of trustworthy currency, brought the Panic into the Southwest, but planters continued buying land when they could, desperately hoping to make up in volume for prices that refused to rebound—thanks to the surplus that they now produced. When prices continued to fall, planters in Alabama and Mississippi could not make enough on cotton to pay the loans they had taken out to buy land and slaves. The Bank's contraction and the restrictions on land office money further reduced public land sales; speculators who had bought land at peak prices couldn't sell it, and recent purchasers asked Congress to let them forfeit undeveloped land in return for the cancellation of remaining payments. Through 1818 and 1819, westward migrants continued to arrive in Missouri, but the hard times followed them; in 1820 the tide slowed and the new state's inflated economy, built on the expectation of continuing immigration, quickly deflated; by the end of 1821 only a single chartered bank remained open in the three states of Indiana, Illinois, and Missouri. In Tennessee, Kentucky, and Missouri, state politics became focused on the question of debtor relief, and what began as local realignments would turn into a national political upheaval that ushered in the era of Jacksonian Democracy.

In the more populous East, the Panic of 1819 revealed itself in the numbers of failing businesses and unemployed workers; in the West, the two most telling statistics are these: by the summer of 1819, "$800,000 in specie [had] been drawn from Ohio . . . for the Bank of the United States," with nearly as much drained from Kentucky, and by the summer of 1820, there was a total of $21,173,489.87—one and one-half times the entire federal budget—owed to the United States Treasury for land west of the Allegheny Mountains, unlikely to be paid.[2]

At the same time that wagons loaded with silver were making their way east from Chillicothe to Philadelphia, James Flint was traveling through Kentucky from Lexington to Cincinnati. In December 1818 he told his readers, "Tavern keepers, grocers, and others receive the money of the banks nearest them, although they know the banks will not pay specie for them. They see that without the rags now in circulation they would have very little money. Everyone is afraid of bursting the bubble." He found western banknotes depreciated as much as 30 percent below their face value. When the depression arrived in the Northwest, Flint suspended his letters; number 14 is dated March 10, 1819, and number 15 resumed almost a year later, on February 27, 1820—when he remarked, as he passed through the town of Mount Vernon, Ohio, that it was "the place of the Owl Creek Bank, well known among the paper manufacturers of this country." While Flint's correspondence was suspended, Hezekiah Niles was reminding *his* readers that he had recently posed a question about those western banknotes: "From an Indiana paper we learn that some person named *Bigelow*, who has a bank in Jeffersonville, pays his notes with those of some other man named *Piatt*. What does Piatt do with his notes?" Now the *Register* printed a response from the St. Louis *Enquirer*, edited by Thomas Hart Benton (soon to be Missouri's first U.S. senator): "We answer Mr. Niles' question by informing him that Mr. Piatt redeems his notes with notes of the Vincennes steam mill (sawing mill)—and if Mr. Niles wants to know [with] what lumber the mill redeems its notes, we answer Piatt's.—This is not intended as a joke, but is the literal statement of two travelers from the Atlantic states, by way of Cincinnati and Vincennes."[3]

This was just the sort of story Niles loved, illustrating both the venality of bankers and the unsophisticated character of the West. But the Steam Mill Company, in Vincennes, was in fact a "bank of issue," just as the Chemical Manufacturing Company (later Chemical Bank of New York and now JP-Morgan Chase) was, back in cosmopolitan New York; and Beach and Bigelow's Exchange Bank of Indiana, the private bank in Jeffersonville of "some person named Bigelow," was more dependable than most of the chartered banks, faithfully redeeming all of its notes even after it closed. Niles was revealing his own provincialism when he scoffed at "some other man named Piatt"; John Piatt, sometimes called "the Girard of the West," was the richest man in Cincinnati—if not the entire Northwest—and his bank was the oldest in Ohio. That was not enough to save him from the Panic, and after the BUS contraction his bank indeed struggled to redeem its notes with those of any other bank it could get, until it failed in late 1819 or early 1820. Piatt went to debtors' prison, where he died in 1822.[4]

Ohio had been the first western state laid out for sale under the Ordinance of 1787, and by the 1820 census its population was nearly 600,000, greater than Massachusetts. Only 35,000 people lived in towns over a hundred; nearly a third of them lived in Cincinnati, which was the fastest growing city in the country—until the Panic. The nine-story steam mill there turned out seven hundred barrels of flour per week. It had cost $120,000 to build and was the tallest building west of the mountains. "Cincinnati," Flint wrote in 1818, "is no sooner seen than the importance of the town is perceived. A large grist mill, three large steam boats on the stocks and two more on the Kentucky side of the river, and a large ferry boat, wrought by horses, were the first objects which attracted my attention." He continued, "On the shore, the utmost bustle prevails. . . . Merchants' shops are numerous and well-frequented. The noise of carriage wheels in the street, and of the carpenter, the blacksmith, and the cooper make a busy din. Such an active scene I never expected to see in the back woods of America."[5]

Cincinnatians did not think of themselves as living in the backwoods. The Bell, Brass, and Iron Foundry (opened in 1816) employed 120 men; William Henry Harrison was a trustee of the Cincinnati Manufacturing Company, which owned the mill. Steubenville, population two thousand, did not think it was the backwoods, either. The commercial center of a wool-producing region, it boasted woolen, cotton, and paper mills, twenty-seven shops, sixteen taverns, and—of course—two banks. In 1816 the Miami Manufacturing Company had opened a large cotton factory at the town of Freeport, on the Little Miami River. Chillicothe (the state's first capital) was, like Cincinnati, home to a branch of the BUS. It also had a courthouse, an academy, two churches, two newspapers, several steam-powered mills, a brewery, a tannery, numerous merchants—and three more banks. Already, in November 1818, Flint noticed that one had shut its doors.[6]

That fall, the economic life of the state began slowly grinding to a halt. Although Flint was impressed by its bustle, Cincinnati had seen its imports decline from over $1.6 million in 1817 to barely $500,000 in 1819. The first instinct of the populace was denial. The Cincinnati *Inquisitor*, on January 12, 1819, reprinted an editorial from the New York *Gazette*: "Trade will regulate itself. Banks will soon become more useful, and merchants more wise. . . . There is no real distress in the country and we hope to hear no more about it." As summer came on, despite the mounting evidence of depression, the Cincinnati *Liberty Hall* still insisted, "As yet we have felt little of it here. Our city is improving almost beyond example—we have had no bankruptcies—no imprisonment for debt; but we need not expect to escape the general shock." But the same paper, a month earlier, had reported rising unemployment.[7]

The Cincinnati banks had refused the BUS demand for specie payment, and the Bank was now calling in its loans and draining silver from the state. This monetary assault could not have come at a worse time. Wheat and wool were the state's main exports (primarily down the Ohio and Mississippi to New Orleans). Now wheat that had commanded $1.00 or $1.50 per bushel in 1815 was down to seventy-five cents, on its way to a low of twenty cents. Flour that had sold for anywhere from $6.50 to $12.00 per barrel dropped to $2.50 or $3.00. In 1820 Adam Hodgson was in Virginia, where wheat prices had also collapsed. "I have been assured," he wrote, "on the authority of several persons who have passed through Kentucky and Ohio this autumn, that in many cases the farmers would not cut their wheat, but turned their cattle into it." By then, land prices around Marietta had depreciated 90 percent; farmhands could be hired for next to nothing, but farmers weren't hiring. Prices were so low that they would not cover freight costs, and land speculators were being jailed for inability to pay judgments against them. The price of wool fell to the point that, like wheat, it was not worth processing; farmers slaughtered and ate their sheep instead of shearing them. Although prices would at last begin to rise in 1821, wool was not shipped in quantity from Steubenville to eastern mills again until 1825.[8]

When Flint returned to Cincinnati in 1819 he found a changed city. "The town does not now present anything like the stir that animated it about a year and a half ago. Building is in a great measure suspended, and the city which was lately overcrowded with people, has now a considerable number of empty houses. . . . Many merchants and labourers find it impossible to procure employment." The 1819 *Cincinnati Directory* gave the population as 10,283; it had doubled in the past five years, but the U.S. census the next year found it shrinking at 9,642. In 1820 the foundry closed, leaving over a hundred men out of work, and in October the Rochester *Telegraph* printed a letter from Cincinnati asserting that there was "distress as beyond conception. Marshall and sheriff sales are almost daily." Flint commented that unemployment was so high that many town-dwellers had moved out to the woods; the following year in Indiana he reported that he had encountered 1,500 men looking for work since hard times had begun. The BUS, already hated for its attack on the city's banks, had begun foreclosing as businesses failed. According to documents of the U.S. Senate, the Bank of the United States wound up the owner of half of the city's real estate: coffeehouses, warehouses, stores, stables, ironworks, residences, and vacant lots, as well as some fifty thousand acres of farmland in Ohio and Kentucky. By 1823 defaulted real estate loans in Cincinnati exceeded $2.5 million. (In 1825 the BUS opened a second branch in Cincinnati to handle the actual banking; the first branch office was turned into a real estate liquidation agency.)[9]

Although the Cincinnati banks had refused specie to the BUS, they kept providing it to local customers while they could. Ohio required its banks to do so. Nevertheless, of the twenty-five or more banks operating in the state in the autumn of 1819, only six or seven still redeemed in silver. The legislature had also outlawed banknotes of less than one dollar and had made it a misdemeanor to accept a note at less than face value (an unenforceable law that was repealed in the next session). The difficulties caused by depreciated notes are illustrated in the account book of the Miami Manufacturing Co. Their cotton mill on the Little Miami burned in September 1819; although the timing seemed suspicious, there was no formal arson investigation. After the fire, the owners made an effort to collect the many accounts due—a prolonged, frustrating effort, as it turned out. The company accepted banknotes issued by the Miami Exporting Company, one of Cincinnati's four major banks, at fifty cents on the dollar. Notes issued by Piatt's Bank (about to go under) and the Lebanon Miami Bank were taken at between fifty and sixty-three cents on the dollar. Some accounts were settled in produce, including sides of bacon that were sold at Cincinnati. Throughout the Northwest, barter was returning as banknotes lost their value. While some items—coffee, tea, leather, iron, and gunpowder—were only available for money, for other purchases the acceptable alternatives included fur, deerskins, linen, and even feathers. Harvest workers, shoemakers, tailors, and most back-country laborers were now paid in grain.[10]

Anger at the banks was not limited to the BUS. Gorham Worth, the former BUS cashier at Cincinnati and bitter critic of Cheves, wrote to his friend Thomas Sloo, "Damn the Banks, and the Witch that begot them! . . . All things are changed, the rich have become poor, the poor distrust, one universal state of embarrassment exists; 'tis want, and fear, and prosecution and suspense and terror and dismay and bankruptcy and pauperism on all sides and on all hands." Piatt's Bank "bursted all to flinders" at the end of 1819; in October 1820, Flint noted from Cincinnati that "two of the banks have given up business altogether, and two others are struggling for existence. Their money is 33½ and 60 per cent. under par." Corroborating Benton's letter to Niles, he added, "One of these establishments has been in the habit of giving in exchange for its own notes, those of another paper shop at a considerable distance; when the paper, so obtained, is presented at the second, it is taken in exchange for the money of a third bank still farther off. At the third the bills are exchanged for those of the first. This is in reality making banks equally solvent with their neighboring institutions."[11]

William Greene, secretary to Ohio governor Ethan Allen Brown, told the governor in 1820,

One thing seems to be universally conceded, that the greater part of our mercantile citizens are in a state of bankruptcy—that those who have the largest possession of real and personal property . . . find it almost impossible to raise sufficient funds to supply themselves with the necessaries of life—that the citizens of every class are uniformly delinquent in discharging even the most trifling of debts.[12]

Indiana had less than one-quarter of Ohio's population, and Illinois perhaps a third of that; they had no urban centers like Cincinnati, but their residents were also prostrated by the Panic's effects. Hodgson reported that in Illinois, where wheat and corn were the only cash crops, "At present I am told that the expense to convey flour from Illinois, and selling it in New Orleans, would leave little or nothing for the grower of the wheat." Indiana began the year 1819—its third year as a state—with $4,451.18 in the state treasury; it collected revenue through "sundry sheriffs" of $7,399.51, and spent $11,792.90½, including $346.00 for "wolf scalps." The year-end balance was $57.78½. Two years further into the depression the state opened the year with a deficit and only avoided ending even deeper in debt by depositing $10,000 in state treasury warrants—credit extended to the state by the state. Across the Ohio River, Kentucky ended 1819 claiming a balance of $54,000, but with $47,000 in uncollected revenue and unpaid government debts of $62,000, the surplus was an illusion.[13]

Thomas Douglas had arrived in southern Indiana from Connecticut a year before statehood. He would later become the chief justice of the Florida Supreme Court, but in 1817 he was a young merchant in Jefferson County, fully as optimistic as the rest of his new state:

> Soon after my arrival in Madison, in addition to my Store I established a tin and button manufactory, and entered pretty largely, for a man of my means, into land speculation. Lands were then sold at $2.00 per acre, one fourth to be paid down, and the residue in three annual payments. Most emigrants entered to the extent of their means, relying on sales for means of future payments, in the expectation of receiving a profit on such sales, but the consequence was, that there were more sellers than buyers, and a debt accumulated to the Treasury of the United States which became extremely embarrassing and alarming.[14]

There might have been more buyers had it not been for two things that discouraged them. First, of course, was the steady decline in the price of wheat. Second was the difficulty in obtaining land office money. Legally, it was up to the Treasury secretary to decide which banks' notes would be accepted in payments to the Land Office. Between 1814 and 1817, when no banks outside New England were redeeming in specie, the decision had been left to the local offices, who best knew the condition of their neighboring banks; the banks the secretary designated as federal depositories accepted any currency that the offices approved. After 1817, when specie redemption was ostensibly practiced almost everywhere, the BUS branches became the depositories except in areas like Illinois or Tennessee where there were no branches. Secretary Crawford rewarded his allies or shored up local support—with an eye to the 1824 election—by designating favored banks, even removing deposits from the BUS branch in Savannah to the Bank of Darien. In Illinois, the bank of Crawford's ally Jesse Thomas was given the authority to choose the notes it would accept as the westernmost depository bank; Thomas naturally rejected those of his only competitor, the Bank of Edwardsville (run by his political rival, Ninian Edwards). During the period of bank expansion, depositories otherwise welcomed almost all notes, but after the contraction began in 1818, land office money had to be acceptable to the BUS.

Banks that refused BUS demands for specie found their notes rejected for land purchases, but so did some others that were still attempting to redeem. John Sering, cashier of the Farmers and Mechanics Bank in Madison, Indiana, complained to Crawford on June 14, 1820, that his bank had "continued the payment of specie until its notes, with all the western paper, were refused in payment of land; which . . . caused a general depreciation of all western paper." The president of Indiana's only other chartered bank, the Bank of Vincennes, had already warned Crawford the previous year that western farmers "cannot get for their produce one dollar of the kind of money that will be received in payment of their debts due to the United States." That spring James Flint observed, "Of upwards of a hundred banks that lately figured in Indiana, Ohio, Kentucky, and Tennessee, the money of two is now only received at the land office in payment for public lands. Many have perished and the remainder are struggling for existence." No wonder that he added, "The merchant, when asked about the price of an article, instead of making a direct answer, usually puts the question, 'What sort of money have you got?'"[15]

In 1819 President Monroe chose James Madison's close friend Edward Coles to be register of the land office at Edwardsville, in Illinois's Madison County, across the Mississippi from St. Louis. In August, Coles wrote to Josiah Meigs, the Land Office commissioner, "Little or no land, except immediately in the vicinity of the scite [sic] of the New Seat of Govt. of this State, has sold above two dollars an acre; and I will further add, if the list of Land Office Money be not enlarged, much of the little that has been sold will be forfeited." Samuel Finley, of the Chillicothe land office, had also warned that "such money, as will be received in the Branch Bank of the United States and in the Land Office here is not really to be had."[16]

Without money to make purchases there could be no land sales—a dilemma for Crawford, who badly wanted western land receipts but did not trust western currency. Ohio sales dropped by more than 75 percent from 1818 to 1820; significant immigration to the state would not resume until 1824. Little land was sold in Indiana, and only at the minimum price. The Corydon *Gazette* in Indiana considered the shortage of land office money a calamity for the state. Without some extension of acceptable currency, the paper predicted, executions of foreclosures would reach the amount of all the money and receivable notes in the entire state. "Infancy will be thrust out to nakedness and starvation, and age to despair and death." In the Jeffersonville district some two hundred quarter-sections were forfeited from inability to make payments. Hibbard, in his *History of Public Land Policies*, estimates that fully half of the men in the Northwest states were in debt to the federal government for land.[17]

Thomas Douglas recalled, "At the great crisis of the money market which occurred [in 1819] I found myself with a debt of upwards of $30,000 with little available cash to meet it. As, however, the pressure and failure were general everywhere, I had little difficulty, with the property I had on hand, in arranging with most of my creditors." Some, however, "pressed their claims to judgment and execution, and my library, and even my household furniture, were all sold by the Sheriff. I did not even claim what was by law exempt from execution. When my creditors saw that, even the hardest of them relented, and I settled every claim that was presented." The experience led Douglas to study law. He was quickly elected judge in Jefferson County—even before he was admitted to the bar, in 1822.[18]

In the spring of 1819 the Bank of the United States had been owed $6.3 million in the state of Ohio alone; by the spring of 1822 that debt had been reduced to less than a million, largely by foreclosure. In 1821 Henry Clay—the Bank's primary lawyer in Ohio—was able to report to Langdon Cheves, "I have therefore the satisfaction to inform you, that we have obtained two hundred eleven judgments, in cases issuing from the Cincinnati office alone, and that there were only about twenty cases continued . . . owing to some peculiar circumstances." He added a word of caution, however: "Our currency is continuing in Kentucky to get worse." The *National Intelligencer*—a paper that supported Crawford's candidacy—copied editorials from the Cincinnati *Liberty Hall* and the Chillicothe *Gazette* suggesting that Clay, understood to be the means by which the BUS took possession of much of Cincinnati, was a traitor to westerners who "would seem justified, wherever in their power, to remunerate the author of this mischief with a coat of tar and feathers." (Clay was not unique in adapting his principles to financial necessity—among those who assisted him in his suits on behalf of the Bank was Gorham Worth, the fired Cincinnati branch cashier who had earlier compared Langdon Cheves to Satan.)[19]

Ohio had benefited from the high export price of wheat in 1816 and 1817; after it fell, societies were formed there, as in the East, to encourage local manufacture and consumption. At the urging of William Henry Harrison (one of the state's largest industrial stockholders), Ohio passed a law to exempt textile mills, ironworks, and glassworks from taxation. County fairs added prizes for glassware, flannel, and broadcloth to the traditional awards for livestock, fruits, and vegetables. The congressional delegations from all three northwestern states backed the failed tariff of 1820 and were unanimous in their support of the successful tariff of 1824. Despite all efforts, true recovery in the region— measured by purchasing power and general commercial activity—would be delayed until 1825. That year the Erie Canal opened and construction of the National Road resumed, on the Ohio side of the river at last.[20]

Before the hard times arrived, the south shore of the Ohio River had looked every bit as promising as the north. Cincinnati might be the commercial center on the north bank, but Kentucky had both the river port of Louisville and—farther inland—Lexington. The War of 1812 had brought prosperity to both, and in his 1819 *Sketches of Louisville*, Henry McMurtrie described a boomtown that was about to go bust. He marveled that lots on the principal streets that had sold for $700 before the war began were, five years later, selling for $300 *per foot* of street frontage; but McMurtrie warned that the inflated price was due to "banks, rag money, speculators, shavers, *et id omne genus*." With steamboats now plying the Ohio, Louisville had grown used to crowds of strangers passing through. Then hard times came down the river, and the traffic dried up. In September 1820, when Flint visited, tavern keepers spoke to him of their decreased business now that travelers had become fewer.[21]

In the bluegrass country Flint had seen evidence of monetary troubles in 1818: "Small bills are in circulation of a half, a quarter, an eighth, and even a sixteenth of a dollar. These small rags are not current at a great distance from the place of their nativity. A considerable portion of the little specie to be seen is of what is called cut money"—Spanish coins chopped into fractions.

"This practice prevents such money from being received into banks, or sent out of the country in the character of coins, and would be highly commendable were it not for the frauds committed by those who clip the pieces in reserving a part of the metal for themselves." Flint was disturbed that a farmer from Mount Sterling, thirty miles east of Lexington, would pay thirty-six dollars for a coat imported from England, when the corn he grew sold for twenty-five cents a bushel. "The farmer then, who wears such a coat, must pay a hundred and forty-four bushels for it—a quantity sufficient to be bread for twelve men for a whole year." He was baffled by an economy in which "a chemical manufacturer, at Pittsburg, buys salt petre imported from India, cheaper than he can procure the spontaneous product from the caverns of Kentucky."[22]

But in the city of Lexington, the downturn had been under way for some time. In 1815, *Niles' Register* had confidently declared that "the manufacturing establishments of this town, have reached an eminence which ensures their permanent prosperity and usefulness," but there was no competing with the flood of cheap imports. Property values for the city of Lexington had reached their peak in 1816 at \$3,136,455 and were on their way down to less than half that figure; they would not get back even to \$2 million until 1830.[23]

The postwar failure of the hemp industry triggered the collapse. The established firm of Morris, Boswell, and Sutton closed in December 1817; the Warfield Company followed shortly, and Thomas January, in business more than twenty-five years, failed in 1819. Mills processing not only hemp but cotton and woolen textiles, iron, and paper—some employing over a hundred workers—gradually shut down, unable to compete with British manufactures dumped below cost. The tariff of 1816 could not save Lexington; the Kentucky Society for the Encouragement of Domestic Manufactures was founded there in 1817, and Lexington's own Henry Clay urged Congress to pass a more restrictive tariff in 1820. By then, only a single cotton-bagging plant remained open, and when the Baldwin tariff bill was defeated, the Lexington *Public Enquirer* framed its front page in black and proclaimed, "Mourn, O ye sons and daughters of Kentucky. O ye inhabitants of the United States, put on sackcloth and ashes, for the great enemy of your independence has prevailed. You must still remain tributary to the workshops of Europe. Your factories must remain prostrate. Your agricultural production must lie and rot on your hands."[24]

Lexington would not rebound as Pittsburgh, Cincinnati, and Louisville would. In 1819 the *Gazette* published the gloomy news that "an house and lot on Limestone Street," the city's most desirable address, "for which $15,000 had been offered some time past, sold under the officer's hammer, for $1,200. An house and lot, which I am informed was bought for $10,000 after $6000 had been paid by the purchaser, was sold under a mortgage for $1,500, leaving the original purchaser (besides his advances) $3,500 in debt." In 1820 the Carolina *Centinel* printed a letter from Lexington stating that factories representing half a million dollars in capital were idle: "A deeper gloom hangs over us than was ever witnessed by the oldest man. The last war was sunshine, compared to these times."[25]

Clay's investments in his hometown nearly ruined him; he too had endorsed the notes of friends who then defaulted, leaving him liable for thousands of dollars. He made up his mind to step down as Speaker of the House in order to concentrate on his legal practice. He told John Quincy Adams that he had been offered a retainer of $5,000 by the BUS—a figure that matched Adams's salary as secretary of state, the same position he would one day offer Clay in his own administration. (In fact, the Bank paid him $6,000.)[26]

Clay went enthusiastically to work on behalf of the Bank. Besides his activity in Ohio, he filed numerous suits in his home state of Kentucky, to the detriment of his popularity there as well. He was determined to win cases for the Bank and thus to pay his own substantial debts, but he was willing to compromise when a friend and colleague was involved. He told Cheves that he had been placed in "somewhat an embarrassing situation" by agreeing to sue his old ally Richard Mentor Johnson, now senator from Kentucky, who owed the Bank around $200,000. Although he maintained "a firm determination to discharge my duty" to the Bank, he persuaded Cheves to agree to an exception to its usual policies, allowing Johnson to turn over real estate to the Bank in return for wiping out his debt. Clay assured Cheves that the property's value was far more genuine than "the enormous & fraudulent valuations" of much property he filed suit over in Cincinnati—and he warned that Johnson simply lacked the money to pay the debt otherwise. As a result, Clay was able to report that he had succeeded in winning a judgment in the Bank's favor, and Johnson survived to become Martin Van Buren's vice president.[27]

The people of Kentucky were divided in their attitude toward banks in general, but they were nearly unanimous in their hostility toward Clay's employer, the Bank of the United States. Contraction was particularly severe in the Ohio valley: along with Pittsburgh and the two Ohio branches, the branch offices of the Bank in Louisville and Lexington were warned by Cheves against issuing more notes, and when additional capital was allocated to most branches in 1819—$1.5 million each to New York and Charleston—none was allocated to those offices. At the beginning of that year, Niles quoted an unnamed Kentucky newspaper, which calculated that the two branches together were owed $2,690,700:

> This is the *trifling* sum which the people of Kentucky are called on to pay in *specie*; for the notes of these branches have long since vanished. Indeed we believe that all the U.S. bank paper, bank of Kentucky paper and specie circulating in the state, would not be sufficient to redeem this debt. . . . Add to this the *millions* due to the land offices, which must now be paid in specie or U.S. Bank paper, and our situation becomes truly appalling.[28]

Of all the cities where the Bank had branches, the most extreme curtailment of loans had been at Louisville, reaching nearly 50 percent of all loans outstanding. Lexington's *Kentucky Reporter* accused the banks and the government of having conspired to promote irresponsible land speculation, and acerbically commented, "Nearly all the money that is paid, goes over the mountains; the government has but little use for it in the western country." As silver left the state, public meetings began calling on the banks to suspend specie payment and issue more paper—and stop calling in loans.[29]

The first of these meetings took place in Frankfort. In May the state's leading banks had met there, pledging that they would not suspend specie payment. Then, barely two weeks later, a group of prominent citizens gathered and asked the banks to do just that. Among them was John Pope, a former senator who had just represented the Bank of Kentucky at the banks' May meeting. The Frankfort Resolutions, reported in the newspapers of Philadelphia and New York, took note of the scarcity of money and the serious unemployment in the state. They blamed the banks for their expansionist excesses, which had led to a run on specie, and called on them now to "suspend specie payments and make moderate paper issue." Amos Kendall's *Argus of the West* and the Lexington *Herald* insisted that most of the state's residents opposed the resolutions, which they condemned for "shielding the extravagant debtor," but popular meetings passed similar resolves in six counties; contrary resolutions, demanding specie redemption, were passed in six others. Louisville now insisted on specie redemption, but the city would find itself so short of any money by 1822 that the city government would print inconvertible scrip in denominations between six cents and a dollar. Amounting to $47,000, they quickly lost all value; the city collected and burned them in 1826.[30]

The banks did suspend, despite their pledges not to, but they also continued to call in loans until, one by one, they began to shut down. Finally, in 1821, the Bank of Kentucky itself failed, undercut by the Bank of the Commonwealth, a state-owned bank created by the legislature to issue the paper so much in demand (which also immediately depreciated). Before that happened, one Kentucky bank had sent its representative to exchange $30,000 of its paper for "Tennessee or other current paper," and a day or two later had gone out of business. "Those [the agent] had swindled were in pursuit of him," Niles reported, "determined to take the law in their own hands, breathing vengeance for the trick played upon them. Yet the directors who sent out this agent are called honorable men."[31]

It is a measure of the desperation of the times that anyone would accept an offered exchange of Kentucky paper—or that anyone would seek out Tennessee notes for the exchange. Both states were transformed by the Panic—not just in their economies but in their politics as well. Robert Remini, biographer of both Clay and Jackson, believes that "the development of the Relief and Anti-Relief Parties in Kentucky was the most dramatic example" of the effects of the depression, while "the single event that decisively shaped the future course of Tennessee's politics as it entered the decade of the 1820's—just as it did in many other states—was the Panic of 1819."[32]

In the hills of eastern Tennessee, Knoxville's Bank of Tennessee was able to continue redeeming its notes in specie because it had issued fewer of them and had not loaned so much as the Nashville banks. The Knoxville *Reporter*, accordingly, blamed economic distress on speculation, luxury, and people's desire to live beyond their means. In middle Tennessee, the state's center of both commerce and land speculation, a different view prevailed. The Murfreesboro *Courier* there maintained that "a fall in foreign markets, and the domestic scarcity of a circulating medium" were to blame, not the debtors' "imprudence."[33]

Middle Tennessee was cotton-growing country. Most of the Tennessee land speculation—and much of the Tennessee banks' currency—had been directed to Alabama; the rich soil of that state's Madison County was a southern extension of the middle Tennessee cotton land that Andrew Jackson was already farming at the Hermitage. In Alabama all local attention was on the record-setting land sales, first handled at Milledgeville, Georgia, and then at Huntsville itself, on the Big Bend of the Tennessee River. Sales continued even after the price of cotton fell. But on June 12, 1819, the Huntsville *Alabama Republican* noted that in the East, "extraordinary pressures in the mercantile part of that community" had begun, moving west and south "until the whole union [had] become embarrassed by the failures of mercantile houses and the depreciation of the paper currency." It was the first notice of the Panic of 1819 in any Alabama newspaper. News traveled slowly before railroad or telegraph, and the next week a director of Huntsville's Planters and Merchants Bank, John M. Taylor, wrote from New Orleans to Daniel Boardman back in Huntsville that he had heard "of the immense and unparallelled [*sic*] fall in the price of cotton" only after his firm of Taylor and Foote had purchased "a very large quantity of cotton at the highest prices from local planters." The company would have to liquidate its assets to repay its creditors. The collapse of prices would also leave Willis Pope, son of the powerful LeRoy Pope, $80,000 in debt.[34]

John Williams Walker, Willis Pope's brother-in-law, sympathized with those who were brought down by their speculation, even one who was a BUS director. His boyhood friend Larkin Newby had been appointed to the board of the Fayetteville, North Carolina, branch bank, in 1817. On January 2, 1820, having heard of Newby's losses, Walker wrote to assure him that if need be he would look after Newby's wife and children in the crisis that had thrust "its Medusa front into all our faces, and fastens its incubus on all classes of the community." When he saw "the failure of a man such as you—so prudent, so industrious, and so enterprizing," Walker told Newby, "I tremble for myself and my friends, whose heads are still above water. Some are already sunk and gone. Others are still tottering—and a breach overwhelms them." As Walker saw it, "The mania of speculation was epidemic."[35]

Walker was another of those native Virginians whose parents had moved to Georgia when he was a child. He had been a student along with John C. Calhoun at Moses Waddel's small but famous academy, and Walker entered Princeton as a junior, along with his lifelong friend, Thomas Percy. Walker was already showing symptoms of the tuberculosis that would take his life at the age of thirty-nine. Perhaps he recognized that his days were numbered; he was a young man in a hurry who impressed everyone he met with his energy. He quickly won an appointment as a territorial judge and became a charter trustee of the Planters and Merchants bank; in 1819, he was chosen to be Alabama's initial U.S. senator.[36]

By that time the depression was arriving in the Southwest, and Walker and his neighbors had suffered the combined impacts of the disastrous fall in the price of cotton and the Tennessee banks' specie suspension, which created a severe shortage of land office money. Walker and Percy had married daughters of the wealthy and influential LeRoy Pope, head of Huntsville's Planters and Merchants Bank; Pope's son Willis now made the unwise decision to dissolve his partnership in the firm of Jackson and Pope and buy out his partner's share, believing he could do better on his own. He asked his brothers-in-law to endorse his notes to Jackson, and of course they agreed. Willis Pope showed none of his father's business acumen, at a time when even good businessmen were failing. Moreover, his ethics were suspect; he was later publicly accused of having forged a note in 1819 for $6,408 and of "endeavoring by all sorts of quibbles, prevarications, and subterfuges known to the law, to elude a repayment in sound funds." Walker had left for Washington to take his seat in the Senate; Percy wrote to him regularly to keep him apprised. In March 1820 he told Walker that he had "held a long talk with Willis, & he assures me that neither you, nor I, shall suffer by him." Fortunately, LeRoy Pope's connections were influential enough to get his son's debtors to pay up, so that Walker did not suffer Jefferson's fate. Percy, however, found it best to avoid going into the town of Huntsville, "for I shall be asked for money & it is what I have not got." Walker was at the same time characterizing the economic crisis to Newby as "a fearful and fiery trial, ruining many and shaking more: but the purgation will be complete." He expressed relief that "I was not quite so mad as some of my neighbors. I bought no high-priced lands." But he acknowledged that "I went into Bank—where a planter ought never to go" and contracted a debt. (It was, of course, his father-in-law's bank, and he was one of the directors.) The Panic, he told Newby, had injured "all classes of the community," both the gambler and the innocent victim. He ended the letter, "Should God vouchsafe to deliver me from this peril, I shall take especial care hereafter how I expose my little barque to so tempestuous a sea."[37]

Many of Walker's neighbors were swamped by that sea, including a number who could hardly be called speculators. James Irwin farmed 150 acres in Madison County without slaves, but he owed money to two merchants in Huntsville—a farmer's inescapable advance against the next crop. He also owed money to his neighbor David Maxwell, who farmed 160 acres with a single slave. Unable to pay his debts, Irwin lost his farm in December 1819. Another northern Alabama farmer, William Harris, had bought land at the height of the 1818 to 1819 boom. He wrote to his brother, "You know that the d——d land cost me $26,000." By 1820, in debt and finding that "it is almost impossible to raise money by the sale of property," he sacrificed it for $10,800. A few months later he told his brother, "The embarrassment of mind I have suffered for some time . . . causes reflections which almost unmans me, those feelings I hope you never may experience." He closed the letter, "Show this to no person but the family." Harris was so humiliated by his losses that he left Alabama to start over in Tennessee.[38]

Notices of sheriffs' sales in the *Alabama Republican* peaked in late 1819 and 1820. There were at least twenty sales advertised between April 1819 and November 1820. In January 1820 the paper carried the news of the suicide of Llewellyn Jones. A well-known man "in affluent circumstances," he was said to be a cousin of Martha Washington and a veteran of Valley Forge. He had come south in 1809 from Tennessee among the first settlers of the Big Bend area, bringing four slaves to begin clearing 640 acres. Six years later he owned one thousand acres, two town lots, and thirty-four slaves; he gave his plantation the romantic name of Avalon. But on January 27, 1820, Percy wrote to tell Walker, "Llewellen Jones put a period to his existence last night by hanging himself." Two days later the *Republican* reported that Jones, having lately purchased a "beautiful country seat near Huntsville," had hanged himself from "one of the joists" in his "unfinished country house." Jones had taken his life "in despair at the bad bargain he had made" in a land purchase he now could not pay for.[39]

Percy also told Walker that the Cypress Land Company, the consortium of Tennessee speculators founded by John Coffee whose shareholders included Andrew Jackson and the ubiquitous LeRoy Pope, had called on the purchasers of its lots in Florence to settle their notes with Pope by the end of the month; those who did not would "be sued indiscriminately." Four public auctions at Huntsville between July 1819 and January 1820 attracted few bidders, although private sales continued at the two-dollar minimum price. In February 1820 James Walker, brother of the senator, wrote to tell him, "In the uncertainty, the lands belonging to the Government will not sell for more than one fourth what they did two years ago—indeed there is not funds enough in the country to buy all that is offered even at $2 an acre." Cahaba, farther south in the "Black Belt" (so-called for its rich, dark soil) had been chosen as the capital of the new state in 1820. Land sales at the Cahaba office in 1820 had yielded $801,029.37 in the first quarter, but only $37,724.64 in the second and a mere $6,051.97 in the third. The fourth quarter sale was cancelled.[40]

LeRoy Pope's Planters and Merchants Bank was suffering now that the Tennessee banks had stopped redeeming their notes. Pope wrote to Crawford to complain that merchants in New York "collected their Tennessee debts in Tennessee paper, which was then exchanged at a great discount for ours, with which they drew the specie, unless we supplied them with eastern funds." Unable to withstand the drain, Planters and Merchants finally suspended specie payment in 1820, and its notes fell to the same level of depreciation as the Tennessee banks' paper. Southern Alabamians depended on Georgia banks for currency, along with the small Tombeckbe Bank in St. Stephens and the Bank of Mobile; those two banks were able to continue paying specie, but to the outrage of their directors the state agreed to accept the unredeemable Huntsville notes in payment of taxes and issued treasury bonds payable in Huntsville paper. The governor, Thomas Bibb, was a director of both the Planters and Merchants Bank and the Cypress Land Company.[41]

With the depression Huntsville acquired a second newspaper—the *Democrat*—which styled itself "the voice of the people." It launched a campaign against the Planters and Merchants Bank, accusing the bank and its president of abusing the poor—specifically, of arranging for cotton to be shipped to New York, where it was sold for sound money, and then exchanging the proceeds for deeply discounted Planters and Merchants notes, a practice termed "shaving." The charge seemed that much more plausible after LeRoy Pope was dismissed from his other office of federal pension agent for the same "shaving"—receiving federal pension payments in BUS notes and then paying out the depreciated notes of his bank to the pensioners. The coup de grace would be administered in 1825 when the bank's charter was annulled for failure to redeem in specie. A BUS branch was opened in Mobile over vociferous protests in 1826, and the Tombeckbe Bank gave up the ghost in 1827, just ahead of its president, Israel Pickens—like Walker, a victim of tuberculosis.[42]

By then the depression had lifted somewhat, although the price of cotton remained at all-time lows. Other than a state-owned bank created by the legislature (which finally began making low-interest loans in 1824, in inconvertible notes), debtor relief never got off the ground in Alabama—the biggest debtors were too closely intertwined with the unpopular banks—but the state took greater advantage than any other of the land relinquishment law that Walker would get through Congress in 1821. When the sale of federal land on credit was ended by the land law of 1820, the *Alabama Republican* declared, "We hazard nothing in venturing the assertion that of the debt of 7 or 8 millions [in the Tennessee Valley] which will be due at the expiration of five years from the purchase, not $100,000 will *ever* be paid." At that point, the price of cotton, which had briefly risen from fifteen cents to eighteen, was falling again; investors in Alabama altogether owed more than $11 million to the U.S. Treasury, more than half the nation's entire land debt, but relinquishment cut that debt by more than 50 percent. The passage of the relinquishment bill was Senator Walker's greatest (and last) accomplishment for his state.[43]

Financial relationships in the Southwest were complex; networks of indebtedness stretched far beyond bank loans and debt to the land office. In Alabama, and even more in Mississippi (where there was only one bank) borrowing could take the form of drafts, bills of exchange, or personal promissory notes, which could then be passed along in payment of the creditor's own debts. This "accommodation paper" was particularly popular among planters, but it was also common in towns, among merchants and artisans. For instance, Thomas Cain was a watchmaker and jewelry merchant who purchased a town lot in Huntsville in 1817 and a second in 1819, where he built his shop. He owed several notes to a neighbor, Simon Dance; when hard times put pressure on debtors, Dance assigned the notes to a Philadelphia merchant to whom *he* owed money. In 1820 Cain had to sell the first lot (his home) to pay the Philadelphian, but he kept the shop and his business survived.[44]

Accommodation paper, which let borrowers meet debt by transferring other debts owed to them, was a way to cope with the shortage of hard currency. Financial relations in Alabama and Mississippi often depended on face-to-face transactions, and planters kept accounts in their pocketbooks. A planter who was traveling on business might write to his wife and direct her to look for a particular note in the pocketbook he had left at home. The collapse of cotton prices set off a chain reaction of obligation, and the stricter requirements of bank loans began to be applied to these informal arrangements as the pressure of debt increased. In Mississippi, hundreds of collection suits were filed after 1819 at the Adams County courthouse in Natchez. In 1820 alone there were claims filed for 202 promissory notes, fourteen bills of exchange, seven due bills, thirty-two open accounts, and eleven simple loans. As late as 1826 the hard times lingered in the cotton country and the backlog of debt led to 209 claims for promissory notes, seven for bills of exchange, three for due bills, forty for open accounts, two for bonds, and three for simple loans; in more than three-quarters of the claims the amount was less than $500, and fewer than one in twenty was over $2,000.[45]

Jonathan Thompson, a Natchez planter and attorney, died in 1823 deeply in debt to his partners in a Louisiana plantation; he had mortgages on thirty-three slaves and two mortgages on his land, but he was owed approximately $59,000 by a total of forty-six individual debtors, of which $52,049 was marked "doubtful" in the Adams County probate ledger. His case illustrates the financial difficulties of those who came to the lower Mississippi and acquired land and slaves on credit. Thompson, who had come south from Massachusetts, began borrowing money from Winthrop Sargent, the former territorial governor, in early 1819, starting with a $3,400 loan. In July, with cotton prices in freefall, he borrowed more, and soon he owed Sargent more than $13,000. When Sargent died in August of 1823, Thompson gave a promissory note to his partner, James Trask (another Massachusetts native), and asked him to pay the debt to Sargent's estate. Shortly thereafter Thompson himself died, without repaying the note to Trask—which Trask in turn claimed from Thompson's estate.[46]

These complicated debts were necessary because the credit contraction that had begun in 1818 made it difficult for planters to borrow from banks. Thompson had tried and failed to get a loan from the Bank of Mississippi on behalf of his partner's brother, Israel Trask. As he explained to James Trask in September 1818, "I returned here to indorse [sic] with your brother's name and my own, but it would not answer . . . owing as I understand to the extraordinary course now pursued by the bank [of the United States] at New Orleans which makes them careful here how they put any of their means in the power of the banks there." In December, Trask wrote to Thompson, "Finding an opportunity here of raising the money wanted by my brother . . . I have this day drawn on you at 60 days for the amount, say $15,000 in favor William Kenner and company"—the partners' New Orleans factor—"which please accept, and I shall place timely funds in your hands to withdraw the same at maturity." While the market was booming, such arrangements were an easy way to operate in a shortage of currency; when prices fell, informal arrangements between partners or friends wound up in court.[47]

The cautious Bank of Mississippi was by then run by another northern transplant, the wealthy cotton planter Stephen Duncan, born in Pennsylvania. Duncan's plantations, however, were unencumbered; he had inherited from the families of both his first and second wives, daughters of original settlers. Although he did borrow from his own bank in 1817 to purchase a hundred slaves, his position as a director protected him even as the bank called in other loans; in fact, he and the other stockholders continued to earn dividends from the bank. Even so, in July 1822 he was forced to ask his brother-in-law, Thomas Butler, "to loan me . . . for 60 days—the sum of 500 doll. My funds are entirely exhausted and I have several debts to pay— and wd. be glad to borrow 500 doll. for a couple of months." Duncan had recently loaned large sums of money to other relatives (including $46,671 to a different brother-in-law in July 1821) and was lending money to neighbors while buying more land at depressed prices. In the autumn of 1822, only two months after borrowing $500 from Butler, he managed to pay $20,000 in cash for a plantation of 1,000 arpents (about 850 acres) called Saragossa, five miles south of Natchez.[48]

Such byzantine arrangements suited the planter Duncan, but the bank president Duncan was far more straitlaced. Following the BUS contraction, his bank restricted credit just as those in other states did. The Bank of Mississippi was conservative to the point that even while cotton prices remained painfully low in the 1820s the bank paid its investors dividends of ten dollars and even eighteen dollars per share. Mississippi had not experienced such an extravagant land bubble as Alabama had, and distance kept the state from depending on the Tennessee or Kentucky banks whose failures made an impact on northern Alabama. The New Orleans branch of the BUS had issued fewer notes than other western branches, and with less paper in circulation Mississippi was somewhat less vulnerable to deflation, even though there was no escaping the fall in prices of cotton and land. His land unmortgaged and his investments diversified, Duncan rode out the storm; he would oppose secession in 1861 and move to New York City, where his investments outside of Mississippi enabled him to live comfortably until his death in 1867.[49]

The Natchez planters sold their cotton through New Orleans and were part of a community that extended along both banks of the Mississippi River. Most land tenure derived from old French or Spanish grants, a fact reflected in the habitual use of the arpent—an old European unit of about .85

acres—to measure land. Besides the BUS branch, there were three incorporated banks in New Orleans, but the charter of the Louisiana Bank ran out in
1819 and the Planters Bank suspended operations in 1820. That left the Bank
of Orleans, chartered in 1811. The Louisiana State Bank was then chartered
by the legislature in 1818 to provide currency for the commercial city; it had
five rural branches as well. The Louisiana State Bank was so cautious in its
loan policy that a legislative committee in 1819 urged it to be more liberal.
(The state was a major stock-owner.) When the suggestion was ignored, the
state senate attempted to replace its officers with more malleable men. In
the decade after the panic, New Orleans would become a major banking
center: the nation's second busiest export city was also the primary entry for
Mexican silver, and by the 1830s six local banks and the BUS branch were
again issuing large amounts of currency backed by extensive capital reserves.
The popular, bilingual Citizens Bank ten-dollar note, with the word "Dix"
printed in large letters across the back, is often said to be the reason the deep
south came to be called "Dixie Land"; it and other Louisiana currency regularly circulated as far north as New York. But in 1819 New Orleans banking
was contracting.[50]

Louisiana's leading banking historian, George D. Greene, finds "virtually
no evidence concerning 'the Panic of 1819' in Louisiana, and its effect was
probably quite limited." Greene employs a very narrow definition of the
Panic, and closer examination casts some doubt on his conclusion. (He does
admit, in a note, that "there were some business failures among the leading
New Orleans merchant houses in 1819 and succeeding years.") The Planters
Bank failed in 1820 with six years still left on its charter, and the Louisiana
State Bank was forced to close four of its five out-of-town branches by 1825,
giving its debtors a limit of four years to repay their loans. As in Alabama,
Tennessee, and Kentucky, a state-owned bank would be created to provide
debtor relief. (Rothbard confuses it with the Louisiana State Bank, which
was partly state-owned; the entirely public Bank of Louisiana was, however,
a separate institution, created in 1824. Neither was connected to the Louisiana Bank, which had closed in 1819.) The new bank also had rural branches,
and it received the reluctant support of Gov. Thomas Robertson as an alternative to "stop laws, paper money, and other similar quackery."[51]

Robertson's predecessor, Gov. Jacques Villeré, like many elected officials,
downplayed the economic troubles at first. At the beginning of 1819, just
before the fall in cotton prices reached New Orleans, he acknowledged that
"commerce indeed has for some time experienced and still does experience

pecuniary embarrassments," which he attributed to "the speculating and enterprising spirit which animates and marks the character of our citizens."
In the immediate aftermath, the experience of Louisiana's "speculating and
enterprising" planters was much the same as that of their neighbors across
the river. William T. Palfrey had recently begun planting in St. Mary Parish,
south of New Iberia; in the winter of 1818/19, he expressed his satisfaction
that the price of land was rising and cotton prices were at a record high, but
cotton prices soon plunged and land prices followed. By autumn picking season, Palfrey was worried. His cotton "never looked as well as it does now,"
but the price was "so unfavorable" that his slaves' value had fallen too. He
feared a "depression in the amount of Dollars." By spring 1820 it was worse;
despite an abundant crop, he had to keep borrowing. Palfrey survived the
depression, but many of his neighbors were not so fortunate.[52]

John Taylor, the Alabama cotton merchant, had been in New Orleans
when he learned that the "immense" drop in prices had wiped out his company, Taylor and Foote. Every time brokers in the city thought the price had
hit bottom, it would drop again, from thirty-four cents to twenty and fourteen and even nine cents per pound by 1823. When crops failed to return any
profit, planters were suspicious of their factors, who often extended credit
against the expected return on their cotton. Robert W. Chinn was a partner
in the firm of Chinn and Johnson, factors in New Orleans. At the end of February 1822, he wrote to his client, Louisiana planter William S. Hamilton,
after he discovered that the latest drop had left Hamilton owing him more
money than he could pay: "I did not think when I addressed you yesterday
on the subject of accts. that yr. situation was so embarassing [sic] and that the
difficulty of paying was so great with you, or I assure you, not withstanding
my own wants, I should not have mentioned the subject." Chinn's delicacy
was for naught; the next year Hamilton was selling through Dicks, Booker,
and Co. They too wrote to tell him that the price had again fallen, so low
that they had sold his fifty bales at a half cent per pound below the minimum
price he had set them: "This may be improper, and you have a right to claim
the half cent . . . [but] we were convinced that more than the 12 cents offered
could not be obtained. . . . We hope you will be satisfied that we consulted
your interest, if we disobeyed your instructions." Hamilton, never able to get
out of debt after the Panic, went through five different factors in New Orleans between 1819 and 1828 in a futile effort to sell at a profit.[53]

Hard times arrived in the Southwest when the price of cotton fell and
banks began their contraction of credit; they lingered for years as cotton

surpluses kept the price from recovering even after the British resumed their purchases. The Panic came latest of all to Missouri. There, growth not only stopped but temporarily reversed: St. Louis would lose a third of its population between 1821 and 1823.[54]

In the boom times, even as late as 1819, no part of the country seemed more appealing to settlers than the Missouri territory, distant and still primitive as it was. In 1818 Patty Lippincott wrote from St. Louis to her brother, Isaac Swift, in Ravenna, Ohio—a place that had itself been the frontier only a few years earlier. "Perhaps it will suit you to reside here, land is very cheap and good, both in Missouri and Illinois Territory two-dollars per acre, we live in town but hope to be able to purchase land after a while." Her husband, Thomas Lippincott, continued the letter. They had been in Missouri only "a few weeks," but he was in the full flush of enthusiasm:

> I am convinced that if you could see this country, and become acquainted with the manner in which money can be made—or rather property acquired—you would need no urging to close your business in Ohio and come immediately to this country. The soil is perhaps as good as any in the world—you smile—and so did I, on reading what I conceived the extravagant accounts of this often-termed "Terrestrial Paradise"—But really I am convinced that although such were my opinions, yet "the half was not told me."

Patty confessed that she found St. Louis itself a "dissipated disagreeable place," and by the end of the year they had moved to the hamlet of Milton, Illinois, where they opened a store; a few years later Milton was a "deserted and ruined village," abandoned after a wave of malaria that took the life of Patty Lippincott.[55]

Missouri had residents of long standing like Auguste Chouteau, founder of St. Louis, who owned huge French and Spanish land claims and hoped to make a fortune selling land to people like the Lippincotts. It had also attracted more recently arrived entrepreneurs like Moses Austin of Connecticut, who made and lost a fortune in lead mining, and Thomas Hart Benton, of North Carolina by way of Tennessee. Both invested in banks and speculated in land; Benton edited the St. Louis *Enquirer*, which tirelessly boosted the prospects of the region. A cousin of Henry Clay's wife, Lucretia, Benton had been named for her father, Col. Thomas Hart. After a shootout with Andrew Jackson, Benton had thought it wise to leave Nashville; he wrote to his friend Preston Blair that he had arrived in St. Louis in 1815 with $400 and was "comfortably established." In 1819 he told Blair that if he had come with $20,000 he would be worth a quarter of a million: "Ground around St. Louis then [1815] selling for thirty dollars an acre, sells at this day for two thousand." Moses Austin had been one of the founders of the Bank of St. Louis; Benton was among the stockholders who removed the bank's scheming cashier, John B. N. Smith, and later seized the bank and padlocked its doors. The bank's failure ruined Austin, who then traveled to San Antonio, in the province of Mexico he called Tejas, and received permission to bring emigrants there in 1820 (a plan characterized by Matthew Carey as "the emigration of American citizens to a Spanish Colony, seeking asylum from the distress they suffer in their own country"). He contracted pneumonia and died on the way back in June 1821, making a deathbed plea to his son to carry out the plan. The son, Stephen F. Austin, became known as the father of Texas.[56]

The War of 1812 had slowed the growth of Missouri, but soon more migrants followed Benton and Austin; one of them, the Baptist missionary John Mason Peck, wrote that "in the winter, Summer, and autumn of 1816 they came like an avalanche. . . . Caravan after caravan passed over the prairies of Illinois, crossing the 'great river' at St. Louis." The population of that town was about 1,500 in 1815 and over 2,000 by 1816. Two years later Patty Lippincott estimated it at "about two thousand five hundred, half Americans" and half French-speakers; the 1820 census would count 4,598, putting St. Louis ahead of Lexington and Louisville even before Missouri statehood. Another missionary, the Harvard-educated Congregationalist Timothy Flint, recalled immigrants pouring into the territory in 1817 and 1818 with wagons full of children, and wives and slaves walking alongside, an image that reminded him of the Old Testament Israelites. "It is to me a very pleasing and patriarchal scene. It carries me back to the days of other years, and to the pastoral pursuits of those ancient races, whose home was in a tent, wherever their flocks found range." In the minds of the immigrants, "the hills of the land of promise, were not more fertile in milk and honey than are the fashionable points of immigration."[57]

Peck and his family, like the Lippincotts, rented a single room in St. Louis while eagerly eying the surrounding farmland. For it they paid the exorbitant rent of twelve dollars per month; Peck was unhappy to find that everything was more expensive in Missouri: butter was thirty-five or fifty cents a pound, sugar the same, and coffee seventy-five cents. He blamed the inflated prices on the Ohio and Kentucky banknotes—"shinplasters," he called them—circulating in great numbers. The rising prices reflected the boom times in St. Louis: at least a hundred houses were built in 1818, in such demand that occupancy averaged eight or ten people; by 1821 the city boasted 306 log or frame houses, seventy-seven made of stone, and seventy-five of brick. In 1818 pine lumber was up to eight dollars per board foot, ten times the going rate in Pittsburgh and twice what St. Louis had paid the previous year. The Missouri *Gazette* that year reported that common laborers would not work for less than $1.50 per day and asserted that many had earned enough in a year's time to buy 160 acres. Land between St. Louis and nearby St. Charles had sold in 1808 for twenty-five to fifty cents per acre; by 1818 it sold for at least eight dollars and as much as twelve dollars per acre. By the end of that year Chouteau and J. B. C. Lucas had sold seventy-eight lots in St. Louis for just over $25,000. Lucas, in less than ten years, had turned a profit of 1,200 percent on his early land speculations—and had so far sold only one-quarter of what he had.[58]

In 1818 St. Louis was big enough to establish a police department; a chief of police was hired, along with an assistant and a constable for night duty, and a force of six patrolmen. James Barnes announced the opening of a hat factory in the town of Franklin, promising beaver felt hats made "in the most elegant and durable manner"; he planned to hire five or six apprentices. The *Gazette* was looking forward to the construction of woolen mills, since so many of the immigrants had brought "considerable" flocks of sheep. When John Paxton published the first *Directory* of St. Louis in 1821, he listed forty-six merchants, fifty-seven "groceries" (primarily saloons), twenty-eight carpenters, thirteen boat makers, three newspapers (the *Gazette*, the *Register*, and the *Enquirer*), twenty-seven lawyers, thirteen physicians, a brewery, a tannery, a nail factory, and three soap and candle works; more than half had arrived since 1817. The majority of the city's inhabitants were single men, many of whom would depart when the hard times arrived. Paxton claimed that the fur trade made up $600,000 of St. Louis's annual commerce of $2 million, but that trade had actually begun to decline in the last year. Paxton spoke with pride of the "elegant . . . fine brick cathedral" that had replaced the old log church. He proclaimed St. Louis a place where "both scholar and courtier could move in a circle suiting their choice and taste." That was something of a stretch: Christian Wilts complained that no one bought books at his general store and thought his supply of Shakespeare would last fifty years. Scholars and courtiers were both rarities in Missouri.[59]

The year 1819 came and went, but Missouri seemed to be immune to the depression that was spreading across the country—although the police chief and his assistant were laid off as an economizing measure. The *Gazette* noted in late fall of 1819 that many immigrants "of the wealthier type" continued to arrive, so that "to borrow, to buy and sell again to the newcomer" was still the popular practice. The Tallmadge Amendment created an uproar in Congress but not so much in Missouri; residents were united in insisting on the right to make their own decision on slavery, just like any other state, and the territorial delegate in Washington, John Scott, mentioned neither that controversy nor the economic crisis in his reports home; letters to his constituents were devoted to his efforts to secure "adjustment" of land claims and the right of preemption in Howard County, up the Missouri River, and to the much-anticipated public land sales.[60]

Speculators looked westward to vast public lands, but merchants in St. Louis knew that the city's prosperity depended on the river trade. There was much excitement in August 1817 when the *Zebulon Pike* became the first steamboat to dock at St. Louis, but by 1819 steamboat traffic on the Mississippi had become commonplace, and the first steamboat had already ventured up the Missouri River. Timothy Flint, with a New Englander's practical eye, declared, "The advantage of steamboats, great as it is everywhere, can no where be appreciated as it is in this country. The distant points of the Ohio and the Mississippi used to be separated from New Orleans by an internal obstruction, far more formidable in passing, than the Atlantic. If I may use a hard word, they are now brought into juxtaposition." And the other Flint, the Scottish visitor, wrote that he had spoken in Kentucky to a traveler from Missouri who described the sale of public lands there in 1818, "exposed by auction, in quarter sections of 160 acres each. A considerable part of them are sold at from three to six dollars per acre. . . . Land dealers are very vigilant in securing for themselves great quantities of the best land."[61]

The sales were not always brisk and never approached the level of Alabama, but the immigrants kept coming. In November 1819 the *Enquirer* reported 120 wagons per week, for nine or ten weeks, passing through St. Charles on their way up the Missouri to Boon's Lick. Timothy Flint counted a hundred migrants in a single day at St. Charles, in wagons drawn by six horses, followed by about a hundred cattle. The train stretched three-quarters of a mile. He would look back on 1817 and 1818 as the time when "the rage for speculation was the highest. . . . I question if the people of Missouri generally thought there existed higher objects of envy than Chouteau and a few other great land-holders of that class." At first the migrants all wanted to go to Boon's Lick; then the favored destination was Salt River.

> In the year 1819, the current set in another direction. The Kentuckians and Tennesseans were moving their droves of cattle to a point on the Illinois. I could not exactly make out for two or three days the name of the destined country. They pronounced it as though it were Moovistar, or as my children phrased it, 'Moving Star.' On being better informed, we were told that the country was denominated from some poor sand-banks near the river, 'Mauvaise Terre,' or 'Poor Land.'

But the market refused to believe that there was any poor land. One tract was put up at auction with no more precise location than that it lay thirty miles north of St. Louis: "A general laugh ran through the crowd assembled at the court house door. But a purchaser soon approached, who bid off the tract . . . undoubtedly with a view to sell it to some more greedy speculator than himself."[62]

The thicket of old and overlapping claims complicated everything. There were Spanish grants, French grants, New Madrid warrants, preemption rights, and more. Timothy Flint was amused by the obsession over them all:

> The discussion, the investigation of these claims, the comparative value of them . . . the prospect of confirmation of the unconfirmed titles, the expectation of one from the eloquence of members of congress who would espouse the interest of his claim, of another from his determined and declared purpose to carry his claims by bribery—conversations upon these points made up the burden of the song in all social meetings. They were like the weather in other countries, standing and perpetual topics of conversation.

Although the U.S. attorney general declared New Madrid warrants to be nontransferable in 1820, the Missouri General Assembly—which included many with vested interests in them—was still objecting as late as 1825: "Should the patents to the land be withheld, it would . . . cause the ruin of many of our most worthy and respectable citizens."[63]

Among those who speculated in New Madrid warrants were Moses and Stephen Austin; with the Bank of St. Louis failing and the family's Spanish claim to mining land disallowed, Stephen wrote to his brother-in-law, "I advise you to return as quick as possible with all the money you can and buy Madrid claims." In his journal he noted that he had "given power of attorney to W.M. O'Hara to purchase any amount of Madrid Claims and locate them for our joint account, and I have received a power from him to lay out towns and sell lots on the claims we hold jointly." Towns were being laid out with abandon by many imaginative speculators. Richard Venables promoted the town of Mexico, supposedly named by emigrants heading for the Austins' destination; it would actually come into being ten years later. Other promoters named their anticipated towns Alexandria and Monroe. The projected communities of Wocondo, Belfast, Bainbridge, Missouriton, Monticello, Roche au Pierce, and Washington were all sold off but never developed. Agents of Thomas Hart Benton sold lots in Osage, a town laid out with wide, mile-long streets and "numerous large squares for public buildings." They assured prospective buyers that it was likely to be the new state's capital. Speculators often gambled on the probable (or merely plausible) locations of the state capital or even county seats. Austin himself bought land in Little Rock in hopes that it would become the capital of the new territory to be organized south of Missouri.[64]

In 1819 land sales receipts in the territory were $2,447,336. That amount would not be matched for another fifteen years. Land in Howard County, around the vaunted Boon's Lick, sold for an average of four dollars per acre in early 1819; in Franklin County, just west of St, Louis, "about every quarter that is good [sold] from $4 to $12 per acre." And in June the *Gazette* reported speculators selling land around St. Louis for twenty dollars per acre, with half down in silver and the remainder financed at 10 percent with two acceptable securities.[65]

But Missouri was not under some special enchantment, and the hard times that had struck the rest of the country were approaching. "The first impediment" to development had already become visible to Timothy Flint, "and went on increasing in force, until I left the country" in 1819:

> This was in the sudden reduction of prices in the Atlantic country, the pressure of the times, and the sudden failure of numerous banks of the western country. For a while immigrants kept arriving, bringing with them the money with which they bought their lands. . . . But the moment the pressure began to operate, in preventing the people who were disposed to remove to the country from selling their lands, the tide was arrested.[66]

There were plenty of signs that the boom could not last, but few in Missouri were willing to see them. The auctions at the St. Louis land office in August and September 1818 had been much anticipated, although the crowds were less than expected and much of the offered land went unsold. Better-attended spring sales brought lower than predicted prices, although immigrants were still numerous. The *Gazette*, like other newspapers, looked on the bright side, observing that the sales "must be encouraging to emigrants, as the price is very low compared with that of lands not more fertile in other parts of the southern and western sections of the union." But the *Gazette* had already taken note of the depression beginning in those sections. News required weeks to get to Missouri, but in February 1819 the paper had reported,

> In the East was proposed the all too familiar suggestion of relief through a law forbidding the export of specie; of pressure to prevent any more imports of 'the needless trappings of luxuries'; to abandon speculation, which had often led the youth astray; that the rich men spend their surplus money in encouraging industry at home; that the middle class must learn to live within their income; that young men must depend upon productive labor and not their wits for a livelihood; and that all must refrain from aping the establishment of nations of Europe.

This was the first published notice in Missouri of the nation's economic troubles, but it was followed by signs of increasing anxiety: in April the *Intelligencer* suggested the best use for the proposed new town sites was to plow them under and plant corn; in July the *Gazette* declared that "the signs of the times are alarming: a dark and dreadful cloud hangs over our country, which may break to the ruin of many," and the *Intelligencer* warned that it would be wise to spend less and lay something aside for a rainy day.[67]

Missouri public land sales in 1819 had reached nearly 900,000 acres; in 1820 they would be less than 76,000. The St. Charles *Missourian* began publishing lists of tax delinquents in July 1820; the list of August 12 would include the name of Richard Venables, the promoter of the town of Mexico, who owed taxes on properties amounting to 16,000 acres. The *Enquirer* avoided negative news as long as it could, but by 1821 the depression was undeniable: even the *Enquirer* had to admit in March that "acute distress was written . . . on the countenances of most men," and the next week the *Gazette* declared, "The evil beginning in the Atlantic cities has gradually extended itself to this state and produced a pecuniary embarrassment and distress, both public and private, heretofore unknown among us." In July, the *Missouri Republican* sounded like any newspaper in Philadelphia or Baltimore: "We have seen men of integrity and sensibility destroyed by the sense of degradation consequent on commitment to jail."[68]

The poor 1820 land sales were undeniable evidence that the flood of immigrants had not only ebbed but was drying up; prices dropped abruptly. Timothy Flint recalled,

> They took a sudden, I might call it figuratively, a perpendicular fall. For they fell from an estimation above their real value, through all the stages of depreciation, to an estimation probably far below their proper value. Hundreds of speculators, who had embarked all their means, and a still greater degree of credit in their speculations, and who might have sold their lands in the fortunate moment and been independent, retained them, through greediness, until they sank at once upon their hands and many were ruined; and as always happens . . . could not fail to drag down multitudes with them in their fall.[69]

In August 1821, the sheriff of St. Louis County advertised 14,271 acres and 105 town lots to be sold for nonpayment of taxes; the collector of Howard County, in the Boon's Lick country, had 8,311 acres and fourteen town lots to sell. The *Gazette* noted that few attended or had means to attend the sheriffs' sales. Those who had bet everything on the prospect of more people coming to Missouri now began to leave the state. The population of St. Louis dropped by 35 percent; of those who remained, so many voters were disqualified for failure to pay taxes that the vote to adopt a city charter in 1823 was only 107 to 90 and the mayoral election saw a total of only 192 votes cast. Merchants were closing their doors; after the failure of the surrounding banks and the collapse of land sales, they could not get the cash they needed to pay their eastern suppliers. Half of the major firms in St. Louis closed between 1821 and 1823—only the "groceries" selling liquor by the drink prospered. The failures included Christian Wilt & Co. (with all the unsold volumes of Shakespeare); the general merchants Waddle & Blanchard, John Lindell, Nathaniel Payne, and S. R. Ober; and the druggist David Tuttle. Only a year earlier their advertising had filled the pages of the newspapers—Wilt often took a full column in the *Gazette*—but now more than two dozen merchants went out of business; many of them had joined in the land speculation, to their sorrow.[70]

The Bank of St. Louis, poorly managed and victimized by its cashier, had failed in 1819. Benton used the *Enquirer* to cast suspicion on a number of prominent Kentuckians he accused of conniving in the corruption—including Richard Mentor Johnson, who seemed to have a weakness for sketchy financial schemes. Moses Austin, for whom the bank failure was the last straw, had been arrested for debt. He published this notice in the *Gazette* on March 22, 1820:

> My creditors are hereby notified that on Saturday the 25th inst., between the hours of ten in the forenoon and three of the clock in the afternoon of the said day, I shall make application . . . to be permitted to take the benefit of the several laws of this territory concerning insolvent debtors, and to be released from my imprisonment.[71]

Austin would make his application at his home in the town of Herculaneum—ironically named for the city destroyed along with Pompeii in another, much earlier, catastrophe. Austin was freed and then departed for Texas, but he was only one of many imprisoned for debt before the new state ended the practice in 1821. The *Intelligencer* had urged the reform, pointing out that most of the jailed debtors were not big speculators and that "the small dealers and the poorer class of men, who form a large majority" had already lost everything they had. The *Gazette* noted that "such is the depreciation of the value of property, that the accumulated labor of years is not now sufficient to pay a trifling debt, and property some years since which could have sold for eight to ten thousand dollars will scarcely, at this time, pay a debt of five hundred."[72]

Few in Missouri were in a hurry to put the blame on speculators; to do so would have placed most of the population at fault. Inevitably, anger was directed at the banks, which were accused of both irresponsible expansion and heartless contraction. A letter published by the *Enquirer* on March 17, 1821, is representative:

> Almost three years ago there was a considerable emigration to the state, and large quantities of the notes of the banks of Kentucky, Ohio, North and South Carolina, and Tennessee were brought to and circulated in this state. . . . [If] the notes of the Bank of Missouri beyond what is now in circulation is [sic] taken into consideration, it probably amounted to nearer ten hundred thousand dollars. The Banks of Ohio were first discredited and its notes withdrawn from

circulation; then followed all the rest, and the Bank of Missouri was compelled to limit its issue.

The writer estimated the sudden decrease in the circulating medium to be as much as nine-tenths, at the very least four-fifths. Five months after the letter was published, the Bank of Missouri shut its doors. The next month, a letter appeared in the *Gazette* signed "Stockholder of the Bank of St. Louis":

> Not many days since, citizens of this town witnessed an obscure individual receiving, with the execrations of society, ten lashes and standing in the pillory, also condemned to be in jail until he should pay a fine of double the amount, for [mis]using the money entrusted to him. . . . And yet the directors of the Bank of Missouri, who have appropriated somehow, I will not say to themselves, $152,000 of public money and upwards of $29,000 belonging to private individuals, which had been placed with them for safekeeping, are still caressed and respected in society.[73]

Responses to the depression in Missouri included a number of efforts to diversify the economy. Agricultural societies were organized in 1821 and 1822 to encourage regular trade fairs and a home market for the state's produce. As Missouri's first U.S. senator (and a paid agent of Astor's American Fur Company), Benton persuaded Congress to end the system of government factors and open Indian trading up to private individuals; St. Louis was the logical depot for trade up the Missouri River. In 1821 the Santa Fe Trail began leading enterprising traders to the old Spanish city, by then an administrative outpost of the new Mexican government. William Becknell, from the town of Franklin, had headed across the Kansas plains with a small group of men, looking for trade with either Indians or Mexicans. Since currency was nearly unavailable, he hoped to trade for Mexican silver. Becknell encountered a detachment of Mexican soldiers who told him his merchandise would be welcome in Santa Fe, where supplies had been short since Mexican independence. He sold everything he had brought in November at high profits and returned to Missouri with the good news. Annual caravans followed, bringing somewhere between $100,000 and $200,000 in much-needed silver back to Franklin.[74]

With the exception of Alabama, no part of the country had attracted so many people so quickly as Missouri. In the ensuing collapse, no part of the country, not even Cincinnati, was more severely stricken. No other city lost population at the rate that St. Louis did. Missourians' hopes had been the highest, and their disappointment was the most complete. But because Missouri was still so new, recovery would come more easily—far more so in St. Louis than in Lexington. Still, it would take time. Of Missouri's eventual 114 counties, nineteen were rapidly organized between 1816 and 1821, but only five more from 1821 through 1824.[75]

Despite the calm that followed the Missouri Compromise, the tide of immigration to Missouri would not be so high again for a decade. Through 1822, businesses continued to advertise their willingness to accept produce in payment of debts, listing beef, pork, tobacco, lard, salt, sugar, beeswax, honey, and country linen as acceptable substitutes for money. Timothy Flint acknowledged both the intensity of the blow and the stubbornness of the people, on both the Illinois and Missouri sides of the Mississippi: "There was probably no part of the United States more severely pressed than these two states. Improvement not only came to a stop but seemed to retrograde. . . . I witnessed the meeting of two families on the St. Charles Road, the one going to Boon's Lick, and the other coming from it. They had formerly been neighbors in Kentucky." One family was absolutely convinced that the future lay in Missouri; the other had had enough of it and was headed back east. They debated for some time, but neither could shake the other's conviction, and at last they continued on their ways, in opposite directions.[76]

RELIEF?

While it was easy to blame the Bank of the United States, no one really understood what was causing the hard times that had descended upon the country; there was likewise no agreement on what to do about them. As president, John Quincy Adams would call for unprecedented federal initiatives in many areas; in 1819 he was convinced that there was no remedy "but time and patience." Thomas Jefferson's political philosophy has often been characterized as "the government that governs least, governs best"; nevertheless, he told Adams's father that he hoped "our legislators have wisdom enough to effect a remedy." The New York *Evening Post* disagreed: "The laws of trade will restore things to an equilibrium, if legislatures do not rashly interfere in the natural course of events." Conservatives were certain that the cure was a return to the frugality and industry of bygone days, and a committee of the Presbyterian Church in 1819 declared the only solution lay in "the principles and duties of our holy religion, which are not less conducive to the temporal welfare of men, than to their eternal happiness."[1]

Ever since the New Deal, each modern economic downturn evokes the immediate question of what the government is going to do—and it goes without saying that government means the *federal* government. The early nineteenth century was a different world; during two terms in office, President Monroe rarely commented on the nation's economic woes, and no one really expected him to. The presidency had not yet been declared a bully pulpit, and a century before radio there was certainly no tradition of "fireside chats." The president delivered his annual message to Congress in writing; there would not be a State of the Union address between Jefferson and Woodrow Wilson. The Federal Reserve was likewise a century in the future. There was no federal policy on unemployment, no federal office that kept economic statistics. It is true that the Bank of the United States had five directors appointed by the president of the United States—but the other twenty were elected by its private shareholders. Even the Treasury secretary told the BUS president Langdon Cheves that his first responsibility was to provide dividends to his stockholders. Secretary Crawford always had his eye on the political consequences of any event, but in 1819 his primary duty was to respond to the drop in national revenue: he could choose to ask Congress to cut the military budget, which he did, or ask them to raise the tariff, which he did not. There was not much other federal spending and little other revenue now that land sales had fallen off.

That is not to say that there was no governmental role to be played. Poor relief had long been understood to be a responsibility of local government—although the scope of the Panic would challenge that assumption, leaving the destitute to depend more and more on what are now called non-governmental organizations. Regulation of banking, such as there was, fell entirely to state governments. To the extent the Supreme Court permitted, so did the laws covering debts and bankruptcies, given the absence of a federal bankruptcy law, which Congress refused to pass. The depression years would see debates in almost every state legislature over creating publicly owned loan banks, ending imprisonment for debt, and limiting the forced sale of debtors' property by means of stay laws and minimum appraisal laws. The national government continued to mint silver and gold coins (too valuable to spend), but its only official response to the debased paper currency was to refuse to accept payment in notes that were not redeemable in specie. There was one thing, however, that only the Congress could take any action on: the enormous debt run up by Americans who had bought land from the United States on credit.

As early as 1810 Albert Gallatin had stated his conviction that public lands should only be sold for cash, but Congress had not wanted to hear it; Republicans were committed to making land ownership easy for small farmers. By 1819, with perhaps half the population of Ohio in debt to the Unites States Treasury, Surveyor General Edward Tiffin wrote to Land Commissioner Josiah Meigs, "I cannot forbear saying, that, I much fear a Spirit of disaffection &&& toward the general government is arising in the West sufficient to alarm its fast friends and certainly requires vigilance. . . . At least it is enough to admonish the government to make no more Debtors, but change the system of disposing of public lands."[2]

The next year, with very little land office money in circulation, Congress closed the barn door behind the runaway horse and voted on April 24, 1820, to end land sales on credit—at the same time reducing the minimum purchase from 160 to 80 acres and the minimum price from $2.00 per acre to $1.25. On the one hand, this improved the position of bankers and spec-ulators, who could still offer buyers several years over which to finance a purchase; on the other hand, the prospect of outright ownership of 80 acres for $100 was tough competition for the investor with 160-acre parcels to sell, on which he had already paid at least $80 and still owed $240 or more. The government's cash requirement, the difficulty of getting bank loans, and the dismal prices of wheat and cotton reduced land sales from $13.6 million in 1818 to $1.7 million in 1820, a bitter pill for the Treasury Department at a time when revenue from duties on imports was at its lowest since the war.[3]

The House Committee on Public Lands would continue to struggle with relief for debtors. In 1828 the committee's chairman looked back a decade and described buyers who had "found that they, in common with the com-munity around them, had been deceived by the mere *appearance* of prosper-ity. . . . The price of cotton continued to fall, till, it did not bring one third of the price upon which their calculations to pay their land debts had been based." Southern congressmen were all too aware of that reality in 1820 as they prepared to vote to end credit sales. On the 20th of February, Alabama's John Williams Walker pointed out to the Senate that extensions on payments for land had become so automatic that acreage purchased when Ohio land was first put up for sale, twenty years earlier, was still not fully paid for. The total now due to the U.S. Treasury was nearly $22 million—"a fearful sum." Prices had shot up so fast that purchases at auction in Alabama "seemed to have been made under the influence of a sort of delirium." The Yazoo scrip issued by the federal government had been partly to blame, although no more than the creation "in Kentucky and Tennessee, [of] about seventy banks, whose paper was profusely scattered over the country."[4]

Kentucky's own Sen. Richard Mentor Johnson, personally in debt to the BUS, offered an amendment to the public lands bill that would allow debtors to retain as much of their land as their payments had already covered, forfeit-ing the remainder in return for cancellation of the debt. The great speculative purchases had been made in 1818 and 1819, and in most cases three-quarters of the payments remained to be made, but desperate buyers would rather give up three-quarters of their land than face losing it all through foreclosure. Walker spoke in favor of the amendment, pointing out that relinquished land could be resold by the Land Office (albeit at far lower prices), thus providing much-needed revenue for the government. When New York's Sen. Rufus King objected that no bidder "would be found mad enough" to bid against the prior owner, Walker pointed out that the same would be true if land were forfeited, without relinquishment. And the prior owners were by no means all speculators: "It was the most discreet men sometimes who gave the highest prices." Walker himself "had known, for example, as high as seventy-eight dollars per acre given for land by those who bought it with the full intention themselves to cultivate it." Indeed, "The most prudent, calculating men in the country were swept away by the delirium of the moment." If land sales on credit were to end abruptly, he believed, the government had the obligation to "interpose for the relief of the late purchasers." King and most of the Senate remained unconvinced. The amendment failed, with only the votes of Alabama, Kentucky, Illinois, and one senator each from Indiana and South Carolina. Walker voted to end credit sales anyway. But he was not ready to give up on relinquishment.[5]

Later in the summer the Land Office revealed that buyers of Alabama land owed over $11 million of the debt still outstanding, with little prospect of paying it. In October Charles Tait, a former Georgia senator and an Alabama investor, warned Walker, "I believe that it is generally understood that we cannot pay for our land if the present laws are enforced," and he asked him to seek an extension that would divide the remaining payments into eight annual installments. In November, even President Monroe—usually silent on the subject of the nation's devastated economy—suggested in his annual message that "a reasonable indulgence" for public land debtors might be in order, since "the purchases were made when the price of every article had risen to its greatest height, and the installments are becoming due at a period of great depression." Two days after Monroe's statement, Johnson again introduced a resolution to allow land debtors to relinquish prorated portions while keeping title to the rest. Similar resolutions quickly followed from Senators Noble (Indiana), Thomas (Illinois), and Walker. Now even Hezekiah Niles, a perennial critic of land speculation, endorsed a relinquishment law—although he predicted that only the poorest lands would be relinquished while the best were retained.[6]

Alabama Attorney General Henry Hitchcock wrote at once to Walker to suggest that if Crawford—already a presumed candidate for the presidency in 1824—would support relinquishment, he would help his chances in Alabama. Crawford needed no one to point that out to him; he had probably encouraged Monroe's suggestions and had proposed a plan of proportional relinquishment, forgiveness of approximately a quarter to a third of debt, and the extension of repayment to ten installments, without interest. At year's end Walker again addressed the Senate on behalf of a bill by which buyers could relinquish land which the federal government would then resell, returning to the original buyers all proceeds above $1.25 per acre, up to the original price. Those who wished to retain their land would receive payment extensions, and those who paid all of what they owed would receive a discount of three-eighths the purchase price, plus interest.[7]

The speech, delivered on December 28, 1820, was the longest and most important of Walker's brief career. (He had been elected only one year earlier and illness would force him to resign less than two years later; he would die the following spring.) He told the Senate, "Remember that you are told from high authority that the total currency of the Union has been suddenly reduced from one hundred and ten to forty-five millions of dollars." Cotton, he noted, had fallen from twenty-five to ten cents per pound, and the notes of all those Kentucky and Tennessee banks were no longer accepted by the Land Office: "You have repudiated the seventy banks, and the planter who owes you must exchange one hundred dollars in those vile rags for eighty-five dollars of such as will pass muster in the land office. . . . Individual petitions, nay whole states supplicate your clemency. Seven of these new States and two Territories await with solicitude the fate you are preparing for them." Once again characterizing the economic crisis as monstrous, he closed, "It is for you to determine whether they shall be stifled by the horrible incubus of this debt."[8]

It was an era in which eloquent speeches could change senators' minds, and Walker's succeeded. One week later the Senate's Public Land Committee reported out a bill that closely followed Crawford's suggestions and promised what Walker was asking for. The bill swept through the Senate by a vote of 36 to 5 and passed the House easily, 97 to 40. New England representatives barely opposed it, 14 to 13, but it carried in the Southeast by a two to one ratio and in the Middle Atlantic by four to one. The West—where its effects would mainly be felt—was nearly unanimous, with only three eastern Tennessee representatives voting no.[9]

The relinquishment law was welcomed warmly in western states. The Steubenville *Western Herald* wrote on May 17, "Whatever may be said of the conduct of Congress in other respects, the people of the West cannot but feel grateful for the attention that has been paid to their interests." The gratitude cooled as the law's complexity delayed its implementation. Cincinnati's *Liberty Hall* had written on May 9 that the new law was "hailed with much satisfaction by the people of the western country," but on June 18 that paper feared that it was "likely to be inoperative for the want of instructions from the Secretary of the Treasury respecting the construction which is to be given to it." Crawford was beside himself as the political capital he had won began to evaporate; the law was simply too complicated, and three months after its passage Commissioner Meigs was still trying to create the necessary forms, which were not mailed to land offices until the end of June. It was mid-August before the slow mails brought them to Franklin, Missouri, and Cahaba, Alabama—and the law required that claimants file them by September 30.[10]

Twelve days before that deadline, the Cahaba receiver, Alexander Pope, wrote to Meigs, "Scarcely a day has passed since we commenced doing business but what I have stood up at my desk from 8 or 9 o'clock in the morning until 9 o'clock in the evening receiving and examining the papers handed in for record, and this too in a crowd frequently of 20 or 30 persons asking questions at the same time." Congress, again at the urging of Senator Walker, extended the Relief Act for a year, and then extended it again in 1823 and 1824. Although the law was an administrative nightmare, it succeeded in reducing the huge debt that had been run up in the land boom and at the same time kept much of the land in the hands of the original buyers. Several districts in Ohio, Indiana, and Illinois registered forfeitures of over 100,000 acres each, and in the Huntsville district over 400,000 acres were relinquished. Within the first year that the law was in effect, half of the debt in the state of Alabama was wiped off the books. In Alabama and Missouri, in particular, most of those who relinquished land continued to farm it, in hopes of eventually repurchasing it. On May 19, 1826, the *Southern Advocate* would report that, just as Rufus King had predicted, neighbors did not bid against neighbors for their old property—but outside "sharpers" appeared who threatened to bid prices up unless they were paid a bribe. Many farmers regained their land, but some paid the sharpers as much as they paid the government at the new auctions. King, if he saw the article, made no comment: the last of the Founders to hold federal office had retired from the Senate and would die the following April.[11]

What more could—or should—the federal government do? Manufacturing interests wanted higher tariffs, but the failure of the Baldwin Tariff in 1820 dashed their hopes: it passed the House easily but was defeated in the Senate. (A protective tariff would finally be passed by a narrow margin in 1824, over strong southern opposition.) Western states urged internal improvements that might invigorate their economies, but Monroe vetoed a bill to extend the National Road beyond Wheeling in 1822, demonstrating that he, like Madison before him, believed that such federal activity required a constitutional amendment. (He would change his mind in 1824 after two more years of hard times in the West.) There remained the perennially controversial subject of the currency. While many in and out of Congress believed the only hope was a return to hard money, there was also strong support for a re-expansion of paper—perhaps directly by the U.S. Treasury. Thomas Law was an influential English-born resident of Washington, D.C., whose name unfortunately called to mind John Law, the man behind the previous century's infamous Mississippi Bubble. Under a variety of pseudonyms, he published essays in the *National Intelligencer* advocating a nonconvertible national paper currency. (Although the editors of the pro-administration *Intelligencer* publicly disagreed with him, Law was a friend of Gallatin, Crawford, Calhoun, and Adams, and the *Intelligencer* printed his essays on a regular basis.) A few weeks after the Spencer Committee criticized the BUS but recommended no action, Congress passed a resolution calling on the secretary of the treasury to respond to both monetary approaches—hard money and paper—by reporting to the next Congress "such measures as in his opinion may be expected to procure and retain a sufficient quantity of gold and silver coin in the United States, or to supply a circulating medium, in place of specie." Crawford would spend nearly a year putting his Currency Report together.[12]

On the fourth day after the new Congress assembled in December 1819, the House heard from one of its newest members—but one with a long history in government. Charles Pinckney III had been, along with Rufus King, among the youngest delegates to the Constitutional Convention. He had since served briefly in the Senate and then three times been elected governor of South Carolina, but this would be his only term in the House. Pinckney, who claimed to be the author of the Constitution's clause forbidding states to issue paper money and restricting legal tender to gold or silver, surprised his new colleagues by announcing that in one week he "would introduce a bill to be entitled 'An act to establish a circulating medium for the United States, and to sustain the credit thereof.'" Pinckney said he was waiting a week for Congress to receive Crawford's report on the subject.[13]

Pinckney was confused. The treasury report delivered the next week was simply the annual update on revenue and expenditures, amounting to only three pages; Crawford's Currency Report was still not ready. Pinckney never did introduce his bill, the details of which (if he had indeed gotten that far) remain unknown. Crawford's thorough, meticulous response to Congress's directive was finally delivered two months later, on February 12, 1820. Crawford acknowledged that the government's specie reserves were inadequate to make gold or silver a practical circulating currency for the nation, but—after a detailed and sympathetic consideration—he concluded that a government-issued paper currency would do more harm than good: "The evils which are felt in those sections of the union where the distress is most general will not be extensively relieved by the establishment of a national [paper] currency." The "sufferings" produced by the existing financial system, he decided, would have to continue until values settled at their "natural level," and "until this be effected, an abortive attempt, by the substitution of a paper currency, to avert the evils we are suffering, will produce the most distressing consequences."[14]

Nothing more would be heard about federal efforts to relieve the depression. Indiana's lone congressman, Thomas Hendricks, informed his unhappy constituents that Crawford's report was "against the policy of an issue of treasury notes or government paper . . . to arrest the evils we are suffering." Moreover, he continued, "For these evils, public opinion is the best, and perhaps the only effective corrective." But around the country, public opinion was far from united. "The necessities of the times have been fertile of expedients," wrote Hendricks, both "to supply a deficit of currency and to restore credit to the circulating medium of the country." He spoke from personal experience. In Hendricks's home state of Indiana, the State Bank (formerly the Bank of Vincennes) had been issuing notes unredeemable in specie, and the federal government was about to remove its deposits. Rep. Hendricks, along with Sen. James Noble, was an investor in the bank. The bank's insurgent opponents, who would become the leaders of Indiana's Jacksonian Democrats, were insisting on specie redemption or a repeal of the bank's charter, and in the 1820 elections the voters demanded hard money by a wide margin. Other states swung in the opposite direction. John Quincy Adams had already noted with disapproval in his diary: "County meetings have been held in the Western States and in some of the Atlantic States, and petitions for special calls of their Legislatures and of Congress are in circulation, the objects of which is to obtain suspensions of specie payments by law—an execrable device."[15]

Indiana, New York, and Massachusetts revealed strong sentiment for canceling banks' charters if they refused to redeem in specie, and the Pennsylvanian Stephen Simpson demanded, in Duane's *Aurora,* "the total prostration of the *banking* and *funding* system" by the use of nothing but gold and silver coins, but most other states heard growing demands to re-expand currency. One idea was to prop up the notes of nonredeeming banks by devices such as Alabama's legislation that made them acceptable for payment of local taxes and requested—unsuccessfully—that the land offices and the Treasury Department accept them, too; another approach, followed in Tennessee, Kentucky, Missouri, and Illinois, was to create state-owned banks and require that creditors either accept their notes (also nonredeemable) or else wait as long as two years before the state would execute a judgment for debt. In one state after another, relief parties began to organize, advocating one or both of these approaches.[16]

In Tennessee, both of the established factions found themselves elbowed aside by a third group, led by Felix Grundy. Grundy had given up a successful political career in Kentucky to seek his fortune in Tennessee. He had led the failed attempt to bring a BUS branch to the state in 1817; two years later, sensing the public mood, he reversed his field and returned to politics as the leader of an anti-banking reform group made up of debtors. Grundy had no wish for conflict with either of the other factions if he could succeed by cooperating with both. Freshly elected to the Tennessee legislature, he won passage in 1819 of the Endorsement Law. This was a plan that managed to protect both debtors and bankers: the former would receive a two-year stay of any judgments for debt unless their creditors were willing to accept at face value the depreciated notes of the state-chartered banks—one of which was run by the Overton group and one by Jackson's adversary, Andrew Erwin. Governor Joseph McMinn vetoed the Endorsement Act, but the legislature overrode the veto, and the voters elected a new pro-relief governor. Following Crawford's Currency Report, as both the independent Nashville Bank and Erwin's Farmers and Merchants Bank slid toward failure, Grundy went a step further: he proposed a state loan office to issue nonredeemable currency at 6 percent, along with a stay law that would require creditors to accept loan-office notes or wait two years for execution.

One of the few men in middle Tennessee to speak out against Grundy's relief proposals was Andrew Jackson, who compared them to the notorious Mississippi Bubble. Jackson argued that a loan office could hardly be constructive when the hard times were the result of "the large emissions of paper by the banks." He called a public meeting to denounce the plan and sent a hostile "memorial" to the legislatures. The Hero of New Orleans was still the most admired man in Tennessee, but Jackson's meeting and message did not please the state's many debtors; the state senate called his language offensive and tabled his memorial. Then they set up the loan office as a state-owned bank, making only noncommercial loans, with its notes backed by public lands.[17]

The newly elected governor, William Carroll, was no more a friend to banking than Jackson. He declared that the only true remedy for the economic distress was industry and economy on the part of the citizens, but he took no public position on the new state bank. Neither did the state supreme court, although it ruled the stay law unconstitutional in 1821. That year Jackson warned his brother-in-law, John Donelson, "Have nothing to do with the new rags of the state for be assured it will be a reign of immoral rule, and the interests of speculation alone will be consulted during the existence of the new dynasty."[18]

In Pennsylvania, the Raguet committee had recommended a state loan office in 1819, authorized to lend $1.5 million, although Raguet himself would soon shift to a hard-money philosophy. The proposal was backed by Gov. William Findlay's pro-banking New School Republicans but blocked in the House by William J. Duane and his allies, now known as the Old School; in 1820 Findlay became the second governor chased from office in the wake of the Panic. More states, farther west, turned to loan offices and state-owned banks but with little success. Illinois had, like Alabama, failed to raise sufficient capital to open a semi-public bank, so the legislature followed up by converting Jesse Thomas's Bank of Illinois into a completely state-owned institution. Gov. Shadrach Bond vetoed, but as in Tennessee his veto was overridden. The Bank of Illinois began making $1,000 loans in 1821 and Bond too was replaced at the next election, by Edward Coles. Illinois also petitioned the U.S. Treasury, unsuccessfully, to accept the new notes at the land offices. Then, as the notes rapidly depreciated and even state officials refused to accept them at par, the legislature took the embarrassing step of authorizing state auditor's warrants with which to pay their own salaries.[19]

The "county meetings" that Adams decried had begun in Kentucky in the summer of 1819. The resolutions that had passed in Frankfort, and those that echoed them or contradicted them in other counties around the state, all centered around the "scarcity of money" and the question of nonredeemable currency. The controversy over debt relief galvanized the state. Many influential Kentuckians were, like Clay, both debtors and creditors at the same time. A significant part of the establishment agreed with Clay on the sanctity of contracts and looked askance at the behavior of the state's many new banks. Most Kentuckians, however, resented the BUS, which was simultaneously draining specie from Lexington and Louisville and severely restricting its own issue of banknotes at those branches. The rapidly growing Relief Party was itself divided. Some, like Amos Kendall, wanted a return to hard money; more, following Francis Preston Blair, believed the solution lay in expanding paper currency. Both sides agreed that legislative action had to be taken to protect the state's many debtors. The anti-relief conservatives also disagreed among themselves, but they were united in their disapproval of any interference between debtors and creditors and in their opposition to any state-sponsored expansion of currency.

Kentucky's Relief Party won control of the legislature in 1819 and passed a stay law similar to Tennessee's Endorsement Act. It, too, was vetoed by the governor, Gabriel Slaughter; once again, the legislature overrode the veto and Slaughter was replaced by a pro-relief governor, John Adair. In November 1820, despite Kendall's resistance, the pro-relief legislature created the Bank of the Commonwealth—another state-owned bank. Its charter was opposed in the legislature by John Pope; as a director of the Bank of Kentucky, Pope had first promised to redeem notes in specie and then advocated suspension of specie payment at Frankfort; now he reverted to his original stance. When the Bank of the Commonwealth began issuing notes, Pope's Bank of Kentucky refused to accept them and cut back on the issue of its own notes, which it promised to redeem—eventually, but not immediately. The Bank of Kentucky's contraction created even more demand for the paper of the new Bank of the Commonwealth, which quickly issued the $3 million worth of currency authorized by its charter, despite opening with barely $7,000 in capital—money it spent on printing presses, ink, and paper. (Bray Hammond, in *Banks and Politics*, observes that Alexander Hamilton had recommended a ratio between specie reserves and notes of one to five; Kentucky, in Hammond's words, was "stretching it toward a ratio of nothing to infinity.") The notes of this new bank also rapidly depreciated, and within a year they held barely half their value. Still, combined with the state's stay law, they managed to preserve a significant number of debtors from disaster; they also drove the Bank of Kentucky to suspend operations, and by 1822 they were worth so little that the best that could be said about them was that they were not worth counterfeiting.[20]

Both Clay in Kentucky and Jackson in Tennessee stood out against public opinion in opposing debt relief. Kendall, only recently the tutor to the Clay children and now editor of the *Western Argus*, told his former employer, "The Relief Party are very jealous of you. It is important that this jealousy should not break out into public expression and criticism. . . . In this situation I can do much to suppress their jealousy to you." Clay was unable or unwilling to provide the financial support Kendall wanted; he stuck with the BUS, and Kendall turned against first the Relief Party and then Clay, eventually joining the Jackson camp. Jackson's anti-bank sentiments were so well-known that his resistance was soon forgiven by the advocates of relief, who got little good out of the state-owned banks. In the 1824 presidential election each candidate would carry his adopted state, but nationally Jackson's anti-bank views gained him votes, while Clay's association with the BUS cost him.[21]

In the years following 1818 every state west of the Appalachians except Mississippi and Louisiana passed some kind of legislation restricting bank charters, but the problem remained: how were people to pay the debts they had already incurred? Alabama, Tennessee, Indiana, Illinois, Missouri, and Kentucky all created state-owned banks or loan offices to issue currency unbacked by specie. But greater access to depreciated currency could only help those debtors who were able to keep borrowing, and it was no help if creditors refused to accept the notes. Therefore, additional proposals were made in almost every state to preserve property from foreclosures, from sheriff's sales, and from executions of judgments against debtors. Some of these were passed by legislatures but vetoed by governors; in a few cases, it was the governors who took the initiative only to have the legislatures block them; and in many cases, bills were passed and signed into law only to be declared unconstitutional by state courts. Some form of debt relief was made law in twelve states, mostly in the West but including Rhode Island, Vermont, Maryland, and Pennsylvania. Five states—Pennsylvania, Maryland, Ohio, Kentucky, and Indiana—required minimum appraisals to be set by neighbors, below which a debtor's property could not be sold. Cleveland, Ohio, was still only a village of six hundred, but it supported two competing newspapers that disagreed on all important questions. Debt relief was one that would divide almost every western community; the Cleveland *Register* demanded state relief from "rapacious" creditors, but the *Herald* called for the repeal of the minimum appraisal law and was outraged that creditors were obliged to accept such miscellaneous property as watches, dogs, and barrels, at inflated appraisals, or else wait at least six months to collect debts.[22]

Laws staying execution of judgments for debt up to two and a half years on a variety of conditions (usually if creditors refused depreciated banknotes in payment) were passed by eight states: Vermont, Maryland, Kentucky,

Tennessee, Louisiana, Indiana, Illinois, and Missouri (but not Ohio; Rothbard mistakenly says so, and many subsequent writers pass along his error). Almost every state legislature debated debt relief, and laws came close to passing in Delaware, New Jersey, North Carolina, and even that most financially conservative of states, Virginia.[23]

Few states had experienced as much speculation as Missouri, where the expectation of endless immigration had been an article of faith. The state had roughly equal numbers of creditors and debtors, with many Missourians falling into both categories simultaneously. In Missouri, as in Pennsylvania and North Carolina, it was the governor who took the lead in calling for debt relief. Alexander McNair summoned his state legislature into a special session in 1821 to pass a stay law. According to the *Gazette*, legislators hoped that in time both credit and markets would improve, enabling many landowners to reclaim their lost property. The special session reserved from sheriffs' sales for each family one cow, one calf, one bed, a spinning wheel, a loom, and other personal property. Here, as in Kentucky, the Relief Party controlled both executive and legislature—barely. In November, meeting again, they passed further stay laws and a minimum appraisal law, but the margin was close: the laws passed by five votes in the House and two in the Senate. As in Kentucky, the courts ruled them unconstitutional, in 1822.[24]

The legislature not only passed the stay law but created a state loan office as well. It would issue nonconvertible paper money in denominations ranging from fifty cents to ten dollars, receivable for payment of taxes, salaries, auditors' warrants, and certain other debts. Its bills were immediately discounted, but they were popular, and counterfeiting was the sincerest form of flattery: enterprising Missourians managed to redeem $193,647 worth—even though only $184,788 were legally printed. In the 1822 election participation was reduced among those who could not pay tax bills; consequently, the antirelief forces won a majority and repealed the loan office, and in 1830 the U.S. Supreme Court finally ruled it unconstitutional.[25]

When the courts threw out Missouri's laws, the relief movement there collapsed, but when the Kentucky Court of Appeals overturned that state's stay law, the pro-relief legislature voted first to dissolve the court and then to create a new one, appointing Preston Blair as its clerk; when the old court refused to step down, Blair broke into its offices and seized its records. In the decade that followed, Kentucky's pro- and anti-relief factions evolved into the New Court and Old Court parties. Pro-relief (now New Court)

Gov. Joseph Desha was reelected in 1824 by a margin of two to one. In the paradoxical politics of the times, Andrew Jackson—about to be nominated for the presidency by Tennessee's Relief Party—made this comment on the Kentucky relief and court controversies:

> The conduct of Kentucky with regard to the Judiciary is to me the most alarming and flagitious, and augurs (if persisted in) the destruction of our republican government—for let me tell you, that all the rights secured to the citizens under the constitution is [sic] worth nothing, and a mere buble [sic] except guaranteed by an independent and virtuous Judiciary, and shall the Demagogues of Kentucky succeed in destroying that independence, they place the Judiciary in the hands of those designing Demagogues, and the Judiciary will become the mere tools of oppression of the people, and wielded by these men for their wicked purposes.[26]

Less than three weeks later Jackson accepted the Tennessee General Assembly's unanimous nomination to be president of the United States. Grundy, surely the quickest man in Tennessee to recognize a trend, was the legislature's spokesman in securing his acceptance. By 1828 most of Kentucky's Relief Party would abandon their state's favorite son, Henry Clay, tainted by his work for the BUS, and hop on the Jackson bandwagon—including William T. Barry, Jackson's eventual postmaster general, who as the new court's chief justice must be considered one of the primary "Demagogues." Jackson's personal popularity among westerners who clamored for debt relief, paradoxical though it was, proved irresistible to those Kentucky politicians whom historian Charles G. Sellers has dubbed "Jackson Men with Feet of Clay."[27]

The Northwest, which would turn its back on Clay and give all its electoral votes to Jackson in 1828 and 1832, had long supported direct debtor relief. Ohio had had a minimum appraisal law on the books at statehood in 1803. During the sixteen years that followed, millions of acres there had been purchased from the federal government, and—thanks to congressional extensions—half of the population still owed payments. Illinois had a stay law since 1813 requiring creditors to accept notes of Illinois banks at par; in 1821, after both Illinois banks suspended specie payment, the law was revised to include the new state-owned bank, and all pending executions for debt were postponed for nine months. The 1821 law also granted a right of replevy: owners could reclaim property if they were able to make full payment within three years. In Indiana, the legislature passed a similar stay law (including exemptions of some personal property) in 1819, over a single dissenting vote, and added minimum appraisal laws in 1820 and 1821 that remained in force until 1824.[28]

The relief movement was by no means limited to the West, but it met with more resistance in the East. Although Virginia planters had always struggled with debt, where banking and money policy were concerned there was no more conservative state south of New England. Gov. James Preston addressed the legislators on December 6, 1819: the debtors' troubles, he insisted, were caused by "imprudence, extravagance, love of ease, and inordinate desire to grow rich quickly"; his solution was a return to industry and economy. The next month, Rep. Thomas Miller told the General Assembly that the fault lay with the banks, who had been responsible for the rise in prices when they expanded credit and who were now to blame for the falling prices when they contracted. Miller told his colleagues, most of whom were in debt themselves, that "extravagance" and laziness were not the causes; the problem was that planters had borrowed when tobacco was at twelve dollars and wheat at two dollars but were repaying their debts with tobacco at five dollars and wheat at one dollar—and the price of imported woolens, sugar, and coffee unchanged or even rising. In consequence, they now risked losing their farms. Minimum appraisal laws had been enacted by the House of Burgesses from time to time during the colonial years; Miller called for one in January 1820, which would have been Virginia's first since independence. His bill was defeated by a substantial margin in February; a stay law came much closer in 1821, but still went down in a vote of eighty-four to ninety-five. Virginia would continue its conservative policies. So would North Carolina, where it was the governor, John Branch, who urged the legislature to pass stay and minimum appraisal laws. This they declined to do, with an exception for former Cherokee lands purchased from the state.[29]

Maryland was a different story. There the economy had begun to decline in 1816, when the fledgling textile industry was badly hurt by cheap imports. In Baltimore, one of the chief exporting cities, the 1817 decline in wheat sales abroad came on top of the losses by importers. Those factors, coupled with a rash of unwise speculation in the midst of the banking crisis, led to a shocking series of bankruptcies in 1819. The demand for debtor relief was strong enough that the state first abolished debtors' prison and then followed with a stay law—plus exemption from forced sale for household goods up to fifty dollars.[30]

In New York, Gov. DeWitt Clinton had already asked the legislature to abolish imprisonment for debt; in 1817 they did do so in cases amounting to less than twenty-five dollars, but chose to retain prison time for failure to pay larger sums. Pennsylvania (alone) spared all women debtors, and by 1823 it had joined New York, Vermont, and New Hampshire in ending imprisonment for petty debts. Kentucky, Ohio, and North Carolina waived jail for all debtors who turned over their property to creditors, and the new states of Indiana, Mississippi, Alabama, and Illinois included similar provisions in their constitutions, although they were prevented by *Crowninshield* from discharging debts. Ferris Pell, who would later be prosecuted not for debt but for fraud, wrote in 1819, "Fraud is a crime. And imprudence may be so excessive, as to justify suspicion of fraud, and inquiry by a competent tribunal. But neither imprudence that is not fraudulent, nor misfortune, is a crime, and when the law regards and punishes them as such, the law becomes criminal itself."[31]

Pennsylvania was another state where the governor advocated more debtor relief than the legislature was first inclined to grant. Although the economy had been struggling since the end of the war, battling factions could not agree on a course of action. In 1818 Governor Findlay's proposed minimum appraisal law was rejected; William J. Duane warned that such a law would interfere with the revival of "credit or confidence." Condy Raguet's Senate committee also rejected direct debt relief as both impractical to enforce and an infringement of the sanctity of contract, although the committee did recommend establishing a loan office. (Findlay's New School administration endorsed that idea, but Duane and the anti-bank Old School faction blocked it.) While advocates of relief were uniting politically in other states, they could not find common ground in fractious Pennsylvania; in the election of 1820 Philadelphia voters could choose among a conservative Federalist, a moderate Federalist, an Old School Republican, a New School Republican, and a baffling variety of minor party candidates. To Nicholas Biddle, the unsuccessful New School candidate for Congress in 1818 and 1820, it was "a perfect chaos of small factions." By 1821, however, times were hard enough that the legislature was ready at last to come together to ease the laws on execution of debt, and Pennsylvania finally passed a minimum appraisal law.[32]

In Federalist New England, the state governments of Massachusetts, Connecticut, and New Hampshire chose not to interfere in their citizens' financial difficulties. Although the case of Hannah Crispy made imprisonment for debt controversial in Boston, no New England state ended the practice until Vermont in 1830 and Connecticut in 1837. Rhode Island law had essentially treated bank debtors as guilty if accused, requiring immediate debt execution when a bank gave notice, with no provision for a hearing. (Banks, however, were entitled to a trial if *they* were accused of failing to pay a debt.) When textile mills around the state began closing, the summary bank process law was repealed in late 1818. Vermont stood out from the rest of the region. The one New England state without a seaport, its economy had long depended on farming (and smuggling across the Canadian border), and after the string of abnormally cold years, farmers were in debt. Vermont had become the first New England state with a Republican-majority legislature in 1812; the popularly elected House of Representatives voted for stay laws in 1818 and 1820, but they were defeated in the more conservative Senate, where representation (as in Massachusetts) reflected property value rather than population. But the depression dragged on there, and a stay law was finally passed in 1822. The circuit court quickly declared it unconstitutional.[33]

Of the debt-relief laws passed by the various states, most existed only briefly, and it is hard to find a national political figure who endorsed them. Clay, Adams, Calhoun, and Jackson condemned stay laws; Benton was not yet a national figure, but he was in the process of evolving, becoming a hard-money man and turning against loan offices like Missouri's at the same time that he shifted from support of slavery to its opposition. Crawford disapproved of debtor relief in general, but he blamed the hard times at least as much on a plague of local banks as on indolence or extravagance, and he was not sorry to see legislation that might bring an end to some of them. In his 1820 Treasury Report he paraphrased what he had told Cheves nearly a year earlier: "If, in affording a shield to the debtor, against the legal demand of his creditor, the axe shall be applied to the root of the evil, by the annihilation of banks where they ought never to have existed"—that is, "in the small inland towns and villages"—then he could see a silver lining: "The interference however doubtful in point of policy or principle, may, eventually, be productive of more good than evil." In reality, before debtor relief laws had appeared in very many states, most of the banks Crawford had in mind were closing or had already failed. And among the banks that still remained to fall victim to stay laws or loan offices were such relatively responsible institutions as the Bank of Missouri, the Bank of Tennessee, and the Bank of Kentucky.[34]

The federal government made public land laws, and the states—within limits set by the courts—had control over banking and the execution of debt; that much was certain, although there was intense disagreement about which policies should be adopted. When it came to individuals who were left completely destitute by the depression—the unemployed, the homeless, and those who had lost everything—a once-clear responsibility was quickly becoming less so. As a rule, states were not inclined to accept the burden. New York, with significant portions of both its revenues and its poor coming from abroad, had been atypical; from 1807 to 1817 "one third of the auction duties were applied to the support of the foreign [i.e., immigrant] poor, varying from $12,000 to $20,000 annually. . . . In support of the Common Poor, nothing." But in 1817 the state adopted a new law under which that revenue "was withdrawn for the purpose of being applied to the construction of canals"—DeWitt Clinton's great project—"and an annual payment of $10,000 substituted." The following year, Clinton's annual message to the legislature recommended stopping all contributions entirely.[35]

Poverty had always been a fact of life; Matthew 26:11 was everywhere taken for granted: "The poor you will always have with you." Charity was a virtue enjoined upon all churchgoers, but it had also been a traditional obligation of towns and cities—the immediate community—rather than the more distant state. However, the challenges to the economy after the War of 1812 brought an increased demand for aid that taxed municipal resources. By 1817 over 15,000 people in New York City—more than one in eight residents—required some sort of public or private charitable relief. The almshouse population had been 1,043 in 1816; that number then increased by half the next year and reached 1,896 residents by 1820. The debtors' prison held 95 in 1816 and 300 only a year later. By 1820 there were 423 inmates, and the city's Common Council joined the Humane Society to petition the state to end imprisonment for debt.[36]

In 1817, a year of worsening depression in New York, the Society for the Prevention of Pauperism was founded; the Rev. John Stanford would be the director for its six-year existence. In his fourth annual report in 1821, Stanford stated that 10,000 people in the city were completely destitute and another 12,000 to 13,000 received some sort of charitable assistance, at a time when New York City's population was 120,000. The New York *Advertiser* declared, "Under the severe and universal pressure every man feels, many suffer and all are anxious to obtain relief." The newspaper reminded readers that it was "the responsibility of every man to exert himself as far as lies within his power to quiet public distress and to assist in carrying his friends and neighbors through the days of depression."[37]

That feeling that all were in this together would not last; it was already eroding even as the *Advertiser* asserted the civic duty to assist in alleviating the distress that "every man feels." By 1819 the New York Common Council was opposed to the practice of distributing public charity to any but the inmates of the almshouse, but the council was finding the numbers of the poor far greater than jail or almshouse could handle; reluctantly it approved grants to the Humane Society for the next three years to provide food, purchased at a reduced price through the almshouse, for the "outdoor" poor. The Humane Society of New York City had been founded shortly after the Revolution. (The modern Humane Society of New York, an animal welfare group, dates to 1904 and is unrelated.) Originally focused on rescuing debtors from prison, the society inspired numerous similar groups at first, but many of them closed down operations in the years following 1819, offering reasons like those given by the Brooklyn Humane Society; its directors announced that they had become "convinced by painful experience that institutions of this nature have a direct tendency to beget, among a large portion of their fellow citizens, habits of imprudence, indolence, dissipation, and consequent pauperism." Public opinion was beginning to blame the poor for their own poverty.[38]

The Humane Society did keep up its soup kitchens, even as other aid was cut back. Soup, often supplied by the city's butchers, was a popular way to stretch donations; in 1819 Baltimore had no fewer than twelve locations at which it was dispensed, and Philadelphia provided every pauper a pint per day. In contrast to New York and Pennsylvania, where outdoor aid was being reduced or eliminated, the mean numbers receiving outdoor relief in Virginia counties and cities increased by 4 percent between 1816 and 1821 and then by another 15 percent as the agricultural depression lingered until 1828. Economic historian Clyde Haulman believes that Virginia's compassion and generosity "went well beyond that shown by the middle Atlantic states," and "during the 1820's support for the poor across the state was at odds with the pattern of relief found in the Northeast and along the mid-Atlantic coast." Even as "other areas of the country responded to the crisis by tightening their belts . . . per-capita spending on the poor increased in Virginia." Demands for relief were highest in the Tidewater area of the state, a region that was, like New York City, dependent on the export trade in commodities—tobacco in particular.[39]

In the deep south, the Natchez Hospital, a semi-public institution created in 1805 to care for the poor, was swamped by demand and ran out of funds by the end of 1819; it was unable to reopen for more than a year. The city of New Orleans had been in the habit of allotting fifty dollars per month to the poor before 1817; in the twelve months of 1821 it spent a total of $3,000, plus sixty cords of wood for winter heating and cooking. A particular motive for this generosity is suggested by historian Barbara Bellows:

> The leitmotif of the Southern public relief system was to give definition to the role of the white laborer in the urban economy. Even in indigence and unemployment, a distinction had to be made between the white hireling and the black slave if the grand illusion of white supremacy was not to be eroded at its base. . . . Fear of strangers, vagrants, and vagabonds better describes the antipathy aimed at some indigents of the city, rather than horror at their personal conduct.

In Charleston, where there had long been a large number of free African Americans, free people of color had organized their own charitable societies as early as 1790, when mixed-race refugees from St. Domingue formed the Brown Fellowship Society. Observing "complexional distinctions within that caste," the Society of the Free Dark Men of Color was created the following year; by 1813 there were three more organizations providing aid to "impoverished and orphaned free black children." All of these gradually closed after Denmark Vesey's planned slave rebellion was exposed in 1822, as Charleston cracked down on free blacks in general.[40]

Initially, the sense of civic duty reinforced religious teachings to help neighbors in need, but towns and cities had never experienced such high demand or a need that lasted so long. As both financial resources and morale were strained, it was a natural reaction in both North and South to turn against "the other"—strangers, vagrants, and of course immigrants. The dubious assertion of New York's Mayor Cadwallader Colden was quoted in the *Second Annual Report* of the Society for the Prevention of Pauperism: "The shipment of the poor to the United States is a means of getting rid of them, which has been adopted by a public authority in several parts of Europe." Colden called on the state government to prohibit landing ships' passengers without first posting bond that they would not become public charges; otherwise, "We would be overwhelmed with the poor and miserable of all Europe."[41]

Throughout 1819 newspapers published accounts of political and economic upheaval in England that threatened to send waves of emigration to the

United States. As unsold exports piled up, English cotton mills—which had already reduced their purchases of American cotton—were finally laying off workers. In June Niles reported that "the manufacturing districts are dreadfully distressed. At Leicester, within ten days, it is said that 5000 persons were thrown out of employ—*though the price of cotton was expected to decline further.* . . . It appears that 11,000 persons emigrated to America from [Belfast] last season, amongst whom were upwards of *seven hundred families.*" In August, Niles reported "alarming intelligence from Leeds" of worker unrest and declared that 35,000 people had gathered at Glasgow to petition for means to emigrate to North America.[42]

There is no question that emigration to America was suddenly interesting in Great Britain after peace was restored in 1815. The great surge from Ireland was still decades in the future, but English capitalists were already employing agents to buy up both farmland and urban real estate in the United States. They had laid out whole towns in the Northwest like Wanbrough and Albion in the western Illinois region that was becoming known as English Prairie, and James Flint's letters were aimed squarely at prospective English and Scottish emigrants. However, contrary to the fears of Mayor Colden, they targeted farmers, artisans, and members of the middle class—the poor, after all, lacked resources to buy the lots that were being offered for sale by English promoters like Morris Birkbeck and George Flower. But by the spring of 1819, Flint was urging caution, and another British traveler, Emanuel Howitt, was actively discouraging Britons from coming to America: "The voice of disappointment will certainly have arisen above that of wild and romantic adventure and made itself heard. Such is the present state of tidings here, that neither farmers nor mechanics can succeed. The vast number of sheriff's sales are a sufficient proof. . . . This is definitely not the time for emigration."[43]

The anonymous British author of *Things As They Are, or America in 1819* sailed back to Liverpool from New York on board the ship *Magnet*, which carried 164 returning emigrants: "a pretty striking proof of the situation of America." He grimly declared, "As many as can get back to England, although they know that they are quitting starvation to encounter misery and oppression, are coming [back] again." Others who chose to remain in New York often sought assistance from the British consul, James Buchanan, who offered them land grants in Canada. (Neither the future president nor the Baltimore merchant, this Buchanan was an Ulster Scot.) Financial aid to recent Irish immigrants from the Friendly Sons of St. Patrick doubled between March 1819 and March 1820.[44]

Whether immigrant or native, the poor were encountering more and more reluctance to offer public support unless they accepted incarceration at a workhouse or poor farm. Josiah Quincy published a report to the Massachusetts General Court, warning against any "provision for the poor, by supplies or money, at their own houses. The result of the experience of England is unequivocally stated to be, that supplies were expended by the men, in ale, and by the women for tea and sugar; that when given in articles of food and clothing, they were sold to obtain luxuries." But Quincy was also uncomfortable with the alternative of "pauper auctions," a phenomenon that had begun to appear, especially in New England, in the late eighteenth century. Communities would invite private individuals to bid for the opportunity to take in the impoverished in return for their involuntary labor. New Hampshire's Gov. William Plumer called this "the most eligible and cheapest method," and two towns in New York reported that their poor relief costs dropped by one-half to two-thirds when they switched from outdoor relief to pauper auctions, but in 1823 New York's Secretary of State John Van Ness Yates blamed the system for a number of deaths at the hands of negligent "caretakers." Both auctions and the involuntary indenture of children were decried by critics as "private enterprise in human stock," but both continued.[45]

Poor relief was becoming a subject of intense interest to the legislatures of Massachusetts and New York as well as city governments from Philadelphia to Petersburg, Virginia. While costs were always a primary concern, the poor were beginning to be described as a social problem, a potential source of civil disturbance, and the proper objects of moral reformation. Government bodies were eager to reduce their expenses for the poor, but at the same time they wanted to maintain control over them. Again and again the decision was to eliminate outdoor relief or any assistance that was given to individuals or families who were not being kept in poorhouses—renamed "workhouses"— with the expectation that the requirement of labor (and the administration of moral education) would inspire the unemployed to find work. In Massachusetts, the 1821 Quincy Report recommended terminating all poor relief "except on condition of admission into public institutions"; in 1823 New York's Yates Report went one step further, suggesting that the able-bodied poor between the ages of eighteen and fifty should receive no public assistance under any circumstances, and that the old, the young, and the infirm should be restricted to institutional relief—the county poorhouse.[46]

These policies were eagerly adopted in Mid-Atlantic states, where the unemployed were numerous, and in New England, where the Puritan tradition was strong. Southern states, like Virginia, had so far been more flexible and in many ways more compassionate. Now, as budgets were strained, pressures for reform were appearing in the South, too. In Petersburg the bill for poor relief in 1820 to 1823 had reached $5,000 per year, three times the former expenditure, and the city concluded that the proper response was to be more severe. In 1823, after Massachusetts but ahead of New York, Petersburg put an end to outdoor relief. The next year the city council made the additional, predictable decision, "that the Poorhouse establishment of this town be hereafter considered & used as a Workhouse."[47]

Haulman, after his close examination of the Panic in Virginia, believes that eventually "the Panic and its aftermath destroyed the sense of community consensus that had been so prevalent in the 1780's and 1790's among the elite" of Richmond and Petersburg, regarding responsibility for the collective welfare. But the Petersburg council was satisfied with its parsimony. By refusing to help "outpaupers," they reduced costs dramatically; many of the poor, it turned out, would rather take their chances than give up their freedom or dignity and enter the poorhouse. By 1825, just two years after the policy was adopted, expenditures on poor relief (with little help from the painfully slow improvement in the economy) were down to one-third what they had been in 1823.[48]

Philadelphia found the same satisfactory effect of ending outdoor relief. Overall expenditures declined as the economy there improved, but real expenditures per recipient also decreased more than 20 percent between 1820 and 1829. In New York, where the numbers of desperate poor increased by over 22 percent between 1819 and 1822, poor taxes per one thousand of population declined at the same time by 26 percent in New York City and by 21 percent in the rest of the state. And in Rhode Island, where the number of paupers was also rising sharply with mill unemployment, the Newport Asylum cut expenditures by one-third from 1819 to 1820 and continued to cut them through 1824.[49]

The line between rationalization and sincere principle is a fine one at best, but there was a new belief taking hold in the country. "In truth, however unamiable or unfeeling the declaration may appear," said the New York *American*, "it is nevertheless our conviction that all purely charitable institutions except hospitals for the insane, tend to aggravate evils which it is their purpose to relieve." The rationalist eighteenth century had given birth to organizations like one in South Carolina, founded in 1764 to relieve "every poor person without distinction," and Philadelphia's Society for Inoculation of the Poor Gratis (1774), and the Humane Society of New York City in the 1780s; in the new republican nineteenth century, the conviction that anyone could succeed through hard work and self-discipline had its inevitable corollary: that failure must be (as state governors now declared from Virginia to Tennessee to New York) the result of laziness and dissolution.[50]

When public spending on relief decreased, private and religious philanthropies were left to fill in. During the bitterly cold January of 1821, the mayor's office in New York—now on record against funding outdoor relief—received $2,553 from the city's churches to supply the city's poor with winter fuel. The Roman Catholic Asylum in Manhattan had taken in five orphans in 1817; in 1819 it was caring for twenty-eight. Across the country hundreds of evangelical benevolent organizations combined monetary with spiritual support for children, women, and the infirm; they included such very specialized charities as the Protestant Half Orphan Society, the Ladies Association for the Benefit of Gentlewomen of Good Family Reduced in Fortune Below the State of Comfort to Which They Have Been Accustomed, and the National Truss Society for the Ruptured Poor. Other benefactors of the poor appeared from decidedly secular directions. In Virginia, the Petersburg Benevolent Mechanic Association was founded with the stated objective of helping "distressed widows and orphans" who did *not* live in the poorhouse. Ronald G. Walters, in *America's Reformers 1815–1860*, places such workingmen's organizations, providing aid for the families of artisans and skilled laborers, "at the opposite extreme from Protestant missionary activities." While many of these groups questioned the effectiveness of religion as a means of social change, the leaders of the Mechanics Union of Trade Associations, the first citywide journeymen's organization in Philadelphia, were members of the Universalist Church, which denied that man was inherently sinful or needed conversion to escape suffering in this life or damnation in the next. That was a long way from the evangelical perspective of the Second Great Awakening. Workingmen's organizations sometimes entered into direct conflict with the evangelical movement, especially when the latter insisted that individual sin was the entire explanation of workers' distress. A writer in the Philadelphia *Mechanics' Free Press* objected indignantly, "When you have complained of oppression, they have told you such was the dispensation of Providence, and you must be obedient."[51]

Both municipalities and private philanthropies supported thousands left destitute by the Panic of 1819, and they shared the same ambiguous attitude toward their beneficiaries. Ohio's Gov. Thomas Worthington urged—unsuccessfully—that additional poorhouses open in his state; more typical was New York's Gov. DeWitt Clinton, who told his legislature, "Pauperism increases with the augmentation of the funds applied to its relief. The fruits of industry are appropriated to the wants of idleness; a laborious man is taxed for the support of an idle beggar." His legislature agreed and in the next session passed a resolution against any public aid to the poor, maintaining that "once on the public bounty" the poor would "spurn the industry of their ancestors." They were riding a new wave of popular conviction that would recur in the tales of welfare queens in Cadillacs that became the political currency of the 1980s and 1990s; in 1996, 65 percent of those surveyed said the worst thing about welfare was not the cost but that "it encourages people to adopt the wrong lifestyle and values." In 1823 the Society for the Prevention of Pauperism, only six years old, reorganized as the Society for the Reformation of Juvenile Delinquents. Groups that had seen their mission as feeding or housing the poor were changing their focus to the promotion of personal habits of frugality and moral virtue. Matthew Carey, still fighting against Philadelphia's abolition of outdoor poor relief, was a lonely voice from the pre-Panic past: "Many citizens entertain an idea that in the present state of society in this city, every person able and willing to work may procure employment; that all those who are thus employed, may earn a decent and comfortable support; and that the whole, or at least the chief part of the distress of the poor, arises from idleness, dissipation, and worthlessness." Nothing, he argued, could be further from the truth. Very few—other than the poor themselves—publicly agreed.[52]

The successful termination of the War of 1812, followed by unprecedented economic activity, had reinforced the conviction that America was uniquely favored by God. A heightened sense of civil religion encouraged the old Puritan belief that the virtuous would be rewarded in this life—a conviction expressed in John Adams's rhetorical question to Jefferson, "Will you tell me how to prevent riches from becoming the effects of temperance and industry?" Along with that conviction came the belief that the inverse was also true, that poverty was the punishment for moral weakness. Ronald Walters finds a turn away from charity following the next Panic in 1837: "Prompted by their own financial difficulties and by rising fear of disorder from the lower classes, many middle class people withdrew from programs to aid the needy. The ranks of paupers swelled at the very moment sympathy and aid for them disappeared." But this turn had already begun following the earlier Panic of 1819. It simply recurred with the next depression, and with each one that followed—through the Great Depression of the 1930s. The certainty that only the undeserving were poor made it easy for Treasury Secretary Andrew Mellon to encourage Herbert Hoover to "liquidate labor . . . liquidate the farmers"—advice that shocked the Quaker president and would be mocked in the 1939 film *The Wizard of Oz*: after learning that Dorothy has melted the Wicked Witch with a bucket of water, the Wizard responds, "You liquidated her, eh?"[53]

Mellon also assured Hoover that the Depression would have a beneficial effect on people's behavior: "High costs of living will come down. People will work harder, live a more moral life." This moralization of economic disaster also dates from the Panic of 1819. Taken aback by their experience after 1819, Americans were reversing the previously accepted understanding: namely, that the community should take responsibility when its members suffered adversity. Business failures, which had not long since been seen as an acknowledged risk from which so many successful entrepreneurs had recovered, were now blamed on a lack of those character traits that ensured success: self-discipline, perseverance, and hard work. Poverty, like insolvency, was increasingly blamed on personal habits rather than social and economic conditions. Just before shifting its attention to juvenile delinquency, the Society for the Prevention of Poverty declared that "intemperance, ignorance, and idleness are the prolific parents of pauperism and that every exertion should be made to exterminate those dangerous vices by inculcating religion, morality, sobriety, and industry . . . among the indigent and laboring people."[54]

The older Calvinist doctrine of predestination could still be heard in the remarks of the Rev. Charles Burroughs, speaking at the dedication of the new poorhouse in Portsmouth, New Hampshire. He saw a sharp line between honest poverty, "an unavoidable evil . . . in the wise and gracious Providence of God," and undeserving pauperism, "the consequence of willful error, of shameful indolence, of vicious habits. It is a misery of human creation, the pernicious work of man, the lamentable consequence of bad principles and morals." Those for whom God had ordained poverty might still deserve charity, even if those who had brought poverty upon themselves did not. However, a different perspective was growing more and more influential in American popular religion: an individualistic ideology promoted by the revivalism of the Second Great Awakening that rejected Calvinism and emphasized personal responsibility for seeking salvation—and avoiding poverty. The section of western New York that had lately boomed and then "busted" became known as the "Burned-Over District" after the continuous revivals there that left few residents unconverted. During the five years after hard times began in 1816, more towns in New York held revivals—and larger numbers joined churches—than in any previous period. The distinction between the deserving and undeserving poor began to evaporate if poverty, like damnation, could be avoided by a conversion of the heart. Soon, contrary to republican tradition, poverty was no longer "a corporate moral obligation but an individual moral deficiency. Simply put, poor people lacked spiritual and moral direction."[55]

In Southern cities as well, the change in attitude toward the poor seemed to be associated with the spread of the Second Great Awakening. Suzanne Lebsock, author of *The Free Women of Petersburg*, says,

> We do know that organized benevolence preceded the revivals. . . . By 1821 a Dorcas society [of the town women] had gathered to aid the poor. Then came the revival. In 1822 Methodists and Presbyterians together succeeded in stirring up Petersburg's first dramatic religious awakening [after which] there were indeed new indications that a substantial segment of the townspeople supported sterner standards.[56]

The conjunction of the Panic of 1819 and the Second Great Awakening transformed attitudes toward charity for more than a century to come, but their combined impact was not limited to poor relief. The historians Lois Banner and Martin Wiener describe an increased interest on the part of evangelical Christians in "social control" over a wide range of activities. The Hicksite separatists, who split the Society of Friends, followed Elias Hicks in the 1820s in denouncing the evils of banks, the Erie Canal, and politics; conversely, the Second Great Awakening also led others to embrace political action for religious ends. The leading historian of the Whig Party, Michael Holt, locates that party's origins in the moralization of financial success or failure that appeared after the Panic of 1819: "The majority of the middle and upper classes in rural areas, small towns, and large cities supported the Whigs—especially in relatively prosperous areas involved in the production and exchange of goods for sale. . . . Whigs portrayed themselves as the party of probity, respectability, morality, and reason." Speaking the language that the evangelical middle class had begun applying to the undeserving poor, Whigs would characterize Democrats as "lawless and lazy drunkards, a contemptible and dangerous rabble." Democrats, in turn, would describe Whigs as "bigoted and self-righteous religious fanatics intent on imposing their ethical values on others."[57]

These charges and countercharges became standard political rhetoric in the campaigns of Jackson, Clay, Van Buren, and Harrison, but they were first heard before either the Whig or the Democratic Party had declared itself. During the depression years from 1818 to 1821 working men and small farmers, at odds with the politically dominant merchants, manufacturers, and bankers, forced constitutional conventions in Connecticut, Massachusetts, and New York. (The same phenomenon would be repeated following the Panic of 1837 in other states.) Between 1790 and 1820, the prerequisite of property ownership for voting rights had been abandoned in the constitutions of fourteen states. In 1821 reformers at the Massachusetts convention demanded a broader franchise there too. Conservatives pushed back by raising the specter of armies of paupers led to the polls by the caretakers of the poorhouses. Josiah Quincy, who had just delivered his report on pauperism to the legislature, now told the convention that "extreme poverty—that is pauperism—is inconsistent with independence." He and his supporters maintained that by accepting public assistance, the poor "made a voluntary surrender of their liberties" and were no longer free men in the sense that voting required.[58]

Quincy was apparently oblivious to the paradox that he had just denied financial aid to paupers because they had chosen poverty of their own free will but wished now to deny them the vote because, citing the British legal authority William Blackstone, paupers "had no will of their own." Alexander Keyssar, in *The Right to Vote*, remarks on "the almost obsessive incantation of Blackstone's phrase" at the different states' constitutional conventions. He also points out the inconsistency when Josiah Quincy and John Adams (his ally on this question) insisted that paupers "should not vote because they would threaten the interests of property—that is, that they would have *too much* will of their own. . . . The well-to-do feared not that the poor would have no will of their own but precisely the opposite."[59]

The influence of hard times on the new fear of paupers' voting is evident from the dates that different states moved specifically to disenfranchise the poor. Immediately after the Revolution most states still retained property requirements for voting, but only New Hampshire, in 1792, specifically excluded paupers. Then, gradually, property requirements began to be dropped. But in the years of economic turmoil between 1810 and 1831, following the stress of the embargo and running through the Panic and its aftermath, South Carolina, Maine, Massachusetts, Virginia, and Delaware all decided that good government required that the poor be explicitly banned from voting. No other states would then act until the next Panic and depression arrived at the end of the 1830s, when Rhode Island, New Jersey, and Louisiana also singled out paupers for exclusion. The fear subsided—and other crises distracted—until the Panic of 1873, after which the southern states of Arkansas and Texas excluded paupers, apparently in an effort to keep some freed slaves from voting. (Several southern states exempted Confederate veterans from voting restrictions.) Only after the Panic of 1893 did poll taxes become standard across the South, effectively excluding the poor without naming them through the mid-twentieth century.[60]

John Quincy Adams's formula of "time and patience" was not to be a lasting answer—in less than twenty years a second panic threw the country into depression and inspired the same debates again. By then there was no more Bank of the United States—its charter was allowed to expire in 1836—and the Van Buren administration would be the scapegoat. Once again banks suspended specie redemption and then failed. States that had not taken legislative action after the first panic did so this time: Alabama, Illinois, and Virginia passed stay laws, and minimum appraisal laws were revived in Ohio, Indiana, Illinois, Michigan, and Mississippi. And once again, courts overturned them. People again went to prison for debt in most states.[61]

The Civil War would finally bring federally issued paper money, but the public still demanded its convertibility into specie until the gold standard was abandoned during the Great Depression in 1933 and paper dollars finally ceased to be exchangeable for silver in 1968. Congress created a Federal Reserve system in 1913 and finally produced a series of federal bankruptcy laws, beginning in 1841 with frequent revisions after that. Nothing, however, could prevent recurring panics, depressions, or recessions. Easy credit could still inflate a speculative bubble in the first decade of the twenty-first century just as it did in the second decade of the nineteenth century.

While some habits continued unchanged after 1819, there were others that could not survive it. Civic and religious reactions to the Panic of 1819 eroded the eighteenth-century tradition of community responsibility for the poor, cutting back poor relief in general and ending outdoor relief entirely for a century to come. The new hostility toward the poor was the beginning of a long-lasting trend. In the view of the social historian Stanley Katz, "It is only a slight exaggeration to say that the core of most welfare reform in America since the early nineteenth century has been a war on the able bodied poor: an attempt to define, locate, and purge them from the rolls of relief"—and from the voting rolls, as well. More than a century after America's first great depression put this trend in motion, it still permeated public attitudes during America's greatest depression. Harry Hopkins, Franklin D. Roosevelt's right-hand man, was struck by the persistence of it even in the relief agencies of the New Deal. "Under the philosophy of this ancient practice," he wrote in 1936, the able-bodied pauper was presumed to be "in some way morally deficient. . . . Every help which was given him was to be given in a way to intensify his sense of shame."[62]

The redefinition of poverty as moral failure that began with the Panic of 1819 was so successful that it convinced the poor themselves. In his history of the Depression years, *Freedom from Fear*, Douglas Kennedy writes, "Social investigators in the 1930's repeatedly encountered feelings of guilt and self-recrimination among the unemployed, despite the transparent reality that their plight owed to a systemic economic breakdown. . . . In a culture that ascribed all success to individual striving, it seemed to follow axiomatically that failure was due to individual inadequacy."[63]

THE POLITICS OF CORRUPTION
AND THE CORRUPTION OF POLITICS

For a nation struggling to cope with economic catastrophe, the first instinct was to point fingers and the second instinct was to look for solutions; who was to blame, and what could be done? Perhaps the lazy and improvident deserved to suffer for their moral failures, but there were also the greedy and the ruthless who seemed able to manipulate events: bankers, speculators, and politicians. Corrupt individuals might be pursued through criminal prosecution, but what about a political system that invited corruption? Victims of the Panic looked to their legislatures for relief, but their faith in their elected officials had been shaken. Lawmakers who took payoffs and conferred special favors on their friends were not the ones to restore the national virtue. People who had lost their own investments in the Panic of 1819 were inclined to blame the shadowy figures who seemed to manipulate the economy, unrestrained by law or morality—bank directors, land speculators, or even the secretary of the U.S. Treasury. To the western farmers, the laid-off mill hands, and the many clerks, artisans, and mechanics who lost their jobs, it was clear that they had done nothing to deserve their fates and could do nothing to redress the wrongs they had suffered—unless they demanded a role in the political process.

It was a fundamental principle of Jeffersonian republicanism that governments derived their just powers from the consent of the governed. Government had to be changed in order to be purified, and government could only be changed by the electorate. In state after state, Americans began to demand a broader-based politics, and to achieve the necessary change they were willing to accept a more combative, divisive partisanship. Thanks to the Panic of 1819, the Era of Good Feeling was ending as soon as it began.[1]

If legislatures were giving the newly chartered banks a license to print money, it was inevitable that money would find its way back to the legislatures.

By 1819, in addition to growing charges of corruption, state representatives faced outrage if they passed debtor relief and outrage if they did not. Governors and their administrations changed, but many citizens chafed at how little difference it seemed to make. After Pennsylvania's Governor Findlay was defeated by Duane's reformers in 1821 the legislature sent him straight to the U.S. Senate. DeWitt Clinton was governor of New York from 1817 to 1822; at the end of his term the New York *Statesman* complained, "There has been no accountability in our public agents from the highest to the lowest," but Clinton was reelected in 1825 and remained in office until his death in 1828. John Eaton's pseudonymous *Letters of Wyoming*, promoting Andrew Jackson's presidential campaign in 1824, gave voice to popular disgust with the nation's political morality: "We are not as we once were . . . virtue is on the wane." Eaton, along with much of the country, was expanding the target from financial to political immorality, railing at "intrigue," "management," and "corruption" in the Monroe administration. If the government of a virtuous people was corrupt, the only answer was for the people to take over the government. "Rotation in office" became one of the popular demands of the reformers.[2]

Jefferson had declared the election of 1800 to be the inception of a republican revolution, but in the next two decades revolution settled into routine. At the presidential level, the first four decades in the United States were a period of stunted political development, and the aging revolutionary generation maintained an exclusive hold on the nation's highest office. By 1816 James Monroe was a visible anachronism, wearing knee breeches and a three-cornered hat to his inauguration. Yet Monroe was reelected in 1820 with only a single dissenting electoral vote, despite his seeming indifference to the economic crisis—evidence that political leadership was distant from the lives of everyday people. Barely a hundred thousand popular votes were cast that year by a nation of over nine million. Very few Americans voted at all in the early nineteenth century, and fewer still voted for the president. Presidential electors might be chosen by the legislature or the voters, with most states going back and forth. Between 1789 and 1824, only Maryland and Virginia held a popular vote for electors in all ten presidential elections, while New York, Delaware, and South Carolina left the choice to the legislature all ten times. U.S. senators were also appointed by state legislatures until the Seventeenth Amendment to the Constitution in 1913. The elections that really mattered were those for the U.S. House of Representatives—and for state assemblies.

Before the Panic of 1819, only Pennsylvania and New York—where big-city interests struggled against rural majorities—experienced much in the way of organized political competition. In most states, apportionment of legislatures lagged behind western settlement, and the eastern areas predictably controlled the assemblies. Important questions about patronage or the granting of privileges and charters were often settled behind closed doors, frequently through compromises that avoided an awkward public vote. Local oligarchies chose candidates to run in elections that were lopsided or uncontested. Consensus and "harmony of interests" were emphasized. After the Panic, all of this would end in Tennessee, Kentucky, and Missouri with the conflict over debtor relief, and in states as different as Alabama and Massachusetts contested elections between sharply opposed factions also became common for the first time.

During the economic boom, people had been too busy making money to worry much about making public policy. But the boom had also introduced an intensified belief in the benefit of competition, a belief that proved fatal to commercial monopolies after court cases like *Gibbon v. Ogden* and soon challenged local political monopolies as well. The economic revolution came first, but the political revolution followed close behind. New conflicts were arising between incompatible interests, waiting only for the pressure of hard times to bring them to public debate. Tariffs, internal improvements, and slavery had previously been debated in terms of political principles. As they became defining economic concerns of different regions of the country, ambitious politicians like Webster and Calhoun were forced to reverse their earlier positions. The conflicting interests of manufacturers and merchants, wage-earners and employers, and creditors and debtors led to heated political rivalries and bitter partisan contests, especially as the more democratic constitutions of the new states increased pressure on the older states to expand their suffrage.[3]

The right to rule that the wealthy had taken for granted was coming under attack: after New Hampshire set the example by removing its property ownership restriction for voters, eight new states entered the Union with no property requirement for voting. The older states had been reluctant to extend the franchise, but by 1819 the new challenges they faced were pushing them to adapt. The Panic year was a turning point in the rise of American democracy. Previously, the republican habit had been economic participation by all but political participation by relatively few. As Sean Wilentz points out, "In 1819 the American economy, red hot with postwar expansion, melted down. . . . Quickly, outcries for widened democracy became attached to collisions of class caused by the economic disaster. The greatest political effect was to invigorate the city and country democracies, with a revived focus on economic and financial issues."[4]

The appearance of distinctly issue-oriented political movements shook the political establishment. The very idea of political parties in a republic had been anathema to the Founders; Federalists and Republicans had accused each other of putting the interests of a faction ahead of the good of the whole. Jefferson's inaugural address had reminded his countrymen, "We are all Republicans, we are all Federalists" (if not a conviction, then at least a sincere hope), but by 1822 even Jefferson was acknowledging the inevitability of factionalism. Kentucky's split into new parties over the issue of debtor relief seemed healthy to Jefferson, and in July he wrote to the chief justice of Kentucky's new court, William Barry, wondering whether for Republicans, "the surrender of our [Federalist] opponents, their reception into our camp, their assumption of our name . . . may be a good or an evil." To Barry, a highly partisan politician who would later control the great flow of patronage as Jackson's postmaster general, Jefferson declared, "I consider the party division of whig and tory the most wholesome which can exist in any government, and well worth being nourished."[5]

Barry's own Relief Party in Kentucky could have become the nucleus of a national party aligning debtors against creditors, had people remained in one category or the other; but in the United States people were alternately debtors or creditors, and often were both at once—including leading political figures like Clay and Jackson. But formally organized parties were less than a decade away. The short-lived Anti-Masonic Party would hold the first national party convention in 1831; Jacksonians had effectively launched the Democratic Party in the 1828 campaign, and the Whigs would soon thereafter give the country a competitive two-party system that would endure until the Civil War. But the politics of mass participation got its first real impetus from a series of state constitutional conventions called between 1816 and 1821 in response to the pressures of boom and bust.

The first such convention was attempted before the economic distress could galvanize popular support, and it never got off the ground. Proposed by the Virginia House of Delegates, it was supported in the *Enquirer* by Thomas Ritchie, a leader of the enduring Old Republican faction, the "Richmond Junto." Virginia's constitution, written in 1776, had apportioned seats in its assembly by county rather than by population and had restricted suffrage to property owners. Jefferson's suggestion that the state therefore grant every white male fifty acres was dismissed as whimsical. The advancing frontier had brought a growing population to the western part of the state, and advocates of an 1816 convention were out to weaken the disproportionate grip of the older Tidewater region. They succeeded in passing bills for western bank charters and internal improvements, but their plans for constitutional reform were stymied when the state senate—controlled by that Tidewater elite—killed the proposal. Virginians would have to wait another twenty-five years for their convention, but the genie of constitutional revision was out of the bottle. By 1818 the hard times were pressing on New England, and that year Connecticut called a convention to revise its 180-year-old constitution.[6]

The Connecticut convention originated in the long-simmering resentment directed by Republicans and Episcopalians, in particular, against the Federalist/Congregationalist power structure. Connecticut was, along with Massachusetts, a vestige of the Puritan theocracy that had ruled New England since 1620; the Congregationalists were still the legally established church, supported by state tax revenues. (The so-called Standing Order of Connecticut was so conservative—and entrenched—that the state would not ratify the Bill of Rights, with its prohibition of an established church, until 1939.) Connecticut was also the hard core of Federalism and had reacted to the election of Jefferson by passing a notorious "stand-up" law in 1801, requiring that votes be cast publicly, by voice. The state had been home to the reactionary Hartford Convention that had flirted with secession during "Madison's War" of 1812; while Hartford society had stopped just short of giving aid and comfort to the enemy, immediately after peace was declared the city hosted a festive ball in honor of the Royal Navy that had spent the past three years blockading the New England coast. But like the rest of the country, even hidebound Connecticut was under economic pressure to change.

Between November 1817 and April 1818 at least sixteen towns in Connecticut petitioned the legislature to call a constitutional convention. By that time only Rhode Island had a larger share of its population engaged in manufacturing, and the mill and factory owners were much more inclined than the mercantile elite to support the Republican agenda, including the Tariff of 1816. Most mill employees owned no real estate and were thus ineligible to vote; they joined with the state's religious minorities to demand more liberal suffrage and more nearly equal rights and privileges for all Christian denominations. Their unlikely leader was Oliver Wolcott Jr., the former Federalist secretary of the treasury. Wolcott had split with his party to support the war effort, and he had become part-owner of several textile mills. In 1817 he was elected governor by the Tolerationist Party, which had just succeeded in wresting control of the legislature from the Federalists.

The Connecticut convention was divided over the question of suffrage in a rapidly changing social order. One of the delegates, perhaps eyeing Wolcott, warned the convention, "It ought to be remembered, sir, that manufacturers are rapidly increasing; and employers may bring them in regiments to the polls." Wolcott and his supporters succeeded in ending both the property requirement and religious establishment, but in a corollary that foreshadowed the actions of other northern states, they also put an end to voting by free blacks, whether landowners or not. White workingmen and tenant farmers would, in the coming years, underline the equality they claimed with the wealthier property owners by asserting their shared racial superiority. That pattern would become most familiar in southern states, but it was embraced first in Connecticut, New Jersey, and New York; as soon as the next panic arrived in 1837, Pennsylvania followed their example.[7]

With the newly enlarged electorate, the establishment Standing Order could read the writing on the wall. Connecticut's all-Federalist congressional delegation retired *en masse*. Only Rep. Jonathan Moseley managed to be reelected—by switching to the Republican Party. Over the past twenty years, six different Federalists had held office for six terms or more, but in the next twenty years, turnover would be constant: only two representatives would be elected more than three times. Following the Connecticut convention, Wolcott published his belief that "At no period have the . . . people been more tranquil and united, than at this time," although he worried that "the suspension of business is so universal as to menace a subversion of public industry." Tranquility would vanish in the worsening depression and the Missouri crisis. But even after the Missouri Compromise seemed to restore sectional calm, the damage done by the Panic left both modest farmers and workingmen unsettled. The nation's next two state conventions would be directly driven by the concerns of this "middling interest," who were neither at the top nor the bottom of the economic ladder.

Amid the uncertainties caused by debt and the fluctuating currency, artisans felt threatened from above and below as employers turned to cheaper production methods that could employ less-skilled labor. In 1820, New York coach maker Abraham Quick complained that responsible craftsmen were under assault by new competitors who were eager to cut corners and make fast profits, men "without any regards for their reputation or respect for their Creditors," who would sell cheaply made products "at any price which of-fered to convert them to cash." Journeyman tailors, used to making their customers' clothing to order, objected to the master tailors' new practice of hiring women, at much lower wages, to sew "slops"—cheaply produced clothing, ready-made in set sizes. As "country" Democrats were gaining political experience through the struggles over debtor relief, workingmen's political parties formed in cities. Craftsmen, shopkeepers, and workingmen began to call themselves the "middling interest" to distinguish themselves from both the "better sort"—the ruling landowners, merchants, and factory owners, and the "meaner sort"—servants, itinerant laborers, and sailors. The middling interest, frustrated by the hard times, were the primary beneficia-ries of the constitutional reforms in Connecticut, and they threw their sup-port behind similar reforms in Massachusetts and New York.[8]

The Massachusetts constitution had been drafted by John Adams in 1780. Forty years later, the unpredictable Josiah Quincy joined forces with Joseph T. Buckingham, a political leader of the middling interest, to pursue its revi-sion. Their goal was the reformation of laws governing debt, militia service, and suffrage. Buckingham, whose ambitious hopes would be dashed, was a self-made printer who had been hard hit by the Panic of 1819. Quincy came from a line of Harvard-educated merchants and lawyers; his father had been co-counsel with Adams in defending the British soldiers accused in the Bos-ton Massacre, and his grandfather was a friend of Benjamin Franklin. Quin-cy's goals for revising the constitution were a good deal more conservative than Buckingham's, and he would be satisfied with the results.

Quincy was a self-described "raving Federalist." His position on the War of 1812 was 180 degrees from that of Oliver Wolcott; at the beginning of the war he told Henry Clay that southerners and westerners "are not to set up a standard for duty and discourse for my part of the country. While I have a tongue or pen, the ignorant part of the nation shall not assume to itself with impunity, to lord over the intelligent, nor the vicious over the virtuous." Clay considered challenging him to a duel but concluded that it would be a waste of time to try to call out a Yankee. Quincy's self-assurance did not diminish with age; as the least popular president of Harvard since the seven-teenth century, he would expel the entire sophomore class after the riot of 1834.[9]

Quincy's reform aims were limited, but any reform offended the octo-genarian John Adams, the honorary chairman of the convention when it convened in November 1820. A more flexible conservative was the young Daniel Webster, recently relocated from New Hampshire. The reformers did succeed in ending the freehold voting requirement, but Quincy was ambivalent on the question of broadening the franchise. The next year, opposing a city charter for Boston with balloting by wards, he would declare the "pure democracy of the town meeting more suited to the character of the people of New England," and like Connecticut conservatives he feared the impact of the growing number of industrial laborers. He warned the delegates, "Let the gentlemen from the country consider, how it may affect their rights, liberty, and properties, if in every county of the Commonwealth there should arise, as in time there probably will, one, two, or three manufacturing establishments, each sending as the case may be, from one to eight hundred voters to the polls depending on the will of one employer, one great capitalist."[10]

Adams warned that suffrage reform was a head-on assault against property by mere numbers, and delegate Warren Dutton gave his opinion that, "In this country, where the means of subsistence were so abundant and the demand for labor great," anyone who failed to acquire property must be "indolent or vicious." The Boston "middling interest" was pressing for *some* voice in response to the hard times, and the upshot was a patchwork of compromise: suffrage was extended to all male taxpayers after a one-year residence, but the constitution retained Adams's 1780 rule that senate districts reflect taxable property rather than population. To Adams's disgust, the test oath for officeholders was ended, but the Congregationalists remained the established, tax-supported church. When the convention adjourned in January, Adams was unhappy with even modest changes, but Quincy and Webster were not disturbed; Webster said, "We have got on as well as we expected." The reform leader Buckingham understood the reasons for Webster's satisfaction; when he was asked what the convention had achieved, his reply was, "Nothing—absolutely nothing."[11]

New York followed Massachusetts, in the autumn of 1821. The legislature had approved a convention in November 1820, part of a strong reaction by the middling interest as DeWitt Clinton's increasingly arrogant, ostensibly Republican administration began supporting Federalist programs. The governor cast the deciding vote in the state's Council of Revision to veto the convention, on the grounds that only the people could call one. The Bucktail reform faction lacked the necessary two-thirds majority to override, but they immediately passed a second measure calling for a referendum, and in April the voters endorsed the convention by a three-to-one margin. It met from August through November, chaired by the vice president of the United States, former governor Daniel Tompkins. Among the delegates was the convention's driving force, Martin Van Buren, along with such venerable Federalists as Rufus King and Chancellor James Kent; James Tallmadge, who had left the House of Representatives shortly after precipitating the Missouri crisis, was a Clintonian delegate.

Just before the convention, Van Buren wrote to King to reassure him that he had no intention of overturning the social order; the conflict, brought to a head by the Panic, was really between "the yeomanry of the state" and a "nefarious band of speculators" who had "preyed upon the very vitals of the government," and whom Van Buren blamed for the depression that gripped New York. As in the other recent state conventions, the most divisive issue was the property requirement for voting, opposed by urban artisans and shopkeepers and the state's numerous tenant farmers. Chancellor Kent and the Van Rensselaer brothers, with their vast landholdings upstate, led the conservatives. Kent darkly warned that the poor were out to "share the plunder of the rich," and insisted that the freehold requirement alone protected the solid citizens "against the caprice of the motley assemblage of paupers, emigrants, journeymen manufacturers, and those undefinable classes of inhabitants which a state and city like ours is calculated to invite." He lectured Van Buren's restive yeomanry in language that the Panic had made familiar across the country: "There is a constant tendency in human society and the history of every age proves it; there is a tendency . . . in the debtor to relax or avoid the obligation of contracts; in the majority to tyrannize over the minority and trample down their rights; in the indolent and profligate to cast the whole burthens of society upon the industrious and the virtuous." The middling interest, gladly denying the vote to paupers, had no sympathy for the indolent and profligate, but to Kent's surprise they did not see themselves in those terms. They acknowledged that there were many debtors among them still, but they also insisted that they were industrious and virtuous—and that they *were* the majority. Kent had accurately predicted that they would disregard the minority's rights; although the chancellor was thinking of the wealthy, the minority of free blacks turned out to be the victims. The delegates added New York to the list of states granting suffrage to white taxpayers who owned no real estate—but at the same time the convention voted to *increase* the property requirement for free black voters.[12]

How much difference did the reforms make? In 1818 only five House districts in Massachusetts had competitive races (in which the winner garnered under 60 percent of the votes); in 1824 there were nine. New York saw an even more dramatic change, going from seven competitive districts to twenty-one. Moreover, in New York's 1818 election, six candidates had easily won 90 percent or more of the vote; in 1824 that number was reduced to two. By the end of 1821—the lowest point of the depression—twenty-one out of twenty-four states had taken steps to remove the property requirement for voting; only the deeply conservative states of Virginia, North Carolina, and South Carolina had done nothing. (In South Carolina, three of nine congressmen ran unopposed in 1818 and five did in 1824; in Virginia more than half were unopposed in 1818 and a third still were in 1824.) Those were also states where banking had never been allowed to expand as it did elsewhere, and where debtor-relief movements had found little support. In 1824 only six states (all but one of them northern free states) granted suffrage to African Americans, and five of the original thirteen had taken measures to restrict or repeal free blacks' right to vote. In the years following 1812 six more states had entered the union with manhood suffrage provisions in their constitutions—for white males only. The question of votes for women, even if they were property owners or taxpayers, was never seriously raised.[13]

The labor historian David Montgomery has argued that the changes made in this period, by adding thousands of craftsmen, artisans, and mechanics to the voting rolls, led inevitably to changes that benefitted working people. He says that the "wage contract" joined the freehold as a "badge of participation in the polity." But the extension of suffrage that followed the Panic of 1819 was certainly not meant to strengthen the poorly paid mill hands and factory operatives who had lately learned how precarious their own wage contract could be. The middling interest—the farmers who rented their fields, the shopkeepers and journeymen—remained at odds with both rich and poor, and never intended to embrace the "meaner sort." David Bull, a New York convention delegate, echoed Massachusetts's Quincy: "the whole body of every manufacturing establishment . . . are dead voters, counted by the head, by their employers," but he was sure that "the farmers in this country will always outnumber all portions of our population." To him, the idea that unskilled laborers "may rise, in the majesty of their strength, and usurp the property of the landholders, is so unlikely to be realized that we may dismiss all fear arising from that source." If he had not been so confident, he admitted, he would "hesitate in extending the right of suffrage." Chancellor Kent nevertheless insisted that because "the disproportion between men of property and of no property is daily increasing," New York City was "destined to become the London of America. And can the gentleman say, that no danger is to be apprehended from those combustible materials which such a city must ever enclose?" Even Van Buren, whose Bucktail faction depended on the urban vote, assured New Yorkers that he opposed "universal suffrage" and that the convention's reforms were aimed only at extending suffrage to the respectable middle levels of society. (He would grow more democratic after abandoning the unsuccessful Crawford campaign to support Jackson in 1828.)[14]

Factional conflict was clearly on the rise. The ideal of a "harmony of interests" was cracking everywhere under the economic strain of 1819; its disintegration can be clearly traced in the experience of Boston, a city that was struggling to comprehend its own diversity of interests. In an essay entitled "The Fragmentation of a Great Family: The Panic of 1819 and the Rise of the Middling Interest in Boston 1818–1822," Andrew Cayton points out that "while notions of organicism had long since lost favor" in the factional politics of New York and Pennsylvania, "it took the Panic of 1819 to discredit them in Boston."[15]

In Massachusetts the Federalist governor John Brooks devoted his 1820 annual message to the "depression and embarrassments" for which he saw no solution but his "unwavering belief . . . in the power of just laws and virtuous habits." Boston's Republican newspaper, the *Patriot*, declared that the great issue in the 1820 election of the Board of Selectmen was "the present embarrassed state of our *merchants*; the distressed condition of our *tradesmen*; and the universal complaint among every class of our citizens." In the previous year's legislative election, the Federalist *Columbian Centinel* had warned that Republicans "desire changes for themselves, and not the benefit of the whole," while the *Patriot* insisted that the Federalists would ignore what was best for the "whole" of the people, being driven by "private motives." Both parties in Boston had then appealed to the welfare of "the whole," rather than the interests of one party's constituents. Now, as the state's middling interest was calling for constitutional reform, the election for selectmen elicited somewhat sharper warnings, but each party continued to claim that it was looking out for the welfare of the whole, damning the opposition as the tool of special interests. The *Patriot* urged the election of Republicans "who will look with a vigilant eye to the interests of the whole community, and not to that of any particular order, sect, or profession." The *Centinel*, sensing that Federalists were losing their traditional passive support by shopkeepers and craftsmen, warned that Republicans were seeking "power and dominion . . . for their own benefit," not "the promotion of the common welfare." Ominously, however, its editors had to admit, "General laws must, sometimes, operate inconveniently to individuals."[16]

As the "depression and embarrassments" in Massachusetts wore on—and even after the state had extended the franchise to all taxpayers—there was resentment that the "opulent citizens" seemed able to evade taxes that fell more heavily on the middle class. A Committee on Tax Assessment, headed by the young merchant Lewis Tappan, concluded that it was indeed true that "the richer classes are not proportionately taxed with those of smaller property." A movement was developing to incorporate Boston as a city separate from Suffolk County, whose justices of the peace had kept merchants and landowners in control of Boston's Court of Sessions (the town administration). Although its commerce had been surpassed by first Philadelphia and then New York, Boston had grown dramatically; the population increased fourfold between 1780 and 1820, but even with over 40,000 inhabitants, the "town" was still administered as if it were an eighteenth-century village. No longer a compact community, Boston was now clearly divided into neighborhoods: Beacon Hill for the comfortable merchant class, South Boston for the less well-off. Old ordinances only served to rub in socioeconomic distinctions, like the one that decreed that two-story houses could not be made of wood, but only the more expensive brick or stone.[17]

Boston's middling interest now resolved to look out for its own welfare, abandoning the old rhetoric of "the good of the whole." The middling interest had already split with the wealthy citizens by supporting auction sales (which lowered prices) despite the objections of large merchants whose profits were reduced. In January 1822 they carried the vote for a city charter that would concentrate their voting power by electing city officials by ward rather than at large. Josiah Quincy had campaigned against the charter, hoping that preserving the old town system would also mean preserving the old outwardly unified power structure, but when Quincy ran in the city's first mayoral election, he failed to receive a majority and withdrew rather than face a runoff. The middling interest that upended Boston politics in 1822 were victims of the hard times after the Panic, but just as at the convention in 1820/21, the adversaries of the rich were not the allies of the poor. In the 1822 mayoral vote, Quincy had carried the four wealthiest wards, and his Republican opponent had taken the six wards in the middle range of wealth—but the two poorest wards gave their votes to third and fourth parties, factions that were politically more radical. The "harmony of interests" in Boston—the "welfare of the whole"—had been permanently fragmented, and in the post-Panic years factions would consistently militate for their own particular interests.[18]

Boston's middling interest made up the audience in the 1820s for Lyman Beecher's sermons against the "Harvard" Unitarianism of the city's upper classes. When Beecher moved to Cincinnati to head the Lane Seminary, he would find that Ohio had gone through a similar process of fragmentation. No distinct reform party had arisen as had happened across the river in Kentucky, but in Ohio as in Massachusetts, one historian has written, the "Panic of 1819 . . . splintered forever the assumptions on which the government of Ohio had been constructed in 1802: a democratic society produced not a natural harmony but a natural cacophony of interests." According to Steubenville's *Western Spy*, the people were resolved "to submit no longer to the abuses of the banking system" or to the class that ran it, and in 1820 and 1822 new voters in many states showed up in record numbers to turn out incumbent officeholders. They were determined not to replace them with anyone remotely connected to banking or speculation. Even William Henry Harrison, Ohio's once and future favorite son, was defeated for Congress by the little-known James Gazlay, who had managed only a sixth-place finish the year before in a contest for the state legislature. Harrison's history of large-scale land speculation made him briefly unpopular; it did not help matters that he had arranged to have his son appointed receiver at the Vincennes land office. In the factional upheavals, Gazlay would be defeated after a single term by James Findlay, the Jacksonian mayor of Cincinnati. When Findlay repudiated Jackson in 1832, he too would be defeated—and in 1840 the district would give Harrison a landslide vote for president. By then, however, the movement for popular participation—and the polarization that began after the Panic of 1819—had produced something new: a contest between two bitterly opposed, thoroughly organized national parties, complete with memorable slogans, campaign songs, and scurrilous unauthorized biographies.[19]

The Second Party System, Whigs and Democrats, was the product of the divide that had grown out of the Panic of 1819: popular anger at the bankers and wealthy easterners protected by privileges and charters, who were blamed for the losses of farmers and workingmen, was countered by the indignation of a respectable middle class who blamed economic troubles on laziness and self-indulgence and demanded positive government activity in the form of tariffs and internal improvements. "Consistently," writes Michael

Holt, "Whigs took the pro-corporation, pro-banking, and pro-paper money side in their votes and in their rhetoric, while over time more and more Democrats clustered on the opposite side."[20]

Jackson's 1828 campaign against John Quincy Adams has been called the birth of modern politics, but even before the post-Panic depression had lifted it was becoming clear that politics was changing. With the expanded suffrage creating a new participatory politics, the presidential election of 1824 was the first in which popular votes were extensively reported and recorded. The economic factionalism that grew out of the depression ensured that politics would be partisan as well. Republican politicians might still speak of conciliation and the "harmony of interests," but in the coming decades compromise became so difficult that Henry Clay would be celebrated as a political magician when he was able to produce it. Consensus inevitably gave way to conflict since each faction believed its opponents were threatening liberty itself. The clashes arising in 1819 set American politics on the path to becoming the blood sport one Mississippi congressman would shortly describe to another: "As a general rule, about one half of those who vote look upon the privilege as worthless unless they can use it to gratify a personal hostility, or religious antipathies, or to inflict injury on what they hate." This would be the political legacy of the Panic of 1819.[21]

Even before Monroe was elected in 1816, the presidential campaign for 1824 was under way. In December 1815, when Gallatin had written to John Quincy Adams that "there is at this moment less apparent party agitation than I had known for a long time," William Crawford was indecisively beginning his pursuit of the nomination. He withdrew his name two months before the Republican congressional caucus the following spring but then allowed it to be raised at the last minute. The 1816 caucus chose Monroe by a close vote, 65 to 54, and Crawford learned a lesson about hesitation. He would concede Monroe the traditional two terms, but from that moment he fixed his eye on 1824 and never let up. As secretary of the treasury, he was presumed to be the front-runner. Adams held the office of secretary of state, which had been the stepping-stone for Madison and Monroe, but Adams was a recent convert from Federalism, and the party caucus distrusted him. The powerful ambition of John C. Calhoun and Henry Clay would launch each of them on the first of their several fruitless campaigns for the nation's highest office. In 1819, Andrew Jackson was the darkest of dark horses. That year Clay accused him, on the floor of the House, of turning a police action against the Seminoles on the Florida border into an invasion of foreign soil—and of violating international law by court martialing and executing two English civilians. Behind the closed doors of the cabinet, Crawford and Calhoun called for his censure, convinced that Jackson had disobeyed Monroe's orders and exceeded his authority by seizing the Spanish fortress at Pensacola. In the past, such opposition at high levels would have kept even a military hero's name from being suggested; soon, the rising tide of outrage against corruption in general and corrupt politics in particular would make past practices irrelevant. Resentment of the deal-making political establishment would undercut Crawford's anticipated anointing by the congressional caucus; anger at both the Bank of the United States and the establishment would coalesce around the best-known public figure *outside* the government. A century and a half before Carter, Reagan, or Trump, Andrew Jackson became the first candidate to run against Washington, D.C.[22]

The election of 1824 would prove to be unique in American history, the only time the clear leader in both the popular *and* electoral vote has been denied the White House. The anything-goes atmosphere of the postwar years had left all of the candidates open to accusations of corruption, proven or not, and the election would culminate in the notorious "corrupt bargain" in the House of Representatives, where the election was decided in the absence of an absolute majority in the electoral college. Political maneuvering by the powerful Speaker, Henry Clay, enabled Adams—second in the electoral vote—to secure a majority of states in the House. Adams may actually have been the most morally upright of the candidates, but when he made Clay secretary of state, the apparent payoff would permanently tarnish both men.

Well before that, it was obvious that the Federalist Party was headed for extinction: when the Sixteenth Congress met in March of 1819, of forty-six Senate seats the Federalists held only ten (soon falling to eight), and of 183 representatives, all but twenty-five were Republicans. In 1820, for the first time, there would be no Federalist nominee for the presidency. Two years earlier Rufus King, the Federalists' final presidential candidate in 1816, had weighed the political prospects:

> As yet nothing of interest has occurred in Congress; the apathy which appears to exist must not be regarded as evidence that no strong passions are concealed, and waiting only for the occasion to show themselves. An opposition will arise. The President has no zealous friends nor enemies; but as a sufficient number of rivals may be pointed out, the quiet aspect of things will not continue.

King went on to mention Crawford, DeWitt Clinton, and John Quincy Adams as possible rivals for the succession, and concluded, "I think it is quite impossible as yet, to determine what new controversies or parties, are likely to arise." Republicans sensed the same uneasy calm before the storm, and in 1820, after the Panic led to nationwide depression, Calhoun told Adams that he saw "a general mass of disaffection to the government, not concentrated in any particular direction, but ready to seize upon any event and looking out anywhere for a leader." Adams presciently responded, "Government can do nothing . . . but transfer discontents, and propitiate one class of people by disgusting another."[23]

There was already plenty of disaffection and discontent within the Republican Party. The Missouri crisis had set northern anti-slavery men against southerners; the Baldwin tariff in 1820 split the East and the West, and nearly every issue separated the National Republicans—Clay, Adams, and (still) Calhoun—from the Old Republicans who favored Crawford and whose spokesmen were John Randolph and Philip Barbour in Congress, Thomas Ritchie in the press, and John Taylor of Caroline in long, abstruse books. Tensions were intense enough to inspire personal violence: escalating conflict would cause Clay and Randolph to take up pistols in 1826; Randolph, by then in the Senate, could not restrain his own tongue, calling Clay a "Judas" who had "crucified" the Constitution and characterizing his relationship with Adams in terms of two characters from Henry Fielding's popular novel *Tom Jones*: "the coalition of Blifil and Black George . . . the combination unheard of till then, of the Puritan and the Blackleg." Clay might have shrugged off being called Judas, but the term "Blackleg" implied cheating at cards; that was intolerable. A challenge was delivered and accepted, shots were exchanged, but Randolph's coat was the only casualty.[24]

As King had observed, the bland President Monroe had neither strong supporters nor enemies. There were opponents of the administration, but no personal invective was aimed at Monroe, who appeared to be a figurehead; reluctant to make policy on any controversial issue, he regularly consulted the retired James Madison for advice on Latin America, the Florida disputes, the tariff, and internal improvements. He appeared oblivious to the economic distress that wracked the nation.[25]

In November 1818 the president had told Congress that the economy presented "ample cause for satisfaction," forecasting a budget surplus and increased sales of public lands—presumably on the advice of his treasury secretary. But Crawford was even then telling Congress that instead of an $8 million surplus, the government was facing a deficit of $1.5 million, thanks to a decline in import duties after the tariff of 1816. Crawford recommended severe reductions in the administration's budget. He knew that imports had rebounded a year after the tariff (collection of duties always trailed by a year), and he could see that income from land sales was skyrocketing, but he had an ulterior motive. As he well knew, the largest budget item by far was the War Department; its secretary, Calhoun, also had his eyes on 1824, and Crawford saw an opportunity to discomfit a serious rival. When the Panic hit in 1819, it caught both Monroe and Crawford by surprise, but Calhoun confided to Adams that he suspected Crawford—among others—of using the incipient depression to manipulate the public mood. He worried about the "vague but widespread discontent, caused by the disordered circumstances of individuals, but resulting in a general impression that there was something radically wrong in the administration of the government," and in his department in particular.[26]

Adams's suspicions of Crawford were no less than Calhoun's, and they only increased; at the beginning of 1820 he wrote in his diary,

> Every act and thought of Crawford looks to the next Presidency. All his springs of action work not upon the present but upon the future, and yet his path in the Department is now beset with thorns, from which he shrinks, and which I think he will not ward off with success. In short, as the first Presidential term of Mr. Monroe's administration has hitherto been the period of the greatest national tranquility enjoyed by this nation at any portion of its history, so it appears to me scarcely avoidable that the second term will be among the most stormy and violent.

Tranquil the politics may have seemed, but Adams had already noted that "the merchants are crumbling to ruin, the manufacturers perishing, agriculture stagnating, and distress universal in every part of the country. The revenue has not yet been, but must very sensibly and very soon be affected by this state of things."[27]

The revenue was indeed affected; Crawford may have meant to exaggerate the threat of a deficit, but he wound up underestimating it by more than $2 million. Revenue for 1816 (collected mainly in 1817) had been $36 million. It rose for 1817 but then dropped to $26 million in 1818, $21 million in 1819, $15 million in 1820, and $13 million in 1821; it would remain under $20 million until 1822. Inevitably there was a widespread demand for government retrenchment. There has never been a time when politicians have not been eager to put themselves on record against government waste, and both Old Republicans and the remaining Federalists were happy to expose it in Monroe's administration. Their first target was the "bloated" federal payroll. In reality, federal employment was minuscule outside the military and the local post offices. In Washington, the Post Office Department had a payroll of twenty-six individuals; State Department staff totaled fourteen (plus three clerks in the Patent Office), the same number as the U.S. Mint and the General Land Office (which also employed fifty-one more people in land offices across the country). The Navy Department had fifteen civilian employees, the War Department twenty-one. The largest federal department within the nation's capital was Crawford's own Treasury Department: its secretaries, clerks, and messengers numbered only ten, but there were also 140 comptrollers, auditors, and revenue agents.[28]

Congressional insistence on slashing this payroll presented Crawford with a challenge—and an opportunity. There were a number of congressmen, many unallied with Crawford, who thought the War Department's spending was out of control. William Plumer Jr., a representative from New Hampshire, wrote to his father (the state's governor) that "[Calhoun's] schemes are too grand and magnificent, and he labors too much for show and effect. If we had a revenue of a hundred millions, he would be at no loss how to spend it." With revenue only a fraction of that amount, Crawford's allies in Congress seized the chance to clip Calhoun's wings—and force decisions that would upset his following among influential army officers. They quickly cut the Indian Affairs budget by half and the fortifications budget by two-thirds. The House Ways and Means Committee slashed the War Department appropriation from $6 million to $3 million and held it there through 1825; the authorized strength of the army was likewise halved, from twelve thousand to six thousand. Major General Andrew Jackson (not yet aware of Calhoun's criticism of him behind cabinet doors) wrote to the secretary of war, "The government should be d————d. It is certainly true that the Military committee in the Senate have and will be wielded by the present Secretary of the Treasury. Their object will be to affect you, and draw the attention of the nation from his corruption and intrigue."[29]

Not all of the budget cutters were Crawfordites—Plumer disliked Crawford a good deal more than he did Calhoun—but Calhoun was convinced that Crawford was behind the attack on his department. He was able to fend off a proposal to abolish the military academy at West Point, but he had to carry out the very unpopular order to remove six thousand veterans from the pension rolls. He also had no choice about reducing the number of officers by half, with inevitable reductions in rank for many who were kept on. He could retain only one of the army's two major generals, and Jackson was junior to Gen. Jacob Brown; well aware of Jackson's sensitivity and appreciating his influence, Calhoun now persuaded Monroe to appoint the general governor of the new Florida Territory, even though he had recently urged that Jackson be censured for his conduct there. That solved one problem, but there were many more—some of his own making.[30]

Calhoun was quite right that his woes were in part due to Crawford's malign influence, but now there was no denying the revenue shortfall, which strengthened the hand of Old Republican radicals. Men like Randolph and Philip Barbour were eager to reduce the size of the federal government as a matter of principle, and they had consistently opposed the internal improvement and tariff bills that Calhoun had aggressively promoted in Congress. The reaction to the Panic of 1819 included a growing repugnance toward all the excesses that had led up to the collapse, excesses that now carried a strong odor of corruption. Calhoun was not accused of personal immorality; he was among the most rigid puritans in Washington, already becoming known as the "cast-iron man." But he had turned a blind eye to highly questionable dealings in the War Department, and the chickens were coming home to roost.

Just as the early nineteenth century tolerated bankers' financial chicanery that today would be manifestly illegal, so the behavior of public officials was not yet circumscribed by many of the norms that are now taken for granted. It was assumed that the attorney general would take on private legal work; his salary was accordingly lower than that of other cabinet officers. (Like both Clay and Webster, William Wirt was retained by the Bank of the United States.) Clay, Webster, and Benton were doing nothing out of the ordinary when they accepted fees or loans from businesses that would be affected by their legislation. Nepotism was accepted as a matter of course; sons were regularly employed in government by their fathers, and clouds of brothers-in-law seemed always to receive appointments and favors. But even by the ethical standards of the day, the 1810s and 1820s were tainted by corruption on an unprecedented scale; Monroe's administration, taken as a whole, may have been the most corrupt in the early history of the United States.[31]

Charges of corruption would dog all of the candidates in 1824. Plumer's criticism of Calhoun grew out of the profligate spending and dubious morality of department subordinates and contractors. War and Treasury were "the two most venal departments of the government," in the opinion of Robert Remini, "which is saying a lot considering the condition of the others." Crawford and Calhoun, if not personally involved, willingly looked the other way. Two of the most flagrant examples, and the subjects of Plumer's immediate complaint, were the construction of Fortress Monroe and the ill-fated Yellowstone Expedition—two projects that Calhoun personally promoted, both thrust before the public eye as a result of the Panic.[32]

Fortress Monroe was to be built at Old Point Comfort, the strategically vital entrance to the Chesapeake Bay; had it been there in 1814, the British might not have been able to capture and burn Washington, D.C. In the still-inflating economy of early 1818, the contract for supplying the massive granite foundation was awarded to Elijah Mix, one of the innumerable brothers-in-law who seemed to haunt every official who had money to spend—in this case, Calhoun's chief clerk, Major Christopher Vandeventer. Mix, to no one's surprise, was in over his head; with supply costs rising, Vandeventer agreed to purchase one-quarter of the contract. Showing circumspection unusual for the place and time, he first asked Calhoun for his approval, and the secretary, unwisely, made no objection. There was no legal obstacle, but the ethics were clearly questionable. Encouraged by Calhoun's acquiescence, Vandeventer then purchased another quarter interest. Mix had made his bid near the height of the financial boom; when the Panic arrived and prices tumbled, the contract was suddenly profitable. Vandeventer sold his shares, pocketing a substantial return on his brief investment.[33]

An anonymous letter was sent to Monroe, followed by an exposé in the Washington *Gazette* (both apparently planted by Crawford); a congressional investigation followed, in which the deals were made public. Calhoun refused to be intimidated by his cabinet rival and retained Vandeventer in his office, with no official reprimand. Despite clumsy attempts by Mix to suggest that Calhoun was knowingly complicit from the start, the investigating committee found no credible evidence that he "connived at such participation in any of his subordinate officers"; the committee concluded that Mix was "utterly destitute of the slightest claim to be believed upon his oath."[34]

The Vandeventer/Mix affair was overshadowed, however, by a far more public scandal in the War Department, one that clearly involved not only Calhoun but also Richard Mentor Johnson (congressman and future vice president) and eventually President Monroe. This was the Yellowstone Expedition, plagued from the start by mismanagement, incompetence, and irresponsibility, which resulted in the loss of hundreds of thousands of dollars by the U.S. government. It was without equal at that date as a flagrant example of government corruption and ineptitude. Congress had approved a military expedition up the Missouri River to the Yellowstone River, in the far northwestern reaches of the Louisiana Purchase. The government had very little idea what this vast region contained. Since the Lewis and Clark expedition, only fur trappers had gone there—including troublesome agents of the British Northwest Fur Company—and Calhoun wrote to Jackson in 1818, "I am very desirous by taking strong and judicious posts [on the Missouri] to break British control over the Northern Indians."[35]

As plans got under way, Calhoun experienced an unfortunate lapse of judgment: without inviting any competitive bids, in December 1818 he awarded the supply and transportation contract for the expedition to James Johnson, whose sole qualification was that his brother chaired the House Military Affairs Committee, which oversaw the War Department. Since Richard Mentor Johnson was intimately involved in James's financial operations, this was very close to being a bribe. Calhoun suggested that "the employment of one or two steamboats if there is a reasonable prospect of their success . . . would gain much more interest and éclat to the expedition and would probably impress the Indians and the British." Neither of the Johnsons knew anything about steamboat design or construction, but, following the principle that more is better, they undertook the construction of not one or two, but five of them—broad, heavy side-wheelers. They were also profoundly ignorant of the challenges posed by the uncharted river their boats would ascend. Knowledgeable military officers and rivermen believed that the maximum burden the river would support was eighty tons; the boats the Johnsons constructed were twice that size. An officer on the expedition, Col. Talbot Chambers, characterized their engines as "feeble" and described their draft as nearly twice the four-foot maximum for negotiating the river's shallows and sandbars, noting that one boat, *Expedition*, took five days—with frequent strandings—to just proceed twenty-five miles up the Missouri. Western historian Hiram Chittenden recounts the debacle that followed: "Johnson took little care to see that the equipment was of a character which should ensure a prompt fulfillment of the contract. He provided five steamboats, the *Jefferson*, *Expedition*, *Johnson*, *Calhoun*, and *Exchange*. There is no record that the latter two were able to enter the Missouri at all. The *Jefferson* gave out and abandoned the trip thirty miles below Franklin," becoming the first steamboat ever to sink in the Missouri River. None of the boats got within nine hundred miles of the Yellowstone.[36]

Well before it was known that the expedition was an utter failure, it was clear that the contract for it was a colossal boondoggle. Not only were the Johnsons' stated prices exorbitant, but many costs were left unstated, open to future contingencies—an invitation to fraud. James Johnson was awarded large advances before any of the contracted work was carried out, with no security to the government. Then the Panic of 1819 arrived. The Johnson brothers, like so many entrepreneurs, had borrowed far too much; Richard Johnson's debts to the BUS would lead to his being sued by his Kentucky fellow-congressman, Henry Clay. A number of subcontractors went bankrupt and defaulted on their contracts; the Johnsons demanded further advances in order to secure supplies from new sources. Meanwhile they were fending off their own creditors, who were threatening to seize equipment already delivered to St. Louis. Among those creditors was the Bank of Missouri, and Thomas Hart Benton warned against further advances to the brothers in the pages of the St. Louis *Enquirer*. By the summer of 1819, so much money had been advanced—over $200,000—that the government could not afford to let the expedition collapse. While on a tour of Kentucky, Monroe received an urgent request from Richard Johnson, backed by letters from Andrew Jackson and Kentucky's Gov. Isaac Shelby, and ordered a final advance of an additional $107,000. Calhoun had little choice but to go along.[37]

Back in Washington, Crawford and Clay were highly gratified by the trouble the expedition's well-publicized problems were causing their rival. John Quincy Adams, who personally liked Calhoun but had begun to think of him as an obstacle to his own presidential ambitions, had spoken on December 8, 1819, with Monroe, who told him that Clay was censuring the cost of the expedition in Congress. Once again Adams confided to his diary:

> I had heard here, and even in Boston, obscure intimations of complaint against that expedition and surmises against Colonel Richard M. Johnson and his brother, who are contractors for supplying the troops employed upon it. The honesty of the Johnsons is deeply implicated, and rumors are afoot that advances have been made by the government which will eventuate in a loss of public money . . . which cannot be accounted for according to law.[38]

Monroe assured Adams that the Johnsons had provide adequate security; that was untrue. The money was lost, one more casualty of corruption that might have remained hidden had the Panic not forced it into light. Had the boom continued, the Johnson brothers could have enriched themselves, and the public would have been none the wiser. But soon their conspicuous failure could not escape public notice. Republican Marcus Morton of Massachusetts would speak scornfully of "a government of fraud and deceit." The *National Intelligencer* was usually friendly to the administration (its publishers had the contract for government printing), but even it had to admit that "one of the charges brought against the present administration is a grave neglect and waste of public property," and it added with restrained reproach, "Errors of judgment may have been committed by them as well as other men." The New York *Statesman*, with no printing contract to lose, was more direct: "That scandalous defalcation in our public pecuniary agents, gross misapplication of public money, and an unprecedented laxity in official responsibilities [have] occurred and been suffered under our government for the past six or eight years are faults not to be concealed."[39]

As Republican harmony disintegrated, the prospective candidates for the presidency continued to make their own "obscure intimations" about their rivals' corruption. Calhoun, as it turned out, was by no means the most vulnerable. Clay was accusing the administration of carelessness and waste in the Yellowstone fiasco but was careful not to impugn the morality of Calhoun or the Johnsons. Clay's own drinking and gambling displeased many but hardly fell into the category of corruption; his financial losses in the Panic of 1819, however, put pressure on him that led to troubling conflicts of interest. Clay felt the depression deeply and personally; his own financial reverses forced him to give up the speakership in order to focus on making money through his unpopular representation of the BUS. By February 1821 he proudly informed Langdon Cheves that, while still a member of Congress, he had placed about four hundred suits before the federal courts in Ohio and Kentucky, amounting to nearly $2 million in debts the Bank was trying to collect. In addition to his $6,000 annual retainer, he earned additional fees for cases such as *Osborn v. Bank of the U.S.*, which he argued before the Supreme Court in the fall of 1821, denying Ohio's authority to tax the Bank. He wrote again to Cheves, "I will thank you to place with the Cashier of the Bank the $2000, the residue of my fee for conducting the suit in Ohio, and that which the Bank has had the goodness to allow me for the Supreme Court."[40]

Clay's well-paid work for the Bank was perfectly legal. Still, it hurt him with the multitudes who blamed the Bank for their losses, and his efforts to get Cheves to make exceptions in the case of Richard M. Johnson's debts certainly smacked of favoritism. His disagreement with the relief party in Kentucky, which he tried to keep quiet, was also politically costly although morally unexceptionable. But Clay had acquired a reputation for being slippery, a reputation he could never escape. In 1823 North Carolina's Rep. Romulus Saunders wrote to Bartlett Yancey about Clay's "laxity of principles," and Gen. William Lenoir told his son that he could not support Clay for the presidency because "a man who does not conduct himself morally" was unqualified to take responsibility for "the important business of a Government." The future Whig senator Willie Mangum, who would be a political ally of Clay in later years, now called him "a column that presents so beautiful a Corinthian capital" but "does not rest upon the broad basis of moral confidence." Clay kept taking his retainer from the Bank even after his return to the House in 1822, remaining on the payroll until he became secretary of state, despite doing no more legal work to earn it. Worse still, the sudden pressure of the Panic had led him to accept, while still Speaker of the House, a $20,000 unsecured loan from John Jacob Astor—a huge amount for 1819, when a congressman was paid eight dollars *per diem*. Moreover, it was a loan which he was under no pressure to pay back; it was still outstanding when the next Panic began in 1837 and was at last paid off—by an anonymous benefactor—only in 1845.[41]

Astor found such loans to government officials to be good investments—the more slowly repaid (if at all), the better. He loaned $5,000 to James Monroe, then secretary of state, during the War of 1812; Monroe, in return, rescinded the prohibition on foreigners in the fur trade. (Though he had lived in America for thirty years, Astor was born in Germany and fell under the ban.) Monroe did not repay the loan until he was out of the White House. Lewis Cass, the governor of the Michigan Territory who carried out the rescinding order on Astor's behalf, was himself suspected of accepting a $30,000 bribe from Astor. And Thomas Hart Benton, the newly elected senator from Missouri, was paid a "sizable fee" to look after Astor's interests in Congress; one of his first accomplishments in the Senate was the elimination of the Indian factor system that competed directly with Astor's American Fur Company. Astor was not the only strategic political creditor; while the Bank of the United States saw no benefit in lending to the retired President Madison (known for his probity), it was perfectly happy to make open-ended "loans" to malleable congressmen whose future votes might be helpful. Daniel Webster, notoriously susceptible, expected his annual "retainer" from the

Bank for years after he ceased doing any of its legal work, and Mississippi's Sen. George Poindexter received a $10,000 loan from the Bank shortly before voting for its recharter—and an additional $8,000 a few months after his vote, even though the first loan remained unpaid.[42]

Of all the presidential contenders, Crawford was the most widely believed to be thoroughly corrupt; explosive accusations in 1823 nearly derailed his quest for the White House. Clay's corner-cutting may have been motivated by desperate financial straits; Crawford's motivation was always, as Adams noted, political advantage—a more serious kind of corruption from a republican viewpoint. When Crawford had first set his sights on the presidency back in 1816, he had been unable to prevent the orderly transfer of power to the heir apparent when the congressional caucus nominated Monroe. He was determined that the orderly transfer the next time would lead to his own nomination and election—and he meant to take no chances. Jackson, who was sure that Crawford had tried to destroy his reputation during the controversy over his Florida adventures, wrote a series of "memorandoms [sic]" in 1822, one of which accused Crawford of corruption "in violating the consti[tution] employing a senator to travel over three states to examine the land offices that he might electioneer for him," and "interfering with the states elections of those favorable to his views to the Presidency." The senator in question was Jesse Thomas of Illinois, one of several Crawford supporters who were paid by the Treasury Department ostensibly to inspect land offices while actually working to build support for Crawford's election. Thomas's appointment was a clear violation of Article I, Section 6, of the Constitution, which prohibited members of Congress from concurrently "holding any office under the United States." The appointment as land office inspector was lucrative for Thomas and convenient for Crawford. Crawford also awarded Thomas more mileage money for his travel to Washington than any other Illinois congressman received; in the eyes of Thomas's Illinois rival Sen. Ninian Edwards, the mileage excess was simply a bribe.[43]

Edwards's distaste for Crawford began in the bank expansion that coincided with the land boom before Illinois statehood. As the largest shareholder in the Bank of Edwardsville, he had arranged for Crawford to designate his bank a depository for government funds in the territory. Although he disapproved of Crawford's policy of depositing government funds in favored banks, he preferred that land sale revenue collected in western Illinois be deposited in his own bank rather than in the Bank of Missouri, just across the river in St. Louis. (The only BUS branch west of Louisville was in New

Orleans, 1,200 river miles south.) But Richard and James Johnson, now vocal Calhoun supporters thanks to the Yellowstone contract, were large investors in the Bank of Edwardsville, and Crawford recognized a more useful ally in Jesse Thomas, who was an owner of the Bank of Illinois. He designated that bank a federal depository as well and took the unusual step of permitting Thomas's bank to decide which other banks' notes it would accept from land office receivers—allowing Thomas to blackball his political rival's Bank of Edwardsville. Edwards had no choice but to sell his stock in the bank and end his connection with it "in order to prevent its collapse"; only then did Crawford—having helped Thomas greatly—issue a directive ordering that depository banks now receive the notes of any specie-paying bank in their state. That was too late for the weakened Bank of Edwardsville; it failed in 1821, but the Bank of Illinois survived, reorganized under state ownership.[44]

Calhoun was eager to strike back at Crawford's stage management of the Fortress Monroe and Yellowstone scandalmongering by bringing public attention to these and other allegedly corrupt practices. When the Crawford forces in Congress succeeded in eliminating the Office of Indian Trade, Calhoun helped set up its former superintendent, Thomas L. McKinney, as editor of the Washington *Republican and Congressional Examiner*, newly created to counter the pro-Crawford Richmond *Enquirer*, Washington *Gazette*, Albany *Argus*, and New York *National Advocate*. In January 1823, the *Republican* printed an article written by Edwards under the initials "A.B.," accusing Crawford's supporters in the government printing shop of suppressing parts of documents requested by the House of Representatives the previous year, concerning receipts from public land sales. The tables were suddenly turned; the accused denied any wrongdoing, but there was no denying that sections of Crawford's Treasury Department documents had indeed been deleted before they were sent to the House. One suppressed passage revealed that Crawford had approved making deposits from the Pittsburgh and Chillicothe BUS branches in a struggling Ohio bank, even after it had stopped paying out specie. Another heavily edited document had hidden Crawford's admission that he had approved paying out post road contracts in the depreciated banknotes that the BUS held from that same bank, rather than in BUS notes at par—thus helping the BUS get rid of the notes at face value and letting the troubled bank dodge its inability to redeem them.[45]

This kind of manipulation of "hard" and "soft" currency was a common practice in the Treasury Department, and it often went on without Crawford's involvement; still, he knew about it and did nothing to discourage it.

It was not uncommon in the War Department, either, although Calhoun did try to root it out. Andrew Jackson's own Tennessee militiamen, sent to fight the Creek Indians, had been paid by the U.S. government in notes of the Bank of Chillicothe—which the militiamen discovered were not accepted as cash deposits by Tennessee banks and could not be used to pay taxes or purchase public lands. Two months after the "A.B." letters were published, there was a public scandal when Nashville pension agent Stephen Cantrell was revealed by Tennessee newspapers, reprinted in the *National Intelligencer*, to have used specie, issued to him to make pension payments, to purchase depreciated banknotes with which he paid the claimants, pocketing the difference. Calhoun fired him immediately, but the public only saw another example of government corruption.[46]

The questions being asked about Crawford by the *Republican* and other newspapers would soon be repeated by a House committee created to investigate. Were deposits that by law should have been kept in the BUS in fact going to favored local banks? Was government specie being exchanged for the depreciated paper of those banks? There were rumors that Crawford had bribed Illinois's Gov. Edward Coles, offering to pay him "however he pleased" to look into a suit against the Bank of Edwardsville and to handle claims made by the widow of a land office receiver.[47]

Things were becoming uncomfortable for the presumed front-runner, but Crawford had additional good reasons to get out of town that summer. Washington's weather was miserably hot and humid as usual, and Crawford was becoming seriously ill. (So, that summer, were Clay in Lexington and Jackson at the Hermitage; both were prone to various ailments that occasionally incapacitated them, and Jackson's dueling and brawling had left him carrying two lead bullets that slowly dissolved into his bloodstream. Calhoun had suffered from dysentery in his youth, contracted cholera or yellow fever in 1819, and was also chronically ill, but Adams was the picture of health, despite his habit of bathing in the polluted Potomac; he did his swimming upstream from where Washington's open sewers emptied in.) Crawford was worried by the fevers—yellow fever, cholera, and typhoid—spreading in the nation's capital, and he sought refuge in the Blue Ridge Mountains of Virginia, at the home of his good friend Sen. James Barbour. As Crawford's condition worsened, Barbour made the momentous decision to call in a local doctor. The physician diagnosed heart disease and prescribed digitalis, but he evidently administered an excessive dose. Crawford reacted violently, with the symptoms of a massive stroke. Although Barbour tried to keep the calamity secret, word spread through the surrounding counties; the elderly Thomas Jefferson, who rarely left home anymore, came to visit, convinced that Crawford was dying. Very gradually, however, his condition stabilized. In November, still paralyzed, nearly blind, and almost incapable of speech, he was brought back to Washington, where he lay in bed behind closed shutters. In December, Washington socialite Margaret Bayard Smith expressed her hope that "our friend Crawford will be able to see his Friends. He is now shut up in a dark room and sees very few persons."[48]

The Republican establishment was too deeply committed to Crawford's candidacy to believe that he was permanently incapacitated. There were some hopeful hints of a partial recovery, and Crawford refused to resign his office, remaining secretary of the treasury until 1825. But there were also relapses, and public appearances were out of the question. (He would eventually regain his speech and sight, living on until 1834.) The growing demand for more participatory politics, accelerated by the Panic, had made the congressional caucus unpopular, but Crawford's supporters, particularly the ambitious Van Buren, were now more determined than ever to seal his nomination through that route. Public distaste for wheeling and dealing undermined their effort; Hezekiah Niles declared that he would "rather learn that the halls of congress were converted to common brothels" than see them used for another caucus. In February, only 68 of the 216 Republicans in Congress took part in the caucus: sixty-four voted for Crawford, two for Adams, and one each for Jackson and Nathaniel Macon, but 148 stayed away. It was a dismal showing, but Van Buren pressed on. The vice-presidential nomination was offered first to Clay and then to Adams; both understandably declined, and the caucus finally had to settle on the aging Albert Gallatin: an ominous sign that both the caucus and Crawford were becoming irrelevant.[49]

The rejection of the caucus system in particular and of backroom politics in general was so widespread that a Missouri newspaper proclaimed that "Mr. Calhoun," who had not received a single vote in the caucus, "is, moreover, the candidate of the people—he has not been caucused into notice, but the people are rallying around his standard." That was wishful thinking. As Crawford lost momentum, the other candidates no longer had reason to unite against him, and Margaret Bayard Smith, ever the font of political gossip, reported that "Mr. Clhn [Calhoun] and Mr. A[dams] seem not such good friends as they were. I cannot tell what is the matter but our politicians think they will no longer lend each other a helping hand." Despite the hopeful words from the Missouri editor, too few people rallied around Calhoun's standard; eventually he withdrew, letting it be known that he would settle for the vice presidency. The "people's candidate," it now appeared, was actually Andrew Jackson, and as Calhoun's support dwindled, Jackson's grew.[50]

In the event, the effects of the Panic of 1819 did as much harm to Crawford's candidacy as his physical collapse; the political establishment that he represented had been discredited, party unity was no longer compelling when factions proved determined to pursue their own interests, and Crawford could not escape association with the financial policies that had brought on the lingering depression. The newly energized Democrats in both the rural West and the urban East were looking for new leaders less beholden than Crawford or Clay to the politically and financially powerful. The nation was repelled by the corruption that seemed to swirl around both Calhoun and Crawford as their various surrogates flung mud at one another. Hoping to tamp down the scandal in his administration, Monroe again resorted to the device of sending a troublemaker to a distant posting. He had already gotten Jackson out of the way once by making him governor of the Florida Territory; he tried to make Jackson minister to Mexico in 1823 when the general began to be mentioned as a candidate, but this time Jackson declined. Now Monroe hoped to send Ninian Edwards there instead, correctly suspecting that he was indeed "A.B." In March 1824 Edwards resigned his Senate seat to accept the appointment, and as he left for Mexico City he confirmed the suspicion that he was the author of the letters in the *Republican*. He also published explicit charges that Crawford had mismanaged funds, violated an 1816 congressional resolution by accepting depreciated banknotes, and deceived Congress about the amount. He accused him of misrepresenting the obligation of depository banks, failing to notify Congress when he continued to make deposits in favored banks, and withholding documents requested by Congress.[51]

Crawford denied everything, and Edwards was recalled to face a congressional investigation into the charges before he ever reached Mexico. The investigating committee was dominated by Crawford's friends, and its conclusions supported the "general correctness . . . of his administration of the public finances." Adams dismissed the committee report as a whitewash; Edwards's appointment was rescinded, but when the election was held, Crawford could manage no better than third place behind Jackson and Adams. That was enough, however, to exclude the fourth-place finisher Clay from the constitutionally mandated list of three names sent to the House of Representatives when no one won an absolute majority of electoral votes.

There had been unconvincing accusations of corruption against Adams, too, during the campaign; it was said that as secretary of state he had arranged the Adams-Onis Treaty purchasing Florida to benefit New England insurance companies who had previously paid American claims against Spain. While it is true that the signatures of claimants "On Account of Spanish Spoliation under the Treaty with Spain for the Cession of Florida" included presidents of seven large insurance companies, all were actually based in Pennsylvania and had no apparent connection with Adams. Far more damaging to Adams—and to Clay—would be the "corrupt bargain" by which Clay (through his influence as Speaker) was widely believed to have delivered the necessary House votes to make Adams president, in return for appointment as secretary of state. Calhoun called it "the most dangerous stab which the liberty of the country has ever received," and became the first vice president since Jefferson to enter office in opposition to the new president. He also backed an unsuccessful constitutional amendment to replace the electoral college with popular election of president and vice president, an idea that has surfaced at regular intervals ever since.[52]

Jackson was of course outraged. He had previously gotten along well with Adams (who had been more forgiving of Jackson's Florida excesses than anyone else in the cabinet). Now he fumed, "Was there ever such a bare faced corruption in any country before? . . . The Judas of the West has closed the contract and will receive the thirty pieces of silver." Jackson regularly imputed immorality to every politician except himself; his own record, however, was far from spotless. He had been accused of everything from bigamy to murder (there was something in both charges), including of course willful disobedience of orders in the Seminole campaign in Florida. His execution of two British subjects there, Alexander Arbuthnot and Robert Armbrister, created an international incident; the Liverpool *Mercury* called it "absurdly obvious" that he had violated the laws of war by insisting on their court-martial and forcing their hasty execution: "It is impossible to imagine that 13 or 14 officers, many of high rank, would voluntarily expose themselves to the risk of being disgraced, or that they would conspire together, unjustly, to deprive two obscure individuals of their life." The scandal was sufficiently notorious that, during the angry debate over Missouri, James Tallmadge asked whether opponents of slavery there should expect "the fate of Arbuthnot and Armbrister" at the hands of southerners.[53]

But Jackson's violent habits, even if contrary to law, were not the same as corruption; indeed, they probably won him more support in the South and

West than they cost him elsewhere. With Clay's BUS connection eroding his own following, many once-loyal followers in Kentucky eagerly turned to Jackson. Clay had always had the reputation of a deal-making politician, and the indignant victims of hard times were looking for someone to strike back forcefully against the malevolent "monster" Bank of the United States. Clay's lawsuits for the BUS hurt him, but Jackson's pursuit of his own debtors— he had once brought suit against 129 of them at a stroke—was overlooked or forgiven. In 1820 Calhoun had told Adams that the people were "ready to seize on any event and looking out anywhere for a leader." In 1824, that leader appeared to be Andrew Jackson.[54]

More than any other political figure, Jackson built his career after 1819 by railing against the corruption of the times. He presented himself as the only one who could—to use a phrase from a much later era—"drain the swamp," although the early nineteenth century preferred more classical metaphors: the Lancaster (Pennsylvania) *Journal* declared in 1822, "The Great Augean Stable at Washington wants cleansing, and we know of no other Hercules." His campaign began with his nomination by Tennessee's Relief Party legislators, and it became a crusade against corruption. Politicians, some more radical and some more conservative than Jackson, could not resist the pressure to get on his bandwagon. In Pennsylvania he took support away from Calhoun, and further West he won the endorsement of Clay's erstwhile allies. Cincinnati is the most often cited example of a city where "pronounced popular distress and insurgency against a ruling elite after the Panic of 1819 contributed to a vigorous and impassioned commitment to Jackson in 1824," but there were many others.[55]

It was the aftermath of the Panic that led the Overton faction in Tennessee to engineer Jackson's first state nomination in 1822, and his campaign built on the resentments of the Panic's victims. Those resentments were the focus of John Eaton's pseudonymous *Letters of Wyoming*, the most influential propaganda of the campaign. "Wyoming" described Jackson as another George Washington (who famously could not tell a lie), in sharp contrast to the "degeneracy" of the times embodied in the sophistication of Clay or the devious diplomatic background of Adams: "The metropolist of the Union already vies in aristocratic pomp and empty formalities with the corrupt court of the modern autocrat." The letters played on the hatred and fear of "the cabals of the selfish and intriguing"—the insiders and speculators whom the public blamed for the economic collapse—and they reiterated Jackson's conviction that the worst corruption of all was political: "Look to the city of Washington and let the virtuous patriots of the country weep at the spectacle. There corruption is springing into existence, and fast flourishing" among politicians "in quest of their own interest and promotion."[56]

The impact of corruption on electoral politics would take some time to unfold after 1819, as would the role of the Panic in the sectional division that led inexorably toward the Civil War—a division announced by the twin thunderclaps of the Tallmadge Amendment and *McCulloch v. Maryland*, arriving only three weeks apart in 1819. Although his name was attached to the Supreme Court case, James M'Culloh was only incidentally involved in it. He was, however, a central figure in the shameless corruption that fouled the reputation of the BUS at the very moment that John Marshall's decision made it a lightning rod for sectionalism. That scandal would bring him back into the courts, when he was pursued by the same state attorney general who had argued for Maryland before the Supreme Court, the venerable Luther Martin.

What happened in the Baltimore branch of the BUS was a sign of the times. The ideal of republican virtue seemed to be eroding rapidly. There was, said Niles, an "almost *universal ambition to get forward*," and in an atmosphere where anything appeared possible, where rules were few and ends seemed to justify means, virtue had little chance. In 1817/18, a New Hampshire lawyer named Estwick Evans made what he called a "pedestrious journey," walking westward to Michigan and then south to Louisiana. From frontier outposts like Detroit to sophisticated cities like New Orleans he found the same thing wherever he went: "The love of wealth in this country is making rapid inroads upon the love of principle, and nothing can retard its progress but the exclusive patronage of virtue and talents." By the time Evans published his account of the four-thousand-mile tour, the country was undergoing the collapse of what Condy Raguet called "golden dreams of artificial fortune." The explosion of bank paper and corporate stock in the wake of the War of 1812 was too great an opportunity to resist—especially as runaway speculation in public land was overheating the atmosphere. In 1822, J. D. Steele, traveling through Virginia to North Carolina, wrote in his journal,

> "It is really lamentable & humbling to the pride of integrity—to look at the numerous instances of . . . fraud which have occurred within the last 3 or 4 years— Scarcely is there a large city, or indeed a small one where there is a

Bank—that has not had cause to bewail the aberration from rectitude of some man of (before) unsuspected honesty & one whom the people have delighted to honor— Even now as I passed through Richmond a trial was pending against the state Treas^r as defaulter for $120,000."[57]

Americans were still getting used to having so many banks, with so many banknotes to lend. Such readily available money, eagerly proffered on easy credit, was an irresistible temptation, and many of "(before) unsuspected honesty" were quickly in over their heads. The line between speculation and fraud was blurred, and many people in positions of public trust—treasurers, bankers, customs collectors—violated that trust in the hope that endless expansion would enable them to pay back what they taken, before harm was done. But when the prosperity began to crumble, first in one location and then in another, it took them all down with it.

In 1818 the state treasurer of Kentucky was forced to resign when it was revealed that he was lending state funds to private individuals and pocketing the interest he charged them. The Virginia treasurer whom Steele mentioned had been investing state funds for his own profit; then came the Panic, and he was exposed when auditors discovered a deficit of $101,800. At the same time, just down the street from his office, a clerk at the Farmers Bank of Virginia admitted to embezzling at least $22,000. When Steele arrived in Fayetteville, he found the same thing happening there: "Mr. West, cashier at the U.S. Branch Bank at this place . . . has lately been sent here in place of Mr. Latimer, who became a defaulter to a considerable amount." Randolph Latimer had resigned after receiving repeated letters from the Treasury Department, complaining that returns for Treasury's accounts at his branch had not been received for several months. He does not appear to have been prosecuted. Meanwhile, Langdon Cheves believed the BUS branch in New Orleans had been negligent in collecting balances due from state banks because the cashier of the branch had investments in them. Again, there were no formal charges.[58]

Even bank directors, embarrassed to learn that the public viewed them as swindlers, began to protest when bankers who were clearly dishonest escaped punishment. Nicholas Biddle, newly appointed to the BUS board, wrote to former president James Madison to register his disgust. If a postal employee, he complained, "embezzles or secretes the smallest amount of property confided to him he may be publicly whipped and imprisoned for ten years," while an officer of the BUS "may defraud the institution of millions & escape the criminal law of the United States." Biddle was referring, of course, to the embezzlements of millions of dollars from the Baltimore branch by its president, its head cashier, and one of its directors.[59]

Only forty miles from the nation's capital, Baltimore just then seemed to epitomize everything that was going wrong in the country, from its rising unemployment to its annual epidemics of yellow fever and smallpox. Predictably, the defaulting BUS cashier in Fayetteville had come from Baltimore. Adams commented dourly, "There is not a city in the Union which has so much apparent prosperity or within which there has been such complication of profligacy." Stock in Baltimore's BUS branch amounted to 40,141 shares, legally held in the names of 15,628 persons. In reality, just fifteen individuals controlled three-quarters of it. Around the country three-quarters of all BUS stock was owned by fewer than a hundred investors, but by the Bank's charter, no individual could vote more than thirty shares, no matter how many he might own. Unscrupulous investors quickly figured out how to get around the restriction; Baltimore's George Williams, a national director of the BUS, had purchased one share each in the names of 1,172 individuals, recruited on the streets of Baltimore, who had agreed to let him vote their shares as their attorney. He controlled another thousand the same way in partnership with a clerk in his counting house, James M'Culloh, and branch president Buchanan. (M'Culloh was appointed head cashier, responsible for the branch office's daily activities, and thus, when the State of Maryland sued to collect taxes from the branch, the suit was filed against him.)[60]

In the palmy days of 1817 Williams, Buchanan, and M'Culloh were poised to make themselves rich with the Bank's money. The scandal that would cause the failure of Smith and Buchanan, the prostration of General Smith, and the indictment of the three conspirators began with a violation of the Bank's rule against unsecured loans. The branch president (Buchanan) and head cashier (M'Culloh) quietly approved loans of $429,049 to Buchanan and $244,212 to M'Culloh; to buy his silence they also cut the first teller in for $50,000. They used the money to purchase Bank stock, which was still rising in value. They then sold some of it, borrowed more money, and bought more stock. Very soon the head cashier, who was "absolutely without means" beyond his $4,000 salary, had borrowed $574,001.03 from the Bank. Bank officers Buchanan and Williams, wealthy men already, lent themselves another $2.5 million. By the beginning of 1819 these three had borrowed nearly half of all the money the branch had loaned—and it had loaned more than any other branch of the BUS.[61]

The three spread the Bank's money around freely. Dennis Smith (no relation to Samuel Smith) was president of the Mechanics Bank in Baltimore, from which he had borrowed $800,000. His loan was now due, in specie which he did not have; Mechanics Bank as an institution owed that same amount to the BUS, also in specie. This appeared to be a problem, but Smith also owned several thousand shares of BUS stock. To help him out—and themselves as well—Buchanan and M'Culloh purchased Smith's stock with notes freshly issued by the Baltimore branch, redeemable in specie as all BUS notes were. Smith paid Mechanics Bank, Mechanics Bank paid the BUS, and everyone was happy. But Buchanan and M'Culloh had bought Smith's stock in their own names, not the Bank's. Now, instead of using it to secure their mounting debt, they sold it at the going rate and used the proceeds to buy yet more BUS stock.[62]

The Bank's other directors later maintained that they had no idea what was going on—Buchanan and M'Culloh had full authority on their own to lend the funds of the branch—but BUS president William Jones asked no questions when Dennis Smith, Buchanan, and Williams made him a present of $18,000 in profits on speculation in Bank stock, and between October 1817 and April 1818, Jones himself sold 1,575 shares of stock—issued at $100 per share—at prices ranging from $139 to $153 per share, worth a quarter of a million dollars in all. By 1819 the three Baltimoreans had acquired 18,000 shares of Bank stock, which they listed as security for a loan of $1.9 million from the Philadelphia main office. When they borrowed an additional $1.5 million from the Baltimore branch, this second loan was supposedly secured by the "surplus value" of the same shares, although by then their market price had dropped to less than $100 per share; the "surplus value" did not exist.[63]

The stock price was falling because the Bank had begun its policy of contraction; it fell further when the House committee of Rep. John C. Spencer began investigating the Bank's management. Then the entire house of cards caved in. The public—and the BUS directors in Philadelphia—were shocked to learn how much money the Baltimore branch had loaned. *Niles' Register* began its reporting in italics, underlined, with multiple exclamation points, and then progressed to all capital letters—the contemporary equivalent of enormous black headlines:

Baltimore—eight million, four hundred and eighty-two thousand, three hundred and seventy-nine dollars and seventy-seven cents!!!—WHO HAS GOT IT? Not the people, generally—it is very doubtful if one million, or an eighth of this tremendous amount, is scattered among the regular traders of the city, in aid of regular business. For these, as everybody says, have been squeezed, and squeezed to the limit of leaving mercantile life in them.

The Spencer Committee report in February, despite the newspapers' outrage, stopped short of recommending that the BUS have its charter revoked but strongly condemned its cavalier lending habits—especially at the Baltimore branch. Even after Jones resigned, the directors required only that Buchanan and M'Culloh each furnish $300,000 security for their "loans." In March, M'Culloh (whose new fortune, or what remained of it, was quickly evaporating) went around to sixteen Baltimore merchants; each thought it good policy to endorse the personal note of the head cashier for $12,500. M'Culloh also put up the deed to his own house.[64]

On the day Langdon Cheves took over the BUS presidency, March 6, Marshall's opinion came down in *McCulloch v. Maryland*, throwing out Maryland's tax claim and upholding the constitutionality of the Bank's charter. It was the only good news Cheves would get for a long time. Ten days later he received the details—completely unsuspected, he maintained—of some $3 million loaned by the Baltimore branch without the knowledge of its directors. But the news could not have been the total surprise Cheves claimed. Even Adams, far more removed from the proceedings, had been aware since February that "the Congressional Bank Committee of the last season made a partial discovery of the state of affairs, and it was found that the debts of the house [of Smith and Buchanan] to the bank were enormous."[65]

As March gave way to April, Baltimore merchants began failing—led by Smith and Buchanan. Cheves fired M'Culloh, Buchanan resigned, and General Smith took to his bed. *Niles' Register* reported that "the sensation caused by the removal [of M'Culloh and Buchanan] was astonishing—and the effect of the conduct which it is supposed to indicate, is fearfully anticipated by mercantile men in Baltimore." The next week, Adams (who knew Smith well) wrote,

> For a day or two there was great blustering in the Baltimore newspapers, as if the greatest injustice had been done to M'Culloh, but the mine was blown up ... and a debt of nine hundred thousand dollars appears against the connection, little more than half of which is even supposed to be effectually secured. General Smith is reported to have gone distracted, and to be confined dangerously ill in bed. This explosion has brought on others: the failures are numerous and

for heavy sums. The Presidents and Cashiers of other banks have been playing the same game as Buchanan and McCulloh.[66]

Those other presidents and cashiers would heave sighs of relief when M'Culloh, Buchanan, and Williams got off scot-free, but the rest of the country was disgusted. Niles reported in June that the cashiers of Baltimore's Union Bank and City Bank both resigned; there were runs on those banks and on Dennis Smith's Mechanics Bank before the excitement subsided. It was, according to Niles, "the severest emergency that Baltimore ever experienced," evidently surpassing the British bombardment of Fort McHenry, only five years earlier, that had occasioned the writing of "The Star-Spangled Banner."[67]

The namesake of that fort, James McHenry, had died in 1816, three years before his own Bank of Baltimore was shaken by the Panic. It survived and also weathered the Panic of 1837, failing at last in the Panic of 1857. (Americans were about to discover the business cycle, but their collective financial memories would never reach back more than twenty years.) McHenry's daughter Anna Boyd wrote to her brother John McHenry in August 1819:

> I think, John, one of the most provoking parts of the business is that these destroyers of widows and orphans, affect to consider themselves as persecuted men. McCulloh for example struts about in all the pride and gaiety belonging to an honest heart, and unspotted name boasting as it were; that he is stripped of his feathers, that they are determined to bring him down and have succeeded."[68]

M'Culloh's rather spotted name now became attached to a second case moving through the Maryland courts: the state's prosecution of the three bankers for conspiracy to commit fraud. Luther Martin, Maryland's attorney general for thirty of the past forty-three years, had unsuccessfully represented the state in *McCulloch v. Maryland*. He was preparing his case against M'Culloh, Buchanan, and Williams when he was laid low in August by a stroke from which he would not recover. The prosecution went on without him, and the three "traversers," as they were called, were indicted in Baltimore's City Court for defrauding the BUS of $1.5 million. Their case was moved to rural Harford County when the defense understandably challenged the prospect of a fair trial in Baltimore. There it was thrown out by a two to one vote of the circuit court because conspiracy to defraud did not appear as a statutory offense among the Maryland criminal laws; as would be revealed again and again elsewhere, the law lagged behind the ingenuity of unscrupulous speculators. In 2009 Eric Hilt compared those early cases to what he called "the panic of 2008"; they were the first indication that "the evolution of financial regulations is a game of cat and mouse: regulations are imposed, the firms innovate, and if the innovations result in failures or scandals the regulations are updated and the cycle begins again."[69]

Although the court of appeals sent the case back to Harford County, maintaining that any conspiracy to an improper end was an offense under common law, in 1823 the same judges, by the same vote, found the defendants not guilty. (They had wisely opted for a trial without a jury.) They were, the court declared, simply victims of the financial crash; if their speculation had paid off, it would have made money for the Bank. The chief judge dissented a second time: "The Traversers, in violation of a sacred trust, and under false representations calculated to deceive those who were interested in the due execution of the trust, have taken from the funds of the office a large sum of money, which they converted to their own use, and have failed to return to the Bank a cent of their spoil."[70]

Much the same reasoning that acquitted the trio would be employed, with the same result, in the New York trial of Alfred Pell and his brother Ferris, author of the *Review of the Administration* of DeWitt Clinton and chronicler of the events of 1819 in New York. The brothers were among those charged with conspiracy when nearly a third of the companies listed on the New York Stock Exchange failed in 1826. Niles demanded punishment for the "coldly calculating scoundrels" and a cleansing of "the feculence of Wall Street"—one of the earliest published uses of the street's name to stand for the stock market. The first defendant to go to trial was Jacob Barker, who had helped save the federal government in 1814 with loans of millions of dollars. The prosecution dropped the rest of the cases after Barker's conviction was overturned by New York's unique Court for the Trial of Impeachments and Correction of Errors. This court was an anomalous survivor of the constitutional reforms of 1821, made up of all the state's supreme court justices plus all of the state senate. Barker had retained numerous defense attorneys who happened to be state senators and were thus able to rule on their own case.[71]

The failures of such prosecutions, in such circumstances, only reinforced the public perception that corrupt public officials looked out for corrupt bankers and financiers. Up until 1819 relatively few Americans had actually taken part in the political process—or felt any need to. Now, from the relief wars in the upper south to the awakening of the middling interest in New England, the effects of the Panic sparked the rise in participatory politics and the willingness to organize political factions to protect particular interests. The governing elite—old John Adams in Massachusetts, Chancellor Kent in New York, and the bluegrass aristocracy of Kentucky—bitterly condemned the tyranny of the majority as rule by mere numbers, but a page had been turned in American history.

The expansion of the franchise and the campaign to rescue republican virtue from corruption brought the dawning of the Jacksonian era. The Bank of the United States—engine of growth or monster of greed—remained a central focus as political warfare became a struggle for survival; Jackson would later tell Van Buren, "The Bank, Mr. Van Buren, is trying to kill me, *but I will kill it.*" The Bank, especially following *McCulloch v. Maryland*, came to symbolize the concentration of power that the South and West saw growing in the North and East, and power was universally understood to be the enemy of liberty. Thus 1819 was a watershed year: the corruption in the Bank and Marshall's sweeping new assertion of federal power fell on the country at the same time that the price of cotton collapsed and the Tallmadge Amendment challenged the future of southern slavery. From that point on, American politics would be not only factional but sectional; the South would see the threat of northern encroachment in every tariff or internal improvement bill. In February 1821, Rep. William Hendricks wrote to tell his Indiana constituents that the Panic of 1819, above all, had changed the political landscape: as a result of the "pecuniary embarrassments of the times . . . the interests and necessities of almost every section, have found their way into the Hall, and have advocates on the floor of the House of Representatives."[72]

A HOUSE DIVIDING
The Panic of 1819 and the Growth of Sectionalism

The economic cost of the Panic of 1819 was significantly higher—and the depression lasted much longer—than many modern historians realize. Even so, the economic hard times eventually lifted. As that happened, the debtor relief parties lost their hold on state legislatures, but the political activism awakened by the Panic persisted; indeed, it increased. So too did a more ominous development—cultural and political sectionalism, in the West and especially in the South, recoiling against the economic and political elements of the Northeast that were blamed for the depression. The alienation that was growing would endanger the Union long after the Panic was forgotten.

Since the 1600s, western settlements had been at odds with the East, which had been reluctant to share its political—and financial—power. In the early years of the nineteenth century, western manufacturing regions around Lexington and Pittsburgh had begun to develop a sense of economic independence that was crushed by the onslaught of cheap imports in 1815. Thereafter, protective tariffs were the single most critical interest for the western region. But most westerners were farmers, and land sales in the Northwest had boomed with the price of wheat in 1816 to 1817. The combination of bumper crops and the reimposition of the British Corn Law devastated foreign export prices. Farmers could no longer depend on the easy downriver route to market, especially after southern demand also shrank in the Panic, and internal improvements took on a new urgency in the West. But the final blow came in 1818 with the BUS policy of unrelenting contraction. Heavily indebted westerners watched the region's hard currency disappear over the mountains to the East and were united in their hatred for a common enemy—the monster Bank that, in Benton's vivid image, held their future like a dog that had mouthed a lump of butter, ready to wolf it down at any moment. Kentucky and Ohio fought back with prohibitive taxes on the Bank—taxes that Ohio was still pursuing in *Osborn v. Bank of the United*

States, five years after the *McCulloch* ruling; western anti-banking sentiment would finally propel Jackson into the White House in 1828.

Western sectionalism was born in the hard times of the Panic of 1819. The South's regional identity was formed before that crisis, but the events of 1818 to 1821 solidified the defensive outlook that would characterize southern society and politics for generations to come. Cotton planters' resentment of the middlemen who skimmed profits in New York intensified as the price of cotton slid in late 1818. That winter, the South felt itself under attack by both Congress and the Supreme Court, just as the bottom completely fell out of the cotton market. Southern nationalists who had patriotically supported the Tariff of 1816 felt betrayed, convinced that the tariff drove Britain to shift to India for its raw cotton; nationalists were becoming sectionalists. Old Republicans like Randolph felt vindicated, and southerners would henceforth see tariffs as cynical plots to enrich northern manufacturers at the expense of southern farmers.

Suspicion of the "paper system" and the BUS had begun earlier in the South than in the West, but the anti-federalism of Nathaniel Macon and John Taylor moved into the southern mainstream only with the Panic. Maryland, Tennessee, North Carolina, and Georgia were frustrated in their attempts to tax the BUS, but southerners were particularly alarmed by the breadth of Justice Marshall's decision. States' rights became a southern cause for economic reasons, and almost at once it was reinforced by the anti-slavery attack of Tallmadge's amendment to the Missouri statehood bill. It had been conventional in the South to regret slavery as a "necessary evil," but when the price of cotton fell to half what it had been—and stayed there—the necessity was magnified and the evil was brushed aside. With cotton hovering around the break-even point, the only way out was to make up for low prices with increased production. That was the reason that land auctions in the Southwest did not stop so abruptly as they had in the Northwest. But record land sales in Alabama and Mississippi produced record debts to a suddenly unpopular federal government. In 1811 Rep. Jeremiah Morrow had predicted that the Public Land Act would "engender disaffection of the most dangerous kind—disaffection nerved by the powerful motives of interest," because "the credit at present allowed often induces individuals to make purchases beyond their means." Now, in 1819, Rep. Ephraim Bateman warned (too late) that the "odious relationship, that of creditors and debtors between government and a portion of the people" was bound to be "productive of serious consequences."[1]

Expanded cotton production also meant the expansion of slave labor in the Southwest. The hard times in the wheat-growing upper South had lately made Virginia and Maryland slave-owners eager to sell their "surplus" slaves to these new plantations—and on to Missouri. It was at this point that anti-slavery congressman initiated their campaign against the westward expansion of slavery. Insult was added to injury when southerners were taken aback by the intensity of the speeches in the House attacking the South on moral grounds—coming from congressmen whose true motives, they believed, were more commercial than idealistic.

An indication of the change made by the Panic is the contrast between southerners' defiant reaction to Tallmadge's 1819 Missouri amendment and their conciliatory response to his anti-slavery attack on the new Illinois constitution only three months earlier (before the price of cotton collapsed). Likewise, the Supreme Court's extension of federal power in rulings against Georgia and Virginia had previously excited only the hardliners. But when Marshall appeared to grant absolute impunity to the BUS—after it was already the focus of southern and western anger—and when he implied that there were almost no limits to federal power just as the House claimed the power to stop the spread of slavery, outrage boiled over.

The growth of sectionalism—and the movement for states' rights—can be traced in the evolving challenges to the Bank of the United States. Two votes in Congress illustrate how much southern attitudes changed: the votes to charter the second BUS in 1816 and to renew its charter in 1832. When the initial bill, the work of South Carolina's Calhoun, came up for a vote in 1816 philosophical differences were still possible for southerners—not one southern congressional delegation was unanimous, although every one of them except Virginia came down in favor of the Bank, and even the Virginians opposed it by the narrowest of margins, 11 to 10. However, when Congress voted decisively to renew the charter in 1832 (107 to 85 in the House, 28 to 20 in the Senate), Louisiana would be the sole southern delegation to support renewal, and only one other southern senator would vote to recharter: Mississippi's George Poindexter, who had just received one generous loan from the Bank and was about to receive another.[2]

Before the Panic, opposition to federal power—and to the federally chartered Bank—had come chiefly from Old Republican ideologues with little influence outside Virginia. Before the 1816 charter vote, veteran Anti-Federalists like North Carolina's Nathaniel Macon had revived the arguments they had made against ratifying the Constitution in 1788, and Randolph from the beginning had warned that Calhoun and the Madison administration were abandoning the "federative" character of the Constitution and taking the country in the direction of "consolidation." But in 1816 they had been out of step with the expansionist mood of the South. At that time, Wilson Cary Nicholas (a member of the Richmond Junto, just finishing a term as governor) was pleased to accept the presidency of the Richmond branch of the BUS, and every southern state except Tennessee was happy to be awarded a branch office—two in Kentucky. Even Tennessee's objection was not philosophical but purely a matter of business: when the Tennessee legislature passed its $50,000 tax on *any* bank chartered outside the state, it was understood that Judge John Overton and his brother-in-law, Hugh Lawson White, simply did not want any outside competition for their banks in Nashville and Knoxville.[3]

Other states had equally pragmatic reasons for taxing the Bank—purely economic and neither philosophical nor political. Maryland had been the first, imposing a tax on the Baltimore office just a month after it opened for business, and Maryland would be the first to face a court challenge by the Bank. The state called for a cumbersome tax on each note issued, which could be avoided with an annual payment of $15,000—not out of line with recent precedent: in 1815 Maryland had begun taxing its state banks twenty cents on each thousand dollars of capital, and in 1813 Baltimore banks had been required to pay in a total of $1.12 million to buy shares in a turnpike corporation, at twenty dollars per share. (By 1820 that stock would depreciate to a value of $2.25 per share.)[4]

Maryland set a fine of $500 for each failure to pay taxes on the issuance of banknotes, awarding half the fine to any informer who brought the violation to the state's notice. On May 18, 1818, John James of the city of Baltimore applied to collect $250 as payment for the information that no tax had been paid on notes the head cashier, James M'Culloh, had issued to George Williamson. In nine months the suit passed through the state courts, evolving into *McCulloch v. Maryland* when it was argued before the United States Supreme Court from February 22 to March 3, 1819.[5]

Meanwhile, several other states were also taxing the BUS. In December 1817, a few months after Maryland, Georgia passed a law taxing bank stock 31¼ cents per $100, followed shortly by a resolution clarifying that the law applied only to the BUS, at its Savannah branch. The next year North Carolina imposed a $5,000 tax on the Fayetteville branch. Hezekiah Niles, an energetic enemy of the BUS, encouraged states to "tax the mother bank and the branches out of every resting place except the ten mile square" of the District of Columbia, but there is nothing in the records of the Maryland, Georgia, or North Carolina legislatures to indicate that their goal was anything other than raising revenue, although the Pennsylvania legislature did petition Congress to restrict the Bank's operations to Washington, D.C. The legislatures in Virginia, New York, and Pennsylvania also debated taxing the BUS but decided against it.[6]

The Bank's initial popularity was destroyed by its rigorous contraction, but even before that, a committee of the Ohio legislature had recommended a defensive tax on the BUS in January 1818. The committee report accurately predicted that the BUS branches in Chillicothe and Cincinnati "must very seriously affect the operations of the state banks" there and warned that "the capital introduced into the country through these branches, is directly calculated to wither our agriculture and cramp our manufactures." Still, the Bank had not begun making the demands that would devastate Ohio, and the legislature took no action—yet. But that fall, as shipments of specie left the West for Philadelphia, Kentucky passed a $60,000 tax on the BUS with the clear intention of driving its branches out of Lexington and Louisville. The Supreme Court had already agreed to take up the Maryland case, but twelve days before arguments began, Ohio became the sixth and last state to impose a tax on the bank: $50,000 on each of the two branches. All six states were in the South or the West—the sections most affected by the Bank's contraction.[7]

Through the fall and winter of 1818 there was a steady drumbeat of criticism of the BUS, prompted by the effects of its policy of contracting credit and exacerbated by the behavior of some of its officers, who seemed more interested in enriching themselves than in stabilizing the nation's finances. In October, two unnamed New York congressmen published letters in *Niles' Register*. The author of the first letter declared, "I was one of a number who voted for the incorporation of that *now-swindling monster* . . . I could never have believed that there were men to be found (that called themselves honorable) in the community, that would unblushingly prostitute themselves to the same vile purpose." The second acknowledged, "I voted for the corporation against my own personal interest; but with others, long since regretted that vote."[8]

In its November 7, 1818, issue, the *Register* published a collection of essays critical of both state banks and the BUS. Niles applauded Ohio's proposal to tax the Bank, and urged other states to follow that course: "In it lies the best, or only, hope of safety. . . . The state of Maryland, and I believe Kentucky, have passed laws to tax the Bank of the United States. Similar laws will probably be passed by Pennsylvania, Virginia, and Ohio—and perhaps by some other states. A suit, we are informed, is about to be carried before the superior court of the United States to test the law of Maryland." The justices, who regularly read the *Register,* fully understood that if they found Maryland's tax to be constitutional, the Bank's position would be precarious; the power to tax, as Daniel Webster would remind them, was indeed the power to destroy.[9]

But before the case could reach the Supreme Court, Congress raised the pressure on the Bank. On November 25, New York's Rep. John C. Spencer introduced a resolution calling for an investigation of the Bank's practices; five days later he was appointed chairman of the investigating committee. While the committee deliberated, BUS president William Jones reported on the Bank to the secretary of the treasury; his report was met with first skepticism and then derision when it became public. On January 2, 1819, Niles pointed out some of the contradictions in Jones's attempts to explain how BUS stockholders were able to use the Bank's own notes to pay the second installment on their capital subscriptions—payments the law required to be made in silver or gold. That January 1817 installment had been due four days *before* the Bank's charter permitted it even to begin issuing banknotes—a schedule that was clearly intended to prevent the very form of payment that the stockholders somehow employed. Niles's scorn was unrestrained:

> We have emphatically designated this letter as the production of an "ingenious man"—compelled to recollect the trite saying, that *"public* bodies never feel shame"; whilst we proffer our tribute to the individual whose *official* duty it has been to sign it. We have considered it as the effusion of a *lawyer* at the bar, who having received a fee, was forced "to make a speech," no matter whether it was to the purpose or not to the purpose—and evade those things which he could not deny.

Henry Clay, who had an idea what would be in Spencer's report two weeks before it was released, sent a note to Kentucky's Sen. Martin Hardin on January 4. He admitted that the Bank "has been badly administered. But should we give up the ship, because the crew has misbehaved?"[10]

When the Spencer Committee report was presented to Congress on January 16, it censured the Bank's directors for mismanagement, speculation, and violation of the charter. Indiana's Hendricks called the report "an exposé of a series of improprieties on the part of the directors, not perhaps equaled in the history of any other money institution." But the committee's conclusions were inconsistent and vague, simply calling on the directors to correct past abuses; no crimes were charged, and there was no recommendation that the charter be revoked. When nothing further happened in Congress, criticism of both the Bank and the report grew louder in every part of the country. In February, Rep. John W. Campbell of Ohio wrote home to Allen Trimble, who was about to be elected governor,

> Congress is much perplexed to know what ought to be done with the United States Bank. It now appears to have more friends than it had three weeks ago. Some are for doing nothing on the ground that the stockholders will correct the evil—others say "Spare it," the state banks have done as bad or worse. Some say repeal the charter at once and be done with it. . . . The fear is that nothing will be done.

Ferris Pell, the New York financier, was disgusted:

> The disgraceful policy pursued by the Bank of the United States has tended to widen the gulf of national suffering and heighten the zest of every calamity. In [1817] it enlivened and extended credit, occasioned a flood of paper, gave a hectic excitement to property; and is now, having blackened our national character, and withered thousands of our citizens, by its perfidious laxity, levelling a vital blow at its own existence, by as pernicious a severity.[11]

Many critics believed the Bank was being exploited by unscrupulous investors who were, like the Baltimore trio, speculating in Bank stock. John Quincy Adams, however, was convinced "that the government is the party most interested in the continuance of the Bank and that the interest of the stockholders would be to surrender the charter." He probably had in mind the Bank's value to the treasury; in 1819 it was still expected that the Bank would somehow find the specie with which to redeem the Louisiana Purchase stock. In June, Niles viewed that obligation as the Bank's primary excuse for continuing its policy of contraction, "using its vast power, through government deposits, on the pretext of being compelled to pay about $2,600,000 on the Louisiana loan, to prostrate, not only the whole body of speculators in its own stock, but needlessly to embarrass the good state banks, forbidding them to accommodate their old regular customers." Hendricks, however, believed the Bank had been of little benefit thus far to the government: "It has offered few facilities to the operation of the Treasury. It has not equalized the currency of the country. It has enriched its directors and stock-jobbers, at the expense of others." In actuality, the branch of the federal government with the greatest stake in the survival of the BUS turned out to be the U.S. Supreme Court and its chief justice, John Marshall.[12]

For several years now the court, forcefully led by Marshall, had been the last outpost of federalism. It had handed down a steady stream of decisions upholding the sanctity of contracts, the privileges of corporations, and the power of the federal government over the states. The court had not over-turned an act of Congress since Marshall's first decision, *Marbury v. Madison* in 1801, but it had shown no reluctance to throw out state laws and overturn state courts. In 1810 *Fletcher v. Peck* had declared a state law unconstitutional: the court had overruled Georgia's cancellation of the fraudulent Yazoo land grants. In March 1816, *Martin v. Hunter's Lessee* asserted the power of the U.S. Supreme Court to reverse a decision by the Virginia Supreme Court. That decision came only weeks before the vote to charter the Bank of the United States—a vote in which the majority of Virginia congressmen denied the authority of Congress to charter a corporation.

As the critical year of 1819 began, the court went further in asserting fed-eral authority over states. On February 2, the *Dartmouth College* decision de-nied New Hampshire's right to modify a charter of incorporation. Less than two weeks later, the court overturned New York's bankruptcy law in *Sturges v. Crowninshield*, ruling that the power to regulate bankruptcy was exclusively federal, even if Congress declined to exercise it. The decision came just as the House, passing Tallmadge's Missouri amendment, denied a prospective state's right to decide whether to permit slavery.

John Marshall was a Virginian; he had stepped aside in *Martin v. Hunter's Lessee* because he was himself among the owners of the Virginia real estate that the case involved. (He subsequently sold his stock in the BUS, saying that "a question might be brought before the Supreme Court in which the bank might be concerned.") The holder of over one hundred slaves, he was by no means anti-southern or particularly anti-slavery. But his court's decisions were widely unpopular in the South because each one seemed to go another step further in extending the power of the federal government and denying the sovereignty of the states—often at the very moment that the struggle over sovereignty was highlighted by some controversy unrelated to the case in question. That was never truer than in 1819.[13]

McCulloch, arising just as the economy began to fall apart, moved through the courts with remarkable speed: John James presented his information to Maryland in May 1818, and nine months later the Supreme Court was hearing arguments. The case was argued from February 22 to March 3, 1819, and the decision came down on March 6 in a record three days—an alacrity never matched before or since. (Two or three weeks was a more typical interval at the time. Writing the decision in *Gibbons v. Ogden* occupied Marshall for a month; the *Dred Scott* decision in 1857 took Roger Taney nearly three months after oral arguments concluded.)

Two great questions that could not wait were pressing the court to move so quickly. The Supreme Court was then meeting in the basement of the Capitol. (It would not have its own building until 1935.) As oral arguments began in *McCulloch*, overhead a parallel debate was taking place in Congress, where the Missouri crisis had just burst forth. The historic question of whether the federal government would restrict slavery in a new state still remained unanswered when Congress adjourned—on the same day that arguments concluded in the Supreme Court's chambers below. The second question, less momentous than slavery but just as timely, was the fate of the Bank of the United States: its "perfidious laxity" and "pernicious severity" now seemed to be at the heart of a national economic collapse, but the investigation by the Spencer Committee had proved no more conclusive than the suspended debate over Missouri. The case now before the court could have an enormous impact on both questions: its result could prove fatal to the Bank if the court found for Maryland, and the underlying question was nothing less than the constitutional limitations of federal power over states' rights.

In February 1819, as Marshall's court began to hear arguments in *McCulloch v. Maryland*, a majority in the House of Representatives had just voted to deny Missouri's sovereignty where slavery was concerned. (The Senate had yet to take up the amendment.) It was a critical moment. On one hand, if Maryland prevailed in its claim of sovereignty over the BUS, Marshall's expansion of federal sovereignty over states would come to a sudden halt, and the states would quickly tax the Bank out of Ohio, Kentucky, Georgia, North Carolina, and probably other states as well—maybe out of existence. On the other hand, if the Bank, that hated symbol of centralized power, should win its suit—and if states should be denied the fundamental sovereign power of taxation—what was left of states' rights? If Congress had the authority to charter a bank—a power nowhere mentioned in the Constitution—what might Congress *not* do? And how could an outnumbered South protect what Calhoun would call its "peculiar institution"?[14]

Daniel Webster was the first of three attorneys arguing the Bank's case. He began by paraphrasing a passage from Marshall's *Life of George Washington*. Defending the charter of the First BUS in 1791, Marshall had written, "When a power is delegated to effect particular objects, all the known and usual means of effecting them must pass as incidental to it." Now Webster said, "If [a power] be a fit instrument to an authorized purpose, it may be used, not being specially prohibited." Joining Webster against Maryland were Attorney General William Wirt (employed in his private capacity) and William Pinkney (whom Maryland would nevertheless send to the Senate later that year.) Representing Maryland were Walter Jones, Joseph Hopkinson, and the state's attorney general, Luther Martin, one of the few surviving delegates to the 1787 Constitutional Convention. There he had supported the concept of judicial review, but he had refused to sign the Constitution, fearing that it gave too much power to the central government. Arguing now for Maryland's right to tax and against the broad powers being claimed for Congress, he reached back to the early debates over the Constitution's ratification. There he had found an unexpected ally. He announced that he would read from the records of Virginia's 1788 ratifying convention. At that point, according to Justice Joseph Story, John Marshall sighed and drew in a long breath. Martin then began to quote delegate John Marshall, who had assured the convention that the federal powers were strictly limited: "The powers not denied to the States . . . being possessed of them antecedent to the adoption of the government, and not being divested of them, by any grant or restriction in the Constitution, the States must be as fully possessed of them as ever they had been."[15]

Martin must have relished the irony, but Marshall was not persuaded by his younger, strict-constructionist self; nor was he impressed when Hopkinson argued that the Bank was not a federal agency but rather a private, for-profit company, 80 percent of which was owned by private stockholders—including foreign investors with shares amounting to nearly $3 million. These were not insignificant arguments, but Marshall chose simply to ignore them. The unanimous court upheld the BUS charter and denied Maryland's authority to tax the Bank. But Marshall did not intend to stop there. His aim was to assert the power of Congress to take any "legitimate" action that the Constitution did not specifically prohibit. Martin had argued, on his personal authority as one of the framers, that such a broad interpretation of the Constitution as Marshall now proposed had been dismissed by the 1787 convention as "a dream of distempered jealousy," an imaginary threat that friends of the Constitution need not fear. Now Marshall's sweeping interpretation—in conjunction with the attack on slavery in Missouri—would turn previously nationalist southerners into sectionalists who would come to see almost any use of federal power as a threat to the South.[16]

Marshall declared that the authority given Congress in Article I to enact "all laws . . . necessary and proper" meant much more than most Republicans believed it did: to be "necessary," a given law need not be the only possible way to carry out a power granted in the constitution, nor must the power in question actually be specified there in order to be "proper." Marshall boldly declared, "Let the end be legitimate, let it be within the scope of the constitution, and all means which are appropriate . . . are constitutional." Such a broad reading had not been suggested since the days of Alexander Hamilton, and Republicans—once they caught their breath—were incensed. Story understatedly observed, "This decision excites great interest, and in a political view is of the deepest consequence to the nation." Niles's response was one of the more restrained: "We frankly express *our* opinion, that the writer of the *opinion* in question has not added anything to his stock of reputation by writing it." John Randolph was uncharacteristically at a loss for words, simply calling the decision "wrong, wrong, all wrong." In Richmond, Thomas Ritchie's *Enquirer* began publishing a series of essays attacking the decision.[17]

In the first two essays, "Amphyction" (probably Judge William Brockenbrough, whose brother was president of the Bank of Virginia) denied Marshall's assertion that the *people* had created the federal government, rather than the states—reviving the argument that Patrick Henry had made at the same Virginia convention where Marshall had promised that only enumerated powers could be claimed. Henry had demanded, "Who authorized them to speak the language of We the People, instead of We the States?" "Amphyction" now reiterated the "compact" theory of the Constitution's adoption by sovereign states and warned that Marshall's reasoning opened the door to all kinds of federal projects that both Madison and Monroe had vetoed as unconstitutional; Congress might now spend money on roads and canals, "create boards of internal improvements," and "incorporate companies for a great variety of purposes" never mentioned in the Constitution.[18]

This criticism was mild compared to what was to come, but it impelled Marshall to take the unprecedented step of defending his decision in his own letters to the Philadelphia *Union* and the Alexandria *Gazette*, signed "A Friend of the Union" and "A Friend of the Constitution." The next to weigh in was Virginia's chief justice, Spencer Roane, in four essays signed "Hampden." (It was Roane's ruling that had been reversed in *Martin v. Hunter's Lessee.*) In his four "Hampden" essays he darkly compared the loose construction of *McCulloch* with that "which brought the memorable Sedition act into our code" when Marshall was John Adams's secretary of state. Now Roane blamed not only Marshall but the atmosphere which had brought on the Panic of 1819: a public "sunk in apathy, . . . sodden in the luxuries of banking" who demonstrated a "money-loving, funding, stock-jobbing spirit . . . almost prepared to sell our liberties for a 'mess of pottage.'" To Roane, the Panic and *McCulloch* were closely linked.[19]

Roane's friends and correspondents included Thomas Jefferson and James Madison. In August he sent copies of his essays to Madison; the former president, who refused to make public comments from his retirement, wrote back privately to Roane. Unlike Jefferson, Madison agreed with the court that Maryland lacked authority to tax the federally chartered BUS, but he strongly objected to Marshall's *obiter dictum* that went on to expand the sphere of federal power. As a believer in judicial review, he also noted a possible consequence certainly unintended by Marshall: "Does not the Court also relinquish, by their doctrine, all control on the Legislative exercise of unconstitutional powers?"[20]

One Virginian who was never reluctant to publish his views—at length—was Madison's cousin, John Taylor of Caroline. He had labored for twenty years over *An Inquiry into the Principles and Policies of the United States Government,* completed in 1814, but *McCulloch v. Maryland* inspired a burst of intense activity, and in a matter of months he completed the 344 pages of *Construction Construed and Constitutions Vindicated.* He followed it with two more books in the next two years, *Tyranny Unmasked* and *New Views of the Consolidation of the United States.* Taylor had his own personal history with John Marshall, having squared off in a largely forgotten case that anticipated the arguments of *McCulloch.* Ten years before Marshall's appointment to the Supreme Court, in *The Rev. John Bracken v. the Visitors of William and Mary College,* Taylor had argued for a strict construction of the college's charter, and Marshall had defended the school's more liberal interpretation. Taylor had insisted that a corporation was restricted to doing only that which its charter specified; Marshall had maintained in essence that it could take any legitimate action that its charter did not forbid. Marshall had prevailed before a Virginia Supreme Court of Appeals that, ironically, included Justice Spencer Roane.[21]

The first 290 pages of *Construction Construed* were a point-by-point critique of Marshall's thirty-eight manuscript pages, especially Marshall's idea that almost any means was permissible to a constitutional end: "[E]nds may be made to beget ends, until the co-habitants shall rear a progeny of unconstitutional bastards, which were not begotten by the people." But Taylor had two other targets. The first, which he had attacked exhaustively in his *Inquiry*, was "the paper system." The second was the Tallmadge Amendment. The Panic of 1819, he now believed, had vindicated his 1814 attacks on paper money, and in *Construction Construed* he repeated them, once again employing the metaphor of procreation:

> The great pecuniary favors granted by congress to certificate holders begot banking; banking begot bounties to manufacturing capitalists; bounties to manufacturing capitalists begot an oppressive pension list; these partialities united to beget the Missouri project; that project begot the idea of using slavery as an instrument for affecting the balance of power; when it is put in operation, it will beget new usurpations of internal power over persons and property, and these will beget a dissolution of the union.[22]

No other decision of the Supreme Court would inspire such strong and extended reaction until *Dred Scott* in 1857. Legal historian R. Kent Newmyer ascribes the "apocalyptic" tone of the response to the same two contemporary influences that Taylor focused on. First, he cites "the Panic of 1819 and the onset of the business cycle in American history." The Panic of 1819 had made southerners realize just how precarious their position was. As Marshall complained to fellow justice (and fellow Virginian) Bushrod Washington, even stockholders in the Bank like Richmond branch president Wilson Cary Nicholas—ruined by the Panic—were attacking his decision. The Panic and the shocking misbehavior it revealed had made the Bank a symbol of corruption, mocked in the popular press. (*Aurora*, October 1819: "'Are you not ashamed of yourself?' said a lady to a gentleman, in a playful manner.—'Why should I be ashamed of myself,' rejoined the gentleman, 'I am not a bank director.'") Now Marshall's decision made it the symbol of an overreaching, consolidating federal government as well. Many southern leaders, "previously noted for their moderation and nationalism, now listened with new respect to the voices of extremism: to publicists like John Taylor of Caroline County . . . and to the mesmerizing oratory of John Randolph."[23]

The second timely influence was the Missouri crisis—Taylor's ultimate instance in the extension of federal power "begotten" by *McCulloch*. The governor of Georgia, where the court was already unpopular after *Fletcher v. Peck*, would soon call the Marshall court and the House of Representatives "a combination of fanatics for the destruction of everything valuable in the southern country." Taylor, Ritchie, and Roane agreed. When the Supreme Court Historical Society reenacted the oral arguments of *McCulloch v. Maryland* in 2014, Justice Stephen Breyer told the lawyer portraying Daniel Webster, "What your opponent is worried about is slavery." As Newmyer notes, "The point is not that Virginians perceived an immediate threat to the 'peculiar institution,' but rather that Marshall's opinion invited them to think comprehensively about where they stood in the economic revolution gathering steam across the land." That included the future of cotton planting; the 1819 price was about to fall below the break-even point if slave labor could not expand, and planters were in debt for thousands of newly purchased acres. The *McCulloch* decision and the Missouri crisis were closely linked in southern minds—and both were linked to the Panic of 1819.[24]

Marshall had hoped his decision would strike a decisive blow for nationalism; instead, it energized the states' rights movement that would, just as Taylor foresaw, lead ultimately to secession and Civil War.

Clearly, slavery was the wedge that split the nation, North and South. Always the background for objections to *McCulloch v. Maryland*, it leaped into the foreground in the debate over Missouri. Students are often taught that the intense controversy over Missouri statehood sprang from two factors: the "long-standing" balance of slave and free states and the rapidly growing world demand for cotton, which led southerners to abandon the belief that slavery was a necessary evil and to adopt the conviction that it was a positive good. But a careful examination of the development of the Missouri controversy reveals flaws in both of these popular assumptions and suggests that the unfolding events had much more to do with the developing economic crisis than has been appreciated.

The belief that balancing the number of slave and free states was a principle to which either North or South was committed is an instance of reading history backwards. In retrospect, it is evident that the growing northern population had created a permanent majority in the House of Representatives, leaving the Senate as the South's only defense against the passage of federal laws that might threaten its interests. And the eventual solution in the

Missouri Compromise—tying the admission of the slave state of Missouri to the admission of the free state of Maine—draws modern attention to the pattern of state admissions in the first half of the nineteenth century: an almost (but not quite) regular alternation of slave and free states, ending when California permanently tipped the balance in the Compromise of 1850. But there are several problems with this view. First, it does not seem to have engaged contemporary attention until the prospect of Texas statehood arose in the 1830s; as Matthew Hall reminds us in *Dividing the Union: Jesse Burgess Thomas and the Making of the Missouri Compromise*, "The shibboleth of requiring exactly equal numbers of slave and non-slave states had not yet implanted itself in the American political consciousness." Second, and perhaps more troublesome for the "balance" theory, there actually *was no balance* to be challenged at the time the Missouri bill was brought forward.[25]

In February 1819, when Congress began its acrimonious debate over the admission of Missouri, the Union consisted of twelve states in which slavery was forbidden and eleven in which the practice was allowed. "Balance" would only come about, in passing and unremarked, when Alabama was admitted in December 1819, ten months into the Missouri controversy. Debates in Congress when other states before Missouri were admitted reveal no concern for balance on the part of either region. There were no southern objections when Indiana's entry in 1816 created a majority of free states, nor was there any complaint from northern congressmen when Mississippi's admission gave the South its strategic tie the following year. Illinois's admission did excite contention in the fall of 1818, but there was no southern objection that Illinois was giving free states an 11 to 10 advantage in the Senate. In fact, all of the votes against the admission of Illinois came from anti-slavery northern representatives, who wanted a state constitution that would forbid any *future* amendment to allow slavery (a promise that Indiana's constitution had included but Illinois's lacked). The bill to admit Illinois with the constitution that its people had already approved, flatly forbidding slavery, passed the House by a vote of 117 to 34 with complete southern support, and its approval was unanimous in the Senate.

The failed resistance to Illinois's admission was led by New York's Rep. James Tallmadge, whose amendment to restrict slavery would trigger the Missouri crisis a few months later. But even after the angry debates when that amendment was introduced in February 1819—debates that went so far as threats of personal violence and dire warnings of disunion—Tallmadge himself declared that he had no objection to the planned admission of Alabama as a slave state the following December. The North's numerical advantage in the Senate was given up without a fight. Mississippi's George Poindexter had been one of the few southerners to speak at all when Illinois's admission was debated, and he had endorsed its entry as a free state, entitled to the laws it chose to pass. On November 23, 1818, he declared, "It would be a blessing, could we get rid of [all slaves]; but the wisest and best among us have not been able to devise a plan for doing it." At a moment when cotton prices were soaring and land sales in Alabama were setting records, the Mississippian had expressed his hope that slavery might someday be expelled from the Union— and no southerner rose to defend the institution. During the heated Missouri debate, Tallmadge promised not to oppose slavery in the prospective state of Alabama, expressing his concern that it might be unsafe to ban slavery in that geographic situation:

> I would not ever advocate the prohibition of slavery in the Alabama Territory; because, surrounded as it was by slaveholding states, and with only imaginary lines of division, the intercourse between slaves and free blacks could not be prevented, and a *servile* war might be the result. While we deprecate and mourn over the evil of slavery, honesty and good morals require us to wish its abolition, under circumstances consistent with the safety of the white population.[26]

The election in New York for the Sixteenth Congress had been held in April 1818; Tallmadge, who been elected in 1817 to fill a vacated seat, had not chosen to run for reelection. Thus, when he introduced his Missouri amendment, he was what would later be called a lame duck. Having begun his career as the secretary of Gov. George Clinton, in 1802 he had become an attorney practicing in Poughkeepsie and Manhattan and a political follower of Clinton's nephew DeWitt; he was thus an adversary of Van Buren's Bucktails, whose reforms he would oppose at the state's 1821 constitutional convention. Tallmadge had played a part in New York's final abolition of slavery in 1817, and he modeled his proposal for Missouri on New York's gradual emancipation law. As it happened, the population of African Americans in Missouri in 1819 was about the same as in New York—around ten thousand.[27]

Tallmadge's brief career in the House had been uneventful, simply following the lead of his more experienced New York colleague, John Taylor, another Clintonian. His challenge to the Illinois constitution—restrained, even deferential—was the first time many congressmen had heard his voice. But as his final days in the House wound down, he evidently decided to go out with a bang. He held nothing back in his denunciation of southern slave owners, and when Georgia's Thomas Cobb and Missouri delegate John Scott raised the specter of disunion, he exclaimed, "Sir, if a dissolution of the Union must take place, let it be so! If civil war, which gentlemen so much threaten, must come, I can only say, let it come!" The intensity of his speeches on February 16 and the violence of the reaction seem to have overwhelmed him, and he did not speak again until the penultimate day of the Fifteenth Congress, when the House received the Senate's rejection of his amendment. He urged the representatives to table the Missouri statehood bill, and to his satisfaction they voted once again to make the restriction of slavery an absolute condition of admission, before adjourning.[28]

The Senate's vote to reject the Tallmadge Amendment was much closer than is often assumed. The usually scrupulous Robert Remini says that "the Senate shot it down by the overwhelming vote of 31 to 7," but that is entirely misleading. In fact, Tallmadge's proposal had two sections, which the Senate took up separately. The critical first clause, prohibiting the introduction of any more slaves into Missouri, was defeated 22 to 16, and only because it was opposed by five northern senators: both of the new Illinois senators, Edwards and Thomas, along with the Massachusetts Federalist Harrison Gray Otis, Pennsylvania's Abner Lacock, and William Palmer of Vermont. (Like Tallmadge, the latter three did not seek reelection.) Had they voted in favor, the amendment would have passed even if the three absent southern senators had been there to vote "no." In that case the Missouri admission bill would have landed on President Monroe's desk with the expansion of slavery prohibited—but with nothing done to free the ten thousand slaves already there. It was the second clause of the amendment—gradual emancipation of only the *children* of slaves born *after* admission, upon reaching the age of twenty-five—that was defeated 31 to 7, opposed by many northern senators unwilling to go on record as voting to leave present Missouri slaves in bondage for life.[29]

The Senate rejected the Tallmadge Amendment on February 28; the next day, it also voted against restricting slavery in the Arkansas Territory—already narrowly rejected in the House as well—by the closer vote of 19 to 14. On March 4 the Senate adjourned, and the Fifteenth Congress was done, leaving the Missouri question to its successor—the Sixteenth Congress that had already been elected but would not meet until December 1819.

When Tallmadge first spoke up to challenge Illinois's admission in November 1818, cotton was still at record-high prices, Spencer's committee had not yet begun to investigate the BUS, and land sales were booming. *McCulloch v. Maryland* had not yet reached the Supreme Court. Less than four months later, when Congress adjourned without passing the Missouri statehood bill, the price of cotton was in free fall, land sales had stalled in the Northwest (although not yet in Alabama), and Chief Justice Marshall was putting the finishing touches on a *McCulloch* decision that would outrage southerners in particular, opponents of the Bank in general, and advocates of states' rights above all. That March the economic collapse of 1819 was just sinking in on many Americans, and sectionalism in politics was not yet set in concrete. In early 1819 it was still possible for public figures from all regions to hold positions that were not dictated wholly by geography. John Quincy Adams would later regret that the Tallmadge Amendment had not become law, but as late as July 1819 he wrote, "On this particular question I did not approve of the attempted restriction upon the State of Missouri because I believe it not compatible with the Constitution of the United States or the Louisiana Treaty," and he criticized Crawford for trying to capitalize on southern resentment of the amendment. By the time the new Congress assembled in December to take up the Missouri crisis again, much had changed. The low price of cotton was no longer startling news but a grim, persistent fact of life. Planters in the deep South had made their calculations and determined that the only strategy for coping with low prices and inescapable debts was increased production—by slave labor. With wheat prices also half what they had been, and facing their own mounting debts and the decreasing demand for tobacco, slave owners in Maryland and Virginia saw no alternative but to sell slaves to those planters—and to Missouri.

The first Missouri debate had taken place in the midst of the unfolding Panic of 1819, literally surrounded by it in Congress: the last item of business in the House before Tallmadge's amendment had been a memorial from George Williams, protesting his innocence in the unfolding scandal at the Baltimore branch of the BUS; after the final vote to permit slavery in the Territory of Arkansas—and the rejection of John Taylor's last-ditch proposal to ban slavery everywhere north of latitude 36°30'—the next thing the House of Representatives had turned to was a motion to rescind the Bank's charter for mismanagement. But it soon became clear that Congress would do nothing about the Spencer Committee's report on the Bank, and critics of *McCulloch* despaired that the Supreme Court had now made it impossible for the states to do anything either. Although Ohio stubbornly moved forward to collect its tax despite that decision, Tennessee abandoned its prohibitory tax law. Migrants kept arriving in Missouri, but land sales there slowed, and prices remained low in the uncertainty about what the next Congress would do. In the autumn, Jefferson wrote his letter telling John Adams that "the paper bubble is now burst." Adams replied, "Congress are about to assemble, and the clouds look Black and thick—Assembling from all points threatening thunder and lightning." Adams foresaw a mosaic of interrelated dangers: "the Missouri slavery—the encouragement of manufactures by protecting duties or absolute prohibitions—the project of a Bankruptcy Act, the plague of Banks." Three weeks later, Jefferson acknowledged them all, but he insisted that "the banks, bankrupt law, manufactures . . . are nothing." (He had not revealed his own dire financial straits to Adams.) "These are occurrences which like waves of a storm will pass under the ship. But the Missouri question is a breaker on which we lose the Missouri country by revolt, & what more, God only knows."[30]

Jefferson, who truly feared that Missourians might form an independent republic if denied statehood, also chose not to tell the Federalist Adams what he and Madison both darkly suspected: that the northern challenge over Missouri was part of a conspiracy to revive the moribund Federalist Party. But for most southerners, the Missouri crisis was overshadowed by Marshall's rescue of the hated Bank and by the blank check he had written to the federal government. Missourians themselves worried about their own land speculations in the event that the anticipated flood of immigration should dry up and leave them in debt for land they could not sell, and southerners and westerners in general reacted to all these challenges by rallying around states' rights.[31]

The Northeast was itself struggling with business failures and unemployment, worried that even falling cotton prices could not keep its mills profitable, given the diminished demand for their products in the South and West. Northerners who listened to revivalists in the Burned-Over District or at Yale College—or to Unitarian ministers in Boston—dug in and declared moral war on the evils of slavery, which they had also come to see as a threat to the wages of workingmen who might move west, and which, moreover (thanks to the Constitution's three-fifths clause) increased the southern share of power in Congress, obstructing the passage of a protective tariff.

In that charged atmosphere, older men imagined themselves refighting the battles of their youth. Jefferson wrote to Barry about the distinction between "whigs" and "tories," using the language of the American Revolution to voice his fears of the resurgence of his old Federalist enemies. One of the last of those Federalists, Rufus King, revived his old attacks on the three-fifths clause, which he had railed against thirty years earlier at the Constitutional Convention. He was convinced that the Republican Party held the balance of power only because the South's enslaved population increased southern numbers in both Congress and the electoral college when each slave was counted as three-fifths of a person in apportioning a state's representation.

Younger politicians, more concerned with the future than the past, had a different view. The most emotional attacks on slavery in Congress had just come from Republicans, like Timothy Fuller of Massachusetts and Arthur Livermore of New Hampshire, and the restriction movement was led by the New York Republicans Tallmadge and Taylor, allies of Clinton against Van Buren. Astute observers saw in the Missouri conflict the splitting up of the Republican hegemony and the consequent jockeying for power at both the state and national levels—one more factor along with the Panic of 1819 in the demise of the Era of Good Feeling.

That is not to say that the opponents of slavery were not sincere in their moral fervor, or that the southern resistance was not heartfelt in its indignation. But the political ramifications were easy to see. Most restrictionists were National Republicans aligned in general with Clay or Adams, but those two supported Missouri's right to make its own choice on slavery. With his eye on the 1824 election, Clay for one was reluctant to offend New York's Bucktail and Pennsylvania's Old School factions, whose rivals were leading the restriction movement, or residents of the new western states who were already unhappy with his support of the Bank. Calhoun and Adams (before the coming campaign drove a wedge between them) agreed in private that Crawford's vocal pro-slavery response to the crisis was part of his "canvass for the presidency" in the South. Calhoun was walking a fine line, aware that his home state of South Carolina was adamantly pro-slavery but still hoping to win Pennsylvania's nomination in 1824 with New School support. He did his best to stay out of the public debate, but when pressed he privately acknowledged his belief that "a conspiracy either against our property, or just weight in the Union . . . might and probably would lead . . . directly to disunion." That same belief was much more publicly declared by Old Republicans like Barbour and Randolph, although they spoke less about slavery than about the growing power of the federal government over the states, especially after *McCulloch v. Maryland.* John Van Atta, in his recent study of the Missouri crisis, concludes that "Tallmadge's initiative carried more far-reaching and radically statist implications than it might seem looking back today. . . . To many southerners . . . northern attempts to restrict slavery smacked of growing federal power, combined with virulent anti-southern feeling. At the very same time, the Bank of the United States had come to symbolize the dangers of national consolidation." *McCulloch v. Maryland* would have been incendiary in any case, but the Panic of 1819 fanned the flames.[32]

The challenges facing the new Congress in the fall were previewed in its difficulty replacing Clay as Speaker of the House. The two leading candidates were Rep. William Lowndes and Rep. John Taylor. Both had voted for the Bank charter and the Bonus Bill, along with Clay and Calhoun. Both had supported the Tariff of 1816, against Webster. But Lowndes was from South Carolina and Taylor was from New York, and they had taken opposite positions on the Tallmadge Amendment. After twenty-two ballots, that was what it came down to, and Taylor won the dubious privilege of presiding over the Missouri debates—as well as the other controversies that lay before the Sixteenth Congress.

There were many. On the second day of the new year, John Quincy Adams called on John C. Calhoun after church.

> I had an hour of conversation with him upon topics of great public interest. . . . There are several subjects upon which the public mind in this country is taking a turn which alarms me greatly for the continuance of the Union—the bank; the currency; the internal improvement question; the extension or repression of slavery; the conflicting ambitions of the great States of New York and Virginia, and the workings of individual ambition, mingling with all these controversial topics. It seems to me that we are at the eve of a great crisis, of which scarcely anyone is yet aware.[33]

Missouri was not the first or even the second of the topics Adams listed, but the next day he wrote in his diary, "The Missouri question thrills in every Southern nerve. It is yet in a state of chaos in my mind." Adams, the ultimate Washington insider, might have been surprised to learn that south and west of the District of Columbia, Missouri was not the first or even the second thing on many people's minds. There was indeed a fervent anti-slavery movement in the northeastern cities, but in Alabama, southern nerves were thrilling more to fears about the economy. By now the real estate boom was crashing there, as it had in the Northwest, and in February Thomas Percy wrote to his brother-in-law John Williams Walker, Alabama's newly sworn-in senator, "The great interests of the nation: the Spanish relation, the more momentous Missouri question . . . were not thought of or talked about by anyone." All was overshadowed by the economic Panic. The same was true that month in the depressed commercial center of Baltimore; there the *Patriot* reported, "The people do not yet participate in the unhappy heat of zeal and controversy, which has inflamed their Senators and Representatives." And Charles Pinckney III, who had taken his seat in December of 1819, now told the House of Representatives, "At the time I left, or sailed, from the city I here represent [Charleston, South Carolina], scarcely a word was said of the Missouri question; no man there even supposed that one of such magnitude was before you."[34]

Nevertheless, it was indeed before them, and the new Congress picked up where the old one had left off. Three days into the December session, Speaker Taylor stepped down from the chair to move an amendment to the Missouri statehood bill, reviving Tallmadge's restriction of slavery. On January 3, the day that Adams confided his own uncertainty to his diary, the House voted statehood for Maine, bypassing the usual requirements that it first organize a territorial government and submit a constitution. Massachusetts had given the constitutionally required approval for its northern district to separate, but it had imposed a narrow time limit: if Maine did not achieve statehood by March 4, it would revert to being a district of Massachusetts. This fact was not lost on Henry Clay. Though no longer Speaker, he was determined to find a resolution to the crisis, both for the nation's sake and for his own; as a slave-owning southerner who was identified with such "national" ideas as tariffs, internal improvements, and—of course—the Bank, his own political ambitions depended on mending the sectional split that had appeared and now threatened to grow wider and deeper. As early as December 30 Clay had implied to Massachusetts's Rep. John Holmes that Maine's statehood might depend on Missouri's—and vice versa. Holmes and Rep. Ezekiel Whitman, who both hoped to represent Maine, heard the clock ticking. The House plowed ahead as it had in the last session, but the Senate got the message, with Virginia's James Barbour suggesting that the two statehoods be linked; Holmes wrote to Massachusetts state senator William King, after meeting with Monroe and Sen. Barbour, that "Barbour and several others thought it is best that the *Mother* should have *twins this time*." On January 18, two weeks after the House approved statehood for Maine, the Senate gave no indication that it was inclined to take up the Maine bill separately from Missouri; on that date, Illinois's Sen. Jesse Thomas (a Crawford client and an opponent of restriction) made the surprising motion to revive Taylor's failed proposal to ban slavery north of latitude 36°30'—but this time, exempting the state of Missouri.[35]

Thomas's idea was to offer northern congressmen a fig leaf for abandoning the Tallmadge (now Taylor) Amendment, but they were not eager to accept it. Neither house could produce a majority willing to go on record as both accepting slavery in Missouri and banning it elsewhere—while simultaneously making Maine a state. That package was the compromise that the Monroe administration fervently desired, but it seemed unattainable. Monroe's own influence as president was never strong, and reactions to both the Bank and the economic collapse had diminished it even more in his native Virginia and the rest of the South. But Monroe (and the Bank) had powerful friends in Pennsylvania and New York, as well as some new and unexpected support in the freshman class of both the House and the Senate.[36]

In Pennsylvania, Monroe had a valuable ally in Nicholas Biddle, the ambitious lawyer he had just appointed to the Board of Directors of the BUS. Biddle had come into the Bank in the housecleaning that replaced William Jones with Langdon Cheves (a South Carolina nationalist who objected to the restriction of slavery in Missouri). Biddle's timely reports to Monroe helped steer the Missouri Compromise through the shoals of Pennsylvania politics in 1820, and he was largely responsible for persuading Reps. Samuel Moore, Thomas Rogers, and Daniel Udree to support it when it threatened to come undone in 1821. Both times, the Panic of 1819 showed its influence.

Then there was the vice president. Daniel Tompkins, as governor of New York during the War of 1812, had gone personally into debt while raising funds to equip the state's militia, cosigning loans from New York banks. His efforts to seek repayment had been delayed first by his careless record keeping and then by the Panic. Moreover, he too had invested unwisely in real estate and found himself unable to make his loan payments. Like others who were stuck with land debts they could not repay, he had borrowed when money was plentiful, but the Panic had driven down prices. Tompkins, badly in need of a $75,000 loan, had already turned to drink; now he turned to Langdon Cheves and the BUS. After two weeks of ineptly presiding over Missouri debates in the Senate, the vice president abruptly left Washington for his home in New York, where his former patron, DeWitt Clinton, had succeeded him as governor of the state. Now Clinton was the patron of Tallmadge and Taylor; he rightly suspected that Tompkins meant to pressure New York

Republicans to back the compromise, encouraged by the helpful Cheves, who had quickly arranged his loan and incurred his gratitude.[37]

Tompkins was a long-standing member of the New York Manumission Society, and as governor had sponsored and signed New York's final 1817 emancipation act, but as Monroe's vice president and now as Cheves's (and the Bank's) debtor, he had multiple incentives to pursue compromise—and there were multiple targets for his efforts. Tompkins's brother Caleb, congressman from New York's third district, had been among the first to support the amendment introduced by Tallmadge, his neighbor from the fourth district. Representing Manhattan's second and sixteenth districts were Henry Meigs and Henry Storrs. Storrs, a Federalist in his second term, had been a classmate of Calhoun at Yale. Meigs, a freshman Republican, happened to be the son of Josiah Meigs, the General Land Office commissioner who was now dealing with the precipitous decline in land revenues from Alabama and Missouri—and both his brother and his sister lived in Georgia. Now Reps. Tompkins, Storrs, and Meigs were possible compromise votes. It is unclear today how much influence the vice president had, but restrictionists evidently believed it was significant; they reviled him as "that miserable Sycophant who betrayed us to the lords of the South . . . that smallest of small men Daniel D. Tompkins." In December 1820 eight New England members of the electoral college (including Daniel Webster) punished him by casting their vice-presidential votes for Richard Rush instead, although all of them but William Plumer Sr. voted for Monroe's reelection. (Tompkins's alcoholism had dimmed his reputation in Washington, but he remained sufficiently respected in New York to be chosen to chair the 1821 constitutional convention.)[38]

Compromise seemed to be blocked by the lack of a majority who would vote for *both* parts, but it could succeed with a majority for *each* part. Biddle, Tompkins, and other pro-compromise agents did not need to achieve complete conversions. If enough northern votes could not be won over to admit Missouri with slavery, some members might at least be willing to absent themselves from the voting and thus open a path for the statehood vote. But the compromise would fail unless enough southerners could be persuaded to do the inverse—a few voting to prohibit slavery in the northern Louisiana territory (in return for Missouri's unrestricted admission), and enough staying away from the vote to allow a majority of those present to pass the 36°30' limitation. Here again a complex web of personal connections was critical, also depending on key freshmen. At the center was the now-forgotten senator from Alabama, John Williams Walker.

Walker did not need Percy's letter to tell him that his constituents were more worried about debt than about Missouri; however, he saw that the two issues were inextricably linked. Walker's greatest concern was the relinquishment amendment for purchasers of federal lands; it would not pass for another year, but at the moment there was real doubt whether the public land bill would even come up for a vote. Sen. James Barbour, as president pro-tempore, exercised the power over scheduling wielded today by the majority leader; when Missouri statehood seemed in jeopardy on March 1, he announced that until the compromise passed, "he did not feel in the humor to present the legislation on the [public land] bill, which at any other moment he would have regarded as a very important one." (Once the compromise was achieved, it would take only a week for the Senate to pass both that bill and a bill to suspend sale of forfeitures for failure to complete payment.)[39]

Walker and his Alabama colleague, William Rufus King, were thus determined to remove the obstacle to their state's economic rescue. But Walker saw the importance of the Missouri Compromise for its own sake too. Raised in Georgia, he had gone north to college, graduating from Princeton in a class that would produce three governors, a U.S. representative, and four senators. Princeton president Samuel Stanhope Smith taught his students to be nationalists: he insisted that they learn the Constitution by heart and he made *The Federalist* required reading. In the Senate in 1820, when most southern senators (and both of Indiana's) voted against Thomas's 36°30' amendment, it was Walker and King who provided the southern votes required for passage. In the House, Walker's Princeton schoolmate John Cuthbert of Georgia was persuaded to cast one of the few southern votes essential to pass the Thomas Amendment when forty-two other southerners voted no. Meigs, Storrs, and a scattering of other northerners voted for Missouri statehood without restriction; Caleb Tompkins and just enough others were absent, and the compromise was achieved. Another of Walker's Princeton schoolmates, New Jersey's freshman Sen. Samuel Southard, would cast a key vote for the final 1821 Missouri settlement, and he may have persuaded his father, Rep. Henry Southard, to vote for it as well in his final term in the House, despite having voted for the Tallmadge Amendment in 1819.

In the North, the compromise was widely seen as a southern victory. Several congressmen who supported it were denied reelection; Connecticut's

Sen. James Lanman was burned in effigy at Hartford. In New York the *Advertiser* proclaimed that *"the freedom of our country has been sacrificed,"* and Rufus King wrote bitterly to his son that renegades had "fought under the black flag." He complained bitterly that "Meigs & Storrs of N.Y. . . . boldly voted with the slave States" and that "Tompkins of N.Y. fled the question." King's assessment that "the slave states have triumphed over us" seems to have been based on his frustration that the three-fifths clause would remain in effect; he did not, in the letters he wrote immediately afterward, express any concern about the Missouri slaves themselves but characterized the vote as a lost opportunity "to establish the equal rights of the citizens of the free states."[40]

Not everyone agreed. New York's John Taylor wrote to his wife, "We have gained all that was possible . . . an ample recompense for all the time and labor it has cost us." The Chester (Pennsylvania) *Village Record* declared, "We announce, with unfeigned satisfaction, that the 'perplexing question'— the 'disheartening question'—of the admission of Missouri is decided. . . . For once the South has been outgeneraled; and forced to do right, in spite of all their pride and prejudices, and all their preconceived opinions and resolutions."[41]

Indeed, many southerners felt defeated. John Randolph, who had proclaimed, "God has given us Missouri and the devil shall not take it from us," now called the compromise a "dirty bargain," and joined thirty-four southern congressmen voting against the final bill. Ritchie, in the *Enquirer*, mourned the outcome: "Instead of joy, we scarcely ever recollect to have tasted a bitterer cup." When Missouri's first senators, Thomas Hart Benton and Daniel Barton, arrived in Washington, they settled into the orbit of such Old Republicans as Virginia's Randolph and John Taylor of Caroline, who would shortly be sent to the Senate. Benton was already distancing himself from their support of slavery—he later claimed that in 1820 he had been "equally opposed to slavery agitation and slavery extension"—but he was drawn to their denunciations of the BUS and the "paper system." The majority in the House now turned against the restrictionists, and after only one year as Speaker, New York's Taylor was replaced by Philip Barbour, the Old Republican from Virginia.[42]

The precarious compromise was nearly derailed over the winter of 1820/21 when Missouri presented a state constitution forbidding "free negroes and mulattoes from coming to and settling in this state." Northern congressmen objected that *this* restriction would deny their states' black citizens the Constitution's guarantee to each citizen of "all Privileges and Immunities of

Citizens in the several States," and they threatened to deny statehood after all, refusing to count Missouri's 1820 electoral votes. Now Henry Clay began to earn his reputation as the Great Compromiser, assembling a committee that would cobble together a second compromise, finalizing admission on the vague condition that Missouri could pass no laws infringing on the "privileges and immunities" of any citizen. Charles Pinckney observed trenchantly that until the free states "by an alteration of their constitution or laws" admitted blacks "to a full participation of all the political rights of their white citizens," northern criticism of Missouri was mere hypocrisy. Once again, the administration turned to Biddle to help assure the necessary northern votes. He was able to turn three Pennsylvania representatives who had voted against the original compromise and may have swayed Pennsylvania's Walter Lowrie in the Senate. Clay's second compromise passed, and Missouri's electoral votes were added to Monroe's total. (Underlining Pinckney's jab, Connecticut and New York rescinded or restricted black suffrage later that year, and Indiana, Illinois, Iowa, and Oregon would eventually adopt the same exclusion of free blacks that Missouri had attempted.)[43]

The entire debate on Missouri, in the three successive Februaries of 1819 to 1821, took place in the deepening depression following the Panic of 1819. Clay's February 1821 announcement of the successful second compromise is document 502 in the *American State Papers* of the Sixteenth Congress; document 500 is the resolution sent to the Senate by the Ohio legislature, asserting their right and intention, despite *McCulloch v. Maryland*, to tax the BUS. The next thing the Senate turned to in February after approving the second compromise was the public land bill with Walker's relinquishment amendment. This time it passed.

The Missouri Compromise may have seemed a sign that sectionalism could be overcome, but the truth was that the divisions in both houses of Congress were now almost completely sectional, and the margins on critical questions were only three or four votes. Jefferson was quick to predict that the compromise's calming of sectional division would be temporary: "It is hushed indeed for the moment, but this is a reprieve only . . . and every new irritation will make it deeper and deeper." The lingering effects of the collapse of cotton prices and the festering resentment of *McCulloch v. Maryland* remained. The unresolved problem of slavery had been only briefly brushed aside. As the upper South had shifted more and more to wheat farming, the "redundant" slave population there had begun to be sold to southwestern cotton planters; after 1819, the price of those slaves fell along with the price of cotton, but states like Virginia and Maryland would remain dependent on the western extension of slavery to the hemp fields of Missouri and the expanding cotton plantations of Alabama and Mississippi.[44]

In the deep South, the dream that slave labor would produce fabulous wealth from high cotton prices had been replaced by the conviction that only slave labor could stave off bankruptcy. Ever-greater yields were the only way, given the new reality of low prices, that deeply indebted landowners could keep their heads above water, and between 1820 and 1830 the production of cotton would more than double. Greed is said to be a powerful motivation but fear an even stronger one. In the depression that refused to loosen its grip on the cotton South, it was more fear than greed that made threats to slavery intolerable—and made sectionalism inevitable. That was the work of the Panic of 1819.

The intense, *ad hoc* anti-slavery movement inspired by the Missouri question dispersed as quickly as it had arisen, and for a while the issue of slavery receded from public attention; eyebrows were raised when Attorney General Wirt ruled in 1823 that land bounties promised to veterans of the War of 1812 applied to black veterans as well as white, but nothing came of it. Both North and South were shocked in 1822 by the intended carnage of the Denmark Vesey conspiracy, and David Walker's 1829 *Appeal to the Colored Citizens of the World* inspired a strong reaction in southern states but was rejected as too radical by most anti-slavery northerners. However, other reasons for sectional division were aggravated by the effects of the Panic of 1819. Internal improvements seemed vital to economic revival in the West but appeared dangerous to the South, requiring increased revenues to pay for them at a time when the collapse of cotton made southerners fearful of the protective tariffs demanded by the North and the West. Southerners who had voted for the Tariff of 1816 had reaped no benefits for their region; indeed, after Britain briefly turned to India for cotton in 1818, they were convinced that tariffs were a mortal threat to an export market that now depended on increased sales of cheap cotton—and would be wiped out should the British again stop buying. And *McCulloch*, on the heels of the Supreme Court decisions of *Fletcher v. Peck* and *Martin v. Hunter's Lessee*, had fired concern about the growth of a federal power that seemed directed expressly against southern states like Virginia and Georgia.[45]

McCulloch had linked both the hated Bank of the United States and the unpopular U.S. Supreme Court to the bogey of national consolidation. At the same time, internal improvements were also becoming tied in the southern mind to the threatening doctrine of loose construction of the Constitution. Calhoun, like other southern nationalists, was realizing that there was no future in resisting sectionalism, but it would be a few years before he became its leading advocate. Maryland's Alexander Hanson, Virginia's Henry St. George Tucker and South Carolina's William Lowndes had joined him in supporting the Bank charter and the 1816 tariff; their nationalism would erode as the economy began to suffer. Just enough southerners had followed Calhoun's lead on the 1817 Bonus Bill for internal improvements that it too had passed—with Hanson's vote, but without Lowndes or Tucker. Madison then vetoed it as unconstitutional. When Clay tried to revive it in 1818, Nathaniel Macon warned his fellow North Carolinian Bartlett Yancey (who had voted for the 1817 version), "The states having no slaves may not feel as strongly as the states having slaves about stretching the Constitution, because no such interest is to be touched by it." A month later, he was even more explicit: "If Congress can make canals, they can with more propriety emancipate." This time a series of three resolutions in favor of internal improvements was defeated in the House, with the South Carolina, Maryland, and Georgia delegations divided and Virginia, North Carolina, Tennessee, and Mississippi opposed. In the words of John Lauritz Larson, "By the spring of 1818 the problem of internal improvements embodied the question of liberty and power" for more and more southerners. The number would increase as the depression that had already struck the West spread through the South.[46]

When the first signs of economic decline had appeared in reduced revenue from import duties, Crawford had urged his southern partisans in Congress to cut federal spending. Now western states were making the opposite argument. As the depression wore on, internal improvements joined protective tariffs as a fundamental issue of Panic-fueled western sectionalism. All along the Ohio valley there were calls for projects that would revive commerce and industry: a canal around the falls at Louisville, canals to the Great Lakes, and new roads into the interior. Cincinnati had been settled by southerners, but on these questions it was thoroughly western. The Cincinnati *Liberty Hall* in September 1819 reported a "large and respectable" public meeting, one of the many taking place that autumn across the country. While gatherings in the northeast were focused on slavery in Missouri, the Cincinnati meeting was called to endorse all of the proposed internal improvement projects and to urge the federal government to subsidize them. As the Panic withered commerce, more and more states sought internal improvements that required the support of the Army Corps of Engineers, the nation's only organized engineering service: canals in Virginia, Ohio, and Illinois, and road projects in Maine, New York, Iowa, Tennessee, Georgia, Mississippi, and Louisiana. Calhoun, the secretary of war, still supported them all.[47]

Kentucky was also firmly in the western camp. As soon as the compromise had passed, Kentucky's Richard Mentor Johnson once more rose to speak. Echoing Alexander Hamilton's praise in *Federalist* No. 7 of "the spirit of enterprise, which characterizes the commercial part of America," Johnson asked, "Shall Congress invigorate this spirit of enterprise, which characterizes the States and the people of the States, by timely and reasonable appropriations, or shall we refuse our aid, and thus indirectly condemn, and positively protract that system which will give to this nation so much wealth, so much power, and so much union?" Johnson then introduced a resolution to investigate federal cooperation with Ohio, Pennsylvania, Virginia, Kentucky, and Indiana to improve navigation of the Ohio River, including a congressional stock subscription for the Kentucky Ohio Canal Company. The resolution passed, but with resistance coming from both the South and the Northeast, the Roads and Canals Committee produced no legislation. The greater national union that Johnson had earlier forecast was in fact disintegrating when it came to internal improvements.[48]

Old Republicans like Macon had always been leery of federal projects. With the conjunction of *McCulloch* and Missouri, internal improvements proposals in Congress were increasingly seen by southerners in a new light, as further assertions of unlimited federal power in an area that Madison and Monroe had both considered beyond the limits of the Constitution—and thus as further undermining of the principle of limited government that protected the institution of slavery. In 1822, the Roads and Canals Committee did suggest five urgently needed national projects: an Atlantic coastal waterway; a Washington, D.C., to New Orleans road; canals going around the falls of the Ohio and connecting that river with the Great Lakes and the Potomac; a canal between the Susquehanna and the Finger Lakes of New York; and canals to link the Tennessee River with the Savannah, Alabama, and Tombigbee Rivers. Four of the five would have benefitted depressed slave states, but all were blocked by southern opposition. Two years later, Randolph warned southerners against the General Survey Bill, endorsed by Monroe: "If congress possess the power to do what is proposed in this bill, they may not only enact a sedition law—for there is precedent—but they may emancipate every slave in the United States—and with stronger color of reason than they can exercise the power now contended for."[49]

Even then, Calhoun did not give up his nationalist ambition to "conquer space"; he not only urged the passage of the General Survey Bill, but, in his final months as secretary of war, he camped along with the army engineers who surveyed the route of the Chesapeake and Ohio Canal through the wilds of western Pennsylvania. He hoped to see the Great Lakes country "firmly united to that of the Western Waters, and both with the Atlantick States, and the whole intimately connected with the center." But in Calhoun's home state, with cotton below fifteen cents a pound, South Carolina planters who faced growing competition from Alabama and Mississippi saw no benefit in internal improvements; no federal construction money was being spent in South Carolina, and the irascible Prof. Thomas Cooper at South Carolina College accused Calhoun of spending "the money of the South to buy up influence in the North." In North Carolina, Archibald Murphey's long campaign for internal improvements had been abandoned; Murphey was headed for debtors' prison, and an electioneering ballad expressed the prevailing attitude toward those who still wanted the legislature to spend their shrinking funds on roads and canals:

> So therefore let it be our care
> To keep these men away from there
> Who build their castles in the air,
> Who dream they can vast things perform
> And in a breath God's works reform![50]

The question of slavery pitted the North against the South and divided the West; opposition to internal improvements united the North and South against the West. As if that were not enough discord, there was a third source of sectionalism that split the North and set the West against the South: in the same way that the Panic led westerners to seek federal spending for internal improvements and southerners to oppose it, the depression energized both the proponents and the adversaries of a protective tariff. The Tariff of 1816 had been only moderately protective; after imports had rebounded through 1818, Matthew Carey held a well-attended Convention of the Friends of National Industry early in 1819 in New York City, to call for stronger protection. In May Adams recorded, "I received this day a printed copy of the seventh address from the Society at Philadelphia for the Protection of Domestic Industry, urging a petition to the President for an immediate call of Congress to change the tariff and pass prohibitory laws." And in 1820 Pittsburgh's Henry Baldwin, chairman of the House Committee on Manufactures, introduced a strongly protective tariff bill that would pass the House easily and fail in the Senate by a single vote.[51]

In September 1819 the New York *American* accused protectionists of exaggerating the impact of the Panic because they had an axe to grind, but it was plain that the depression was growing worse. In February 1820, Congress began debating currency reform, land sales, spending cuts, a national bankruptcy law—and the tariff. Baldwin's tariff was proposed in response not only to the distress of manufacturers but also to Crawford's projection of a $5 million deficit. It called for raising rates nearly 10 percent on manufactured goods in order to protect industry, and increasing the duties on coffee, tea, sugar, and salt in order to produce revenue. The proposed tariff came out of Baldwin's committee and has always borne his name, but its chief spokesman was Henry Clay, whose evolving "American System" advocated both internal improvements to promote domestic commerce and tariffs to protect domestic industry. After nearly two years of depressed grain exports, Clay did not have to convince westerners that they should focus on the domestic market. But despite more than a year of low cotton prices and a continuing decline in tobacco exports, he had no success persuading southerners to give up their dependence on sales abroad.[52]

The Baldwin tariff passed the House the same way the Tallmadge Amendment had, on a sectional vote that left the South embittered. The Virginia Agricultural Society of Fredericksburg, in an 1820 memorial to Congress, declared its opposition in the language of John Taylor of Caroline, asserting that "hostility resulting from true republican principles, to partial taxation, exclusive privileges, and monopolies created by law, was the primary cause of our glorious and ever-memorable revolution" in 1776. Virginia's Rep. William Archer quoted the seventeenth-century English revolutionary Richard Rumbold, rejecting the idea that "some men came into the world with saddles on their backs and others booted and spurred to ride them." He warned any who hoped "to mount upon the backs of the Southern people, that they would find their seats neither pleasant nor so entirely secure but that they might chance to encounter a fall, from the effects of which it might not be so easy to recover." Nevertheless, demonstrating the western states' commitment to protectionism, Baldwin's bill won the support of Kentucky, Ohio,

Indiana, and Illinois, as well as the middle Atlantic states and the cotton-milling states of Rhode Island and Massachusetts. Kentucky and Tennessee shared their experience with the debt relief conflicts, but they differed on internal improvements and the tariff. Tennessee, which grew cotton, joined the other southern states in opposition; Kentucky, which did not, aligned with the other Ohio valley states of the West. The tariff received no House votes at all from Maryland, Virginia, or any state south of Kentucky. And like the Tallmadge Amendment, it faced near-unanimous southern opposition in the Senate. That body had already postponed construction of the Cumberland Road in the name of economy; on May 4 it disappointed the West again, defeating the tariff by a single vote, 22 to 21.[53]

After 1819 Hezekiah Niles was a tireless advocate of protective tariffs, and when the Baldwin bill was defeated, Niles demanded that the voters punish its opponents. He had no luck persuading the constituents of Lowndes, Barbour, or Virginia's William McCoy, who had all voted yes in 1816 but no in 1820. In April Niles blamed the nation's economic collapse on "the mighty mass of paper afloat," but he added that it "had been hurried on, or driven into a *heap*, by the want of a sound *political economy* in our government." He had in mind above all the dependence on cotton exports. "Those who, from the high price of their agricultural products *abroad*, were always opposed to supporting *home* manufactures, (we are sorry to say), will soon feel the necessity of regarding the *home* market." When cotton planters continued to oppose raising the tariff, Niles suggested at the end of July the prohibition of all goods made from East Indian cotton or "manufactured beyond the Cape of Good Hope," still hoping to win southern support. He also advocated higher duties on imported goods made of flax, hemp, or wool—with which western growers competed, as well as paper and pig iron—which Pennsylvania produced. The benefit, he argued, would be felt by southern cotton planters, by wool and grain growers in the middle and western states, and by the eastern unemployed, as well as "all who depend on a circulating currency" which would be strengthened if specie were not leaving the country to pay for imports.[54]

Baldwin's Committee on Manufactures remained convinced that a protective tariff was essential for economic recovery, although southern congressmen continued to block its every effort. On January 15, 1821, the committee again declared that free trade was the cause of the nation's continuing economic distress. Without a tariff, they warned, America's wealth "flows in a torrent-like stream beyond its jurisdiction, never to return." With a tariff, wealth would become "a steady gentle current, meandering through every occupation within the great circle of national industry, giving use and value to every production, floating it to every market."[55]

But Clay had been right about the breakdown of "political connexions." In 1821 Virginia's Philip Barbour replaced New York's ineffectual John Taylor as Speaker of the House, and he saw to it that no tariff bill came to the floor for a vote. The other John Taylor, in Virginia's Caroline County, again took up his pen, declaring in the bluntly titled *Tyranny Unmasked* that "the government will be implored to sustain abuse, monopoly, exclusive privilege, and extravagance" by northern sectionalists, "and as its administrators always get a share of the spoils, they will be extremely charitable." After his death in 1824, his disciple John Randolph would carry on his defense of slavery and his attacks on abusive federal power—represented by internal improvements, the Supreme Court, and the BUS, as well as tariffs.[56]

In the Carolinas even that old advocate of internal improvements, Archibald Murphey, was taking up Taylor's ideas. Murphey worried, not without reason, that North Carolina's specie was being drained northward when the state's banknotes were presented for redemption by northern speculators—and when Carolinians voluntarily sent it off to purchase goods in "distant markets" like New York. As historian Daniel Dupre observes, "From the perspective of North Carolina in the depths of the depression, 'home' and 'abroad' were defined by the state's borders." Thomas Cooper, who had been recruited from England to teach at the University of Virginia by Jefferson, left Charlottesville in 1820 to take up a post at South Carolina College. In 1824 he published *Consolidation*, a short work of political economics second only to Taylor's much longer books in its influence on the South. Internal improvements, the tariff, and the opinions of John Marshall had convinced Cooper that "the power of the president of the United States, the power of the Congress of the United States, and more than all, the power of the Supreme Court of the United States (the most dangerous body in the Union) has increased, is increasing, and ought to be diminished."[57]

For two years Barbour kept the tariff from a vote in the House, where southern numbers would have been insufficient to prevent its passage. But late in 1823 Clay returned to the Speaker's chair for a final term before becoming secretary of state. He promptly appointed Pennsylvania protectionist John Tod to chair the Committee on Manufactures (Baldwin had left the House in 1822), and the committee reported out a bill that set duties on iron, woolens, cotton fabric, and hemp at 35 percent—the steepest rate yet. With the depression slow to lift in the West, representatives like Missouri's John Scott were eager to protect not only American industry but, as Scott told his constituents, American republican virtue: "By a too frequent, open, and unrestricted intercourse with foreign nations, we imbibe their manners, contract their vices, give in to their luxuries, and lose that Republican simplicity, on which our government is based." Now Tennessee voted as a western state; Andrew Jackson, sent briefly to the Senate as a prelude to his presidential campaign, supported both tariff and internal improvements in 1824—with the South backing Crawford, he had little choice but to embrace a western perspective, especially when he hoped to win votes in Pennsylvania, Ohio, Indiana, and Illinois. But Calhoun, preparing to abandon his immediate presidential ambitions for what would be a term of vice presidential opposition, was making his long swing from nationalism to southern sectionalism. Appeals to patriotism no longer resonated in South Carolina. As a congressman, Calhoun had championed the tariff in 1816; as secretary of war he was silent on the tariff in 1820; but in 1824, as vice president-apparent, he encouraged South Carolinians George McDuffie in the House and Robert Hayne in the Senate to oppose the tariff. He had come to see protective tariffs as part of the Adams-Clay policy that, with the help of the Supreme Court, was becoming the law of the land—strengthening power (of the central government) but weakening liberty (of the states), especially in the South.[58]

Virginians were relentless in their opposition. Barbour, no longer able to prevent a vote, now declared a protective tariff every bit as unconstitutional as internal improvements. A tariff was legitimate only to raise revenue for national defense; beyond that, federal authority could not favor one region or economic interest at the expense of another. It was an argument that John Randolph had already made. In 1816, Randolph had said, "I will not lay a duty upon the cultivator of the soil to encourage exotic manufactures," and in the heat of debate he had called the tariff "a scheme of public robbery." He now mocked the 1824 tariff's support in the West: "The merchants and manufacturers of Massachusetts and New Hampshire repel this bill, while men in hunting shirts, with deerskin leggings and moccasins on their feet, want protection for home manufactures." But Randolph was not up to date. Webster, who had opposed the previous tariffs on behalf of New England shipping interests, had since seen the direction of his region's future—with the guidance of the Boston Associates. He voted in favor of the Tariff of 1824 and those that followed. The "men in hunting shirts" of Virginia's own western counties were increasing faster than Randolph's Tidewater and Piedmont constituency; the Old Dominion's congressmen had been unanimous against the tariff in 1820, but despite lopsided pro-Tidewater apportionment, one of them would vote for the Tariff of 1824 and three would support the Tariff of 1828, which set the highest duties in history. In 1824 the tariff passed not only in the House but in the Senate, thanks to the growing strength and sectional unity of a West that could now count both Tennessee and Kentucky. There was nothing left for the South but to fall back on Barbour's argument for strict construction and on Patrick Henry's Antifederalist compact theory of the Constitution—"We the States"—with its implied threat of secession.[59]

From the southern point of view, of course, sectionalism was a *northern* phenomenon. As vice president, Calhoun wrote to Bartlett Yancey, "I do not doubt, that the more daring sperits [*sic*] that guide the councils of the [northern] coalition, count the slave question, as among the ways and means of uniting what is called the free states." The Tallmadge Amendment, the sweeping assertions of *McCulloch v. Maryland*, and the protective tariffs all seemed to the South a coordinated effort to advance the interests of northern finance, commerce, and manufacturing—running roughshod over what Taylor, Cooper, and (eventually) Calhoun insisted was the true meaning of the Constitution. Struggling with an agricultural depression that stretched on and on, southerners came to believe that anti–slavery arguments were employed in a cynical attempt to drum up public support in the North for economic subordination of the South.[60]

By the late 1820s the Panic of 1819 had run its course, although its effect on the nation had not. Because it had been without precedent—and because it had descended on different parts of the country at different times and in different ways—the depression and its causes were difficult for people to apprehend, let alone comprehend. As is so often the case, an economic catastrophe that seems inevitable in retrospect was utterly astonishing when it happened. But from the vantage point of two hundred years later, it takes on a too-familiar pattern: money was cheap, banks were too eager to lend, and inexperienced investors were in a rush to get in on the profit-making. Before long there were more sellers than buyers, loan payments could not be made, and the bubble burst.

American exceptionalism was already firmly rooted in what was, after all, the world's only self-invented republic, blessed with what seemed like inexhaustible resources and enjoying a social and economic mobility unknown anywhere else on earth. But the self-sufficiency that seemed to develop during the embargo and the War of 1812 was an illusion. The United States was inextricably tied to the world economy. Like Great Britain or China, the United States was dependent on a flow of precious metal from Mexico and South America that was now unable to keep up with the demand for circulating currency. Almost overnight America had taken the lead in the creation of banks (with their flood of banknotes) and the innovation of limited-liability corporations. But the reality was that America remained above all a producer of raw materials. When foreign demand for agricultural commodities shot up (especially in Great Britain) Americans rushed to buy land on which to grow more. Conversely, the American market for manufactured goods was critical to the factories of Europe (especially in Great Britain). When fears of postwar unemployment and resulting unrest drove English industries to overproduce, the wave of cheap imports swept away many of the "infant industries" of New England, New York, and Pennsylvania and battered new western cities like Pittsburgh and Lexington. When European grain harvests recovered and English mills turned to other sources of raw cotton, American prices tumbled—and millions of borrowed dollars could not be repaid.

Price deflation, widespread unemployment, business failures, and bank closures were baffling new experiences. The search for explanation seemed to lead to the Bank of the United States, and the Bank has been blamed ever since for first feeding the frenzy by allowing easy credit and then bringing down the house of cards with rigid policies of contraction. There is no question that the Bank magnified both the bubble and the crash, but it was not responsible for creating either the commercial depression in the Northeast that came with the dumping of imports in 1815 or the swarm of state-chartered (and unchartered) banks that was already flooding the country with unsupported banknotes well before the BUS opened in 1817. Most of the initial deposits on public land purchases were paid with those banknotes. Treasury Secretary Crawford had no training in economics (who did?) and he was torn between the desire to raise federal revenues by promoting land sales and the fear of encouraging a potentially worthless currency by accepting those notes. As John Quincy Adams complained, Crawford was often more concerned by the political than the financial consequences. The contraction, begun in 1818, was unavoidable given the scarcity of specie everywhere and the impending obligation to redeem Louisiana Purchase bonds in silver or gold. The Bank succeeded in evading that obligation in 1818 and 1819, but the country could not escape the falling price of wheat after 1817 or the collapse of cotton at the end of 1818. These were triggered by sudden changes—the rebound after the "volcano weather" and the English shift to Indian cotton—but they continued because supply now outstripped demand, thanks to the crop yields of the vast public lands purchased and planted in both the Northwest and Southwest.

It was no surprise that American manufacturers and wool growers would clamor for protective tariffs. It was predictable that grain farmers, now dependent on the domestic market, would demand more canals and better roads. And it was only natural that cotton planters, already possessed of incredibly fertile lands, would try to make up for lower profits by increasing volume. These were simply matters of economic self-defense, but they had the inescapable consequence of hardening sectional interests for decades to come. There were other consequences that were less direct. Outrage at the banks (not only the BUS) launched state campaigns for debtor relief that grew into a national movement for mass-participation politics and political parties. That movement gained steam from the Panic's revelation of shocking corruption, both financial and political, in the anything-goes atmosphere of the boom times. Jefferson's Republican Revolution was evolving into the era of Jacksonian Democracy. When the "middling interest" took control, their moral indignation was not directed only against the corrupt elite. Reinforced by the individualist doctrines of the Second Great Awakening, many who were just able to keep their own heads above water explained others' economic failure as the result of moral failure, and a long-standing tradition of municipal care for the poor was abruptly replaced by the equation of poverty with laziness and self-indulgence. The indigent were isolated socially and politically as the expanding franchise explicitly excluded paupers. In a seeming paradox that was not lost on Charles Pinckney and other southerners, northern states like Connecticut and New York took steps to disenfranchise African Americans even as they mounted a moral and political attack on the extension of slavery from the South into the West.

The slave question would not go away; neither would the demand for higher tariffs, although 1828's improbably passed "Tariff of Abominations" would be, as John Randolph put it, concerned with only one manufacture: the manufacture of Andrew Jackson's presidency. Vice President Calhoun, however, decided that this latest tariff was a mortal threat to the South, and that Jackson's determination to enforce it was an assault on the Constitution. That decision led him to resign his second term as vice president in order to expound the doctrine of nullification. With that, Calhoun completed his transformation from committed nationalist to thoroughgoing sectionalist. So, ironically, did another South Carolinian: Langdon Cheves.

The savior of the Bank of the United States when he took the helm in 1819, Cheves, like most Jeffersonians, had voted against the recharter of the First BUS. At the time, he had suggested that a national bank might yet be framed that he could support; he clearly did not believe that a federal charter was necessarily in conflict with the Constitution. In 1812, as a War Hawk who shared a boardinghouse in Washington with Clay, Lowndes, and Calhoun, he supported heavy import duties to pay for the war; when Clay went to negotiate the Treaty of Ghent in 1814, it was Cheves who was chosen to succeed him as Speaker of the House. He returned to private life at the end of that year, turning down both Madison's offered nomination as secretary of the treasury and Monroe's to the Supreme Court, but in 1817 he readily accepted appointment as a director of the new BUS branch in Charleston. When he was elected president of the Bank in 1819, he aggressively took charge, never doubting that he was the man for the job.[61]

Cheves had appeared as much a nationalist as Calhoun, but after 1822 he too joined wholeheartedly in the southern resistance to consolidation. He shared his state's outrage at the Tariff of Abominations, but he believed Calhoun's idea of nullification by a single state was simply impracticable; instead, he called for a southern convention to oppose both the tariff and Jackson's threats of force. In later years Langdon Cheves would insist that he had only accepted the presidency of the BUS out of a sense of duty and was glad to be out of it. In 1836 the Bank's charter expired, and the following year Cheves told the Charleston *Mercury* that he now considered the Bank of the United States "inexpedient, unnecessary, and dangerous." Moreover, he insisted with a straight face, "I have always believed it was unconstitutional." Who could gainsay him? Calhoun chose not to. Neither Webster nor Clay had been interested in Cheves's political opinions, so long as they were paid well for their services, and both were well accustomed to reversing their own positions. Jones, Crawford, Girard, Madison, and Monroe were all dead. Niles had been incapacitated by a stroke and had retired from public life. Biddle was busy pursuing his scheme to corner the cotton market—but the price of cotton was about to crash again, and another public land bubble would shortly burst, leaving thousands of speculators hopelessly in debt again. The Panic of 1837 was beginning.[62]

NOTES

Introduction

1. Howe, *What Hath God Wrought?*, 126–27; Feller, *Public Lands in Jacksonian Politics*, 10, 16, 20.

2. William Crawford to Langdon Cheves, April 6, 1819, in *Report of the Condition of the Bank of the United States*, 68.

3. North, *Economic Growth of the United States*, appendix III, table 1; Pittsburgh *Gazette*, Feb. 5, 1819; Carey, "The New Olive Branch," in his *Essays on Political Economy*, 330.

4. Eight-reale Spanish coins were the famous "pieces of eight." The smallest acceptable fraction of cut money was one-eighth or a "bit"—hence "two bits" for twenty-five cents—and the New York Stock Exchange continued to list stock prices in eighths of a dollar from 1817 until 1997 (although the United States never minted a coin in that denomination). "Clipped money," on the other hand, referred to currency debased by the criminal practice of shaving metal off the edge.

5. Noyes, *Family History in Letters and Documents,* 1:344–45; Rammelkamp, "Thomas Lippincott," 254.

Chapter One: The Legacy of Napoleon

1. Callender, *Prospect Before Us*, 2:57; Hazard, *Jonny-Cake Papers*, 232–33; Jefferson to John Holmes, April 22, 1820, in Jefferson, *Memoirs,* 4:322. No one anticipated the electoral college tie between Jefferson and his running mate, Aaron Burr, which would briefly through the outcome in doubt and would necessitate the passage of the 12th Amendment.

2. Adams, *History of the United States During the Administrations of Thomas Jefferson,* 2:26–27.

3. Jefferson to Livingston, April 18, 1802, in *Founders Online.*

4. De Cesar and Page, "Jefferson Buys Louisiana Territory"; Beckert, *Empire of Cotton*, 106–7; June 19, 1803, NP I.4.A.13, Northbrook Papers, Baring Archive, cited in Beckert, *Empire of Cotton*, 107. Barings finally went out of business in 1995, when the bad investments of a rogue employee, Nick Leeson, cost the bank £827 million—dwarfing the disastrous speculation that occurred with the money of the Second Bank of the United States in 1819.

5. De Cesar and Page, "Jefferson Buys Louisiana Territory."

6. Flint, *Letters from America*, 272–73; *Niles' Weekly Register*, Oct. 12, 1822, 92, 95.

7. Friedman, "Bimetallism Revisited," 88; Niles' *Weekly Register*, Feb. 27, 1819, 22–24; April 3, 1819, 159–60; Gallatin, *Considerations on the Currency*, 16; Raguet, *Treatise on Currency and Banking*, 207–8.

8. Adams, *Memoirs*, 4:399–400, 402–3.

9. *Niles' Register* Aug. 7, 1819, 399; White, *Money and Banking*, 33–34; Flint, *Letters from America*, 269 (Aug. 15, 1820).

10. Gallatin, *Considerations on the Currency*, 10. See TePaske, *New World of Gold and Silver*; Bakewell, *Mines of Silver and Gold*.

11. Gallatin, *Considerations on the Currency*, 9; Silver Institute, "Silver in History"; Rodriguez, *Down from Colonialism*, 15; Ward, *Mexico*, 1:306–91; Henderson, *Mexican Wars for Independence*, 124, 32; Coulson, *History of Mining*, 140; Anderson, "Frontier Economic Problems in Missouri," 68.

12. *Journal of the Senate of ... New-York, 42nd Session*, 67; Wolcott, *Remarks*, 12.

13. Hao, "Chinese Teas to America," 21.

14. Hao, "Chinese Teas to America," 22–24, table 6; Dallas to Rep. J. W. Eppes, Ways and Means Chairman, Feb. 29, 1815, House Document No. 84 (1815), quoted in Elliott, *Funding System of the United States and of Great Britain*, 619.

15. Raguet, *Treatise on Currency and Banking*, 7n; *Niles' Register*, Nov. 7, 1818, 175.

16. Ellis, *Aggressive Nationalism*, 163; Haulman, "Panic of 1819," 22; Schur, "Second Bank of the United States and Inflation," 132.

17. Duryea, "William Pitt, the Bank of England, and the 1797 Suspension of Specie Payments"; Smith and Cole, *Economic Fluctuations*, 24–25; Mitchener, "Classical Gold Standard," 88. See also Feaveryear, *Pound Sterling*; Hawtrey, "Bank Restriction of 1797," 53–54; Sumner, *History of American Currency*, 232–33.

18. Allen, *Global Financial System*, 33–34.

19. Neal, "Financial Crisis," 55; Bordo and White, "Tale of Two Currencies," 313; *Niles' Register*, May 8, 1819, 190; Gayer, Rostow, and Schwartz, *Growth and Fluctuation of the British Economy*, 1:133–34.

20. Smith and Cole, *Economic Fluctuations*, 29; Gayer, Rostow, and Schwartz, *Growth and Fluctuation of the British Economy*, 1:159–67.

21. Reprinted by the *National Intelligencer*, May 20, 1815, quoted in Peterson, *Great Triumvirate*, 46.

22. Gallatin to Jefferson, Dec. 18, 1807, in *Founders Online*. See Miller, "Smuggling into Canada"; Gordinier, "Versatility in Crisis."

23. North, *Economic Growth of the United States*, 55; Salem *Gazette*, Aug. 12, 1808, quoted in Gray, *William Gray of Salem*, 43–44n; Wolcott, *Remarks*, 11; Sears, "Philadelphia and the Embargo of 1808," 354.

24. Report *to Congress 1810, in ASP: Finance*, 2:426.

25. White, *Memoir of Samuel Slater*, 74.

26. Coxe, *Statement of the Arts and Manufactures*, 9–10, 23–25, and *Supplementary Observations*, liv–lxi. See Sears, "Philadelphia and the Embargo of 1801," 355–59.

27. *United States Gazette*, Oct. 8, 1808, quoted in Sears, "Philadelphia and the Embargo of 1801," 355.

28. [Samuel Relf,] Editor of Philadelphia *Price Courant* [*sic*] to Thomas Jefferson, Library of Congress manuscript, quoted in Sears, "Philadelphia and the Embargo of 1801," 357.

29. Ingersoll, *View of the Rights and Wrongs*, 49; Matson, "Matthew Carey's Learning Experience," 462. See Wright, *Economic History of the United States*, 201–2.

30. Stettler, "Growth and Fluctuation of the Antebellum Textile Industry," 116.

31. See McLane, *Documents Relating to the Manufactures*; Meyer, *Roots of American Industrialization*, 95; Day, "Early Development of American Cotton Manufacture," 452; Atock and Piersall, *New Economic View*, 122; Stettler, "Growth and Fluctuation of the Antebellum Textile Industry," 117.

32. Wolcott, *Remarks*, 11–12.

33. Smith and Cole, *Economic Fluctuations*, 25; *ASP: Finance*, 2:404; Bonelli, *Response of Public and Private Philanthropy*, 10.

34. Stettler, "Growth and Fluctuation of the Antebellum Textile Industry," 118; Smith and Cole, *Economic Fluctuations*, 28; Widmer, "War of 1812?"

35. Morris to Rufus King, Nov. 1814, quoted in Ketcham, James *Madison*, 589.

36. Gallatin, *Considerations on the Currency*, 44; Report of the Commissioners of the Sinking Fund, reprinted in *Niles' Register*, Feb. 19, 1820, 428; Wilentz, *Rise of American Democracy*, 204; Smith and Cole, *Economic Fluctuations*, 28.

37. Remeni, *Andrew Jackson and the Course of American Empire*, 88–90; Hofstadter, *American Political Tradition*, 66–67, 76.

38. See Hammond, *Banks and Politics in America*; Fenstermaker, *Development of Commercial Banking*; Weber, "Early State Banks"; *Reports of the Secretary of the Treasury*, 2:481–525.

39. Blackson, "Pennsylvania Banks and the Panic of 1819," 338, 345. See Fenstermaker, *Development of Commercial Banking*; Weber, "Early State Banks."

40. Blackson, "Pennsylvania Banks and the Panic of 1819," 344–45; Carey, *Autobiography*, 233.

41. Blackson, "Pennsylvania Banks and the Panic of 1819," 338; Matson, "Matthew Carey's Learning Experience," 466; Hammond, *Banks and Politics*, 227–28; *Bank Returns*, Ms. in Archives of the Commonwealth of Massachusetts, quoted in Smith and Cole, *Economic Fluctuations*, 28.

42. Bonelli, *Response of Public and Private Philanthropy*, 11; McMaster, *History of the People of the United States*, 4:294–95; *Niles' Register*, "Supplement" to vol. 7, 175.

43. Albert Gallatin in *ASP: Finance*, 3:331–32; Hammond, *Banks and Politics*, 228.

44. Wright, *Economic History of the United States*, 227; "Federal 1814 Government Spending," https://www.usgovernmentspending.com/fed_spending_1814USmn.

45. Smith and Cole, *Economic Fluctuations*, 147; Matson, "Matthew Carey's Learning Experience," 468–69; Bezanson, Gray, and Hussey, *Wholesale Prices in Philadelphia*, 1:353.

46. Brougham, *Speeches*, 274.

47. Ibid.; *Niles' Register*, Dec. 28, 1816, 284.

48. Albion, *Rise of the Port of New York*, 12; *ASP: Commerce*, 2:647; North, *Economics Growth of the United States*, 78–80, 228; *Historical Statistics of the United States*, series V–1, V–8, V–192, Y–338, Y–353.

49. Coxe, *A View of the United States of America*, quoted in Watts, *Republic Reborn*, 257; Thompson, "Auction System in New York," 155.

50. Thompson, "Auction System in New York," 156. See Cohen, "'The Right to Purchase Is as Free as the Right to Sell,'" 25–65.

51. Buck, *Development and Organization of Anglo-American Trade*, 141–45; Dangerfield, *Era of Good Feelings*, 176–77; Cimenti, "In Light of Failure," 52, Cayton, "Fragmentation of a 'Great Family,'"148.

52. Thompson, "Auction System in New York," 156–57.

53. Rothbard, *Panic of 1819*, 236; Bishop, *History of American Manufacturers*, 2:258; Matson, "Matthew Carey's Learning Experience," 472–73.

54. Meyer, *Roots of American Industrialization*, 93, 108–9; Rothenberg, "Invention of New England Capitalism," 88; Morris, *Dawn of Innovation*, 97; Matson, "Matthew Carey's Learning Experience," 469.

55. Matson, "Matthew Carey's Learning Experience," 468–69; Philadelphia Society for the Promotion of American Manufactures, *Circular*, 3; Fleming, *History of Pittsburgh and Environs*, 2:473–74; Carey, *New Olive Branch*, 133; *Niles' Register*, Feb. 22, 1817, 428; Wade, *Urban Frontier*, 180–81.

56. Cochran, *Frontiers of Change*, 64; Wittlinger, "Early Manufacturing in Lancaster County"; Boston *Daily Advertiser*, June 28, 1821, quoted in in Cayton, *"Fragmentation,"* 149.

57. *ASP: Finance*, 3:449–50; Pell, *Review of the Administration*, 81–82.

58. Tucker, "America's Debt Through the Eyes of the Founders"; Dallas to Eppes, Feb. 20, 1820, in *ASP: Finance,* 2:911.

59. Ware, *Early New England Cotton Manufacture,* 71; Cochran, *Frontiers of Change,* 64.

60. *ASP: F*, 3:140–44; *Circular Letters*, 3:1040.

61. *Annals of Congress*, 14th Congr., 1st sess., HR 312; Calhoun, *Papers*, 1:350.

62. Stettler, "Growth and Fluctuation of the Antebellum Textile Industry," 119; Coxe, *An Addition, of December 1818,* 7; Pittsburgh *Mercury*, Aug. 1, 1820, quoted in Wade, *Urban Frontier*, 180–81; Cochran, *Frontiers of Change*, 76; Carey, *New Olive Branch*, 126.

63. *Niles' Register*, Dec. 5, 1818, 265.

Chapter Two: Three Revolutions

1. April 26, 1820, in Clay, *Speeches*, 1:226.

2. Chew, "Certain Victims of an International Contagion."

3. Appleby, "Popular Sources of American Capitalism," 440; Ellis, "Market Revolution," 149.

4. Bremer, "Frontier Capitalism," 82–83. See Hurt, *Agriculture and Slavery*, 64–66; Duden, *Report on a Journey to the Western States of North America*, 256–57.

5. Rothenberg, "Invention of New England Capitalism," 95.

6. Ellis, "Market Revolution," 160, 93; Katz, *In the Shadow of the Poorhouse*, 4.

7. Tucker, *Samuel Slater and the Origins of the American Textile Industry*, 92; Meyer, *Roots of American Industrialization*, 105; Fuller, *Introduction to the History of Connecticut as a Manufacturing State*, 14; Tharp, *Appletons of Beacon Hill*, 103; Morris, *Dawn of Innovation*, 95.

8. Morris, *Dawn of Innovation*, 97; Stettler, "Growth and Fluctuation of the Antebellum Textile Industry," 122–24; Meyer, *Roots of American Industrialization* 11, 96.

9. Cochran, *Frontiers of Change*, 51, 60, 65; Knowles, *Mastering Iron*, 4; Doerflinger, "Rural Capitalism in Iron Country," 9, 30–31.

10. Abernethy, *Formative Period in Alabama*, 109.

11. Sheldon, *Life of Asa G. Sheldon*, 128–29.

12. Trimble, *Autobiography and Correspondence*, 60–61.

13. Smith and Cole, *Economic Fluctuations*, 20; Cochran, *Frontiers of Change*, 41–42. See Ellis, *Short History*, 174.

14. North, *Economic Growth of the United States*, 52–53.

15. Flint, *Recollections*, xix–xvi, xxii, 76–78.

16. *Niles' Register*, Jan. 23, 1819, 416; Jerome, *History of the American Clock Business*, 43, 46–47.

17. Cochran, *Frontiers of Change*, 54.

18. Taylor, *Transportation Revolution*, 10–11; "Richest Americans in History," *Forbes*, Aug. 24, 1998.

19. Jefferson to U.S. Congress, December 2, 1806, in *Founders Online*; Larson, "'Bind the Republic Together,'" 367–87. See Ellis, "Market Revolution," 154–55.

20. Madison, "Seventh Annual Message (December 5, 1815)," https://millercen ter.org/the-presidency/presidential-speeches/december-5-1815-seventh-annual -message (accessed Dec. 25, 2016); Calhoun, *Speeches*, 2:190.

21. *Niles' Register*, May 8, 1819, 187–88.

22. Elizabeth (NJ) *Journal*, April 22, 1819, in *Circular Letters*, 3:1070–71.

23. Cochran, *Frontiers of Change*, 46, 48; Puls, *Samuel Adams*, 157–58; Pred, *Urban Growth and the Circulation of Information*, 36–48; *Niles' Register*, Dec. 5, 1818, 268.

24. John, *Spreading the News*, 3–5; Rothbard, *Panic of 1819*, 21n; Kielbowicz, *News in the Mail*, 3, 71; Appleby, "Popular Sources of American Capitalism," 456; Howe, *What Hath God Wrought?*, 227.

25. Cochran, *Frontiers of Change*, 46; Ware, *Early New England Cotton Manufacture*, 16; Ellis, *Short History*, 180; McMaster, *History of the People of the United States*, 3:462–63.

26. Meyer, *Roots of American Industrialization*, 29–32; Wright, *First Wall Street*, 119–20; *Niles' Register*, Dec. 5, 1818, 267.

27. Haulman, *Virginia and the Panic of 1819*, 18; Meyer, *Roots of American Industrialization*, 30; Hammond, *Banks and Politics*, 188; Cochran, *Frontiers of Change*, 46, 48; Boggess, *Settlement of Illinois*, 114.

28. La Rochefoucauld-Liancourt, *Travels* (London: R. Phillips, 1799), 2:37, quoted in Haulman, *Virginia and the Panic of 1819*, 17; *Niles' Register*, Dec. 12, 1818, 267.

29. Wright, "Specially Incorporated Transportation Companies," 978; *Niles' Register*, Oct. 24, 1818, 139; Feb. 20, 1820, 475; Shaw, *Erie Water West*, 87–88, 132. See Sheriff, *Artificial River*.

30. *Niles' Register*, Oct. 17, 1818, 125–26.

31. Letter dated St. Louis, July 19, 1819, quoted in Chittendon, *History of the American Fur Trade*, 567–68.

32. *Niles' Register*, Dec. 5, 1818, 267.

33. Hunter, *History of Industrial Power*, 2:371.

34. Entry of April 26, 1819, in Adams, *Memoirs*, 4:351; Gudmestad, *Steamboats and the Rise of the Cotton Kingdom*, 16; Wade, *Urban Frontier*, 162.

35. Gudmestad, *Steamboats and the Rise of the Cotton Kingdom*, 16, 17, 20, 23; Howe, *What Hath God Wrought?*, 214.

36. McMurtrie, *Sketches of Louisiana*, 193, 199; Gudmestad, *Steamboats and the Rise of the Cotton Kingdom*, 24, 25, 148. See Schab, "Woodhawks and Cordwood."

37. Gudmestad, *Steamboats and the Rise of the Cotton Kingdom*, 23; Bruchey, *Cotton and the Growth of the American Economy*, 80; Boggess, *Settlement of Illinois*, 119.

38. Morris, *Dawn of Innovation*, 111; Hunter, *History of Industrial Power*, 2:371; Stiles, *First Tycoon*, 84.

39. *Niles' Register*, Jan. 9, 1819, 384; Flint, *Letters from America*, 286; Gudmestad, *Steamboats and the Rise of the Cotton Kingdom*, 24.

40. Sylla and Wright, "Corporation Formation," 654.

41. Seavoy, *Origins of the American Business Corporation*, 257.

42. *Trustees of Dartmouth Coll. v. Woodward*, 17 U.S. 4 Wheat. 518 (1819).

43. *Niles' Register*, Feb. 20, 1819, 477; Richmond *Examiner*, June 1, 1819.

44. Wright, "Corporate Entrepreneurship," 206; Kamoie, *Irons in the Fire*, 137–38; Brazy, *American Planter*, 16.

45. Wetherill, *Story of the Philadelphia Stock Exchange*, 11; Barnes, *History of the Philadelphia Stock Exchange*, 9; Vitiello, *Philadelphia Stock Exchange*, 54–55.

46. Vitiello, *Philadelphia Stock Exchange*, 56.

47. Rousseau and Sylla, "Emerging Financial Markets," 10–11.

48. Watson, *Observations*, 18–19.

49. Taylor, *Transportation Revolution*, 281; Bloodgood, *Treatise on Roads*, 97; Klein, "Voluntary Provisions of Public Goods?" 792.

50. Pell, *Review of the Administration*, 30; Durrenberger, *Turnpikes*, 104, 125; *Annals of Congress*, 15th Congr., 1st sess., House of Representatives, 1377; Cochran, *Frontiers of Change*, 47.

51. Gudmestad, *Steamboats and the Rise of the Cotton Kingdom*, 25–27; Wright, "Corporate Entrepreneurship," 200.

52. Cochran, *Frontiers of Change*, 47; Gudmestad, *Steamboats and the Rise of the Cotton Kingdom*, 25–26, 27.

53. Wright, "Specially Incorporated Transportation Companies," 973–74 (table 1).

54. Ibid., 976; Sylla and Wright, "Corporation Formation," 657–58; Atack and Passell, *New Economic View of American History*, 122.

55. Wright, "Corporate Entrepreneurship," 210–11; Evans, "Blast from the Past."

56. Watson, *Liberty and Power*, 15–16; Rousseau and Sylla, "Emerging Financial Markets," 7.

57. Rousseau and Sylla, "Emerging Financial Markets," 10, 27.

58. Morison, *Maritime History*, 25; Bodenhorn, *History of Banking*, 36–37.

59. Sylla and Wright, "Early Corporate America," 22.

60. Pell, *Review of the Administration*, 83.

Chapter Three: Volcano Weather

1. Stromboli, off the coast of Sicily, would become familiar after Jules Verne's 1864 *Journey to the Center of the Earth*, but there do not appear to have ever been any steamboats named for it.

2. Evans, "Blast from the Past"; Eddy, "Before Tambora," 7.

3. Post, "Economic Crisis of 1816–1817," 248.

4. Thorp, *Business Annals*, 155–57.

5. Chenoweth, "Ships' Logbooks and 'The Year Without a Summer'"; Post, "Economic Crisis of 1816–1817," 331; London *Times*, July 7, 1816; Maye, "Volcanic Eruption with Global Repercussions."

6. Fay, *Corn Laws and Social England*, 78; Gayer, Rostow, and Schwartz, *Growth and Fluctuation of the British Economy*, 1:115; Barnes, *History of the English Corn Laws*, 157–62.

7. Klingaman and Klingaman, *Year Without a Summer*, 40–41, 45; Wood, *Tambora*, 52; London *Times*, Sept.3 and 7, 1816.

8. Entry of July 19, 1816, in Adams, *Memoirs*, 3:404–5.

9. Klingaman and Klingaman, *Year Without a Summer*, 225–26; London *Times*, Nov. 16, 1816; Halévy, *Liberal Awakening*, 16.

10. Tooke, *History of Prices*, 2:19–20.

11. Milham, "The Year 1816," 563; Goodrich, *Peter Parley's Recollections*, 1:79.

12. Klingaman and Klingaman, *Year Without a Summer*, 65; Jerome, *Life*, 31, 32; Thomas, *Travels through Western Country*, 105, 82.

13. Records of Prof. Charles Dewey, Williams College, cited in Klingaman and Klingaman, *Year Without a Summer*, 56, 103; *Niles' Register*, Aug. 10, 1816, 385–86; Klingaman and Klingaman, *Year Without a Summer*, 155.

14. Jefferson to Gallatin, Sept. 8, 1816, in Jefferson, *Papers*, Retirement Series, 10:379–80.

15. *Niles' Register*, Aug. 10, 1816, 385; *National Intelligencer*, Sept. 3, 1816; *Carolina Courant*, Oct. 10, 1816.

16. *Enquirer*, Aug. 31 and Sept. 14, 1816; Georgetown (SC) *Gazette*, reprinted in Norfolk *American Beacon*, Sept. 16, 1816; Norfolk *Pilot*, Sept. 11, 1816, quoted in Boggess, *Settlement of Illinois*, 110. See Skeen, *1816: America Rising*, 5.

17. *American Beacon*, July 18, 1816; Niven, *John C. Calhoun*, 68; Malone, *Jefferson*, 6:301, 302; Jefferson to Patrick Gibson, Sept. 10, 1818, in *Founders Online*.

18. Boggess, *Settlement of Illinois*, 108; Flint, *Letters from America*, 94 (Oct. 19, 1818); *Niles' Register*, Nov. 7, 1818.

19. *Niles' Register*, Oct. 9, 1819, 96; Sept. 25, 1819, 64.

20. Heidler and Heidler, *Henry Clay*, 145; Flint, *Recollections*, 283. See *Orleans Gazette and Commercial Advertiser,* May 18, 1819.

21. Goodrich, *Peter Parley's Recollections*, 1:79; Sheldon, *Life of Asa G. Sheldon*, 146–47; Skeen, *1816: America Rising*, 6; Cole, *Wholesale Commodity Prices*, 161; Pitkin, *Statistical View*, 108–15.

22. Richmond *Enquirer*, Sept. 7, 1816; Jefferson to Gallatin, Sept. 10, 1818, in *Founders Online*.

23. *Times* of London, Aug. 14, 1816; Taylor, *Transportation Revolution*, 210; Amherst (NH) *Farmer's Cabinet*, quoted in Klingaman and Klingaman, *Year Without a Summer*, 104–5.

24. Klingaman and Klingaman, *Year Without a Summer*, 237–39; Mussey, "Yankee Chills, Ohio Fever," 442.

25. Mussey, "Yankee Chills, Ohio Fever," 446; Klingaman and Klingaman, *Year Without a Summer*, 244; *Niles' Register*, supp. to vol. XV, 16.

26. Smith, *History of The Prophet Joseph Smith,* 65, 69.

27. *Historical Statistics of the United States*, Part 1:24–37; Klingaman and Klingaman, *Year Without a Summer*, 218; Howe, *What Hath God Wrought?*, 80.

28. Flagg, "Pioneer Letters," 154–55.

29. Dippel, *Eighteen Hundred and Froze to Death*, 144; *American Mercury*, Oct. 21, 1817; New York *Commercial Advertiser*, Dec. 17, 1819.

30. *16th Census of the United States: Population*, 1:18, 20–21; Greve, *Centennial History of Cincinnati*, 1:500; North, *Economics Growth of the United States*, 62; Taylor, *Transportation Revolution*, 9.

31. Zanesville *Messenger*, Oct. 16, 1818, quoted in Stommel, *Volcano Weather*, 96–97; Douglas, *Autobiography*, 44–45.

32. Smith, *Recollections*, 85; Pocock, "Popular Roots of Jacksonian Democracy," 495; James Kimball, *A Journey to the West in 1817, Historical Collection of the Essex Institute* 8 (1868): 235, quoted in Cayton, *Frontier Republic*, 116.

33. Flint, *Letters from America*, 68, 72, 87; Birkbeck, *Notes on a Journey*, 31.

34. St. Louis *Gazette*, Oct. 20, 1816, quoted in Rohrbough, *Land Office Business*, 70; *Niles' Register*, Dec. 5, 1818, Jan. 2, 1819.

35. *Niles' Register,* Oct. 17, 1818, 125–26.

36. Birkbeck, *Notes on a Journey*, 71, 105; Biggs, *To America in Thirty-nine Days*, 12.

37. Dec. 5, 1811, in *ASP: Public Lands*, 2:256; *Circular Letters*, 3:1075–76.

38. Lebergott, "Wage Trends, 1800–1900," 450, 452.

39. Wolcott to Nicholas, Jan. 24, 1797, in *ASP: Public Lands*, 1:74. See Rohrbough, *Land Office Business*, 22.

40. Rohrbough, *Land Office Business*, 30–31.

41. Haynes, "Formation of the Territory," 1:183.

42. General Land Office Letters Sent, Miscellaneous, Oct. 21, 1808, quoted in Rohrbough, *Land Office Business*, 45, 49–50; Ketcham, *James Madison*, 625.

43. Gallatin to James Findley, Nov. 6, 1802, quoted in Rohrbough, *Land Office Business*, 31–32.

44. Gallatin to Jefferson, Jan. 6, 1807, in Gallatin, *Writings*, 1:326–27.

45. *ASP: Public Lands*, 3:420. See Rohrbough, *Land Office Business*, 58–59.

46. Badollet to Tiffin, Dec. 20, 1815, Reynolds to Tiffin, June 3, 1814, Badollet to Tiffin, June 1, 1814, and Badollet to Meigs, Nov. 18, 1814, all quoted in Rohrbough, *Land Office Business*, 103, 60.

47. Abernethy, *Formative Period in Alabama*, 65; Howe, *What Hath God Wrought?*, 126.

48. General Land Office Letters, Vincennes, March 1, 1817, Dec. 12, 1816, July 5, 1817, quoted in Rohrbaugh 131.

49. Birkbeck, *Notes on a Journey*, 26; *Western Intelligencer* Feb. 28, 1818; *Herald*, reprinted in the *National Intelligencer*, Sept. 24, 1818. See Rohrbough, *Land Office Business*, 127, 131–32.

50. USGS, "New Madrid 1811–1812 Earthquakes."

51. Rohrbough, *Land Office Business*, 106.

52. Ibid., 135.

53. Rector to Meigs, Oct. 18, 1819, quoted in Rohrbough, *Land Office Business*, 139–40; *Alabama Republican*, Oct. 30, 1820. See

54. Ewing to Crawford, Jan. 9, 1819, in *ASP: Finance* 3:735; Treasury Report, Feb. 14, 1822, in *ASP: Finance*, 3:718.

55. Biddle Memorandum, no date, Nicholas Biddle Papers, Library of Congress, quoted in Schlesinger, *Age of Jackson*, 76.

56. Glaeser, "Nation of Gamblers," 15; Cole, "Cyclical and Sectional Variations," 52, 41, 43–44. See Rohrbough, *Land Office Business*, 91–92.

57. Barnes, *History of English Corn Laws*, 157–62; Oct. 18, 1816, in Adams, *Memoirs*, 3:453; Tooke, *History of Prices*, 2:14; *Times* of London, July 13 and 27, 1816; *Farmers' Register*, Oct. 2, 1816. See Klingaman and Klingaman, *Year Without a Summer*, 224.

58. Barnes, *History of English Corn Laws*, 162; Fay, *Corn Laws and Social England*, 79; Gayer, Rostow, and Schwartz, *Growth and Fluctuation of the British Economy*, 1:141; Haulman, *Virginia and the Panic of 1819*, 11; Rothbard, *Panic of 1819*, 20; *Historical Statistics 1789–1945*, 245–48.

59. Boles, *Black Southerners*, 72; Cole, *Wholesale Commodity Prices*; North, *Economics Growth of the United States*, table A–IX, 250. See also Wright, *Political Economy of the Cotton South*.

Chapter Four: Alabama Fever

1. Fischer and Kelly, *Bound Away*, 127; Howe, *What Hath God Wrought?*, 158; "List of Purchasers of Lots in the Town of Florence," Accounts: Land, Cypress Land Company, 1818–1834, Coffee Papers, Alabama Department of Archives and History, cited in Dupre, *Transforming the Cotton Frontier*, 45; Ketcham, *James Madison*, 623.

2. "Report of the Committee on Inland Navigation," North Carolina Senate, 1815, quoted in Murphey, *Papers*, 2:20–21; Raleigh *Star*, Sept. 6, 1816; Ruffin, *Papers*, 1:198, quoted in Rohrbough, *Land Office Business*, 9.

3. Hammond, quoted in Dattel, *Cotton and Race*, 48.

4. Cole, "Cyclical and Sectional Variations," 45.

5. *Niles' Register*, Jan. 30, 1819.

6. Tait to Walker, Oct. 16, 1820, Walker Papers, Alabama Department of Archives and History, quoted in Bailey, *John Williams Walker*, 120. See Rohrbough, *Land Office Business*, 125.

7. General Land Office Letters, Huntsville, Feb. 21, 1818, and April 10, 1818, quoted in Rohrbaugh,122; *Niles' Register*, Oct. 17, 1818, 125; Nov. 7, 1818, 199.

8. Pittsburgh *Gazette*, reprinted in *Niles' Register*, Sept. 19, 1818; Fort Claiborne *Courier*, reprinted in Huntsville (AL) *Republic*, May 1, 1819.

9. Letter from Sec. of Treasury, July 31, 1820, quoted in Rohrbaugh, *Land Office Business*, 127; *ASP: Public Lands*, 5:378–80, 513; *Niles' Register*, Jan. 30, 1819, 423.

10. Taylor, *Transportation Revolution*, 198; Weems, "Bank of Mississippi," 773.

11. Brazy, *American Planter*, 9–11, 24.

12. Abernethy, *Formative Period in Alabama*, 53, 65; Bailey, *John Williams Walker*, 120.

13. *ASP: Finance*, 3:494.

14. Crawford to John Taylor, Oct. 26, 1818, Treasury Department Letters to Land Offices, 1801–1833, NARA, quoted in Rohrbough, *Land Office Business*, 138.

15. Pope to Meigs, Jan. 2, 1818, quoted in Rohrbough, *Land Office Business*, 119.

16. *ASP: Public Lands*, 7:548.

17. Remini, *Andrew Jackson and the Course of American Empire*, 135; Jackson, *Papers*, 4:176–78, 78–79.

18. General Land Office Letters, Huntsville, Nov. 26, 1818, April 22, 1819, quoted in Rohrbaugh, *Land Office Business*, 124.

19. North, *Economics Growth of the United States*, 68, 75–76.

20. Abernethy, *Formative Period in Alabama*, 108–9.

21. Ibid., 110–11.

22. Baines, *History of the Cotton Manufacture*, 347; Mitchell, *British Historical Statistics*, 331.

23. Beckert, *Empire of Cotton*, 408–9; Dattel, Cotton and Race, 27, 29; Otto, *Southern Frontier*, 84–85.

24. Bruchey, *Cotton and the Growth of the American Economy*, 95, 104–10. See Woodman, *King Cotton*, 29; McLane, *Documents Relative to the Manufactures*, 1:929; Hammond, *Cotton Industry*, appendix 1.

25. Glaeser, "Nation of Gamblers," 13; North, *Economics Growth of the United States*, 75.

26. Coxe, "Addition," 9; Haulman, *Virginia and the Panic of 1819*, 11; Cole, *Wholesale Commodity Prices*, 206–07.

27. Beckert, *Empire of Cotton*, 125; Coxe, "Addition," 4, 10.

28. Ibid.

29. *Niles' Register*, Jan. 30, 1819.

30. *Aurora*, April 6, 1819, reprinted in *Niles' Register*, April 24, 1819.

31. *Niles' Register*, May 8, 1819, 180; May 22, 1819, 220; Aug. 28, 1819, 437–38; Pell, *Review of the Administration*, 82.

32. *Niles' Register*, May 8, 1819, 173–74.

33. Ibid., 179; Dodge, *Cotton*, 74, 76; *Niles' Register*, Sept. 11, 1819, 29; Barnes, *History of English Corn Laws*, 309; Calhoun, *Papers*, 7:198, 218.

34. Coxe, "Addition," 6; *Niles' Register*, March 18, 1820, 51; Pitkin, *Statistical View*, 108, 111, 117; Haulman, *Virginia and the Panic of 1819*, 187n.

35. Corbin to Madison, Oct. 10, 1819, in *Founders Online*; Deyle, *Carry Me Back*, 42; Hodgson, *Remarks During a Journey*, 178.

36. Haulman, *Virginia and the Panic of 1819*, 65–66; *Niles' Register*, Oct. 9, 1819, 85; Hodgson, *Remarks During a Journey*, 185, 39. See Phillips, *American Negro Slavery*, 371; Conger, "South Carolina and Early Tariffs."

37. Dattel, *Cotton and Race*, 46.

38. Hodgson, *Remarks During a Journey*, 190.

39. Corbin to Madison, Oct. 10, 1819, in *Founders Online*.

40. Williamson and Cain, "Measuring Slavery in 2011 Dollars." See Fogel, *Without Consent or Contract*, 60–81.

41. Gray, *History of Agriculture*, 2:893–905; Hammond, *Cotton Industry*, appendix I; Stettler, "Growth and Fluctuation of the Antebellum Textile Industry," 129; Cole, *Wholesale Commodity Prices*, table 4.

42. Tadmon and Johnson, 225; *Niles' Register*, April 15, 1820, 115; Dattel, *Cotton and Race*, 52.

43. Cole, "Cyclical and Sectional" table 4; North, *Economics Growth of the United States*, 72; Dattel, *Cotton and Race*, 67–68.

44. Glaeser, "Nation of Gamblers," 15; Madison to Rush, April 21, 1821, in *Founders Online*; North, *Economics Growth of the United States*, 69, 71, 73; Cole, "Cyclical and Sectional" table 4.

45. *Western Intelligencer*, Feb. 28, 1818.

46. Rothbard, *Panic of 1819*, 19–20.

47. Ibid.

Chapter Five: Bank Expansion

1. Richmond *Enquirer*, April 18, 1820; *Journal of the House of Delegates* 1820–21, 10.

2. Washington to Jefferson, Aug. 1, 1786, in *Founders Online*; Jefferson to Edward Carrington, May 27, 1788, in ibid.; John Adams to F. A. Vanderkemp, Feb. 16, 1809, in Adams, *Works*, 9:610.

3. Jefferson to Gallatin, Oct. 16, 1815, in *Founders Online*; John Adams to Jefferson, March 12, 1819, in ibid.; Madison, *Papers*, 9:158; Taylor, *Inquiry into the Principles and Policy*, 275.

4. Jefferson, quoted in Malone, *Jefferson*, 6:306; "Seventy-Six," *Cause of, and Cure for Hard Times*, iv.

5. *Niles' Register*, Jan. 9, 1819, 364.

6. Entry of July 16, 1819, in Adams, *Memoirs*, 4:401.

7. *Aurora*, January 9, 1807; Jarvey, *Robert Y. Hayne and His Times*, 87.

8. *Niles' Register*, Jan. 9, 1819, 361–62.

9. Jefferson to Gallatin, Oct. 16, 1815, in *Founders Online*; Trimble, *Autobiography and Correspondence*, 108; Washburn, *Autobiography and Memorials*, 31–31.

10. Russell, *Freedom versus Organization*, 302–3.

11. Fleming, *Louisiana Purchase*, 18; Richard Ellis, "Market Revolution," 156.

12. Nevins, *History of the Bank of New York*, 30–31; Bodenhorn, *History of Banking*, 41–42.

13. John Farmer and Jacob Moore, *Gazetteer of the State of New Hampshire* (Concord, NH, 1823), quoted in Appleby, "Popular Sources of American Capitalism," 454; Hammond, *Banks and Politics*, 167–68; McCabe, "Banking," 59–64; *Liberty Hall*, Jan. 26, 1818; Finley, *Autobiography*, 273; *Niles' Register*, July 10, 1819, 322.

14. Fenstermaker, *Development of American Commercial Banking*, 8; Unger, *Last Founding Father*, 296; Weber, "Early State Banks," 449, 440–43; Gallatin, *Considerations on the Currency*, 97–100.

15. *Circular Letters*, 3:1073.

16. Dewey, *State Banking Before the Civil War*, 182–86. See Hammond, "Long and Short Term Credit."

17. Ellis, "Market Revolution," 156; Fenstermaker, *Development of Commercial Banking*, xiii; Hammond, *Banks and Politics*, 188, 192.

18. Clark and Hall, *Legislative and Documentary History*, 500; Gallatin, *Considerations on the Currency*, 3:286–87; Rousseau and Sylla, "Emerging Financial Markets," 6. See Fenstermaker, *Development of Commercial Banking*, 66–68.

19. Weber, "Early State Banks," 345; *Western Spy*, Sept. 13, 1816; Fenstermaker, *Development of Commercial Banking*, 22; Huntington, *History of Banking and Currency*, 38.

20. Smith and Cole, *Economic Fluctuations*, 27; Fenstermaker, *Development of Commercial Banking*, 22.

21. *Watchman*, Dec. 3, 1818; Huntington, *History of Banking and Currency*, 66; Norton, *History of Knox County*, 182.

22. Coover, "Ohio Banking Institutions," 312–13.

23. Norton, *History of Knox County*, 183, 190, 196. See Porter, *Politics and Peril*, 52.

24. Hammond, *Banks and Politics*, 173.

25. Ibid., 178; Jenks, "First Bank in Michigan," 53; Dexter is the subject of Jane Kamensky's *Exchange Artist*.

26. Gouge, *Short History of Paper Money*, 141.

27. Abernethy, *Formative Period in Alabama*, 103–4.

28. Pickens to Calhoun, August 9, 1818, in *Territorial Papers*, 8:396.

29. Haines and Sylla, *History of Interest Rates*, 317–26; Brazy, *American Planter*, 21–22.

30. Carey, *Reflections on the Present System of Banking*, 6; Morgan to Sergeant, Jan. 22, 1816, Sergeant Papers, Historical Society of Pennsylvania, quoted in Blackson, "Pennsylvania Banks and the Panic of 1819," 341–42; *Washington Reporter*, April 21, 1817.

31. Peck, *Forty Years*, 84; Sallee, "Branch Banking in Missouri."

32. Federal Reserve Bank of St. Louis, "A Foregone Conclusion"; Scharf, *History of St. Louis City and County*, 2:1385; Primm, *Lion of the Valley*, 106–7.

33. Flint, *Letters from America*, 223–24 (March 10, 1820; Adams, *Memoirs*, 4:396 (June 24, 1819); Wolcott, *Remarks*, 12–14.

34. Fenstermaker, *Development of Commercial Banking*, 10.

35. Meyer, *Roots of American Industrialization*, 61; Morris, *Dawn of Innovation*, 106. See Dalzell, *Enterprising Elite*, 95–108; Lamoreaux, *Insular Lending*, 1–30, 52–83.

36. *Niles' Register*, Feb. 26, 1820, 147; Oct. 17, 1818, 125–26.

37. Jarvey, *Robert Y. Hayne and His Times*, 85; Bodenhorn, *History of Banking*, 34. See Greenspan, "*Our Banking History*."

38. Schur, "Second Bank of the United States and Inflation," 119; Gallatin, *Considerations on the Currency*, 46–47; Crawford, in *ASP: Finance*, 3:493; Walters, "Origins of the Second Bank of the United States," 118; Kaplan, *Bank of the United States*, 44.

39. *ASP, Finance*, 3:5, 10–11, 19; Minute Book No. 6, Bank of North America, Historical Society of Pennsylvania, quoted in Blackson, 339; *United States Gazette* (Philadelphia), Feb. 22, 1816; Kaplan, *Bank of the United States*, 44–46. See Walters, "Origins of the Second Bank of the United States," 115–22.

40. Calhoun, *Works*, 155–58, 161–62; Clarke and Hall, *Legislative and Documentary History*, 680–84. See Hammond, *Banks and Politics*, 236.

41. Clarke and Hall, *Legislative and Documentary History*, 655.

42. *Annals of Congress*, 14th Congr., 1st sess., 1219, 281. See Catterall, *Second Bank of the United States*, 23.

43. *Niles' Register*, April 13, 1816, 98.

44. July 20, 1817, in *ASP: Finance*, 4:807; March 7, 1817, in ibid., 4:774. See Hammond, *Banks and Politics*, 253.

45. McMaster, *Life and Times of Stephen Girard*, 2:314.

46. Catterall, *Second Bank of the United States*, 22; Bogen, "Scandal of Smith and Buchanan," 128.

47. McMaster, *Life and Times of Stephen Girard*, 2:314–15; Catterall, *Second Bank of the United States*, 40. See Hammond, *Banks and Politics*, 257; Walters, "Origins of the Second Bank of the United States," 115-17, 119.

48. Remini, *Andrew Jackson and the Course of American Freedom*, 27; Wilentz, *Rise of American Democracy*, 27; Wright, *First Wall Street*, 72; Gouge, *Short History of Paper Money*, 110; Eckert, "William Jones," 175–76; Jones to Madison, October 1814, Madison Papers, Library of Congress, quoted in Eckert, "William Jones," 177; Ketcham, *James Madison*, 589; Leon Schur allows that while "Jones's management of the Bank was pedestrian, . . . [w]hat the customary account fails to bring out clearly is the great magnitude of the task expected of Jones and the Bank, and the great opposition to their attempts to carry out this task." ("Second Bank of the United States," 118).

49. Wilentz, *Rise of American Democracy*, 206; Catterall, *Second Bank of the United States*, 29.

50. *Niles' Register*, Jan. 2, 1819, 345.

51. Dewey, *State Banking Before the Civil War*, 175–80; Hammond, *Banks and Politics*, 254.

52. Hidy, *House of Barings*, 70–71; Boyd, "John Sergeant's Mission to Europe," 228–31; Hammond, *Banks and Politics*, 255; Astor to John Savage, Nov. 25, 1817, John Jacob Astor Papers, NYPL, in Bonelli, *Response of Public and Private Philanthropy*, 12.

53. Schur, "Second Bank of the United States," 119; *ASP: Finance*, 4:759; Catterall, *Second Bank of the United States*, 23–24; Blackson, "Pennsylvania Banks and the Panic of 1819," 340; *ASP: Finance*, 3:232.

54. William Jones Papers, Pennsylvania State Historical Society, in Knodell, *Second Bank of the United States*.

55. *ASP: Finance*, 4:524, 509.

56. Hammond, *Banks and Politics*, 256; Catterall, *Second Bank of the United States*, 32; Johnson, 853–54; *ASP: Finance*, 3:308.

57. Catterall, *Second Bank of the United States*, 36–37.

58. *ASP: Finance*, 4:769, 820; Hammond, *Banks and Politics*, 248; *Niles' Register*, May 17, 1817, 185; Catterall, *Second Bank of the United States*, 37–38.

59. Catterall, *Second Bank of the United States*, 28–29. See Hammond, *Banks and Politics*, 300–325; Howe, *What Hath God Wrought?*, 375. BUS notes were not technically legal tender; even notes of the Bank of England did not attain that official distinction in Britain until the 1830s, but in both countries coins were so rarely seen that notes of those banks functioned as the equivalent.

60. Astor to Gallatin, March 14, 1818, Albert Gallatin Papers, New-York Historical Society, quoted in Dangerfield, *Era of Good Feelings*, 179–80.

Chapter Six: Bank Contraction

1. Simon, *On the Nature and Elements*, 18; Hausman and Hausman, "Berkeley's Semantic Dilemma," 231; Dostoevsky, *Demons*, trans. Pevear and Volokhonsky, 718.

2. *Niles' Register*, Sept. 18, 1819, 69.

3. E.g. Kindleberger and Aliber, *Manias, Panics, and Crashes*, 137; Catterall, *Second Bank of the United States*, 61.

4. House of Representatives Report 460, 22nd Congr., 1st sess. (April 30, 1832), 351–52; Schur, "Second Bank of the United States," 118, 127, 133; Catterall, *Second Bank of the United States*, 57, 61; Adams, *Memoirs*, 4:241–42. See Howe, *What Hath God Wrought?*, 143–44; Rothbard, *Panic of 1819*, 11–17. Crawford has his defenders; Walter Buckingham Smith thinks his letters and reports reveal "breadth and statesmanlike quality" (*Economic Aspects of the Second Bank of the United States*, 10), although the excerpts he quotes do not all support that judgment—e.g., a letter assuring Cheves that "the first duty of the Board is to the stockholders; the second is to the nation" (58); Smith also acknowledges that Jones "with some justice, blamed the federal government for many of the troubles of the Bank in 1818" (113).

5. House of Representatives Report 460, 22nd Congr., 1st sess. (April 30, 1832), 351–52; Crawford to Biddle, May 30, 1823, U.S. Treasury Letters to Bankers, vol.

6, quoted in Smith, *Economic Aspects*, 105; Kindleberger and Aliber, *Manias, Panics, and Crashes*, 187.

6. *ASP: Finance*, 3:335.

7. July 3, 1817, in *ASP: Finance*, 4:540.

8. Ibid., 3:326, 3:387. See Catterall, *Second Bank of the United States*, 62.

9. *ASP: Finance*, 3:367; *Annals of Congress*, 15th Congr., 2nd sess. 331, 1363; *Niles' Register*, Sept. 5, 1818, 25, 59–60; Sept. 19, 1818, 61. See Schur, "Second Bank of the United States," 126.

10. *ASP: Finance*, 4:859–60. One of the largest and—for a while—most trusted banks in Cincinnati was the bank of John Piatt, which was not chartered by the state, but by November 1819 its notes were considered worthless. See Otter, *History of My Own Times*, 130n.

11. Catterall, *Second Bank of the United States*, 52; *ASP: Finance*, 4:855; Schur, "Second Bank of the United States," 130.

12. *ASP: Finance*, 3:324.

13. Ibid., 3:496.

14. Catterall, *Second Bank of the United States*, 30; Dangerfield, *Awakening of American Nationalism*, 83.

15. Jan. 30, 1819, in King, *Life and Correspondence*, 6:200–201; Boyd, "John Sergeant's Mission to Europe," 226–31; Wilkins, *History of Foreign Investment*, 61.

16. Entry of Oct. 12, 1818, in Adams, *Memoirs*, 4:131–32.

17. Entry of October 19, 1818, in ibid., 4:139; Catterall, *Second Bank of the United States*, 52, 56; Hiday, *House of Baring*, 72; *ASP: Finance*, 3:338–39.

18. *National Intelligencer*, reprinted in *Niles' Register*, Dec. 12, 1818.

19. *Niles' Register*, Jan. 30, 1819, 417; King, *Life and Correspondence*, 6:197–98.

20. *Niles' Register*, Feb. 20, 1819, 478.

21. Dabney, *Liberalism in the South*, 84.

22. Cheves, quoted in Gouge, *Short History of Paper Money*, 107; McMaster, *Life and Times of Stephen Girard*, 2:351. Jones was convinced that Cheves had intrigued to replace him, but Walter Smith believes "the office sought Cheves, not the reverse"; see Friendly Monitor, *Brief Review of the Origin*, 32; and Smith, *Economic Aspects*, 285n.

23. Gouge, *Short History of Paper Money*,107–8, 105. See Smith, *Economic Aspects*, 285–86n.

24. Ibid., 106.

25. Crawford to Cheves, April 6, 1819, Cheves Papers, quoted in Smith, *Economic Aspects*, 119–20; entry of March 25, 1819, in Adams, *Memoirs*, 4:311.

26. Entry of April 5, 1819, in ibid., 4:324–25; Cheves to Crawford, April 2, 1819, in Monroe Papers, Library of Congress Manuscript Division.

27. Gouge, *Short History of Paper Money*,109.

28. Entries of April 20 and 24, 1819, in Adams, *Memoirs*, 4:344–49.

29. Entry of May 6, 1819, in Adams, *Memoirs*, 4:359; *Niles' Register*, May 22, 1819, 226.

30. Entry of June 24, 1819, in Adams, *Memoirs*, 4:395.

31. Entry of May 27, 1819, in ibid., 4:375.

32. *Niles' Register*, June 5, 1819, 256; June 26, 1819, 298.

33. Dec. 24 and 22 1819, in Cox, "Selections from the Torrance Papers," 26–27; U.S. Congress, *Bank of the United States*, House Executive Document 147, 22nd Congr., 1st sess. (1831–32), 46, quoted in Blackson, "Pennsylvania Banks and the Panic of 1819," 352.

34. *Report of the Bank of the United States to the Committee of Ways and Means*, Jan. 28, 1833, 11.

35. Cheves to Crawford, Oct. 27, 1819, in *ASP: Finance*, 4:912–13, 4:900.

36. Executive Document 2, 2nd Congress, 1st session, quoted in Schur, "Second Bank of the United States," 128.

37. Smith, *Economic Aspects*, 49 (chart IV); Rothbard, *Panic of 1819*, 18; Schur, "Second Bank of the United States," 130–34.

38. U.S. Congress, *Bank of the United States*, House Executive Document 147, 5, quoted in Blackson, "Pennsylvania Banks and the Panic of 1819," 352; *Niles' Register*, March 11, 1820, 35; Gallatin, *Considerations on the Currency*, 45–51; Smith, *Economic Aspects*, 40, 119, 286.

39. Gallatin, *Considerations on the Currency*, 56; Federal Deposit Insurance Corporation, "Statistics at a Glance," https://www.fdic.gov/bank/statistical/stats/; Blackson, "Pennsylvania Banks and the Panic of 1819," 339; Hammond, *Banks and Politics*, 228.

40. *National Advocate*, Oct. 26, 1815, quoted in Hammond, *Banks and Politics,* 179; *Niles' Register*, Aug. 28, 1819, 454.

41. *ASP: Finance*, 4:856.

42. Catterall, *Second Bank of the United States*, 63; *ASP: Finance*, 4:867; Kendall, *Autobiography*, 204.

43. *Niles' Register*, Dec. 5, 1818, 256.

44. Trimble, *Autobiography and Correspondence*, 117.

45. *Niles' Register,* Dec. 12, 1818, 283; Dec. 19, 1818, 290.

46. Flint, *Letters from America*, 133, 136.

47. Raquet, April 18, 1821, quoted in Ricardo, *Minor Papers on the Currency Question,* 199–201.

48. Entry of May 27, 1819, in Adams, *Memoirs*, 4:375; Albany *Argus,* June 29, 1819, quoted in Fenstermaker, *Development of Commercial Banking*, 12; *Niles' Register*, Jan. 16, 1819, 385.

49. Letter of Dec. 30, 1830, in Flint, *Letters from America*, 133; *Niles' Register*, Sept. 11, 1819, 20. See Knox, *History of Banking*, 485–86.

50. Crawford to John Taylor, Oct. 26, 1818, Treasury Department Letters to Land Offices, 1801–1833 (National Archives), quoted in Rohrbough, *Land Office Business*, 138.

51. June 7, 1819, in *ASP: Finance*, 4:882.

52. *ASP: Finance*, 4:956; *Niles' Register*, June 12, 1819, 258, 260; July 17, 1819, 341; July 24, 1819, 359; July 3, 1819, 311; July 31, 1819, 373; Aug. 28, 1819, 434.

53. *Journal of the Senate, New York*,42nd sess., 69; Hammond, *Banking and Politics*, 180; Knox, *History of Banking*, 549; Richmond *Enquirer*, June 15, 1819, quoted in Rothbard, *Panic of 1819*, 93.

54. *Niles' Register*, Sept. 4, 1819, 19–20; Oct. 30, 1819, 139; Oct. 9, 1819, 84.

55. Ibid., June 22, 1820, 338; Catterall, *Second Bank of the United States*, 84.

56. Weber, "Early State Banks," 445; Greer, "Economic and Social Effects," 229; Gallatin, *Considerations on the Currency*, 103–6.

57. Report on Currency, Feb. 12, 1820, in *Reports of the Secretary of the Treasury*, 2:481–85.

58. Ibid.

59. Adams, *Memoirs*, 4:498.

Chapter Seven: Hard Times in the East

1. Knight's *Popular History* was not published until 1856, but the author had been thirty-four years old in 1825; see Lepler, *Many Panics of 1837*.

2. Jefferson to Rush, Jan. 22, 1819, in *Founders Online*.

3. Adams to Jefferson, Dec. 21, 1819, in ibid.

4. London *Courier*, May 11, 1820, reprinted in *Niles' Register*, July 29, 1820, 387.

5. *Niles' Register*, April 10, 1819, 114; May 22, 1819, 209; Oct. 23, 1819, 116.

6. Mintz and McNeil, "Growth of Political Factionalism"; Lebergott, "Labor Force, Employment, and Unemployment, 1929-39: Estimating Methods"; Johnston and Williamson, "What Was the U.S. GDP Then?"; North, Economic Growth of the United States, 233, 234 (tables A–VIII, C–VIII); Lebergott, "Labor Force, Employment, and Unemployment, 1929–39."

7. Appleby, "Popular Sources of American Capitalism," 441, 453; *Niles' Register*, Dec. 5, 1818, 245.

8. Peterson, *Great Triumvirate*, 102–4; *Niles' Register*, Dec. 4, 1819, 209; April 8, 1820, 97; Taylor, *Transportation Revolution*, 201.

9. Flint, *Letters from America*, 202–3; Gross, Newman, and Campbell, "Ladies in Red," 35–36. See Sobol, "Charging the Poor," 497, 486.

10. *Niles' Register*, July 24, 1819, 356; Nov. 6, 1819, 146; Flint, *Letters from America*, 273; Margo, *Wages and Labor Markets*, 70–73.

11. Adams, *Memoirs*, 4:375, 395–96.

12. Rezneck, "Depression of 1819–1822," 33; Gras, *Massachusetts First National Bank of Boston,* 44-49; Ware *Early New England Cotton Manufacture,* 65–72; *ASP: Finance,* 4:395–49; Dodge, *Memorial,* 96, 102–4.

13. Wolcott, *Remarks*, 4, 5; Stettler, "Growth and Fluctuation of the Antebellum Textile Industry," 121, 127; Troy Company Papers, to Laidlaw and Allen, Dec. 14, 1818, to Shaw and Tiffany, March 11, 1819, Quarterly Accounts 1818–1823, quoted in Ware, *Early New England Cotton Manufacture,* 68.

14. Haulman, *Virginia and the Panic of 1819*, 90.

15. Sheldon, *Life of Asa G. Sheldon*, 102–3.

16. David Stoddard Greenough Papers, Massachusetts Historical Society, quoted in Kidd, "To Be Harassed by My Creditors," 173.

17. Massachusetts Department of Labor, "Historical Review of Wages and Prices, 1782–1860," Sixteenth Annual Report (Boston, 1885), 3:317–28, cited in Rothbard, *Panic of 1819*, 23; Wolcott, *Remarks*, 4; Josiah Quincy, quoted in Katz, *In the Shadow of the Poorhouse*, 7.

18. Flint, *Letters from America*, 42–43, 30–31 (July 24, 1818).

19. Jones & Cline to Thomas W. Williams, May 3, 1819, Williams Papers, New York Public Library, cited in Bonelli, *Response of Public and Private Philanthropy*, 13; *National Advocate*, May 1819, reprinted in *Niles' Register*, May 8, 1819, 179; June 26, 1819, 291.

20. *Minutes of the Common Council* 10:515, 527–28, 400, 11:475–77, quoted in Bonelli, *Response of Public and Private Philanthropy*, 97–98.

21. *Evening Post*, Aug. 7, 1819, *National Advocate*, June 16, 1820; Bonelli, *Response of Public and Private Philanthropy*, 18; Wilentz, *Chants Democratic*, 50; Hinks, *To Awaken My Afflicted Brethren*, 67.

22. Wilentz, *Chants Democratic*, 50; "An Emigrant," in *Things as They Are*, 15; *Niles' Register*, Aug. 7, 1819, 385; Sept. 4, 1819, 16; New York *American*, Sept. 1, 1819; Stanford Annual Reports 1815–1821, Stanford Miscellaneous Papers, New-York Historical Society, quoted in Bonelli, *Response of Public and Private Philanthropy*, 82.

23. *Argus*, 19 1819, reprinted in *Niles' Register*, Oct. 30, 1819, 138; *Niles' Register*, Jan. 30, 1819, 418; Feb. 26, 1820, 445; Anne W. Cary to Sarah Tuckerman, July 15, 1818, in Curtis, *Cary Letters*, 258; Samuel Hopkins quoted in Carey, "Address to the Farmers," in his *Essays in Political Economy*, 419.

24. Carey, *The New Olive Branch*, 319–21; Carey, *Essays on Banking*, 25; *Republican*, Sept. 11, 1818, quoted in Blackson, "Pennsylvania Banks and the Panic of 1819," 342; *Journal of the Senate of the Commonwealth of Pennsylvania*, Vol. 30, *1819*, 223. See Matson, "Matthew Carey's Learning Experience," 473.

25. *Journal of the Thirtieth House of Representatives of the Commonwealth of Pennsylvania*, 476–88. See Carey, *New Olive Branch*, 133.

26. Flint, *Letters from America*, 50–59 (Aug. 5-7, 1818); Bezanson, Gray, and Hussey, *Wholesale Prices in Philadelphia*, 2:185.

27. McMaster, *Stephen Girard*, 2:356.

28. Carey, *New Olive Branch*, 133; Kidd, "To Be Harassed by My Creditors," 177.

29. Rebecca Gratz to Maria Gist, Nov. 17, 1821, Sept. 10, 1826, in Gratz, *Letters of Rebecca Gratz*, ed. David Phillipson (Philadelphia: Jewish Publication Society, 1929), 91–92, quoted in Kidd, "To Be Harassed by My Creditors," 177–78; Sandage, *Born Losers*, 27–30.

30. Matthew Carey Papers, Edmund Carey Gardiner Collection, Historical Society of Pennsylvania, quoted in Kidd, "To Be Harassed by My Creditors," 172; Rezeck, "Depression of 1819–1822," 32; "Report of the committee Appointed . . . on the Subject of the Distressed and Embarrassed State of the Commonwealth," in Hazard, *Register of Pennsylvania*, 4:136; *Niles' Register* 1 April 1820 (but note the date), 96; Carey, "New Olive Branch," in his *Essays on Political Economy*, 321.

31. *Niles' Register*, Oct. 9, 1819, 85; Jan. 30, 1819, 418; Jan. 9, 1819, 364; Hodgson, *Remarks During a Journey*, 44, 46 (Dec. 24, 1820).

32. Licht, *Getting Work*, 2; Flint, *Letters from America*, 274 (Aug. 15, 1820).

33. *Aurora*, Sept. 8, 1819, quoted in Matson, "Matthew Carey's Learning Experience," 478; Rezneck, "Depression of 1819–1822," 31; Hazard, *Register of Pennsylvania*, 4:168–69; *Niles' Register*, Oct. 23, 1819, 116; Aug. 21, 1819, 419; Oct. 16, 1819, 112; Sullivan, *Industrial Worker in Pennsylvania,* 79; and Sullivan, "Decade of Labor Strife," 124.

34. *Niles' Register*, Feb. 5, 1820, 390; Aug. 28, 1819, 440; Sept. 4, 1819, 16; Hodgson, *Remarks During a Journey*, Dec. 24, 1820, 43–44; Sullivan, *Industrial Worker in Pennsylvania*, 68, 72.

35. *Forges and Furnaces Collection*, 20, 27, 42, 52, 54.

36. *Cramer's Pittsburgh Almanack* (Pittsburgh: Cramer, Spear and Eichbaum, 1817), 36; Flint, *Letters from America*, 84–86; *Gazette*, Feb. 5, 1819, Jan. 11, 1820, quoted in Wade, *Urban Frontier*, 167; Hazard, *Register of Pennsylvania*, 4:168–69; Carey, New Olive Branch, 330; Pittsburgh *Statesman*, quoted in Wade, *Urban Frontier*, 168.

37. Carey, "Address to the Farmers," in his *Essays on Political Economy*, 419, 421.

38. McMaster, *Stephen Girard* 2:366, 368.

39. Maryland State Archives, "Brookeville 1814."

40. Entries of May 24 and 30, 1819, in Adams, *Diary*, 5:370, 384.

41. Hodgson, *Remarks During a Journey*, Dec. 13, 1820, 38; *Niles' Register*, Oct. 30, 1819, 129; July 31, 1819, 369; June 26, 1819, 291; Oct. 23, 1819, 115.

42. *American*, Oct. 1817; *Series of Letters and Other Documents*, 101.

43. *Niles' Register*, Sept. 16, 1820, 41; Smith, *Economic Aspects*, 124; *Federal Gazette* 20 Aug. 1822; Coil, "Baltimore Society for the Prevention of Pauperism," 77; "O.B.," in *Federal Gazette*, Oct. 31, 1822; Olson, *Baltimore*, 64.

44. *Niles' Register*, Sept. 16, 1820, 41; [Maryland] Governor and Council (Pardon Papers), Petition for William Fry, October 5, 1822, MSA s1061–22, MdHR5401–21, and Petition of James Brightwood, December 12, 1821, MSA s1061–21, MdHR 5401–21, quoted in Grivno, *Gleanings of Freedom*, 136; "Daybook of a Journey to North America," in Billingmeir and Picard, *The Old Land and the New*, 222, 227.

45. Flint, *Letters from America*, 264–65 (Aug. 15, 1820).

46. See Hinks, *To Awaken My Afflicted Brethren*, 27–28, 30–31, 63–64.

47. Jefferson to Adams, Nov. 7, 1819, in *Founders Online*. See Malone, *Jefferson and His Time*, 6:312.

48. Hodgson, *Remarks During a Journey*, 139.

49. North, *Economics Growth of the United States*, 191; Smith, *Economic Readjustment of an Old Cotton State*, 22. Nine of Massachusetts's representatives were reassigned to Maine with the latter's statehood in 1820, but the total for the pair increased by two.

50. Fischer and Kelly, *Bound Away*, 127.

51. McMaster, *Stephen Girard*, 2:356.

52. Kidd, "To Be Harassed by My Creditors," 173.

53. H. G. Jones, "Archibald De Bow Murphey," in *Dictionary of North Carolina Biography*, 4:346; Blanchard D. Robinson, "Thomas Ruffin," in ibid., 5:266–67; Kidd,

"To Be Harassed by My Creditors," 178–82; Murphey to Ruffin, Aug. 13, 1820, and Sept. 30, 1829, in Murphey, *Papers*, 1:173–74.

54. Jefferson, *Notes on the State of Virginia*, 197; Sloan, *Principle and Interest*, 218.

55. Richmond *Enquirer*, June 1, 1820.

56. Petersburg Personal Property Book, Virginia State Library 1809, 1817, quoted in Lebsock, *Free Women of Petersburg*, 177; ibid., 215.

57. Berry, " Rise of Flour Milling in Richmond," 401; Haulman, *Virginia and the Panic of 1819*, 150, 62, 94, 98–99, table 5.9; *Niles' Register*, Nov. 20, 1819, 185.

58. *Enquirer,* June 19, 1818; *Niles' Register*, May 8, 1819, 180; *Enquirer,* May 21, 1819, quoted in Haulman, *Virginia and the Panic of 1819*, 39.

59. Hodgson, *Remarks During a Journey*, 37–38 (Dec. 13, 1820).

60. Malone, *Jefferson and His Time*, 6:302–03; Jefferson to Gibson, July 30, 1818; Nicholas to Jefferson, Sept. 14, 1818; Gibson to Jefferson, Feb. 18, 1819; Jefferson to Gibson, April 22, 1819, in *Founders Online*.

61. Nicholas to Jefferson, May 10, 1819, in ibid.

62. Jefferson to Nicholas, May 14, 1819; and Nicholas to Jefferson, May 20, 1819, in ibid.

63. Nicholas to Jefferson, June 1, 1819, in ibid.

64. Jefferson to Richard Rush, June 33, 1819; Nicholas to Jefferson, June 28, 1819; and Jefferson to Nicholas, July 2, 1819, in ibid.

65. Nicholas to Jefferson, Aug. 5, 1819, in ibid.

66. Jefferson to Nicholas, Aug. 17, 1819, in ibid.

67. Malone, *Jefferson and His Time*, 6:314.

68. Ketcham, *James Madison*, 616; Brant, *James Madison*, 6:446.

69. Biddle to Madison, April 26, 1825, in *Founders Online*; Catterall, *Second Bank of the United States*, 111.

70. Madison to Biddle, May 2, 1825, in *Founders Online*.

Chapter Eight: Hard Times in the West

1. Smith, *Economic Aspects*, 40; Benton quoted in Turner, *Rise of the New West*, 107.

2. *Niles' Register*, June 26, 1819, 298; *ASP, Public Lands* 3:645.

3. Flint, *Letters from America*, 136, 306; *Niles' Register*, Nov. 13, 1819, 164.

4. Esary, "First Indiana Banks," 146; Baird, *History of Clark County, Indiana*, 72; Hand, "Cincinnati's Richest Man Died in Debtor's Prison." See Landy, *Cincinnati Past and Present*. Piatt, like Girard, had advanced funds to the federal government during the War of 1812; but unlike Girard, he was not reimbursed. Not until 1875, more than sixty years after the obligation was incurred, did the Supreme Court finally order the Treasury to pay his heirs the $65,000 he was due—without any interest.

5. Greer, "Economic and Social Effects," 227–28; Cayton, *Frontier Republic*, 113; Flint, *Letters from America*, 149–50.

6. Cayton, *Frontier Republic*, 114, 112; Flint, *Letters from America*, 118–19.

7. Cayton, *Frontier Republic*, 126; Wade, *Urban Frontier*, 171.

8. Cayton, *Frontier Republic*, 128; Hodgson, *Remarks During a Journey*, 32; Utter, *Frontier State*, 2:291–94.

9. Flint, *Letters from America*, 226, 238–39; Cayton, *Frontier Republic*, 127; Rezneck, "Depression of 1819–1822," 30; Sakolski, *Great American Land Bubble*, 178; Senate Document 96, 22nd Congr., 1st sess., February 2, 1832, 22–36; Catteral, *Second Bank of the United States*, 67; Smith, *Economic Aspects*, 136.

10. Howells, *Recollections of Life in Ohio*, 137–38.

11. Worth to Sloo in Torrence Collection, Hist. and Phil. Soc. Of Ohio, Wade, *Urban Frontier*, 174; Flint, *Letters from America*, 297 (Oct. 13, 1820).

12. Greene, "New Englander's Impression of Circumstances in 1820."

13. Hodgson, *Remarks During a Journey*, Dec. 13, 1820, 32; *Niles' Register*, Jan. 22, 1820, 340–41.

14. Dodge, *Autobiography*, 46.

15. *ASP: Finance*, 3:739, 735; Flint, *Letters from America*, 219, 225.

16. GLO Letters Received Reg. and Rec., Edwardsville 12: August 5, 1819, Misc., F: June 2, 1819, quoted in Rohrbaugh, *Land Office Business*, 139–40.

17. Hibbard, *History of Public Land Policies*, 100–103, 94; Flint, *Letters from America*, 257.

18. Douglas, *Autobiography*, 46–53.

19. Catteral, *Second Bank of the United States*, 67; Bogart, "Financial History of Ohio," 322; Clay to Cheves, May 5, 1821, quoted in Clay, *Papers*, 3:76; Peterson, *Great Triumvirate*, 67.

20. Utter, *Frontier State*, 2:261–62; Greer, "Economic and Social Effects," 233–34.

21. McMurtrie, *Sketches of Louisiana*, 116; Flint, *Letters from America*, 285 (Sept. 8, 1820).

22. Ibid., 130–31 (Nov. 27, 1818); 135 (Dec. 30, 1818).

23. *Niles' Register*, June 15, 1815, quoted in Wade, *Urban Frontier*, 162; City of Lexington Trustee's Book, June 6, 1816; Kentucky *Gazette*, March 12, 1830, cited in Wade, *Urban Frontier*, 170.

24. Hopkins, *History of the Hemp Industry*, 126; Stanwood, *American Tariff Controversies*, 1:194. See Peterson, *Great Triumvirate*, 66; Wade, *Urban Frontier*, 169–70; Kerr, *History of Kentucky*, 2:600.

25. *Gazette*, reprinted in *Niles' Register*, Oct. 9, 1819, 84; *Centinel*, June 12, 1820, quoted in Rezneck, "Depression of 1819–1822," 31.

26. Peterson, *Great Triumvirate*, 66; Adams, *Memoirs*, 5:305. See Gronert, "Trade in the Blue Grass Region," 321–22; Clay to Jesse Burton Harris, in Clay, *Papers*, 8:399; Remini, *Henry Clay*, 194, 185.

27. Clay to Cheves, July 21, 1821, in Clay, *Papers*, 3:102; Clay to Cheves, Jan. 18, 1821, in Clay, *Papers*, Supplement 83. See Remini, *Henry Clay*, 208.

28. *ASP: Finance*, 4:908; *Niles' Register*, Jan. 16, 1819, 385.

29. Smith, *Economic Aspects*, 127; *Niles' Register*, Sept. 4, 1819, 10.

30. *National Intelligencer*, June 9 and 26, 1819; *Niles' Register*, July 3, 1819, 311; Reuben T. Durrett, *The Centenary of Louisville* (Louisville: J.P. Morton, 1893), 127, cited in Rothbard, *Panic of 1819*, 145.

31. *Niles' Register*, Jan. 15, 1820, 335.

32. Remini, *Andrew Jackson and the Course of American Freedom*, 42, 43.

33. Murfreesboro *Courier*, August 18, 1820, quoted in Dupre, *Transforming the Cotton Frontier*, 66–67; Nashville *Whig*, May 24 and June 14, 1820; Philip Hamer, *Tennessee: A History 1673–1932* (New York: American Historical Association, 1933), 232 ff., cited in Rothbard, *Panic of 1819*, 122–23; *Niles' Register*, Oct. 9, 1819, 84.

34. Dupre, *Transforming the Cotton Frontier*,49–50; Taylor to Boardman, June 25, 1819, Boardman Correspondence 1818–31, Alabama Dept. of Archives and History, quoted in ibid., 50.

35. Williams to Newby, Jan. 2, 1820, Newby Papers, University of North Carolina Library, quoted in Dupre, *Transforming the Cotton Frontier*, 60–61.

36. See Webb and Armbrester, *Alabama Governors*, 21-22, and Bailey, *John Williams Walker*.

37. Letter from "a Virginia merchant" to Clement C. Clay, March 30, 1825, Clement C. Clay Papers, Huntsville (Alabama) Public Library, quoted in Dupre, *Transforming the Cotton Frontier*, 51n3; Percy to Walker, March 15 and Feb. 8, 1820, and Walker to Newby, Jan. 2 and 8 Feb. 8, 1820, Walker Papers, Alabama Department of Archives and History, quoted in Dupre, *Transforming the Cotton Frontier*, 53, 54, 61–62.

38. Dupre, *Transforming the Cotton Frontier*, 56; William Harris to Frederick Harris, Nov. 15, 1820, April 25, 1821, quoted in ibid., 58, 60.

39. *Alabama Republican*, Jan. 29, 1820; Thomas Percy to John Williams Walker, Jan. 27 and Feb. 8, 1820, quoted in Dupre, *Transforming the Cotton Frontier*, 57; Gray, "From a Kingdom in Wales to a Cotton Farm in Alabama."

40. Wallace, "Journey in Time"; Percy to Walker, Feb. 8, 1820, and James Walker to John Williams Walker, Feb. 1820, quoted in Dupre, *Transforming the Cotton Frontier*, 53; *ASP: Public Lands*, 5:384, 385.

41. Abernethy, *Formative Period in Alabama*, 113–14.

42. Huntsville *Democrat*, Oct. 14, 1823, March 30, 1824; Abernethy, *Formative Period in Alabama*, 117, 118–19.

43. Alabama *Republican*, Dec. 1, 1820, quoted in Bailey, "John W. Walker and the Land Laws," 123; *ASP: Public Lands*, 5:645.

44. Dupre, *Transforming the Cotton Frontier*, 55.

45. David, "'In Pursuit of Their Livelihood,'" 227; Adams Co. Court Register, Historic Natchez Foundation, cited in David, "'In Pursuit of Their Livelihood,'" 224, 225. See also Kilbourne, *Debt, Investment, and Slaves*, 16–23; and Woodman, *King Cotton and His Retainers*.

46. David, "'In Pursuit of their Livelihood,'" 236–37.

47. Trask-Ventress Family Papers, Mississippi Department of Archives and History, quoted in David, "'In Pursuit of their Livelihood,'" 229–30.

48. Thomas Butler Papers, LSU Library, quoted in Brazy, *American Planter*, 20; Adams County Deed Records, Natchez, cited in Brazy, 21.

49. Brazy, *American Planter*, 1–25; David, "'In Pursuit of their Livelihood,'" 229.

50. See Caldwell, *Banking History of Louisiana*, 20–62; and Greene, *Finance and Economic Development in the Old South*, 18–21.

51. Greene, *Finance and Economic Development in the Old South*, 19–20, 213; Assembly of Louisiana, 6th Legislature, 2nd session, 92–130, quoted in ibid., 21.

52. Louisiana Senate, 4th Legislature, 2nd session, 13, quoted in ibid., 20; Cooper and Terill, *American South*, 145.

53. Dupre, *Transforming the Cotton Frontier*, 51; Chinn to Hamilton, Feb. 1822, W. S. Hamilton Papers, Wilson Library, UNC Chapel Hill.

54. Primm, *Lion of the Valley*, 119.

55. Noyes, *Family History in Letters and Documents*, 1:343–44; Rammelkamp, "Thomas Lippincott," 253–54.

56. Primm, *Lion of the Valley*, 106; Gracy, "Austin, Moses"; Carey, *New Olive Branch*, 127.

57. Peck, *Forty Years of Pioneer Life*, 84–85; Noyes, *Family History in Letters and Documents*, 343; Flint, *Recollections*, 202.

58. Peck, *Forty Years of Pioneer Life*, 84–85; Primm, *Lion of the Valley*, 104–5.

59. Primm, Lion of the Valley, 98, 108, 109, 89; Franklin (MO) *Intelligencer*, July 2, 1819, and *Missouri Gazette* Oct. 27, 1819, quoted in Anderson, "Frontier Economic Problems in Missouri," 52; Dorsey, "Panic of 1819 in Missouri," 80.

60. Primm, *Lion of the Valley*, 99; *Missouri Gazette*, Oct. 20 and Nov. 3, 1819, quoted in Dorsey, "Panic of 1819 in Missouri," 81; Scott, letter to the Missouri *Intelligencer*, July 16, 1819, Cunningham, *Circular Letters*, 3:1093–94.

61. Primm, *Lion of the Valley*, 108; Flint, *Recollections*, 106; Flint, *Letters from America*, 129 (Nov. 27, 1818).

62. Dorsey, "Panic of 1819 in Missouri," 81; Anderson, "Frontier Economic Problems in Missouri," 41; Flint, *Recollections*, 200–202, 198–99, 203–4, 199.

63. Spanish Land Grant Register; Flint, *Recollections*, 199; *ASP: Public Lands*, 4:155.

64. Austin and Austin, *Austin Papers* 1:337, quoted in Sakolski, *Great American Land Bubble*, 207–8; Anderson, "Frontier Economic Problems in Missouri," 50, 51; Houck, *History of Missouri*, 3:184.

65. Rohrbough, *Land Office Business*, 135; *Gazette*, March 10 and Jan. 27, 1819; Anderson, "Frontier Economic Problems in Missouri," 49.

66. Flint, *Recollections*, 212.

67. *Gazette*, June 9 and Feb. 3, 1819; *Intelligencer*, April 23 and July 16, 1819, quoted in Anderson, "Frontier Economic Problems in Missouri," 48n, 51.

68. Senate Public Document 246, 24th Congress, 3rd session, 5, 8, cited in Rohrbough, *Land Office Business*, 134–35; *Missourian,* July 29 and Aug. 12, 1820, quoted in Anderson, "Frontier Economic Problems in Missouri," 54; *Enquirer*, March 31, 1821; *Gazette,* June 6, 1821; *Republican,* July 25, 1821, quoted in Wade, *Urban Frontier*, 172–73.

69. Flint, *Recollections*, 200–201.

70. Hamilton, "Relief Movement in Missouri," 58; *Gazette*, April 21, 1821; Primm, *Lion of the Valley*, 119, 89.

71. *Enquirer*, Sept. 11, 1819, quoted in Anderson, "Frontier Economic Problems in Missouri," 61; *Gazette*, March 22, 1820, quoted in ibid., 57.

72. *Intelligencer*, April 22, 1820, quoted in Anderson, "Frontier Economic Problems in Missouri," 58; *Gazette*, quoted in Dorsey, "Panic of 1819 in Missouri," 82.

73. Sept. 19, 1821, in Anderson, "Frontier Economic Problems in Missouri," 62.

74. Anderson, "Frontier Economic Problems in Missouri," 69; Remini, *Jackson and the Course of American Freedom*, chap. 2 passim; Bremer, "Frontier Capitalism," 90.

75. The final list includes counties named for all of the first seven presidents except the two Adamses, as well as Clay, Crawford, Benton, Richard M. Johnson, the Old Republican congressmen John Randolph and Nathaniel Macon, and the relief party leaders Felix Grundy and William Barry; Calhoun is missing from Missouri place-names, and Van Buren is the namesake of a town, population 828. Presidents Harrison and Lincoln would eventually have counties named after them, too, and Jackson actually had two counties named in his honor: the second is Hickory County, whose county seat is called Hermitage, after his plantation home.

76. Flint, *Recollections*, 213.

Chapter Nine: Relief?

1. Entry of May 27, 1819, in Adams, *Memoirs*, 4:375; Jefferson to John Adams, Nov. 7, 1819, in *Founders Online*; *Evening Post*, June 15, 1819, quoted in Rothbard, *Panic of 1819*, 31; *Extracts from the Minutes*, 171–72. Exhaustive efforts have failed to find "The government that governs least, governs best" in anything Jefferson said or wrote, but the sentiment is certainly consistent with ideas he often expressed.

2. *ASP: Public Lands*, 1:286–87, 910; *ASP: Finance*, 2:413–14; Rohrbough, *Land Office Business*, 140; Tiffin to Meigs, GLO Letters Received Surveyor General, NW 5: October 31, 1819. See Utter, *Frontier State*, 290.

3. Smith and Cole, *Economic Fluctuations*, 185.

4. Jan. 17, 1828, in *ASP: Public Lands*, 5:377; *Annals of Congress*, Senate, 16th Congr., 1st sess., 445–46.

5. Treat, *National Land System 1785–1820*, 147; Bailey, "John W. Walker and the Land Laws," 123–24, 151–67; *Annals of Congress*, Senate, 16th Congr., 1st sess., 446.

6. *ASP: Public Lands*, 3:645; Bailey, "John W. Walker and the Land Laws," 120; Monroe, "Fourth Annual Message," November 14, 1820, in *American Presidency Project*, http://www.presidency.ucsb.edu/ws/index.php?pid=29462 (accessed May 11, 2017); *Annals of Congress*, Senate, 16th Congr., 1st sess., 17, 22; *Niles' Register*, Jan. 31, 1819, 423; Nov. 25, 1820, 194.

7. Hitchcock to Walker, Jan. 2, 1820, Walker Papers, quoted in Bailey, "John W. Walker and the Land Laws," 123; *ASP: Finance*, 4:597; *Annals of Congress*, Senate, 16th Congr., 2nd sess., 222–36.

8. *Annals of Congress*, Senate, 16th Congr., 2nd sess., 222–36.

9. Ibid., 441; *ASP: Public Lands*, 3:612–16.

10. Rohrbough, *Land Office Business*, 143–44, 145–46.

11. GLO Letters Received, Reg. and Rec., Cahaba 1: Sept. 18, 1821; Rohrbough, *Land Office Business*, 156; *ASP: Public Lands*, 3:645; Dupre, *Transforming the Cotton Frontier*, 55; Abernethy, *Formative Period in Alabama*, 55, 69.

12. Rothbard, *Panic of 1819*, 152; *Annals of Congress*, Senate, 15th Congr., 2nd sess., 1426. See Mooney, *William H. Crawford*, 142–46.

13. *Annals of Congress*, House, 16th Congr., 1st sess., 711. Rothbard (*Panic of 1819*, 161) confuses Charles Pinckney III with his cousin, Charles Cotesworth Pinckney.

14. *ASP: Finance*, 3:494–508.

15. April 10, 1820, in *Circular Letters*, 3:1107–8; Rothbard, *Panic of 1819*, 109–10; entry of June 24, 1819, in Adams, *Memoirs*, 4:395.

16. Simpson writing as "Brutus," *Aurora*, June 24, 1819, quoted in Wilentz, *Rise of American Democracy*, 211.

17. See Hofstadter, *American Political Tradition*, 67; and Remini, *Andrew Jackson and the Course of American Freedom*, 44.

18. Jackson to Donelson, Sept. 3, 1821, Jackson, *Correspondence*, 3:117.

19. Wilentz, *Rise of American Democracy*; Knox, *History of Banking*, 716; Illinois House *Journal* 1820–1821, 236, cited in Rothbard, *Panic of 1819*, 112–15.

20. Hammond, *Banks and Politics*, 282; B. B. Still to John C. Breckinridge, Aug. 16, 1822, cited in Rothbard, *Panic of 1819*, 143.

21. Clay, *Papers*, 3:237.

22. *Niles' Register*, Aug. 10, 1819; *Herald*, March 20, 1821. See Rothbard, *Panic of 1819*, 58–59.

23. See, e.g., Wilentz, *Rise of American Democracy*, 209; and Rothbard, *Panic of 1819*, 80.

24. *Gazette*, July 18, 1821; Missouri General Assembly, *Laws*, 1st General Assembly, Special Session, 1821, 32–34, 2nd Session, 1821, 46–52, 74, cited in Rothbard, *Panic of 1819*, 65–67.

25. Dorsey, "Panic of 1819 in Missouri," 88–90.

26. Jackson to A. J. Donelson, July 5, 1822, Donelson Papers, Library of Congress, quoted in Remini, *Andrew Jackson and the Course of American Freedom*, 27-28.

27. Remini, *Andrew Jackson and the Course of American Freedom*, 38, 39, 44; Sellers, "Jackson Men with Feet of Clay."

28. Indiana General Assembly, *Laws*, 3rd General Assembly, 68, and *Journal of the Senate* 1818–19, 36, Illinois General Assembly, *House Journal* 1820–21, 157, cited in Rothbard, *Panic of 1819*, 59–61.

29. Journal of the House of Delegates 1819–20, 6–9; 1820–21, 126, 140; Richmond *Enquirer*, Feb. 1, 1820; North Carolina Records Survey Project, *Calendar of the Bartlett Yancy Papers*, 4.

30. Matthew Andrews, *Tercentenary History of Maryland* (Baltimore: S.J. Clarke, 1925), 1741, cited in Rothbard, *Panic of 1819*, 50.

31. Rezneck, "Depression of 1819–1822," 44; Peter J. Coleman, "*Sturges v. Crowninshield*," in Hall, *Oxford Companion to the Supreme Court*, 847; Pell, *Review of the Administration*, 78. See *Niles' Register*, Jan. 18, 1823.

32. Pennsylvania General Assembly, *Journal of the Thirtieth House of Representatives* (1819–20), 76–88, *Journal of the Senate* (1819–20), 221–36; Kehl, *Ill Feeling in the Era of Good Feeling*, 12–13; Wilentz, *Rise of American Democracy*, 212–13.

33. Howard K. Stokes, "Public and Private Finances," 3:264–71, 291; Crockett, *Vermont*, 3:181.

34. *Niles' Register*, March 11, 1820, 40.

35. Pell, *Review of the Administration*, 52; Comptroller of the City of New York, *Annual Statement*, 31; Clinton, *Message from the Governor* (1818), 2:914–15, cited in Bonelli, *Response of Public and Private Philanthropy*, 90.

36. Wilson, *Centennial History of the Episcopal Church,* 372, 375–76; Foster, "Urban Missionary Movement," 50; Rev. John Stanford, *Annual Reports of the Society for the Prevention of Pauperism* 1815–1820, Stanford Papers, New-York Historical Society, cited in Bonelli, *Response of Public and Private Philanthropy*, 14; Wilentz, *Chants Democratic*, 26; New York Assembly *Journal*, 42nd Session (1819), 91, 245.

37. New York *Advertiser*, June 28, 1819, quoted in Bonelli, *Response of Public and Private Philanthropy*, 14.

38. New York Common Council, *Minutes*, 10:663–64, 76, 11:134, 460–61, quoted in Bonelli, *Response of Public and Private Philanthropy*, 82–83; Pessen, *Riches, Class and Power*, 264.

39. Rezneck, "Depression of 1819–1822," 31–32; Haulman, *Virginia and the Panic of 1819*, 122, 109, 123.

40. Bellows, *Benevolence Among Slaveholders*, 199; Hinks, *To Awaken My Afflicted Brethren*, 23–24.

41. Society for the Prevention of Pauperism, *Second Annual Report, 1819*, 16, 60.

42. *Niles' Register*, June 5, 1819, 255; Aug. 21, 1819, 429.

43. Flint, *Letters from America*, e.g., letter XVII of May 4, 1820, 224–36; Howitt, *Selections from Letters*, 215, 230.

44. *Things As They Are*, 15; "James Buchanan," in *Dictionary of Ulster Biography*; Bonelli, 85.

45. Quincy, *Massachusetts General Court*, 8; Shaw, *Welfare Debate*, 22–23.

46. Rothman, *Discovering the Asylum*, 155–56; Handler and Hasenfeld, *We the Poor People, 22*; Quincy, *Massachusetts General Court,* 10; Trattner, *From Poor Law to Welfare State*, 58.

47. Shaw, *Welfare Debate*, 24; Haulman, *Virginia and the Panic of 1819*, 122–24; Report of the Overseer of the Poor 1829, Auditor's Item 227, Virginia State Library, and Petersburg Common Council Minutes 1784–1860, Office of the Clerk of the City Council, Petersburg, VA (Sept. 16, 1824), cited in Lebsock, *Free Women of Petersburg*, 213.

48. Haulman, *Virginia and the Panic of 1819*, 104; Lebsock, *Free Women of Petersburg*, 214.

49. Clement, *Welfare and the Poor*, 49; Hannon, "Generosity of Antebellum Poor Relief," 812; Hannon, "Poor Relief Policy," 238–39; Creech, *Three Centuries of Poor Law Administration*, 185–86.

50. New York *American*, Oct. 2, 1819; Trattner, *From Poor Law to Welfare State* 15–46.

51. New York *Patron of Industry*, Jan. 21, 1821, New York *American*, Jan. 21, 1821; Walsh, *Sisters of Charity*, 1:49–50; Howe, *What Hath God Wrought?*, 192; Walters, "Origins of the Second Bank of the United States," 180; Lebsock, *Free Women of Petersburg*, 214–15; Wilentz, *Rise of American Democracy*, 283, 285; *Mechanic's Free Press*, Oct. 16, 1828, quoted in ibid., 285.

52. Cole, "Thomas Worthington," 366; New York *State Assembly Journal* 41st sess., 14, 42nd sess., 607; Deale, "Unhappy History of Economic Rights," 288; Bonelli, *Response of Public and Private Philanthropy*, 50, 140; Carey, "Essay on the Public Character of Philadelphia," quoted in Rothman, *Jacksonians on the Poor*, 171. Deale's *Howard Law Review* article ("The Unhappy History of Economic Rights") offers a thorough survey of American attitudes toward poverty over the past three hundred years.

53. Kidd, "Search for Moral Order," 165; Adams to Jefferson, Dec. 21, 1819, in *Founders Online*; Walters, *American Reformers, 1815-1860*, 176-77; Hoover, *Memoirs*, 3:30. Mellon, a banker by profession, was undoubtedly using the term in the financial sense of converting assets to currency, rather than as the euphemism—only recently coined in the Soviet Union—for mass murder. I cannot speak for the motives of the screenwriters, Florence Ryerson, Noel Langley, and Edgar Woolf, but their 1939 screenplay has obviously reset the story from the late nineteenth century to the contemporary 1930s, and the film's audience would have been much more familiar with Mellon than with Lenin.

54. Haulman, *Virginia and the Panic of 1819*, 122; Kidd, "Search for Moral Order," 162; Society for the Prevention of Pauperism, *Second Annual Report, 1819*, 4.

55. Burroughs, *A Discourse Delivered in the Chapel of the New Alms-House, in Portsmouth, N.H . . .* (Portsmouth, NH: J. W. Foster, 1835), 9; Cross, *Burned-Over District*, 9–11; Bartkowski and Regis, *Charitable Choices*, 36.

56. Lebsock, *Free Women of Petersburg*, 217.

57. Howe, *What Hath God Wrought?*, 230, 193; Holt, *Rise and Fall of the American Whig Party*, 118, 68–69. See Banner, "Religious Benevolence as Social Control"; and Wiener, "Humanitarianism as Control."

58. Keyssar, *Right to Vote*, 61–62.

59. Blackstone, *Commentary on the Laws of England*, 1:165; Keyssar, *Right to Vote*, 10–11 (emphasis added).

60. Keyssar, *Right to Vote*, 343–45.

61. Rezneck, "Social History of an American Depression," 682.

62. Katz, 19; Hopkins, *Spending to Save*, 100.

63. Kennedy, *American People in the Great Depression*, pt. 1, *Freedom from Fear,* 174.

Chapter Ten: The Politics of Corruption and the Corruption of Politics

1. Thomas Jefferson to William Barry, July 2, 1822, in *Founders Online*.

2. Quoted in Parsons, *Birth of Modern Politics*, 92–93; Remini, *Andrew Jackson and the Course of American Freedom*, 397.

3. See Ellis, "Market Revolution" 158.

4. Wilentz, *Rise of American Democracy*, 182, 209.

5. Holt, *Rise and Fall of the American Whig Party*, 31; Jefferson to Barry, July 2, 1822, in *Founders Online*.

6. See Wilentz, *Rise of American Democracy*, 200–201.

7. Keyssar, *Right to Vote*, 32; Wilentz, *Rise of American Democracy*, 183–86.

8. Wolcott, *Remarks*, 4. See Wilentz, *Chants Democratic*, 34, 117–34, 132; Wilentz, *Rise of American Democracy*, 209, 252, 282, 293.

9. Welch, "Josiah Quincy and His School for 'Gentlemen'"; Morison, *Three Centuries of Harvard*, 251.

10. Welch, "Josiah Quincy and His School for 'Gentlemen'"; *Journal of the Debates and Proceedings in the Convention of Delegates* (Boston, 1853), 251–52, quoted in Keyssar, *Right to Vote*, 46–47.

11. *Journal of the Debates*, 247; Wilentz, *Rise of American Democracy*, 187–89; Peterson, *Great Triumvirate*, 104–05.

12. Wilentz, *Rise of American Democracy*, 190–96; Keyssar, *Right to Vote*, 46, 48.

13. Keyssar, *Right to Vote*, 328–38, 45; Wilentz, *Rise of American Democracy*, 201.

14. Montgomery, *Citizen Worker*, 22, 24–50; Keyssar, *Right to Vote*, 47, 45, 69.

15. Cayton, "Fragmentation of a 'Great Family,'" 147.

16. *Patriot*, Jan. 15, 1819; *Columbian Centinel*, Jan. 15, 1819, March 13, 1820; *Patriot*, March 11, 1820, Feb. 20, 1819, March 29, 1820, quoted in in Cayton, "Fragmentation of a 'Great Family,'" 146, 144, 150.

17. Boston Town Records, Sept. 25, 1821, 227–30, cited in Cayton, "Fragmentation of a 'Great Family,'" 154.

18. Welch, "Josiah Quincy and His School for 'Gentlemen'"; Cayton, "Fragmentation of a 'Great Family,'" 150, 165.

19. Cayton, *Frontier Republic*, 129, 133, 134–35; Wilentz, *Rise of American Democracy*, 843 n76. See Gover, *Nicholas Biddle*, 52–70.

20. Holt, *Rise and Fall of the American Whig Party*, 68.

21. Parsons, *Birth of Modern Politics*, 48; Wiley Harris to John F. Claiborne, Aug. 30, 1850, Claiborne Manuscripts, Mississippi Department of Archives and History, quoted in Holt, *Rise and Fall of the American Whig Party*, 119.

22. Gallatin to Adams, Dec. 9, 1819, Gallatin Papers, quoted in Skeen, *1816: America Rising*, 212.

23. King to Jeremiah Mason, Jan. 3, 1818, in Mason, *Memoirs and Correspondence*, 179–80; entry of May 22, 1820, in Adams, *Memoirs*, 5:128–29.

24. *Register of Debates*, 19th Congr., 2nd sess., 3:404. See Remini, *Henry Clay*, 293–95.

25. Ketcham, *James Madison*, 630–31.

26. *Niles' Register*, Nov. 21, 1818, 215; *ASP: Finance*, 3:273–75; Adams, *Memoirs*, 5:128. See Niven, *John C. Calhoun*, 87.

27. Entries of Jan. 8, 1820, and May 28, 1819, in Adams, *Memoirs*, 4:497, 4:375.

28. *Register of Officers and Agents, Civil, Military, and Naval, in the Service of the United States, on the Thirtieth Day of September, 1817* (Washington, DC: Department of State, 1818),9–39.

29. William Plumer Jr. to William Plumer Sr., quoted in Brown, *Missouri Compromise*, 64; Peterson, *Great Triumvirate*, 64; Jackson to Calhoun, July 28, 1822, in Jackson, *Correspondence* 3:164. See Remini, *Andrew Jackson and the Course of American Freedom*, 19.

30. Peterson, *Great Triumvirate*, 93–94; Nevins, *History of the Bank of New York*, 90–92.

31. Remini, *Andrew Jackson and the Course of American Empire*, 15.

32. Ibid., 17.

33. *Report of the Committee . . . on a Letter of John C. Calhoun.*

34. Ibid., 245.

35. Calhoun, *Papers*, 3:61.

36. Nevins, *History of the Bank of New York*, 77; Chittenden, *History of the American Fur Trade*, 1:506.

37. Nevins, *History of the Bank of New York*, 78–79; Calhoun, *Papers*, 3:702–9, 4:38, 74–75, 255.

38. Adams, *Memoirs*, 4:472–73.

39. Letter to John M. O'Conner July 7, 1822, in Van Buren Papers, *National Intelligencer*, May 24 and Aug. 21, 1822, New York *Statesman*, Aug. 6, 1822, all quoted in Remini, *Andrew Jackson and the Course of American Freedom*, 20, 13.

40. *Annals of Congress*, House, 18th Congr., 1st sess., 1962–2001; Clay to Cheves, Feb. 10, 1821, Oct. 22, 1821, in Clay, *Papers*, 3:24–26, 129.

41. Blair to Clay, Oct. 30, 1827, in Clay, *Papers*, 6:1107; Saunders to Yancey, Feb. 1, 1823, Lenoir to Wm B. Lenoir, Feb. 16, 1824, Mangum to Duncan Cameron, Dec. 10, 1823, all quoted in Heidler and Heidler, *Henry Clay*, 170; Remini, *Andrew Jackson and the Course of American Freedom*, 398n23.

42. Remini, *Andrew Jackson and the Course of American Freedom*, 16, 398.

43. Memorandoms [1822], Jackson Papers, Library of Congress, quoted in Remini, *Andrew Jackson and the Course of American Freedom*, 14–15.

44. Dowrie, *Development of Banking in Illinois*, 15; Cutler, "A.B. Controversy," 35.

45. Cutler, "A.B. Controversy," 35–40. See also Cutler, "William H. Crawford."

46. *National Intelligencer*, March 13, 1823; Resch, *Suffering Soldiers*, 151–52.

47. Cutler, "A.B. Controversy," 32; Crawford to Coles, June 14, 1823, Coles Papers, Princeton University Library, cited in Remini, *Andrew Jackson and the Course of American Freedom*, 23.

48. Heidler and Heidler, *Henry Clay*, 163; Smith, *First Forty Years of Washington Society*, 162.

49. *Niles' Register*, Jan. 26, 1822, 333; Mooney, *William H. Crawford*, 258. Gallatin was Swiss by birth but had been living in the United States before the Constitution's adoption and was thus eligible.

50. Jackson, Missouri *Independent Patriot,* Dec. 20, 1823, quoted in Hay, "Case for Andrew Jackson," 139; Smith, *First Forty Years of Washington Society,* 163.

51. Cutler, "A.B. Controversy," 35.

52. Remini, *Andrew Jackson and the Course of American Freedom,* 24; *ASP: FR* Finance?? 5:799; Calhoun, *Papers,* 10:10, 10:27, in Niven, *John C. Calhoun,* 109, 112.

53. *Mercury,* Aug. 20, 1818, reprinted in *Niles' Register,* Oct. 24, 1818, 131; Feb. 16, 1819, *Annals of Congress,* House, 15th Congr., 2nd sess., 1205.

54. Hofstadter, *American Political Tradition,* 67; Adams, *Memoirs,* 5:128–29.

55. Phillips, "Pennsylvania Origins of the Jackson Movement," 502; Ratcliffe, "Crisis of Commercialization," 182. See Ratcliffe, "Role of Voters and Issues in Party Formation"; Stevens, *Early Jackson Party in Ohio,* 3–28, 43–47; Sharp, *Jacksonians Versus the Banks,* 177–78.

56. Calhoun, quoted in Hay, "Case for Andrew Jackson in 1824," 142, 149.

57. *Niles' Register,* Sept. 2, 1815, 238; Evans, *Pedestrious Tour of Four Thousand Miles,* 346; Pennsylvania Senate Report, Jan. 29, 1820, in Hazard, *Register of Pennsylvania,* 4:138; J. D. Steele MS Journal, Huntington Library, quoted in Remini, *Andrew Jackson and the Course of American Freedom,* 16.

58. *Niles' Register,* Feb. 28, 1818, 14; Jan. 22, 1820, 352; *ASP: Finance,* 4:8219; *Letter from the Treasury Department* (1822), 379; Memorandum of May 1819, Cheves Papers, South Carolina Historical Society, quoted in Smith, *Economic Aspects,* 121.

59. Hodgson, letter of July 5, 1819, quoted in Dangerfield, *Era of Good Feelings.*

60. Adams, *Memoirs,* 4:383; Catteral, *Second Bank of the United States,* 39; Bogen, "Scandal of Smith and Buchanan," 128.

61. Catterall, *Second Bank of the United States,* 45–50; *Exhibit of the Losses,* 33–37; Hammond, *Banks and Politics,* 261–62.

62. Bogen, "Scandal of Smith and Buchanan," 129–30.

63. Catterall, *Second Bank of the United States,* 40–41.

64. *Niles' Register,* Nov. 12, 1818, 282; Bogen, "Scandal of Smith and Buchanan," 130–31.

65. Ibid.; entry of May 30, 1819, in Adams, *Memoirs,* 4:383.

66. Entry of May 30, 1819, in Adams, *Memoirs,* 4:383.

67. *Niles' Register,* June 15, 1819, 241–42.

68. McHenry Papers, Maryland State Historical Society, quoted in Bogen, "Scandal of Smith and Buchanan," 132.

69. Hilt, "Wall Street's First Corporate Governance Crisis," 1.

70. Robert Harper, *A Report of the Conspiracy Cases . . .* (Baltimore, 1823), 243, quoted in Bogen, "Scandal of Smith and Buchanan," 131.

71. *Niles' Register,* DATE?; Hilt, "Wall Street's First Corporate Governance Crisis," 14–15, 39.

72. Van Buren, *Autobiography,* 2:625; *Circular Letters,* 3:1138.

Chapter Eleven: A House Dividing

1. *ASP: Public Lands,* 2:256, Dec. 5, 1811; *Circular Letters* 3:1075, March 4, 1819.

2. Louisiana voters had gone for Jackson in 1828 and would again in 1832, but gerrymandered local politics was dominated by New Orleans sugar interests who favored a protective tariff and supported the incipient Whig Party—and the Bank; the Louisiana senators who opposed Jackson's Bank War (Waggaman and Johnson) were transplants from Maryland and Connecticut, respectively, but both died good southern deaths, one in a duel and one in a steamboat explosion.

3. In 1832 White, by then one of Tennessee's senators, would vote against the recharter.

4. Sylla, "How the American Corporation Evolved," 357; Fenstermaker, *Development of Commercial Banking*, 16–20; Ellis, *Aggressive Nationalism*, 5.

5. Bogen, "Scandal of Smith and Buchanan," 129.

6. *Niles' Register*, Feb. 28, 1818; Catteral, *Second Bank of the United States*, 65; *Annals of Congress*, Senate, 16th Congr., 1st sess., 70.

7. *Journal of the House of Representatives, Ohio, 18th General Assembly*, 307–15.

8. *Niles' Register*, Oct. 24, 1818, 129–30. From the hints Niles offered, there were four possible candidates for authorship, but one was almost surely John Taylor, about to become speaker of the House. The other possibilities were William Irving, George Townsend, and Peter Wendover.

9. Ibid., Nov. 7, 1818, 163–64.

10. Ibid., Jan. 2, 1819, 347; Clay, *Papers*, 2:622–23.

11. *Circular Letters*, 3:1046; Trimble, *Autobiography and Correspondence*, 118; Pell, *Review of the Administration*, 82.

12. Adams, *Memoirs*, 5:38–39; *Niles' Register*, June 16, 1819, 257–58; *Circular Letters*, 3:1046.

13. Marshall, quoted in Baker, *John Marshall*, 590. On Marshall's ownership of slaves, see Finkelman, *Supreme Injustice*, esp. chap. 2, "John Marshall, Slave Owner and Jurist."

14. The notorious euphemism seems to date from 1837 and Calhoun's February 6 speech in the Senate on the reception of abolition petitions; the phrase is included in the "Revised Report" of the speech in Calhoun, *Speeches*, 222. It is worth noting that by "peculiar" Calhoun did not mean "odd" or "unusual" but simply particular to the South.

15. Marshall, *Life of George Washington*, 5:296; *McCulloch v. Maryland*, 17 U.S. (4 Wheat.) 316,372 (1819). Story's anecdote was repeated by Alexander Stephens, quoted in Reynolds, "Luther Martin, Maryland, and the Constitution," 318–19. Remarkably, Story did not recuse himself in the *McCulloch* case, although he was a director of the BUS and the president of the Merchant's Bank of Salem.

16. Reynolds, "Luther Martin, Maryland, and the Constitution," 318.

17. Story to Sarah Story, March 7, 1819, in Story, *Life and Letters*, 1:325; *Niles' Register*, March 20, 1819, 57; Reynolds, "Luther Martin, Maryland, and the Constitution," 318.

18. Baker, *John Marshall*, 606; *Enquirer*, March 30, 1819; Henry, June 4, 1788, quoted in Elliot, *Debates in the Several States*, 3:22. See Gunther, *John Marshall's Defense*, 52–77.

19. Ibid., 134, 112. See Miller, "John Marshall in Spencer Roane's Virginia." Roane was Patrick Henry's son-in-law and Thomas Ritchie's father-in-law.

20. Madison to Roane, Sept. 2, 1819, in *Founders Online*.

21. Smith, *John Marshall*, 147–48.

22. Taylor, *Construction Construed*, 84, 298.

23. Newmyer, *John Marshall and the Heroic Age*, 332–35; Marshall to Bushrod Washington, March 27, 1819, in Marshall, *Papers*, 281; *Niles' Register*, Oct. 9, 1819, 84; Heidler and Heidler, *Henry Clay*, 145.

24. Gov. George Troup, quoted in Latner, *Presidency of Andrew Jackson*, 13; Borkoski, "What Does Necessary Mean?"; Newmyer, *John Marshall and the Heroic Age*, 334.

25. Hall, *Dividing the Union*, 125.

26. *Annals of Congress*, House, 15th Congr., 2nd sess., 308, 1203. See Van Atta, *Wolf by the Ears*, 45–47.

27. Freehling, *Road to Disunion*, 1:144.

28. *Annals of Congress*, House, 15th Congr., 2nd sess., 1204, 1436–38.

29. Remini, *The House*, 107. Otis, as a representative in 1800, had denounced a petition from black Philadelphians opposing the fugitive slave law and asking for gradual abolition as "mischievous"; its subjects were "properly and only objects of legislation in the several states" (*Annals of Congress,* House, 6th Congr., 1st sess., 230).

30. *Niles' Register*, March 20, 1819, 77; Adams to Jefferson, Nov. 23, 1819, Jefferson to Adams, Dec. 10, 1819, all in *Founders Online*.

31. See Scherr, *Thomas Jefferson's Image of New England*, 259.

32. Adams, *Memoirs*, 5:5–12; Calhoun, *Papers*, 5:413; Van Atta, *Wolf by the Ears*, 64–65. See also Niven, *John C. Calhoun*, 82, and Remini, *Andrew Jackson and the Course of American Empire*, 41–42.

33. Jan. 2, 1820, Adams, *Memoirs*, 4:495.

34. Ibid., 4:496; Percy to Walker, Feb. 8, 1820, in Dupre, *Transforming the Cotton Frontier*, 53; *Baltimore Patriot*, in Sydnor, *Development of Southern Sectionalism,* 131; *Annals of Congress*, House, 16th Congr., 1st sess., 1310.

35. Hall, *Dividing the Union*, 148–49; Remini, *Henry Clay*, 181; Van Atta, *Wolf by the Ears*, 92; Holmes quoted in Forbes, *Missouri Compromise and Its Aftermath*, 66.

36. See Forbes, *Missouri Compromise and Its Aftermath*, 63–74.

37. Ibid., 71–73, 118.

38. Moore, *Missouri*, 182, 183.

39. *Annals of Congress*, Senate, 16th Congr., 1st sess., 463–64, 489.

40. *Niles' Register*, Feb. 26, 1820, 441; New York *Advertiser*, March 7, 1820; King to J. A. King and Charles King, March 5, 1820, in *Life and Correspondence*, 6:291, to J. A. King, March 4, 1820, in ibid., 6:289; to Oliver Wolcott, March 3, 1820, in ibid., 6:288. Sen. Mark Hatfield, in *Vice Presidents of the United States*, 77, mistakenly says that King accused Daniel Tompkins of having "fled the field," although King was clearly referring to the vice president's absent brother, Caleb Tompkins, in listing absent congressmen who "fled the question." Unfortunately, the U.S. Senate website repeats his error ("Daniel D. Tompkins, 6th Vice President," *U.S. Senate*, www.senate.gov, accessed Oct. 20, 2017), as does Paul Finkelman, in *Slavery and the*

Founders, 119; Finkelman compounds the error by misspelling Tompkins's name and misidentifying him as a senator.

41. John Taylor to Lucy Taylor, March 2, 1820, quoted in Hall, *Dividing the Union*, 185; Chester *Record*, March 7, 1820.

42. Moore, *Missouri Controversy*, 93; Hart, *Essentials of American History*, 301; Richmond *Enquirer*, March 7, 1820; Taylor, *Construction Construed*, 298; Benton, *Thirty Years' View*, 9; Wilentz, *Rise of American Democracy*, 287. See also McLeod, "Political Economy of John Taylor," 407; Shalhope, *John Taylor of Caroline*, 182–202; Lenner, "John Taylor and the Origins of American Federalism," 412–20.

43. *Congressional Globe*, vol. 17, 30th Congr., 1st sess., appendix, 726–27; Farnam, *Chapters in the History of Social Legislation*, 220; *Abridgement of the Debates in Congress*, 6:710–11; *Annals of Congress*, 16th Congr., 2nd sess., 1139.

44. Jefferson to John Holmes, April 27, 1820, in *Founders Online*. See Wilentz, *Rise of American Democracy*, 222–23.

45. *Official Opinions of the Attorneys General*, 1:602.

46. Macon to Yancey, March 8, 1818, printed in *North Carolina University Magazine* 7(1858):95; Macon to Yancey, April 15, 1818, ibid., 95-96; Larson, 118.

47. Wade, *Urban Frontier*, 187–88; Larson, *Internal Improvements*, 137; Calhoun, *Papers*, 4:10–13, 107, 219–20, 294, 327, 342, 381, 411, 450, 503, 511–12, 528, 539–40, 641; 5:43–44, 169; 8:372–73.

48. *Annals of Congress*, Senate, 16th Congr., 1st sess., 442.

49. *Annals of Congress*, House, 17th Congr., 1st sess., 1684–85, 18th Congr., 1st sess., 1307–8; Larson, *Internal Improvements*, 138.

50. Calhoun, *Papers*, 10:421–29, 514–15, 309, 347–54; Niven, *John C. Calhoun*, 106; Malone, *Public Life of Thomas Cooper*, 295; Cooper to Gulian C. Verplanck, May 15, 1827, quoted in Wilentz, *Rise of American Democracy*, 291–92; "Voice of the Illiterate," quoted in Watson, *Liberty and Power*, 63.

51. Haulman, *Virginia and the Panic of 1819*, 147; Adams, *Memoirs*, 4:370.

52. *Annals of Congress*, House, 16th Congr., 1st sess., 1926–46; Peterson, *Great Triumvirate* 73.

53. *ASP: Finance*, 3:447–48;, *Abridgment of the Debates of Congress*, 6:634 (April 26, 1820. Thomas Jefferson (Archer's cousin) made Rumbold's words famous in his final public letter, written just before his death in 1826, but apparently no historian has yet proposed that Archer's 1820 speech may have suggested it to him. See Adair, "Rumbold's Dying Speech."

54. *Niles' Register*, April 10, 1819, 114; July 31, 1819, 369–70.

55. *ASP: Finance*, 3:598, in Dupre, "Panic and Political Economy," 266–67.

56. *Tyranny Unmasked*, 113, quoted in Dupre, "Panic of 1819 and the Political Economy," 287.

57. Murphey to Col. William Polk, July 24, 1821, quoted in Dupre, "Panic of 1819 and the Political Economy," 266; ibid., 268; Cooper, *Consolidation*, 6. See Malone, *Public Life of Thomas Cooper*, 296.

58. *Circular Letters*, 3:1260–61; Niven, *John C. Calhoun*, 108, 135; Jenkins, *Life of John Caldwell Calhoun*, 18–19. See Peterson, *Great Triumvirate*, 74–75.

59. *Annals of Congress*, House, 18th Congr., 1st sess., 959–66, House, 14th Congr., 1st sess., 1328; House, 18th Congr., 1st sess., 2370.

60. Calhoun, *Papers*, 10:253. See Niven, *John C. Calhoun*, 127.

61. "Cheves, Langdon (1776–1857)" in *Biographical Directory of the United States Congress, 1774–Present*, http://bioguide.congress.gov/scripts/biodisplay.pl?index =c000350 (accessed Sept. 10, 2017); Lindquist, "Langdon Cheves," 27, 20; King, *Henry Clay and the War of 1812*, 178.

62. Charleston *Mercury*, Oct. 5, 1830, quoted in Freehling, *Prelude to the Civil War*, 203; Charleston *Mercury*, Aug. 18, 1837, reprinted in *Niles' Register*, Sept. 2, 1837, 9.

BIBLIOGRAPHY

Newspapers and Periodicals

Alabama Republican (Huntsville, AL)
American (Baltimore)
American (New York)
American Mercury (New York)
American Beacon (Norfolk)
Argus (Albany)
Aurora (Philadelphia)
Carolina Centinel (New Bern, NC)
Columbian Centinel (Boston)
Commercial Advertiser (New York)
Courier (Ft. Claiborne, AL)
Courier (London)
Daily Advertiser (Boston)
Democrat (Huntsville, AL)
Enquirer (Richmond)
Enquirer (St. Louis)
Evening Post (New York)
Farmer's Cabinet (Durham, NH)
Farmers' Register (Petersburg, VA)
Federal Gazette (Washington, DC)
Gazette (Georgetown, SC)
Gazette (Pittsburgh)
Gazette (Salem, MA)
Gazette (St. Louis)
Herald (Cleveland)
Herald (Kaskaskia, IL)
Independent Patriot (Jackson, MO)
Intelligencer (Franklin, MO)
Irish Times (Dublin)
Journal (Elizabeth, NJ)
Kentucky Gazette (Lexington, KY)

Liberty Hall (Cincinnati)
Mechanic's Free Press (Philadelphia)
Merchant's Magazine and Commercial Review (New York)
Mercury (Charleston)
Mercury (Pittsburgh)
Messenger (Zanesville, OH)
Missouri Republican (St. Louis)
Missourian (St. Charles, MO)
National Advocate (New York)
National Intelligencer (Washington, DC)
Niles' Weekly Register, AKA Niles' Register (Baltimore)
Orleans Gazette and Commercial Advertiser (New Orleans)
Patriot (Boston)
Patron of Industry (New York)
Pilot (Norfolk)
Price-Courant (Baltimore)
Price Courant (Philadelphia)
Record (Chester, PA)
Register (Cleveland)
Reporter (Washington, PA)
Republican (Greensburg, PA)
Republican (Westmoreland)
Statesman (New York)
Statesman (Pittsburgh)
Times (London)
United States Gazette (Philadelphia)
Watchman (Dayton)
Western Argus (Frankfort, KY)
Western Intelligencer (Kaskaskia, IL)
Western Spy (Cincinnati)
Whig (Nashville, TN)

Archival Sources

Coxe, Tench. "An Addition, of December 1818, to the Memoir [of February and August 1817] on the Subject of the Cotton Culture, the Cotton Commerce, the Cotton Manufacture of the United States." Historical Society of Pennsylvania, Coxe Family Papers. Microfiche 1819 no. 43761, 43762.

Forges and Furnaces Collection, 1727–1921. Collection 212. Philadelphia: Historical Society of Pennsylvania, 2005. https://hsp.org/sites/default/files/legacy_files/migrated/findingaid212forgesandfurnaces.pdf

General Records of the Department of the Treasury (cited as Treasury Records). Records Group 56.2.2 General Records of the Office of the Secretary 1789–1977, Letters Received, Microfilm Record M174. National Archives and Records Administration.

James Monroe Papers. Library of Congress Manuscript Division.

Nicholas Biddle Papers. Library of Congress Manuscripts Division.

Steele, J. D., Manuscript Journal, 1820–1829. Huntington Library collection.

Government Documents and Records

Abridgement of the Debates in Congress from 1789 to 1856. New York: Appleton, 1858.

American State Papers: Commerce and Navigation. 2 vols. Buffalo, NY: Heine, 1998.

American State Papers: Finance. 5 vols. Buffalo, NY: Heine, 1998.

American State Papers: Miscellaneous. 2 vols. Buffalo, NY: Heine, 1998.

American State Papers: Public Lands. 8 vols. Buffalo, NY: Heine, 1998.

[*Annals of Congress.*] *Debates and Proceedings in the Congress of the United States.* 42 vols. Washington, DC: Gales and Seaton, 1834–1856. https://memory.loc.gov/ammem/amlaw/lwaclink.html

Comptroller of the City of New York. *Annual Statement of the Funds of the Corporation of the City of New York.* New York: Trow, 1845.

Congressional Globe. 46 vols. Washington, DC: Blair & Rives, 1834–1873. https://memory.loc.gov/ammem/amlaw/lwcglink.html.

Hazard, Samuel G., ed. *Hazard's Register of Pennsylvania.* Vol. 4. Philadelphia: Geddes, 1827.

Historical Statistics 1789–1945, A Supplement to the Statistical Abstract. Prepared by the Bureau of the Census with the Cooperation of the Social Science Research Council. Washington, DC: Government Printing Office, 1949. https://census.gov/library/compendia.

Historical Statistics of the United States, Colonial Times to 1970 (Bicentennial Edition). https://census.gov/library/publications/library/compendia

House of Representatives Report 460, 22nd Congress, 1st session (April 30,1832). https://fraser.stlouisfed.org/title/3622.

Journal of the Assembly of the State of New York at Their Forty-First Session. Albany, NY: J. Buel, 1818.

Journal of the Assembly of the State of New York at Their Forty-Second Session. Albany: J. Buel, 1819.

Journal of the Debates and Proceedings in the Convention of Delegates Chosen to Revise the Constitution of Massachusetts. Boston: Daily Advertiser, 1853.

Journal of the House of Delegates [Virginia] 1819–1820. Richmond, VA: Thomas Ritchie. 1820.

Journal of the House of Delegates [Virginia] 1820–1821. Richmond, VA: Thomas Ritchie, 1821.

Journal of the House of Representatives of the State of Ohio, Eighteenth General Assembly. Columbus, OH: Columbus Gazette, 1819.

Journal of the Senate of the Commonwealth of Pennsylvania. Vol. 30, *1819.* Harrisburg: James Peacock, 1820.

Journal of the Senate of the State of New-York, Forty-Second Session. Albany, NY: J. Buel, 1819.

Journal of the Thirtieth House of Representatives of the Commonwealth of Pennsylvania. Harrisburg: James Peacock, 1820.

A Letter from the Treasury Department, Accompanied with all the Correspondence between the Secretary and the Banker . . . between the 1st of January 1817 and the 8th of May, 1822, 18th Congress, 1st session, Document No. 140. Washington, DC: Gales and Seaton, 1822.

Official Opinions of the Attorneys General of the United States. vols. Washington, DC: Government Printing Office, 1791–1848.

Quincy, Josiah. *Massachusetts General Court, Committee on Pauper Laws.* Boston: Russell and Gardner, 1821.

Register of Officers and Agents, Civil, Military, and Naval, in the Service of the United States, on the Thirtieth Day of September, 1817. Washington, DC: Department of State, 1818.

Report from the Select Committee on East India Produce. London: House of Commons, 1840.

Report of the Bank of the United States to the Committee of Ways and Means of the House of Representatives, January 28, 1833. fraser.stlouisfed.org/title/3673.

Report of the Committee . . . on a Letter of John C. Calhoun . . . House Reports, 19th Congress, 2nd session, Number 79. Washington, DC: Gales and Seaton, 1827.

Report of the Debates and Proceedings of the Convention of the State of New York . . . 1821. Albany, NY: Hosford, 1821.

Reports of the Secretary of the Treasury of the United States. 7 vols. Washington, DC: Blair and Rives, 1837.

Territorial Papers of the United States. Edited by Clarence E. Carter and John P. Bloom. 28 vols. Washington, DC: Government Printing Office, 1934–75.

United States Reports. 567 vols. to date. Washington, DC: Government Printing Office, 1790–.

Primary Sources

Adams, John. *Works of John Adams.* Edited by Charles Francis Adams. 10 vols. Boston: Little, Brown, 1854.

Adams, John Quincy. *Memoirs of John Quincy Adams, Comprising Portions of His Diary from 1795 to 1848.* Edited by Charles Francis Adams. 12 vols. Philadelphia: Lippincott, 1874–1877.

Austin, Moses, and Stephen F. Austin. *The Austin Papers.* Edited by Eugene C. Barker. 2 vols. Washington, DC: Government Printing Office, 1924–28.

Baines, Edward, Sir. *History of the Cotton Manufacture in Great Britain.* London: Fisher, Fisher and Jackson, 1835.

Benton, Thomas Hart. *Thirty Years' View.* 2 vols. New York: Appleton, 1854.

Biggs, Joseph. *To America in Thirty-nine Days.* Idbury, UK: Village Press, 1925.

Billingmeir, Robert H., and Fred A. Picard, trans. and eds. *The Old Land and the New: The Journals of Two Swiss Families in America in the 1820s.* Minneapolis: University of Minnesota Press, 1965.

Birkbeck, Morris. *Notes on a Journey in America.* London: Ridgway, 1818.

Bloodgood, S. de Witt. *A Treatise on Roads, Their History, Character, and Utility.* Albany, NY: Steele. 1838.

Brougham, Henry. *Speeches of Henry, Lord Brougham.* London: Lea and Blanchard, 1841.

Burroughs, Charles. *A Discourse Delivered in the Chapel of the New Alms-House, in Portsmouth, N.H. . . .* Portsmouth, NH: J. W. Foster, 1835.

Calhoun, John C. *Papers of John C. Calhoun.* Edited by W. Edwin Hemphill, Robert Meriwether, Clyde Wilson, et al. 28 vols. Columbia: University of South Carolina Press, 1959–2003.

———. *Speeches of John C. Calhoun Delivered in the Congress of the United States from 1811 to the Present Time.* Edited by John Crallé. New York: Harper Brothers, 1843.

Callender, James T. *The Prospect Before Us.* 2 vols. Richmond, VA: Printed by the Author, 1800.

Carey, Matthew. *Autobiography.* Brooklyn, NY: Research Classics, 1942.

———. "Essay on the Public Charities of Philadelphia." Philadelphia: Clark and Raser, 1830.

———. *Essays on Banking.* Philadelphia, 1816.

———. *Essays on Political Economy.* Philadelphia: Carey and Lea, 1822.

———. *The New Olive Branch.* Philadelphia: M. Carey and Sons, 1820.

———. *Reflections on the Present System of Banking in the City of Philadelphia.* Philadelphia: M. Carey, 1817.

Circular Letters of Congressmen to Their Constituents, 1789–1829. Edited by Noble E. Cunningham. 3 vols. Chapel Hill: University of North Carolina Press, 1978.

Clarke, M. St. Clair, and D. A. Hall. *Legislative and Documentary History of the Bank of the United States.* Washington, DC: Gales and Seaton, 1832.

Clay, Henry. *Papers of Henry Clay.* Edited by James F. Hopkins, Mary Hardgreaves, et al. 11 vols. Lexington: University Press of Kentucky, 1959–92.

———. *Speeches of Henry Clay.* Edited by Calvin Colton. 2 vols. New York: A. S. Barnes, 1857.

Cooper, Thomas. *Consolidation: An Account of Parties in the United States, from the Convention of 1787 to the Present Period.* 2nd ed. Charleston, SC: Times and Gazette, 1830.

Cox, Isaac J., ed. "Selections from the Torrance Papers, VI." *Quarterly Publication of the Historical and Philosophical Society of Ohio* 6 (1911): 1–44.

Coxe, Tench. *Statement of the Arts and Manufactures of the United States for the Year 1810 [and Supplementary Observations].* Philadelphia: Cornman, 1814.

———. *A View of the United States of America.* Philadelphia: Hall, 1794.

Cramer's Pittsburgh Almanack. Pittsburgh, PA: Cramer, Spear and Eichbaum, 1817

Curtis, Caroline G., ed. *The Cary Letters.* Cambridge, MA: Riverside Press, 1891.

Dabney, Virginius. *Liberalism in the South.* Chapel Hill: University of North Carolina Press, 1932.

Dodge, Bertha S. *Cotton: The Plant That Would Be King.* Austin: University of Texas Press, 1984.

Dodge, David L., *Memorial of David L. Dodge, Consisting of an Autobiography.* Boston: Whipple, 1854.

Dostoevsky, Fyodor. *Demons: A Novel in Three Parts.* Translated by Richard Pevear and Larissa Volokhonsky. New York: Vintage, 1995.

Douglas, Thomas. *Autobiography of Thomas Douglas, Late Judge of the Supreme Court of Florida.* New York: Calkins and Stiles, 1856.

Duden, Gottfried. *Report on a Journey to the Western States of North America.* 1829. Reprint, Columbia: University of Missouri Press, 1980.

Elliot, Jonathan. *Debates in the Several States of the Adoption of the Federal Constitution.* 5 vols. Washington, DC: Published by the author, 1836.

———, ed., *The Funding System of the United States and of Great Britain.* Washington, DC: Blair and Rives, 1845.

Evans, Estwick. *A Pedestrious Tour, or Four Thousand Miles, through the United States and Territories during the Winter and Spring of 1818.* Concord, NH: Joseph C. Spear, 1819.

An Exhibit of the Losses Sustained at the Office of Discounts and Deposit Baltimore, under the Administration of James Buchanan, President, and James W. McCulloh, Cashier. Baltimore: Thomas Murphy, 1823.

Extracts from the Minutes of the General Assembly of the Presbyterian Church in the United States of America, A.D. 1819. Philadelphia: Thomas and William Bradford, 1819.

Finley, James B. *Autobiography of James B. Finley, or Pioneer Life in the West.* Edited by W. P. Strickland. Cincinnati: Cranston and Curtis, 1854.

Flagg, Gershom. "Pioneer Letters of Gershom Flagg." Edited by Solon J. Buck. *Transactions of the Illinois State Historical Society* 15 (1910): 138–83.

Flint, James. *Letters from America, 1818–1820.* 1822. Reprinted as vol. 9 of *Early Western Travels 1748–1846*, edited by Reuben Gold Thwaites. Cleveland: Arthur H. Clark, 1904.

Flint, Timothy. *Recollections of the Last Ten Years, Passed in Occasional Residences and Journeyings in the Valley of the Mississippi.* Boston: Cummings, Hilliard, 1826.

Founders Online: Correspondence and Other Writings of Six Major Shapers of the United States. National Archives, National Historical Publications and Records Commission. https://founders.archives.gov.

"Friendly Monitor." *A Brief Review of the Origin, Progress, and Administration of the Bank of the United States.* [Philadelphia]: [1819].

Gallatin, Albert. *Considerations on the Currency and Banking System of the United States.* Philadelphia: Carey and Lea, 1831.

———. *Writings of Albert Gallatin.* Edited by Henry Cochran. 3 vols. Philadelphia: Lippincott, 1879.

Goodrich, Samuel Griswold. *Peter Parley's Recollections of a Lifetime.* New York: Miller, Orton, and Mulligan, 1856.

Gouge, William. *A Short History of Paper Money and Banking in the United States.* Philadelphia: T. W. Ustick, 1833.

Greene, William. "A New Englander's Impression of Circumstances in 1820: Letters by William Greene." Edited by Rosamund Wilson. *Bulletin of the Historical and Philosophical Society of Ohio* 7, no. 2 (1949): 116–22.

Hazard, Thomas R. *Jonny-Cake Papers.* Boston: Printed for subscribers, 1915.

Hodgson, Adam. *Remarks During a Journey through North America in the Years 1819, 1820, and 1821* . . . New York: S. Whiting, 1823.

Hoover, Herbert. *Memoirs of Herbert Hoover.* 3 vols. New York: Macmillan, 1952.

Howitt, Emanuel. *Selections from Letters Written during a Tour through the United States in the Summer and Autumn of 1819.* Nottingham, UK: J. Dunn, 1820.

Ingersoll, Charles Jared. *A View of the Rights and Wrongs, Power and Policy of the United States of America.* Philadelphia: Conrad, 1808.

Jackson, Andrew. *Correspondence of Andrew Jackson.* Edited by John S. Bassett. 7 vols. Washington, DC: Carnegie Institute, 1926–35.

———. *Papers of Andrew Jackson.* Edited by Harold Moser et al. 10 vols. to date. Knoxville: University of Tennessee Press, 1980–.

Jefferson, Thomas. *Family Letters of Thomas Jefferson.* Edited by Edwin M. Betts and James A. Bear Jr. Columbia: University of Missouri Press, 1966.

———. *Memoirs, Correspondence, and Papers of Thomas Jefferson, Late President of the United States.* Edited by Thomas Jefferson Randolph. 4 vols. London: Colburn and Bentley, 1829.

———. *Notes on the State of Virginia.* Edited by David Waldstreicker. Boston: Bedford St. Martin's, 2002.

———. *Papers of Thomas Jefferson,* Retirement Series. Edited by J. Jefferson Looney. 13 vols. to date. Princeton: Princeton University Press, 2004–.

———. *Works of Thomas Jefferson.* Edited by Paul L. Ford. 12 vols. New York: Putnam's, 1904.

Jerome, Chauncey. *History of the Clock Business for the Past Sixty Years, and Life of Chauncey Jerome.* New Haven, CT: F. C. Dayton, 1860.

Kendall, Amos. *Autobiography of Amos Kendall.* Edited by William Stickney. Boston: Lee and Shepard, 1872.

King, Rufus. *Life and Correspondence of Rufus King.* Edited by Charles R. King. 6 vols. New York: Putnam, 1894–1900.

Lederer, David Friedrich. "Report of the Famine and Hyperinflation of 1816 and 1817." August 17, 1817. From the Bürger-und Notabilienbuch. https://www .physics.ohio-state.edu/~palmer/Geradstetten/Report%20of%20the%20Fam ine%20and%20Hhe%20Hyper-Inflation%20of%201816%20and%201817 .pdf

Lloyd, James T. *Lloyd's Steamboat Directory and Disasters on the Western Waters.* Cincinnati: James Lloyd, 1856.

Madison, James. *Papers of James Madison.* Congressional Series. Edited by William T. Hutchinson et al. 17 vols. Chicago: University of Chicago Press, 1962–77; Charlottesville: University of Virginia Press, 1977–91.

Marshall, John, *Life of George Washington.* 5 vols. Philadelphia: C. F. Wayne, 1804.

———. *Papers of John Marshall.* 9 vols. Edited by Charles F. Hobson. Chapel Hill: University of North Carolina Press, 1974–.

Mason, Jeremiah. *Memoirs and Correspondence of Jeremiah Mason.* Edited by George Stilling Hilliard. Cambridge, MA: Riverside Press, 1873.

McLane, Louis. *Documents Relative to the Manufactures in the United States*. 4 vols. 1833. Reprint, New York: Burt Franklin 1969.

McMurtrie, Henry. *Sketches of Louisville and Its Environs*. Louisville, KY: S. Penn, 1819.

Murphey, Archibald. *Papers of Archibald Murphey*. Edited by William H. Hoyt. Raleigh: E. M. Uzzell, 1914.

"Nathaniel Macon and Bartlett Yancey." North *Carolinia University Magazine* 7(1858):89-100.

Noyes, Emily, ed. *A Family History in Letters and Documents, 1667–1837*. St. Paul, MN: Privately printed, 1919.

Otter, William. *History of My Own Times*. Edited by Richard B. Stott. Ithaca, NY: Cornell University Press, 1995.

Peck, John Mason. *Forty Years of Pioneer Life*. Philadelphia: American Baptist Publication Society, 1864.

Pell, [William] Ferris. *A Review of the Administration and Civil Police of the State of New York*. New York: Conrad, 1819.

Philadelphia Society for the Promotion of American Manufactures. *Circular*. Philadelphia, 1817.

Pitkin, T. *A Statistical View of the Commerce of the United States of America*. New Haven, CT: Durrie and Peck, 1835.

Raguet, Condy. *A Treatise on Currency and Banking*. Philadelphia: Griggs and Elliott, 1840.

Rammelkamp, Charles. "Thomas Lippincott: A Pioneer of 1818 and his Diary." *Journal of the Illinois State Historical Society* 10, no. 2 (1917): 237–55.

Report of the Condition of the Bank of the United States by the Committee of Inspection and Investigation. Philadelphia: William Fry, 1822.

Ricardo, David. *Minor Papers on the Currency Question, 1809–23*. Edited by Jacob Hollander. Baltimore: Johns Hopkins University Press, 1932.

———. *The Works and Correspondence of David Ricardo*. Edited by Pierro Sraffa. 11 vols. Cambridge: Cambridge University Press, 1951–73.

Ruffin, Thomas. *Papers of Thomas Ruffin*. Edited by J. G. de Roulhac Hamilton. 2 vols. Raleigh, NC: Broughton, 1918–20.

A Series of Letters and Other Documents Relating to the Late Epidemic of Yellow Fever, Published by Authority of the Mayor. Baltimore: William Warner, 1820.

"Seventy-Six." *Cause of, and Cure for Hard Times: Containing a Definition of the Attributes and Qualities Indispensable in Money as a Medium of Commerce*. New York: Privately printed, 1819.

Sheldon, Asa. *Life of Asa G. Sheldon, Wilmington Farmer*. Woburn, MA: Moody, 1862.

Simon, T. Collyns. *On the Nature and Elements of the External World*. London: Churchill, 1847.

Smith, John Jay. *Recollections of John Jay Smith*. Philadelphia: Lippincott, 1892.

Smith, Lucy Mack. *History of the Prophet Joseph Smith, by His Mother*. Salt Lake City, UT: Improvement Era, 1902.

Smith, Margaret Bayard. *First Forty Years of Washington Society.* Edited by Gaillard Hunt. New York: Scribner's, 1906.

Society for the Prevention of Pauperism. *Second Annual Report, 1819.* New York: Conrad, 1820.

Story, William W., ed. *Life and Letters of Joseph Story.* Boston: Little, Brown, 1851.

Symmes, John C. *Correspondence of John Cleves Symmes.* Edited by Peter Thompson, Beverley W. Bond, et al. New York: Macmillan, 1926.

Taylor, John. *Construction Construed and Constitutions Vindicated.* Richmond, VA: Shepherd and Pollard, 1820.

———. *An Inquiry into the Principles and Policies of the United States Government.* Fredericksburg, MD: Green and Cady, 1814.

———. *Tyranny Unmasked.* Washington, DC: Davis and Ford, 1822.

Things as They Are, or America in 1819. Manchester, UK: J. Wroe, 1819.

Thomas, David. *Travels through the Western Country in the Summer of 1816.* Auburn, NY: Rumsey, 1819. Reprint, Darien, CT: Hafner, 1970.

Thompson, Abraham. "Auction System in New York." *Merchants' Magazine and Commercial Review* 10 (1844): 154–58.

Tooke, Thomas. *History of Prices, and of the State of the Circulation.* 2 vols. London: Longmans, 1838.

Trimble, Allen. *Autobiography and Correspondence of Allen Trimble, Governor of Ohio.* Columbus, OH: Old Northwest Genealogical Society, 1909.

Van Buren, Martin. *Autobiography of Martin Van Buren.* Edited by John Clement Fitzpatrick. Washington, DC: Government Printing Office, 1920.

Ward, H. G. *Mexico in 1827.* 2 vols. London: Colbourn, 1828.

Washburn, Ichabod. *Autobiography and Memorials.* Edited by Henry Cheever. Boston: Lothrop, 1878.

[Watson, Elkanah]. *Observations on the real, relative and market value of the turnpike stock of the State of New York. By a Citizen.* New York: S. Gould, 1806.

White, George S. *Memoir of Samuel Slater.* Philadelphia, 1836.

Wilson, James Grant, ed. *Centennial History of the Episcopal Church, 1785–1885.* New York: Appleton, 1886.

Wolcott, Oliver. *Remarks on the Present State of Currency, Credit, Commerce, and National Industry: In Reply to an Address at the Tammany Society of New-York.* New York: Wiley, 1820.

Yancey, Bartlett. *A Calendar of the Bartlett Yancey Papers.* Raleigh: North Carolina Historical Society, 1940.

Secondary Sources

Abernethy, Thomas P. *The Formative Period in Alabama, 1815–1828.* Rev. ed. Tuscaloosa: University of Alabama Press, 1965.

Adair, Douglass. "Rumbold's Dying Speech, 1685, and Jefferson's Last Words on Democracy, 1826." *William and Mary Quarterly,* 3rd ser., 9 (1952): 521–31.

Adams, Henry. *History of the United States During the Administrations of Thomas Jefferson.* 9 vols. New York: Scribner's, 1889–91.

Alberts, Robert C. *The Golden Voyage.* Boston: Houghton Mifflin, 1969.

Albion, Robert G. *The Rise of the Port of New York, 1815–1860.* New York: Scribner's, 1930.

Allen, Larry. *Global Financial Systems, 1750–2000.* London: Reaktion Books, 2001.

Anderson, Hattie M. "Frontier Economic Problems in Missouri 1815–1828." *Missouri Historical Review* 34, nos. 1 & 2 (1939–40): 38–70, 182–203.

Andrews, Matthew P. *Tercentenary History of Maryland.* Chicago: Clarke, 1925.

Appleby, Joyce. "The Popular Sources of American Capitalism." *Studies in American Political Development* 9 (1995): 437–57.

Atack, Jeremy, and Peter Passell. *A New Economic View of American History from Colonial Times to 1940.* 2nd ed. New York: Norton, 1994.

Bailey, Hugh. C. "John W. Walker and the Land Laws of the 1820's." *Agricultural History* 32 (1958): 120–26.

———. *John Williams Walker: A Study in the Political, Social, and Cultural Life of the Old Southwest.* Tuscaloosa: University of Alabama Press, 1964.

Baird, Lewis. *Baird's History of Clark County, Indiana.* Indianapolis: Bowen, 1909.

Baker, Leonard. *John Marshall: A Life in Law.* New York: Macmillan, 1974.

Bakewell, Peter. *Mines of Silver and Gold in the Americas.* London: Routledge, 1997.

Banner, Lois. "Religious Benevolence as Social Control,." *Journal of American History* 60 (1973): 34–41.

Barnes, Andrew. *History of the Philadelphia Stock Exchange, Banks, and Banking Interests.* Philadelphia: Baker, 1911.

Barnes, D. G. *History of the English Corn Laws, from 1660–1846.* London: Routledge, 1930.

Bartkowski, John P., and Helen A. Regis. *Charitable Choices: Religion, Race, and Poverty in the Post-Welfare Era.* New York: New York University Press, 2003.

Beckert, Sven. *Empire of Cotton: A Global History.* New York: Knopf, 2014.

Bellows, Barbara Lawrence. *Benevolence Among Slaveholders: Assisting the Poor in Charleston, 1670–1860.* Baton Rouge: Louisiana State University Press, 1993.

———. "Tempering the Wind: The Southern Response to Urban Poverty, 1850–1865." PhD diss., University of South Carolina, 1983.

Bernstein, Peter L. *Wedding of the Waters: the Erie Canal and the Making of a Great Nation.* New York: Norton, 2005.

Berry, T. S. "The Rise of Flour Milling in Richmond." *Virginia Magazine of History and Biography* 78 (1970): 387–408.

Bezanson, Anne, Robert Gray, and Miriam Hussey. *Wholesale Prices in Philadelphia 1784–1861.* 2 vols. Philadelphia: University of Pennsylvania Press, 1936.

Bishop, Leander. *History of American Manufacturers from 1608 to 1860.* 2 vols. Philadelphia: E. Young, 1866.

Bjork, G. "The Weaning of the American Economy." *Journal of Economic History* 24, no. 4 (1964): 541–60.

Blackson, Robert M. "Pennsylvania Banks and the Panic of 1819: A Reinterpretation." *Journal of the Early Republic* 9, no. 3 (1989): 335–58.

Bodenhorn, Howard. "Capital Mobility and Financial Integration in Antebellum America." *Journal of Economic History* 52, no. 3 (1992): 586–610.

———. *A History of Banking in Antebellum America: Financial Markets and Economic Development in an Era of Nation-Building.* New York: Cambridge University Press, 2000.

Bogart, Ernest L. "Financial History of Ohio." *University of Illinois Studies in the Social Sciences* 11 (1912): 1–358.

———. "Taxation of the Second Bank of the United States by Ohio." *American Historical Review* 17, no. 2 (1912): 312–31.

Bogen, David S. "The Scandal of Smith and Buchanan." *Maryland Law Forum* 9 (1985): 125–32.

Boggess, Arthur C. *The Settlement of Illinois.* Chicago: Chicago Historical Society, 1908.

Boles, John B. *Black Southerners 1619–1869.* Lexington: University Press of Kentucky, 1984.

Bonelli, Vincent F. *The Response of Public and Private Philanthropy to the Panic of 1819 in New York City.* New York: Dorrance, 2004.

Bordo, Michael D., and Eugene N. White. "A Tale of Two Currencies: British and French Finance during the Napoleonic Wars." *Journal of Economic History* 51, no. 2 (1991): 303–16.

Borkoski, Kali. "What Does Necessary Mean? And Who Decides?" *Supreme Court of the United States Blog,* October 17, 2014. http://www.scotusblog.com/2014/10/what-does-necessary-mean-and-who-decides-reenacting-mcculloch-v-maryland/

Boyd, Julian P. "John Sergeant's Mission to Europe for the Second Bank of the United States, 1816–1817." *Pennsylvania Magazine of History and Biography* 58 (1934): 213–31.

Brant, Irving. *James Madison, Commander in Chief.* Indianapolis, IN: Bobbs-Merrill, 1961.

Brantley, William H. *Banking in Alabama.* Birmingham, AL: Oxmoor, 1961.

Brazy, Martha Jane. *An American Planter: Stephen Duncan of Antebellum Natchez and New York.* Baton Rouge: Louisiana State University Press, 2006.

Bremer, Jeff. "Frontier Capitalism: Market Migration to Rural Central Missouri 1815–1860." In *Southern Society and Its Transformation, 1790–1860,* edited by Susannah Delfino et al., 79–101. Columbia: University of Missouri Press, 2011.

Brown, Kenneth. "Stephen Girard's Bank." *Pennsylvania Magazine of History and Biography* 66 (1942): 29–55.

Brown, Richard H. *Missouri Compromise, Political Statesmanship or Unwise Evasion?* Boston: Heath, 1964.

Bruchey, Stuart. *Cotton and the Growth of the American Economy: 1790–1860.* New York: Random House, 1967.

Buck, N. S. *Development and Organization of Anglo-American Trade, 1800–1850*. New Haven, CT: Yale University Press, 1925.

Caldwell, Stephen A. *A Banking History of Louisiana*. Baton Rouge: Louisiana State University Press, 1935.

Carstensen, Vernon, ed. *The Public Lands: Studies in the History of the Public Domain*. Madison: University of Wisconsin Press, 1962.

Catterall, Ralph. *The Second Bank of the United States*. Chicago: University of Chicago Press, 1903.

Cayton, Andrew. "The Fragmentation of a 'Great Family': The Panic of 1819 and the Rise of the Middling Interest in Boston." *Journal of the Early Republic* 2, no. 2 (1982): 143–67.

———. *Frontier Republic: Ideology and Politics in the Ohio Country*. Kent, OH: Kent State University Press, 1986.

Chenoweth, Michael. "Ships' Logbooks and 'The Year Without a Summer.'" *Bulletin of the American Meteorological Society* 77 (1996): 2077–93.

Chew, Richard S. "Certain Victims of an International Contagion: The Panic of 1797 and the Hard Times of the Late 1790s in Baltimore." *Journal of the Early Republic* 25, no. 4 (2005): 567–70.

Chittenden, Hiram M. *History of the American Fur Trade in the Far West*. 2 vols. 1905. Reprint, Lincoln: University of Nebraska Press, 1986.

Cimenti, J. "In Light of Failure: Bankruptcy, Insolvency, and Financial Failure in New York City, 1770–1860." PhD diss., City University of New York, 1992.

Clark, Christopher. *The Roots of Rural Capitalism: Western Massachusetts, 1780–1860*. Ithaca, NY: Cornell University Press, 1990.

Clement, P.F. *Welfare and the Poor in Nineteenth-Century Philanthropy 1800–1854*. Rutherford, NJ: Fairleigh Dickinson Press, 1985.

Cochran, Thomas C. *Frontiers of Change: Early Industrialism in America*. New York: Oxford University Press, 1981.

Cohen, Ira. "The Auction System in the Port of New York, 1817–1837." *Business History Review* 45, no. 4 (1971): 488–510.

Cohen, Joanna. "'The Right to Purchase Is as Free as the Right to Sell': Defining Consumers as Citizens in the Auction-House Conflicts of the Early Republic." *Journal of the Early Republic* 30, no. 1 (2010): 25–65.

Coil, Blanche. "The Baltimore Society for the Prevention of Pauperism, 1820–1922." *American Historical Review* 61, no. 1 (1955): 77–87.

Cole, Arthur H. "Cyclical and Seasonal Variations in the Sale of Public Lands 1816–1860." *Review of Economic Statistics* 9 (1927): 41–53.

———. *Wholesale Commodity Prices in the United States, 1700–1861*. Cambridge, MA: Harvard University Press, 1938.

Cole, Frank T. "Thomas Worthington." *Ohio Archeological and Historical Publication* 12 (1903): 339–74.

Conference on Research in Income and Wealth. *Trends in the American Economy in the Nineteenth Century*. Princeton, NJ: Princeton University Press, 1960.

Conger, John L. "South Carolina and Early Tariffs." *Mississippi Valley Historical Review* 5, no. 4 (1919): 415–25.

Conkin, Paul. *Prophets of Progress: The American Economy in 1815.* Bloomington: Indiana University Press, 1980.

Cooper, William, and Thomas E. Terrill. *The American South: A History.* New York: Knopf, 1990.

Coover, A. B. "Ohio Banking Institutions 1803–1866." *Ohio Archeological and Historical Publication* 21 (1912): 296–320.

Coulson, Michael. *The History of Mining: The Events, Technology, and People Involved in the Industry that Forged the Modern World.* London: Harriman House, 2012.

Cowen, David J. "Financing the War of 1812." *Financial History* 104 (Fall 2012): 32–42.

Creech, M. *Three Centuries of Poor Law Administration: A Study of the Legislature in Rhode Island.* New York: Columbia University Press, 1936.

Crockett, Walter H. *Vermont: The Green Mountain State.* 3 vols. New York: Century History, 1921.

Cross, Whitney R. *The Burned-Over District.* Ithaca, NY: Cornell University Press, 1950.

Cunningham, Noble. *The Presidency of James Monroe.* Lawrence: University of Kansas Press, 1996.

Cutler, E. Wayne. "The A.B. Conspiracy." *Mid-America* 51 (1969): 24–37.

———. "William H. Crawford: A Contextual Biography." PhD diss., University of Texas, 1971.

Dalzell, Robert F. *Enterprising Elite: The Boston Associates and the World They Made.* Cambridge, MA: Harvard University Press, 1987.

Dangerfield, George. *Awakening of American Nationalism, 1815–1828.* New York: Harper and Row, 1965.

———. *Era of Good Feelings.* New York: Harcourt, Brace, 1952.

Dattel, Gene. *Cotton and Race in the Making of America.* Chicago: Ivan R. Dee, 2009.

David, Elbra. "'In Pursuit of their Livelihood': Credit and Debt Relations among Natchez Planters in the 1820s." In *Southern Society and Its Transformation, 1790–1860,* edited by Susannah Delfino et al., 217–46. Columbia: University of Missouri Press, 2011.

Davis, Lance E. "Stock Ownership in the Early New England Textile Industry." *Business History Review* 32, no. 2 (1958): 204–22.

Day, Clive. "Early Development of the American Cotton Manufacture." *Quarterly Journal of Economics* 39, no. 3 (1925): 450–68.

Deale, Frank. "The Unhappy History of Economic Rights in the United States and Prospects for Their Creation and Renewal." *Howard Law Review* 43 (2000): 281–342.

De Cesar, Wayne T., and Susan Page. "Jefferson Buys Louisiana Territory, and the Nation Moves Westward." *Prologue Magazine* 35, no. 1 (Spring 2003). https://www.archives.gov/publications/prologue/2003/spring/louisiana-purchase.html.

Dewey, Davis R. *State Banking before the Civil War.* Washington, DC: Government Printing Office, 1832.

Deyle, Steven. *Carry Me Back: The Domestic Slave Trade in American Life.* New York: Oxford University Press, 2005.

Dictionary of North Carolina Biography. Edited by William S. Powell. Chapel Hill: University of North Carolina Press, 1979–96.

Dippel, John V. H. *Eighteen Hundred and Froze to Death.* New York: Algora, 2015.

Dodge, Bertha S. *Cotton: The Plant that Would Be King.* Austin: University of Texas Press, 1984.

Doerflinger, Thomas. "Rural Capitalism in Iron Country: Staffing a Forest Factory, 1808–1815." *William and Mary Quarterly* 59 (2002): 3–38.

Dorsey, Dorothy B. "The Panic of 1819 in Missouri." *Missouri Historical Review* 29, no. 2 (1935): 79–91.

Dowrie, George. *The Development of Banking in Illinois, 1817–1863.* Urbana: University of Illinois, 1913.

Dupre, Daniel S. "Ambivalent Capitalism on the Cotton Frontier: Settlement and Development in the Tennessee Valley of Alabama." *Journal of Southern History* 56 (1990): 215–40.

———. "The Panic of 1819 and the Political Economy of Sectionalism." In *The Economy of Early America: Historical Perspectives and New Directions*, edited by Cathy Matson, 263–93. University Park: Penn State University Press, 2006.

———. *Transforming the Cotton Frontier: Madison County, Alabama, 1800–1840.* Baton Rouge: Louisiana State University Press, 1997.

Durrenberger, Joseph A. *Turnpikes: A Study of the Toll Road Movement in the Middle Atlantic States and Maryland.* Valdosta, GA: Southern Stationery and Printing Co., 1931.

Duryea, Scott. "William Pitt, the Bank of England, and the 1797 Suspension of Specie Payments: Central Bank War Finance During the Napoleonic Wars." *Libertarian Papers* 2 (May 2010): #15. http://libertarianpapers.org.

Eckert, Edward C. "William Jones: Mr. Madison's Secretary of the Navy." *Pennsylvania Magazine of History and Biography* 96 (1972): 167–82.

Eddy, John A. "Before Tambora: The Sun and Climate, 1790–1830." In *The Year Without a Summer?*, edited by C. R. Harrington, 7–11. Ottawa: Canadian Museum of Nature, 1992.

Ellis, David, et al., eds. *A Short History of New York State.* Ithaca, NY: Cornell University Press, 1957.

Ellis, Richard E. *Aggressive Nationalism: McCulloch v. Maryland and the Foundation of Federal Authority in the Young Republic.* New York: Oxford University Press, 2007.

———. "The Market Revolution and the Transformation of American Politics, 1801–1837." In *The Market Revolution in America: Social, Political, and Religious Expressions*, edited by Melvyn Stokes and Stephen Conway, 149–76. Charlottesville: University of Virginia Press, 1996.

Ellison, T. *The Cotton Trade of Great Britain.* London: E. Wilson, 1886.

Engerman, Stanley, and Robert Gallman, eds. *The Cambridge History of the United States.* Vol. 2, *The Long Nineteenth Century.* New York: Cambridge University Press, 1996.

Esary, Logan. "The First Indiana Banks," *Indiana Quarterly Magazine of History* 6 (1910): 144–58.

———. "State Banking in Indiana, 1814–1873." *Indiana University Bulletin* 10 (1912): 219–305.

Evans, G. H. *Business Incorporations in the United States, 1800–1943.* New York: National Bureau of Economic Records, 1948.

Evans, Robert. "Blast from the Past." *Smithsonian,* July 2002.

Farnam, Henry. *Chapters in the History of Social Legislation in the United States to 1860.* Washington, DC: Carnegie Institute, 1938.

Fay, C. R. *The Corn Laws and Social England.* Cambridge: Cambridge University Press, 1932.

Feaveryear, Albert. *The Pound Sterling: A History of English Money.* Oxford: Oxford University Press, 1931.

Federal Reserve Bank of Philadelphia. *The Second Bank of the United States: A Chapter in the History of Central Banking.* Philadelphia: Federal Reserve Bank of Philadelphia, 2010. https://www.philadelphiafed.org/-/media/publications/economic-education/second-bank.pdf

Fehrenbacher, Don E. *Sectional Crisis and Southern Constitutionalism.* Baton Rouge: Louisiana State University Press, 1995.

Feller, Daniel. *The Public Lands in Jacksonian Politics.* Madison: University of Wisconsin Press, 1984.

Fenstermaker, Joseph Van. *The Development of American Commercial Banking, 1782–1837.* Kent, OH: Kent State University Press, 1965.

Field, Alexander. "Uncontrolled Land Development and the Duration of Depression." *Journal of Economic History* 52, no. 4 (1992): 785–805.

Field, Edward. *State of Rhode Island and Providence Plantations at the End of the Century: A History.* 3 vols. Boston: Mason, 1902.

Finkelman, Paul. *Slavery and the Founders: Race and Liberty in the Age of Jefferson.* New York: Routledge, 2014.

———. *Supreme Injustice: Slavery in the Nation's Highest Court.* Cambridge, MA: Harvard University Press, 2018.

Fischer, David, and James Kelly. *Bound Away: Virginia and the Westward Movement.* Charlottesville: University of Virginia Press, 2000.

Fleming, George Thornton. *History of Pittsburgh and Environs.* 6 vols. New York: American Historical Society, 1922.

Fleming, Thomas. *The Louisiana Purchase.* Hoboken, NJ: J. Wiley, 2003.

Flinn, M. W. "The Poor Employment Act of 1817." *Economic History Review* 14 (1961): 82–92.

Flynn, Dennis O. "Silver in a Global Context, 1400–1800." In *Cambridge World History,* edited by J. H. Bentley et al., 6:213–40. Cambridge: Cambridge University Press, 2015.

Fogel, Robert. *Without Consent or Contract: The Rise and Fall of American Slavery.* New York: Norton, 1989.

Forbes, Robert Pierce. *The Missouri Compromise and Its Aftermath: Slavery and the Meaning of America.* Chapel Hill: University of North Carolina Press, 2009.

Foster, Charles. "The Urban Missionary Movement 1814–1837." *Pennsylvania Magazine of History and Biography* 75/76 (1951): 47–65.

Fowler, P. H. *Historical Sketch of Presbyterianism within the Bounds of the Synod of Central New York.* Utica, NY: Curtiss & Childs, 1877.

Frankel, J. "The 1807–1809 Embargo against Great Britain." *Journal of Economic History* 42, no. 2 (1982): 291–308.

Freehling, William W. *Prelude to the Civil War: The Nullification Controversy in South Carolina 1816–1836.* New York: Oxford University Press, 1965.

———. *The Road to Disunion,* Vol. 1, *Secessionists at Bay, 1776–1854.* New York: Oxford University Press, 1991.

Freyer, Tony. *Producers versus Capitalists: Constitutional Conflict in Antebellum America.* Charlottesville: University of Virginia Press, 1994.

Friedman, Milton. "Bimetallism Revisited." *Journal of Economic Perspectives* 4 (1990): 85–104.

Fuller, Grace Pierpont. *Introduction to the History of Connecticut as a Manufacturing State.* Northampton, MA: Smith College Studies in History, 1915.

Gayer, Arthur, W. W. Rostow, and Anna Schwartz. *The Growth and Fluctuation of the British Economy, 1790–1850.* 2 vols. London: Oxford University Press, 1953.

Gifford, Daniel. "A Society for Everything: Remaking America's Charitable Landscape during the Second Great Awakening." *O Say Can You See? Stories from the National Museum of History,* March 3, 2016. http://americanhistory.si.edu/blog/charity-second-great-awakening.

Glaeser, Edward L. "A Nation of Gamblers: Real Estate Speculation and American History." National Bureau of Economic Research Working Paper 18825, Feb. 2013. http://nber.org/papers/w18825.

Goodrich, Carter. *Canals and Economic Development.* New York: Columbia University Press, 1961.

Goran, Thomas P. *Nicholas Biddle: Nationalist and Public Banker, 1786–1844.* Chicago: University of Chicago Press, 1959.

Gordinier, Glenn. "Versatility in Crisis: The Merchants of the New London Customs District Respond to the Embargo of 1807–1809." PhD diss., University of Connecticut, 2001.

Gracy David B., II. "Austin, Moses." Texas State Historical Association, http://tshaonline.org/handbook/online/articles/fau12 (accessed 30 March 2017).

Gras, Norman Scott Brien, *Massachusetts First National Bank of Boston, 1784-1934.* Cambridge, MA: Harvard University Press, 1937.

Gray, Edward. *William Gray of Salem, Merchant: A Biographical Sketch.* Boston: Houghton Mifflin, 1914.

Gray, Jacquelyn Procter. "From a Kingdom in Wales to a Cotton Farm in Alabama." Huntsville History Collection. http://huntsvillehistorycollection.org/

hh/index.php?title=From_a_Kingdom_in_Wales_to_a_Cotton_Farm_in_ Alabama (accessed April 2017).

Gray, Lewis C. *History of Agriculture in the Southern United States to 1860*. 2 vols. Washington, DC: Carnegie Institute, 1933.

Greene, George D. *Finance and Economic Development in the Old South: Louisiana Banking, 1804–1861*. Stanford, CA: Stanford University Press, 1972.

Greenspan, Alan. "Our Banking History" Remarks by Chairman Alan Greenspan Before the Annual Meeting and Conference of the Conference of State Bank Supervisors." Nashville, TN, 2 May 2, 1998. Federal Reserve Board. http://www.federalreserve.gov/boarddocs/speeches/1996/19980502.htm

Greer, Thomas H. "Economic and Social Effects of the Panic of 1819 in the Old Northwest." *Indiana Magazine of History* 44 (1948): 227–43.

Greve, Charles. *Centennial History of Cincinnati*. Chicago: Biographical Publishing, 1904.

Grivno, Max L. "Chased Out on the Slippery Ice: Rural Wage Laborers in Baltimore's Hinterland, 1815–1860." In *Southern Society and Its Transformation, 1790–1860*, edited by Susannah Delfino et al., 131–53. Columbia: University of Missouri Press, 2011.

———. *Gleanings of Freedom: Free and Slave Labor Along the Mason-Dixon Line, 1790–1860*. Urbana: University of Illinois Press, 2014.

Gronert, Theodore. "Trade in the Blue Grass Region, 1810–1820." *Mississippi Valley Historical Review* 5, no. 3 (1918): 313–23.

Gross, Karen, Marie Stefanini Newman, and Denise Campbell. "Ladies in Red: Learning from America's First Female Bankrupts." *American Journal of Legal History* 40 (1996): 1–40.

Gudmestad, Robert. *Steamboats and the Rise of the Cotton Kingdom*. Baton Rouge: Louisiana State University Press, 2011.

Gunn, L. Ray. *The Decline of Authority: Public Economic Policy and Political Development in New York State, 1800–1860*. Ithaca, NY: Cornell University Press, 1988.

Gunther, Gerald, ed. *John Marshall's Defense of McCulloch v. Maryland*. Stanford, CA: Stanford University Press, 1969.

Ha, Songho. *The Rise and Fall of the American System: Nationalism and the Development of the American Economy, 1790–1837*. London: Pickering and Chatto, 2009.

Haeger, John D. *The Investment Frontier: New York Businessmen and Economic Development of the Old Northwest*. Albany: State University Press of New York, 1981.

Haines, Sidney, and Richard Sylla. *A History of Interest Rates*, 3rd. ed. New Brunswick, NJ: Rutgers University Press, 1991.

Halévy, Elie. *The Liberal Awakening*. New York: Barnes and Noble, 1961.

Hall, Mathew W. *Dividing the Union: Jesse Burgess Thomas and the Making of the Missouri Compromise*. Carbondale: Southern Illinois University Press, 2015.

Hamer, Philip. *Tennessee: A History 1673–1932*. New York: American Historical Association, 1933.

Hamilton, W. J. "The Relief Movement in Missouri, 1820–1822." *Missouri Historical Review* 22, no. 1 (1927): 51–92.

Hammond, Bray. *Banks and Politics in America from the Revolution to the Civil War.* Princeton, NJ: Princeton University Press, 1957.

———. "Long and Short Term Credit in Early American Banking." *Quarterly Journal of Economics* 49, no. 1 (1934): 79–103.

Hammond, Matthew. *The Cotton Industry; An Essay in American Economic History; Part I. The Cotton Culture and the Cotton Trade.* New York: Macmillan, 1897.

Hand, Greg. "Cincinnati's Richest Man Died in Debtor's Prison." *Cincinnati Magazine,* October 24, 2016. http://www.cincinnatimagazine.com/citywiseblog/john-h-piatt/

Handler, Joel F., and Yeheskal Hasenfeld. *We the Poor People: Work, Poverty, and Welfare.* New Haven, CT: Yale University Press, 1997.

Hannon, J. U. "The Generosity of Antebellum Poor Relief." *Journal of Economic History* 44, no. 3 (1984): 810–21.

———. "Poor Relief Policy in Antebellum New York State: The Rise and Decline of the Poor House." *Explorations in Economic History* 22, no. 3 (1985): 233–56.

Hao, Yen-P'ing. "Chinese Teas to America—A Synopsis." In *America's China Trade in Historical Perspective,* ed. Ernest R. May and John K. Fairbank, 11–31. Cambridge, MA: Harvard University Press, 1986.

Hart, Asa Bushnell. *Essentials in American History: from the Discovery to the Present Day.* New York: American Book Co., *1905.*

Haulman, Clyde. "Panic of 1819: America's First Great Depression." *Financial History* 96 (Winter 2010): 22–24.

———. "Virginia Commodity Prices during the Panic of 1819." *Journal of the Early Republic* 22, no. 4 (2002): 675–88.

———. *Virginia in the Panic of 1819: The First Great Depression and the Commonwealth.* London: Pickering and Chatto, 2008.

Hausman, Alan, and David Hausman. "Berkeley's Semantic Dilemma: Beyond the Inheritance Model." *History of Philosophy Quarterly* 13, no. 2 (1996): 221–38.

Hawtrey, R. G. "The Bank Restriction of 1797." *Economic Journal* 28, no. 109 (1918): 52–65.

Hay, Robert P. "The Case for Andrew Jackson in 1824: Eaton's 'Wyoming Letters.'" *Tennessee Historical Quarterly* 29, no. 2 (1970): 139–51.

Haynes, Robert V. "The Formation of the Territory." In *A History of Mississippi,* edited by Richard A. McLemore, 1:174–216. Jackson: University of Mississippi Press, 1973.

Heidler, David S., and Jeanne T. Heidler. *Henry Clay: The Essential American.* New York: Random House, 2010.

Hempton, David. *Methodism: Empire of the Spirit.* New Haven, CT: Yale University Press, 2005.

Henderson, Timothy. *Mexican Wars for Independence.* New York: Farrar, Straus, and Giroux, 2009.

Hibbard, B. H. *A History of Public Land Policies.* New York: Macmillan, 1924.

Hidy, Ralph W. *The House of Baring in American Trade and Finance: English Merchant Bankers at Work, 1763–1861.* Cambridge, MA: Harvard University Press, 1949.

Hilt, Eric. "Wall Street's First Corporate Governance Crisis: The Panic of 1826." National Bureau of Economic Research Working Paper 148292, April 2009. http://www.nber.org/papers/w14892.

Hinks, Peter P. *To Awaken My Afflicted Brethren: David Walker and the Problem of Antebellum Slave Resistance.* State College, PA: Penn State Press, 2010.

Hobsbawm, Eric J. *Industry and Empire: The Making of Modern English Society.* Vol. 2, *1750 to the Present Day.* New York: Pantheon, 1968.

Hofstadter, Richard. *American Political Tradition and the Men Who Made It.* New York: Knopf, 1948.

Holt, Michael. *Rise and Fall of the American Whig Party.* New York: Oxford University Press, 1999.

Hoover, Herbert. *Memoirs of Herbert Hoover.* 3 vols. New York: Macmillan, 1952.

Hopkins, James F. *A History of the Hemp Industry of Kentucky.* Lexington: University Press of Kentucky, 1951.

Houck, Louis. *A History of Missouri from the Earliest Explorations . . .* Chicago: Donnelly, 1908.

Howe, Daniel Walker. *What Hath God Wrought? The Transformation of America, 1815–1848.* New York: Oxford University Press, 2007.

Howells, William C. *Recollections of Life in Ohio, 1813–1840.* Cincinnati: Robert Clarke, 1895.

Hubbard, R. Glenn, ed. *Financial Markets and Financial Crises.* Chicago: University of Chicago Press, 1991.

Hunter, Louis C. *History of Industrial Power in the United States.* 3 vols. Charlottesville: University of Virginia Press, 1991.

Huntington, Charles C. *A History of Banking and Currency . . . in Ohio Before the Civil War.* Columbus: F. J. Heer, 1915.

Hurt, R. Douglas. *Agriculture and Slavery in Missouri's Little Dixie.* Columbia: University of Missouri Press, 1992.

Huston, James. *Securing the Fruits of Labor.* Baton Rouge: Louisiana State University Press, 1998.

Irwin, Douglas. "New Estimates of the Average Tariff of the United States, 1790–1820." *Journal of Economic History* 63, no. 2 (2003): 506–14.

Jarvey, Theodore D. *Robert Y. Hayne and His Times.* New York: Macmillan, 1909.

Jenkins, John S. *The Life of John Caldwell Calhoun.* Auburn, NY: John Beardsley, 1850.

Jenks, William L. "The First Bank in Michigan." *Michigan History* 1, no. 1 (1917): 41–62.

John, Richard R. *Spreading the News: The American Postal System from Franklin to Morse.* Cambridge, MA: Harvard University Press, 1995.

Johnson, Paul. *Birth of the Modern: World Society 1815–1830.* New York: HarperCollins, 1991.

Johnston, Louis, and Samuel H. Williamson. "What Was the U.S. GDP Then?" *Measuring Worth,* 2018. http://measuringworth.org/usgdp/

Kamensky, Jane. *Exchange Artist*. New York: Penguin, 2008.

Kamoie, Laura Croghan. *Irons in the Fire: The Business History of the Tayloe Family and Virginia's Gentry, 1700–1860*. Charlottesville: University of Virginia Press, 2007.

Kaplan, Edward. *The Bank of the United States and the American Economy*. Westport, CT: Greenwood, 1999.

Katz, Michael. *In the Shadow of the Poorhouse: A Social History of Welfare in America*. 2nd ed. New York: Basic Books, 1996.

Kehl, James A. *Ill Feeling in the Era of Good Feeling: Western Pennsylvania Political Battles, 1815–1825*. Pittsburgh: University of Pittsburgh Press, 1956.

Kennedy, Roger. *Mr. Jefferson's Lost Cause: Land, Farmers, Slavery, and the Louisiana Purchase*. New York: Oxford University Press, 2002.

Kerr, Charles. *History of Kentucky*. Chicago: American Historical Society, 1922.

Ketcham, Ralph. *James Madison: A Biography*. Charlottesville: University of Virginia Press, 1990.

Keyssar, Alexander. *The Right to Vote*. New York: Basic Books, 2009.

Kidd, Sarah. "'To Be Harassed by My Creditors Is Worse than Death': Cultural Implications of the Panic of 1819." *Maryland Historical Magazine* 95, no. 2 (2000): 160–89.

———. "The Search for Moral Order: The Panic of 1819 and the Culture of the Early Republic." PhD diss., University of Missouri, 2002.

Kielbowicz, Richard. *News in the Mail: Press, Post Office and Public Information 1700–1860s*. Westport, CT: Greenwood, 1989.

Kilbourne, Robert H. *Debt, Investment, and Slaves*. Tuscaloosa: University of Alabama Press, 1995.

Killenbeck, Mark K. *McCulloch v. Maryland*. Lawrence: University of Kansas Press, 2006.

Kindleberger, Charles C. *Financial Crises: Theory, History, and Policy*. New York: Cambridge University Press, 1982.

———. *Manias, Panics, and Crashes: A History of Financial Crises*. 6th ed. London: Palgrave Macmillan, 2011.

King, Quentin S. *Henry Clay and the War of 1812*. Jefferson, NC: McFarland, 2014.

Klebaner, B. J. *Public Poor Relief in America, 1790–1860*. New York: Arno, 1976.

Klein, Daniel B. "The Voluntary Provision of Public Goods? The Turnpike Companies of Early America." *Economic Inquiry* 28, no. 4 (1990): 788–812.

Klingaman, William, and Nicholas Klingaman. *The Year Without a Summer: 1816 and the Volcano that Darkened the World and Changed History*. New York: St. Martins, 2013.

Knodell, Jane Ellen. *The Second Bank of the United States: "Central" Banker in an Era of Nation-Building*. Abingdon, UK: Routledge, 2016.

Knowles, Arne. *Mastering Iron: The Struggle to Modernize an American Industry, 1800–1868*. Chicago: University of Chicago Press, 2013.

Knox, John. *A History of Banking in the United States*. New York: Bradford Rhodes, 1903.

Kotar, S. L., and J. E. Gessler. *The Steamboat Era*. Jefferson, NC: McFarland, 2009.

Kukla, John. *A Wilderness So Immense: The Louisiana Purchase and the Destiny of America*. New York: Knopf, 2003.

Kulikoff, Allan. *Agrarian Origins of American Capitalism*. Charlottesville: University of Virginia Press, 1992.

Labbé, Dolores E., ed. *The Louisiana Purchase and Its Aftermath 1800–1830*. Lafayette: Center for Louisiana Studies, 1998.

Labsock, Suzanne. *Free Women of Petersburg*. New York: Norton, 1985.

Lamb, H. H. *Climate, History, and the Modern World*. London: Routledge, 1995.

Lamoreaux, Naomi. *Insider Lending: Banks, Personal Connections, and Economic Development in Industrial New England*. New York: Cambridge University Press, 2010.

———. "The Structure of Early Banks in Southeastern New England: Some Social and Economic Implications." *Business and Economic History* 13 (1984): 171–84.

Landy, James. *Cincinnati Past and Present*. Cincinnati, OH: Elm Street Printing, 1872.

Larson, John L. "'Bind the Republic Together': The National Union and the Struggle for a System of Internal Improvements." *Journal of American History* 74, no. 2 (1987): 367–87.

———. *Internal Improvements: National Public Works and the Promise of Popular Government in the Early United States*. Chapel Hill: University of North Carolina Press, 2001.

Latner, Richard B. *The Presidency of Andrew Jackson: White House Politics 1829–1837*. Atlanta: University of Georgia Press, 1979.

Leach, Richard H. "George Ticknor Curtis and Daniel Webster's 'Villainies.'" *New England Quarterly* 27, no. 3 (1954): 391–95.

Lebergott, Stanley. "Labor Force, Employment, and Unemployment, 1929-39: Estimating Methods." *Monthly Labor Review* 67, no. 1 (July 1948): 50-53. https://www.bls.gov/opub/mlr/1948/article/pdf/labor-force-employment-and-unemployment-1929-39-estimating-methods.pdf.

———. "Wage Trends, 1800–1900." In Conference on Research in Income and Wealth, *Trends in the American Economy in the Nineteenth Century*, 449–500. Studies in Income and Wealth 24. Princeton, NJ: Princeton University Press, 1960.

Lehman, J. David. "Explaining Hard Times: Political Economy and the Panic of 1819 in Philadelphia." PhD diss., University of California, Los Angeles, 1992.

Lenner, Andrew C. "John Taylor and the Origins of American Federalism." *Journal of the Early Republic* 17, no. 3 (1997): 399–423.

Lepler, Jessica N. *The Many Panics of 1837*. New York: Cambridge University Press, 2013.

Licht, Walter. *Getting Work: Philadelphia 1840–1950*. Cambridge, MA: Harvard University Press, 1992.

Lindquist, Elizabeth. "Langdon Cheves." MA thesis, University of Chicago, 1927.

McCabe, James. "Banking." In *Encyclopedia of Louisville*, ed. John E. Kleber, 59–64. Lexington: University of Kentucky Press, 2015.

McCusker, John J. *How Much Is That in Real Money? A Historical Price Index for Use as a Deflator of Money Values in the Economy of the United States*. Worcester, MA: American Antiquarian Society, 1992.

McLeod, Duncan. "The Political Economy of John Taylor." *Journal of American Studies* 14, no. 3 (1980): 387–406.

McMaster, John Balch. *History of the People of the United States.* 8 vols. New York. Appleton, 1896.

———. *The Life and Times of Stephen Girard, Mariner and Merchant.* 2 vols. Philadelphia: Lippincott, 1918.

Majewski, John. *A House Dividing: Economic Development in Pennsylvania and Virginia before the Civil War.* New York: Cambridge University Press, 2000.

Malone, Dumas. *Jefferson and His Time.* 6 vols. Boston: Little, Brown, 1948–81.

———. *The Public Life of Thomas Cooper.* New Haven, CT: Yale University Press, 1926.

Margo, Robert. *Wages and Labor Markets in the United States 1820–1860.* Chicago: University of Chicago Press, 2000.

Marichal, Carlos. *Bankruptcy of Empire: Mexican Silver and the Wars between Spain, Britain, and France, 1760–1810.* Cambridge: Cambridge University Press, 2007.

Martin, Scott, ed. *Cultural Change and the Market Revolution in America, 1789–1860.* Lanham, MD: Rowman and Littlefield, 2005.

Maryland State Archives. "Brookeville 1814." https://msa.maryland.gov/brookeville/ (accessed Nov. 9, 2016).

Mathias, Frank F. "The Relief and Court Struggle: Half-Way House to Populism." *Register of the Kentucky Historical Society* 71, no. 2 (1973): 154–76.

Matson, Cathy. "Capitalizing Hope: Economic Thought and the Early National Economy." In *Wages of Independence: Capitalism in the Early American Republic,* edited by Paul A. Gilje, 5–10. Madison, WI: Madison House, 1997.

———. "Matthew Carey's Learning Experience: Commerce, Manufacturing, and the Panic of 1819." *Early American Studies* 11, no. 3 (2013): 455–85.

Matthews, Ronald E., and Janet Lane. *Is Charity a Choice: Protestant Evangelicals, Charitable Choice, and the Feeding of the Poor.* Newcastle, UK: Cambridge Scholars, 2012.

Maye, Brian. "A Volcanic Eruption with Global Repercussions—An Irishman's Diary on 1816, the Year without a Summer." *Irish Times,* August 19, 2016.

Meyer, David R. *The Roots of American Industrialization.* Baltimore: Johns Hopkins University Press, 2003.

Milham, Willis. "The Year 1816: The Causes of Abnormalities." *Monthly Weather Review* 52, no. 12 (1924): 563–70.

Miller, H. Nicholas. "Smuggling into Canada: How the Champlain Valley Defied Jefferson's Embargo." *Vermont History* 38, no. 1 (1970): 5–21.

Mintz, Stephen, and Sara McNeil. "Growth of Political Factionalism and Sectionalism." *Digital History* ID 3531. http://digitalhistory.uh.edu/disp_textbook. cfm?smtid=2&psid=3531

Mitchell, B. R. *British Historical Statistics.* Cambridge: Cambridge University Press, 1988.

Mitchener, Kris James. "The Classical Gold Standard." In *Routledge Handbook of Major Events in Economic History,* edited by Randall E. Parker and Robert Whaples, 88–102. London: Routledge, 2013.

Mohl, Raymond. *Poverty in New York, 1783–1825*. New York: Oxford University Press, 1970.

Montgomery, David. *Citizen Worker: The Experience of Workers in the United States with Democracy and the Free Market during the Nineteenth Century*. New York: Cambridge University Press, 1994.

Mooney, Chase C. *William H. Crawford 1772–1834*. Lexington: University of Kentucky Press, 1974.

Moore, Glover. *The Missouri Controversy, 1819–1821*. Lexington: University of Kentucky Press, 1953.

Morison, Samuel Eliot. *Maritime History of Massachusetts 1783–1860*. Boston: Houghton Mifflin, 1921.

———. *Three Centuries of Harvard, 1636–1936*. Cambridge, MA: Harvard University Press, 1936.

Morris, Charles R. *The Dawn of Innovation: The First American Industrial Revolution*. New York: Public Affairs, 2012.

Murphy, Richard C., and Lawrence J. Mannion. *The History of the Friendly Sons of St. Patrick in the City of New York, 1784 to 1955*. New York: Dillon, 1962.

Murry, G. S. "Poverty and Its Relief in the Antebellum South: Perceptions and Realities in Three Selected Cities: Charleston, Nashville, and New Orleans." PhD diss., Memphis State University, 1991.

Mussey, Barrows. "Yankee Chills, Ohio Fever." *New England Quarterly* 22, no. 4 (1949): 435–51.

Neal, Larry. "The Financial Crisis of 1825 and the Restructuring of the British Financial System." Federal Reserve Bank of St. Louis *Review* 80, no. 3 (May–June 1998): 53–76.

Nevins, Allan. *History of the Bank of New York and Trust Company, 1784 to 1934*. New York: Privately printed, 1934.

Newmyer, R. Kent. *John Marshall and the Heroic Age of the Supreme Court*. Baton Rouge: Louisiana State University Press, 2001.

———. "John Marshall, *McCulloch v. Maryland*, and the Southern States Rights Tradition." *John Marshall Law Review* 33, no. 4 (2000): 875–937.

Niven, John. *John C. Calhoun and the Price of Union*. Baton Rouge: Louisiana State University Press, 1988.

North, Douglass C. *The Economic Growth of the United States, 1790–1860*. Englewood Cliffs, NJ: Prentice-Hall, 1961.

Norton, A. Banning. *History of Knox County from 1779 to 1862 Inclusive*. Columbus, OH: Nevins, 1862.

O'Brien, Michael. *Conjectures of Order: Intellectual Life in the Old South*. 2 vols. Chapel Hill: University of North Carolina Press, 2004.

Olson, Sherry H. *Baltimore: The Building of an American City*. Baltimore: Johns Hopkins University Press, 1980.

Otto, John S. *Southern Frontiers 1607–1860: The Agricultural Evolution of the Colonial and Antebellum South*. Westport, CT: Greenwood, 1989.

417

Parks, J. H. "Felix Grundy and the Depression of 1819 in Tennessee." *Publication of the East Tennessee Historical Society* 10 (1938): 19–42.

Parsons, Lynn Hudson. *The Birth of Modern Politics: Andrew Jackson, John Quincy Adams, and the Election of 1828.* New York: Oxford University Press, 2009.

Pease, Theodore C. *The Frontier State.* Urbana: University of Illinois Press, 1987.

Perkins, Edwin J. "Langdon Cheves and the Panic of 1819: A Reassessment." *Journal of Economic History* 44, no. 2 (1984): 455–61.

Pessen, Edward. *Riches, Class and Power: America Before the Civil War.* New Brunswick, NJ: Transaction Publishers, 1973.

Peterson, Merrill. *The Great Triumvirate: Webster, Clay, and Calhoun.* New York: Oxford University Press, 1988.

Phillips, Kim T. "The Pennsylvania Origins of the Jackson Movement." *Political Science Quarterly* 91, no. 3 (1976): 498–508.

Phillips, Ulrich. *American Negro Slavery.* Baton Rouge: Louisiana State University Press, 1966.

Pocock, Emil. "Popular Roots of Jacksonian Democracy: The Case of Dayton, Ohio, 1815–1830." *Journal of the Early Republic* 9, no. 4 (1989): 489–515.

Porter, Kenneth W. *John Jacob Astor: Business Man.* 2 vols. New York: Russell and Russell, 1966.

Porter, Lorle. *Politics and Peril: Mount Vernon, Ohio in the Nineteenth Century.* Zanesville, OH: New Concord Press, 2005.

Post, John D. "The Economic Crisis of 1816–1817 and Its Social and Political Consequences." *Journal of Economic History* 30, no. 1 (1970): 248–50.

———. *The Last Great Subsistence Crisis in the Western World.* Baltimore: Johns Hopkins University Press, 1977.

Pred, Allan. *Urban Growth and the Circulation of Information: The United States System of Cities, 1790–1840.* Cambridge, MA: Harvard University Press, 1973.

Primm, James Neal. *Lion of the Valley: St. Louis, Missouri, 1764–1980.* 3rd ed. St. Louis: Missouri Historical Society, 1998.

Puls, Mark. *Samuel Adams, Father of the American Revolution.* New York: Palgrave, Macmillan, 2006.

Ratcliffe, Donald J. "The Crisis of Commercialization: National Political Alignments and the Market Revolution, 1819–1844." In *The Market Revolution in America: Social, Political, and Religious Experiences 1800–1880,* edited by Melvyn Stokes and Stephen Conway, 177–201. Charlottesville: University of Virginia Press, 1996.

———. "The Role of Voters and Issues in Party Formation: Ohio, 1824." *Journal of American History* 59, no. 4 (1973): 847–70.

Redlich, Fritz. *The Molding of American Banking: Men and Ideas.* New York: Hafner, 1947.

———. "William Jones and His Unsuccessful Steamboat Venture of 1819." *Bulletin of the Business Historical Society* 21, no. 5 (1947): 125–36.

———. "William Jones' Resignation from the Presidency of the Second Bank of the United States." *Pennsylvania Magazine of History and Biography* 71, no. 3 (1947): 223–41.

Reinhart, C., and K. Raogoff. *This Time is Different: Eight Centuries of Financial Folly.* Princeton, NJ: Princeton University Press, 2009.

Remini, Robert. *Andrew Jackson and the Course of American Empire.* New York: Harper and Row, 1977.

———. *Andrew Jackson and the Course of American Freedom.* New York: Harper and Row, 1981.

———. *Henry Clay: Statesman for the Union.* New York: Norton, 1993.

———. *The House: A History of the House of Representatives.* New York: Smithsonian Books/Harper Collins 2006.

Reynolds, David S. *Waking Giant: America in the Age of Jackson.* New York: Harper Collins, 2008.

Reynolds, William L. II. "Luther Martin, Maryland, and the Constitution." *Maryland Law Review* 47, no. 1 (1987): 291–321.

Rezneck, Samuel H. "The Depression of 1819–1822: A Social History." *American Historical Review* 39, no. 1 (1933): 28–47.

———. "The Social History of an American Depression, 1837–1843." *American Historical Review* 40, no. 4 (1935): 662–87.

Riesman, Janet A. "Republican Revisions: Political Economy in New York After the Panic of 1819." In *New York and the Rise of Capitalism*, edited by William Pencak and Conrad Wright, 1–44. New York: New-York Historical Society, 1989.

Roberts, R., and D. Kynaston. *The Bank of England: Money, Power, and Influence 1694–1994.* Oxford: Oxford University Press, 1995.

Robbins, R. M. *Our Landed Heritage: The Public Domain 1776–1936.* Princeton, NJ: Princeton University Press, 1942.

Rodriguez, Jaime. *Down from Colonialism: Mexico's Nineteenth Century Crisis.* Berkeley: University of California Press, 1983.

Rohrbough, Malcolm J. *The Land Office Business: The Settlement and Administration of American Public Lands, 1789–1837.* New York: Oxford University Press, 1968.

Rothbard, Murray. *The Panic of 1819: Reactions and Policies.* New York: Columbia University Press, 1962. Reprint, Auburn, AL: Ludwig Mies Institute, 2007.

Rothenberg, Winnifred Barr. "The Invention of New England Capitalism: The Economy of New England in the Federal Period." In *Engineers of Enterprise: An Economic History of New England*, ed. Peter Temin, 69–106. Cambridge, MA: Harvard University Press, 2000.

Rothman, David J. *The Discovery of the Asylum: Social Order and Disorder in the New Republic.* Boston: Little, Brown, 1971.

———. *Jacksonians on the Poor: Collected Pamphlets.* New York: Arno Press, 1971.

Rousseau, Peter, and Richard Sylla. "Emerging Financial Markets and Early U.S. Growth." *Explorations in Economic History* 42, no. 1 (2005): 1–26.

Russell, Bertrand. *Freedom versus Organization 1814–1914.* New York: Norton, 1934.

Sakolski, A. M. *The Great American Land Bubble: The Amazing Story of Land-Grabbing, Speculations, and Booms from Colonial Days to the Present Time.* New York: Harper, 1932.

Sallee, Frank. "Branch Banking in Missouri." *Missouri Law Review* 49, no. 4 (1984): 791–815.

Sandage, Scott. *Born Losers: A History of Failure in America.* Cambridge, MA: Harvard University Press, 2005.

Schab, David. "Woodhawks and Cordwood: Steamboat Fuel on the Ohio and Mississippi Rivers, 1820–1860." *Journal of Forest History* 21, no. 3 (1977): 124–32.

Scherr, Arthur. *Thomas Jefferson's Image of New England: Nationalism Versus Sectionalism in the Young Republic.* Jefferson, NC: McFarland, 2016.

Schlesinger, Arthur. *Age of Jackson.* Boston: Little, Brown, 1945.

Schoen, Brian. *The Fragile Fabric of Union: Cotton, Federal Politics, and the Global Origins of the Civil War.* Baltimore: Johns Hopkins University Press, 2009.

Schonhardt-Bailey, Cheryl. *From the Corn Laws to Free Trade: Interests, Ideas, and Institutions in Historical Perspective.* Cambridge, MA: MIT Press, 2006.

Schur, Leon M. "The Second Bank of the United States and the Inflation after the War of 1812." *Journal of Political Economy* 68, no. 2 (1960): 118–34.

Sears, Louis M. "Philadelphia and the Embargo of 1808." *Quarterly Journal of Economics* 35, no. 2 (1921): 354–59.

Seavoy, Ronald. *The Origins of the American Business Corporation, 1784–1855.* Westport, CT: Greenwood, 1982.

Sellers, Charles. "Banking and Politics in Jackson's Tennessee, 1817–1827." *Mississippi Valley Historical Review* 41. no. 1 (1954): 61–81.

———. "Jackson Men with Feet of Clay." *American Historical Review* 62, no. 3 (1957): 537–51.

———. *The Market Revolution: Jacksonian America, 1815–1846.* New York: Oxford University Press, 1991.

Shalhope, Robert. *John Taylor of Caroline.* Columbia: University of South Carolina Press, 1980.

Sharp, James Roger. *The Jacksonians Versus the Banks.* New York: Columbia University Press, 1970.

Shaw, Greg. *The Welfare Debate.* Westport, CT: Greenwood Press, 2007.

Shaw, Ronald. *Erie Water West.* Lexington: University of Kentucky Press, 1966.

Sheriff, Carol. *Artificial River: The Erie Canal and the Paradox of Progress 1817–1826.* New York: Hill and Wang, 1996.

Silver Institute. "Silver in History." http://silverinstitute.org/silver-in-industry/

Skeen, C. Edward. *1816: America Rising.* Lexington: University of Kentucky Press, 2003.

Sloan, Herbert E. *Principle and Interest: Thomas Jefferson and the Problem of Debt.* New York: Oxford University Press, 1995.

Smart, William. *Economic Annals of the Nineteenth Century.* 2 vols. 1911. Reprint, New York: Kelley, 1964.

Smith, Alfred G. Jr. *Economic Readjustment of an Old Cotton State, South Carolina 1820–1860.* Columbia: University of South Carolina Press, 1958.

Smith, Jean. *John Marshall, Definer of a Nation.* New York: Macmillan, 1998.

Smith, Walter Buckingham. *Economic Aspects of the Second Bank of the United States.* Cambridge, MA: Harvard University Press, 1953.

———, and Arthur Cole. *Economic Fluctuations in American Business, 1790–1860.* Cambridge, MA: Harvard University Press, 1935.

Stanwood, Edward. *American Tariff Controversies in the Nineteenth Century.* Boston: Houghton-Mifflin, 1903.

Stettler, Henry. "Growth and Fluctuation of the Antebellum Textile Industry." PhD diss., Purdue University, 1970.

Stevens, Henry. *The Early Jackson Party in Ohio.* Durham, NC: Duke University Press, 1957.

Stiles, T. J. *The First Tycoon: The Epic Life of Cornelius Vanderbilt.* New York: Knopf, 2009.

Stilwell, Lewis D. *Migration from Vermont.* Montpelier, VT: Academy Books, 1948.

Stokes, Howard. "Public and Private Finance." In Field, *State of Rhode Island . . .,* 3:171–322.

Stoll, Steven. *Larding the Lean Earth: Soil and Society in Nineteenth Century America.* New York: Hill and Wang, 2002.

Stommel, Henry M. *Volcano Weather: The Story of 1816, the Year Without a Summer.* Newport, RI: Seven Seas Press, 1983.

Stott, Richard B. *Workers in the Metropolis: Class, Ethnicity, and Youth in Antebellum New York City.* Ithaca, NY: Cornell University Press, 1990.

Sullivan, William. "A Decade of Labor Strife." *Pennsylvania History* 17, no. 1 (1950): 23–38.

———. *The Industrial Worker in Pennsylvania, 1800–1840.* Harrisburg: Pennsylvania Museum Commission, 1955.

Sumner, William Graham. *History of American Currency with Chapters on the English Bank Restriction and Austrian Paper Money.* New York: Holt, 1884.

Sydnor, Charles. *The Development of Southern Sectionalism, 1819–1848.* Baton Rouge: Louisiana State University Press, 1948.

Sylla, Richard. "Early American Banking: The Significance of the Corporate Form." *Business and Economic History* 14 (1985): 105–23.

———. "How the American Corporation Evolved Over Two Centuries." *Proceedings of the American Philosophical Society* 158, no. 4 (2014): 354–63.

———. "U.S. Securities Markets and the Business System, 1790–1840." Federal Reserve Bank of St. Louis *Review* 80, no. 3 (1998): 83–103.

———, and Robert E. Wright. "Corporation Formation in the Antebellum United States in Comparative Context." *Business History* 55, no. 4 (2013): 653–69.

———, and Robert E. Wright. "Early Corporate America: The Largest Industries and Companies before 1860." *Financial History* 103 (Summer 2012): 21–25.

———, Jack W. Wilson, and Charles P. Jones. "U.S. Financial Markets and Long-Term Economic Growth, 1790–1989." In *American Economic Development in Historical Perspective*, edited by Thomas Weiss and Donald Schaefer, 28–52. Stanford, CA: Stanford University Press, 1994.

Tadiman, Michael. *Speculators and Slaves: Masters, Traders, and Slaves in the Old South*. Madison: University of Wisconsin Press, 1989.

———, and Walter Johnson. *Soul by Soul: Life Inside the Antebellum Slave Market*. Cambridge, MA: Harvard University Press, 1999.

Taussig, E. F. *Tariff History of the United States*. 1931. Reprint, New York: Kelley, 1967.

Taylor, George R. *The Transportation Revolution*. New York: Rinehart, 1951.

Taylor, Philip E. "The Turnpike Era in New England." PhD diss., Yale University, 1934.

TePaske, John J. *New World of Gold and Silver*. Edited by Kendall W. Brown. London: Brill, 2010.

Tharp, Louise. *The Appletons of Beacon Hill*. Boston: Little, Brown, 1973.

Thorp, Willard. *Business Annals*. New York: National Bureau of Economic Research, 1926.

Trattner, Walter. *From Poor Law to Welfare State: A History of Social Welfare in America*. 10th ed. New York: Simon and Schuster, 2007.

Tucker, Barbara. *Samuel Slater and the Origins of the American Textile Industry, 1790–1860*. Ithaca, NY: Cornell University Press, 1984.

———, and Kenneth H. Tucker. *Industrializing Antebellum America: The Rise of Manufacturing Entrepreneurs in the Early Republic*. New York: Palgrave Macmillan, 2008.

Tucker, Rich. "America's Debt Through the Eyes of the Founders.". *Heritage Foundation* no. 4065, October 8, 2013. http://thf_media.s3.amazonaws.com/2013/pdf/ib4065.pdf.

Unger, Harlow Giles. *The Last Founding Father: James Monroe and a Nation's Call to Greatness*. New York: Da Capo, 2009.

United States Geological Survey. "New Madrid 1811–1812 Earthquakes." https://earthquake.usgs.gov/earthquakes/events/1811-1812newmadrid/summary.php.

Utter, William T. *The Frontier State, 1803–1825*. Columbus: Ohio State Archeological and Historical Society, 1942.

Van Atta, John. *Wolf by the Ears: The Missouri Crisis, 1819–1821*. Baltimore: Johns Hopkins University Press, 2015.

VanBurkleo, Sandra F. "'The Paws of the Banks': The Origin and Significance of Kentucky's Decision to Tax Federal Banks, 1818–1820." *Journal of the Early Republic* 9, no. 4 (1989): 457–87.

Vitellio, Domenic. *The Philadelphia Stock Exchange and the City It Made*. Philadelphia: University of Pennsylvania Press, 2010.

Vogt, D. C. "Poor Relief in Frontier Mississippi." *Journal of Mississippi History* 51, no. 2 (1989): 181–99.

Wade, Richard C. *The Urban Frontier: The Rise of Western Cities, 1790–1830*. Cambridge, MA: Harvard University Press, 1959.

Wallace, Harry E. "Journey in Time: History of the Shoals." Florence (AL) *Times-Daily*, February 25, 1999.

Walsh, Marie. *The Sisters of Charity of New York 1809–1909.* 2 vols. New York: Fordham University Press, 1960.

Walters, Raymond, Jr. "The Origins of the Second Bank of the United States." *Journal of Political Economy* 53, no. 2 (1945): 115–31.

Walters, Ronald G. *American Reformers, 1815-1860.* New York: Macmillan, 1978

Ware, Caroline. *The Early New England Cotton Manufacture: A Study in Beginnings.* Boston: Houghton Mifflin, 1931.

———. "The Effect of the American Embargo, 1807–1809, on the New England Cotton Industry." *Quarterly Journal of Economics* 40, no. 4 (1926): 672–88.

Watson, Harry. *Liberty and Power.* New York: Hill and Wang, 1990.

Watts, Steven. *The Republic Reborn: War and the Remaking of Liberal America, 1790–1820.* Baltimore: Johns Hopkins Press, 1987.

Weber, Warren E. "Early State Banks: in the United States: How Many Were There and When Did They Exist?" *Journal of Economic History* 66, no. 2 (2006): 433–55.

Welch, Claude E. "Josiah Quincy and His School for 'Gentlemen.'" Harvard *Crimson* 21, September 1959.

Weems, Robert C. "The Bank of Mississippi: A Pioneer Bank of the Old Southwest, 1809–1844." PhD diss., Columbia University, 1951.

Welsh, Samuel L., and Margaret Armbrester. *Alabama's Governors: A Political History.* Tuscaloosa: University of Alabama Press, 2014.

Wetherill, Elkins. *Story of the Philadelphia Stock Exchange.* New York: Newcomen Society, 1976.

White, Horace. *Money and Banking.* Boston: Ginn, 1902.

Widmer, Ted. "The War of 1812? Don't Remind Me." Boston *Globe*, April 20, 2014.

Wiener, Martin. "Humanitarianism as Control." *Rice University Studies* 67 (1981): 1–84.

Wilentz, Sean. *Chants Democratic: New York City and the Rise of the American Working Class, 1788–1850.* New York: Oxford University Press, 1984.

———. *The Rise of American Democracy: Jefferson to Lincoln.* New York: Norton, 2006.

Wilkins, Mira. *History of Foreign Investment in the United States to 1914.* Cambridge, MA: Harvard University Press, 1989.

Williamson, Samuel, and Louis Cain. "Measuring Slavery in 2011 Dollars." *Measuring Worth*, 2018. http://measuringworth.com/slavery.php.

Winston, J. E., and R. W. Colomb. "How the Louisiana Purchase Was Financed." *Louisiana Historical Quarterly* 12 (1929): 189–237.

Wittlinger, Carleton. "Early Manufacturing in Lancaster County." PhD diss., University of Pennsylvania, 1952.

Wood, Gillen D'Arcy. *Tambora: The Eruption that Changed the World.* Princeton, NJ: Princeton University Press, 2014.

Woodman, Harold D. *King Cotton and His Retainers: Financing and Marketing the Cotton Crop of the South, 1800–1925.* Lexington: University of Kentucky Press, 1968.

Wright, Chester. *Economic History of the United States.* New York: McGraw Hill, 1941.

Wright, Gavin. *The Political Economy of the Cotton South*. New York: Norton, 1978.

Wright, Robert. "Corporate Entrepreneurship in the Antebellum South." In *Southern Society and Its Transformation, 1790–1860*, edited by Susannah Delfino et al., 195–214. Columbia: University of Missouri Press, 2011.

———. *Corporation Nation*. Philadelphia: University of Pennsylvania Press, 2013.

———. *The First Wall Street: Chestnut Street, Philadelphia*. Chicago: University of Chicago Press, 2005.

———. "Specially Incorporated Transportation Companies in the United States to 1860: A Comprehensive Tabulation and Its Implications." *Journal of Business and Economics* 5, no. 7 (2014): 972–89.

Zarnowitz, Victor. *Business Cycle: Theory, History, Indicators, and Forecasting*. Chicago: University of Chicago Press, 1996.

Ziegler, Philip. *The Sixth Great Power: Barings 1762–1929*. London: Collins, 1988.

INDEX